Financial Wisdom

Volume I

Personal Finance and Career Skills to Guide Teens and Young Adults on Their Journey to Success and Happiness

FINANCIAL WISDOM™
PREPARATORY INSTITUTE

Financial Wisdom

Volume I

Personal Finance and Career Skills to
Guide Teens and Young Adults on
Their Journey to Success and Happiness

Published by Financial Wisdom Preparatory Institute, LLC
Culver City, CA
USA
http://financialwisdompi.com/
contact@financialwisdompi.com

ISBN: 978-0-9834686-0-8

Library of Congress Control Number: 2011925463

Printed in the United States of America

About Dr. Joetta Forsyth

Dr. Joetta Forsyth received her Ph.D. in Business Economics from Harvard with concentrations in finance and industrial organization. Her Ph.D. was awarded through a joint program with the Harvard Business School and Economics Department. She has a B.A. and M.A in Economics from the University of Chicago. In addition to years of experience in business, Dr. Forsyth was a finance professor at the University of Michigan and the University of Southern California before joining the faculty at Pepperdine's Graziadio School of Business and Management as a finance professor.

Why Dr. Forsyth Wrote This Textbook and Founded Financial Wisdom Preparatory Institute

At various points during my introductory college finance course, I was fond of making a short speech about something I felt was truly important. One of those speeches was my "Teach Your Children Well" speech, which I would give after showing my students techniques for financial planning.

I would start by asking my students how many of them had children, and then summarize all of the things that caring parents do for their children; send them to a good school, watch who they spend time with, feed them nutritious food, make sure they get exercise, and so forth. Despite this, it is astonishing how little time the typical parent spends teaching their kids how to handle their money. What an important skill to have!

I would ask my students (who did not have to answer) how many had made a big financial mistake that caused them serious harm. Hands would shoot up. I would tell them that financial problems affect much of daily life and are even a major contributor, if not the most important contributor, to divorce. I then advised my students to put in the time to give their kids financial training in order to protect their welfare, happiness, security, and maybe even their families. Someday, later in life, their financially wise and content children would thank them with deep gratitude.

The financial crisis that we have all been enduring has been a non-ending nightmare. The widespread abuse that occurred in mortgage lending is clear. Compounding the problem was the lack of understanding people had about taking out a mortgage, and what was in their own best interest. How terribly, terribly, tragic. How much devastation would have been avoided if people had financial training and understood the risks that they were taking? How many dreams, families, lives, have been shattered? The grievous consequences can be seen on every block in every city.

What Financial Wisdom Prep Does

In addition to publishing groundbreaking textbooks on personal finance for young adults, Financial Wisdom Preparatory Institute promotes young adult financial literacy in several ways.

Educators: High school teachers can take highly interactive online courses with small class sizes. These courses provide rigorous training in personal finance. Instructional methods, materials, and lesson plans for teaching finance to young adults are also provided.

Parents/Homeschoolers: Financial Wisdom will offer small, highly interactive courses for parents in personal finance, and how to instruct their child in personal finance. Parents will be given teaching materials and lesson plans for their child.

Testing: Standardized testing of students will be offered. This can be particularly helpful to homeschooled children who receive the benefit of independent, standardized grading of their achievements.

For more information visit: http://financialwisdompi.com

Acknowledgements

There are many who have encouraged me along the way, including my family, and especially my son. My friend Linnea McCord has been a tremendous help in numerous ways, and has unfailingly encouraged me.

I was very fortunate to have received invaluable editing assistance from Kelly Barron.

Domenica Trevor and Toni Hull also provided superb editing assistance.

Integrity

It is imperative that financial educators be as free of conflicts of interest as possible. Asking someone who sells consumer financial products and services to teach personal finance is like asking a used car salesman to teach about buying cars. You may end up learning the most effective method possible for lining their pockets with your money. Therefore, Financial Wisdom Preparatory Institute has an integrity policy to address conflicts of interest:

It is the policy of Dr. Joetta Forsyth and Financial Wisdom Preparatory Institute that during their employment with Financial Wisdom Prep, no employees compensated by Financial Wisdom Prep sell consumer financial products or services, nor receive compensation from any business or individual that sells or promotes consumer financial products or services.

Disclaimers

This textbook is for educational purposes only. Each person will have their own unique financial circumstances. When making any important financial decision, consult with the appropriate financial or tax advisor, or legal counsel. This textbook is updated periodically and may not contain the latest information on tax rules, accounting rules, etc. It is also the responsibility of the reader to verify information before making financial decisions. Financial Wisdom Preparatory Institute, LLC is not responsible for any financial decisions you make based on the information you read in this textbook.

Investing is inherently risky. Investment results based on information or advice provided in this textbook may not turn out as intended. Entire investments may even be lost. Losses due to political and economic forces beyond the control of Financial Wisdom Preparatory Institute, LLC are not the responsibility of Financial Wisdom Preparatory Institute, LLC. This applies whether the reader employed advice found in this textbook in the appropriate way, or not.

Textbook Supplemental Materials

This textbook comes with a wealth of spreadsheets and other supplemental materials. Numerous chapters require that the student access these files. Look in the book appendix under "Internet Information" for instructions on how to download the files.

Receiving Volume 2

If you would like to receive an email informing you when Volume 2 is available, please send an email to contact@financialwisdompi.com with "V2" in the subject heading. You email address will not be distributed to anyone, or used for any purpose other than informing you that Volume 2 has become available.

Financial Wisdom

Volume I

Personal Finance and Career Skills to Guide Teens and Young Adults on Their Journey to Success and Happiness

THE FINANCIAL ENVIRONMENT

THE TIME VALUE OF MONEY

THE BASICS OF PLANNING

Career Skills

Risk

Your Credit Score and Good Name

Appendix

Detailed Table of Contents

THE TIME VALUE OF MONEY

The Basics of Planning

Career Skills

Risk

Your Credit Score and Good Name

APPENDIX

Chapter 1
Introduction

Heading for college is one of the most exciting times of a person's life. With the benefit of an excellent high school education, the future looks bright. You have much to be proud of and much yet to achieve.

Have you noticed that two people can start from the same place but end up with very different results? Take two people with similar backgrounds and educations. One accomplishes great things while the other is stifled. One person lives in prosperity and happiness, while the other is miserable and struggling. There is a reason for this — a whole body of knowledge gets passed down in a sporadic way. A lucky few have a high degree of access to this knowledge, some have a little access, and many have none at all. This information is not taught in schools, but it can make all the difference in the world. It is hard earned wisdom learned through life's experiences.

There are also powerful tools for success in the form of technical training. As you head out the door into adulthood you will begin a journey. The purpose of this textbook is to provide you with something essential in this process, gained from those who have gone before. It is a state-of-the-art financial map and compass to speed you on your way.

1.1 A Historical Perspective

In order to understand the importance of personal finance, it is necessary to look to the past for historical perspective. Until the twentieth century, children learned directly from their parents the details of how to succeed in a career through helping with the family business or farm. There were a million little details to learn about successfully running the business. The children were shown how to manage inventory, sell product, raise money to pay for supplies, and keep track of the finances. Eventually they took over the business or started a similar one of their own. Parents also taught their children how to manage their money, build wealth, and provide for themselves and a family. As adults, children stayed near home and had constant access to valuable advice. In school, they were given math problems involving bushels of farm seed or borrowing from the bank.

The contrast with today is remarkable. Most children no longer work at a family business because their parents are employed at companies owned by others. These parents work long hours away from home, and increasingly have to rely on the education system to train their children. This reliance is magnified because children choose not to follow in their parents' footsteps as they pursue their own career interests in entirely different fields. Something vital was lost along the way. The old method for training children went away, and nothing new replaced it. No longer do career skills or money skills get passed down in a systematic way.

Colleges have not stepped up to fill the gap. Their academic traditions of "higher learning" get in the way, along with increased technical demands and the greater specialization of subjects. Medicine is a good example. As the science of medicine has progressed, the amount of technical training that medical students receive has continued to increase. Medical students have branched out into specialties as a result. New doctors may have a great deal of medical knowledge, but they find themselves overwhelmed with all of the complexities of running their offices: recruiting new patients, overseeing and compensating employees, managing the accounting books of the business, avoiding lawsuits, dealing with insurance companies, and on and on.

College professors do not have the incentive to help with the problem. They do not regard it as their job to impart generalized career or money skills to students. They gain prestige and tenure (tenure means they cannot easily be fired) mostly from publishing research. Even most business schools do not teach personal finance. Giving students the many details needed to help their career is time consuming and uncompensated. It is a thankless task, although as I discuss in the Career Skills chapter, if a student actively seeks out the friendlier college professors for advice, many can be coaxed into sparing a little time to help.

Most high schools either do not teach personal finance at all, or at the level needed. This has resulted from high quality financial education and training not being available to high school teachers, who should be taught by someone with a very advanced finance education and an active knowledge of what happens in the real world. It can also be difficult for school administrators to tell if teachers are receiving bad information from so-called "professionals" who are trying to sell financial products and services. If a used car salesman teaches you about buying a car, the information learned may be the most effective way to take money out or your pocket and give it to him. For similar reasons, it is essential that finance instructors be free of conflicts of interest, including the motive to sell financial products and services. (See the beginning of the textbook for a summary of my background, and my policies regarding integrity.) Much worse, some high schools have been bamboozled by finance industry types into teaching information that is downright harmful.[1]

---

[1]I have been horrified to discover that some high schools encouraged their students to get actively involved in trading stocks. Turning students into stock-churning, fee-generating, day traders is disastrous. The schools might as well have sent them on a field trip to Las Vegas, complete with requiring them to bring bags of coins for the slots along with their bag lunches.

What has happened is, generation after generation has made the same mistakes over and over again. Basic technical training needed to manage money does not get taught. Warning signs never get put up in front of financial road hazards and dangerous drops. People fall time and again and have the financial equivalent of maiming injuries. There are people who have had their lives destroyed on every block, and nothing has been done. And if people do not know how to handle themselves financially, how can they be vigilant voters who carefully oversee the politicians who take and spend their money? It is time for a change.

1.2 What This Textbook Is Not

This textbook is not about promoting a career in "business." There is no conspiracy to talk you into putting on a three-piece suit and working at a bank. However, it is important to realize that any career requires having business skills.

Famous performers are a good example. They must sign contracts, protect their rights to their work, promote themselves through marketing campaigns, and make sure that the people who are collecting the sales proceeds pay them what is due. Some of the most successful performers have a sharp sense of business.

Oprah Winfrey is a wonderful example of what can happen when someone who is a gifted entertainer is also savvy about business. The owners of art galleries are another example, and must run their businesses in addition to being art experts. They must promote their studio, protect their inventory from theft and damage, raise money to buy new works, keep accounting books and file taxes. Philanthropists are others who must raise money, monitor how funds get spent on the needy, buy supplies such as emergency food or medicine, see that the supplies get delivered (too often powerful and corrupt people steal charitable donations and supplies), and negotiate with foreign governments. Whether you want to be an author, television news reporter, or famous artist, you will need career skills relating to business.

This textbook is not about getting rich. There are people with enormous amounts of money who are very unhappy. Others have very little money but lead satisfying lives. Focusing on the size of a bank account to the detriment of all else is a recipe for a barren existence. There is also no secret, magic formula guaranteed to make you rich. Anyone who makes claims to the contrary is trying to sell you something. Instead, you will be trained to take control of your money for your own benefit. What you will learn will help you accumulate wealth, but it is no fail-safe checklist for becoming the next Donald Trump.

This textbook is not part of a simplistic advice program. I assume that you have a very strong educational background, and that you are motivated and high achieving. I offer demanding and rigorous training in personal finance at a very high level, based on the latest academic research combined with down on the ground, part of the action, street smarts. You will also hear story after story from real life that contain lessons of value. Many will be fascinating, fun, even humorous. All are designed to impart someone else's hard earned lessons of wisdom, and to spare you from learning those same lessons the same way. Many will be inspirational.

I will not give you a set formula that you are expected to follow. Everyone has different feelings and preferences. Financial mistakes are not about wanting the wrong things. Most people like to have beautiful or valuable possessions, as well as the monetary freedom to enjoy themselves. Financial mistakes are exactly that – mistakes. They are about not knowing what is in your own interest. If you understand personal finance clearly, then you will make the best decisions given who you are.

1.3 What This Textbook Does

This textbook focuses on two main topics; career skills and personal finance. For those of you who plan on having a career, this textbook provides sophisticated principles for success. There are also a number of pitfalls that can stifle or ruin a career. Having a poor reputation is an obvious example. In this new information age we live in, this problem is of serious concern like never before.

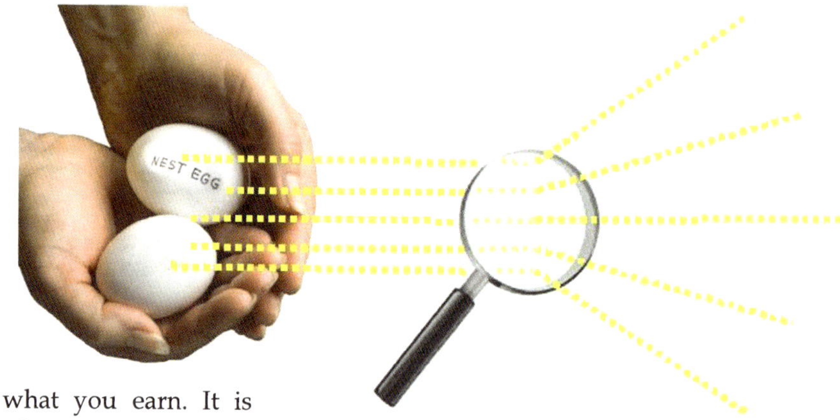

Everyone needs to know how to manage their personal finances. Clearly people of great wealth need to know how to manage their money. However, even people who have chosen to live with modest means and dedicate their lives to helping the poor need to know how to make every penny count. Regardless of who you are, if you work hard for a living you will want to make the best use of what you earn. It is remarkable that people spend long hours toiling at a career, yet give little though to the best use of their earnings. Personal finance is about magnifying whatever you have to promote your own goals and happiness.

The impact of personal financial knowledge can be enormous. It can mean the difference between being safe, comfortable, and happy, to being desperate, anguished, and living in fear. It is possible that you could earn half as much as someone else, and yet end up owning a home and retiring early, while his wealth and possessions stay stuck at a low level and he has to work in old age.

A big financial mistake can be disastrous. My students do not have to answer, but when I ask how many have made a serious financial mistake that has had a terrible effect on their lives, many hands shoot up. Another, more subtle problem occurs when people make smaller, cumulative mistakes that never get corrected over the course of their lifetime. The damage can be just as severe.

Imagine young children being sent out on their own to live. It is easy to guess what would happen. They do not know enough to take care of themselves, and they would quickly fall prey to avaricious adults. In some cases, the ill intentions of the adult would be obvious. In others, the situation would be more insidious. The child may cling tightly to someone they regard as a benefactor, who is in fact exploiting her badly. Adults with kind hearts would watch in frustration as she refused to let go.

When people leave home with good educations, they have the advantage of a great deal of knowledge that will allow them to earn a high income. However, most people never receive financial training. They work hard to earn money, but they are close to helpless, if not completely helpless, when it comes to knowing what to do with it. They accumulate a tempting pile and seek out help from people more knowledgeable than themselves — who in turn make money from them. It can be very difficult to tell if they are being helped or harmed. The situation is ripe for exploitation.

When you turn eighteen you lose many of the legal protections of a child. Taking on the concerns of an adult and leaving home also separates you from the advice and protection of your parents. As an adult, there are people who would not blink to take your money. If you are youthful and inexperienced, they will use your assumption of being protected against you. It just makes you a more appealing target. Making the situation worse, you may not be in the habit of questioning adults. However, you are legally an adult too, and must make the important transition to protecting yourself from other adults; including asking tough questions when called for.

I refer to financially dangerous predators as "WWISLS" (pronounced "whistles" for weasely, wily, smiling, liars) and they are out there. Other people are simply financial sales people. They have no idea if a financial product is good or bad for you, but are simply told what to say and what to sell. The general public also lacks financial training. Mixing this lack of training with bad practices in the finance industry is like mixing fire and gasoline. One only has to look at the mortgage crisis, which precipitated the recent financial crisis, to see the devastation that results. No fire, flood, or earthquake can compare in terms of economic damage. Thousands upon thousands have lost their homes and are financially destroyed. Banks became destabilized, leading to the greater financial crisis and mass unemployment that has harmed everyone.

Some people seem to lead charmed lives. Even with modest resources they somehow always reach their goals. They grow in success and wealth, while leading a relaxed and happy existence. Others seem to be forever practicing bad alchemy. Despite enormous resources and advantages they have trouble getting what they want. They are always stressed out and struggling, and the more they struggle, the more they flounder.

Your life and career are a journey. On any journey, success depends on having a good map. A map does not dictate where you have to go, but it does help you reach your goals. A map may also open up new possibilities that you had not even considered. You may discover that what you thought was worthwhile is not, while some newly discovered opportunity is what you had really wanted after all. Journeys also involve a process of self discovery. With a really good map you can take charge. To others, you will seem to magically appear at places when there is no magic involved. You simply have a map and they do not. You will also discover special hidden places you can call your own.

This textbook will also teach you mathematical formulas and how to use spreadsheets. The reward will be understanding the underpinnings of the financial activities that you undertake, rather than having to rely on someone else. What seems mysterious and complicated to most others will be clear. You will also have powerful tools for planning and anticipating where you are headed. Nothing is guaranteed in life. But having a map will give you a much better idea of what to expect and a plan for where you will end up.

A guidebook is also a powerful tool. There is tremendous wisdom to be found in the tales of difficulty and success of those who have travelled the same terrain that you are about to cover. What an advantage it is to be able to call upon the lessons learned, and the experiences gained of those who have gone before. I will never forget visiting the Accademia Gallery in Florence, Italy. I had read in a guidebook that upon request, they would give a discreet, unadvertised tour of one of their basements. Touring that basement was one of the highlights of my entire trip. Practice drawings by Michael Angelo were sketched directly on the wall and depicted the human body at different points as it went through motion. It was a fascinating chance to look at a great master in the process of learning his craft. Without the guidebook I would have never known about the tour. I was told recently that they no longer allow tourists to visit the basement.

This textbook then, is meant to be a map and guidebook. Like a map that contains distances and elevations, mathematics is required. Like a guidebook, there are many stories and experiences. How you use it is up to you. However, instead of seceding power over your wealth to others, you will be able to keep control. When you do hire advisors for assistance, you will be able to watch them closely. After all, you will have access to much of the same knowledge and tools that they do. You will gain power over your own life. Armed with knowledge you will be a force to be reckoned with.

1.4 Topics to Be Covered

You will be amazed at how much better you understand how the world out there works after reading this textbook. You will start this journey by learning about businesses and institutions. These are the places where people earn their living and conduct their daily lives outside the home. You shall also learn about financial markets and financial securities such as stocks and bonds. Do you want to understand the news? When you are done with this textbook you will have a much better comprehension of what is being discussed about the economy. In order to understand what is happening in the world, in order to have a career and invest money for the future, it is necessary to learn the basics of businesses and institutions.

There are three chapters in the textbook that I think of as "broccoli" chapters. The first one is on tax codes. While it may not be the most pleasant of chapters, working through it will reduce suffering later. Taxes (and death) cannot be avoided. Chapter Three helps by introducing the topic in a way that makes doing taxes later a whole lot less painful.

The next topic is personal financial statements. The balance sheet gives you a "snapshot" of where you stand in terms of accumulating wealth. The income statement is a kind of progress report. Personal financial statements can also provide you with warning that you are headed for trouble. The ocean may seem very calm right before a tsunami wipes out a town. Financial statements can serve as an early warning system that trouble is heading in. Concepts such as "solvency" and "liquidity" are introduced. By tracking your solvency and liquidity, you can avoid becoming financially destitute.

The topic of "managing cash and budgeting" covers basics such as writing checks and owning bank accounts. It also goes over how to create a budget. It is a common story that when people begin working they spend way beyond their means. They are excited at receiving a paycheck, and do not understand all of the things that they need to set their money aside for. They try to imitate other people at their place of employment who are above them in rank and income. They find themselves in their mid-thirties deep in debt, with no savings and no ability to buy their own place to live. By creating a budget you are taking control of your finances. You can see what the consequences of your spending are, and you can also prioritize what is important from what is not. You will also be able to adjust your spending so that you can achieve goals that are important to you in the future. This chapter is also an opportunity to discover how you will be able to live once you leave college.

The time value of money is the foundation of personal finance. The time value of money addresses interest rates, investing in debt (including savings accounts), and borrowing. By the time you are done with the topic, you may very well understand a loan better than the employee who is offering it to you. Banks will no longer be intimidating places, but rather places to show off your knowledge. You will be able to tell how much you will accumulate in the future in savings accounts and other accounts that pay interest. You will understand the basics of mortgages. You will also be able to see through a number of abusive loan practices, and understand just how much interest you are really paying on a loan. You will be able to compare different loans and investment accounts more effectively.

The next step involves learning how to budget using Excel®. You will take into account borrowing or saving as covered in the time value of money. You will consider different scenarios and begin to learn forecasting by creating short-term forecasts of your own hypothetical finances. You will also discover the wealth-destroying consequences of borrowing to consume.

The next two chapters are the final broccoli chapters – saving for retirement and financing college. Retirement may seem like a far-off concern, but it is necessary to start saving while young in order to ensure you are not destitute in old age. Ignoring advantageous retirement plans is like throwing money away. In addition, whether you are preparing for college, or already in college, there are many strategies that can be used to finance college, and anyone should be able to attend a good college with enough thought and effort. The next topic is long-term forecasting in Excel. This is where you will discover tools for looking into the future and seeing where you will be. You will have the chance to create a forecast of your entire life, based on possible career plans.

Most people spend money on a daily basis, often without a lot of thought. Suppose that someone earns twice as much as you do, but squanders half their money on things that they do not really value. You spend every dime in the most effective way possible. As a practical matter, you are both just as wealthy. Personal finance is not just about how money comes in; it is also about how money goes out. I have developed a framework that you can use to spend money in a very effective way. Eventually this framework will become second nature when you consider spending, just like a pitcher does not consciously think about physics equations when throwing a ball. I will also show you common pitfalls involving spending.

The next topic directly addresses career skills, although many of the chapters also contain information that is helpful to your career. Many things can affect how successful you are. The chapter covers principles that can be applied anywhere; including networking, researching situations ahead of time, and finding individuals to work with that have a reputation for honesty and reliability. You will learn many savvy skills and strategies that will put you way ahead of the game.

Personal finance would not be complete without a discussion of how borrowing to invest increases risk for an investor. You shall also discover that investors are misled because investment funds borrow to invest themselves, creating misperceptions about their performance. Borrowing to invest money can also lead a person into financial distress and default.

Credit scores are collected on people. They are like a grade of your financial responsibility. When you borrow, your credit score is accessed, and the interest rate on your loan will reflect your score – if you get the loan at all. The affect on your wealth can be enormous. When you apply for a job you may be asked for your credit score and a bad score will ruin your chances. Credit scores are also used for setting rates on automobile insurance, other kinds of insurance, and a host of other activities. Not only that, bad financial mistakes can be reflected in your score for a very long time; sometimes, forever.

Financial distress is a traumatic event. It is also a major reason for divorce and even suicide. Most people do not realize how prevalent it is because people do not talk about it. The chapter on financial distress refers to it as "dark matter" and discusses how to avoid financial distress, as well as the best ways to cope with the situation.

Identity theft involves someone taking out financial transactions in your name for the purpose of stealing. Your credit score and good name can be destroyed. Someone who is accused or convicted of a crime may even pretend to be you, and could cause you to get arrested. The identity theft chapter covers a number of good habits to develop to avoid identity theft, as well as steps to be taken if you are a victim. I finish with a discussion of maintaining a good public appearance, and the many ways that your appearance to the public can be permanently marred. I also discuss strategies on making yourself look as good as possible to potential employers, college admissions officers, the public, your community, and your family.

1.5 Conclusion

You are beginning a journey that will take you far. Hopefully, this textbook will give you a big head start. While everyone else is lining up at the starting line, you will begin halfway down the track.

This text book will also help you build your life's story one chapter at a time. Make it a masterpiece full of adventure, and be sure to bring your financial roadmap and enjoy the ride.

Note: The people depicted in photographs throughout the book are models, and not the actual people being referred to in the text. Many photographs were also modified to suit the situation being discussed. To see if a picture has been modified, refer to the book appendix.

THE FINANCIAL
ENVIRONMENT

Chapter 2

Businesses, Institutions, & Financial Securities and Markets

The underpinnings of daily life involve interacting with businesses and institutions. This can include anything from buying groceries to attending college. If you plan on a career, much of your day will be spent working as an owner or employee. You may not think of yourself as a future business person, but most professions require organized businesses. Whether you dream of owning your own art gallery, starting a philanthropic foundation, becoming an author, or leading a multinational bank, businesses and institutions provide the architecture on which these dreams are built.

2.1 Companies and Institutions

I will start with a discussion of businesses, which vary in size and what they sell, whether it is products, services, or information. Businesses also vary in how they are controlled, and how they are treated by law.

All businesses are owned by someone, but what does ownership imply? Having ownership suggests that those who own the business make profits or lose money according to how their business does. Ownership also gives them say over how the business is operated. However, as you shall observe, this is not so simple. Large public corporations can have thousands of owners, many of whom do not follow the day-to-day operations of the business. These owners rely on elected representatives, called a board of directors, to see that the managers who run the firm act in the company's best interests.

Owners have placed their own money into their business, but they need to develop patience because the company's earnings go to pay many expenses first. Employees must be compensated, taxes paid, suppliers who provided goods or services to the business reimbursed, and creditors repaid that made loans to the company. The owner is last in line. Only when everyone else is paid does the owner receive any profit that is left.

Loans to the business are also referred to as debt and involve the owner or manager of the business signing a contract (which is a legal agreement) with the person or company making the loan, referred to as a "creditor. "The contract between the two specifies when the money needs to be paid back, and the timing and size of interest payments. Interest is the profit that a lender makes from lending to the company. The contract may have other restrictions as well, referred to as "covenants." An example may be that the owner cannot increase their own salary until the debt is paid off. Although creditors cannot tell the owner what to do — the owner still makes the decisions — the owner is bound by the debt contract. Failing to meet the contract could result in the business ending up in court, referred to as going bankrupt, and the company being taken away from the owner and given to the creditors. The company can also sell debt contracts called bonds, which companies or individuals buy. The buyer is in effect making a loan to the company when they buy the bonds, i.e., the company receives money when they sell the bonds, and are required to pay money back at some point, just like with loans.

Strange Facts

When someone starts a business the concept usually grows out of a successful hobby, is related to a skill or knowledge the owner has, or fills a need in the market. Items or services sold generally support each other in order to appeal to the same customer base and increase sales.

So what were they thinking?[2]

- *Mapleton Taxidermy and Cheese Store* (Ontario, Canada)
- *Porter's Fireworks and Firewater* - Liquor and Fireworks (Evanston, WY)
- *Wimbrough & Sons* - Septic Tanks – Burial Vaults (Portsmouth, VA)
- *Dave's Soda and Pet City* (Springfield, MA)
- *Video Magic* – Movies and Tanning (Marietta, OK)
- *Cadwell's Ice Cream, Cadwell's Towing Service* (Marshall, MO)
- *Auto Vendors* – Cars and Pool Tables (Visalia, CA)
- *Golf Ball Outlet and Fireworks Megastore* (Hardeeville, SC)
- *King Arthur's Barber Shop and Shoe Repair* (Jacksonville, FL)

Basic Issues of Ownership

In order to understand the types of businesses that exist, it is necessary to understand basic issues of ownership. The first issue has to do with something called "limited liability." Take the owner of a hotdog stand. It turns out that very harmful bacteria called salmonella were in the hotdogs that the owner bought from a supplier. The owner was unaware that the hotdogs had salmonella. He cooked them and sold them to customers. One of those customers became very sick and lost function in one kidney. The customer sued the owner in court for damage to his health, and a jury found the owner liable (required to pay the person suing; known as the "claimant"). The damages the owner was required to pay equaled $400,000. The hotdog stand was only worth $20,000. The owner's house was taken away from him, as was his car, and all his other property, which did not add up to the total of $400,000. To make up the difference, the owner's wages were "garnished," meaning that if he works for a company, a percent of his wages will be taken away and given to the claimants.

This owner did not have limited liability. With limited liability, the claimants would only have been able to take the hotdog stand. They would not have been able to take the owner's personal assets (property) such as the house and car, and they could not have garnished his wages. Clearly, limited liability would have been very advantageous to the owner.

Another issue that owners face is taxes. With some kinds of businesses, federal and state governments take a percent of the profits as business taxes; however, the government is not finished. When the profits of the business get paid to the owner, the owner then has to give a percentage of this profit to the government in the form of personal taxes. This is referred to as "double taxation." The same dollar of earnings of the business is taxed twice. Other businesses have something called "flow-through" taxation. In this case, the business is not taxed at all. Rather, the

2 From http://www.11points.com/Personal-Misc/11_Businesses_Selling_Two_Hilariously_Unconnected_Items; http://www.waymarking.com/waymarks/WM5BEA_Golf_Ball_Outlet_and_Fireworks_Megastore_Hardeeville_SC.

owner of the business pays personal taxes on the earnings of the business. Clearly, flow-through taxation is a major advantage.

Businesses also face differences in who can be an owner, and therefore, who can fund the company (give the company money). In some types of businesses just about anyone can be an owner, while in other businesses, some categories of institutions are excluded. "Institution" refers to an organization of some kind that is considered important to society. Colleges are referred to as educational institutions. A financial institution is a company that is involved in the functioning of the financial markets in an important way. An example could be an insurance company, which protects people or businesses. They take payments from people or businesses, and if a bad event called a "hazard" specified in the insurance contract happens, the insurance company gives the person or business a payment. An example is life insurance. If the person specified in the contract dies, their designated beneficiary receives the insurance payment.

Banks are considered financial institutions. They take cash deposits from customers, as well as borrowing money from others, and lend the money to individuals and businesses. They are highly regulated by the government.[3] These are just a few of the many examples of institutions. Owners typically wish to have access to as many institutional investors as they can because they can benefit from the large sums of money that institutional investors control. Therefore, they may shy away from forming as a type of business entity that is not allowed to have institutional investors.[4]

Owners As Shareholders

Some owners control businesses directly, while other businesses have owners who are shareholders. Those shareholders purchase stock in the company. Owners are said to have "equity" in their companies. Corporations sell stock certificates (shares) to the public, and then people or businesses buy and sell the shares of stock among themselves. Stock certificates typically give shareholders one vote per certificate.[5] Shareholders vote for the board of directors, who are their elected representatives. The "board" oversees the managers who run the business and are required by law to act in the company's interest. The company's interest is generally interpreted to be the shareholders' (owners') interest, although there may be exceptions to this.[6] When the company makes profits, the shareholders are entitled to these profits, typically in proportion to how many shares they own. However, the managers of the company may choose to keep the profits inside the company to invest in the business. Shareholders face less risk than many direct owners in businesses because they have limited liability. This may come as small consolation to someone who put all of their life savings into one stock, only to have it become worthless.

---

[3] Although some would argue that given the current financial crisis, banks were not regulated enough.

[4] Another example of an institutional investor is a pension fund, which holds people's savings for retirement and pays people recurring payments called a "'pension" in retirement. State employee pension funds such as California's, called CALPERS, are quite large. College endowments (money donated to colleges from philanthropists) are another example of an institutional investor.

[5] As you shall learn, this is not always the case.

[6] This issue is controversial. Some argue that the company's interest can diverge from the shareholders' interest in the eyes of the law. However, there are numerous reasons why self-interested boards may not act in the shareholders' interests (or the "company" for that matter), and corresponding examples to point to.

Key Takeaway: Business owners come in many varieties. Some directly control their business, while others are shareholders and vote for a board of directors to oversee management. Owners make or lose money with the business and are the last ones to get paid. With some kinds of businesses there are two layers of tax, known as double taxation. First the business is taxed, and then the owners get taxed on any money that they receive. Other businesses have only a single layer of tax, known as flow-through taxation. Just the owners pay taxes. Limited liability protects the owners of some businesses, but not others. Limited liability means that if the company is sued, the owners' personal assets cannot be taken.

Legal Business Entities

After having established principles of ownership in businesses, I can now proceed to how the law defines businesses. Keep in mind that the laws governing businesses vary from state to state, therefore it matters in which state a business is established (incorporated) under the law. Owners can decide under which legal form they wish to establish their business and in which state.[7] They can also change the incorporation of their business, which may be more or less difficult depending on their current incorporation.

C Corporations

A "C corporation" is typically a large company whose stock is traded in the stock market. Some examples would be Google Inc. and Apple Inc. An unlimited number of people can own shares in a typical C corporation, including people with very little money, and almost all C corporations have investors who are not considered to be "qualified investors" in the eyes of the law. It is possible that uneducated, low income individuals have their entire life savings invested in a C company. Therefore the government goes to great lengths to protect shareholders, particularly from self-interested managers of the business who may mislead shareholders, harm the business, or even steal.

The person in charge of board meetings is called the chairman of the board. The board is elected by the shareholders and is supposed to monitor the managers of the company. The top manager in charge of running the company is called the chief executive officer (CEO). The CEO is often the chairman of the board as well. This may pose a conflict of interest, because the CEO may act in their own interest as a company manager, while their position on the board requires that they act on behalf of shareholders to monitor managers. (Conflicts of interest are a recurring problem in the financial world, and are important in the law as well. I shall discuss this in detail when I cover the role of financial advisors in Volume 2.) The person below the CEO who is in charge of the financial activities of the company is called the chief financial officer (CFO). Table 2-1 summarizes ownership in a C corporation, along with other business forms under the law (which will be discussed shortly).

C corporations have limited liability. Otherwise, we would see far less trading of stocks in the stock markets because investors who may buy the shares would be worried that they could have their personal assets taken away in a lawsuit. (It would be ill-advised to buy the shares without investigating the company thoroughly first.) However, C corporations do have two layers of tax. The corporation's profits are taxed, and then any profits distributed to shareholders are taxed again at the personal level.

[7] Although in practice it can be difficult to incorporate in a state in which the business does not reside.

Table 2-1
Legal Corporate Entities

Business Form	C Corporation	S Corporation	Sole Proprietorship/ Partnership	Limited Liability Company (LLC)
Limited Liability	Yes	Yes	No	Yes, theoretically. Uncertain in practice.
Flow Through Taxation	No	Yes	Yes	Yes
Ownership Restrictions?	No, typically with non-accredited investors, some exceptions	Yes, typically with accredited investors	No	No
Costly or Difficult?	No to some extent, but mostly yes	No	Yes	Yes
Institutional Ownership?	Yes	No	No	Yes

An important advantage of a C corporation is that institutions can own shares in a C corporation, which gives the company access to a very large source of funding. Another advantage is that just about anyone can own shares in a C corporation. To own shares just requires a call to a stockbroker (to be discussed later) who will buy them on your behalf. There are some exceptions: a foreigner cannot own a large amount of shares in a defense contractor or in a company that is considered vital to U.S. interests.

C Corporation Regulations

C corporations are simple in that it is easy to become an owner in a C corporation, but that is where the simplicity ends. C corporations are heavily regulated. For instance, they are required to file quarterly reports with the Securities and Exchange Commission, known as the SEC. The SEC oversees the activities of publicly traded companies in relation to their stocks and bonds. Company reports have to be signed by accounting auditors, which can be a very expensive process. Auditors certify that the financial statements detailing the financial condition of the company are correct. These financial statements are then made available to investors and the general public.

C corporations are required to submit reports to the shareholders, known as proxy statements, once a year before the annual shareholders' meeting. Shareholders meet once a year to vote on the board of directors and certain important matters of the company that may arise from time to time, such as issuing new stock or merging with another company.

C corporations also have to publish "prospectuses" when they sell new financial securities to the public in the form of extra stock certificates or bonds. Prospectuses describe the condition of the company and give the intended use of any money raised. There is also a law known as "fair disclosure." Fair disclosure requires that if managers have something important to say about the company, they have to make what they say available to all the shareholders at the same time. This prevents some shareholders from having an advantage over other shareholders by having quicker access to information. There are also many rules that a corporate board has to follow in order for the stock to be listed on a stock exchange.

To make things even more complicated, the Sarbanes-Oxley Act has many requirements for corporations. Sarbanes-Oxley or "SOX" was enacted in response to the Enron scandal.[8] Top managers are also required to report to the SEC when they buy or sell shares in the company, and they are not allowed to trade if they know important information about the company that is not publicly known. Otherwise, they could be convicted of insider trading which is considered a felony.

Wal-Mart Stores, Inc.

Sam Walton (1918-1992) started with a single store in 1962 and soon added additional stores as part of a franchise arrangement. He hired his brother Bud to be his first assistant manager paying him around $50 a month, poverty wages even then.

Walton left the franchise arrangement to become more independent. On the opening day of his store in Springfield, Missouri, he used an outdoor display of a mountain of watermelons and donkey rides for the children to entice new customers. It was an excessively hot day and soon the watermelons began to burst, and the donkeys did what donkeys do! Before long the parking lot was covered in watermelons and donkey-doo.[9]

In spite of that fiasco, Sam Walton continued adding stores. Wal-Mart incorporated October 31, 1969, and began to be publicly traded (to be discussed below) in 1970. They had over 400 billion in sales in 2008.

For several reasons Wal-Mart has become a controversial company. People believe that when Wal-Mart stores open, they hire employees at lower wages, and force smaller, local businesses to close. They also believe that Wal-Mart changes local cultures by importing American culture into other parts of the world when they move in. However, customers and employees have their own view, because people line up to shop and apply for jobs at Wal-Mart. The Wal-Mart Corporation is now one of the largest corporations in the world.

S Corporations

S corporations are similar to C corporations in that they issue shares, but they are required to be closely held. Only 100 investors can own shares in an S corporation. This can be a disadvantage because the company has limited ability to find new investors. However, the benefit is that they get flow-through taxation. And typically, they require their investors to be considered qualified legally, also known as being "accredited." The idea behind accredited investors is that if owners are able to absorb losses, then they do not need the protections that unqualified investors need. Therefore, it is not necessary for the government to saddle a corporation with all of the costly regulations that

[8] Enron went bankrupt and was handed over to its creditors who suffered large losses. The stock became worthless. Many employees lost their jobs. A number of Enron employees had their retirement savings in Enron stock, which became worthless as well. The CEO and CFO were found guilty of committing fraud and sent to jail. The chairman of the board was charged with fraud, but he died before he could be tried.

[9] http://walmartstores.com/AboutUs/288.aspx

corporations otherwise have. S corporations typically require their investors to be accredited in order to avoid costly regulations. There are a number of rules for becoming an accredited investor. For individuals, they have to have net worth (to be explained later – a measure of wealth) of $1 million, or make at least $200,000 per year. Finally, S corporations have limited liability, just like C corporations.

Partnerships and Sole Proprietorships

A partnership is very different from a C corporation or S corporation. In order to start a partnership you simply have to get together with a friend and open your doors for business. (Of course, you have to register your business with numerous government agencies just like any business). You own equity and control the company directly, rather than owning shares. A sole proprietorship is simply when you start a business by yourself and it is like a partnership. Sole proprietorships and partnerships do not have limited liability and the personal assets of the owners are at risk if the company gets sued. They do have flow-through taxation. Any person can start a partnership, although some professions impose their own limitations on who can be a partner. For instance, in the legal profession only lawyers can be partners at a law firm.

It sounds like it would be simple to start a partnership; however, this is not the case. There are many things that the partners need to agree on ahead of time. For instance, what if one partner wants to retire before the other one does? How would they handle such a situation? Another situation to worry about is what would happen if one of the partners dies. Would the surviving spouse be allowed to participate in the business? What would happen to the ownership stake of the deceased? Would the surviving partner sell off the business and give the deceased partner's proceeds to the surviving spouse, or continue to run the business alone and decide when profits are paid out? If the partners do not agree on a myriad of issues in advance and write them down in a legal document, they could end up suing each other for years. A surviving spouse could also be left destitute. There are standard contracts which can make it easier for the partners to come to an agreement in an economical way. Institutions cannot form partnerships, although they can form something called a "joint venture."

Limited Liability Companies

S corporations are like C corporations because the owners hold stock. Similarly, limited liability companies (LLCs) are like partnerships because they are owned directly. LLCs have an advantage over partnerships because they have limited liability. However, this must be taken with a grain of salt. In some states, with California being an example, judges are notorious for stripping the owners of an LLC of their limited liability. The owner thinks they are protected, but the business gets sued and the judge decides that the owner's assets are available to the person suing. A common reason this happens is because the owners mix their private lives with their business. An example would be using the same bank account to pay for business expenses and personal expenses. It is very important for owners of an LLC to keep their business activities completely separate from their personal activities.

Although there are no restrictions on who can start an LLC, they are not simple for the same reason that partnerships are not simple. Institutional ownership in an LLC is discouraged but not impossible.

The Chocolate Factory [10]

At 3-years old, Elise Macmillan stood next to her grandmother and learned how to make candy. Instead of just a fun childhood project, it became a serious endeavor of the little girl's to experiment making great chocolates. Her mother would find celery sticks in the microwave with bits of chocolate chips melted on top.

When Elise was 10, children were given the opportunity to sell their wares at a local marketplace in Denver. People loved her confections and she began receiving phone orders for more. Her brother Evan, thirteen-years-old, knew something about computers and developed a business plan for them and a website. They borrowed $5,000 and set up a business in the family kitchen. Elise's candies were made in the images of farm animals, like pigs in mud, and they called it The Chocolate Farm. By the time she was sixteen, they had moved into a large facility and were grossing $1 million a year and had 40 employees.

As of the date of this writing, their website has only one line: "We've been acquired! For questions, please email questions @ chocolatefarm." (Owners often dream of their business being acquired by a company that has lots of cash, sometimes getting rich in the process.)

Nonprofits

A final type of business is called a "nonprofit." These kinds or organizations are not formed to provide profits to the owners. Rather they have some other purpose for society, often associated with charity. They are not allowed to pay out profits, but retain their profits inside the company for use in furthering their goals. Some are controlled by "members" who vote on candidates for the board while others are controlled directly by a board, without member votes. Nonprofits must apply to the IRS to be considered a nonprofit for tax purposes. If the IRS approves of the purpose of the nonprofit, the earnings of the nonprofit are not subject to income tax as long as these earnings come from the approved purpose. However, nonprofits may be subject to other kinds of tax. Foundations are typically thought of as having investment funds that they donate to other charities, although the word "foundation" can be applied to any nonprofit.

Challenge

Think about a hobby or skill, and create an idea for a business. Would you choose a corporation, a partnership, sole proprietorship, or nonprofit? What would be the advantages and disadvantages? Just for fun, what two ideas would you pair to create a business and why?

[10] "Generation Next: Elise & Evan Macmillan, 14 & 16," http://www.entrepreneur.com/magazine/entrepreneursstartupsmagazine/2002/may/51398-11.html; Al Lewis, "Why Russell Stover plowed the Chocolate Farm," May 17, 2006, http://blogs.denverpost. com/lewis/2006/05/17/why-russell-stover-plowed-the-chocolate-farm; Thomas Fields-Meyer, "Teen Titans," People, Nov. 08, 2004, http://www.people.com/ people/archive/article/0,,20145944,00.html; http://www.chocolatefarm.com.

Table 2-2 lists the world's largest businesses.

Table 2-2
The World's Largest Companies

Rank	Company	Country	Industry
1	General Electric	United States	Multiple Businesses (Conglomerate)
2	Royal Dutch Shell	Netherlands	Petroleum
3	Toyota Motor	Japan	Automobiles and Trucks
4	ExxonMobil	United States	Petroleum
5	BP	Britian	Petroleum
6	HSBC Holdings	Britian	Banking
7	AT&T	United States	Telecommunications Services
8	Wal-Mart Stores	United States	Retail Stores
9	Banco Santander	Spain	Banking
9	Chevron	United States	Petroleum
11	Total	France	Petroleum
12	ICBC	China	Banking
13	Gazprom	Russia	Petroleum
14	PetroChina	China	Petroleum
15	Volkswagen Group	Germany	Automobiles and Trucks

Source: *Forbes* "The Global 2000" Special Report, April 8, 2009, http://www.forbes.com/lists/2009/18/global-09_The-Global-2000_Rank.html, accessed May 25, 2009.

Challenge

The biggest companies tend to be in certain, specific industries. Why those industries? What sort of challenges do you think would be associated with running companies of this size? What kind of business entity would you expect them to be?

Saving Feet

In Ethiopia, walking on the volcanic ash in the soil can cause a horrible foot disease called Podoconiosis. There is a single remedy to avoid this condition – shoes. In many third world countries shoes are difficult to come by, especially shoes that fit. Blake Mycoskie planned to give 300,000 pairs of shoes away in 2009 to needy children, but there was a catch – he needed to sell just as many.

Blake wears colored strings around his wrists to signify the third world countries to which he's traveled. With his handsome, grunge, actor-like looks and unruly brown hair, the barely 30 year-old entrepreneur decided to use his skills to make money as a way to help people. He started college as a tennis player, but injured his Achilles tendon. Eventually Blake created businesses such as a door-to-door laundry service for college students, a company in Nashville targeted to the music industry, and ventures in reality television and online drivers' training.

In 2006 Blake travelled to Argentina to learn polo, and two things caught his attention while there. For at least 100 years farmers had been wearing Alpargata, a traditional rope-soled shoe. The other was the poverty-stricken, bare-foot children with their horrible foot infections from cuts and bruises. He returned to LA with 200 pairs of shoes and an idea – to create a company that would allow him to give away one pair of shoes for every pair sold. From his apartment in Venice, California, he sold 10,000 shoes and then later that year returned to Argentina to give away 10,000 pairs. The company then setup headquarters in Santa Monica, California.

After that, Blake learned about the foot disease in Ethiopia and has expanded his efforts. In the 3 short years of TOMS Shoes existence, the business has already given away over 140,000 pairs of shoes.[11]

Key Takeaway: There are many ways to form a business, with important advantages and disadvantages to consider. Some offer tax advantages, while others have limited liability. Each form of business presents its own challenges in terms of complexity, and the ability to raise money from investors to grow.

---

[11] "Gratis Internet CEO Rob Jewell Attends Annual Summit Series – Recognized as a Top Entrepreneur under 35," Nov. 26, 2008, http://www.gratisinternet.com/Press/Release/?13; "Blake Mycoskie," The Huffington Post, http://www.huffingtonpost.com/blake-mycoskie,; "Saving the World, One Shoe at a Time," Oct. 22, 2008, http://www.huffingtonpost.com/blake-mycoskie/saving-the-world-one-shoe_b_136836.html;. "Gossip Rocks," Dec. 14, 2008, http://www.gossiprocks.com/forum/news/90958-blake-mycoskie-hes-handsome-rich-helps-children-third-world.html. Emily Lerman, "PhiLAnthropist Interview: TOMS Shoes Founder Blake Mycoskie Plans to Give Away 300,000 Pairs in 2009," LAist, Arts & Events, April 15, 2009, http://laist.com/2009/04/15/what_happens_when_you_travel.php.; TOMS Web site, http://www.tomsshoes.com/content.asp?tid=227; "Podoconiosis," http://tomsshoes.phpwebhosting.com/podo.

2.2 Financial Securities and Markets

One of the most important ways in which you can insure a prosperous future is to invest your savings wisely. The impact of investment decisions can be enormous. Where you put your money may mean the difference between financial prosperity and poverty. However, this task is a daunting one. There is a dizzying array of financial securities (also called financial instruments) that can be invested in, and the list of securities is constantly growing. In the following pages I will discuss the most common varieties, while putting off a detailed discussion of investment strategies until Volume 2.

Stocks

Shareholders receive money from a business in one of two ways. The first is by receiving dividends, which are payments by the company to the shareholders. Dividends are paid once every quarter, and are taxed at the capital gains tax rate which is currently 15% (or 5% if you have low income). The other way is for the company to buy back shares from shareholders. In this case the stockholder has to surrender the shares in order to receive money from the company. When a stockholder sells shares, they will sell them above or below what they paid for them. If they sell them for more than they paid for them, they have made a profit and have what is called a capital gain. If the stock was held for more than a year, they pay the capital gains rate. If the stock was held for less than a year, capital gains are taxed at the personal income tax rate which can be as high as 35% in 2010. If the stock is sold for less than what was paid for it, there is a "capital loss." I shall discuss the tax treatment of capital gains and losses in further detail in the next chapter.

Are you a bull or a bear? Bulls are optimistic about the stock markets, while bears are pessimistic. Should emotion be a part of investing?

Sometimes there are preferred shareholders. They are referred to as preferred because they get paid before common shareholders (but after creditors). Just like with common shareholders, if there is not enough money the company can simply decide not to pay dividends, but they have to cut the common dividend before they can cut the preferred dividend. Unlike with common shareholders, the preferred shareholders typically receive a fixed dividend, which can be an advantage in down times.[12] However, when times are good, the company will only raise the dividend for the common shareholders, who get the leftovers. If a company defaults on its debt, during bankruptcy proceedings the court is supposed to see to it that the creditors get paid first, then the preferred shareholders if there are any, then finally the common shareholders, who often get nothing.

Stockbrokers conduct stock transactions for a fee on behalf of the investors who hire them. If you wish to trade stocks or other securities, you will have to contact a stockbroker. Stockbrokers have to pass an exam given by the government called a Series 7 exam, and acquire a license. Currently, stockbrokers do not have a fiduciary duty to their clients, although there is currently a proposed regulation to change this. "Fiduciary duty" means that they have to put

[12] "Participating" preferred is an exception. Preferred dividends are increased in tandem with common dividends.

their clients' interests above their own. Other advisors, such as personal tax accountants and financial advisors, are considered to have a fiduciary duty.

Stocks can be traded on stock exchanges, or in the over-the-counter market. Stock exchanges are physical locations where stock is traded among individuals or companies. These trades do not involve the company that originally issued the stock.[13] Therefore, when investors trade it is referred to as the "secondary market." This is like people buying and selling used cars. The original company that made the car has nothing to do with the resale. The "primary market" is when the company sells shares to investors. This is like buying a new car from the car manufacturer.

When a stock is traded on an exchange, it is said that the stock is "listed" on the exchange. The exchange has to agree to have the stock listed. The best known stock exchange in the United States is the NYSE Euronext in New York City. Most of the stocks of the largest companies are traded there. The NASDAQ is an electronic exchange where brokers are connected by a computer network. Companies traded on the NASDAQ tend to be smaller in size, but there are more of them. The NASDAQ sets rules for how stocks can be listed and traded over their network. In response to competition from the NASDAQ and other electronic exchanges, the NYSE Euronext also began to offer electronic trading. The over-the-counter market involves networks of stockbrokers and dealers who buy and sell unlisted stocks.

Stock exchanges set rules for how listed companies will be governed. For instance, they will have rules for the board of directors, including the need to have outsiders oversee CEO compensation and financial statement reporting. The Securities and Exchange Commission (SEC) oversees the process of companies selling stock to investors, the trading of stock among investors, and the activities of stock exchanges.

Debt

There are two different types of debt. The first type is negotiated between the company and an individual, or with another company such as an insurance company or bank. The lender gives the company money and specifies when the money has to be returned. When the company returns the money that was lent, it is considered to be returning "principal," which is not taxed. The company also pays the lender interest, which is extra money so that the lender can make a profit. Interest paid to individuals is taxed at the personal income tax rate. If the money is paid to a corporation, it pays the corporate income tax rate. This type of lending can be very flexible, and the terms of the loan, including restrictions on the part of the borrower called "debt covenants," can be negotiated.

Bonds

Another type of debt involves selling bonds, which are simply debt contracts offered by the company. Debt contracts can also be called "debt instruments." The company decides on what to put in the contract, including terms of payment and restrictive covenants. The company then sells the bonds, and the price they receive will depend on how much investors like the terms in the contract. When the buyer pays for the bonds, they are in effect lending the company money with the price of the bond as the loan amount. This is also true of other kinds of debt. (When a company signs a debt contract, they are in effect selling it like a bond, and the loan amount is the price received.) When a bond finally gets paid off, it is said to have "matured."[14] (Stocks do not mature, and could theoretically be held in the markets forever.) Bonds have to be registered with the SEC.[15] Loans are not overseen by the SEC, which can be an advantage.

[13] Although sometimes the company may go to the stock market to buy back shares.
[14] There are rare instances of bonds that never mature.
[15] An exception to this is if the bonds are sold in a "private placement" to a select group of institutions.

The federal government also borrows money, and is in fact the biggest borrower in the world. Particularly large sums of debt are owed to Japan and China. Federal government debt is typically considered very safe because the federal government can either tax people or print money to pay off their debt, although there have been startling discussions of late that the safety of federal government debt may be in some doubt. One type of federal debt is called a "treasury bond," "treasury note," or "treasury" for short. These bonds have a maturity ranging from one month to thirty years. Maturities of less than one year are called T-bills. Maturities over a year to ten years are called T-notes, and maturities over ten years are called T-Bonds. States and local governments are not allowed to tax the interest investors receive from U.S. treasuries.

There are also GSEs (government sponsored enterprises) and other types of quasi-government agencies (hybrid government-private organizations) that borrow money. GSEs are not officially part of the government, but implicitly have the backing of the government in investors' eyes. Fannie Mae and Freddie Mac are examples of GSEs. They buy mortgages, which are loan contracts signed by home owners that contain a promise to pay, and resell them to investors with a guarantee that they will pay the investor if the homeowner defaults on the mortgage. Those guarantees became a problem when defaults on mortgages started rising recently. In the current financial crisis, Fannie and Freddie were given bailout money by the federal government to keep them solvent (out of bankruptcy). I shall discuss their role in the financial crises in more detail in a later chapter.

State and local governments also borrow money. The bonds they issue are called municipal bonds and are not taxed by the federal government. They are often not taxed at the local level as well. Municipal bonds ("munis") typically have a company that guarantees payment to investors. This is called a third party guarantee. If the municipal government defaults on the bonds the third party has to come up with the payment. Historically, municipal bonds have been considered to be very safe. However, in the current financial crisis municipal governments are having trouble raising the money that they need because of political resistance to raising taxes, and a lack of investor confidence in third party guarantees.

The Money Market and the Capital Market

The "money market" refers to debt that matures in a year or less. Traditionally, the money market has been considered to be very safe. The reason for this is that investors in the money market do not like taking risks and will only buy debt that is very safe. (Often companies will temporarily invest money that they need to pay their employees or their taxes. That money earns interest during the short time it goes unused. Companies are unwilling to take risks with that money.) Historically, defaults on debt in the money market have been rare. However, during the current financial crisis, money market instruments affected by mortgage defaults began to fail, causing the money market to virtually shut down.

The capital market is debt that matures in over a year, and stocks which do not mature. This is where long-term funding comes from. Debt in this market can be riskier, as are stocks. In fact, the stock in a company is always riskier than the debt because the debt gets paid first. There are rating agencies that rate the likelihood of bonds defaulting. During the current financial crisis these rating agencies came under criticism for not predicting the high default rate of bonds backed by mortgages.

Mutual Funds

Investors can buy shares in mutual funds, which take money from investors and buy a variety of stocks, bonds, and other financial investments. Each share an investor owns entitles him to a portion of the profits. Mutual funds offer investors the option to buy shares in different portfolios (groups of securities), such as a portfolio that tracks stocks in the S&P 500 index. S&P 500 corporations are very large companies that Standard and Poor's Company chooses to include in their large 500 company index. An index tracks how a theoretical portfolio of stocks in the index would perform. There are a number of indices that companies promote. For instance, Dow Jones & Company has an index of large companies called the "Dow Jones Industrial Average Index." Mutual funds also put together other kinds of portfolios, such as portfolios of T-bills, corporate bonds, and stocks in mature companies, energy companies, foreign companies, etc.

Some mutual funds allow investors to buy the mutual fund's shares directly. This enables investors to avoid having to contact a broker and consequently pay extra fees. Mutual fund shares can only be bought and sold once a day, which makes them less liquid than stock, which can be traded frequently throughout the day. (Liquidity refers to the ability to easily sell something quickly, and will be discussed in a later chapter.) However, mutual funds make it easy to own an interest in a large number of securities at once. This is referred to as "diversification", and is an important investing principle. By diversifying you are not just relying on a few companies, which can lower your risk substantially. (I will spend a considerable amount of time on this in Volume 2.) Without mutual funds, investors must acquire securities individually, and can accumulate substantial brokerage fees to obtain a diversified portfolio. Mutual funds reduce this expense by creating one large portfolio that individuals can own a share in.

Derivatives and Futures

Derivatives are complex financial instruments whose value depends on another security. A stock is not a derivative. Its value comes from an ownership stake in a company. A stock option is a derivative. A stock option is a contract that gives someone the right to buy or sell a specific stock in the future at a set price. An option's value comes from another security – the stock, and it is therefore a derivative. There are many derivatives. For instance, "collateralized debt obligations" (CDOs) that get their value from mortgages have been pointed to as being at the heart of the current financial crisis. Futures (and forward) contracts involve an agreement to buy commodities or financial securities in the future. Some are based on indices. There is a large variety of possible futures commodities and indices, including frozen orange juice, pork bellys (bacon), gold, oil, agricultural products, housing indices, etc. Futures are traded on futures exchanges. I will put off a discussion of derivatives and futures until Volume 2.

Hedge funds are big investors in derivates and futures. Hedge funds only have qualified investors. In fact, the idea behind a hedge fund is similar to the idea behind an S corporation. Hedge funds are not saddled with all of the regulations that mutual funds have because their investors are qualified. Investors in hedge funds are required to commit to keep their money in the fund for a substantial amount of time. In addition to funding from these equity investors, hedge funds borrow heavily and buy a variety of securities, including very risky ones. They may pursue very complex strategies, and rely on intricate mathematical modeling. They have been very loosely regulated in the past. However, there is a push to have them register with the SEC and receive regular examinations, as well as face restrictions on their activities. There are also mutual funds that own portfolios of hedge funds, giving access to smaller, non-qualified investors. Whether this is a good idea remains controversial.

Private Investments

Wealthier individuals and institutions can invest in various organizations that fund private businesses. Venture capital is an example. Venture capitalists (VCs) receive funding from investors, which they use to take ownership stakes in new businesses. Typically, an entrepreneur will get money from "friends and family" such as college buddies, fathers-in-law, etc. However, this money can quickly dry up. The next step is to try to convince an "angel investor" to contribute money in return for an ownership stake. An angel investor is simply a wealthy individual who likes to tinker in new businesses. When this money runs out, the next step is to go to a venture capitalist. Venture capitalists often specialize in funding new businesses at different stages of their life. A number of their business may not work, but they are hoping that the ones that succeed will earn tremendous amounts of money like an Apple. Some may fund very new startups, while others fund businesses that are nearly ready to go public. ("Going public" refers to a private business selling stock for the first time and becoming a publicly traded corporation. Their initial stock sale is referred to as an initial public offering, or "IPO.")

Venture capitalists demonstrate that financial firms specialize. In their case, they are specialists at recognizing good business ideas, and helping new businesses take shape and find customers. They like to take their companies that are successful public, because they are not interested in running a more mature, developed business. (Financial institutions in general have specialties.) Finally, it is important for an entrepreneur to realize that each time they ask for more funding from a venture capitalist, the VC takes a larger ownership stake in the company. The entrepreneur may end up owning very little of the company they founded by the time they are done!

Private equity firms borrow heavily, and also receive funding from equity investors to acquire the public stock of companies. They are doing the reverse of an IPO, in that they are taking a public company private by buying up the stock. They can also invest in already private businesses. Once they acquire a business they try to improve the business to make a profit. Perversely, some private equity companies have themselves been going public lately.

How Can You Be Fired from Your Own Company?

Steve started college, but then decided to demonstrate an independent streak, so he dropped out – so that he could "drop in." By dropping in he was free from required courses and able to attend the classes that truly excited and interested him. He didn't have money for a dorm room, so he slept on the floor in the rooms of his friends and picked up food money from turning in soda bottles. One of the courses that interested him turned out to be calligraphy, where he learned all about the beauty of sans and sans serif fonts and the history of typography – a skill with seemingly limited career opportunities.

In his parents' garage, at the age of 20, Steve Jobs and Steve Wozniak started Apple – and that interest in fonts and typography became the heart of the design of the computer. After ten years of hard work and the assistance of an angel investor, Apple grew to be a $2 billion company with over 4,000 employees.

A year later, at the age of 30, after they had just released what Jobs felt was their finest creation, the Macintosh, he was fired. He had hired someone to run the company with him, but the two of them had a difference of opinion about the future of the company, and the Apple board of directors sided with the other guy. An often unpleasant shock to company founders is that when a company becomes public, the shareholders are the owners, and the founder becomes – a mere employee.

Jobs was devastated and publicly humiliated. Everyone knew that he been deposed from his own company, and he felt like he had failed the previous generation of entrepreneurs by dropping the baton that they had passed to him.

After awhile, Steve realized that this was still what he loved to do and so he started over. In the next five years he created Next and Pixar. Pixar created the first animated computer film "Toy Story"® and is the most successful animation studio in the world. In an amazing turn of events, Apple bought Next and Jobs returned to Apple.[16]

[16] Steve Jobs, speaking at Stanford University commencement, http://www.evancarmichael.com.

> ***Key Takeaway:*** There are many types of financial securities. They fall broadly into the categories of debt, stock, derivatives, and futures. Stockbrokers assist individuals in trading securities. Each type of security has its own conditions and risks. Mutual funds sell shares in portfolios to investors, including small investors, and purchase securities for the portfolios. Wealthier individuals can invest with hedge funds that invest in derivatives and other risky securities, or companies that own private businesses. These include venture capital firms and private equity firms. Venture capital firms help start new businesses, with the typical goal of turning the business into a public corporation. Private equity does the opposite – typically public companies are taken private in order to improve them.

Challenge

If you were given $10,000 to hold for 18 months, what would you do with it and why?

2.3 Inflation

I will end this chapter with a discussion on inflation. Goods, services, and wages rise over time due to inflation. Inflation happens over the long-term because money is created by the federal government and put into the economy. When you have more dollars chasing the same number of goods, the price level rises. (This can happen unevenly, with price increases showing up in some places faster than others.) However, inflation does not necessarily mean that people are better or worse off inasmuch as there is simply more printed money in the economy.

Imagine that there was no inflation and there was a frost in Florida. If the price of an orange rises, this would be a "real" price increase that reflects the fact that there is a shortage of oranges. The price of an orange rises in comparison to other goods and services. When inflation is thrown into the mix, people may not be sure if the real price of the orange is going up – it is becoming more expensive compared to other goods and services – or if it is caused by inflation, which causes prices to rise in general. This confusion comes from the uneven arrival of inflation for different goods and services.

People also get upset because they negotiated contracts before prices rose. Suppose you signed a contract with your employer that specified your wages would go up by 3% for the year. It turns out that inflation was 5%. Your earning power fell because you did not anticipate inflation correctly. On the other hand, your employer would be upset if inflation turned out to be 1%. Sometimes inflation happens because people confuse a real price increase with inflation. For instance, if there is an oil crisis and many industries raise prices because they must buy oil at a higher price, people may think this is due to inflation (which tends to persist) and begin to build these price increases into their behavior, such as demanding a larger wage increase in their employment contract.

The ultimate problem with inflation is that it confuses people. Prices are at the heart of our economy. Prices must be correct for the economy to work well. They determine where resources go including goods and services. Inflation creates confusion about prices, which in turn leads to inefficiency in the economy. This problem is made worse by contracts and other situations where prices do not change easily. For example, restaurants may delay increasing prices because of the cost of making new menus.[17]

Wealth can also be unexpectedly shifted between groups for no good reason. For instance, when you discovered that inflation was 5%, you had to work for a lower wage for the year in terms of buying power, which transferred wealth from you to your employer (who is able to raise prices to customers by 5% but only increased your wage by 3%). Some of these arbitrary wealth transfers can be massive. For instance, many debt contracts have fixed payments. With inflation, these payments fall in terms of lost buying power, benefiting debtors while harming lenders. People with fixed-rate mortgages can enjoy a massive benefit from unexpectedly high inflation, while shareholders and private owners of companies that lend, and people seeking new mortgages and loans from damaged financial institutions are harmed.

If high inflation in the United States occurs, there could be another, potentially very harsh cost. The world uses the United States dollar as a "reserve currency." Many transactions around the world are conducted in dollars. This is extremely beneficial to the United States, because foreigners essentially buy our dollars (which are just printed pieces of paper, after all) with goods and services. With high inflation in the United States, the world may decide to stop using the dollar as a reserve currency, because the dollars we are selling are losing their value rapidly, and confusing the price of transactions overseas. Not only would the United States not be able to sell dollars anymore, but the veritable ocean of dollars that are held around the world would come flooding back to the United States, creating very severe inflation.

The Federal Reserve is an independent government agency responsible for overseeing the financial system. An important task of the "Fed" is to control inflation. The Fed does this by buying and selling T-bills, referred to as open market operations. When the Fed buys T-bills it is taking money and sending it out into the economy, which has the effect of lowering interest rates. This makes it easier for businesses and consumers to get loans and stimulates the economy, but it can also cause inflation. When the Fed sells T-bills it takes money from the seller and therefore pulls money out of the economy. This keeps inflation under control, but depresses the economy because it increases interest rates. The Fed is constantly walking a tightrope, trying to keep inflation in check without damping the economy.[18]

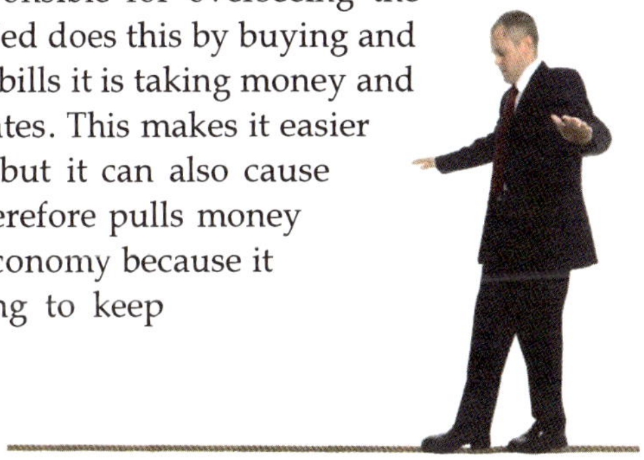

17 Mankiw, Gregory. "Small Menu Costs and Large Business Cycles: A Macroeconomic Model of Monopoly, Quarterly Journal of Economics 100, no. 2 (May, 1985): pp. 529-537.

18 When the Fed buys T-bills there is another effect that stimulates the economy. By removing T-bills from the economy, the Fed is reducing the number of borrowers in the economy. With the same number of lenders and fewer borrowers, borrowers are able to negotiate lower interest rates. This increases borrowing by business, which leads to business investment. When the Fed sells t-bills, the opposite effect occurs.

Key Takeaway: Inflation is a general increase in prices that results from the government putting more money into the economy. Real price increases are due to circumstances that are particular to industries such as bad weather destroying crops, an accident that keeps goods from getting to the market, or other events. Inflation harms the economy by creating confusion about prices, which are essential to the functioning of the economy. Inflation also causes arbitrary wealth transfers between different groups. The Fed walks a tightrope, conducting open market operations to manage inflation while trying not to depress the economy.

Challenge

If there is high inflation, what actions may you take to protect yourself?

2.4 Conclusion

Congratulations. You have mastered the basics of the financial environment. You are now ready to explore that environment in greater detail. This chapter included a lot of information, and led you through a wide ranging overview of the greater business and financial world at large. Hopefully, you have found that many of the complicated sounding terms you hear bandied about in the news and elsewhere are really not so complicated after all. You are now better able to understand the news and participate as an informed citizen in elections. You are also ready to delve into the topic of personal finance.

Key Terms:

Angel investor
Bankruptcy
Bond ratings
Bonds
C corporation
Capital gains
Capital losses
Capital market
Claimant
Commodities
Conflict of interest
Covenants
Creditor
Debt
Default
Diversification
Dividends
Double taxation
Dow Jones Industrial Average Index
Equity
Federal Reserve
Fiduciary duty
Financial instruments
Financial securities
Flow-through taxation
Forward contracts
Friends and family
Futures contracts
Government sponsored enterprises (GSEs)
Hedge funds
Index funds
Inflation
Institutions
Insurance
Interest
IPO
Joint venture
Limited liability
Limited liability company (LLC)
Liquidity
Market indices
Money market
Municipal bonds (munis)
Nonprofit
Open market operations
Partnership
Primary market
Private equity
Qualified investor
Quasi-government agencies
S corporation
S&P 500 Index
Secondary market
Stock
Stockbroker
Suppliers
T-Bills
Treasury bonds
Venture capital

End of Chapter Questions

1. What are the main differences between creditors and owners of a business?
2. How are shareholders different from other owners of a business?
3. What are C corporations, S corporations, partnerships, and LLCs? Describe the advantages and disadvantages of each type of legal business entity.
4. Explain who the chairman of the board, the CEO, and the CFO are.
5. How are stocks and bonds different?
6. Who is the biggest borrower in the United States?
7. What is the difference between the money market and the capital market?

8. What is a mutual fund, and what is the main advantage of investing in a mutual fund?
9. What is a venture capitalist?
10. What is a hedge fund?
11. What is double taxation and flow-through taxation?
12. What is a nonprofit?
13. What are the main advantages of municipal bonds?
14. What is a capital loss and gain?
15. What is bankruptcy?
16. Who is a stockbroker?
17. What are derivatives?
18. What are futures and forwards?
19. What is the Federal Reserve?
20. What is an open market operation?
21. What causes inflation?
22. What problems does inflation create?
23. Who gets harmed by inflation and who benefits?
24. What is limited liability?
25. Is it easy or difficult to form a partnership?
26. When someone sells a bond, are they borrowing or lending?
27. When it comes to financial markets, what is the difference between a "bull" and a "bear"?
28. What is a private equity company?
29. Why may it be important to not mix your personal life with your business?
30. What is a stock exchange? What are two major exchanges? What does it mean for a company to be listed? What does it mean for a stock to trade "over-the-counter"?

Chapter 3

Tax Codes

3.1 The Basics of Tax Codes

As your begin to earn income you become a producing member of society contributing to the gross domestic product (GDP). GDP measures income-producing activities in the United States. Total government spending as a percentage of GDP in 2009 was above 40%. And that must be paid for with taxes. Many people who have below-average income do not pay income taxes at all. Over the course of your life, having graduated from a top school there is a chance that 50¢ or more of every dollar that you earn will go to taxes. There are many ways that people are taxed, from federal and state income taxes and sales and property taxes to car registration fees. There are also hidden taxes, such as duties on imports, that you pay through higher prices on goods and services. Given that so much of your hard-earned pay will go to taxes, it is worth learning about the tax codes to make sure you do not pay more than you owe.

Most of us approach the subject of taxes with dread. But the reality is that it is a subject that cannot be avoided: ignorance is not bliss. Not understanding the basics of the tax codes could cost you a fortune. There is software that will help you with filling out taxes. However, if you do not understand taxes you could be paying much more than necessary. Many of the financial activities that you undertake should be guided by tax considerations.

There are four approaches to paying taxes: hide income and break other laws, aggressively avoid taxes and stretch the rules, know the rules well and do what is allowed without pushing boundaries, or pay taxes in a simple way, like ordinary people do.

Some enjoy tinkering with taxes. They regard it as a puzzle or a contest: The other side sets up the rules, and it becomes a game to outwit them. In this chapter you will read about some of those people who tried to outsmart the Internal Revenue Service (IRS), including a Nobel Prize winner in economics who ran circles around the IRS for years. (The IRS is responsible for collecting federal taxes.) He had developed what he thought was an infallible tax shelter — until an accomplished fellow Nobel laureate testified against him in tax court.

There are arguments to be made for being more aggressive or less so in your approach to reducing your taxes. Some people may feel that those who earn a higher-than-average income face a heavy tax burden. They feel that the tax laws already assume that they are taking advantage of every tax break that they can find and that punishment is built into the laws. Others may think that it is wrong to use their access to superior information and sophisticated advisors to get out of paying taxes. After all, taxes pay for firefighters, police, national defense, some social services, etc., and some believe they should pay their fair share without trying to take advantage of ways to avoid taxes. I leave this to your personal moral standards with a strong admonishment not to play chicken with the law. The consequences can be severe.

Even If the President Is Your Brother

Billy Carter was a good ol' down-home Southern boy, with his thick, black-framed glasses and an ever-present beer can. Billy wasn't shy about saying exactly what he thought, and he could come up with some loo loos. Billy got himself in big trouble with the IRS. Yes, he was the younger brother of President Jimmy Carter, but that didn't seem to mean anything. The IRS said he owed taxes on money he earned from speaking engagements. Billy's defense was that he couldn't produce the documents that would clear him because the Feds had all his papers; he was under investigation after he'd accepted a $220,000 loan from the Libyan government. The Feds couldn't seem to understand why he had ties to Libya.

Billy lived in the small town of Plains, Georgia, where he and President Carter grew up. Plains had become a regular tourist attraction with Billy Carter in residence, and folks would come from all over to see him with his famous beer can and hear his homemade homilies. As his legal and tax bills piled up, Billy resorted to selling off all his property - including his service station, the home where he had raised some of his children, and a softball field. The property went for cheap auction prices, just enough to cover his taxes and a bank loan.

He was eventually cleared of wrongdoing, but by then he had lost everything and moved to Haleyville, Alabama, to become a salesman for a mobile home manufacturer. And Billy's service station in Plains? A civic group that eventually bought the property transformed it into a museum in 2008.[1]

It is also important to know that tax codes change constantly. The tax cuts signed into law by President George W. Bush will expire in 2010, and the following year could see very substantial changes. Therefore, I will not go through an endless list of current tax rates and amounts. During the current economic crisis, the tax laws can be expected to be in particular flux. The focus of this chapter will be to explain the basic structure of the personal tax codes and to point out issues and strategies related to managing taxes. I will not discuss corporate taxes, and I will save a detailed discussion of a number of related issues, such as estate planning, for Volume 2. I shall also focus on federal taxes, which tend to be the most onerous and complex. Realize, however, that individuals are taxed in a variety of ways, at the federal, state, and local level. In any event, most people do not find delving into tax codes enjoyable. The solution? Let us just get it over with at the beginning. If you eat your broccoli, you can proceed to the main course and, eventually, dessert. (A disclaimer — I refuse to eat broccoli, cooked cabbage, or Brussels sprouts! But I do pay attention to the tax laws.)

[1] Ed Magnuson, Evan Thomas, Christopher Ogden, "The Burden of Billy," Time, August 4, 1980; Wendell Rawls, "Plains Property of Billy Carter Sold in Auction," The New York Times, June 28, 1981; Richard Fausset, "Carter gas station historic?" Orlando Sentinel, November 18, 2009.

Key Takeaway: The tax codes are complicated, and constantly changing. Understanding how the tax codes work will better prepare you for making wiser financial decisions and make you more informed when dealing with taxes. It is not a good idea to try to outsmart the IRS.

Challenge

Do a little research about tax scams and tax scammers. Which one is the most outrageous?

Tax Rates

Table 3-1 presents IRS tax rates for 2009, called the "ordinary income rate." These can be found at the IRS Web site: http://www.irs.gov/. Your tax rate will depend on your filing status: single, head of household, married filing jointly, or married filing separately. In order to be considered a head of household, you must meet certain conditions regarding being single and having a dependent.

Let us look at the rate for single taxpayers. Up until \$8,350 in income, you have a tax rate of 10% applied to the part of your income that is subject to tax. From \$8,350 through \$33,950, this next income is taxed at the 15% rate. For income over \$33,950 but below \$82,250, you are taxed at the 25% rate, and so on. For instance, suppose you earn \$89,000. Your taxes would be:

$$[(\$8{,}350-\$0)\cdot.10] + [(\$33{,}950-\$8{,}350)\cdot.15] + [(\$82{,}250-\$33{,}950)\cdot.25] + [(\$89{,}000-\$82{,}250)\cdot.28]=\$18{,}640.$$

As you earn more income, the next bracket of income (income between two amounts) that you enter is taxed at a higher rate. It is important to distinguish between the average taxes that you pay and your marginal tax rate. Chart 3-1 illustrates this. Note that it is not drawn to scale.

Your average taxes are $\frac{\$18{,}640}{\$89{,}000} = .21$. This is lower than your marginal tax rate, which is .28. Your marginal tax rate is the rate applied to the next dollar of income you earn. Right now you are in the 28% bracket. Marginal rates are important for making decisions, and are the main focus in financial planning. Suppose that you decided to work additional hours to earn a few extra dollars of overtime. Your extra earnings will be taxed at your marginal rate, and this is what will influence your decision about whether it is worth working overtime for the extra pay.

Who's the Vampire?

Sword flashing, fangs bared, Wesley Snipes fought the IRS as a blood-sucking enemy - or at least an income-sucking enemy - in a battle for freedom from taxes. Like many of us, the star of the *Blade* trilogy and *White Men Can't Jump* did not like paying taxes. So he stopped. Was he fighting evil vampires or misled by even more evil bloodsuckers?

In 2000 Snipes met the distinguished-looking, grey-haired, smiling Eddie Ray Kahn, founder of the American Rights Litigators and its successor Guiding Light of God Ministries. Those enterprises had been deemed by the government as promoters of tax scams. One of Kahn's repudiated arguments was that only a foreign source of income is taxable. If only! Kahn's arguments had already been struck down by various courts by the time Snipes became ensnared.

Snipes used the groups' accountant, Douglas P. Rosile, who had lost his professional license in both Florida and Ohio, to file some of his tax returns. After Snipes met Kahn he did not pay income taxes or payroll taxes from 1999 to 2004 - a time in which he earned more than $10 million per contract for two *Blade* sequels. In fact, he went so far as to file claims for a refund of $12 million for his 1996 and 1997 taxes and drew fake checks to pay the U.S. Treasury. (Nothing like writing bogus checks to call attention to the fact you are not paying taxes.) Snipes was indicted for tax fraud and conspiracy in 2006.

The actor's lawyers were able to convince the jury that he was duped into believing that he did not have to pay the taxes. But in February 2008, Snipes was defanged and his crusading sword was broken over the judge's knee. He was convicted of three misdemeanors and sentenced to three years in prison for failure to file tax returns — not bad, considering he was facing sixteen years. He is also still liable for up to $17 million in back taxes plus penalties and interest. Kahn and Rosile were convicted of fraud and conspiracy; Kahn got ten years, Rosile got four and a half.

The moral of this story? Protect yourself from creatures of the night. Double check the backgrounds of advisors and verify licenses. These ghouls are happy to charge you fees for fraudulent, too-good-to-be-true tax advice, and you may just end up in a deep dark hole. [2]

[2] "Wesley Snipes Gets 3 Years for Not Filing Tax Returns," *The New York Times,* April 25, 2008; David Cay Johnston,"Wesley Snipes Cleared of Serious Tax Charges," *The New York Times,* Feb. 2, 2008; Kevin Graham, "Snipes Receives 3 Years," *St. Petersburg Times,* April 25, 2008; Linton Weeks, "Wesley Snipes Fights Taxman To a Draw; Action Star Found Guilty Only of Lesser Charges," *The Washington Post*, Saturday, February 2, 2008.

Table 3-1
2009 Federal Tax Rate Schedules

Bracket Beginning Income				
Single	Head of Household	Joint Married	Separate Married	Tax Rate
$0	$0	$0	$0	**10%**
$8,350	$11,950	$16,700	$8,350	**15%**
$33,950	$45,500	$67,900	$33,950	**25%**
$82,250	$117,450	$137,050	$68,525	**28%**
$171,550	$190,200	$208,850	$104,425	**33%**
$372,950	$372,950	$372,950	$186,475	**35%**

Chart 3-1
2009 Federal Single-Taxpayer Tax Rate Schedule

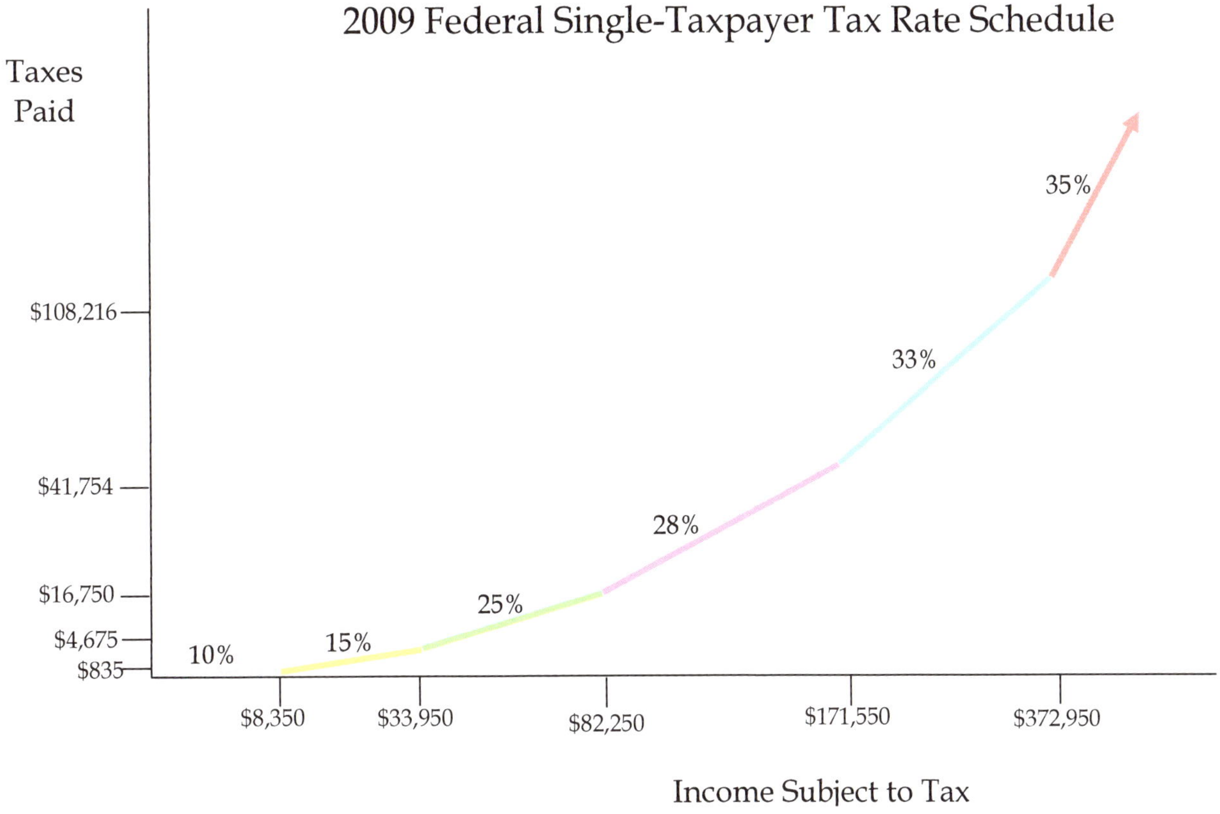

> ***Key Takeaway:*** As your income grows you move into progressively higher tax brackets, and your average taxes will be below your marginal tax rate. When making income and overtime decisions, it is important to understand the marginal rate at which you will be taxed.

> **Challenge**
>
> Research current salaries for a career you are interested in pursuing, and figure out the rate at which you may be taxed.

3.2 Navigating Tax Codes

An example of a tax form is in the appendix. You will find it useful to follow the form as I discuss the "basic" structure of the tax codes. I will also start building Chart 3-2. The chart can be used as a road map when filling out taxes. Notice that "basic" is in quotes. There is nothing basic, or more to the point, simple about the tax codes. In fact, there are thousands of pages of tax codes, and it is not possible for typical individuals to know all of the rules. This, of course, is a bonanza for tax specialists as overwhelmed taxpayers flood their offices before the April 15 tax-filing deadline for individuals. Knowing the basics about taxes and about choosing good tax specialists can save you money and financial headaches later.

In order to understand Chart 3-2, a discussion of tax specialists is necessary. Tax specialists may sound somewhat insane to someone who overhears one of their conversations. In pinstripe suits and clicking their calculators, they decry adding to income while delighting in expenses and losses. While they may seem a bit unhinged, there is a method to their madness. For income tax purposes, <u>reported</u> income is bad because it creates taxes, while reported items that reduce income, such as losses, will lower taxes. In this spirit, items with red boxes are associated with higher taxes, while items in green are associated with lower taxes.

<u>Adjustments to Gross Income</u>

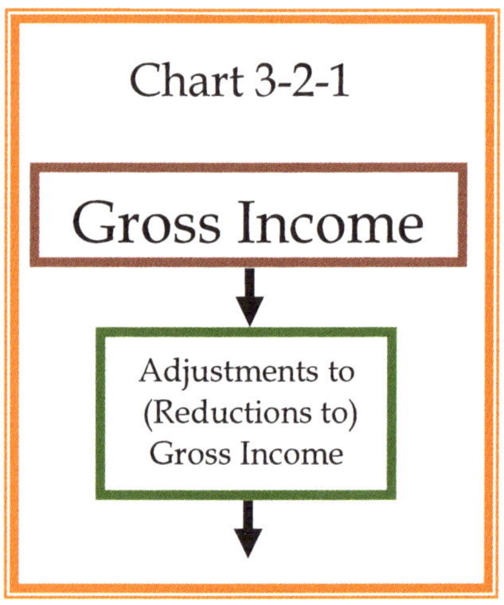

Chart 3-2-1 starts with "gross income" and "adjustments to gross income." Gross income includes, unless specifically excluded by law, all compensation and income received, whether monetary (in the form of money) or in the form of property or services. On joint returns, the two spouses report their combined income. Contributions as an employee to a retirement plan are taken out of income.

Business income is included in gross income, and is business revenue minus expenses. It is reported in Schedule C. Employer contributions to pension and profit sharing plans (payments for employees' retirement) are taken out. Insurance payments are also removed, including employee health insurance.

Several types of income have their own tax rates and reporting requirements. If you earn wages as an employee (earned income or "active income,") your employer reports this to the government and mails you a W-2 form, which summarizes your compensation, withholding, and other information needed to calculate your taxes. If you are self-employed, you use a Schedule C form to report your income. Note that if you are an employee, your employer withholds your FICA (Federal Insurance Contributions Act) and income tax contributions; you must fill out a W-4 form, which tells your employer how much to withhold. Withholding means that your employer takes part of your pay and sends it to the government before you receive your paycheck. FICA taxes pay for Social Security and

Medicare. Social Security benefits include retirement payments, disability benefits (payments you receive if you are physically unable to work for an extended period of time), and payments to survivors if you die. Medicare provides for hospitalization benefits after you reach retirement age. Your employer must match the FICA taxes you pay, so the government actually gets twice your FICA contributions. After a certain income level, Social Security is not taxed on extra earnings. If you are self-employed, as your own employer you have to pay the employee and employer portion of FICA taxes (doubling the tax you are responsible for), and make sure you are paying estimate payments, which are a quarterly estimate of the taxes you owe.

Passive income comes from income-generating activities in which an individual does not actively participate. Examples can include royalty payments from owning songs or apartment rent that goes to a non-managing owner. Passive income can be associated with tax shelters. Passive losses may be used only to offset income from passive sources.[3] Finally, there is miscellaneous income that does not fall into any of the previous categories and which carries its own rules, such as prize winnings. Certain kinds of income are not taxable; these include gifts and inheritances below a certain limit, and compensation for injury and sickness such as worker's compensation and some disability-to-work payments.

What If You Are Heading for the Moon?

Hurtling into outer space, enveloped in the deep black of the galaxy outside of Earth's atmosphere, Apollo 13's Jack Swigert sat between fellow astronauts Jim Lovell and Fred Haise, watching the blue planet grow ever smaller. It was April 13, 1970, and everything was going well. Back on Earth, Joe Kerwin at Mission Control was making conversation with the astronauts about current events. Kerwin paused before asking if they had filed their taxes yet.

Somewhat panicked, Swigert cut in. "How do I apply for an extension?" The ground crew hooted. "It ain't too funny," the astronaut insisted. "Things happened kinda fast down there and I do need an extension."

Kerwin told Swigert that the astronaut was giving Mission Control a good laugh. "Well," grumbled Swigert, "I may be spending time in another quarantine when we get back, besides the medical one they're planning for us."[4]

The next day an oxygen tank on the spacecraft ruptured and Apollo 13's mission to the moon was transformed into a life-and-death race for home before the oxygen ran out, the crew froze to death, or a miscalculation of the craft's trajectory hurtled it out of Earth's range.

The drama captured the attention of the world. The historic mission was made into an Academy Award-winning movie that starred Kevin Bacon as Swigert, Tom Hanks as Lovell, and Bill Paxton as Haise. Another dramatic touch? During the ordeal in space, Swigert learned he had been pardoned by President Richard Nixon for missing the April 15 tax-filing deadline.

[3] Passive losses can be used as deductions in the future (carried forward) against future passive income.
[4] Jim Lovell and Jeffrey Kluger, "Preempted," *LOST* magazine, December 2006-January 2007, No. 11.

> ***Key Takeaway:*** A new employee must fill out a federal W-4 form for the employer to determine how much income tax to withhold. Employees and employers must also make FICA contributions. The self-employed must make employee and employer FICA contributions and pay estimate payments.

Challenge

Which tax rate do you think is most applicable to the amount that needs to be withheld from your paycheck: your marginal rate or your average rate?

Portfolio Income

Portfolio income comes from investments in stocks and debt such as bonds, and consists of dividends, capital gains, and interest.[5] The government requires that companies that pay you portfolio income report your income to the government. You will also receive 1099 forms from those companies that you must use in reporting earnings. Interest income comes from holding debt, or mutual fund shares that are invested in debt, and is taxed at the personal income tax rate. You will receive a 1099-INT form. Dividend income is reported on form 1099-DIV form, and is taxed at the long-term capital gains rate (except foreign dividends which get taxed at the ordinary income rate).

Capital Gains and Losses

Capital gains require their own analysis. When discussing investing, it is useful to distinguish between securities (which are pieces of paper that promise payment) and real assets (which are physical objects). The tax terminology is different. Real property is real estate, and personal property is everything else that is a physical object. Intangible assets cannot be touched, such as a trademark.[6] Capital gains can occur for financial investments and other kinds of investments. Real and personal property capital gains are taxed at the higher rate of 28% (or 15% for low-income individuals).[7] Tax laws also distinguish between long-term capital gains on investments held over a year, and short-term capital gains on investments held less than a year. Long-term capital gains are taxed at the 15% rate (5% for low-income individuals), while short-term capital gains are taxed at the higher income tax rate. A capital gain is the difference between the price of an asset and the basis. The basis for a financial asset is the purchase price. If an asset is real, the basis can be increased by the cost of improvements to the property. The IRS does not want to discourage people from improving their property. This would happen if they were taxed on the higher price they receive as a result, without taking into account that they had to spend money to achieve that higher price.[8] The more that you are able to increase your basis the less tax you pay, since capital gains are the sale price minus the basis.

---

[5] Repayment of principal is not considered income or capital gains and is not subject to tax.

[6] A trademark indicates that goods or services come from the same source. They are owned.

[7] See http://www.irs.gov/taxtopics/tc409.html.

[8] Depreciation can lower the basis, but depreciation was used to lower taxes in earlier years.

I've Been Trapped!

$$C = S \cdot N(d_1) - E \cdot e^{-R_F T} \cdot N(d_2),$$

$$d_1 = \frac{\text{Log}\left(\frac{S}{E \cdot e^{-R_F T}}\right) + \frac{1}{2}\sigma^2 T}{\sigma\sqrt{T}},$$

$$d_2 = d_1 - \sigma\sqrt{T}.$$

On a hot midsummer day in 2003, Myron Scholes, winner of the Nobel Prize in Economics, sat in the witness chair. He was defending his honor, defending the millions of dollars he could lose along with those of his partners from the now-defunct hedge fund Long Term Capital Management, defending his own genius. Based on mathematical formulas and models only rocket scientists can appreciate (the Black-Scholes model is based on mathematics used by rocket scientists), and like a rocket gone awry, Long Term Capital came crashing to Earth and needed to be bailed out before it threatened the world financial system — a precursor of the current financial crisis. What Scholes was counting on in the courtroom was that no one would be able to understand the complicated tax shelter he designed so Long-Term and his partners could evade taxes.

Scholes, wizened and with grey-streaked hair, nudged his eyeglasses higher. A bead of perspiration formed on the bridge of his nose - possibly from the heat, or possibly in response to the lengthy interrogation by government attorney Charles P. Hurley. Responding to Hurley's questions in a nasal voice, Scholes allowed a hint of humor, a hint of arrogance, a hint of condescension to come through. He was the genius. His role was to seem genuine, unconcerned, in control. Hurley, a street-smart prosecutor who was there to bring Scholes down, could not compete with Scholes' genius for mathematics or speak a language riddled with terms few could grasp. Instead, Hurley took a wily approach.

Hurley asked Scholes about his knowledge of taxes; Scholes denied having any real knowledge of taxes. Hurley entered into evidence the textbook *Taxes and Business Strategy*, of which Scholes was a principal author and from which he taught graduate students at Stanford University. Scholes now had to confess he has some knowledge of taxes. Step by step, Hurley dropped bread crumbs and lead Scholes through a line of questioning that caused him to admit that everything Long-Term Capital based its tax shelter on was disallowed. Inwardly, Hurley smiled: *Gotcha!* Scholes, finally realizing what had happened, blurted out, "I've been trapped here."

Then, the coup de grace. To fight an economic titan, bring in your own. Joseph Stiglitz, who received the Nobel Prize in Economics in 2001, testified that the transactions used for Long-Term Capital's tax deductions had basically "no economic value." The final nail in the coffin was hammered home. Later, in a decision of nearly 200 pages, Judge Janet Bond Arterton gave Long-Term Capital, and specifically Scholes, an old-fashioned thrashing on behalf of the IRS.

Two Nobel laureates demolished Long-Term Capital's tax shelter, and one of them was Scholes himself. No matter how smart you are or how dumb they are, there is probably still someone smarter or wilier. When you break the tax laws, or any law for that matter, you may discover that you have outsmarted yourself.[9]

A capital loss occurs when the sales price minus the basis is negative, and it can generate a small tax break. A wash sale occurs when someone sells a financial security at a loss and then repurchases the same or a similar security within thirty days. The IRS wants to prevent people from selling and then buying back securities for the sole purpose of generating capital losses to reduce taxes, and therefore prevents a tax deduction on wash sales.

---

[9] David Cay Johnston, "Economist Questioned on Tax Shelter Role," *The New York Times*, July 10, 2003; Kara Scannell, "Nobel Winner Stiglitz Says Deals at LTCM Had `No Economic Value'," *The Wall Street Journal*, July 18, 2003; Lynnley Browning, David Cay Johnston, "Hedge Fund Is Censured and Ordered to Pay Taxes," *The New York Times*, Aug. 28, 2004.

A house can be a substantial way to avoid capital gains taxes. If a home is your principal residence,[10] then as long as you wait two years after purchase to sell, you can avoid paying capital gains taxes of up to $500,000 if you are married, and $250,000 if you are single. Note that it is important to keep records of improvements that you make to your house, including receipts, so that you can increase the basis of your house (and reduce reported capital gains). Capital losses (because of a low sale price) on a principal residence cannot be used to reduce taxes.

The calculation of capital gains or losses can be somewhat involved, as seen in Chart 3-3. First, the sum of long-term capital gains and losses on assets needs to be calculated. (Some assets will have capital gains; others will have losses.) Then the same calculation needs to be made for short-term gains and losses. Next, the sum of long-term gains and losses, and short-term gains and losses needs to be added together. If on net you have had a capital gain, then long-term capital gain taxes or income taxes are applied. If on net you experienced a capital loss, then up to $3,000 can be used to offset taxable income. If any is left over, it can be saved and used in future years (carried forward) to offset any capital gains. Once capital gains are offset, any leftover can reduce income up to the $3,000 limit. Be sure to offset capital losses; they cannot be used once you die. (When you die you still have to have a tax form completed!)

Note that it may be worthwhile to wait to sell assets at a loss. Suppose that you have generated capital gains for this year. If you sell assets for a capital loss, they will be used to offset capital gains, and will only offset taxes charged at the 15% rate (the left square at the bottom of Chart 3-3). On the other hand, if you wait and you do not have capital gains next year, your capital losses can be used to offset income, which is taxed at a higher rate (the green box).

Returning to the road map, Chart 3-2-1 showed that once gross income has been calculated, the next step was to make adjustments that reduce gross income. Educator expenses can be taken out, such as when a professor buys a textbook as part of their job. Health savings accounts are another example.[11] Moving expenses to take a new job qualify to reduce income if you move far enough. A portion of student loan interest can be taken out. Self-employed people can take out retirement plan contributions.

Key Takeaway: Capital gains of less than a year are taxed at a higher rate than longer-term capital gains. After summing up total capital gains or losses, capital gains get taxed; capital losses can be used only sparingly to reduce taxes.

Challenge

Suppose you bought a house for $500,000 and then did $150,000 in upgrades. If the value of your house is now $600,000, what impact did the upgrades have on your taxes?[12]

[10] It can be possible to have a second home qualify under certain circumstances.

[11] Health savings accounts are a way for people to save taxes on health expenses, and will be discussed in Volume 2.

[12] None. Even without the upgrades, your capital gain is under the limit for married couples or singles ($500,000 or $250,000).

Chart 3-3

Capital Gains Taxes

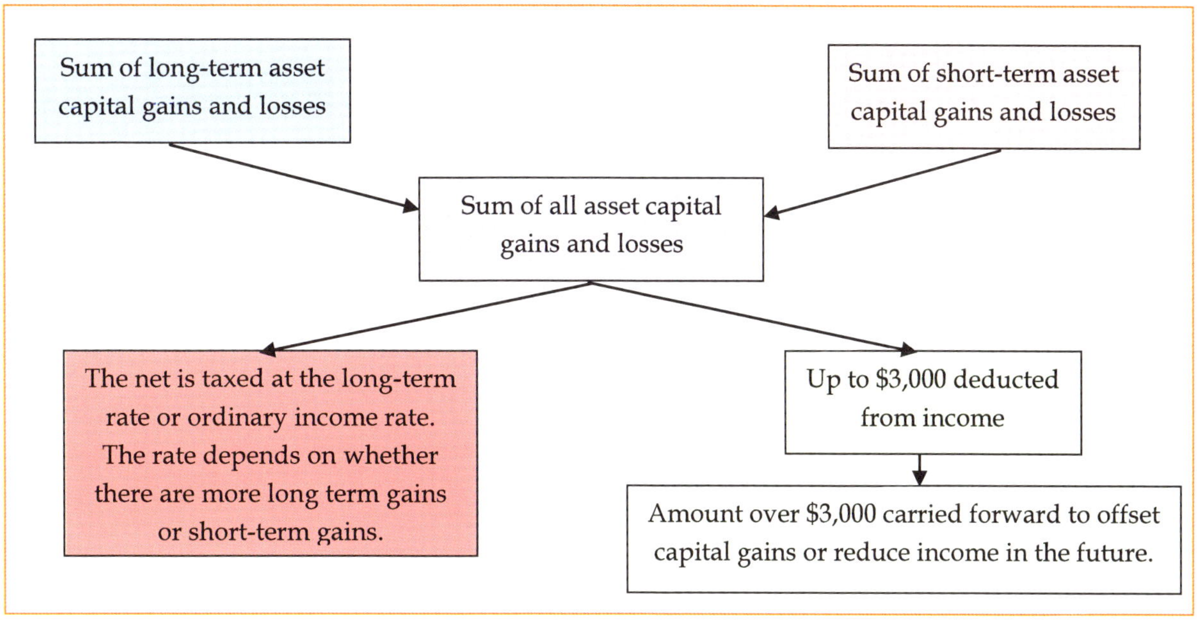

Deductions

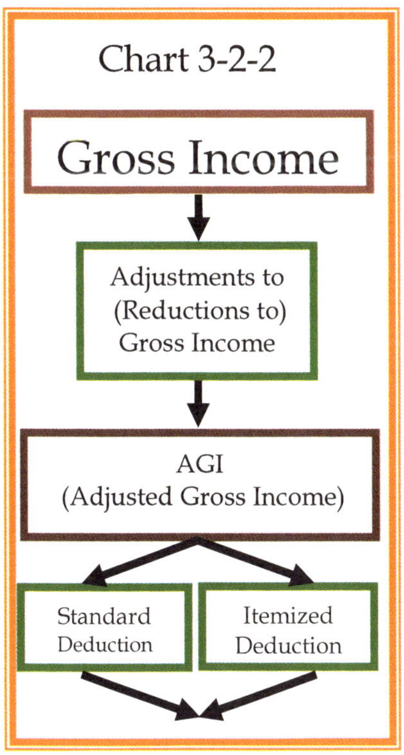

Once adjustments to gross income have been made, you are left with adjusted gross income (AGI). The next step is to decide whether to take the standard deduction or to itemize deductions, as seen in Chart 3-2-2. The standard deduction is a fixed amount based on tax status (single, head of household, etc.), which is adjusted for inflation each year. The alternative is to itemize deductions. This tends to be preferable for individuals who pay higher income taxes, especially in high-tax states. Ultimately, which path to take depends on which method will produce the highest deduction, and is up to the person filing the taxes.

There are a number of itemized deductions. But in some instances, what is being deducted has to amount to a minimum percentage of AGI and will only count after that percentage. In other cases there are caps on how much can be deducted. Such itemized deductions include medical expenses; charitable contributions; state, and local income and property taxes; qualifying interest expenses including mortgage interest; theft and casualty losses.

Medical expenses are a very broad category, and include expenses such as medical insurance and lodging while receiving medical care away from home. However, only medical expenses greater than 7.5% of AGI can be deducted. (As you shall see, there are tax strategies that can help you make use of this deduction.)

The law concerning charitable contributions is in flux. At present, cash contributions to qualifying (acceptable for charity purposes under the law) nonprofit organizations are limited to 50% of AGI, with additional limits to private foundations. Deductions above the limit can be carried forward for five years. The laws concerning giving real property such as art are more complicated, and should be considered before such a donation is made. Mileage while using a car for charitable purposes is deductible.

State and local income and property taxes can be deducted. Sales taxes can be deducted instead of local income taxes, which can be very beneficial for residents of states that do not have income taxes. Sales and FICA taxes cannot be deducted. Some interest expenses can be deducted. A very important deduction that can often create substantial tax savings is interest on a mortgage. However, it is important to investigate restrictions on deductibility. For instance, borrowing cannot exceed $1 million, home equity loans cannot exceed $100,000, and the home must be qualified as a residence. I will discuss these issues after you have explored something called an "amortization schedule" for a mortgage, which breaks out how much of a mortgage payment is principal (the return of principal is not considered a taxable event) and interest. If you borrow to make an investment, the interest is tax deductible with certain restrictions. Borrowing to participate in passive activities is deductible with restrictions.

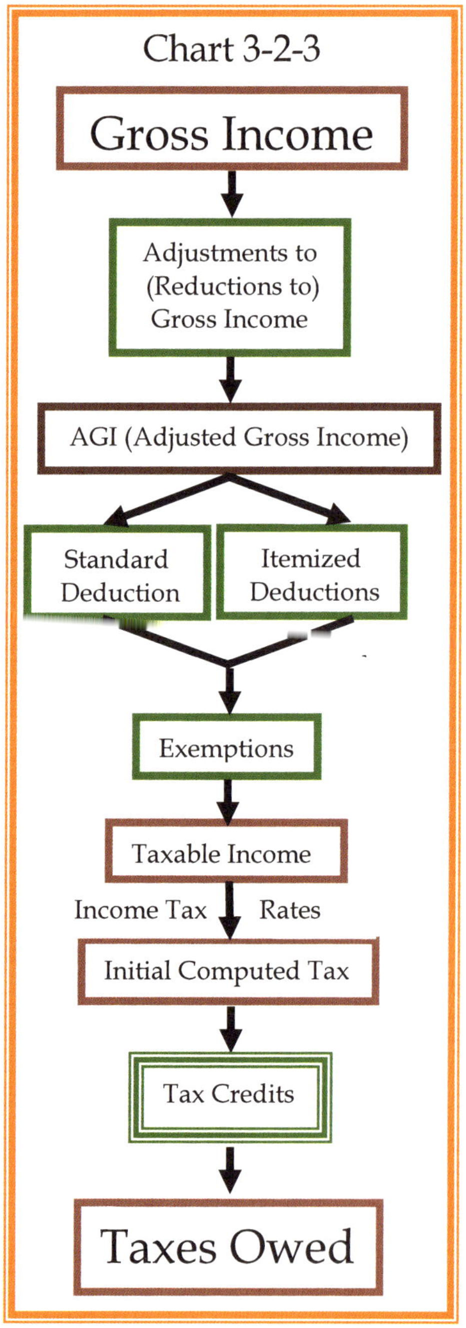

Chart 3-2-3

The IRS allows individuals to make deductions when they have suffered a significant casualty loss or reduction in value of their property. Casualty losses fall into two categories: those resulting from nature or accidents, such as flood and fire, and from theft or vandalism. If you have such losses and they have not been reimbursed by your insurance company, you can deduct them if they are above 10% of AGI. Each separate loss can be deducted only for amounts over $100. Different rules apply if you live in an area declared a federal disaster area by the president.

Finally, there is a grab bag of other deductions. Employee expenses are an example. These include travel expenses and 50% of meals.

Exemptions

At this point you have calculated your income after deductions. As seen in Chart 3-2-3, it is now time to subtract any exemptions that you are allowed. An exemption is a fixed amount per person that is adjusted each year for inflation. In 2009 it was $3,650 per person. You get one personal exemption for yourself, another for a spouse if you are filing jointly, and one for each dependent claimed. A dependent is defined by the tax codes, but in general a dependent is a minor child that is relying on you for financial support. There are sometimes other situations where someone can be claimed as a dependent: An important case is an adult child who is a college student. The child can be claimed as long as certain conditions are met. In this case, it is important for the child and parent to coordinate their taxes, since the child cannot take an exemption on his own taxes. Note that in the past, high-income taxpayers had to reduce or eliminate their personal exemption depending on their income. At the moment, however, this is being phased out.

Key Takeaway: Items such as educator expenses and health savings accounts are subtracted from gross income to get adjusted gross income. If you have enough deductions you may choose to itemize, otherwise the IRS offers you a standard deduction. People can also take exemptions, which are fixed amounts, for themselves and dependents. It is important for college students to coordinate exemptions with their parents.

Challenge

What kind of tax deductions may you have the year you take your first job out of college?

Tax Credits

You are now at your taxable income. It is time to apply the tax tables to compute your tax. Be sure to follow instructions. If you have high income, you have to fill out specific tables in order to compute your tax. Once this tax is computed, you have several steps left before your final tax bill is calculated. An important step is to consider possible tax credits. These are worth their weight in gold, and are unlike deductions. For instance, if you have AGI of $100,000, are in the 28% tax bracket, and take a $100 deduction for medical expenses, the differences in your taxes is: [tax before] – [tax after] = [100,000·(1-.28)] – [(100,000-**100**)·(1-.28)] = 100·.28=$28. A deduction saves you your tax-bracket percentage times the deduction. Tax credits are different because each dollar of credit comes directly out of your taxes (is 100% deductible).

If you got a $100 tax credit, your taxes would be directly reduced by $100. One example of a tax credit is when the government does not tax you if you reside abroad and have already paid income taxes in a foreign country. Note that the rules are different depending on whether you live in a country that has signed a tax treaty with the United States; you should investigate your tax situation if you are considering working abroad. Some tax credits do not have to be carried forward if they cause your income tax to go negative – you get a check in the mail (they are refundable). Some credits for higher-income individuals, however, are phased out.

Homeowners can get a partial tax credit for expenditures to increase the energy efficiency of a home. Purchasers of hybrid cars can also get a credit. Full or partial care credits for disabled dependents – adults or minors – are available if the taxpayer can demonstrate certain expenditures were necessary because the taxpayer was working, looking for a job, or going to school full time. An "earned income credit" is available to very low-income individuals. There is a child tax credit that can be taken for each child, but gets phased out for high-income individuals. Table 3-2 summarizes the three major categories that reduce taxes.

Key Takeaway: Tax payers are allowed certain tax credits, which can be quite valuable because they are taken directly from taxes. Some are phased out for high-income individuals.

Table 3-2
Summary of Major Categories That Reduce Taxes

Category	Description
Gross Income	All compensation and income received. Employee contributions to a retirement account are removed. For businesses, this is revenue minus expenses.
Adjustments to Gross Income reduce gross income	Examples include educator expenses and health savings accounts.
Deductions reduce income before tax rates are applied.	The standard deduction is a fixed amount. An alternative is to take itemized deductions. Among these are medical expenses, charitable contributions, state and local income and property taxes, qualifying interest expenses, theft and casualty losses.
Exemptions reduce income before tax rates are applied.	These are a fixed amount applied to everyone equally, regardless of income. They are adjusted each year for inflation. You get one personal exemption for yourself, another for a spouse if you are filing jointly, and one for each dependent claimed.
Credits directly reduce taxes.	This is a grab bag of tax credits, including ones to promote home energy efficiency and the sale of hybrid cars, for a disabled dependent of a job seeker, and for low-income people.

The Alternative Minimum Tax

Once you have taken your credits, it is time to calculate your tax. At least, that is the way it worked in the past. However, Congress decided that too many very high-income individuals were finding clever ways to avoid paying taxes and instituted the "alternative minimum tax" (AMT). It was initially intended to apply only to extremely wealthy individuals. But it was not adjusted for inflation, and as price levels and wages rose more and more people - including middle-class taxpayers - became subject to the tax. The AMT is a parallel method of computing taxes. It generally allows fewer deductions, but has a bigger exemption and a lower tax rate than the top bracket. This is intended to keep high-income individuals from excessively using deductions to lower their taxes.

As the final Chart 3-2 illustrates, start with income after deductions and add back some of those deductions, including state and local taxes and various other items. You must also add back "preference items" that received preferential treatment, such as municipal bond interest. Then subtract the AMT personal exemption, which is phased out for high-income individuals. Then apply a 26% or 28% rate on income above a certain level. This is your AMT tax. Your final calculation is to compare your AMT tax with the taxes you computed using the standard method. You must pay whichever is higher. In Chart 3-2, the AMT tax tipped the scale and became the required final tax.

The tax codes can contain nasty surprises. Someone who never paid the AMT may suddenly see a big jump in taxes when the AMT kicks in. For example, when dot.com executives exercised stock options given to them by their companies, they were allowed to buy shares on the cheap – below the price of the stock (I will discuss options in Volume 2). Say an executive exercising his options bought stock for $100 that was worth $300, making a theoretical profit of $200 (the profit is not realized until the executive sells the stock). The executive got a further tax break if he held the stock for one year. The AMT rules were different, however, and the executive owed taxes immediately on the $200 difference. Suppose the next year, when the taxes were due under AMT, the stock that the executive held was worthless because the dot.com went bust. Not only is the executive out of a job, but he owes AMT taxes on the $200 from the previous year and cannot sell his worthless stock to pay the tax. When the dot.com bubble burst, executives found themselves destitute: They lost their jobs, they lost their pensions, and under AMT they found themselves owing the IRS hundreds of thousands of dollars on money they never received.

Key Takeaway: When making financial decisions, make sure you understand the tax implications. Potential hidden problems, including the AMT, can come as a nasty surprise.

Chart 3-2

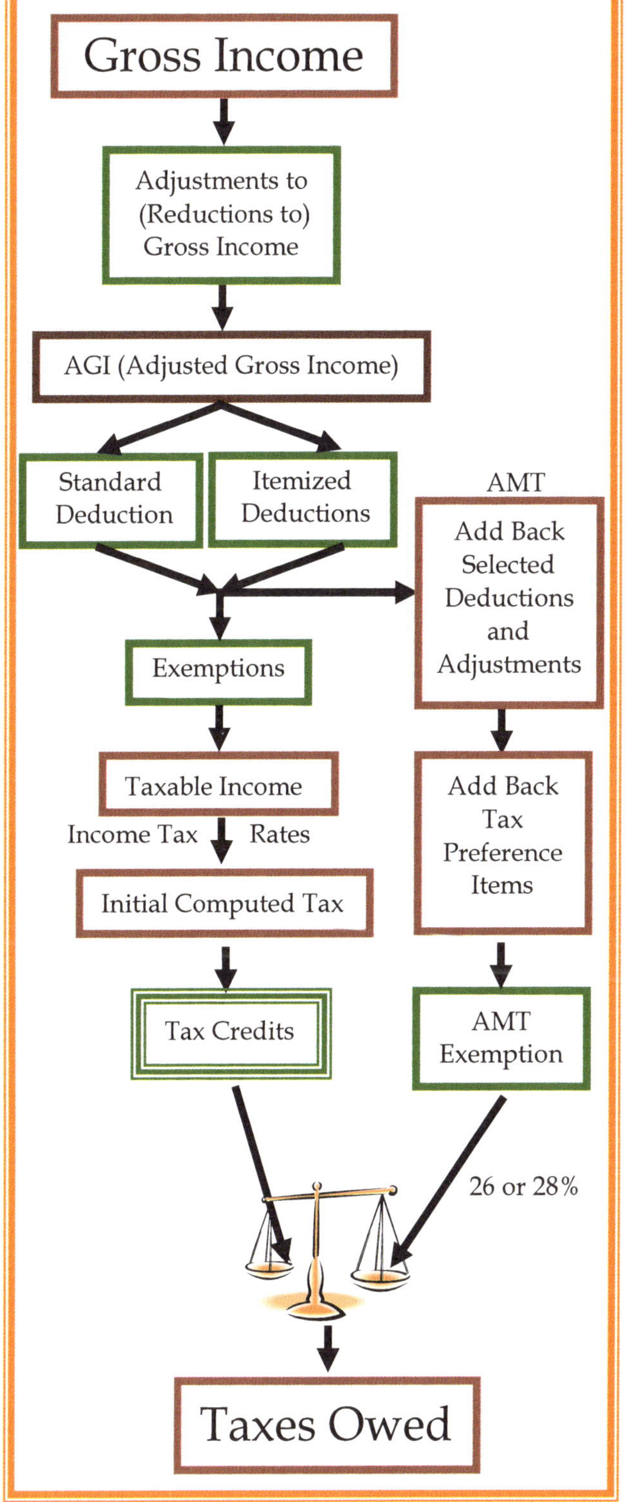

Fiction but True

Do You Have a Ticking Time Bomb in Your House and Don't Know It?

Imagine discovering a hidden door in your house. When you open it, you find a bomb with a timer counting down — it's too late. A similar situation can happen to your financial house with unexpected taxes.

In 2001, with the ink on his computer science degree still wet, Douglas got his dream job as vice president for a start-up dot.com that had developed an exciting Internet search engine that would leave all the others in the dust. Being a start-up, Seek-and-Find could not afford to pay as large a salary as Douglas had hoped for; he was counting on earning enough to quickly repay his college loans. In lieu of a higher salary, Seek-and-Find offered him stock options; their value was at a premium and in the future would by far surpass their current worth. Of course he was busy and didn't consult with a tax accountant, but he couldn't lose.

Douglas and his beautiful fiancé, Jenny, finally got married. They decided to go ahead and exercise his stock options - after all, it was like money in the bank, albeit paper. When they figured out their financial worth including the stock options, Douglas discovered he was a millionaire — on paper. He splurged, trading in his wreck of a car for a shiny silver BMW Z4. Jenny preferred a SUV. They bought an upscale four-bedroom house with a pool, not too far from the new sleek office building where he would be working.

One sunny morning Douglas drove to work, where he was surprised to find a parking lot full of local news media vans. After fighting past a sea of shouting reporters he was even more surprised to learn his company was filing for bankruptcy. Apparently, there was a glitch in Seek-and-Find's technology that made the search engine susceptible to viruses and hackers, and overnight word had spread across the Internet. Seek-and-Find was out of business.

Douglas was deeply in debt, had a portfolio full of worthless stock, and had just lost his income. Douglas and Jenny lost their home and their cars were repossessed. But they still owed enormous taxes on the value of the stock options he exercised, even though that stock was now worthless.

During the late 1990s and early 2000s, many people caught up in the dot.com bust found themselves living through this terrible nightmare. The government has since enacted legislation to remedy the problem, entitling those who paid the tax on valueless exercised stock options to a refund over a two-year period and abating taxes for those still making payments.

In the years since 2001, Douglas and Jenny faced bankruptcy and depression; the stress almost drove them to divorce. It took them years to get back on their feet, but even though their taxes and penalties will be refunded, how will they recover from the emotional toll? How many times has Douglas asked himself: "What would have happened if I had taken the time to investigate the full tax, legal, and income implications before I declared myself rich, and lived accordingly?"[13]

---

[13] Fictional, based on actual accounts.

Taxes and Starting a New Job

When you take a job for the first time, your employer will give you a bewildering form called the "W-4" that is used to tell your employer how much income to withhold from your paycheck. Your employer sends this withheld money to the federal government (and to the state, if yours has an income tax). Because earners must make contributions to cover their taxes on a monthly or, at minimum, quarterly basis, this process keeps you from facing penalties. If you receive regular payments that have not been subject to withholding – if you are self-employed, for example, or have investment income – you must take it upon yourself to send withholding on these payments to the government.

In order to figure out your withholding, you must know if you can take the dependent exemption for yourself. You should discuss this with your parents. Both of you cannot simultaneously declare you as a dependent. It is also especially important to check your withholding if you have more than one job or if your spouse works, because the extra income earned from your second job could bump you into a higher tax bracket. In other words, the withholding from your paycheck is based on the lower tax bracket associated with your paycheck, but your tax bracket is higher because of other income and so not enough has been withheld. Withholding also varies by state. California has withholding for disability.

The W-4 has instructions to help you fill it out. Fortunately, since you have read this chapter you know the meaning of "tax exemptions," 'filing status," and an array of other terms. You can also go to the IRS Web site (http://www.irs.gov), click on the "individual" button, and scroll down until you see "IRS Withholding Calculator." This is a handy tool for figuring out how much needs to be withheld and is updated regularly. An alternative is to visit an accountant. If you can afford it, this can be a worthwhile use of funds when you are getting started in a new job. Whenever your circumstances change, it is a good idea to get solid tax advice.

3.3 Conclusion

There are important tax laws having to do with saving for college, saving for retirement, and leaving an inheritance. I put off a discussion of these issues until I get to these topics in Volume 2. In addition, I put off a discussion of tax-savings strategies. You have taken a broad look at the tax codes, which are actually quite complex. It is not possible for any typical individual to keep up with all of them. It is important that you have a basic understanding of tax codes or you could end up spending a great deal in taxes. However, it is also important to get regular checkups with a tax expert. This can be necessary even if you have a relatively low income and simple taxes. Your expert will make sure you are taking advantage of all the tax savings available, and recommend strategies for tax savings in the future. This is especially important if your life circumstances change - if you get married, have a child, or are preparing to retire. The fees you pay for tax advice are even tax deductible.

One final admonition is in order. In Volume 2 I will discuss how financial advisors have conflicts of interest (they may increase the money they make by steering you in the wrong direction). Tax advisors can have these conflicts just like any financial advisor. Look out for tax advisors who charge high fees for complex or odd-sounding schemes while promising you the moon. When you get into trouble with the IRS, such advisors walk away with their pockets full. Several major accounting firms have gotten into serious trouble for convincing their clients to undertake convoluted schemes to save taxes. Their clients ended up having to pay big fines in addition to the taxes they owed. Be suspicious of anything that sounds labyrinthine. My accountant once told me, "If you do not understand what I am telling you, I am either lying or I do not know what I am talking about."

Key Takeaway: Taxes are complicated and the regulations change from year to year. It is wiser to understand the full tax implications of choices you make before the tax bill is due and get good quality advice from a reputable advisor, especially when circumstances change.

Challenge

How do you view taxes — as a puzzle or as a headache? What can you do in your personal life to minimize tax frustration and maximize tax benefits?

Key Terms:

1099 Form
Adjustments to gross income (AGI)
Alternative minimum tax (AMT)
Asset basis
Average tax rate
Carried forward
Earned or active income
Estimate payments
Exemptions
FICA
Filing status
Gross income
Head of household
Itemized deductions
Long-term capital gains
Marginal tax rate
Medicare
Passive income
Personal property
Portfolio income
Real property
Short-term capital gains
Social security
Standardized deduction
Tax credits
W-2 form
Withholding

End of Chapter Questions

1. What is the difference between your average tax rate and your marginal tax rate?
2. Your taxable income is 180,000 and you file as head of household. What is your calculated tax? (Ignore possible AMT taxes.)
3. What is the difference between active and passive income? Are they treated differently for tax purposes?
4. What is the basis of an asset?
5. What is the difference between short-term capital gains and long-term capital gains?
6. What are the main items included in gross income?
7. What are two adjustments to gross income?
8. How is the standardized deduction different from itemized deductions?
9. What is the FICA tax and what does it pay for?
10. What are exemptions?
11. What are tax credits, and how are they different from deductions?
12. What is the AMT?
13. Why are more and more people subject to the AMT?
14. How do business expenses affect taxes?
15. If something is an adjustment to income rather than a deduction, how may this be an advantage?

16. You sold three stocks during the current tax year. You paid $100 for a stock three years ago and just sold it for $110. You also bought stock one month ago for $50 and just sold it for $62. You also bought stock for $10 two months ago and just sold it for $2. Do you have net capital gains or losses? What is your net capital gains or losses? Will you apply the long-term capital gains rate to the net or your income tax rate?

17. You sold four stocks during the current tax year. You paid $6,000 for stock two years ago and sold it for $4,000. You paid $8,000 for stock three months ago and sold it for $3,000. You paid $5,000 for stock six months ago and sold it for $6,000, and you paid $11,000 for a stock four years ago and just sold it for $13,000. Do you have a net capital gain or loss? How will you calculate taxes?

18. What is withholding?

19. What is a W-4 form. Who gives it to you and what must you specify in the form?

20. When filling out a W-4 form, will it matter that you have a spouse and a second job? If so, how?

21. What rate is currently applied to stock dividends?

22. Are capital gains taxes applied to the sale of a home? If so, how?

23. How can state and local income taxes come into play in calculating your federal tax?

24. Why is it desirable to be considered a head of household. Can any single person file this way?

25. How do charitable contributions affect taxes?

26. Are medical expenses deductable?

27. Name several tax credits.

28. Why may high income individuals not be able to receive a tax credit?

29. What is a W-2 form?

30. What is an important tax aspect of paying a mortgage?

Appendix

Form **1040** Department of the Treasury—Internal Revenue Service
U.S. Individual Income Tax Return **2009** (99) IRS Use Only—Do not write or staple in this space.

Label	For the year Jan. 1–Dec. 31, 2009, or other tax year beginning , 2009, ending , 20			OMB No. 1545-0074
(See instructions on page 14.) L A B E L	Your first name and initial	Last name		**Your social security number**
Use the IRS label.	If a joint return, spouse's first name and initial	Last name		**Spouse's social security number**
Otherwise, please print or type. H E R E	Home address (number and street). If you have a P.O. box, see page 14.		Apt. no.	▲ You **must** enter your SSN(s) above. ▲
	City, town or post office, state, and ZIP code. If you have a foreign address, see page 14.			Checking a box below will not change your tax or refund.
Presidential Election Campaign	▶ Check here if you, or your spouse if filing jointly, want $3 to go to this fund (see page 14) ▶			☐ **You** ☐ **Spouse**

Filing Status

Check only one box.

1 ☐ Single
2 ☐ Married filing jointly (even if only one had income)
3 ☐ Married filing separately. Enter spouse's SSN above and full name here. ▶
4 ☐ Head of household (with qualifying person). (See page 15.) If the qualifying person is a child but not your dependent, enter this child's name here. ▶
5 ☐ Qualifying widow(er) with dependent child (see page 16)

Exemptions

6a ☐ **Yourself.** If someone can claim you as a dependent, **do not** check box 6a
b ☐ **Spouse**
c **Dependents:**

(1) First name Last name	(2) Dependent's social security number	(3) Dependent's relationship to you	(4) ✓ if qualifying child for child tax credit (see page 17)
			☐
			☐
			☐
			☐

If more than four dependents, see page 17 and check here ▶ ☐

d Total number of exemptions claimed

Boxes checked on 6a and 6b
No. of children on 6c who:
• lived with you
• did not live with you due to divorce or separation (see page 18)
Dependents on 6c not entered above
Add numbers on lines above ▶ ☐

Income

Attach Form(s) W-2 here. Also attach Forms W-2G and 1099-R if tax was withheld.

If you did not get a W-2, see page 22.

Enclose, but do not attach, any payment. Also, please use **Form 1040-V.**

7	Wages, salaries, tips, etc. Attach Form(s) W-2		7	
8a	**Taxable** interest. Attach Schedule B if required		8a	
b	**Tax-exempt** interest. **Do not** include on line 8a	8b		
9a	Ordinary dividends. Attach Schedule B if required		9a	
b	Qualified dividends (see page 22)	9b		
10	Taxable refunds, credits, or offsets of state and local income taxes (see page 23)		10	
11	Alimony received		11	
12	Business income or (loss). Attach Schedule C or C-EZ		12	
13	Capital gain or (loss). Attach Schedule D if required. If not required, check here ▶ ☐		13	
14	Other gains or (losses). Attach Form 4797		14	
15a	IRA distributions 15a	b Taxable amount (see page 24)	15b	
16a	Pensions and annuities 16a	b Taxable amount (see page 25)	16b	
17	Rental real estate, royalties, partnerships, S corporations, trusts, etc. Attach Schedule E		17	
18	Farm income or (loss). Attach Schedule F		18	
19	Unemployment compensation in excess of $2,400 per recipient (see page 27)		19	
20a	Social security benefits 20a	b Taxable amount (see page 27)	20b	
21	Other income. List type and amount (see page 29)		21	
22	Add the amounts in the far right column for lines 7 through 21. This is your **total income** ▶		22	

Adjusted Gross Income

23	Educator expenses (see page 29)	23		
24	Certain business expenses of reservists, performing artists, and fee-basis government officials. Attach Form 2106 or 2106-EZ	24		
25	Health savings account deduction. Attach Form 8889	25		
26	Moving expenses. Attach Form 3903	26		
27	One-half of self-employment tax. Attach Schedule SE	27		
28	Self-employed SEP, SIMPLE, and qualified plans	28		
29	Self-employed health insurance deduction (see page 30)	29		
30	Penalty on early withdrawal of savings	30		
31a	Alimony paid b Recipient's SSN ▶	31a		
32	IRA deduction (see page 31)	32		
33	Student loan interest deduction (see page 34)	33		
34	Tuition and fees deduction. Attach Form 8917	34		
35	Domestic production activities deduction. Attach Form 8903	35		
36	Add lines 23 through 31a and 32 through 35		36	
37	Subtract line 36 from line 22. This is your **adjusted gross income** ▶		37	

For Disclosure, Privacy Act, and Paperwork Reduction Act Notice, see page 97. Cat. No. 11320B Form **1040** (2009)

Tax and Credits	38	Amount from line 37 (adjusted gross income)		38
	39a	Check if: ☐ **You** were born before January 2, 1945, ☐ Blind. ☐ **Spouse** was born before January 2, 1945, ☐ Blind. **Total boxes checked ▶ 39a** ☐		
Standard Deduction for—	b	If your spouse itemizes on a separate return or you were a dual-status alien, see page 35 and check here ▶ 39b☐		
• People who check any box on line 39a, 39b, or 40b **or** who can be claimed as a dependent, see page 35.	40a	**Itemized deductions** (from Schedule A) **or** your **standard deduction** (see left margin)		40a
• All others:	b	If you are increasing your standard deduction by certain real estate taxes, new motor vehicle taxes, or a net disaster loss, attach Schedule L and check here (see page 35) ▶ 40b☐		
Single or Married filing separately, $5,700	41	Subtract line 40a from line 38		41
Married filing jointly or Qualifying widow(er), $11,400	42	**Exemptions.** If line 38 is $125,100 or less and you did not provide housing to a Midwestern displaced individual, multiply $3,650 by the number on line 6d. Otherwise, see page 37		42
Head of household, $8,350	43	**Taxable income.** Subtract line 42 from line 41. If line 42 is more than line 41, enter -0-		43
	44	**Tax** (see page 37). Check if any tax is from: a ☐ Form(s) 8814 b ☐ Form 4972		44
	45	**Alternative minimum tax** (see page 40). Attach Form 6251		45
	46	Add lines 44 and 45 ▶		46
	47	Foreign tax credit. Attach Form 1116 if required	47	
	48	Credit for child and dependent care expenses. Attach Form 2441	48	
	49	Education credits from Form 8863, line 29	49	
	50	Retirement savings contributions credit. Attach Form 8880	50	
	51	Child tax credit (see page 42)	51	
	52	Credits from Form: a ☐ 8396 b ☐ 8839 c ☐ 5695	52	
	53	Other credits from Form: a ☐ 3800 b ☐ 8801 c ☐	53	
	54	Add lines 47 through 53. These are your **total credits**		54
	55	Subtract line 54 from line 46. If line 54 is more than line 46, enter -0- ▶		55
Other Taxes	56	Self-employment tax. Attach Schedule SE		56
	57	Unreported social security and Medicare tax from Form: a ☐ 4137 b ☐ 8919		57
	58	Additional tax on IRAs, other qualified retirement plans, etc. Attach Form 5329 if required		58
	59	Additional taxes: a ☐ AEIC payments b ☐ Household employment taxes. Attach Schedule H		59
	60	Add lines 55 through 59. This is your **total tax** ▶		60
Payments	61	Federal income tax withheld from Forms W-2 and 1099	61	
	62	2009 estimated tax payments and amount applied from 2008 return	62	
	63	Making work pay and government retiree credits. Attach Schedule M	63	
If you have a qualifying child, attach Schedule EIC.	64a	**Earned income credit (EIC)**	64a	
	b	Nontaxable combat pay election 64b		
	65	Additional child tax credit. Attach Form 8812	65	
	66	Refundable education credit from Form 8863, line 16	66	
	67	First-time homebuyer credit. Attach Form 5405	67	
	68	Amount paid with request for extension to file (see page 72)	68	
	69	Excess social security and tier 1 RRTA tax withheld (see page 72)	69	
	70	Credits from Form: a ☐ 2439 b ☐ 4136 c ☐ 8801 d ☐ 8885	70	
	71	Add lines 61, 62, 63, 64a, and 65 through 70. These are your **total payments** ▶		71
Refund	72	If line 71 is more than line 60, subtract line 60 from line 71. This is the amount you **overpaid**		72
Direct deposit? See page 73 and fill in 73b, 73c, and 73d, or Form 8888.	73a	Amount of line 72 you want **refunded to you.** If Form 8888 is attached, check here ▶☐		73a
	▶ b	Routing number ▶ c Type: ☐ Checking ☐ Savings		
	▶ d	Account number		
	74	Amount of line 72 you want **applied to your 2010 estimated tax** ▶	74	
Amount You Owe	75	**Amount you owe.** Subtract line 71 from line 60. For details on how to pay, see page 74 ▶		75
	76	Estimated tax penalty (see page 74)	76	

Third Party Designee

Do you want to allow another person to discuss this return with the IRS (see page 75)? ☐ **Yes.** Complete the following. ☐ **No**

Designee's name ▶ Phone no. ▶ Personal identification number (PIN) ▶

Sign Here

Joint return? See page 15. Keep a copy for your records.

Under penalties of perjury, I declare that I have examined this return and accompanying schedules and statements, and to the best of my knowledge and belief, they are true, correct, and complete. Declaration of preparer (other than taxpayer) is based on all information of which preparer has any knowledge.

Your signature	Date	Your occupation	Daytime phone number
Spouse's signature. If a joint return, **both** must sign.	Date	Spouse's occupation	

Paid Preparer's Use Only

Preparer's signature ▶	Date	Check if self-employed ☐	Preparer's SSN or PTIN
Firm's name (or yours if self-employed), address, and ZIP code ▶		EIN	
		Phone no.	

Form **1040** (2009)

Chapter 4

Personal Financial Statements

You may not think of yourself as being like a public corporation, but in many ways you are., This will become more apparent as you earn income, pay taxes, save your earnings, accumulate assets both short-lived and long-lived, and have liabilities. (Liabilities mean that you owe money, and can come in the form of loans, taxes due, and other obligations.) These are the same things that corporations do. Public corporations also have to file financial statements in order to report their economic condition to shareholders. And just as financial statements are invaluable for understanding the financial circumstances of corporations, they are also invaluable to the individual.

There are two main concerns that a financially wise person should address throughout their lives; am I financially safe, and what is my progress towards accumulating wealth? Financial statements address these questions. I now turn to how a personal financial statement may look. Nicholas James has a number of characteristics of interest.[1]

Nick James

Nicholas "Nick" James is the grandson of the famous singer, Lucilla Reyes, who created several hit jazz albums with a Latina flair in the 1950s. He is cheerful, optimistic, attractive, and generous to his friends. He is also physically fit due to a love of bicycle racing. Nick grew up listening to his grandmother's jazz songs, and imagining a world of possibilities. Recently, he graduated from college, and as a result of growing up immersed in the entertainment industry, took a high-paying job producing special effects for music videos and commercials. Nick is also lucky. He inherited his grandmother's townhouse in Encino California that she used to stay in when she had to visit Los Angeles. It has an old fashioned, but still valuable home theater, and several vintage cars in the garage that were also left to Nick, along with a trust fund that makes regular payments to him.

Nick's personal financial statements are more complicated than most people's because he is relatively affluent, and he is active about investing his money in a variety of assets. This allows for a more thorough analysis of personal financial statements. Your personal financial statements may be simpler and quicker, especially when you first get started. However, if you are prosperous in the future, yours may look something like Nick's.

[1] Nicholas James is a hypothetical person created for teaching purposes.

4.1 The Balance Sheet

Throughout your lifetime you will own assets. An asset is something that has value. Something has value when it can be sold for money.[2] Assets can be real (a house), or financial (a stock certificate). They include short-term assets such as a certificate of deposit (a kind of bond or "debt instrument") issued by a bank that matures within a year, or long-term assets such as a car or house. A loan is an asset to the person making or holding the loan – they expect to receive payment.

A liability is money that is owed. (The person whom you owe the money to considers it to be an asset.) A liability could be any money that you personally owe, including payment due to the government in the form of taxes. Typically, a person borrows in order to buy at least some of their assets, possibly not for their entire life, but certainly in the beginning. Borrowings and other obligations which must be paid off are referred to as "liabilities."

A balance sheet can be thought of as a "snapshot" of how you are doing. It asks the question, "If I sold off everything that I own and pay off my debts and obligations, how much will I have left over?" It represents how much wealth you are accumulating. This is a particularly important question when thinking about retirement. At some point, most people stop working when they reach old age. They must then live off of the wealth that they have accumulated. They do this by selling their assets (or getting payments from assets such as receiving rent payments from an apartment building they own). Before they can enjoy this money, they must pay off their creditors. The balance sheet tells us what progress an individual is making towards accumulating wealth.

Key Takeaway: Individuals undertake many of the same activities that corporations do. And just like with corporations, a balance sheet can be a useful tool for understanding an individual's financial condition. A balance sheet takes a look at a point in time. It compares the value of assets owned with liabilities, which represent money owed. The difference represents how much would be left over if all assets were sold and liabilities paid off. This is a measure of wealth, and is an important metric of prosperity in retirement.

4.1.1 Assets

Table 4-1 illustrates the part of a hypothetical balance sheet for Nick that lists his assets. This is the "asset side" of the balance sheet. Nick's assets are broken down and listed as current assets and long-term assets. Current assets are assets that he plans on holding for less than a year. The first asset is cash and equivalents, of which he has $20,000. This is currency that he has in his possession, as well the balance in his checking account with the bank. This balance is considered cash because Nick can use it like cash by writing a check or using a debit card. Typically, people cycle through their cash and replace it on an ongoing basis within a year, and it is considered a short-term asset. Depending on the amount he spends, $20,000 may be too much to have either in a checking account or his wallet. The reason is that cash does not earn interest. It may be better to put that money into an investment that earns a profit. As long as the investment is easy to sell, if his checking account gets too low he can liquidate the investment (sell it, or "cash out") and put the sales proceeds into his checking account. In the interim, as an investment the money is earning a profit. Of course, this requires that Nick monitor his checking account to avoid running out of money. I will discuss this issue in further detail in the next chapter.

---

[2] There are assets that have value to you personally but not to others. These assets are referred to as having "sentimental value." To avoid complication I will not consider these.

Table 4-1
The Assets in Nick James's Balance Sheet, 12/31/2009

Assets		
Current Assets		
	Cash	20,000
	Short-Term Financial Assets	80,000
	Short-Term Personal Property	30,000
	Other Short-Term Assets	15,000
	Total	145,000
Long-Term Assets		
	Long-Term Financial Investments	740,000
	Retirement Accounts	140,000
	Long-Term Property	820,000
	Other Long-Term Assets	220,000
	Total	1,920,000
	Total Assets	2,065,000

The next current asset item is "short-term financial assets." Nick has $80,000 in short-term financial assets. These are financial securities that Nick will own for less than a year. There are numerous examples of short-term financial assets. His savings account at a bank is a short-term asset because he can remove his money at any time. A certificate of deposit (CD) from a bank is another example. If it matures in a year or less it is a short term asset. When he buys a CD from a bank, he pays money for the CD, and at the time of maturity, the bank pays him back his money plus interest. His account at a mutual fund is another example. Typically people can remove money when they wish, although some mutual funds have a penalty for early withdrawal. Nick has also made a short-term loan to a friend who was in a car accident and needs a new car, and Nick expects to get paid back when his friend is reimbursed from the auto insurance company.

Nick has $30,000 in "short-term personal property", which is personal property with some value that he expects to not have in a year. This could be clothing, books, or electronics. In his case, he plans to sell his grandmother's home theater, freeing up an additional room in his house for a home office.

It is important to note that corporations have strict rules about how they account for assets and other items in financial statements, and a bonus of this chapter is that you will have a leg up on understanding financial statements if you ever own a business or have to learn about accounting statements as part of a business education. However, the rules for businesses are different. In the case of assets, businesses typically include the amount they paid for the assets, minus a schedule dictated by the government for how the value of the assets declines over time (a depreciation schedule). These rules are there to protect investors from management, who may mislead investors into thinking assets are worth more than they actually are. Nick is constructing his balance sheet for himself. As long as he does not have rose colored glasses on, he does not have to worry about misleading himself and can construct his financial statements as he wishes.

However, human beings tend to be too optimistic (such as Nick's housekeeper, whom I shall discuss in a minute). He should be careful to be realistic about the "market value" of his assets, that is, the amount that he could sell them for, minus the cost of selling them (such as eBay fees). Corporations are required to write down the value of assets if they decline in value. Writing up the value of assets is restricted. All of this causes the value of assets, as reported by corporations in their financial statements, "the book value of assets," to stray from the market value. You as an individual do not face these same restrictions, and are free to record your assets at their estimated market value. A conservative approach, which I recommend, is to assume that most purchases such as clothing, small-valued electronics, and knickknacks are essentially worthless if sold. They should not be included in assets.

The market value of financial assets could decline or rise. For instance, the market value of your mutual fund account declines because the securities held in the mutual fund portfolio decline in value. Another unfortunate example may be a loan that you made to someone. This is an asset because they owe you money. If you believe that they will not pay you back or that you will only get part of your money back, the market value of the loan (which is what you could sell it to someone else for) will have declined.

"Other short-term assets" are any asset that does not fit into another category, and that Nick does not expect to hold for more than a year. Nick has $15,000. Consistent with his unfailing good luck, this includes prize winnings from a raffle that have not been paid to him yet. He is also expecting to get paid within the next year from suing his irresponsible neighbor for running over his expensive racing bike. Unfortunately, she "drives" her car like she is in a demolition derby.

"Long-term financial investments" includes financial assets that he will hold for more than a year. One example is stock that he intends to hold for more than a year. This stock recently declined in value and is listed based on what it can currently be sold for. An intended investment in a private equity fund is also included, in which he will not be allowed to withdraw his money for over a year. Nick decided to become a more sophisticated investor and had been attending investment conferences. At a particularly opulent one, complete with table after table of spectacular hors d'oeuvres, Nick met a financial agent who steered investors to a private equity fund (earning the agent fees from the fund in the process). Nick was impressed by the agent's knowledge of the finance industry and urbane manner. Plus, private equity funds had been earning large profits for investors. Nick signed a contract committing him to invest in the private equity fund in one month, and he expects to receive the shares when he pays. He will not be able to withdraw his money for a long time. Hedge funds and venture capitalists also have these kinds of requirements not to withdraw money. I will discuss private equity, venture capital, and hedge funds in more detail in Volume 2.

Nick has also made a loan to a good friend from college who wanted to start a business providing information technology services to government agencies. Some of that loan was supposed to be paid back to Nick this year, but because of the California budget crisis, his friend's business will not get paid on its first state contract until the following year. In total, he has $740,000 in long-term financial investments.

Each month Nick has money withheld by his employer and put into a 401(k) retirement account which he adds to "retirement accounts." This category would also include accumulated social security benefits. However, it may be difficult to estimate the value of his social security contributions. He has accumulated $140,000 so far in retirement accounts (which I will discuss in more detail in a later chapter).

"Long-term property" includes physical property that Nick intends to hold for more than a year. He has $820,000 worth of long-term property. Two common examples of physical property are cars and real estate. Note that most cars will lose their market value over time as they age.[3] Nick owns expensive vintage cars that have increased in value. Real estate will typically increase in value (but not necessarily, as can be seen in the current financial crisis). His new entertainment system is also included. Nick lists it for less than he paid for it because electronic equipment typically falls in value immediately after it has been purchased. Last, but not least, Nick has the townhouse his grandmother left him.

"Other long-term assets" is a more esoteric category. It may include royalty payments, which are payments for the right to use something owned by another. In Nick's case, he owns the rights to some of the songs his grandmother created. Each time a radio station plays one of the songs, they have to make royalty payments to him. (Michael Jackson actually purchased the rights to the Beatles' songs, and received royalties when their music was played.) The market value of money in the trust fund left to him by his grandmother is also included in this category. A trust fund is set up legally so that someone can contribute money to someone else. I shall discuss this in more detail in Volume 2. Nick has $220,000 in other long-term assets.

"Total assets" is the sum of current assets and long-term assets. It represents the total value of assets that have accumulated over the course of his lifetime. This number will change each day, as the market value of his assets changes day to day. Of course, he will not want to track his balance sheet from day to day, but he should look at it periodically, such as once a year. He has $2,065,000 in total assets.

Key Takeaway: Include assets that you own in your balance sheet. Their value is what they can be sold for minus selling expenses. Ignore small items, or items that will lose their value quickly. Some assets are short-term because you expect to sell or spend them within a year. Assets you hold for more than a year are long-term.

Challenge

Do you own any assets? What are they? Are they short-term or long-term?

4.1.2 Liabilities

Liabilities come from owing money. Unfortunately, there are many ways that this can happen. Borrowed money is a liability. Other examples include owing taxes, owing the cable company, or expecting to lose a lawsuit and being forced to pay money to another party. Table 4-2 illustrates the "liabilities and net worth" side of Nick's balance sheet. I start with liabilities.

[3] In fact, cars immediately drop quite a bit in value as soon as they are driven off the lot because they go from being a "new" car to a "used" car.

Table 4-2
The Liabilities and New Worth in Nick James's Balance Sheet, 12/31/2009

Liabilities and Net Worth		
Current Liabilities		
	Payments Due	40,000
	Accrued Expenses and Obligations	320,000
	Short-Term Debt Due	5,000
	Current Portion of Long-Term Debt	50,000
	Total	415,000
Long-Term Liabilities		
	Long-Term Debt Obligations	706,000
	Other Long-Term Obligations	80,000
	Total	786,000
Total Liabilities		1,201,000
Net Worth		864,000
Liabilities and Net Worth		2,065,000

Current liabilities have to be paid within the coming year. "Payments due" represents payments for goods and services already received. Most of the time individuals are required to prepay for goods and services. For instance, apartment rent is paid ahead of time. As long as an individual can terminate a contract, such as an apartment lease, they are not obligated to pay in the future, and it is not a liability. A cell phone bill is for past services (it cannot be gotten rid of by cancelling the contract) and is a liability, as is a cable bill. On the other hand, Nick was required to leave a deposit with the cell phone company when he first initiated service, and the deposit is refundable when he terminates service. (Nick had a bad credit score, which will be discussed in a later chapter.) The deposit is therefore an asset. Another example of a liability would be his owing money for legal services rendered. Payments due in the balance sheet is $40,000. This is relatively large, in part because he owes attorneys.

Nick has $320,000 in "accrued expenses and obligations." These are payments due within the next year, but not for goods or services directly received. The biggest item for most individuals is taxes due. Over the course of the year, Nick has been accumulating taxes on his salary because he has withheld less than he owes. (If he withheld more than he owed this would be an asset because he would expect a refund.) He will also have to pay property taxes. Of course, he may benefit from goods or services that the government provides, but these have not been directly purchased by him. If he owed the government for being allowed to use federal property for cattle grazing, this would go under payments due because it is directly related to a service.

Another example of accrued expenses and obligations would be owing money to the person who successfully sued him. Nick's housekeeper was on the gymnastics team in high school and insisted that she could stand on a ladder to clean his windows. Nick was worried that she would get hurt, but she adamantly insisted she could do it. Nick agreed because he did not want to insult her athletic ability. Later she fell, broke her shoulder, and chose to sue Nick. He was fuming mad and decided to fight her in court. The court ruled that it was Nick's responsibility to keep her safe regardless of what she said. Therefore, the housekeeper won. Nick did not have umbrella insurance (to be discussed in Volume 2), and owes the money. Of this, $10,000 is due within a year. Finally, Nick committed to invest $300,000 in a private equity fund within the next month and it is also included in accrued expenses and obligations. As you shall see, this was a big mistake.

The "short-term debt due" on Nick's balance sheet is $5,000. This may include any loan that matures in a year or less. Nick bought an expensive entertainment system. He took out a loan with the seller that he has to pay off in one year.

Short-term debt is different from the "current portion of long-term debt." Remember that debt payments come in two forms. The money that was lent has to be paid back. This is referred to as principal. Extra money on top of this is interest, which is the profit that the lender makes. Nick took out a mortgage on his townhome, and committed to pay back some of the money this year, while the rest of the money will be returned in later years. "Current portion of long-term debt" refers to the principal that Nick will pay back in the next year on the long-term debt contract. As will be explained later, interest payments do not show up here, but in a financial statement called the income statement. Nick also has long-term student loans, some of which are due within a year.

Credit cards are considered revolving consumer loans, because if Nick pays back some of the principal he can immediately go out and borrow it again. Theoretically, he could always owe the credit card company. For the purpose of the balance sheet snapshot the current portion is the principal he is required to pay back within the next year as of today. Of course, this could change in the future depending on what he does.

Nick is also paying off his mortgage, and will pay substantial principal within the next year. However, he also likes expensive furniture, and has charged up large charges on credit cards, some of which will need to be paid back this year. In total, over the course of the next year he will pay $415,000 in short-term obligations. Now that you have learned about current liabilities you can already see a hint of trouble to come: Nick's current assets are less than his current liabilities.

"Long-term debt obligations" includes the return of principal on debt that occurs after one year. Nick has $706,000, which is mostly mortgage payments, along with credit card debt and student loans. "Other long-term obligations" includes payments that he has committed to make that are not debt. Nick will owe $80,000 in two years due to being sued. In total, he will pay $786,000 later than a year from now. Combining current liabilities and long-term liabilities, Nick will owe a total of $1,201,000.

The difference between Nick's total assets and his liabilities is referred to as his "net worth." Nick's net worth is a measure of how wealthy he is. If he were to sell all of his assets and use the proceeds to pay off all of his liabilities, he would have $864,000 left over.

Nick will want his net worth to be as high as possible when he retires, so that he will have plenty of resources to live on. (Notice that mathematically, liabilities and net worth have to equal total assets, since net worth is total assets minus total liabilities. This is how a balance sheet gets its name — because total assets have to equal total liabilities and net worth.)

The balance sheet is a snapshot of a person's financial position at a particular point in time. However, it is important to aim towards having a high net worth for retirement. Therefore, being able to forecast what the balance sheet will look like in the future is very important. You shall spend a great deal of time learning how to forecast throughout this textbook; however, I will put off this topic for the moment.

Key Takeaway: In your balance sheet, include all of your liabilities. Liabilities are money that you owe. If you have not received goods or services yet, then do not include those payments. Principal on debt should be included, but not interest. Principal involves returning the money that was borrowed. Interest is the extra payment that allows the lender to earn a profit.

Challenge

Do you have liabilities? What are they? Are they short-term or long-term? What do you think your net worth is? Balance sheets tend to look particularly bad right after a person graduates from college. Why would this be?

4.1.3 The Balance Sheet and Financial Solvency

Theoretically, net worth is the amount that would be left over after all assets are sold and liabilities paid off. You can also think of net worth as a cushion or safety net. What if your liabilities were greater than your assets? You could not sell assets to pay off your liabilities and may become bankrupt. As you failed to pay your liabilities, your creditors would start seizing your assets. You would be forced into filing bankruptcy with the courts in order to have the process brought under control, and you could end up with everything being taken away: home, car, family heirlooms – everything.

So how much net worth do you need to feel safe? One approach is to look at worst case scenarios. In the current financial crisis, it is not uncommon for stocks to lose most, if not all of their value. The stock market declined overall by more than half its value from its peak in 2007, to its trough in 2009.[4] Housing prices took a similar tumble in some areas. A worst case scenario would assume that asset values fell by the worst amount seen historically, and maybe even a little more. After going through each of his assets, Nick decided that the worst case would look like Table 4-3 below.

[4] Based on the S&P 500 Index.

Table 4-3
Nick James's Worst Case Balance Sheet

Assets		
Current Assets		
	Cash	20,000
	Short-Term Financial Assets	60,000
	Short-Term Personal Property	10,000
	Other Short-Term Assets	15,000
	Total	105,000
Long-Term Assets		
	Long-Term Financial Investments	610,000
	Retirement Accounts	70,000
	Long-Term Property	555,000
	Other Long-Term Assets	200,000
	Total	1,435,000
	Total Assets	1,540,000
Liabilities and Net Worth		
Total Liabilities		1,201,000
Net Worth		339,000
Liabilities and Net Worth		1,540,000

Each item on the asset side of the balance sheet is reduced based on historical worst case scenarios. Note that some assets can decline more than others. Total liabilities are left the same, since these payments are required under all circumstances.[5] This reduces net worth to $339,000, which is a much smaller number. However, it is still positive, suggesting the Nick will not become "insolvent" in a bad downturn. Insolvent means that his net worth is negative. If this number is negative, Nick will be prudent to take action to reduce his liabilities (possibly by spending less and saving more money, or selling some of his assets at current higher market prices and then paying down the debt).

[5] One exception could be accrued expenses, as taxes payable may fall by a small amount.

Another way of looking at the same issue is by calculating something called a debt ratio. One version of a debt ratio is $\frac{\text{Total Liabilities}}{\text{Total Assets}}$. The debt ratio tells you the proportion of assets taken up by liability claims. The higher the ratio, the less likely it is that you will have sufficient assets in a downturn to pay off liabilities. What constitutes a safe debt ratio depends on the type of assets that you have. If you have assets that are volatile (their value can change a great deal, say by up to 50%), then you would want a debt ratio lower than 50%. If your assets are not volatile (their value could drop by 15% at the most) then you would want a debt ratio below 85%. Nick's debt ratio is 58%. His worst case debt ratio is 78%. He seems to be relatively safe. However, as you are about to see, this is not necessarily the case.

> ***Key Takeaway:*** Someone is insolvent when their liabilities are greater than their assets (their net worth is negative). Insolvency signifies serious trouble since you owe more money than the value of your assets. You may end up bankrupt, with most or all of your possessions taken as a result. It is prudent to construct a worst case balance sheet. This is done by reducing assets by their historically largest drop. If net worth is negative, this means that you would become insolvent in a major economic downturn.

4.1.4 Liquidity

You have seen that the balance sheet and income statement are important for measuring progress towards meeting financial goals. There is another concept that is very important that you can discover from looking at a balance sheet: "liquidity." If liquidity is not monitored, Nick could go from prosperous and safe, to bankrupt and destitute in the blink of an eye.

When an asset is liquid, that means it can be sold quickly without having to resort to offering a significant discount. For instance, suppose that you want to sell stock in a company and that stock is actively traded on a stock exchange. In addition, the amount that you want to sell is only a small fraction of what is traded every day. You are insignificant compared to all of the buyers and sellers of the stock. You can simply call your broker and ask him to sell your stock immediately, which will not affect the stock price in the overall market.

On the other hand, suppose that you want to sell $200 million worth of stock, and only about $5 million of that company's stock is traded in a typical day. If you try to sell all of your holdings at once, there will not be a lot of buyers available. You may have to offer the stock at a steep discount off of the current price in order to induce people to come into the market and buy. In this case, you holdings are "illiquid."

In order for an asset to be liquid, the owner needs to have a small holding in comparison to the size of the market. Another way of saying this is that there needs to be plenty of potential buyers of the asset. Also, there has to be a mechanism to sell the asset quickly. Stock markets allow the rapid trading of stocks.

But what about a house? I shall go into greater detail in Volume 2 about all of the steps that need to be taken in order to sell a house. To name just a few, the house has to be fixed up to be as presentable as possible and any needed repairs made. To get the house ready for sale, Nick needs to hire a plumber to fix several plumbing problems. Next, a broker typically needs to be found to assist in selling the house. The buyer in turn needs to secure mortgage financing from a bank. The bank has to investigate the buyer, and needs to verify the value of the house. (This is necessary in case the buyer defaults and the bank has to seize the house.) The buyer has to hire an engineer to inspect the house, and hires a company to conduct a title search on the house. This is necessary to make sure that the IRS or anyone else does not have a lien (claim) on the house.

All of this should illustrate that selling a house can be time consuming and complicated. If the seller is under intense pressure to sell quickly, they will have to offer a very steep discount. This is because they will have to induce someone who has a lot of cash (and does not need a time consuming bank loan) to come in and buy. The buyer is taking a risk because they do not have the time to do a careful title search, engineering inspection, etc. The buyer will therefore demand a very steep discount off the price of the house.

You have seen that net worth is a measure of solvency. A higher net worth makes it less likely that liabilities become greater than assets in a downturn, leading to bankruptcy. It turns out that the issue of liquidity is also very important. Table 4-4 illustrates a liquidity schedule, and lists Nick's assets from a liquidity perspective. It is broken down by how long it would take to sell his assets without offering a steep discount off the price.

Some assets simply cannot be sold before a certain point in time. Others may be sold sooner, but with a (potentially large) loss in value. A asterisk (*) denotes the assets that can be sold sooner, but at a discount. Cash and money in Nick's savings account would be immediately available. He would also be able to sell a large amount of assets within one week. For instance, he could redeem his non-restricted mutual fund accounts. Notice that some of this was listed as a long-term financial investment because he had not been intending to sell it within a year; however, in an emergency he could. There is also an active market for used cars, where used car dealers stand ready to buy and sell. Therefore, his cars are also listed there. If his cars are extremely rare and valuable, it will take much longer to sell them because they will have to be sold at a special auction, or through some other time-involving means.

The old home theater system and other assets that Nick had been intending to sell within a year are listed as being saleable within one month (possibly through an online auction site). In an emergency he could also sell the entertainment system that he had recently purchased. Since he had not been planning on selling it, the entertainment system was listed under long-term property. He also expects to receive raffle winnings within a month. Moving along, he made a loan to a friend who will pay him back in three months.

Table 4-4
Nick James's Liquidity Schedule Assets

Time	Asset		Amount	Place in Balance Sheet
Immediate	Cash		20,000	Cash
	Savings Account		10,000	Short-Term Financial
	Total		30,000	
One Week	Money Market/Stock Accounts at Mutual Fund		5,000	Short-Term Financial Assets
	Stock at Mutual Fund Intended to Be Held for Over a Year		60,000	Long-Term Financial Investments
	Cars		80,000	Long-Term Property
	Total		145,000	
One Month	Old Home Theater	*	30,000	Short-Term Personal Property
	Entertainment System	*	5,000	Long-Term Property
	Raffle Winnings		5,000	Other Short-Term
	Total		40,000	
Three Months	Loan Made to a Friend		5,000	Short-Term Financial Assets
Nine Months	Certificates of Deposit		20,000	Short-Term Financial Assets
	Successful Lawsuit Proceeds		10,000	Other Short-Term Assets
	Restricted Account at Mutual Fund	*	40,000	Short-Term Financial Assets
	House	*	735,000	Long-Term Property
	Value of Royalty Payments		120,000	Other Long-Term
	Total		925,000	
Long-Term	Private Equity Investment		300,000	Long-Term Financial Investments
	Trust Fund from Grandmother		100,000	Other Long-Term Assets
	Small Business Loan		380,000	Long-Term Financial Investments
	Retirement 401K Account	*	50,000	Retirement Accounts
	Social Security		90,000	Retirement Accounts
	Total		920,000	

Nick has a large amount of assets that he could sell, or that will mature within nine months. His certificates of deposit will mature within nine months. He is also owed money from a successful lawsuit. He purchased shares in a mutual fund over four years ago that carried a stiff 10% penalty for early withdrawal before five years. That restriction will expire within nine months. The biggest item is his house. If priced reasonably, during normal times it should sell within nine months.[6] Of course, it would be painful indeed for him to end up in the position of selling his house because he was having trouble paying his obligations. The pain will only be magnified if a spouse or children are involved. To make it worse, he may have to pay a penalty for paying off his mortgage early.

The last item listed is the value of royalty payments. When someone has a claim to regular payments for some reason, it can sometimes be possible to sell those rights to someone else. There is a market for royalty rights, and it is expected that they could be sold within nine months.

The final category is long-term assets that cannot be sold easily. Included is the private equity investment that Nick committed to and is pending. The investment has early withdrawal restrictions. There is a chance he may be able to sell the rights to his investment, but he may have difficulty. Sometimes payments from a trust fund can be assignable (saleable to someone else). However, his grandmother provided, perhaps wisely, that he cannot sell the rights to those payments. Nick was shocked to find this out — he had been planning on using the money to help pay for the private equity investment. He had a friend who sold the rights to a trust fund that was assignable, and Nick assumed that he could do the same. Nick should have consulted with an attorney, rather than relying on a friend.

Finally, Nick is expecting to receive proceeds from a loan that he made to a friend who was starting a new business, but the loan is not due for several years. Nick had been promised that part of that loan would be paid within a year but the payment was delayed because of the California financial crisis, and his friend simply does not have the money yet.

Nick would face substantial penalties (10%) for withdrawing his 401K funds early in addition to paying substantial taxes on the withdrawal, which will significantly reduce the amount of cash that he could receive. His social security benefits are not accessible at all.

> ***Key Takeaway:*** Some assets are liquid while others are not. If an asset is liquid, it can be sold quickly without a significant reduction in price. Assets that are listed under "long-term assets" because they are not intended for sale can be liquid, while short-term assets can be somewhat illiquid.

Now that a liquidity schedule for Nick's assets has been established, it is time to look at obligations that must be paid, as shown in Table 4-5. Within a week he has to pay bills for goods and services received. However, assets available immediately, plus assets available within one week exceeds this by $135,000. This is reported in the surplus (deficit) column. It is calculated as all assets available up to that time, minus obligations coming due. Presumably Nick will use his cash and some of the money in his savings account to pay bills.

[6] During a financial crisis, the liquidity of houses and other assets will fall. I discuss this later.

Table 4-5

Liquidity Schedule Liabilities and Overall Surplus or Deficit

Time Until Due	Liability	Amount	Surplus (Deficit)
One Week	Payments Due	40,000	
	Total	40,000	135,000
One Month	Private Equity Payment	300,000	
	Mortgage Principal	3,500	
	Total	303,500	(128,500)
Three	Owes from Law Suit	10,000	
	Mortgage Principal	13,000	
	Total	23,000	(146,500)
Nine	Taxes Due	10,000	
	Loan on Entertainment System/ Student Loans	5,000	
	Mortgage Principal	25,500	
	Total	40,500	738,000
Long-Term	Credit Card Principal/ Student Loans	21,000	
	Mortgage Principal	693,000	
	Owes From Lawsuit	80,000	
	Total	794,000	864,000

The private equity placement is a big problem. Nick needs $300,000 in cash in one month to fulfill his commitment. Unfortunately, he has not planned ahead, and money that he assumed he would get from the business loan and trust fund is not available. To add to this, he has to pay $3,500 in principal on his mortgage. The result is trouble. Nick cannot sell or liquidate enough assets to cover this obligation. He has a short-fall of $128,500. If he cannot find some way to raise the cash, Nick faces bankruptcy. By month three the situation has worsened. Only $5,000 will come in from the car loan to a friend. On the other hand, he must continue to make principal payments on the mortgage, as well as paying damages awarded against him in a lawsuit.

By nine months time, Nick's situation has reversed itself, resulting in excess funds. He will continue to have to pay off the principal on his mortgage, as well as the $5,000 loan he took out on the entertainment system. However, by that point he will have been able to sell a substantial amount of his assets. Nick was able to avoid selling his house, which is worth $735,000 by the thin margin of $3,000. (His surplus is $738,000.) He survived the tough one-three month period by talking the private equity company into letting him delay his investment for eight months. (However, there had been no guarantee that they would have agreed to a delay.)

A slight dip in the value of his assets would have tipped him into having to sell the house. He did have to sell his vintage cars and entertainment system, but he has also learned a valuable lesson for the future. Nick had a number of sleepless nights, and just avoided entering the painful, fear-filled world of bankruptcy. One moment his life seemed bright and full of promise, the next he faced ruin. The good news is that he will be better prepared in the future after suffering a relatively small setback.

Earlier, you saw that Nick's current assets were substantially less than his current liabilities. That was a hint of problems to come. The liquidity analysis added two twists. The first is that you cannot just look at solvency from the perspective of a year versus longer than a year. Current assets and liabilities occur within a year or less. Nick got into trouble within one month.

The second twist is that it is possible that long-term assets can be sold quickly, if unexpectedly. This was the case with some of Nick's investments in stock mutual funds, as well as the house that he has come to regard as a home. It is a painful choice to sells assets quickly, taking a large loss on them in order to prevent bankruptcy. This is referred to as selling at "fire sale" prices. If a business had a fire, the building may be damaged to the extent that the inventory inside is not protected from the elements, or the building may be very unpleasant to customers. The business may sell off its inventory at severely reduced prices under these circumstances.

In general, selling assets at "fire sale" prices refers to some kind of distressed situation where assets get sold off quickly at a steep discount. Think of a personal fire sale as a fast moving forest fire. One minute you own many valuable assets, but because of a liquidity problem, you are forced to rapidly sell asset after asset at severely reduced prices. There can also be unfortunate tax consequences of selling large amounts of assets unexpectedly, including massive capital gains taxes that must be paid the next tax year. For many reasons, fire sales can have a devastating effect on wealth. Think of a liquidity schedule as a way of preventing a fire.

Key Takeaway: If a person is solvent, bankruptcy can still result if liabilities come due before assets can be sold. Even worse, illiquidity can bring on a fire sale, where asset after asset is sold at a steep discount. It is important to keep a liquidity schedule to prevent disaster.

Only when long-term assets are included does the rosy picture of Nick's solvency that was presented before appear. When all assets are sold and liabilities paid, you see his old net worth of $864,000. However, if he had been forced to sell assets at fire sale prices, he would not reach this point and could end up financially destitute. His net worth number contains the assumption that he could take his time selling his assets. When the fire sales are done, very little could be left.

The financial crisis illustrates how the problem can be much worse. Most assets tend to decline in value when times are bad and defaults tend to rise. What situation would Nick be in if his friend with the business loan became seriously ill and declared bankruptcy? Nick has ended up in trouble in the best of times because of poor planning. In order to understand the true risks that he is facing, it is necessary to understand his position in the worst of times.

In Table 4-3, you saw how his balance sheet could look during a financial crisis. To take things a step further, it would be prudent to look at his liquidity during a financial crisis. In fact, a common characteristic of financial crises is that individuals or institutions who thought they were safe discovered that in addition to drastic reductions in the value of their assets, they also had their liquidity drastically fall. Banks are an excellent example of this. They make long-term loans such as mortgages, which are long-term assets for the bank. They raise money by borrowing with short-term debt which must be paid off quickly. When their short-term loans come due, the banks borrow new short-term debt to pay off the principal of the old short-term debt. However, banks may not be able to do this if the market has a crisis of confidence. They cannot borrow to pay off their short-term debt, and they cannot sell their long-term assets (mortgages).

To truly get a picture of the worst case scenario, a liquidity schedule needs to be constructed assuming a severe downturn. When everyone is short on cash, trouble can spread like wildfire. Financial markets may not function well, making it more difficult to sell assets, and potential buyers cannot obtain loans. Once the financial crisis hit, those few people who wanted to buy houses had difficulty obtaining loans – even if they had good credit, because the banks had a liquidity and solvency problem. Those who could borrow found that it took longer to get approved for a mortgage. Finally, people and businesses that owe money may also delay payment or even default. During the current financial crisis, the State of California delayed payment by issuing IOUs, creating further financial problems for the people who were expecting to get paid.

Facing financial distress is very difficult. It is something I shall cover in a later chapter. However, you now have a much better understanding of how to avoid financial distress. When it comes to protecting yourself and your family, you are already much stronger than many.

4.2 The Income Statement

Accumulating wealth is a more cheerful topic. An income statement looks at how net worth changes over a length of time. In other words, if Nick's balance sheet at 12/31/2008 had net worth of $100,000, and his balance sheet at 12/31/2009 had net worth of $150,000, then the change in net worth from the end of 2008 to the end of 2009 would have been $50,000. The change in net worth is a measure of progress towards accumulating wealth as well as financial safety. The income statement breaks out factors that contributed to the change in net worth over some time period. Therefore, an income statement is not a snapshot of one point in time. Rather, it measures what happened over a period of time. In this case, one year.

Chart 4-1

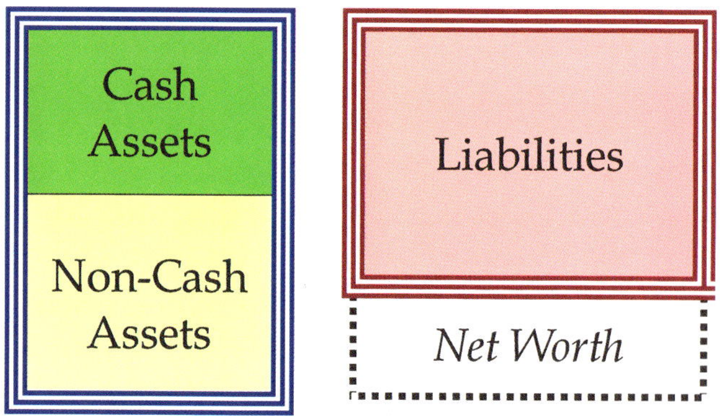

As can be seen in the simplified balance sheet shown in Chart 4-1, changes in assets can come from changes in cash or non-cash assets. Net worth is the difference in the chart height of assets and liabilities. Net worth will increase if cash assets get bigger, non-cash assets get bigger, or liabilities get smaller. If cash or non-cash assets fall, or liabilities rise, net worth will fall.

Before proceeding to the income statement, it will be helpful to discuss how owning securities affects net worth and cash. Investors receive cash from investments in the form of dividends and interest. These payments go directly into cash, and since non-cash assets and liabilities do not change, dividends and interest cause net worth to go up.

Buying securities has a different effect. Buying a security will cause cash to go down by the same amount that non-cash assets go up (financial assets). A cash asset is simply shifted over into a non-cash asset. There will be no change in net worth. Borrowing is the mirror image of investing. Paying interest causes cash to go down (the opposite of dividends or interest earned) without changing non-cash assets or liabilities. This causes net worth to fall. Paying off loans (paying down principal) is the opposite of buying a security. It causes liabilities to fall by the same amount that cash falls, and net worth does not change. (However paying off debt frees you from paying interest in the future, which will increase future wealth. Do not let me discourage you from paying off your debt!)

Securities can also change net worth if the value of the securities changes. Suppose that the value of a person's stockholdings rises, which is the typical situation. Non-cash (financial) assets will increase with no effect on cash or liabilities. Therefore net worth must go up. When people invest wisely, their wealth rises over time.

> ***Key Takeaway:*** The income statement shows how net worth changed over time. Therefore it lists factors that changed assets and liabilities. Earning interest or dividends makes net worth go up, while paying interest makes net worth go down. Buying or selling securities does not change net worth, nor does borrowing or paying off loans. However, paying off loans cancels future interest payments, which will increase future wealth. If the market value of securities goes up, so does net worth, while net worth falls if the market value of securities falls.

It is time to look at Nick's income statement as seen in Table 4-6. Each item in the income statement corresponds to a change in one or more items in the balance sheet that resulted in a change in net worth. An "NC" is included when an item affects net worth through non-cash assets rather than cash.

Table 4-6
Nick James's Income Statement for 2009

Revenues			
	Salary	210,000	
	Payments From a Trust	12,000	
	Royalties	45,000	
	Net Capital Gains (Losses)	(12,000)	NC
	Dividends and Interest Income	33,000	
	Other	16,000	C/NC
	Total Revenue	304,000	
Expenses			
	Recurring Personal Expenses	6,000	
	Benefits (Expenses Only)	8,000	
	Interest Expense	39,000	
	Non-Recurring and Miscellaneous Expenses	95,000	C/NC
	Taxes	115,000	
	Total Expenses	263,000	
Net Income	Net Revenue	41,000	

Revenues increase net worth, either by making assets go up or liabilities go down. Nick's first source of revenue is salary. He is a special effects producer, and earns a high income. He is also receiving monthly payments from a trust fund left to him by his grandmother and regular royalty payments.

Nick experienced a fall of $12,000 in the combined market value of his securities, royalty payments, and trust fund payments. This reduced his net worth. However, Nick received dividends and interest payments of $33,000, which increased his net worth. The "other" category has cash and noncash items that change his net worth. Nick won a law suit and expects to receive $10,000, although he has not been paid yet. This increases his assets and should be reflected as income, but it does not affect his cash for the moment. (When he is finally paid, his net worth will not change — other short-term assets in the balance sheet will fall and cash will rise.) Nick is also waiting to receive $5,000 from winning a raffle, which increases his wealth, but not his cash. (At the point when he actually receives the payments, cash will go up in the balance sheet, other short-term assets will fall, and net worth will not change.) He also received a $1,000 refund from his knee surgeon because he was overbilled the previous year. Since the refund was a surprise, it had not been listed as an asset in his balance sheet. The refund shows up in cash, and also increases his net worth.[7]

After adding up all sources of revenue, in total Nick received $304,000, mostly in cash with some non-cash components. This is an impressive amount for someone fresh from college. However, he had expenses. Expenses are either payments for items that are not assets, or unexpected liabilities that crop up. (As I discussed, payments for assets such as stock do not change net worth.) Expenses make assets go down or liabilities go up, and they reduce wealth.

The first kind of expense is "recurring personal expenses." These are typical expenses that keep repeating as part of daily living. This would include grocery purchases, paid cable bills, payments for haircuts, gym membership fees, and so on. Anytime someone purchases something that is not an asset, their net worth falls. The next expense is "benefits" taken from Nick's paycheck. Benefits used for medical insurance and other items that are not an investments (their value expires) are an expense. Money contributed to his 401(k) plan and to social security is an investment and does not reduce net worth (and is not an expense).

The next expense listed is "interest expense," which reduces net worth (principal payments do not). Most of this comes from the interest paid on Nick's mortgage. However, he has some other debt that also charges interest. Of course, an important difference between mortgage interest and other kinds of interest is that mortgage interest is tax deductible.

Non-recurring and miscellaneous expenses are every kind of expense that is left over. Nick lost $80,000 in a lawsuit by his housekeeper, which he has not paid yet. This has had a very negative effect on his income. It appears in his balance sheet in accrued expenses and obligations and other long-term obligations. It is an expense in his income statement because it increases liabilities and lowers his wealth, but it is not a cash flow since it has not been paid yet. (When he pays it, cash will go down in the balance sheet by the same amount as the corresponding liability, and net worth will not change.) Also, there is a cash flow in non-recurring and miscellaneous expenses of $15,000, because Nick had to repair his home. Finally, taxes are a major expense and have to be removed. Some of the taxes may have already been paid in the form of withholding, causing cash to fall, while some taxes have not been paid and show up as a liability. In either case, net worth goes down.

Net income is total revenue minus total expenses. For 2009, Nick's was 41,000. As seen in Chart 4-2, his net worth at the end of 2008 was $823,000. Adding net income of $41,000 yields his net worth of $864,000 for 2009. Fortunately for Nick, his net income is usually positive and substantial, and his wealth typically grows over time.

---

[7] If he had been aware of the refund, his net worth would previously been higher. He would have had an "other long-term asset" called "refund due" that offset the reduction of $1,000 in his cash from his payment to the knee surgeon.

Chart 4-2
The Relationship Between the Income Statement and the Balance Sheet

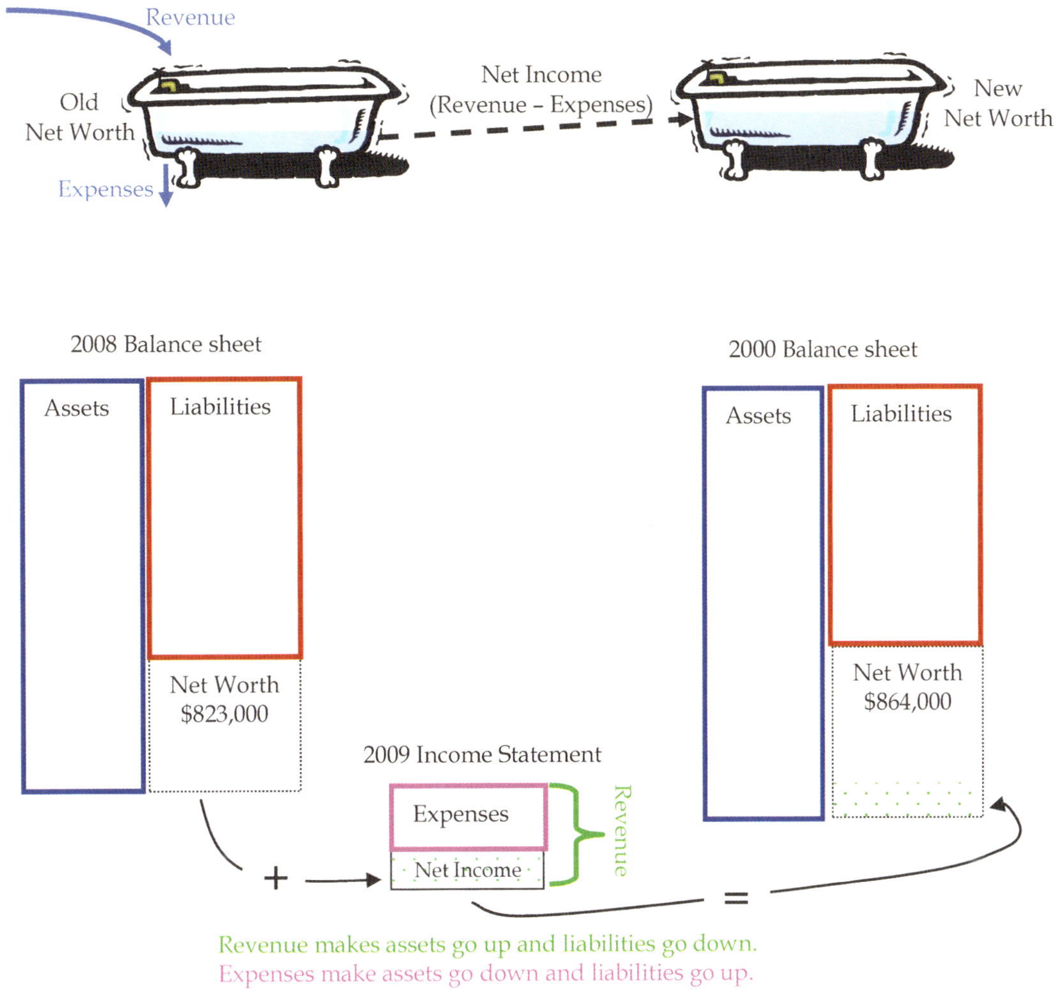

Key Takeaway: Revenues cause net worth to rise. Expenses cause net worth to fall. Some revenues and expenses involve cash rising or falling, while others do not. Net income is the difference between revenues and expenses. Net worth in the previous balance sheet, plus net income, equals net worth in the current balance sheet.

Challenge

What was your income for the year? What do you think your income will be your first year after college?

4.3 Conclusion

Nick made progress of $41,000 for the year. He had a tough time, but managed to emerge relatively unscathed. He learned some valuable lessons, has a lot of earning power, is relatively wealthy for his age, and has a bright future. And now that you have learned about financial statements, hopefully you will not learn the same kind of lessons the hard way.

Financial statements tell you about your financial safety and the progress you are making towards building wealth. Your goal is to accumulate wealth in order to provide for financial security, a comfortable retirement, and other worthy objectives. It is important to consider how wealth will grow in the future. Having wealth connotes a life of contribution and success, and creates the opportunity to give to others.

At some point you may become married. It is important to get your spouse involved in financial planning. There will be a lot less arguments and a lot more joy if you share the same plan. Personal financial statements can help you row in the same direction.

Plan for the worst by creating a "Worst Case Balance Sheet." A solvency schedule should also be constructed. If your assets and investments are simple, it will take but a few moments. Nick had relatively complex personal statements (for illustration purposes). During your early years if you have significant borrowing (such as a mortgage), this is especially vital. Most people get into trouble when they are relatively young. As you accumulate wealth, the need to track solvency and liquidity will decline in importance because your net worth will have become quite large. However, progress towards wealth targets should always be tracked.

It is also vital to analyze how big decisions will affect your financial safety and increase wealth by considering their effect on your financial statements. Nick thought he was safe when he committed to investing in the private equity fund, but he failed to consider his liquidity. Before any large financial decision, issues surrounding solvency, liquidity, and wealth should be worked through carefully.

Key Terms:

Accrued expenses and obligations
Asset side of the balance sheet
Assets
Assignable
Cash flow
Cash out
Current assets
Current liabilities
Current portion of long-term debt
Debt ratio
Equity
Expense
Financial assets
Fire sale
Income
Insolvent
Interest
Liabilities
Liabilities and net worth side of the balance sheet
Liquidity
Long-term assets
Long-term liabilities
Market value
Net revenue
Net worth
Payments due
Principal
Real property
Sentimental value
Short-term assets
Solvency
Total assets
Total expenses
Total liabilities
Total liabilities and equity
Total revenue
Worst case

End of Chapter Questions

1. Given the following information, construct a balance sheet for Trudi for 12/31/2009.

Trudi's Assets and Liabilities 12/31/09				
#	Assets	Value	Worst Case Value	Time Until Sold Without a Steep Discount
1	Mutual fund shares	110,000	85,000	One week
2	Investments in a 401(k) plan	310,000	280,000	Long-term
3	Car	8,000	3,500	One week
4	Cash and checking account	6,500	6,500	Immediate
5	CDs that mature in six months	5,000	5,000	Six months
6	Employer reimbursement for travel within two months	350	350	Two months
7	Savings account	500	500	Immediate
8	Condominium	245,000	185,000	Nine months
9	Assignable trust fund left to you	35,000	28,000	One month
10	Heavy statuette given to you from a moving neighbor that you are planning to sell	500	100	One month
11	Stocks at a brokerage account	14,000	7,000	One week
12	Money market account	8,000	7,700	One week

#	Liabilities	Value	Worst Case Value	Time Due
1	Mortgage	415	415	Every month for year
2	Mortgage	200,000	200,000	More than one year
3	Cable bill	45	45	Two weeks
4	Cell phone bill	95	95	One week
5	Mattress payment to mattress store	700	700	Two weeks
6	College tuition payment promised a cousin	27,000	27,000	More than one year
7	Credit card	12,000	12,000	More than one year
8	Car loan	45	45	Every month for year
9	Credit card	55	55	Every month for year
10	Car loan	2,000	2,000	More than one year
11	Electric and Gas bill	82	82	Two weeks
12	Taxes due	1,200	1,200	Six months

2. Using the information from question 1, construct a worst case balance sheet for Trudi for 12/31/2009.

3. Using the information from question 1, construct a worst case liquidity schedule for Trudi.

4. Given the following information, construct an income statement for Trudi for the year 2009.

Trudi's Revenues and Expenses	
Salary	125,000
Taxes	65,000
Net Capital Gains	12,500
Dividends and Interest Payments	4,000
Interest Expense	14,000
Recurring Personal Expenses	12,000
Prize Winnings	600
Losses From A Kitchen Fire	2,500

5. What is an asset?

6. How do current assets differ from long-term assets?

7. What does it mean for an asset to be liquid? Are current assets liquid?

8. What is a liability?

9. What is the current portion of long-term debt?
10. What is net worth? Why is net worth important?
11. What is a cash flow? What does it mean to have a negative cash flow or a positive cash flow?
12. What two places do changes in net worth come from?
13. What is the purpose of an income statement?
14. How is the timing different for a balance sheet and an income statement?
15. Why do investments not appear in the income statement?
16. What is revenue?
17. How does revenue relate to the balance sheet?
18. How are expenses different from investments?
19. How do expenses relate to the balance sheet?
20. Name examples of items in the income statement that do not affect cash.
21. What is the relationship between revenue, expenses, and net income?
22. How does net income relate to the balance sheet?
23. Why should you look at your balance sheet assuming a worst case scenario for the value of your assets?
24. What is a debt ratio? What does it tell you?
25. Why should you construct a liquidity schedule regularly?
26. Why should you construct a liquidity schedule for your worst case scenario?
27. How do capital gains/losses affect income and cash flow? How do asset sales/purchases affect income and cash flow?
28. There are two overall questions that financial statements address. What are they?
29. What tends to happen to the liquidity of assets during a financial crisis?
30. How liquid is a house? Why?
31. How does paying interest affect net worth? How does borrowing affect net worth? How does paying down debt affect net worth?

Chapter 5

Managing Your Cash and Budgeting

One of the first things that must be learned upon leaving home is how to manage a checking account. Other than the money in your wallet, a checking account is where your immediate cash resides. These days, people frequently make payments with credit cards, but even credit card bills must be paid with cash, and there are a host of other purchases for which credit cards are not accepted. Credit cards also carry with them the temptation to borrow at high rates and can become the financial equivalent of heroin – a topic I will discuss in a later chapter. Budgeting is vital to setting expectations and goals while living within your means.

5.1 Checking and Savings Accounts

Checking accounts are available at banks, savings and loans (also called thrifts), credit unions, and other financial institutions. Savings and loans are similar to banks in that they make loans and take deposits. The role of credit unions, chartered at the state and federal level, is similar to that of savings and loans, but credit unions are owned by their members and make loans and distribute profits to them. Credit unions do not pay federal or state taxes depending on their charter and, as a result, they can typically offer the cheapest rates to borrowers.[1]

NOW accounts are checking accounts that typically pay a small amount of interest but often have minimum balance requirements, and it is usually smarter to have your money earning a higher rate of interest elsewhere. Savings accounts typically pay a small amount of interest and do not allow you to write checks. While some banks allow online transfers between savings and checking accounts, often you must go to the bank to access your funds. It is common to be charged fees on some accounts, and you should find out what those fees are.[2]

An important aspect of these accounts is that they are often insured by the Federal Deposit Insurance Corp. (FDIC), an independent agency of the federal government. The FDIC insures checking, savings, NOW, money market, and certificate-of-deposit accounts for up to $250,000.[3] In addition, retirement accounts with financial institutions are insured. The FDIC's web site is: http://www.fdic.gov/index.html. It is very important to verify that your accounts are insured. If they are not, you may lose everything if your financial institution fails. For a list of FDIC-insured institutions, see the agency's Web site at https://www.fdic.gov/edie/index.html.

---

1 Especially federally chartered credit unions that save the most on taxes.

2 You can avoid a fee if you keep a minimum balance in a checking account. But, of course, you can't earn interest off of this money, while the bank can lend the money out and earn interest.

3 During the recent financial crisis, this limit was increased to $250,000. It is scheduled to return to $100,000 on Jan. 1, 2014.

The FDIC does not insure the money you invest in stocks, mutual funds, life insurance policies, annuities,[4] or municipal securities, even if you purchased these products from the bank that holds your FDIC-insured checking account. Failing to understand this can have tragic results. Financial institutions tend to offer low interest rates on savings accounts and CDs because depositors are generally willing to accept low rates in exchange for the safety of deposit insurance.

Financial institutions offer higher rates on investment products that are not insured. Unwary investors are often lured by the higher rates and do not understand the risks. When Lincoln Savings and Loan, an Arizona thrift, failed during the savings and loan crisis in 1989, many depositors – to their shock – lost their investments in financial products that were not insured by the government. It is also important to realize that when a financial institution (or any business) fails, it can take a very long time to get your money back, even if it is insured.

The Day the Bank Closed

Raymond Tarver, his wife, Louise, and their young daughter lived in Dublin, Georgia, during the Great Depression. In 1929, Raymond, a tall and slender man in his early thirties, had served with the U.S. military during World War I. After the war, he took a position with the First National Bank of Dublin. One morning in 1929, Raymond said, "we three were at the breakfast table when the phone rang. It was one of the fellows who worked at the bank.

"'Tarver, have you heard the news?'

"What news?' said I.

"'Well," he said, 'hurry on down and see.'"

At those words, Raymond recalled, "the seat of my britches almost dropped out." He'd had a "terrible feeling of uneasiness over the bank for some time. Banks had been closing all over the country. There had been a run on our bank some time previous to that, but we tided that over, and since then it had seemed stronger than ever."

Raymond grabbed his hat, hurried downtown, and found a crowd of his fellow employees gathered in front of the bank, "as blank expressions on their faces as I've ever seen," he said. The bank was closed, a notice was posted on the door.

"I didn't worry so much about my losses," Raymond said. "I was so concerned about the other fellows." People were losing their homes and life savings, he said. "The saddest part of it was to see widows who probably had been left a little insurance and had put it all in the bank."

"My job was gone and my savings, too." Raymond said. "Except for the time I served during the war, that was the first day I was without a job since I was just a boy." He went home to break the news to Louise. But "I didn't lose any time worrying, but got my hoe and went to the garden, he said. "Oh, that garden was a lifesaver to me in more ways than one. Some way, you can't worry and watch things grow all at the same time."[5]

[4] I will explain annuities and life insurance policies as investments later.

[5] Raymond Tarver, interview with Federal Writers' Project, "American Life Histories: Manuscripts from the Federal Writers' Project, 1936-1940," Library of Congress. http://lcweb2.loc.gov/cgi-bin/query.

Financial institutions are particularly vulnerable to financial distress and even bankruptcy. The reason has to do with liquidity. Banks typically make loans that mature in a longer length of time than their deposits, and it is this mismatch that causes the problem. Imagine a bank that mostly makes mortgage loans. It may take decades for a typical mortgage to mature and the bank to fully get its money back from the borrower. On the other hand, the bank borrows from investors using short-term debt such as savings deposits and one-year CDs. As customers withdraw deposits and CDs mature, the bank must continue to borrow. For instance, when a $1,000 CD matures and the bank must pay back the investor, the bank sells another CD and uses the proceeds to pay off the first CD. The bank is continually "rolling over" its short-term borrowings.

Suppose, however, that a rumor begins to circulate that the bank is in trouble. Investors will not deposit funds in what is rumored to be a troubled bank—in other words, they refuse to lend the bank money. The bank is in real trouble now, because it cannot easily sell its assets to pay off its existing borrowers. Worse yet, there may be a "run" on the bank, where a mass of fearful depositors rush to withdraw money from checking and savings accounts. The bank cannot raise the required cash, and it fails. Financial institutions are uniquely vulnerable in this aspect: If investors come to believe that a bank is going to fail — for whatever reason, true or not — the bank will fail, even if it was the most solvent bank for miles around before investors began to lose confidence in it. During the Great Depression deposits were not insured. Bank after bank had "bank runs," with frightened depositors mobbing the bank in an attempt to get their money back as the doors were slammed shut in their faces.

Key Takeaway: Banks, savings and loans, and credit unions offer checking and savings accounts. Checking accounts do not pay interest on deposits but you can write checks to make payments; savings accounts pay a small interest rate but do not allow checking. Financial institutions are susceptible to bank runs. The FDIC insures some accounts to reassure depositors. However, not all accounts at a bank are FDIC-insured and it is important to know if your accounts are insured.

Let us start by working through how to write a check:

Jane Wright
224 Oak Lane
Oakfield, MA 02134

231

4/1/2009 **Date**

Pay to the Order of Better Bakers, Inc. **$** 35.24

Thirty Five and 24/100 Dollars

For Mark's Birthday Cake

Jane Wright

:144555666: 5436678915: 00231

When you sign up for a checking account at a bank, you will pay to have checks printed and sent to you. Realize that a check is simply a piece of paper. Checks are numbered consecutively; the number appears in the upper right-hand corner. The numbers at the bottom identify the check for the banking system. The first identifies the bank (144555666); your account number (5436678915) is in the center. The final number identifies the check (as you see, it is the same number that appears in the upper right-hand corner).

Your name and address appear in the upper left-hand corner. Across to the right is space for the date you wrote the check. Beware of "postdating": Say you write a friend a check, but fill in a future date because you do not want the check to be cashed immediately - perhaps because you have not yet deposited the funds in your account that will "cover" that check. Your friend may nevertheless cash the check right away. You are required by law to have the funds in your checking account to cover any check you write. If your account does not contain enough money, your check will "bounce." Suppose you buy a digital music player and pay the store with a check. If the check bounces, your bank will stamp the check "Insufficient Funds" in bold letters and return it to the store's bank. The store is angry. It must contact you and get the money some other way, which can include taking you to court. Bouncing checks can ruin your financial reputation by reducing what is called your credit rating, which I will discuss later. Some frustrated merchants have been known to post bad checks publicly, for all to see.

In the "Pay to the Order of" line, fill in the name of the person or business to whom you are writing the check. In the box to the right of that line, fill in the dollar amount in numerals. On the line below, write out in words the amount of the check; filling in the amount twice can help protect against errors or confusion caused by bad handwriting. It is a good idea to start writing at the far left, and to draw a line through any space that remains on the line. This prevents someone who receives your check from turning "Twenty Five and no/100 dollars" into "Five Thousand, Nine Hundred, Twenty Five and no/100 dollars."

The "For" line, at the bottom left, allows you to make a note about why you wrote the check. Also called the "memo" line, it can be used for your own records (at some point you may get a printout of your check from your bank as documentation) or to provide information to the recipient of the check. Say you write a check to pay a laboratory for a medical test. If it is a common procedure, it is possible that the lab may confuse you with another patient and credit your payment to the wrong person. If you write the customer number as assigned to you by the lab on the memo line of the check, an error like that is less likely to occur.

In some cases a check can be considered a binding legal contract. Suppose you are temporarily living with a friend and, although your name is not on the lease, you have agreed to pay part of the rent. You write a check to the building owner with the words "for October's rent" on the memo line. When your feckless friend leaves without paying the rent, you need time to move out. That check, with its rent notation on the memo line, may give you some legal rights to remain in the building until you find a new apartment. Without such protection, the owner may be able to throw your property out on the street. State laws governing how much legal protection a check can offer vary, so see an attorney before relying on a check as a contract. And remember, this works both ways: A check you receive may have the power of a legal contract, too.

Unless you sign your name at the bottom right-hand corner, your check is worthless. Your signature is your legal word. A big note of caution: *Never* sign a check until you have filled in the amount and the name of the party for whom the check is intended. A situation may arise where you feel obligated to give someone a check to cover an expense even though you do not yet know the exact amount. You may be tempted to fill out the check to the person you owe, sign the check, and leave the amount blank. This is a monumentally bad idea - you have given someone the ability to take as much as they want out of your checking account! Finally, always use ink that cannot be erased or tampered with. Gel ink is best.

A cashier's check, which you purchase from a bank, is another way to pay for something without using cash. The bank takes the money out of your account and guarantees to the person you list on the check that they will get their money from the bank. Someone with whom you are doing business may demand a cashier's check if he does not have the resources to pursue payment on a bounced check.

So how do checking accounts work? Illustration 5-1 demonstrates. Suppose you are planning a surprise birthday party for a friend and it is your job to buy the cake. You order one from Better Bakers that says "You're the bomb." When you pick up the cake on, say, April 1, you give the bakery a check for $35.24. The next day, Better Bakers fills out a deposit slip and puts your check in its bank. The day after that, the bakery's bank sends the check to your bank. (The old-fashioned way to send that check is by "snail mail" – also known as the post office. More often, banks will fax a copy of the check to the other bank, which takes minutes instead of days.)

Illustration 5-1
Check Clearing and Float

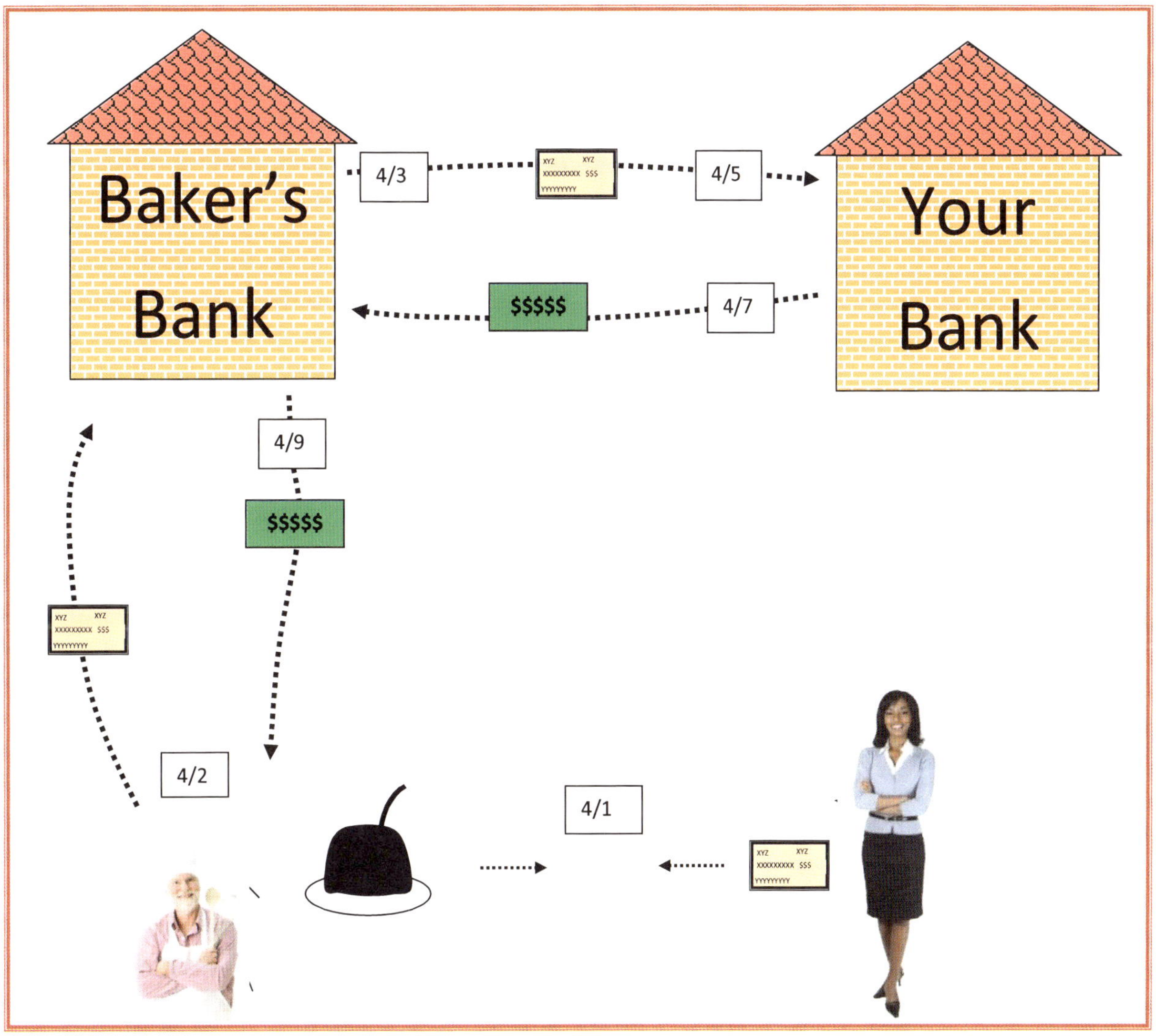

Your bank receives the check on April 5. It takes two days to process (in other words, for bureaucrats to finish the paperwork on) the check.[6] At some point in this process, the amount on the check is officially "debited" against, or subtracted from, your account, and those funds are no longer available to you. By this process, your check has

[6] "Bureaucrat" refers to a worker who writes and enforces rules and procedures or who processes paperwork for the government, a company, or other organization. The term can have a negative connotation brought about from frustration.

"cleared"; the bank has acknowledged that your account has sufficient funds to cover the check. Finally, your bank sends cash to the baker's bank, and that cash is "credited" to the baker's account. It is now April 7. However, the baker cannot get his money yet. His bank has a policy of holding the check for a fixed amount of time before allowing the baker to remove the cash. (This is referred to as the check being "on hold.") Fortunately, these days it generally takes a lot less time for a check to clear.

If you need cash, you can wait in line for a teller or you can use your bank's automated teller machine (ATM). A checking account comes with a debit card, which will have a personal identification number (PIN) assigned to it (sometimes you may choose your PIN). Insert your card into the machine; type in your PIN; and follow the onscreen instructions to withdraw cash, make deposits, print out the current balance in your account, or perhaps transfer money from a savings account to a checking account.

Never give someone else your PIN. The purpose of a PIN is to prevent others from making withdrawals from your account without your permission. Any time you type in your PIN, make sure no one is watching you punch in the numbers; even the bank employee who helps you set up your checking account should not know your PIN.

If you are out of cash and there is not one of your bank's ATM machines nearby, you may use another bank's ATM. But there is a fee - and it can be hefty - for using another bank's ATM. You can also use your debit card to make a purchase. With a debit card transaction, the amount you spend is immediately debited against your checking account. You may be charged a fee to use your debit card, as well.

Another alternative to cash is a credit card. When you present your credit card to a merchant, the credit card company pays the merchant and simultaneously makes you a loan. Typically you will be required to sign a credit card receipt and you may be asked to show identification. In about a month, you receive a bill from the credit card company. If you do not pay the full amount the card issuer begins to charge you interest, and these interest charges can be quite high. I will discuss this in more detail later. Realize that some merchants will take some forms of payment but not others: Some take only cash; others may not accept checks.

Key Takeaway: A check is simply a piece of paper, albeit with possible contractual obligations. You give your word when you sign the check that there is money to back it. Never sign a check without filling in the payee and amount first. You can use debit cards to pay for some purchases and to withdraw cash from ATMs. Find out if fees are associated with your accounts, and never reveal the personal identification number, or PIN, assigned to your card.

It is important to understand the concept of float. One day a woman visited a famous company and purchased a large appliance such as a refrigerator. She paid for it with a check. Back at that time, the store had recently acquired a new-fangled invention that immediately verified whether a check submitted for payment was covered. This woman's check was not. The store manager called the police and the woman was tearfully hauled off in handcuffs for attempting to "pass" a "bad check." She explained that she had plenty of money in her savings account, and that she had intended to go to her bank as soon as she left the store to transfer the money from her savings account into her checking account. By the time the check arrived at her bank, she reasoned, it would be covered. To no avail - since she knew there was not enough money in her checking account to cover the amount of the check she wrote, she had broken the law.

Teenage Conman Travels the World

Frank Abagnale was 16 when he ran away from home after his parents divorced. He quickly resorted to forging checks and managed to do a lot more than just put food on the table. He conned a laundry out of an airline pilot's uniform and spent several years traveling the world in the jump seat of a cockpit. (When invited to take the controls, he would come up with an excuse to decline.) His free-flying ways, for a time, allowed him to get away with forging millions of dollars worth of checks across the United States and around the world, staying in the best hotels all the way. And why stop there? He also impersonated a pediatrician, a lawyer, and a college professor – all with the help of a little forgery.

When he was 21 Abagnale was finally caught, and served prison time in France, Sweden, and the United States. His time in French prison was particularly harrowing: He went from 198 to 102 pounds. His life may have sounded glamorous, but as Abagnale tells it, "I spent birthdays, Father's Day, Mother's Day, Christmases all around the world, alone. I never went to my senior prom or a high school football game. I always knew I'd get caught, and when I was, I relented."[7]

In exchange for a reduced sentence, Abagnale agreed to help the FBI catch forgers. He has helped the bureau for more than 35 years, and one of his sons is an FBI agent. He started his own consulting firm and now makes millions honestly, helping others to root out fraud. With a ghostwriter, Abagnale also wrote *Catch Me If You Can*, a book about his life; it was made into a movie with the same title starring Leonardo DiCaprio.[8]

E.F. Hutton, a stockbrokerage firm, was found guilty of doing something similar, and they were almost put out of business. What they did amounted to check "kiting." This is how it can work: Kathy Kiteflyer keeps a trivial amount of money in two checking accounts. She writes a $10,000 check (the "kite") from her account at Bank A to be deposited in her checking account with Bank B. Suppose that Kathy has clout with the banks (she may own an important business, for instance) and is allowed to withdraw money from Bank B before the $10,000 check has cleared. Kathy takes money out of Bank B and invests it, earning herself interest. Kathy also writes a check from Bank B to Bank A for the same amount. Kathy has her money from Bank B, but her account has not bounced because the bank is holding her check from Bank A. Even when Bank B requests its cash from Bank A, there is a separate check she wrote from Bank B so her account at Bank A does not bounce.

These are not the actual people being discussed.

If nothing is done the checks will eventually bounce. But Kathy keeps juggling balls in the air by writing checks back and forth between the two accounts. She invests the $10,000 she has withdrawn and earns interest, even though there is very little cash in her checking accounts. Check-kiting is a felony and if Kathy is caught she could go to prison. In fact, checks clear much more quickly these days, making this juggling act much more difficult to pull off.

---

[7] David George-Cosh, "This is the Real Frank Abagnale: Famous For His Criminal Past, He Now Teaches How To Combat Fraud," *National Post (Canada)*, Sept. 20, 2006.

[8] http://www.abagnale.com/index2.asp; George-Cosh, *National Post*, Sept. 20, 2006; Duncan Campbell, "Portrait: The Charmer," *The Guardian*, Jan. 23, 2003; Sean Daly, "Old Crimes Do Pay," *Toronto Star*, Friday, Dec. 20, 2002.

Go back to the Better Bakers example. When you wrote the check for the birthday cake, you had to have the cash in your checking account in order to satisfy the law. As far as you are concerned, the money is gone. But your bank still has it, and can earn interest on it. This is perfectly legal. On April 7 your bank sent the amount of the check to the baker's bank. At this point your bank could no longer earn interest on the money. However, the baker's bank could enjoy use of the money until April 9, when the baker finally gained access to it.

In fact, banks take deposits from customers and earn interest on those deposits, even though the customers could come in at any time and demand their money. The bank is betting that that only a small number of customers at any time will want to withdraw cash, so it keeps only a fraction of the deposits on hand and earns interest on the rest by making loans. After the baker's money came in from your bank, the baker's bank may have kept $5 on hand and invested the rest. The bank is legally taking advantage of float. Of course, if all its depositors came in at the same time and demanded their money, that bank would be in big trouble. Sometimes financial services companies such as brokers will hang onto customer's funds, all the while telling them that the money has not cleared.

Key Takeaway: Make sure any check you write is covered. Float is the time between when a payment is made and when the other party receives the money. Banks can legally use float to make money. Check "kiting" is a juggling act that takes advantage of float, and is a felony.

5.2 Managing Checking and Savings Accounts

It is important not to bounce checks – for your reputation, your honor, and your wallet. The best way to guard against that is to keep track of how much money you have in your checking account. The old-fashioned way to do that is to write down in your checkbook the amount of each check, debit card withdrawal, automatic payment, or deposit and keep a running balance. Figure 5-1 shows an example of this process. On April 1, you wrote check number 231 to Better Bakers for $35.24. On April 3, you withdrew $50 in cash from an ATM. One April 4 you used your debit card to purchase groceries. Among other transactions, you deposited a check from your employer who reimbursed you for using your own money to take a potential business client to lunch.

Now note the cable payment. Sometimes when you make regular payments for a service or to repay a loan, the payees will encourage you to arrange for automatic electronic withdrawals – that is, to allow them to remove the payment from your checking account on a specified date and credit it to your bill. Sometimes you may receive a small discount for doing so. Automatic electronic payments allow a company to reduce float and get its hands on your money quickly.

Remember this: if you give a company permission to access your bank account, you rely on its integrity. I was very unhappy with my Internet service, which was provided by a nationally known company, and I was preparing to drop it. I then noticed that the company had triple charged me (money for three months of service was removed from my checking account). I called the company and demanded that the money be put back. A representative told me the company would not do it, but that I would not be charged for the next two months of service. It was not the Internet provider's money – it was mine! I was forced to wait and in effect pay for an extra two months of service before I dropped them. My attitude since then has been, "If you would like my money you can ask nicely. If it is yours I will gladly pay like an honorable person."

Figure 5-1
Checking Account Register

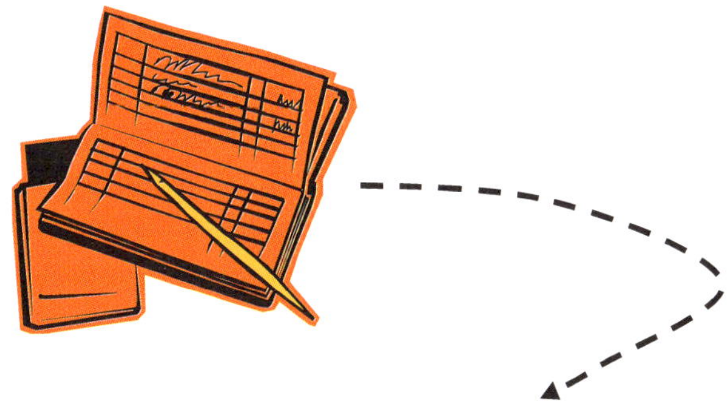

Number	Date	Transaction Description	Payment		X	Deposit		$Balance
231	4/1/2009	Better Bakers (Mark's cake)	35	24				2467.55
ATM	4/3/2009	Cash	50	00				2417.55
DC	4/4/2009	Sally's Supermarket	68	91				2348.54
232	4/5/2009	Brigston's Gas	28	45				2320.09
AP	4/6/2009	Clear As A Bell Cable Company	45	00				2275.09
D	4/8/2009	Pay Check				4500	48	6775.57
D	4/9/2009	Work Expense Reimbursement				58	44	6834.01
ATM	4/12/2009	Cash	100	00				6734.01
233	4/13/2009	Gianni's Italian Restaurant	18	44				6715.57

Unfortunately, to err is human. Each month, your checking account register needs to be reconciled against your bank statement – your bank's record of your account activity. This is important to detect a bank error, your own error, or theft. Figure 5-2 illustrates how to reconcile your account. The first thing to note is that the bank describes some transactions differently than you do. For instance, you record your use of your debit card at Sally's Supermarket as "Sally's Supermarket." The bank's version is "POS Sally's Supermarket." "POS" means "point of sale" – when you used your debit card at the supermarket, the money was withdrawn from your account at the "point of sale."

According to your bank, your account contained $2,502.79 before the Better Baker's transaction. Your ending balance as of the statement date is $6,584.12. This is not the balance that appears in your register, and there are several reasons for that. Some of the transactions listed in your register have not cleared yet – the bank does not know about them or has not yet taken them into account. It is necessary to mark an "X" in your register beside each transaction that has cleared. Your check to Brigston's Gas has not cleared; neither has your check to Gianni's Italian Restaurant or your ATM withdrawal on April 12.

The next step is to add checking transactions listed in the bank statement that are not in your register. Perhaps you forgot to record a transaction – or worse, someone took money from your account without your permission. In this case, you forgot that your monthly car insurance payment was automatically withdrawn on April 12. You add this transaction to your register along with an "X," since it has cleared.

Figure 5-2

Reconciling Your Checking Account

Your Bank Statement					
Number	Date	Transaction Description	Payment	Deposit	$ Balance
				Starting Balance	$2,502.79
231	4/4/2009	Better Bakers	35.24		2,467.55
	4/3/2009	ATM Withdrawal	50.00		2,417.55
	4/6/2009	POS Sally's Supermarket	68.91		2,348.64
	4/8/2009	Deposit		4,500.48	6,849.12
	4/12/2009	Clear As A Bell Cable Company, Inc.	45.00		6,804.12
	4/12/2009	Considerate Car Insurance, Inc.	220.00		6,584.12
				Ending Balance	6,584.12

Number	Date	Transaction Description	Payment		X	Deposit		$Balance
231	4/1/2009	Better Bakers (Mark's cake)	35	24	X			2467.55
ATM	4/3/2009	Cash	50	00	X			2417.55
DC	4/4/2009	Sally's Supermarket	68	91	X			2348.54
232	4/5/2009	Brigston's Gas	28	45				2320.09
AP	4/6/2009	Clear As A Bell Cable Company	45	00	X			2275.09
D	4/8/2009	Pay Check			X	4500	48	6775.57
D	4/9/2009	Work Expense Reimbursement				58	44	6834.01
ATM	4/12/2009	Cash	100	00				6734.01
AP	4/12/2009	Consideration Car Insurance	220	00	X			6514.01
233	4/13/2009	Gianni's Italian Restaurant	18	44				6495.57

To reconcile your account, start with the balance that resulted after the last cleared transaction. This is $6,514.01, after your car insurance payment. Then add back transactions you subtracted that have not cleared and subtract recorded deposits that have not cleared. Here, you need to add back the Brigston's Gas payment and the $100 ATM withdrawal. You must subtract the deposit of the $58.44 reimbursement check. You now have $6,584.02. Whoops: there is a 10¢ gap between the bank's balance and your own figures. So the next step is to check your math. After tedious verification, you find that when you subtracted the check to Sally's Supermarket, you took out 10¢ too much. That figure needs to be entered in your register.

If this seems like an unnecessary hassle, you are right (although it is a useful exercise for understanding reconciling balances). There are several software packages available that make the reconciliation process a snap and also allow you to conduct transactions online. Your bank may offer its own online banking software or Web site. Using some version of reconciliation software is a good idea: It is estimated that nearly 87% of people never bother balancing their checking account.[9] They do not know how much money they have, and could even miss someone systematically stealing from them. You can see a representation of typical software in Figure 5-3.

Figure 5-3
Your Checking Account Software

Number	Date	Transaction Description	Payment	Deposit	C	$ Balance
231	4/1/2009	Better Bakers (Mark's cake)	35.24			2,467.55
		Gifts				
ATM	4/3/2009	Cash	50.00			2,417.55
		Pocket Change				
	4/4/2009	Sally's Supermarket	68.91			2,348.64
		Groceries				
232	4/5/2009	Brigston's Gas	28.45			2,320.19
		Gas				
	4/6/2009	Clear As A Bell Cable Company	45.00			2,275.19
		Utilities: Cable				
DEP	4/8/2009	Paycheck		4,500.48		6,775.67
		Salary				
DEP	4/9/2009	Work Expense Reimbursement		58.44		6,834.11
		Work Reimbursement				
ATM	4/12/2009	Cash	100.00			6,734.11
		Pocket Change				
233	4/13/2009	Gianni's Italian Restaurant	18.44			6,715.67
		Dining Out				

With the software, the register will add and subtract transactions like an Excel spreadsheet, but will look like a paper register. You have to enter the transactions yourself, of course, but this is easier than you think. Instead of laboriously writing down the transaction while standing in line at the store, just stuff the receipt into your wallet. About once a week, pull those receipts out and enter them into the register.

To make it even quicker, the software remembers with whom you transact. You start to enter "Sally's Supermarket" but after you type "Sa," it fills in the rest. Better yet, you have set up categories for transactions, and the software remembers that this transaction goes under "groceries" and automatically enters it in the transaction category cell. It may even remember the last amount you entered for Sally's Supermarket, so that if you spent the same amount you do not have to type it in again. You can type in a comment, too, if you wish.

When entering check numbers, select "next" and the software will fill in the next check number. If that number is out of sequence, you forgot to enter a check into the register. The balance is automatically calculated for you: Notice that the addition mistake made in the paper register with Sally's Supermarket is not there. Data-entry software is accurate and as fast as lightning.

The next step is to download your transactions from the bank. Tell your software about your bank when you set up the software and it can download your transactions. After downloading, you see a screen like the one illustrated

[9] Kevin Risner, "A Balancing Act," *Advertiser-Tribune* (Tiffin, OH), Aug. 30, 2008.

in Figure 5-4. All of your downloaded transactions match, except for the car insurance payment. If someone withdrew money without your permission it would also be a non-matching transaction, alerting you to a problem.

Figure 5-4
Downloaded Transaction Screen

Number	Date	Transaction Description	Payment	Deposit	Match?
231	4/4/2009	Better Bakers	35.24		Y
	4/3/2009	ATM Withdrawal	50.00		Y
	4/6/2009	POS Sally's Supermarket	68.91		Y
	4/8/2009	Deposit		4,500.48	Y
	4/12/2009	Clear As A Bell Cable Company, Inc.	45.00		Y
	4/12/2009	Considerate Car Insurance, Inc.	220.00		N

You tell the software to accept all the payments including the car insurance payment, and the car payment is then added to your register.[10] You are now ready to return to your register, as illustrated in Figure 5-5. A "C" appears next to the transactions that matched the ones that were downloaded from your bank and that you accepted, indicating that they have cleared. The software also tells you the cleared balance according to your register. You tell the software to check your cleared balance with the online bank balance. (You tell the software to reconcile your balance.) Thankfully, they are both equal to $6,584.12 – and your checking account is reconciled. Very little time was spent, and you know where every penny of your money is, which transactions have cleared, and which have not. If you see an old transaction that has not cleared, perhaps it was entered in your register in error.[11]

Key Takeaway: It is important to reconcile your checking account to avoid bouncing checks or failing to notice unauthorized withdrawals. Checking account software makes this process fast and easy. When the cleared balance in the register matches the balance at the bank, the account is reconciled.

Challenge

Do you have your own checking account? If so, try using checking account software to reconcile your account. This will be good practice before you leave home and your checking account becomes more complicated.

[10] You could have skipped entering the transactions yourself and simply downloaded the transactions from your bank. If you do this, you should be careful to check each transaction downloaded from the bank.

[11] To make things easier, you can sort your transactions by whether they were cleared and by the date to find old transactions that never showed up at your bank that need to be deleted. (Deleting an old debit almost seems like free money!) Your software might let you download credit card transactions. If so, set up two separate categories for credit card payments from your checking account (an expense), and credit card payments to your credit card account (an income item). Then your spending categories will appear in a sensible way in spending reports.

Figure 5-5
Your Checking Account Software

Number	Date	Transaction Description	Payment	Deposit	C	$ Balance
231	4/1/2009	Better Bakers (Mark's cake)	35.24		C	2,467.55
		Gifts				
ATM	4/3/2009	Cash	50.00		C	2,417.55
		Pocket Change				
	4/4/2009	Sally's Supermarket	68.91		C	2,348.64
		Groceries				
240	4/5/2009	Brigston's Gas	28.45			2,320.19
		Gas				
	4/6/2009	Clear As A Bell Cable Company	45.00		C	2,275.19
		Utilities: Cable				
DEP	4/8/2009	Paycheck		4,500.48	C	6,775.67
		Salary				
DEP	4/9/2009	Work Expense Reimbursement		58.44		6,834.11
		Work Reimbursement				
ATM	4/12/2009	Cash	100.00			6,734.11
		Pocket Change				
	4/12/2009	Consideration Car Insurance, Inc.	220.00		C	6,514.11
		Insurance: Car				
233	4/13/2009	Gianni's Italian Restaurant	18.44			6495.67
		Dining Out				

A bank employee was embezzling, which is stealing money entrusted to his care and hiding the theft by manipulating financial statements. This was his scheme: When a customer was owed a fraction of a penny, the employee took it instead of crediting it to the customer's account. If a customer is owed interest of $5.426 on a savings account, the bank is supposed to round up and give the customer $5.43. The embezzler was stealing the partial pennies and giving them to himself. A fraction of a cent does not sound like much, but if a bank has $1 billion on deposit, those partial pennies can add up. The embezzler was caught when a little old lady (sounds like a cliché, doesn't it?) complained that she was being shorted on her penny! With your software, you would be able to catch an embezzler, too, without much effort. I recently caught a hamburger restaurant stealing one or two pennies from customers on each purchase. In this case it was the thought that counted — in a bad way.

It is important to keep extra money - a safety stock - in your checking account in case you have expenditures you forgot about or did not anticipate. Some banks provide overdraft protection and will automatically move funds from your savings account when necessary to cover checks; they will also charge you a hefty fee. Some banks will even extend you a loan to cover the shortfall. This way you can keep less of a safety stock in your checking account, putting it instead in an interest-paying savings account. But interest paid on savings accounts tends to be small and the benefit will be modest compared with what the bank charges you for that overdraft loan.

What you do not want to do is bounce checks. Doing so is bad for you, but can be great for the bank - which is why many banks used to automatically cover bounced checks. Suppose over the course of several weeks, you wrote five small checks for a total $18 before you found out you had insufficient funds in your account to cover those checks.

The bank, which automatically covered those overdrafts, charged you a fee of $30 for *each check* you bounced - for a total of $150 in fees. You thought you spent $18, but the total cost to your account was $168! In recent years banks have made as much as $38 billion from these kinds of fees. New rules require banks to ask customers to "opt in" to overdraft protection. The best protection of all (as well as the honorable thing to do): Keep sufficient funds in your checking account.

Keeping a close eye on your cash balances can prove profitable for another reason – you can manage your cash better. Suppose you typically have $10,000 sitting in your account that you do not need for regular expenses. That money, invested elsewhere, can earn you interest: 5% on $10,000 adds up to $500 in a year. Take a couple of minutes every once in a while to balance your checking account and move surplus funds to an investment account - it will pay off.

Another benefit of software is online banking. Suppose you get your cell phone bill in the mail. You do not enjoy addressing envelopes and licking stamps. With online banking, you can fill in your cell phone company and the amount you owe into the register and indicate that you would like a payment sent. The software will prompt you to tell it the company's address if you have not done so already. You should also indicate your customer account number, so the cell phone company will not confuse you with another customer when it receives your payment.[12]

If your bill is the same every month, you can program the software to send a payment for the same amount each month; the fixed amount of monthly apartment rental is a good candidate for this. You can also pay a merchant directly at its Web site, which will ask for checking account or credit card information. In the case of paying credit card bills, I recommend paying at the credit card company's Web site. Once I mailed a check to a credit card company and then left for China. When I got back, I found out that the check had been lost in the mail and it was too late to arrange for a payment before it was considered late. My credit rating took a hit as a result, and it was seven years before the late payment was removed. Talk about seven years' bad luck!

Key Takeaway: Avoid bank fees to cover a checking account. A big source of money comes from moving cash into investment accounts, rather than leaving it in non-interest-bearing checking accounts.

[12] It is not uncommon for merchants and banks to make billing errors because they mistake you with someone who has the same or a similar name. Whenever possible, include account numbers in transactions.

5.3 Budgeting

Budgeting is a lifelong task. Without it you could spend money that you come to badly regret, or even head for financial disaster. Budgeting involves looking regularly at what cash you bring in and where it goes. When you start supporting yourself, budgeting this process and finding resources can be particularly challenging.

Let us look at Jane Wright, who is about to graduate from college and start her first job as a sales associate at Stylish Executive Magazine Inc. Her responsibility is to find potential clients and persuade them to purchase advertising space in the magazine. Her salary is $40,000 a year. This works out to a little over $3,300 per month. Jane looks forward to having this money to spend, which seems like a lot. However, Jane needs to consider how much is going to be withheld from her pay before she can even get her hands on it. Table 5-1 shows what items will be taken out of Jane's check.

Table 5-1
Jane's Take-Home Pay

Item	Type	Amount	Left Over
Salary	Wages, Tips, & Other Compensation	40,000	40,000
401(k)	Deduction	2,000	38,000
Employer Medical/Dental	Deduction	4,200	33,800
FICA	Tax	3,060	30,740
Federal Income Tax	Tax	3,500	27,240
State Income Tax	Tax	1,200	26,040
State Disability Insurance	Tax	240	25,800
Take-Home Pay			25,800
Monthly Take-Home Pay			2,150

A number of items can take a big bite out of her salary. The first is Jane's contribution to her 401(k), plan. (I will discuss retirement plans later.) These contributions are not subject to tax, and are very important so that Jane will be able to retire. Her employer "matches" her contribution so that her contribution is doubled, and it would be like throwing her money away if she did not take advantage of it. Jane is also fortunate that her employer provides her with medical and dental insurance – but medical insurance premiums have been skyrocketing. Next, it is time to take out taxes, including FICA, federal and state income, and because of where she lives, state disability insurance (SDI). When everything is taken out, she will be left with $25,800 for the year. This translates into $2,150 a month that she can spend. For high-income individuals with a lot of benefits, take-home pay could be well less than 50% of their salary!

By the way, be sure to double-check what your company withholds from your paycheck: It is not uncommon for an employer to make a mistake. It is triply important to check bills, especially medical bills - they are frequently littered with mistakes. I can think of recent cable and phone bills where I was overcharged. (I find that mistakes are very rarely in my favor.) Going through bills is tedious but financially rewarding: Think of it as sorting through a dusty old attic to find gems that are hidden away.

As you shall see, $2,150 is not much to live on. But there is another, more immediate problem, Jane is leaving her college dormitory and will move into an apartment. Table 5-2 lists some of the expenditures she must make as she heads out the door. Jane has decided to live with a roommate to reduce her expenses. But the typical apartment owner (or landlord) requires a security deposit of at least one or two month's rent in case the renter fails to make a payment or damages the apartment.[13] Jane needs to come up with half of one month's rent as a security deposit (her roommate provides the other half), plus an additional amount because she owns a pet that could cause damage.

Table 5-2
Jane's Setup Costs

Item	Cost
Apartment Deposit	1,200
Rental Van and Boxes for Moving	250
Initial Furnishings	2,500
Suits and Other Clothing	2,200
Total	6,150

She also has to pay for boxes and a van to move her possessions. There are also an enormous number of things that need to be purchased to furnish her apartment: dishes, pots and pans, cooking utensils, a bed, a sofa, chairs, a dining table and chairs, a dresser, a mirror, pictures, bookshelves, and on and on. Jane hits the online auction markets, but still ends up spending $2,500.

Finally, Jane has to buy suitable business attire; Stylish Executive Magazine expects her to play the part and dress well. Good-quality business suits are extremely expensive, as are executive-quality shirts and blouses. Dress shoes also cost a lot, especially when pairs in black, navy, and brown need to be part of the wardrobe. By the time she is done shopping for clothing, Jane has spent $2,200. Add that to the expenses of moving into her first apartment, and she needs to come up with more than $6,000.

Now is the time to negotiate with her new employer. During the interview process Jane should not ask about her pay or she may not get the job. But once she has gotten an employer's interest and received an offer, Jane should point out that she is just getting started and that her new position requires that she look very sharp. Jane can suggest that a $5,000 "signing bonus" is not unreasonable.[14]

She should also carefully study the job benefits when considering the position. Benefits could comprise a substantial portion of her pay. Another job may have a higher salary, but not offer medical insurance or retirement contributions. (I will discuss this in more detail when I cover retirement forecasting.)

[13] When Jane eventually moves out she will get this back, but of course she will need a deposit on the new place if she continues to rent. Note that landlords are notorious for not giving the deposit back after the person has moved out, and it is often necessary to take them to small claims court.

[14] Employers realize that new graduates face these expenses and will often offer a signing bonus, which is an upfront payment for starting work. Remember that these bonuses are subject to tax, but not other kinds of withholding.

> ***Key Takeaway:*** Even before a college graduate starts a job there are big expenses involved in getting started, including the costs of renting and furnishing an apartment and acquiring a suitable wardrobe. Consider all benefits before taking a job and once you receive an offer, negotiate a signing bonus.

Jane is now ready to start work. But before she does, she puts together a preliminary budget based on her take-home pay. Figure 5-6 illustrates. Jane plans on buying a car. After the down payment (another setup expense) she discovers that she will have $4,800 a year in car payments over five years. Her clothing budget is $800, which works out to $67 per month. She also budgets for eating out. Eating lunch out while she is at work comes to $10 per lunch five days a week. On the weekend, she plans on a smaller dinner that costs $25 and a nicer dinner on Saturday night that costs $35. This works out to $5,720 per year.

Entertainment is budgeted at $1,040 - about $87 per month - and includes movies, concert tickets, etc. If she travels once a year, her entire budget for entertainment will be wiped out. She plans a modest expenditure of $400 for gifts. She expects her grocery bill to be $450 a month and to include household cleaning supplies and personal items from the drugstore. Home furnishings - $600 - include furniture, kitchen supplies, and decor. Jane spends $1,000 a year for car insurance and $200 for renter's insurance, (which covers her property against fire, theft or another calamity). Medical expenses of $200 include payments for medications, doctor's visits, and miscellaneous treatments.

Figure 5-6
Jane's Preliminary Annual Budget

Preliminary Budget for 1/1/2009 - 12/31/2009		
Beauty	800	3.1%
Car Payment, Registration	4,800	18.6%
Clothing	800	3.1%
Contributions to Savings	(9,320)	-36.1%
Eating Out	5,720	22.2%
Entertainment	1,040	4.0%
Gifts	400	1.6%
Groceries	5,400	20.9%
Home Furnishings	600	2.3%
Insurance	1,200	4.7%
Medical Expenses	200	0.8%
Miscellaneous Recurring	3,000	11.6%
Rent	9,600	37.2%
Utilities (Power, Cable, Internet, Cell Phone)	1,560	6.0%
Take Home Pay	25,800	

Miscellaneous recurring expenses deserve some discussion. When Jane bought her clothes, she chose silk blouses because they really made her suits look great. But she now finds that each week she is paying $7 per blouse for dry cleaning: At the end of the year, this will have cost her $1,680! A better choice would have been attractive blouses that can be laundered by hand or in a washing machine. Her friend Mark is also spending a fortune having his cotton shirts starched and pressed. Perhaps it is time for him to learn the finer points of laundry and ironing. A host of other expenses can fall in the category of miscellaneous recurring expenses: gas for the car and car repairs, coins for laundry, shoe repairs, public transportation, unexpected fees.

Jane has made the wise choice to have a roommate. However, she still must come up with $9,600 a year in rent - her biggest expense. (Note that she signed a year's lease. This means that she has committed to live there for a year or suffer adverse financial consequences. What if she loses her job and must move?) Another important benefit of a roommate is sharing utilities. The power bill is $45 per month; cable TV is another $45. Jane's half of both is $45. Added to this her Internet account, which is $40, and her cell phone bill of $45.

So what is left over for savings? Less than nothing! Jane is spending $9,320 more than she earns (her projected savings are negative). It is time to reassess her lifestyle. Thanks to her generous and successful parents, Jane is used to having certain things. However, it is time for her to support herself. She cannot expect to live the way that she is used to right off the bat. A former professor of mine has a Nobel Prize in economics, a professorship at the Harvard Business School, and is presumably very wealthy. He told me that his first job was digging graves with a shovel! There is nothing wrong with living simply when you are young, and successful people everywhere have stories to tell about their modest beginnings when they watched every penny.

The first thing that is clear is that Jane cannot afford a car. Her salary simply will not support it. If she gets rid of the car she saves $4,800 in car payments as well as money for gas, car repairs (which can be substantial), and yearly registration (and she does not have to come up with a down payment). A little extra will be required for public transportation, but car payments and registration go away, $1,000 of her insurance goes away, and gas and car repairs are no longer among her recurring expenses. The lesson: a car is *extremely expensive.* By skipping the car, she saves $6,600 a year - an astounding 25% of her take-home pay.

Of course, doing without a car may not be possible in areas with poor public transportation, although she could try to find a place to live that is near her office. In big cities, it is not uncommon to see high-earning executives on the train simply because it is more convenient. It should also be noted that everything costs more in big cities. It may be the case that while Jane would earn 15% less at a job in a midsized town, she would have 20% more of her take-home pay left over because her rent and other expenses will be so much lower. A midsize city, however, may not have extensive public transportation, making it harder to get by without a car. Consider the living expenses where the job is located when an employer makes you an offer.

Los Angeles is a triple-whammy. It is very difficult to go without a car, expenses are very high, and income taxes are also very high. In Los Angeles, $200,000 may get you a small, rundown condominium in a tough neighborhood. In rural Ohio, however, $200,000 will buy a four-bedroom, two-bath home with a two-car garage.

How a Homecoming Queen Got Rich

Lindsay learned the benefits of saving money at an early age. After years of putting her money away to gather interest, she was able to pay cash for her first home.

Lindsay is 19 years old.

Lindsay was a typical teen enjoying life in rural Ohio: she was a member of her high school cheerleading squad and was crowned homecoming queen her senior year. However, there was something different about her. She started a savings account at age 4 when she won $100 for showing an animal at the county fair. Throughout her childhood she entered 4-H livestock competitions, won thousands of dollars in prizes - and socked it all away.

By age 18 she'd saved $40,000. College seniors who graduated in 2009 carried an average of $23,200 in loan debt. But Lindsay, who continues to live with her parents while studying for a teaching degree, is earning money as a landlord: she rents the house she purchased, which has four bedrooms, two baths and a two-car garage, to relatives. She's putting the monthly rent aside for another house, which she and her fiancé, 22-year-old Heath, plan to move into after they get married. While two-thirds of college graduates face a mountain of debt, Lindsay and her beau plan to buy land and build their dream home at the top of a hill.[15]

Dining out is another spending sinkhole. You can pay $5 for a meal from the grocery store that you cook yourself - or $20 at a restaurant for a similar dish that may be more richly prepared but much less healthy. Eating out regularly simply costs a fortune. Jane realizes that brown-bagging her lunch and dining at less-expensive restaurants on the weekend will save quite a bit of money.

What is so bad about the neighborhood Italian restaurant, where they remember your favorite dish, or grilling hamburgers in the park with friends? (A few months after she started working, Jane hosted a Mexican-themed potluck dinner and invited some of her new colleagues to impress everyone with their favorite spicy dish.) And cutting back on eating out will increase her grocery bill by much less; overall, Jane will save $3,520 a year. Finally, Jane decides that she can find a less-expensive stylist and get her hair done three times a year instead of four. She decides she does not need to spend quite as much money on her weekend wardrobe. Figure 5-7 illustrates her new budget.

Jane is now able to save $1,400 a year. But she is not satisfied. She is 22 and would like to own a modest condominium by the time she is 27. A condo purchase requires the payment of fees and a 20% down payment, totaling $70,000. Jane considers her options. She remembers that there are tutors at her college who charge $35 per hour. Jane was an excellent student and can tutor in math and economics. After consulting with her boss to make sure the company will permit her to earn extra income on the side, Jane decides to tutor at a local university for 12 hours a week. Minus about 35% for taxes and other kinds of withholding, she expects to bring home $1,092 a month . With a month off for school breaks, this adds up to more than $12,000 a year, which supplements the $1,400 she already expects to save.

Including interest earned on her savings, she is now within range to buy her condominium at age 27. Over time as her salary increases, she will be able to buy nicer furnishings and a car. Once she owns a condo, she can save to

---

15 Kathy Lynn Gray, "Frugal Lynn Gray, "Frugal Teen Buys House With 4-H Winnings," *The Columbus Dispatch (Ohio)*, May 17, 2010; Project on Student Debt. "Recent College Grads Face Record Debt and Unemployment," Dec. 1, 2009; http://projectonstudentdebt.org/pub_view.php?idx=523; Karen Blumenthal, "Personal Finance Basics for the Class of 2010." *WSJ*.com, May 23, 2010. http://online.wsj.com/article/SB127457321508095793.html?mod=WSJ_PersonalFinance_PF4.

buy a bigger place. At the same time, she is saving for retirement through her own contributions and those from her employer. Jane is in charge of her life, and is making progress towards accumulating the kind of wealth and lifestyle that her parents have - maybe even better!

Figure 5-7
Jane's New Annual Budget

Final Budget for 1/1/2009 - 12/31/2009		
Beauty	400	1.6%
Car Payment, Registration	-	0.0%
Clothing	600	2.3%
Contributions to Savings	1,400	5.4%
Eating Out	1,200	4.7%
Entertainment	1,040	4.0%
Gifts	400	1.6%
Groceries	6,400	24.8%
Home Furnishings	600	2.3%
Insurance	200	0.8%
Medical Expenses	200	0.8%
Miscellaneous Recurring	2,200	8.5%
Rent	9,600	37.2%
Utilities (Power, Cable, Internet, Cell Phone)	1,560	6.0%
Take-Home Pay	25,800	

Notice that if Jane decides to spend $30 eating out at a restaurant once a week, it will add up to $7,800 over five years. She will have to wait another year to buy her condo. It may seem that Jane is too worried about her money when she considers carefully before spending, but small amounts add up over time and reduce the opportunity to own other, perhaps more worthwhile, possessions. As you shall see, seemingly small expenditures can mean the difference between a safe, happy retirement and an unhappy, desperate retirement.

Key Takeaway: To stay on the right track, a budget is essential. Owning a car and eating out are two major budget busters. Before accepting a job offer, consider benefits, the cost of living in the area, and the availability of public transportation.

Challenge

What kind of lifestyle do you imagine for yourself when you graduate from college?

A person's early years, when they are newly independent, are the most important for setting the foundation for the rest of their life. Unfortunately, these years are also the financially least informed. It is vital to live simply when you are young and to live within your means without borrowing. This is a painful lesson that Jane's friend Brian will learn. He took a slightly higher-paying job without generous retirement benefits or medical insurance. Excited by his new-found income, he decides to buy a car and enjoy nights out at restaurants and clubs. He scoffs at hard-working Jane, who lacks the most stylish of furniture or clothing.

Brian borrowed heavily to purchase clothing and furnishings for his first apartment, where he lives by himself. The fact that he simply needs to swipe a credit card each time he makes a purchase makes it even easier to lose track of his spending. Each year the interest payments on those loans accumulate at a horrific rate, since young workers like Brian do not start out with high credit ratings,[16] adding to the pressure on his earnings to cover his expenses. He is losing ground each year as his debt accumulates. By the time Brian realizes that he has a problem he is thirty and over his head in debt. It will take years to get his situation sorted out and for him to start over from scratch. In the meantime, Jane is enjoying an increasingly prosperous lifestyle, free from worry.

A final benefit of financial software is worth noting. Because categories are associated with register entries, you can generate reports that tell you how much money you are spending in each category. This can be useful for thinking about where you could trim your spending.

5.4 Conclusion

The time to take charge of your money is when you are just getting started in life. This is when most people fall off a financial cliff. As people get older, they get very busy with children and a high-level, but demanding job. They spend every free moment with family and have little time to visit friends. When they do have a little free time, they tend to spend a lot of money on a nice vacation. It is easiest to live simply when you are young and do not have the extra responsibility of raising children. You are happy and carefree, and your friends are too. It is not necessary to spend a lot of money to enjoy life, and with the energy of youth it is easier to get by with few luxuries. In very short order and with a little planning, you will begin to build a prosperous lifestyle.

---

[16] I will explain credit ratings, and why younger adults tend to have a poor one, later. Suffice it to say that a poor credit rating leads to higher interest charges on loans.

Key Terms:

Account fee
ATM
Automatic payment
Bank run
Benefits
Bouncing a check
Budgeting
Bureaucrat
Cashier's check
Check
Check clearing
Check kiting
Checking account
Covering a check
Credit card
Credit rating
Credit union
Crediting (credits)
Debiting (debits)
Deposit insurance
Down payment
Embezzlement
FDIC
Federal Reserve (the Fed)
Float
Holding a check
NOW account
Online banking
PIN
Postdating
Reconciling
Savings account
Savings and loan (thrift)
Security deposit
Signing bonus

End of Chapter Questions

1. Reconcile the following checking account.

Grace Li's Checking Account Register

Number	Date	Transaction Description	Payment		X	Deposit		$Balance
105	8/1/2009	Burton's Shoe Repair	44	13				3492.58
ATM	8/5/2009	Cash	100	00				3392.58
106	8/5/2009	Cell Phone Co.	47	44				3345.14
107	8/12/2009	Natural Foods	224	95				3120.19
D	8/14/2009	Paycheck				3871	72	6991.91
AP	8/19/2009	Better Car Insurance	104	13				6887.78
108	8/22/2009	Cash	40	00				6837.78
Dep	8/24/2009	Birthday Check from Grandma				150	00	6987.78

Grace Li's Bank Statement					
Number	Date	Transaction Description	Payment	Deposit	$ Balance
				Starting Balance	$3,536.71
ATM	8/5/2009	Withdrawal	100.00		3436.71
105	8/6/2009	Burton's Shoe Repair, Inc.	44.13		3392.58
AW	8/6/2009	Clear Cable Services, Inc.	46.85		3345.73
DEP	8/14/2009	Stylish Executive Magazine		3871.72	7217.45
106	8/15/2009	Cell Phone Co.	47.44		7170.01
108	8/23/2009	Withdrawal	40.00		7130.01
50210	8/27/2009	Better Car Insurance, Inc.	104.13		7025.88
				Ending Balance	7025.88

2. What is a checking account? What is a savings account? How do they differ?
3. Where are the most common places to get a checking account?
4. Why are checking and savings accounts typically thought of as being safer than other places where money can be invested?
5. Are all investments offered by an FDIC institution insured?
6. What is a bank run?
7. What are major check-writing no-nos?
8. What is postdating?
9. What is float?
10. What does it mean when a check in on hold?
11. What does it mean when a check clears?
12. What is a PIN?
13. What is an ATM?
14. What is a credit card?
15. What is check kiting?
16. What is reconciling?
17. What is a safety stock?

18. What is overdraft protection?
19. What is online banking?
20. Why is budgeting important?
21. How much of your salary can you expect to take home?
22. What sorts of financial issues can you expect to face when leaving college for your first full-time job?
23. Why are cars so expensive?
24. What is a signing bonus?
25. When considering competing job offers, what types of financial issues are important?
26. Why are banks so susceptible to bank runs?
27. Name some ways to save money when first getting started.
28. Is a check a contract?
29. What is an automatic payment?
30. What is an automatic withdrawal? What problems do they pose?

The Time Value of Money

During your lifetime you will more than likely invest and borrow multiple times. The "Time Value of Money" is one of the main principles behind borrowing and investing. As you shall discover, compounding interest can multiply the value of your investments or magnify the burden of loans. You shall also begin to explore what determines the price of financial securities by examining the nature of interest and where it comes from. This journey into understanding the nature of financial securities will continue into Volume 2. The material is technical and mathematical. It is also the physics of the financial world. The principles behind the math are as unavoidable as gravity and determine the movement of financial markets, just like physical principles lie behind the orbit of the planets around the sun. Physics and finance have a lot of mathematics in common. We shall even discover Einstein's favorite equation. (Just don't let an apple hit you on the head.)

As you work through the Time Value of Money problems in the following chapters, have your financial calculator ready and boot up the matching Excel spreadsheet. The spreadsheets and other supplemental materials for this book are available over the Internet. Go to the Appendix and look under "Internet Information." Be sure to take Microsoft Excel tutorials before starting, and make yourself familiar with Excel. I recommend "Get to know Excel 2007: Create your first workbook" and "Get to know Excel 2007: Enter formulas." To get these, boot up Excel, click on the question mark at the top right, click "Training" and then "Excel 2007 Training Courses."

Chapter 6
Compounding Interest

Imagine that someone wants to borrow $1,000, and promises to pay you back in one year. You trust him completely, and yet you still consider it an inconvenience. The reason is that you would prefer to have your money now. This is the way that just about anyone would feel - people prefer to have access to their money sooner, rather than later. This is called the "time value of money."

6.1 Interest

You make a similar decision if you purchase a CD at a bank. The bank is offering to sell the CD for $952.38. In one year's time you will receive $1,000 when the CD matures (expires). You want to be compensated for having to wait to get your money. At the end of the year, you will receive 5% more than what you paid, i.e., $\frac{1000-952.38}{952.38} = \frac{47.62}{952.38} = .05$, or 5%. This is your compensation for not having access to your money. When the bank pays you the $1,000, of that, $952.38 is principal and $47.62 is interest.

You may not realize it, but you just lent the bank money. The $952.38 that you paid for the CD can be thought of in two ways: either the amount you lent the bank (the loan), or the price of a security. These two definitions are equivalent when buying debt. The fact that the price of the CD was less than $1,000 reflects that it was not worth it to you today to pay $1,000, just to wait and receive $1,000 in a year. The piece of paper that you bought, which was a promise by the bank to pay you $1,000 in a year, was only worth $952.38 to you today. In other words, money in the future is different than money now. You like oranges better than apples. Money in the future is an apple while money today is an orange. The present value (PV) of a cash flow refers to the fact that today, in the present, a promise to receive a cash flow in the future is worth less to you today than the amount that you are promised. A "cash flow" refers to money going in or out. The present value of a $1,000 cash flow receivable in one year is $952.38. The future value (FV) is $1,000 – the amount paid out in the future.

Starting with the interest rate and the present value of the CD, you can figure out the future value. The formula is: $PV \cdot (1+i) = FV$. In other words, if you invest in the CD, in a year you will get your money back (multiply PV by 1), plus you will get interest to compensate you for the time value of money (multiply PV by i). (Interest can also be referred to as "R" or "k.") Putting the two together, you multiply PV by 1+i to figure out how much you will receive in the future. In our example, with a 5% interest rate, $\$952.38 \cdot 1.05 = \$1{,}000$. Note, that without rounding you get $999.999, but the bank rounds this off to the nearest penny.

You can also take the opposite perspective. You may ask yourself, "Based on the interest rate, if the CD pays $1,000 in the future, how much must I pay for it now?" (What is the loan amount or price?) In this case, simply use algebra to invert the equation: $PV = \frac{FV}{1+i}$. Starting with the fact that you know the future value is $1,000 and the interest rate is 5%, $\$952.38 = \frac{\$1{,}000}{1.05}$.

Actually, the interest rate is nothing more than a quick and easy way of stating a price for something. The long winded way of describing the transaction would be "The price of a CD that pays $1,000 in one year is $952.38." The quick way is "A one year, $1,000 CD pays 5% interest." Interest rates are just a shorthand way of describing the price of a debt financial security. Rearranging the formula, you can also solve for the interest rate if you know the present value and future value. The formula is $i = \frac{FV}{PV} - 1$.

I will refer to different time periods using "t." Today is referred to as t=0. Time periods could be years, months, days, or even seconds. I am using a year as our time period for the CD, so the CD matures at t=1, which is one year from today. Assume that cash flows occur at the end of the time period, so that t=1 is at the end of one year from today. Figure 6-1 illustrates the timing of the cash flows. You have already seen the formula for present value and future value, although it is worth going over using reverse polish notation (RPN) on your calculator. RPN takes a short time to get used to, and can dramatically speed up your calculations because it requires fewer keystrokes. (You should also read the manual and understand what a "stack" is.) I assume that you are using an HP12c.

Figure 6-1
Timing of CD Cash Flows

t=	0	1
	952.38	1,000.00

The following symbol means "hit the 'Enter' key": ENTER. A letter highlighted in blue means "hit the blue key before hitting the key," and a letter highlighted in orange means "hit the orange key first." (Actually, it will look somewhat reddish.)

Before you begin, make sure you can see all the way out nine decimal places. You do this by hitting 9. If you see a "BEGIN" in the screen, you have accidentally set it to assume that payments start at the beginning of the time period. Hit END under the "8" key to fix it.

To calculate the future value, you would key in: 952.38 ENTER 1.05 X. To go in the opposite direction and calculate present value, key in: 1000 ENTER 1.05 ÷. Your calculator can also compute values for many transactions using the financial keys, which are the first five keys on the top left. These are, "n," "i," "PV," "PMT" and "FV."

The financial keys can be a very powerful tool for making financial calculations. However, they require a somewhat different method than using a formula. One important difference has to do with cash flows. When you used the present value or future value formulas above, you did not care who was borrowing or lending. The question could be asked, "If the CD pays $1,000 in a year and has a 5% interest rate, what is its price?" It does not matter who the borrower or lender is. However, the financial keys are fussy, and want you to let them know if you are the borrower or the lender.

Suppose you are the one buying the CD. The financial keys demand that you tell them that you are the lender. The present value is entered as a negative cash flow (negative cash flows are money going out) to indicate that you are lending. The future value would then be a positive cash flow to indicate that you are being paid back. If you were the bank (the borrower) you would enter a positive number for the present value, and a negative number for the future value. Unfortunately, the financial keys are very stubborn and insist on positive and negative cash flows. (At some point there is always money going out and money coming in during a financial transaction, regardless of who someone is.)

Another important difference between using a formula and using the financial keys has to do with how interest rates are entered. In formulas, interest rates must be entered as decimals, i.e., .05. When entering interest rates into the financial keys, you must use percentages, i.e., 5. This can cause confusion. In any event, be able to go back and forth between decimals and percentages.

Table 6-1 illustrates how the financial keys are set up:

Table 6-1
Financial Keys

t=0	t=1	t=2	t=3	t=4	t=5	t=6	t=6	t=...	t=n
	PMT	PMT	PMT	PMT	PMT	PMT	PMT	...	PMT
PV									FV

PV refers to the price of a security or an original loan amount. To understand the PMT key, it is necessary to know that there are two types of loans that the financial keys will consider. A mortgage is one type; it requires regular monthly payments, which stop at some point. The PMT key refers to a multiple string of payments on a loan such as those found in a mortgage. The second type of loan is a simple one: where someone borrows, then nothing happens, then it gets paid off. Our CD is an example of this kind of loan.

The FV key refers to a one-time payment in the future, such as what happened with the CD. The "n" key has different meanings depending on the loan. For a simple loan it means the number of times interest is compounded (to be explained shortly). For a loan with recurring payments, it refers to the number of payments. Finally, "i" refers to the interest rate as a percentage. There are five financial keys. If you enter numbers for any four of them, the calculator will tell you the value for the fifth.

How would you use the financial keys to analyze the bank CD? Start by assuming that you know the amount that the CD will pay in a year and the interest rate, and you want to know the price of the CD. To enter a number into a financial key, first hit the number, then the key, realizing that the keys want to know who you are. Pretend to be the bank. The future value is -$1,000, the PMT key is zero since there is no multiple string of payments, "I" is 5 and "n" is 1, since you are looking at a time period of a year, and the CD matures in one year. Note that to change the sign of a number, hit the CHS key above the enter key. Here are the keystrokes: 1 n 5 i 0 PMT 1000 CHS FV.

You now have all of the values entered and are ready to ask for the present value. To get the present value, you can just hit the PV key. The present value is what you expected: $952.38 with rounding. You could have also gone in the other direction. To solve for the future value, you could have entered: 1 n 5 i 952.38 PV 0 PMT. Hitting the FV key would then yield -$1,000 with rounding. If you enter nothing, the default value for PV, PMT, and FV is zero. However, it is best to get in the habit of putting in the zeros since financial keys keep their old values from previous problems if they are not cleared out.

Spreadsheets are extremely powerful tools in finance. There are spreadsheets and other supplemental materials for this book that you can access over the Internet. Go to the appendix for the book and look under "Internet

Information." There you will find instructions for downloading the files that go with this textbook. Take a look at the Chapter 6 supplemental spreadsheet, problem 1, as seen in Figure 6-2. Start with present value: Cell C6 is just entered as a number. Cell D6 contains the future value. The future value formula is shown in the formula bar where cell C1 contains the interest rate.

Figure 6-2
Future Value Formula

	A	B	C	D	E	F
1		i=	0.05			
3		Future Value Problem				
4		t=	0	1		
6			952.38	1,000.00		

D6: =C6*(1+C1)

The cell with the blue border in Figure 6-2 shows what is in the formula bar in the spreadsheet. Note that there is a common source of confusion. A number could be rounded out a large number of places, but the viewer only sees rounding out to 2 places. That is because the display is set to only show 2 places. (Look under "format cell." This is where you control how numbers and cells appear. I set numbers to have commas as well.)

However, for the purpose of calculations, the number continues to be carried out fully. The alternative is to use the Round function in Excel. If I wanted to round the final underlying answer to the nearest penny, the formula would have been "=Round(C6*(1+C1),2)." The "2" refers to the number of places after the decimal point. Suppose I then set the cell to display to the number carried out three places. The number would appear rounded out three places where the last place would be "0." The underlying number would be rounded two places.

The present value version of this problem is on the next spreadsheet (but not shown here). \$1,000 is entered for t=1, and the present value is calculated in cell C6 using the formula shown in the formula bar. It is time to consider a loan for a longer length of time.

6.2 Future Value Over Multiple Time Periods

Suppose an alternative investment has a better interest rate of 7%. You consider investing \$10,000, and would like to know how much you will have accumulated in the investment account at the end of two years. At the end of one year, the future value will be \$10,000·1.07=\$10,700. You then leave your money in again for another year. Starting with \$10,700 at the end of the year and compounding interest again, you will have \$10,700·1.07=\$11,499.00. Since \$10,700·1.07=\$10,000·1.07·1.07, a quicker way of calculating what you would have in two years is $\$10{,}000 \cdot 1.07^2 = \$11{,}499.00$. Using the calculator, it is quicker to start with the 1.07^2 and then multiply by 10,000. The keystrokes for this formula are: 1.07 ENTER 2 y^x 10000 X.

Now try it with the financial keys. Keep in mind that the financial keys remember what was entered last. It is necessary to clear them out. The CLX key clears out the register, but to clear out the financial keys it is necessary to hit CLX. Assuming you are the lender: 2 n 7 i 10000 CHS PV 0 PMT. Hitting the FV key yields \$11,499.00. This time, do not clear out the financial keys. You will see why in a minute.

Our Excel spreadsheet can handle two time periods easily. Looking at Figure 6-3, in Row 5 the amount in the account is equal to the previous cell multiplied by 1+i. Dragging and dropping cell D5 across, by t=2 you have accumulated \$11,449. The interest rate cell was referred to in the formula as "\$C1" and has the dollar sign so that as you drag and drop across, the formula continues to refer to the interest rate cell as C1. If you were to drag and drop down and you did not want the cell address to update, you would have to refer to cell C1 as "C\$1." Normally, the cell location in the formula updates with dragging and dropping, unless the "\$" is left in as a place holder. However, as can be seen in the formula bar for cell E6, it is easy to take 1+i to the second power (Cell E6). You do not need to keep dragging and dropping in order to keep track of how much you are accumulating. The "^" mark means "to the power of." The investment compounded interest twice, corresponding to the final time period of t=2.

Figure 6-3

Future Value Over Multiple Time Periods

	A	B	C	D	E	F	G
1		i=	0.07				
2							
3	Future Value Problem						
4		t=	0	1	2		
5			10,000	10,700	11,449		
6			10,000		11,449		
7							
8			10,000		10,000		

D5: =C5*(1+$C1)

E5: =D5*(1+$C1)

E6: =C6*(1+$C1)^E4

E8: =FV(C1,E4,0,-C8)

Excel has a future value function, as shown in Cell E8. It takes: the interest rate, the number of compounding periods, the payment, and the present value. The interest rate is entered as a fraction (unlike the financial keys) and the present value has to be negative to create a positive future value (the same as the financial keys).

In fact, you could imagine leaving your money in to compound interest for any number of time periods. The formula would be: $FV=PV\cdot(1+i)^n$, where "n" refers to the number of time periods that the money compounds interest.

For instance, suppose you left your money in for thirty-five years. What would you expect to accumulate in the future? $FV = 10{,}000\cdot 1.07^{35} = \$106{,}765.81$. This is quite a large number compared to what you started with. What you are now seeing is the power of compounding. As you earn interest it gets added into the account balance, and during the next time period you earn interest on *that* interest. This makes your money grow at an increasing rate, similar to exponential growth. In fact, you have discovered Einstein's favorite equation - the future value formula. In other words, compounding interest! Figure 6-4 illustrates this. Notice that during the first year, interest of $700 was earned. However, the next year interest earned was $749. The extra $49 came from earning 7% on the previous $700.

You are discovering a key point. The sooner you can invest your money, the faster it will grow and turn into something quite large. This is an argument for saving for retirement when young. And since you have not cleared out your financial keys, you just need to update one key. Hit 35, then the "n" key, then hit the future value key. This time you will get $106,765.81. This is very handy for doing scenarios. For instance, suppose you want to know how much you will have to pay for CDs with different interest rates. Instead of reentering all the keys, simply enter each new interest rate and hit the present value key. However, remember when starting a new problem to clear out the financial keys.

Now, suppose that you plan on putting money into two different accounts and want to know how much in total you will have in two years. You could look at each account separately, and then add the future amounts together at the end. Table 6-2 illustrates this. If you invest $100 in one account at 4% and invest $250 in another account at 4%, you will have $FV = 100 \cdot 1.04^2 = \$108.16$ in the first account, and $FV = 250 \cdot 1.04^2 = \$270.40$ in the second account. In total you will have $108.16 + $270.40 = $378.56.

Table 6-2

Future Value of Two Cash Flows

t=0	t=1	t=2
100		108.16
250		270.40
		378.56
350		378.56

Looking closer, it turns out there is a short cut: $FV = 100 \cdot 1.04^2 + 250 \cdot 1.04^2 = (100 + 250) \cdot 1.04^2$. You could have simply added the two present values together at the beginning and then compounded them up. This short cut is only possible when the timing of the cash flows are the same and the interest rate on the accounts are the same.

Figure 6-4
Compounding Interest

t	Amount Cumulated in Account
0	10,000.00
1	10,700.00
2	11,449.00
3	12,250.43
4	13,107.96
5	14,025.52
6	15,007.30
7	16,057.81
8	17,181.86
9	18,384.59
10	19,671.51
11	21,048.52
12	22,521.92
13	24,098.45
14	25,785.34
15	27,590.32
16	29,521.64
17	31,588.15
18	33,799.32
19	36,165.28
20	38,696.84
21	41,405.62
22	44,304.02
23	47,405.30
24	50,723.67
25	54,274.33
26	58,073.53
27	62,138.68
28	66,488.38
29	71,142.57
30	76,122.55
31	81,451.13
32	87,152.71
33	93,253.40
34	99,781.14
35	106,765.81

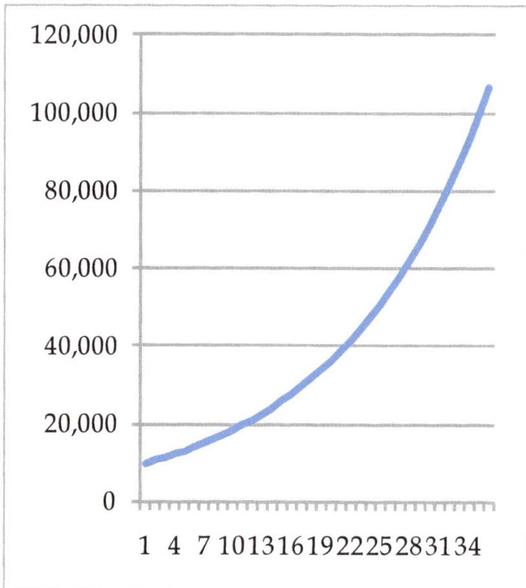

6.3 Future Value In General

In general, if there are multiple cash flows they have to be dealt with separately:

$$=C_0 \cdot (1+i)^n + C_1 \cdot (1+i)^{(n-1)} + C_2 \cdot (1+i)^{(n-2)} + C_3 \cdot (1+i)^{(n-3)} + \dots + C_n$$

For example, suppose that you plan on making a series of deposits in several savings accounts over time, which all have the same interest rate of 6%. You wish to know how much you will have in total at t=3. Table 6-3 illustrates this:

Table 6-3
Future Value of Asynchronous Cash Flows

	t=0	t=1	t=2	t=3
	100	50	80	?
		70		

Cash Flow	Future Value		
100	$100 \cdot 1.06^3$	=	$119.10
50+70=120	$120 \cdot 1.06^2$	=	$134.83
80	$80 \cdot 1.06$	=	$84.80
Sum			**$338.73**

The first $100 compounds interest three times (counting up). The next $50 and $70 can be combined because they occur at the same time and have the same interest rate. They will compound interest twice. The $80 will compound interest once. In total, you will have accumulated $338.73. The spreadsheet solution is illustrated in Figure 6-5, which shows the future value formula for the combined $50 and $70.

Figure 6-5
Future Value of Asynchronous Cash Flows

	A	B	C	D	E	F	G	H
1		i=	0.06					
2								
3			Future Value Problem					
4		t=	0	1	2	3		
5			100			119.10		
6				50				
7				70				
8				120		134.83		
9					80.00	84.80		
10			119.10	134.83	84.80	338.73		
11								

F8: =D8*(1+$C1)^(F4-$D4)

Since you need to count up, the interest rate is taken to the power of (3-1)=2 (Cell F4-D4). Finally, all of the future values are summed down Column F to get $338.73. Notice that there is another way to get the answer. The future value of each cash flow can be calculated below the cash flow in row 10, and then summed across to get the total future value.

6.4 Present Value

Now consider present value when there are multiple cash flows. For instance, suppose one friend owes you $200 at t=2 and another owes you $350 at t=2. The interest rate for both loans was 10%. Table 6-4 illustrates how the present value of the cash flows could be calculated separately, but since they occur at the same time and have the same interest rate, they can also be combined to get the present value. Starting from the future value formula: $FV = PV \cdot (1+i)^2 \rightarrow PV = \frac{FV}{(1+i)^2}$. Therefore, the present value of the $200 is $PV = \frac{200}{1.10^2} = 165.29$.

Table 6-4

Present Value of Two Cash Flows

t=0	t=1	t=2
165.29		200.00
289.26		350.00
454.55		
454.55		550.00

The quickest way to calculate it on your calculator is to start with 1.10, take it to the power of 2, flip it, and then multiply it by 200: 1.1 ENTER 2 y^x 1/x 200 X. Remember that present value tells you what a financial security is worth, or in the case of debt, the equivalent original loan amount. At t=0, theoretically, if you wanted to sell the rights to both loans to someone else, they would pay $454.55.

6.5 General Present Value

When a cash flow is paid in the future, the general present value formula is: PV = $\frac{FV}{(1+i)^n}$. When cash flows occur at different times, the present value needs to be calculated separately. The present values can then be summed. The "..." is a place holder for extra terms that are not written down in the equation below.

$$\mathrm{PV} = C_0 + \frac{C_1}{(1+i)} + \frac{C_2}{(1+i)^2} + \ \ldots \ + \frac{C_n}{(1+i)^n}$$

Now consider the present value of asynchronous cash flows as in Table 6-5. The interest rate is 3%. The top panel in Figure 6-6 shows a method where the present value is calculated in the t=0 cell for each cash flow in the future, and then summed down. The cash flows at t=3 can be combined. Their present value is $1,372.71. The Excel present value function is demonstrated in Cell F11. In total, the present value of all cash flows is $3,286.18. Notice that because you are taking the present value, you are counting down rather than counting up, as in a future value problem.

Suppose the cash flows were payouts from a financial security. The present value of all of the cash flows that the security pays out are equal to the price of the security. In other words, to value a security, take the present value of each cash flow that you expect to receive from the security, and in combination that is what the security is worth.[1]

[1] As you shall see, if you are not sure that you will get paid and interest rates can fluctuate, this adds an extra complication.

Table 6-5
Present Value of Asynchronous Cash Flows

t=0	t=1	t=2	t=3
?	1,000	1,000	1,000
			500

Figure 6-6
Present Value of Asynchronous Cash Flows

	A	B	C	D	E	F	G	H
1		i=	0.03					
2								
3			Present Value Problem					
4		t=	0	1	2	3		
5			970.87	1,000				
6			942.60		1,000			
7						1,000		
8						500		
9			1,372.71			1,500		
10								
11			3,286.18			1,372.71		
12								
13		t=	0	1	2	3		
14				1,000	1,000	1,500		
15		PV		970.87	942.60	1,372.71		
16		Total	3,286.18					
17								

D15: =D14/(1+$C1)^D13

F11: =PV(C1,F4,0,-F9)

C16: =SUM(D15:F15)

The second panel is more convenient in a number of ways. The cash flows are entered directly across in Row 14, and the present values get calculated in Row 15. The present value formula for the cash flow at t=1 is entered into cell D15. Next, drag and drop Cell D15 across through Cell F15. The discounting time period is automatically updated. This can be quite a time saver when there are a lot of cash flows. To get the total present value of all the cells, sum across Row 15 in Cell C16.

In the case of a present value problem with multiple cash flows at the same interest rate, your financial keys can quickly get the answer. For the following problem you need to enter the cash flows in sequence. If there is a cash flow at t=0, it goes into CF_0 under the PV key. Then, cash flows need to be entered in the CF_j key under the payment key. The NPV key calculates the present value when cash flows are not the same in each time period. You would enter: 3 i 0 CF_0 1000 CF_j 1000 CF_j 1500 CF_j NPV.

It is also useful to think about present value in terms of the time value of money. I have already discussed how \$100 two years from now is not worth \$100 today. You shrink the \$100 to reflect what it is worth to you now. For instance, if the interest rate is 4%: $PV = \frac{100}{1.04^2} = 100 \cdot .9245 = \$92.45$. You are multiplying 100 by something less than one to reflect its lower value to you today. This is also referred to as "discounting."

6.6 Conclusion

You have now learned the basics of the time value of money, including interest rates, present value, and future value. In the case of debt, present value refers to how much the debt security was sold for, or equivalently, the loan amount. Future value refers to how much is owed in the future. There are a number of methods to calculate present values and future values. These include using formulas, using the financial keys on a financial calculator, and using spreadsheets. Now that you have the basics, you are ready to work with the more complicated loans and investment problems in the next chapter.

Key Terms:

Compounding
Discounting
Future value
Interest
Present value

Formulas:

The future value of a single cash flow: $FV = PV \cdot (1+i)^n$

The future value of multiple cash flows:

$$= C_0 \cdot (1+i)^n + C_1 \cdot (1+i)^{(n-1)} + C_2 \cdot (1+i)^{(n-2)} + C_3 \cdot (1+i)^{(n-3)} + \ldots + C_n$$

The present value of a single cash flow: $PV = \frac{FV}{(1+i)^n}$

The present value of multiple cash flows: $PV = C_0 + \frac{C_1}{(1+i)} + \frac{C_2}{(1+i)^2} + \ldots + \frac{C_n}{(1+i)^n}$

End of Chapter Questions

1. Why is it that for debt, present value either gives the original loan amount, or the price of a security?

2. What does future value tell us?

3. What does the time value of money refer to?

4. What is discounting?

5. What is compounding?

6. You just put $5,000 into a savings account. The account pays 3% on an annual basis. How much money will have accumulated in the account in six years?

7. You just paid $1,000 for a two-year CD with an interest rate of 4%. A year from now, you will pay $2,000 for a one-year CD with an interest rate of 5%. How much will you receive in total from your CDs when they mature in two years?

8. You are saving to buy a car and you need a down payment of $3,000. You just put money into an investment account that pays 5% interest on an annual basis. You will leave the account alone for two years. When you withdraw your money you have $3,087. How much did you put into the savings account today?

9. You lend money to a friend at 4% interest. Your friend will pay you $540.80 in two years. You lend another friend money at 5% interest. They will pay you $210 in one year. In total, how much did you lend?

10. You paid $4,651.16 for a CD that matures in one year. You will receive $5,000 when the CD matures. What is the interest rate for the CD? (Round your answer out 4 places.)

11. You made three loans. Today, you lent $100 to one friend, and $200 to another friend. A year later (at t=2) you lend another friend $400. All loans had an interest rate of 5%, and all loans are due in four years (at t=4). In total, how much are you owed?

Solve the following problems using only the financial keys on your calculator.
You can double-check yourself using formulas or Excel.

12. You just borrowed $400. The annual interest rate is 7%. In five years when the payment comes due, how much will you owe?

13. You purchased a CD today. The annual interest rate on the CD is 4.5% and it matures in three years, at which point you will receive $5,000. How much did you just pay?

14. You made three loans today. You are owed $500 in one year, $800 in two years, and $1,200 in three years. All three loans have an annual interest rate of 6%. How much did you lend?

Solve the following problems in Excel. For all the problems below
you can double-check yourself using formulas.

15. You will put $8,000 into a savings account today that pays an annual interest rate of 3%. One year from today you will put $9,000 into the account, and two years from today you will put $10,000 into the account. Three years from today, how much will you have in the account?

16. You just borrowed from a friend at an annual interest rate of 4%. You will pay her $350 one year from today, $450 two years from today, $580 three years from today, and then $640 five years from today. How much did you borrow? *(Hint, think of each payment as coming from a separate loan, and then add up how much you borrowed on each loan.)* Double check your answer using your financial keys.

17. You bought a CD that will pay $10,000 in four years, and has an annual interest rate of 5%. You also purchased a CD that will pay $5,000 in two years with an annual interest rate of 3%, and a CD that will pay $1,000 in one year, with an annual interest rate of 2%. In total, how much did you pay?

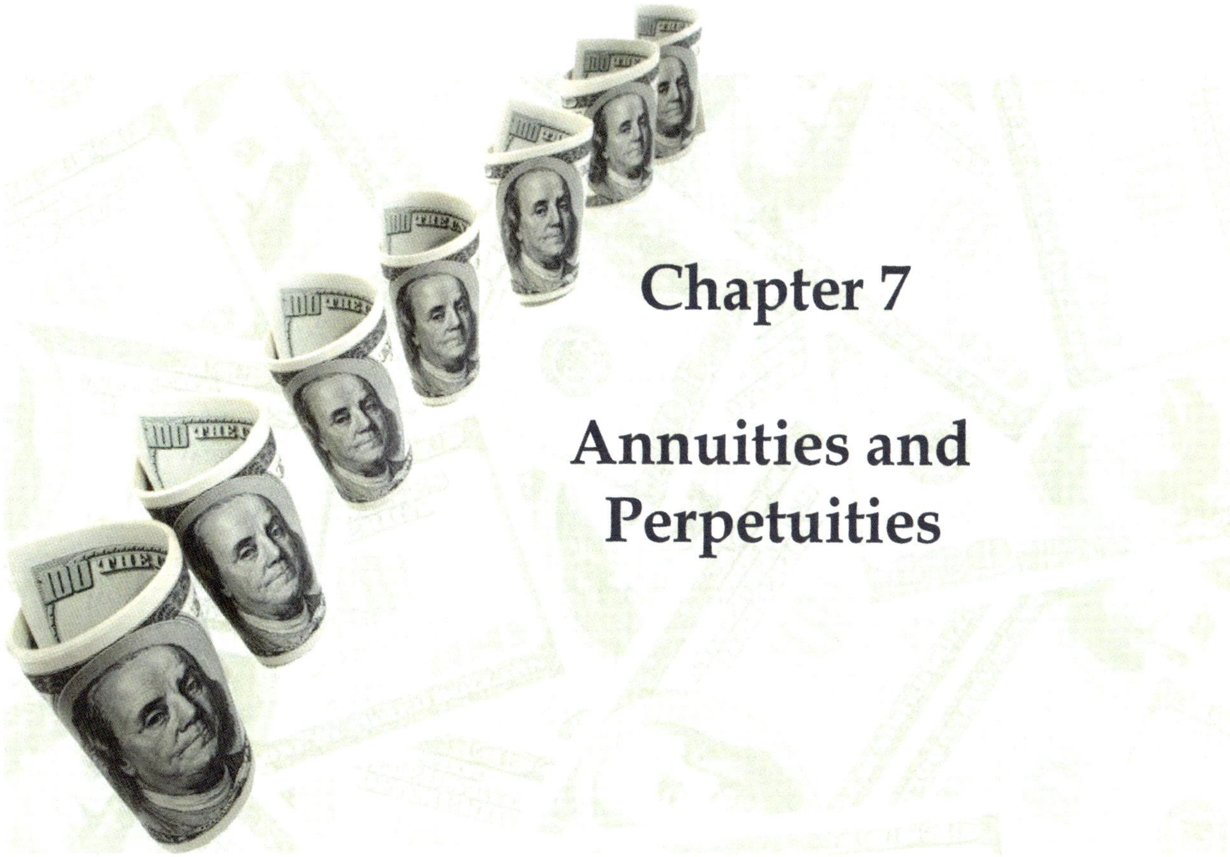

Chapter 7

Annuities and Perpetuities

7.1 Annuities

7.1.1 Present Value

Many consumer loans involve making a constant payment for some length of time, until the loan matures and no more payments are required. From the previous chapter you found that you could take the present value of multiple payments and add them together to arrive at the present value of all the payments. When a loan has more than one payment, exactly the same thing can be done. The present value of the loan (original loan amount or price of the debt security being issued) can be found by adding all of the present values of each payment together. In effect, when a loan has more than one payment, each payment can be considered to be a single loan by itself. When the present value of all the payments in the loan are added up, you arrive at the value of the loan in its entirety, just as if it were a package of multiple loans.

In the circumstance where all of the payments are the same, you have something called a "constant annuity." Mortgages are an example of this. With a fixed-rate mortgage (to be explained in more detail in the next chapter), the same monthly payment is required until the mortgage is paid off and the payments stop. Another example would be a consumer loan to purchase a refrigerator with a 1% monthly interest rate, and monthly payments that last for five years. Figure 7-1 illustrates this. As you work through the problems below, be sure to follow along in the supplemental materials that come with the textbook. (Look in "Internet Information" in the book appendix for instructions for downloading the files.)

Figure 7-1
Refrigerator Loan

	A	B	C	D	E	F	G		BJ	BK
1	i=	0.01								
2	t:	0	1	2	3	4	5		59	60
3			55.61	55.61	55.61	55.61	55.61	• • •	55.61	55.61
4	PV:		55.05941	54.51426	53.97452	53.44012	52.911007		30.91661	30.6105
5	Loan	2,499.95								
6										
7	Annuity Formula:		2,499.95							
8	Excel Function:		2,499.95							
9										

B5: =SUM(C4:BK4)

C7: =(C3/B1)*(1-(1/(1+B1))^60)

C8: =PV(B1,60,-C3,0)

Row 3 has the loan payments, which are $55.61 per month, starting one month after the loan is made. The interest rate that is needed is the monthly interest rate of 1%. This is because payments are monthly, and interest compounds monthly. With annuities, always use the interest rate that matches the timing of the payments. This rate is referred to as the "periodic rate." If payments were quarterly, the periodic interest rate would be the quarterly rate. Notice that even though the loan lasts for five years, "n," the number of payments, is 5·12 = 60. Also, when working with annuities, "n" refers to the number of payments, not the number of times interest is compounded. This makes sense because each cash flow in an annuity compounds interest for a different number of time periods.

In the interest of space, I have left out some of the payments in Figure 7-1, but show the last payments at t=59 and t=60. Another thing to realize about annuity formulas is that they assume the first payment occurs at t=1. If there is an extra payment at t=0, it has to be dealt with separately.

Once you take the present value of each cash flow, you can sum them up in Cell B5, arriving at a present value of $2,499.95. This is what you borrowed. However, it turns out there is a short-cut. When all the payments are the same, there is a formula that allows you to add all the present values up in one fell swoop. This is the present value of a constant annuity formula: $PV= \frac{C}{i} \cdot \left[1- \left(\frac{1}{1+i}\right)^n\right]$. Here, C is the constant payment (cash flow), and "n" refers to the number of payments. "i" is the periodic rate, which in this example is the monthly rate. Cell C7 contains the annuity formula. Annuity formulas are especially wonderful, because instead of creating gigantic spreadsheets for long-term loans, you can calculate the present value in one cell.

Your financial keys also love constant annuities. Since you are no longer working with simple loans where one payment in the future pays the loan off, the FV key is zero. Now it is time to use the PMT key to enter multiple payments. Your keys strokes are: 60 n 1 i 55.61 CHS PMT 0 FV. Then hit the PV key, and out pops $2,499.95. Cell C8 contains the Excel function, where the negative of the payment is included, just as in a calculator. The interest rate is left as a decimal. It is also worth going over the keystrokes using the formula. As you shall see, not all annuities fit in the financial keys. The formula with the numbers plugged in is: $PV= \frac{55.61}{.01} \cdot \left[1- \left(\frac{1}{1.01}\right)^{60}\right]$. The quickest way is to start with 1.01 and work backward and to the left. The keystrokes are: 1.01 ENTER 60 y^x 1/x CHS 1 + 55.61 X .01 ÷.

The next annuity is called a growing annuity. With this kind of annuity, the payments get bigger by the same percent each time period. An example could be restitution payments from a lawsuit. Suppose that a judge orders someone to pay you $1,000 one quarter from today (3 months). Each quarter after that, they must pay you 2% more than the quarter before ("g"=.02). Payments are to last for three years. You decide to try to sell the rights to the payments. Given that the periodic quarterly interest rate is 3%, how much can you sell the payments for? Figure 7-2 illustrates this. (Notice that not all cells are shown, which is why the right edge has an orange border.)

Figure 7-2
Present Value of Growing Annuity Lawsuit Settlement Payments

	A	B	C	D	E	F	G	H
1		i= 0.03			g= 0.02			
2	t=	0	1	2	3	4	5	6
3	Cash Flows		1,000	1,020.00	1,040.40	1,061.21	1,082.43	1,104.08
4				$=C_0*(1+g)$	$=C_1*(1+g)$	. . .		
5					$=C_0*(1+g)^2$	. . .		
6	PV		970.8738	961.4478	952.11338	942.8696	933.7155	924.6503
7	Total PV		11,048.07					
8								
9	Formula		11,048.07					
10								

C9: =(C3/(B1-E1)) * (1 - ((1+E1)/(1+B1))^N2)

Your payment at t=2 will be 2% higher than the one at t=1: 1,000·1.02=1,020. Your payment at t=3 will be 2% higher than your payment at t=2: 1,020·1.02 = 1,040.40 = $1{,}000 \cdot 1.02^2$. This looks like the future value formula for a simple loan, which can cause confusion. The growth rate "g" determines what your payments will be, and has nothing to do with interest. After all, who decided the payments? A judge did. Who sets interest rates? The financial markets do. As can be seen in Figure 7-2, "g" determines what the cash flows are, not how much you earn on those cash flows in a savings account. When it is time to apply discounting, then the interest rate is used. The interest rate reflects the time value of money, as applied to each separate cash flow. g determines what each cash flow is.

There is a formula that can take the present value of all of the cash flows when the cash flows are growing at a constant rate. It is called the present value of a growing annuity: PV= $\left(\frac{C_1}{i-g}\right) \cdot \left[1 - \left(\frac{1+g}{1+i}\right)^n\right]$. This formula is in Cell C9. Cell N2, referred to in the formula, is equal to 12. Notice that unlike with a constant annuity, this formula calls for the cash flow at t=1 since every cash flow is different. The subscript 1 for C_1 tells you that it is the payment at t=1. (With a constant annuity they are all the same.) Also, it is assumed that i>g. I will discuss this more later. Plugging the numbers into the formula: PV= $\left(\frac{1{,}000}{.03-.02}\right) \cdot \left[1 - \left(\frac{1.02}{1.03}\right)^{12}\right]$. Unfortunately, the financial keys cannot handle a growing annuity. However, the keystrokes for the formula are: 1.02 ENTER 1.03 ÷ 12 y^x CHS 1 + 1000 X .03 ENTER .02 - ÷.

Question 1

Now that you have learned the basic principles for taking the present value of an annuity, it is time to practice. Look at a base case first, and then explore permutations to the base case. Starting with the base case: suppose your aunt left you a small inheritance. Starting one month from today, you will receive $100 until two years from today. The periodic monthly interest rate is .005. What can you sell the inheritance for today?[1] (The supplemental materials contain each permutation to follow. I first show the spreadsheet that contains voice comments, then the formula, and then the required financial keystrokes if the financial keys can be used. In the spreadsheet, the voice comments can be heard by clicking on the box next to the spreadsheet.)

Figure 7-3

Present Value of a Constant Annuity with No Cash Flow at t=0

t=	0	1	2	3	4	5	6	7
	0	100	100	100	100	100	100	100
PV of Each Cash Flow*:	0	99.50248756	99.0075	98.5149	98.0248	97.5371	97.0518	96.569
Total PV of the Annuity:	$2,256.29							
*What each payment is worth by itself today								
C_0=	0							
C_1=	100							
g=	0							
Formula:	PV=	$2,256.29						
Excel Function:	PV=	$2,256.29						

Notice that "C_0" is zero, as is "g". (In later problems this will change.) Using the present value of a constant annuity formula: $PV=\frac{100}{.005}\cdot\left[1-\left(\frac{1}{1.005}\right)^{24}\right]$ = $2,256.29. The calculator keystrokes are: 1.005 ENTER 1/x 24 y^x CHS 1 + 100 X .005 ÷. Using the financial keys: 24 n .5 i 100 PMT 0 FV PV. (The present value will be a negative number since the calculator assumes that you must have lent in order to be entitled to these payments. Financial calculators do not assume altruism!)

Question 2

You are ready for your first permutation: your aunt left you a small inheritance. Starting today, you will receive $100 until two years from today. Including today's payment, what can you sell the inheritance for? The difference from the last problem is that you receive a payment immediately. What is the present value of a payment today? The payment is. Also, remember that annuity formulas assume that the first payment starts one time period from today. So how do you deal with the extra cash flow today? You just add it in.

[1] Note that the assumption is that the inheritance is "assignable" and can be sold.

Figure 7-4
Present Value of a Constant Annuity with a Cash Flow at t=0

t=	0	1	2	3	4	5	6	7
	100	100	100	100	100	100	100	100
PV of Each Cash Flow*:	100	99.50248756	99.0075	98.5149	98.0248	97.5371	97.0518	96.569
Total PV of the Annuity:	$2,356.29							
*What each payment is worth by itself today								
C_0=	100							
C_1=	100							
g=	0							
Formula:	PV=	$2,356.29						

Now C_0 is 100, reflecting a cash flow at t=0. This cash flow at t=0 has to be added in separately since the annuity formula ignores it: $PV= 100 + \frac{100}{.005} \cdot \left[1- \left(\frac{1}{1.005}\right)^{24}\right]$ = $2,356.29. The financial keystrokes are the same as before. However, after you calculate the present value, add 100.

Question 3

On to the next problem. Your aunt left you a small inheritance. Starting one month from today, you will receive $100 until two years from today. Each month, your payment will be .2% (.002) larger than the month before. What can you sell the inheritance for today?

Figure 7-5
Present Value of a Growing Annuity, No Cash Flow at t=0

t=	0	1	2	3	4	5	6	7
	0	100	100.2	100.4	100.601	100.802	101.004	101.206
PV of Each Cash Flow*:	0	99.50248756	99.2055	98.9093	98.6141	98.3197	98.0262	97.7336
Total PV of the Annuity:	$2,307.85							
*What each payment is worth by itself today								
C_0=	0							
C_1=	100							
g=	0.002							
Formula:	PV=	$2,307.85						

Now you are back to no cash flow at t=0. However, cash flows are growing, and this is the present value of a growing annuity where g=.2%: $PV= \left(\frac{100}{.005-.002}\right) \cdot \left[1 - \left(\frac{1.002}{1.005}\right)^{24}\right]$ = $2,307.85. The keystrokes are: 1.002 ENTER 1.005 ÷ 24 y^x CHS 1 + 100 X .005 ENTER .002 - ÷. This problem cannot be entered into the financial keys because it is a growing annuity.

Question 4

Your aunt left you a small inheritance. Starting <u>today</u>, you will receive $100 until two years from today. Each month your payment will be .2% (.002) larger than the month before. Including the payment today, what can you sell the inheritance for?

This is the sneakiest problem of all. The question gives you the cash flow at t=0. However, the annuity formula requires the cash flow at t=1, which you must calculate. This is $100 \cdot 1.002 = 100.20$. The formula is: $PV = 100 + \left(\frac{100 \cdot 1.002}{.005 - .002}\right) \cdot \left[1 - \left(\frac{1.002}{1.005}\right)^{24}\right] = \$2,412.46$. The keystrokes are: 1.002 ENTER 1.005 ÷ 24 yˣ CHS 1 + 100 X 1.002 X .005 ENTER .002 - ÷ 100 +.

Figure 7-6
Present Value of a Growing Annuity, a Cash Flow at t=0

t=	0	1	2	3	4	5	6	7
	100	100.2	100.4	100.601	100.802	101.004	101.206	101.408
PV of Each Cash Flow*:	100	99.70149254	99.4039	99.1071	98.8113	98.5163	98.2223	97.9291
Total PV of the Annuity:	$2,412.46							
*What each payment is worth by itself today								
C_0=	100							
C_1=	100.20							
g=	0.002							
Formula:	PV=	$2,412.46						

Question 5

There are many situations in life where you must compare two competing offers. Since these competing offers have cash flows that occur at different times, it is important to put them on the same time basis for comparison. The easiest way to do this is to convert the cash flows of both offers to their present value. You can then compare the two offers directly based on their value today.

The following is an example: You have just won the lottery. Starting today, you will receive $5,000. Each month thereafter you will receive a payment that is .0025 larger than the payment before, so that your payment next month will be .0025 larger than the first one, and so on. You will receive payments until twenty five years from today. The monthly interest rate is .0042. As an alternative, they offer to pay you $1,000,000 immediately. Should you take the series of payments, or take the alternative offer of $1,000,000? Since the alternative offer is as of today, to make the comparison the only thing needed is to convert the string of payments into a present value:

$$PV = 5{,}000 + \left\{\frac{(5{,}000 \cdot 1.0025)}{(.0042 - .0025)} \cdot \left[1 - \left(\frac{1.0025}{1.0042}\right)^{300}\right]\right\} = \$1{,}179{,}933.25 .$$

The string of payments is better. And do not worry if you need money right away. You can immediately sell the string of payments for $1,179,933.25.

0% Promotional Car Offer

A common marketing technique is for car companies to offer loans on their cars at a reduced rate, even 0%. Since you know how to calculate present value, you are in a position to compare competing offers. At the most basic level, the idea is to simply write down the payments associated with each offer and then take their present value. The appropriate interest rate is the rate at which you could borrow in the financial markets, aside from the confounding mix of car price and loan financing.

Start with the 0% offer and figure out the cash flows. Shifty Sam is offering to sell you a specific car model for $20,000. You will be required to put $5,000 down, meaning that you have to pay $5,000 up front out of your own pocket. The rest ($15,000) will be financed with a 0% loan, maturing in three years with monthly payments. At this interest rate, using your financial keys, you can solve for the monthly payments: 36 n 0 i 15000 PV 0 FV PMT. You discover that your payments will be $416.67.

Honest Ed is offering to sell you a car at $18,000. You will have to make a down payment of $3,000. You will also get a loan on the rest at the going market rate of .5% per month. In other words, Honest Ed is selling the car at a lower price, but is not offering the below-market-rate loan.

Note that car dealers are notorious for steering customers to high interest rate banks. In return, the banks give them a cut of the profits. It is best to investigate on your own the best rate you can get. Credit unions tend to have particularly good rates. Using your financial keys you can solve for your payments: 36 n .5 i 15,000 PV 0 FV PMT. You discover that your payments will be $456.33. Figure 7-7 illustrates your payments and their present value.

Figure 7-7
Alternative Car Offers

	t=	0	1	2	3	4	5	6
Honest Ed's		3,000	456.33	456.33	456.33	456.33	456.33	456.33
	PV	3,000	454	452	450	447	445	443
	Total PV	18,000.03						
Shifty Sam's		5,000	416.67	416.67	416.67	416.67	416.67	416.67
	PV	5000	414.597	412.5343	410.4819	408.4397	406.4077	404.3858
	Total PV	18,696.37						

Since Honest Ed's offer is at the market rate of interest, it should not be surprising that the present value of the payments is equal to the car price (it is slightly off due to rounding). Honest Ed's is more interesting. After taking the present value of the down payment, and the payments on the 0% loan at the market interest rate on car loans, the present value is higher. The benefit of the low-interest loan could not offset the fact that the car price was higher. Take Honest Ed's, but watch out for the extended warranty! (They are generally a bad deal because it is not worth the price to have additional future car repairs paid for.)

7.1.2 Future Value

If you put a single cash flow into a savings account, the future value would tell you how much you would have in the future (principal and interest). When working with annuities, future values represent the result of consistent contributions to an interest bearing account. You may use a future value of an annuity problem to ask yourself how much you will have saved to buy a car in three years, or how much you will have saved for retirement in fifty years. And just like present value problems, future value problems have permutations. It is time to work through them.

Question 6

You are saving to buy a 3-D television. Starting one month from today you will put $120 into a savings account. The monthly periodic rate is .4%. How much will you have saved in one year immediately after you put the last payment in? The most direct way to solve the problem is to take the future value of each cash flow (remembering you have to count up instead of down with a future value problem). Then add the future values of all the cash flows to get what you will have saved in total. However, since the payments are constant, you can use the future value of a constant annuity formula: FV= $\frac{C}{i} \cdot [(1+i)^n - 1]$.

Figure 7-8
Future Value of a Constant Annuity, No Cash Flow at t=0

t=		0	1	2	3	4	5	6
		0	120	120	120	120	120	120
FV of Each Contribution*:		0	125.3868774	124.887	124.3898	123.894	123.401	122.909
Total FV of the Annuity:	$1,472.11							
*What each contribution will have compounded up to yield in the future.								

C_0=	0
C_1=	120
g=	0

Formula:	FV=	$1,472.11
Excel Function:	FV=	$1,472.11

Filling in the formula: FV= $\frac{120}{.004} \cdot [1.004^{12} - 1]$ = $1,472.11. The keystrokes are: 1.004 ENTER 12 y^x 1 - 120 X .004 ÷. Since this is a constant annuity, you can use the financial keys: 12 n .4 i 0 PV 120 CHS PMT FV. The future value gives you how much you have saved immediately after you put the last payment in, which in this example is at t=12 (12 months from today). The Excel function is immediately below the formula (see the spreadsheet).

Question 7

On to the next permutation. You are saving to buy a 3-D television. Starting today you will put $120 into a savings account. How much will you have saved in one year immediately after you put the last payment in? Now you have an extra cash flow at t=0 that the annuity formula does not take into account, so you will have to deal with it separately. When you had a present value problem, you simply added it in at the end. However, when you have a future value problem, you have to compound up interest on the first payment since you want to know what the first payment will yield in the future, including compounded interest. To do this, use the formula for the future value of a simple loan from the last chapter. Your formula with the numbers plugged in will be:

$$FV = (120 \cdot 1.004^{12}) + \left(\frac{120}{.004}\right) \cdot [1.004^{12} - 1] = \$1{,}597.99.$$

This looks like the previous example, except that there is the extra cash flow compounded up. Notice that for the simple future value formula for the first cash flow, n is the number of times interest is compounded. In the second part, which takes the future value of the annuity starting at t=1, "n" refers to the number of payments. The keystrokes are: 1.004 ENTER 12 y^x 1 - 120 X .004 ÷ 1.004 ENTER 12 y^x 120 X +. In the case of future value, the financial keys can incorporate the extra cash flow at t=0 by putting it into the PV key. (PV is a one-time cash flow or value at t=0.) The keystrokes are: 12 n .4 i 120 CHS PV 120 CHS PMT FV.

Figure 7-9
Future Value of a Constant Annuity, a Cash Flow at t=0

t=	0	1	2	3	4	5	6
	120	120	120	120	120	120	120
FV of Each Contribution*:	125.8884249	125.3868774	124.887	124.3898	123.894	123.401	122.909
Total FV of the Annuity:	$1,597.99						

*What each contribution will have compounded up to yield in the future.

C_0=	120
C_1=	120
g=	0

Formula:	FV=	$1,597.99
Excel Function:	FV=	$1,597.99

It is a common mistake to forget to compound interest on the cash flow at t=0. One week after I had gone over these formulas with some undergraduates, a student of mine related to me that he had taken my retirement example (where we figured out how much will be saved in the future for retirement) and checked it against his mutual fund company's website—one of the biggest mutual fund companies in the world. He plugged in my example from class with the first payment starting at t=0 and continuing. The amount saved in the future did not agree with what I had calculated in class. After some investigating, he discovered that they had failed to compound interest on the first payment. He fired off an angry email along the lines of "How can I trust you with my money when you can't even..." He did not get a reply to the email, but some time shortly thereafter, the mistake was fixed!

Question 8

You are saving to buy a 3-D television. Starting one month from today you will put \$120 into a savings account. Each contribution will be .3% (.003) larger than the one before. How much will you have saved in one year immediately after you put the last payment in? You now need the formula for the future value of a growing annuity: FV= $\frac{C_1}{i-g} \cdot [(1+i)^n - (1+g)^n]$. Since you have a growing annuity, you are back to entering C_1 specifically in the formula. Plugging in the numbers:

$$FV= \frac{120}{.004-.003} \cdot [1.004^{12} - 1.003^{12}] = \$1,496.43.$$

The keystrokes are: 1.004 **ENTER** 12 y^x 1.003 **ENTER** 12 y^x - 120 X .004 **ENTER** .003 - ÷. Since this is a growing annuity, you cannot use the financial keys.

Figure 7-10
Future Value of a Growing Annuity, No Cash Flow at t=0

t=		0	1	2	3	4	5	6
		0	120	120.36	120.7211	121.083	121.446	121.811
FV of Each Contribution*:		0	125.3868774	125.262	125.1372	125.013	124.888	124.764
Total FV of the Annuity:	\$1,496.43							

*What each contribution will have compounded up to yield in the future.

C_0=	0
C_1=	120
g=	0.003

Formula: FV= \$1,496.43

Question 9

I saved the trickiest for last: You are saving to buy a 3-D television. Starting today you will put \$120 into a savings account. Each contribution will be .3% (.003) larger than the one before. How much will you have saved in one year immediately after you put the last payment in? Remember that you have to put C_1 into the annuity formula, as well as compound up interest on the first payment. Plugging the numbers in: $FV = (120 \cdot 1.004^{12}) + \left(\frac{120 \cdot 1.03}{.004-.003}\right) \cdot [1.004^{12} - 1.003^{12}] = \$1,626.80$.

There are shortcuts for the present value and the future value of an annuity when there is a cash flow at t=0. However, it is often said that when you take a shortcut, you take the long way around. (It is easy to get lost.) I save these shortcuts for the appendix.

Figure 7-11
Future Value of a Growing Annuity, a Cash Flow at t=0.

t=	0	1	2	3	4	5	6
	120	120.36	120.721	121.0832	121.446	121.811	122.176
FV of Each Contribution*:	125.8884249	125.763038	125.638	125.5126	125.388	125.263	125.138
Total FV of the Annuity:	$1,626.80						
*What each contribution will have compounded up to yield in the future.							
C_0=	120						
C_1=	120.36						
g=	0.003						
Formula:	FV=	$1,626.80					

7.1.3 Solving For Interest Rates

When a loan is not an annuity, it is easy to solve for the interest rate. For instance, suppose you Borrow $100 and owe $112.36 in two years. Compounding is annual. To solve for the interest rate:

$$\$100 \cdot (1+i)^2 = \$112.36$$
$$(1+i)^2 = \frac{112.36}{100}$$
$$[(1+i)^2]^{\frac{1}{2}} = \left[\frac{112.36}{100}\right]^{\frac{1}{2}}$$
$$1+i = \left[\frac{112.36}{100}\right]^{\frac{1}{2}}$$
$$i = \left[\frac{112.36}{100}\right]^{\frac{1}{2}} - 1 = .06.$$

When a loan is an annuity, it is not possible to solve for the interest rate using a formula. You must rely on your financial keys or use a spreadsheet function, such as the "rate" function in Excel. Be sure to remember that you have to put in negative cash flows, or you will not get a solution. Looking back at Question 1, the financial keys to solve for the interest rate would be: 24 n 2256.29 CHS PV 100 PMT 0 FV i. With rounding, you get .5%. Even though you do not consider yourself to have a negative cash flow, the financial keys insist on it. They assume that you are not being given something. Plugging in the negative present value is pretending that you are loaning your aunt the money and she is paying you back. (This is necessary to get the answer.) In the last example: 2 n 100 CHS PV 0 PMT 112.36 FV i.

7.1.4 Summary of Annuities

It will be helpful to summarize what you have learned about annuities. Always remember that the annuity formulas value cash flows beginning at t=1. If there is a cash flow at t=0, it must be dealt with separately. "n" is the number of payments. (For simple loans it is the number of times interest compounds.) The periodic interest rate that matches the timing of cash flows must be used. In other words, if you are given an annual interest rate on a loan with monthly compounding, you must convert the rate to a monthly rate. (I will discuss how to do this in the next chapter.)

Present Value

Constant Annuity:

Use the constant cash flow in the formula.
If there is a cash flow at t=0, add it in at the end.

Growing Annuity:

Use C_1 in the annuity formula. (If you are given the cash flow at t=0, you must multiply C_0 by (1+g) to calculate C_1.)
If there is a cash flow at t=0, add it in at the end.

Future Value

Constant Annuity:

Use the constant cash flow in the formula.
If there is a cash flow at t=0, you must <u>calculate the future value</u> of this individual cash flow by compounding up interest and adding it in at the end.

Growing Annuity:

Use C_1 in the formula. (If you are given the cash flow at t=0, you must multiply C_0 by (1+g) to calculate C_1.)
If there is a cash flow at t=0, you must <u>calculate the future value</u> of this individual cash flow by compounding up interest and adding it in at the end.

Figure 7-12
Summary of Working With Annuities

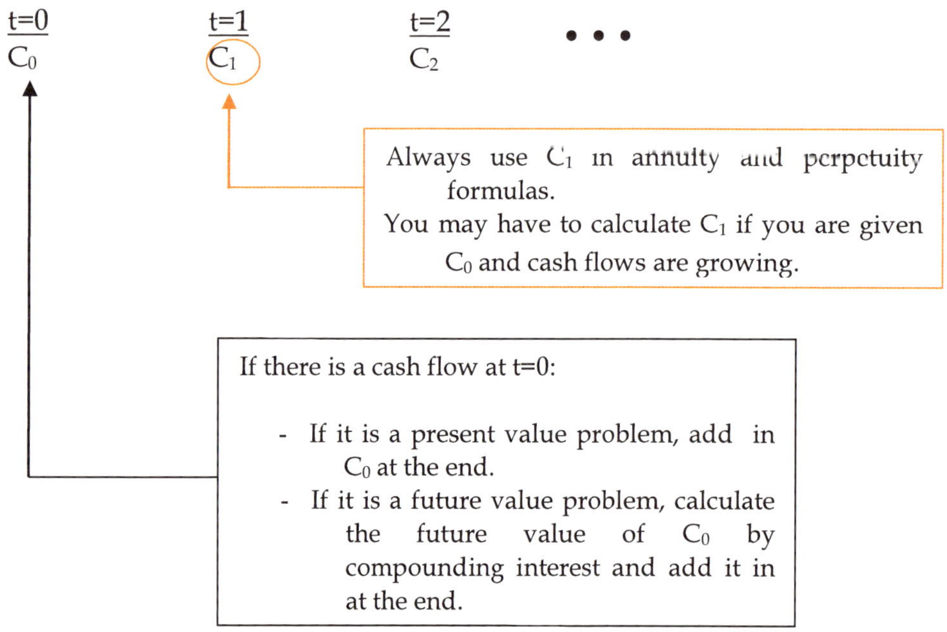

7.2 Perpetuities

There is another kind of annuity - except the payments never stop. This kind of annuity is called a perpetuity. When I introduce perpetuities to my students, sometimes I am asked "Since there isn't anything that exists where payments never stop, how useful is a perpetuity formula?" One of the things I love about teaching finance is that I am almost never asked how something I am teaching is useful, but it does sometimes happen with perpetuity formulas. My answer is that perpetuity formulas are used all of the time. And if you give me a chance to explain them, you will see why.

Imagine that there is a cash flow that starts at t=1 and lasts forever. (There is actually a British consol, a kind of bond that never matures, and keeps on sending payments; theoretically forever.) For example, you expect to receive $100 each quarter forever, starting next quarter. The periodic quarterly rate is 2%. You can use the present value of a constant perpetuity formula to value the payments (and calculate the theoretical price): $PV=\frac{C}{i}=\frac{100}{.02}=\$5,000$. In other words, the promise to pay $100 each quarter forever is worth $5,000 in total.

At this point, a student will often express surprise that a payment that goes on forever could have so little value. To illustrate this, look at Table 7-1, which shows a $1,000 semiannual (every 6 months) perpetuity. Suppose the semiannual rate is 4%.

Table 7-1
$1,000 Perpetuity

t=0	t=1	t=2	t=3	t=4	t=5	• • •	t=300	• • •
	$1,000	$1,000	$1,000	$1,000	$1,000	• • •	$1,000	• • •

The value of all of the payments that go on forever is: $\frac{1,000}{.04}=\$25,000$. However, suppose you want to focus on one of the payments by itself. For instance, you may want to know what the payment at t=300 is worth. When you take the present value of a single cash flow, you use the simple present value formula: $PV=\frac{1,000}{1.04^{300}}=\$0.0077$. In other words, $1,000.00 a hundred and fifty years from now (300 semiannual periods) is essentially worthless. Cash flows that occur very far in the future have very little value, and the further out you go, the faster a cash flow's value heads towards zero.

Perpetuity formulas are used to value securities that last for a very long time. Stocks are an example of this. Stocks can theoretically go on forever. And even if they do not, the perpetuity formula will give an accurate valuation. Yes the perpetuity formula values cash flows after the security's cash flows stop, but these cash flows are so far in the future that they are just about worthless, anyway. So, perpetuity formulas approximate the value of very long-lived securities like stocks very well.

Another kind of perpetuity is a growing perpetuity. The formula is: $PV=\frac{C_1}{i-g}$, $i > g$. Notice that C_1 is used in the formula because all of the cash flows are different. It must be the case that $i > g$, because if not, the perpetuity would be infinitely valuable, and these simply do not exist.

Finally, remember that just like with annuities, if there is a cash flow at t=0 it has to be dealt with separately. And you would never calculate the future value of perpetuities because they go on forever.

7.3 Conclusion

You now have the foundation needed for understanding loans. In addition, you have learned how to take the present value of perpetuities, which will come in handy for valuing long-lived securities, such as stocks, which I will cover in more detail in Volume 2. You now know the basic underpinnings behind how many loans and debt securities are priced. The next step will be to understand interest rates better.

Key Terms:

Annuity
Competing offer
Growing annuity
Periodic rate
Perpetuity

Formulas:

The present value of a constant annuity: $PV= \frac{C}{i} \cdot \left[1- \left(\frac{1}{1+i}\right)^n\right]$.

The present value of a growing annuity: $PV= \left(\frac{C_1}{i-g}\right) \cdot \left[1 - \left(\frac{1+g}{1+i}\right)^n\right]$.

The future value of a constant annuity: $FV= \frac{C}{i} \cdot \left[(1+i)^n- 1\right]$.

The future value of a growing annuity: $FV= \frac{C_1}{i-g} \cdot \left[(1+i)^n- (1+g)^n\right]$.

The present value of a constant perpetuity: $PV= \frac{C}{i}$.

The present value of a growing perpetuity: $PV= \frac{C_1}{i-g}$, $i > g$.

End of Chapter Questions

Annuities

1. You have just won the lottery. Starting today, you will receive $5,000. Each month thereafter you will receive a payment that is .0025 larger than the payment before, so that your payment next month will be .0025 larger than the first one, and so on. You will receive payments until twenty five years from today. The monthly interest rate is .0042. As an alternative, they offer to pay you $1,000,000 immediately. Should you take the series of payments, or take the alternative offer of $1,000,000?

2. You are saving to buy a condo. The condo will cost $500,000, and being responsible you would like to save $100,000, which is 20% of the purchase price. You would like to buy the condo in four years. A savings account has a monthly interest rate of .4%, or .004. You will put $1,850.00 into the savings account today. Each month thereafter, you will contribute the same amount until the final payment four years from today. When you put in the final payment four years from now, will you have saved the $100,000?

3. You are selling a child's game center. Your neighbor tells you that he can give you $200 for it. Alternatively, he can give you $50 right away, and starting next month, $20 each month for 8 months. In other words, you will get 9 payments in total -- $50 right away, and $20 starting one month from today for 8 months. You trust your neighbor to make the payments. The monthly market rate of interest is .005 or .5%. Which offer should you take?

4. You owe the IRS $10,000. You can pay right away, or pay $400 each month for three years (36 total payments) starting next month. The monthly interest rate is .5% or .005. What is the better option – pay 10,000 now, or the monthly payments?

5. You just purchased an annuity from an insurance company, which is a promise to make regular payments to you. You will receive $120,000 one year from now. Each year thereafter you will receive a payment that is 3% higher than the payment you received the year before. Therefore, the payment you receive in two years will be 3% higher than $120,000, and so on. The final payment is in twenty-two years. The annual interest rate for the annuity is 5%. How much did you just pay for the annuity? In addition to the formula, create a spreadsheet.

6. You are sixteen-years-old. You tell your parents that you want to be able to drive the family car, and that you can pay for the added cost of the auto insurance. The current rate for sixteen-year-old boys is $2,000 every 12 months. You explain that you can work part-time and earn $160 "take home" pay per month, paid at the end of each month with the first payment one month from today. You can put your wages into a savings account each month, earning a monthly rate of .75%. Your parents agree to make the first insurance payment immediately, and you agree to make the rest starting at one year from today. Will your current job opportunity allow you to make the insurance payments?

7. You are saving to buy a cabin in the woods. You want to save $140,000 by twelve years from today. A savings account has an annual effective rate of 6%. You will contribute $6,000 today. Each year thereafter you will contribute an amount that is 3% higher than the year before, so that a year from today you will contribute an amount that is 3% higher than what you contributed today, and so on. Will you have enough saved in twelve years? In addition to the formula, create a spreadsheet.

8. You would like to buy a very nice entertainment system in two years. You discover that if you drink coffee made at work (instead of Starbucks) and bring a bagged lunch to work, you will be able to make contributions to a savings account. Starting next month you will put $190 into a savings account with a monthly interest rate of .5%. Each month thereafter your contribution will increase by .33% per month, so that after putting in $190 next month, the month after you will put in .33% more, and so on. The entertainment system costs $5,000. Will you be able to buy the system in two years after you make your final contribution?

9. You are selling an old gaming computer. You neighbor tells you that he can give you $200 for it. Alternatively, he can give you $50 right away, and starting next month, $20 each month for 8 months. In other words, you will get 9 payments in total -- $50 right away, and $20 starting one month from today for 8 months. You trust your neighbor to make the payments. The monthly market rate of interest is .005 or .5%. Which offer should you take?

10. You have just won a lawsuit. They have been ordered to pay you $300,000 today. They come to you with an offer. Today they will pay you $30,000. Each year thereafter for seven years they will pay you 1% more than what they paid you the year before. In other words, your last payment will be seven years from today, and there will be eight payments in total. The first payment will be $30,000, and each payment thereafter will be 1% higher than the previous payment. The effective annual interest rate is 7%. Should you take their offer?

11. You owe the IRS $10,000. You can pay right away, or pay $400 each month for three years (36 total payments) starting next month. The monthly interest rate is .4% or .004. What is the better option - pay $10,000 now, or pay the monthly payments?

Perpetuities

12. A perpetuity pays $3,000 every six months, forever, starting half a year from today. The semiannual interest rate is .05. What is the value of the perpetuity? Permutation: the first payment is today.

13. A perpetuity pays $200 every week, forever, starting next week. Each week the payment is .1% larger than the week before. The weekly interest rate is .23%. What is the value of the perpetuity? Permutation: Your first payment of $200 is today.

Appendix
Annuity Shortcuts with a Payment at t=0

There are shortcuts that can be taken when there are payments at t=0. However, unless you are confident with the annuity material, I recommend that you stick with the longer way that is consistent in the case of present value problems. Firstly, remember that annuity formulas assume that the first payment is one time period away. The trick is to use your imagination and pretend you are standing one time period in the past. Use Question 4 as an example. Looking at Figure 7-6, imagine that you are standing at time period -1 (one time period before today). How would the problem look to you? You would regard it as a growing annuity with no payment at t=0. You would use the formula:

$$PV = \left(\frac{100}{.005-.002}\right)\cdot\left[1-\left(\frac{1.002}{1.005}\right)^{25}\right] = \$2{,}400.461677.$$

The first payment at "t=1" from your perspective, would be \$100. In total now, there would be 25 payments, rather than 24. However, the present value formula would give the value of cash flows at t=-1. (Notice that I carried further out to prevent rounding errors.) To get the true present value, you have to compound up interest one time period. Therefore, the final answer is \$2,500.461677*1.005 = \$2,412.46. Of course, you can do this final step at the end of the calculation without having to write the number out first: $PV = 1.005\cdot\left(\frac{100}{.005-.002}\right)\cdot\left[1-\left(\frac{1.002}{1.005}\right)^{25}\right] = \$2{,}412.46$. I think it is easier to just add in the cash flow at t=0.

Next, consider Question 9. Looking at figure 7-11, you could pretend that you are standing at t=-1 (one time period before today). From this perspective your first payment is \$100, and there are 13 time periods. An added bonus is that since you are calculating what you will have one year from today, by having 13 payments from the perspective of one time ago, you will end up with the right answer without further adjustment. The formula will be:

$$FV = \frac{120}{.004-.003}\cdot\left[1.004^{13} - 1.003^{13}\right] = \$1{,}626.80.$$

This is the final answer without need for more adjustment. This time the short cut is a time saver.

Chapter 8

Interest Rates

8.1 Converting Interest Rates

When working with annuities, it is important to use the periodic rate. This is the interest rate that matches the timing of the cash flows. For instance, if you have a semiannual annuity, then you want to use a semiannual interest rate. However, you may want to compare interest rates on two different investments; one that has monthly payments, and one that has semiannual payments. And not only that, most people typically like to think of interest rates on an annual basis. I now turn to demonstrating how to convert interest rates to a different time basis for comparison.

Figure 8-1 illustrates what would happen if you put $10,000 into a savings account earning 1% interest per month. (These days, you could expect to earn this or less in a year!) Interest is compounded on a monthly basis, and you can see how much the balance in your account grows each month. (Note that this is not an annuity. These are not a series of payments, but rather represent how much your balance grows each month as you compound interest.) By the end of the year, after compounding interest 12 times, your balance is: $\$10{,}000 \cdot 1.01^{12} = \$11{,}268.25$.

On the other hand, suppose that you put $10,000 into another account where interest is compounded annually. At the end of the year you will have $11,268.25. As far as you are concerned, from the perspective of earning interest, the two accounts are equivalent. (Although, of course, your money may be stuck in the annual account and you cannot withdraw it.)

The formula for compounding interest on the annual account is: $\$10{,}000 \cdot (1+i_a) = \$11{,}268.26$. Notice that I have an "a" subscript now to denote the time period that the interest rate is for. Solving: $i_a = (11{,}268.26/10{,}000) - 1 = .126825$ with rounding. This interest rate is equivalent to the monthly rate, because you will have the same amount at the end of the year. You have found a methodology for finding equivalent rates. For short hand, I will refer to this as converting interest rates into different time periods. In this example, I converted a monthly rate into an annual rate.

Figure 8-1
A Monthly Rate Versus an Annual Rate

	A	B	C	D	E	F	G	H	I	J	K	L	M	N
1	i_m=	0.01			i_a= 0.126825									
3	t=	0	1	2	3	4	5	6	7	8	9	10	11	12
4														
5		10,000.00	10,100.00	10,201.00	10,303.01	10,406.04	10,510.10	10,615.20	10,721.35	10,828.57	10,936.85	11,046.22	11,156.68	11,268.25
6		Monthly Formula												11,268.25
7		Annual Formual												11,268.25
8				Monthly Interest:		0.01		Annual Interest:		0.126825				

Take a look at the mathematics:

$$\$10{,}000\cdot(1+i_m)^{12}=\$11{,}268.25 \qquad \text{(Cell N6)}$$

$$\$10{,}000\cdot(1+i_a)=\$11{,}268.25 \qquad \text{(Cell N7)}$$

$$(1+i_m)^{12} = (1+i_a)$$

You can solve for one interest rate in terms of the other:

$$i_a= (1+i_m)^{12}- 1$$

This is the formula in Cell E1. Also,

$$(1+i_m)^{12} = (1+i_a)$$
$$\left[(1+i_m)^{12}\right]^{\frac{1}{12}}= (1+i_a)^{\frac{1}{12}},$$
$$1+i_m= (1+i_a)^{\frac{1}{12}},$$
$$i_m= (1+i_a)^{\frac{1}{12}}- 1$$

When converting one interest rate into another, it is necessary to compare the two time periods. A monthly rate will compound twelve times to get an annual rate. To go the other way from an annual rate to a monthly rate, use a power of 1/12.

To get an annual rate from a quarterly rate: $(1+i_q)^4 - 1=i_a$. Quarterly interest will compound four times to get the annual rate. Or going the other way, $i_q=(1+i_a)^{1/4} - 1$. Suppose you wanted to convert a monthly rate into a quarterly rate. Remembering that there are three months in a quarter (there are four quarters in a year) $i_q=(1+i_m)^3 - 1$, or going the other way, $i_m=(1+i_q)^{1/3} - 1$.

In order to use a formula, the easiest method is to compare the number of times each interest rate will compound in a year: $i_y=(1+i_x)^{\left(\frac{\text{\# times x compounds in a year}}{\text{\# times y compounds in a year}}\right)}-1$. Starting with the monthly example, if i_x is the monthly rate and i_y is that annual rate that you are solving for, $i_a=1.01^{\frac{12}{1}}-1=1.01^{12}-1$. To convert a quarterly rate of 2% to a monthly rate: $i_m=1.02^{\frac{4}{12}}-1=1.02^{\frac{1}{3}}-1=.006623$ with rounding. The keystrokes are: 1.02 ENTER 4 ENTER 12 ÷ y^x 1 −.

Alternatively, looking at the equation there are three months in a quarter, and since you are going from the bigger quarterly rate to the smaller monthly rate, use 1/3. The keystrokes are: 1.02 ENTER 3 1/x y^x 1 − . If you would like to start with the simplified equation in Table 8-1, compare how many times the smaller time period fits in the bigger one. If you are going from an interest rate for the shorter time period to the interest rate for the longer time period, use that number as the power. If you are going in the reverse direction, use 1 over that number. Table 8-1 shows other interest rate conversions.

Table 8-1
Converting One Interest Rate Into Another

i_x	i_y	Equation	Simplified Equation	Result
i_m = .005	i_a	$i_a=1.005^{\frac{12}{1}}-1$	$i_a=1.005^{12}-1.$	.0616778
i_a=.0616778	i_s	$i_s=1.0616778^{\frac{1}{2}}-1$	$i_s=1.0616778^{\frac{1}{2}}-1$	.0303775
i_s=.0303775	i_q	$i_q=1.0303775^{\frac{2}{4}}-1$	$i_q=1.0303775^{\frac{1}{2}}-1$	.015075
i_q=.015075	i_m	$i_m=1.015075^{\frac{4}{12}}-1$	$i_m=1.015075^{\frac{1}{3}}-1$	.005
i_m=.005	i_s	$i_s=1.005^{\frac{12}{2}}-1$	$i_s=1.005^{6}-1$	.0303776

Notice that you started with a monthly rate, which you converted into an equivalent annual rate, which you converted into an equivalent semiannual rate, which you converted into an equivalent quarterly rate, which you converted into an equivalent monthly rate. It should not be a surprise that you ended up back where you started with the same monthly rate.

8.2 Stated Rates Versus Effective Rates

I am about to give you a crazy example, and you will think I have lost my mind. However, before you put the book down and call a psychiatrist, bear with me and you will discover that there is a reason for the wacky example that I am about to show you.

Suppose that I sell bowling balls.[1] You would like to buy one, but to your dismay you discover that I am a little cracked in the head. (Hopefully my bowling balls are not.) Here is how I quote the price: I take the money I want you to give me, divide by 2 and subtract 3. The "price" I quote you is 47 in "Joetta units." After your initial shock, you realize that you know my formula and you say to yourself, "Ok, I just need to figure out how much she wants me to pay her in dollars to buy the bowling ball, and I will never have to deal with her again." At this point, you need to take my nutty formula and undo it. You take the Joetta units of 47, add the 3 back, and then multiply by 2. You discover that I want $100 for the bowling ball. (Originally, ($100/2) − 3 = 47.)

Maybe I am crazy like a fox. Why would I quote prices this way? Because I want to trick you into thinking I am charging you less than what I really am. Unfortunately, this is how interest rates are quoted on consumer loans. They use something akin to Joetta units! A nutty formula is used that makes no sense; that makes it look like you are paying

[1] My first job involved working for a sporting goods wholesaler as a clerk in their warehouse for $4.00 per hour.

less interest on a loan than you actually are. The solution is to have a knee-jerk reaction. Undo the nutty formula to find out what you are really paying.

Now return to the simple example where you put your money into a savings account and let it earn interest for a year. The monthly rate of interest is 1%, and you put $10,000 into the account (see Figure 8-1). Looking at Figure 8-2, the first month (at t=1) you will earn 10,000·.01 = $100 of interest, so that at the end of the first month you will have accumulated $10,100. Of the interest earned, the entire $100 is from your original principal. The next month, you earn interest of $101.00. $100 of that is interest on your original principal. The other $1.00 comes from earning interest on the $100 previous interest earned.

The next month, the same interest is earned on the original principal (your original investment). However, at this point, you get to earn total interest on $10,201. After the $100 interest on the original principal, the rest must be interest that you are earning on previous interest. This is the magic of compounding. It makes your investment grow at an ever increasing rate. Eventually, at the end of the year you have a total of $11,268.25. The increase in your investment came from two places. $1,200 came from interest earned on your original principal. The extra $68.25 came from earning interest on previous interest earned.

Unfortunately, here is where the insanity begins. Consumer loans are quoted using "stated rates." To make it worse, stated rates are based on a nutty formula. But they were not created by the nutty professor; they were enacted into law by your United States Congress in legislation called the – brace yourself – "**Truth in Lending Act**."

Congress mandated that consumer loan interest rates be quoted using something called the APR. The APR (annual percentage rate) takes the periodic rate (in our example .01) and multiplies it by the number of compounding periods in a year.

Suppose that the bank lends you $10,000 for a year with a monthly interest rate of 1% (similar to our previous savings account example, but the bank is lending you money rather than the other way around). The APR for the loan is 12%. If you only owed interest on your original principal, then at the end of the year you would owe 12% ($1,200). Instead, you owe more because of compounding. Why may the Truth in Lending Act be crazy like a fox? For loans, this means that lenders get to quote you a rate that is below what they are really charging you.

The APR ignores compounding. In reality you owe an extra $68.25. What is the annual interest rate that you owe? You already calculated it. It is 12.6825% from Figure 8-1. You are being quoted 12%, but you are in fact paying 12.6825%. Does this make sense? Of course not, you silly goose! Call those helpful healthcare workers in their nice white coats and prepare for the rubber room.

Figure 8-2
Stated Rates Versus Effective Rates – a Monthly Example

$i_m =$ 0.01

t=	0	1	2	3	4	5	6	7	8	9	10	11	12	Total
	10,000.00	10,100.00	10,201.00	10,303.01	10,406.04	10,510.10	10,615.20	10,721.35	10,828.57	10,936.85	11,046.22	11,156.68	11,268.25	11,268.25
Original Principal		10,000.00	10,000.00	10,000.00	10,000.00	10,000.00	10,000.00	10,000.00	10,000.00	10,000.00	10,000.00	10,000.00	10,000.00	10,000.00
Interest on Original Principal		100.00	100.00	100.00	100.00	100.00	100.00	100.00	100.00	100.00	100.00	100.00	100.00	1,200.00
Interest on Interest		0.00	1.00	2.01	3.03	4.06	5.10	6.15	7.21	8.29	9.37	10.46	11.57	68.25
Sum														11,268.25

Unfortunately consumer loans are quoted using stated rates. A stated rate is calculated using a nutty formula. The periodic rate is multiplied by the number of compounding periods in a year. If compounding is quarterly, the quarterly periodic rate is multiplied by 4. If the periodic rate is semiannual, the periodic rate is multiplied by 2. Your knee-jerk reaction should be to undo what they did by dividing by the number of compounding periods in a year. You will then have the periodic rate. The periodic rate is an effective rate. If an interest rate is an effective rate, that simply means that it makes economic sense and will tell you something sensible. Effective rates take compounding into account.

Suppose you have a loan with monthly compounding. Take a look at Table 8-1 again. The first row gives a monthly interest rate of .005, which will be the periodic rate for the loan since it matches the number of compounding periods or payments, depending on if it is a simple loan or an annuity. The equivalent annual rate of .0616778 is not a periodic rate for the loan, but it is an equivalent effective annual rate. Effective rates take compounding into account and reflect reality. An effective rate quoted on an annual basis is called an "Effective Annual Rate," or EAR. You will work with EARs a lot.

Figure 8-3 illustrates how to deal with stated rates. Simply divide by the number of compounding periods in a year. Once you have done this you have the periodic rate. Once you have the periodic rate you can use the compounding formula and methodology demonstrated in Table 8-1 to convert the periodic rate into any effective rate that you want. Often APRs are converted into EARs, but they do not have to be. The periodic rate could be converted into an equivalent rate for any time period.

Table 8-2 illustrates converting APRs into effective rates. In addition to calculating the periodic rate and the EAR, the table also demonstrates how the periodic rate could be used to calculate an effective rate for a time period other than a year. Note that instead of starting from the periodic rate, you could also have taken the EAR and converted it into the other effective rate.

The last line is worth taking note of. The APR of 32% is entirely possible if you are late on a credit card payment. And it is a great demonstration of how APRs mislead borrowers into thinking that they are paying less interest on loans than what they really are. Because the APR is a stated rate, it ignores compounding and will therefore always be below the effective rate. The "default" credit card rate is the APR of 32%. However, the true rate that you are paying, the EAR, is 37.69%. (Pinocchio's nose is quite long on this one.) It turns out that the higher the interest rate and the more frequent the number of compounding periods, the longer Pinocchio's nose becomes. Credit cards have high interest rates, and typically have daily compounding. Therefore, their APRs tend to be quite a bit below the true EAR that the borrower is paying.

Figure 8-3
Periodic, Effective, and Stated Interest Rates

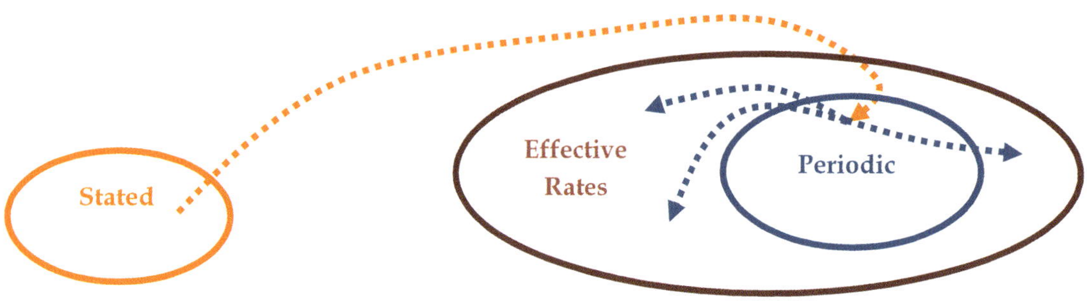

Table 8-2
Converting APRs Into Effective Rates

APR	Loan Compounding or Frequency of Payments	Periodic Rate	EAR	Another Effective Rate
.036	Monthly	$i_m = \frac{.036}{12} = .003$	$1.003^{12} - 1 = .0366$	$i_s = 1.003^6 - 1 = .01814$
.08	Semiannual	$i_s = \frac{.08}{2} = .04$	$1.04^2 - 1 = .0816$	$i_m = 1.04^{\frac{1}{6}} - 1 = .00656$
.05	Quarterly	$i_q = \frac{.05}{4} = .0125$	$1.0125^4 - 1 = .0509$	$i_s = 1.0125^2 - 1 = .02516$
.32	Daily (365)	$i_q = \frac{.32}{365} = .000876712$	$1.000876712^{365} - 1 = .3769$	$i_w = 1.000876712^7 - 1 = .006153$

And now to add to the outrage: It turns out that when people borrow from a bank the loan is quoted to them using an APR, but when they ask about the interest they can earn on a savings account, they are quoted a APY (annual percentage yield). The APY is an effective rate. The bank is quoting the lower stated rate for loans, and the higher effective rate when touting the high interest it offers on its savings accounts. And this was all mandated by Congress! There is no point in getting mad at a loan officer for quoting interest rates to you this way - they are required to by law.

Often times, CDs and other kinds of debt securities do not list their interest rate, but rather have a "YTM." This stands for "Yield to Maturity." This is just the interest rate for the debt under a different name. If you are given a YTM, just use it as "i" in any formula.

8.3 Issues Surrounding Very High Interest Rates and Abusive Loan Practices

It is time to point something out. You have probably grown up in a nurturing, caring environment, and you have spent your life being told to respect adults. The second you turn eighteen and walk out the door, this perspective can do you harm. You are now considered an adult by others, and many will not be shy about taking as much money from you as they can in a business deal. Young adults are nothing more to them than inexperienced, attractive targets, and this is the first day of duck hunting season. Credit card companies are notorious for getting college kids into big financial trouble, all the while extracting huge payments from them.

It is time to change your perspective on yourself and the world. Do not be shy about questioning adults when it comes to business deals and financial transactions. Pluck up your courage and ask questions. After all, you are an adult too. It is now up to you to protect yourself.

Appendix A.1 contains an article on a loan made by a company called Stewart Finance Co. The loan was made to Elsie Williams, a retired hotel maid. The Social Security Administration wanted to encourage poor people to stop using paycheck loan companies (that charge very high fees) and use checking accounts instead, so they arranged for automatic deposits of social security checks. This was especially appealing to low income people, who could get their hands on their money sooner. However, once at Stuart Finance, Else decided to take out one of the loans that they were promoting in order to buy a sofa.

Elsie had cataracts in her eyes, which made it difficult to read the fine print, although most poor people do not understand the fine print anyway, and do not bother. What she did not realize was that they included in the loan an extra amount to purchase death and dismemberment insurance, along with an insurance fee, which she did not need or want. The terms of her loan are in Figure 8-3:

Figure 8-3
Elsie Williams' Loan

Loan for Sofa	204.84
D & D Insurance	73.50
Insurance Fee	10.00
Total Loan	288.34
Montly Payment for Five Months	72

It is time to use what you have learned to see if you can reproduce the APR they quoted Elsie. She had constant payments of $72 for five months, which is an annuity. The loan amount is the present value. The correct formula to use is the present value of a constant annuity:

$$288.34 = \frac{72}{i} \cdot \left[1 - \left(\frac{1}{1+i}\right)^5\right]$$

The interest rate "i" will be the periodic rate. However, when you have an annuity, you cannot use the formula to find the interest rate. You have to rely on your financial calculator. (The calculator is not any smarter than you, it can just "hunt and peck" faster until it finds an interest rate that makes both sides of the equation match.) The financial keys are: 5 n 288.34 PV 72 CHS PMT 0 FV i . The Excel function is =RATE(5,-72,288.34,0). The answer is 7.886124603%. You now have the periodic monthly rate. Using the nutty APR formula: APR=$.07886124603 \cdot 12 = .9463$.

Unfortunately, uneducated people may not understand how high this rate is. What is the effective rate? (From now on convert to percentages, or you may get confused) $EAR = (1.07886124603^{12} - 1) \cdot 100 = 148.65\%$. When is Pinocchio's nose the longest? When the interest rate is high, and when there are a lot of compounding periods. And who pays high interest rates? Poor people. So who do we lie to the most? You've got it.

You are not done yet. Else did not buy the insurance or pay the fee, as far as she knew. She simply borrowed the $204.84 to buy the sofa. Redo the calculation with the loan at $204.84, since this is what she actually got. If you plug 204.84 into the present value key and recalculate the periodic rate, it turns out to be 22.30603627%. Converting this to an EAR and expressing it as a percentage: $EAR = (1.2230603627^{12} - 1) \cdot 100 = 1{,}020.40\%$. This was the effective rate that Else was actually paying.

Every year, many poor people go to "paycheck loan" companies for loans. Visit the site: http://www.mypaydayloan.com/. Click on the "APR disclosure" tab. You will see APR calculations for loans that they make. Take a look at one of their loans. The customer borrows $100 and pays back $125 in seven days. Since it is a simple loan you can calculate the periodic interest rate. It is just: $\frac{\$125}{\$100} - 1 = .25$.

You next need to calculate how many times seven days can compound up in a year, since a year is not an even 52 weeks. The number of compounding periods is 365/7. Using the APR formula: $.25 \cdot \frac{365}{7} \cdot 100 = 1{,}303.57\%$. This corresponds to the APR listed at the website. However, you want the EAR: $\left(1.25^{\frac{365}{7}} - 1\right) \cdot 100 = 11{,}302{,}151.42\%$. Remember the magic of compounding? If you borrow $1 and compound interest at 25% a week, at the end of the year you will owe $11,302,15<u>2</u>.42. (Do not forget to add the original dollar of principal back in or they may charge you interest on it all over again!)

Ethics

Usury laws vary by state. Generally usury laws place a cap on how much interest can be charged. They can also provide for legal relief.

One Side:

Uneducated people are being tricked out of their money. These people do not have the resources to understand the consequences of borrowing at these rates. High interest loans should be outlawed to prevent these people from being hurt. Muhammad Yunus won a Nobel Peace Prize for making small loans to poor people in Bangladesh and elsewhere at low interest rates.

The Other Side:

Individuals should be responsible for their own decisions. Also, the default rate must be very high, and there must be very high administrative costs. This is due to having to take up an employee's time to write a very small loan. Therefore, the personnel cost per loan is very high. (However, my understanding is that paycheck lending is very lucrative.) Finally, these people may have nowhere else to go if they are in a desperate situation and need money. Who are we to dictate to them what is in their own best-interest?

8.4 Floating Rates

A floating interest rate is adjusted based on a published interest rate such as the prime rate or LIBOR. The prime rate is the interest rate charged on loans to the safest business borrowers. LIBOR is the "London Interbank Offered Rate." It is the interest rate that banks in Britain and Europe charge each other for short-term dollar loans.

Suppose that an adjustable interest rate is based on LIBOR. For instance, the rate may be LIBOR + 2%. As LIBOR changes, the rate moves too. The loan may specify a grace period before the initial interest rate can be changed, the number of times a year the interest rate can be adjusted, and the maximum amount that the interest rate can be adjusted. For instance, if LIBOR rises by 5% in one year, and the maximum adjustment amount is 3%, then the floating interest rate can only be adjusted up by 3% for the year. I shall discuss adjustable rates further when I discuss mortgages.

8.5 Nominal Rates Versus Real Rates

So far you have worked with nominal interest rates. These are the interest rates that are written down in a loan contract, or that you can figure out for yourself from the cash flows of the loan. I now turn to the difference between nominal rates and something called a real rate, which takes into account inflation.

As I discussed in Chapter 2, inflation is a general increase in the level of prices over time. Suppose an apple costs $1 today, and prices increase steadily by 3% every year. In five years the price of an apple will be $\$1 \cdot 1.03 \cdot 1.03 \cdot 1.03 \cdot 1.03 \cdot 1.03 = 1 \cdot 1.03^5 = \$1.16$. In other words, and apple will cost $1.16 in the future. The good news is that everything is going up, including salaries, so you should be in a better position to afford the apple.

Notice that this formula looks like the future value formula, but it tells you something completely different—there is no interest being compounded and you are not earning money on an investment. The opposite question is to ask what a dollar in the future would buy you today. Going in the reverse direction: $\frac{1}{1.03^5}=\$.86$. In other words, $1 in the future would buy you what $.86 will buy you today. This is referred to as deflating the dollar amount. Again, while the formula looks similar, this has nothing to do with present value. The formula for deflating a dollar amount in the future is: $\text{Today's Buying Power}=\frac{\text{Future Dollar Amount}}{(1+\text{inflation rate})^{\text{number of time periods}}}$.

Inflation is important for understanding what you earn on your money. Consider the apple example: suppose that you invest $1 and intend to use it to buy an apple in five years. The $1 could buy one apple today. The annual interest rate is 3%. In five years when you withdraw your savings to buy the apple, using the future value formula, you will have $\$1 \cdot 1.03^5 = \$1.16$. Since the apple will cost $1.16, you have not gained in terms of buying power. Your real interest rate is zero. You are doing no better between now and the future.

What is really important is how much an investment will give you in terms of buying power in the future. To discover this, you must take out the rate of inflation. The real rate of interest is what you are gaining in terms of buying power. The formula for the relationship between the real rate of interest and the nominal rate is: $(1+i_{nominal}) = (1+i_{real}) \cdot (1+\text{inflation})$, or, $i_{real} = \frac{(1+i_{nominal})}{(1+\text{inflation})} - 1$. Continuing, $(1 + i_{nominal}) = 1 + i_{real} + inflation + (i_{real} \cdot inflation) \approx 1 + i_{real} + inflation$, since in the absence of very high inflation, $i_{real} \cdot \text{inflation}$ should be very small. With a little algebra the real rate of interest is: $i_{real} \approx i_{nominal} - \text{inflation}$.

Taxes can be especially onerous with inflation. Suppose that the real rate of interest is 2% and inflation is 15%. The nominal rate is 17% (approximately). Suppose you are taxed at 15% on the nominal rate. If you invest $100, at the end of the year you will have earned $\$100 \cdot 1.17 = \$17$. However, you will pay taxes on the interest of $.15 \cdot \$17=\$2.55$, leaving you with $114.45. In effect, your after-tax interest rate is $.17 \cdot (1-.15)=.1445$.

Now remove inflation. Your buying power will decline by 15% because of inflation. Deflating what you have after tax: $\frac{114.45}{1.15} = \$99.52$. After taxes and inflation, your investment has shrunk in value in real terms.

Approximately, your after-tax, real interest rate is: $i_{left\ over} \approx i_{nominal} \cdot (1-\text{tax rate}) - \text{inflation}$. Since $i_{nominal}=i_{real} + \text{inflation}$, $i_{left\ over} \approx (i_{real} + \text{inflation}) \cdot (1-\text{tax rate}) - \text{inflation}$. After a little algebra, the effect of inflation on your after-tax, real interest rate is: $i_{left\ over} \approx i_{real} \cdot (1-\text{tax rate}) - (\text{inflation} \cdot \text{tax rate})$.

It is now clear that inflation multiplies with taxes to reduce what you have left over. Inflation magnifies how taxes reduce buying power from investing, and can drive real, after-tax interest rates negative. The government prints money so that it can spend (causing inflation), and then taxes us on the inflation! And since inflation in combination with taxes can wipe out any gains from investing, it can discourage the creation or expansion of businesses and cause other harm. (People do not bother investing, but rather spend their money, denying businesses the capital they need to expand.)

Even a Suitcase of Money Isn't Worth Much with Rampant Inflation

An American tourist once tipped a chef one dollar for his meal at a Berlin restaurant. Was the chef insulted by receiving a single dollar? Hardly. He called a family meeting and decided to set up a trust fund using the dollar at a local bank.

Such was the topsy turvey world in Germany in 1923 when hyperinflation hobbled the country's economy and the resulting frustration fed the rise of the Nazis. Back then a dollar was equivalent to a trillion marks. Even a wheelbarrow full of bills couldn't buy a newspaper. A loaf of bread cost billions of marks. People burned money to keep warm and used it as wallpaper.

How did it happen? Not all of the reasons are clear, but historians believe that a combination of events created Germany's rampant inflation. The most significant was that it fought and lost costly World War I, and was forced to pay reparations for the damages. That led to the root cause of inflation: an oversupply of money. Printing more and more money caused the cost of goods and services to rise and eventually money became worthless.

By the time German authorities wrangled inflation to the ground, the damage had already been done. Millions had lost their life savings and a devastated and angry middle class turned to Adolf Hitler for answers and inspiration.[2]

Key Takeaway: What is really important about an interest rate is what your interest will buy you in the future after taxes and inflation. The real interest rate takes inflation into account. The after-tax real rate also takes out taxes. Inflation multiplied with taxes can wipe out after-tax real interest rates, even turning them negative.

[2] Michael K. Salemi, "The Encyclopedia of Economics: Hyperinflation," http://www.econlib.org/library/Enc/ Hyperinflation.html; "Millennium Issue: German hyperinflation," *The Economist*, December 23, 1999; http://www.historylearningsite.co.uk/hyperinflation_weima_germany.htm

8.6 Consumer Lending

There are a variety of consumer loans that you may take out over the course of your lifetime, all with different terms. It is important to understand what you are getting into. Some loans have collateral. These are referred to as secured loans. A car loan is an example, where a lender has a lien on the car. If you default on the loan, the lender can seize your car and sell it. If there is anything left over, which is unlikely, you will get the remainder.

There are also unsecured loans. An example would be a revolver loan at a bank, where you can withdraw up to a specified amount, but you can also withdraw less if you choose. If you arrange for a bank revolver, you should expect to be charged an interest rate on the amount that you withdraw, and also a smaller rate on the amount that you did not withdraw (because the bank has to make that money available on short notice).

One of the goals of this textbook is to make you as sophisticated about borrowing as a hard bitten adult with years of experience. Credit cards deserve a discussion all their own, especially since new college students often fall prey to the overuse of high interest rate credit cards.

I have already discussed how credit cards are typically compounded daily and have high interest rates. The APR is well below the true effective rate due to the high interest rate and frequent number of compounding periods. However, typically you will not accrue interest right away. You will receive a credit card statement about once a month with your charges. If you pay them off you will not have to pay interest. (This is not always the case. Be sure to read the fine print.) In effect, the credit card company is making you a short-term, 0% loan. Of course, you have to borrow below the credit limit that the credit card company sets, and realize that they can cancel your card. If you are unable to roll over your borrowings into another card or loan you will be in trouble (use a new loan to pay off the credit card).

Credit cards are unsecured. However, if you default they can refer you to an aggressive collection agency, report negative information to the credit bureaus, and possibly sue you. You could lose bank balances or have your wages garnished (a percent taken by them). You can also have your credit score damaged, with severe financial consequences.

When freshmen first arrived on campus they were confronted with tempting credit card offers complete with offers of free merchandise. The Credit Card Act of 2009 now bans promoting credit cards with free giveaways on or near campus. People under the age of twenty-one must now get an adult cosigner on a card (who also takes responsibility for payment), or prove that they have sufficient income to make the payments.

Many college students still get credit cards, however. Since they typically have no credit history, they are charged a very high rate, although having a cosigner may help. With card in hand, these students begin to spend. They have not been trained in maintaining a budget, and do not understand the consequences of running up a credit card. For every dollar they spend, they must pay that dollar back, plus a hefty interest charge. And since no cash money changes hands, it seems especially effortless to buy purchase after purchase, and dine in restaurant after restaurant, while basking in their new found freedom. By the time these students begin to realize that they have a problem, they are many thousands of dollars in debt. Forget the monkey; they now have a gorilla on their back. Their bright future has been damaged. When they graduate they face all of the expenses of just getting started, while having a massive payment burden month after month. Every spare dime they have goes to making payments. They are not moving forward.

To make it worse, credit card companies often offer teaser rates. These rates start out very low initially, but then reset to a high rate. Students may not notice for a long time that their rate has reset. The credit card companies are also betting that students forget to make payments on time. Students are not used to paying monthly bills regularly and can be forgetful. They are also very distracted when first starting college, with a million new experiences happening.

Students often do not understand the consequences of having their credit rating damaged due to late payments. They very quickly forget to make a payment and their interest rate skyrockets. They may go from a 0% teaser rate to 32% in the blink of an eye, because the teaser rate does not last if they are late by several months.

They will also get late penalties. If they "opted in" for protection against exceeding their credit limit and then run over that limit, they will get charged fees. (Just like checking accounts have fees for covering insufficient funds.)

Some credit card companies in the past even applied a default rate if they found out that someone was late on any bill that they were able to find out about such as a utility bill. (By the way, credit cards offered by stores such as department stores typically carry some of the highest rates.) By the time the student is done, using a credit card to pay for that sandwich could cost $80 after late fees and higher interest rates. The damage could be even worse because their credit rating will be ruined, which will make all loans more expensive for a very long time. I will discuss credit ratings in a later chapter.

If you are under twenty-one years-of-age and have a willing cosigner such as your parents, this will help. However, you could be shifting the burden of your mistakes to your parents. Many parents think credit cards are inappropriate for college students and will not sign. If your parents feel this way, be grateful that they are looking out for you.

Cash advances on a credit card are even worse. With cash advances your balance goes up as you are given cash immediately. However, you get charged very hefty fees. You may be charged a flat rate fee, a percentage of the amount borrowed, or both. In addition, unlike with purchases, you are charged interest immediately on the balance. The credit card companies will also send "checks" in the mail, inviting you to spend them. These checks are typically considered cash advances and come with large fees. They are best left to the paper shredder.[3]

It is also important to read the fine print carefully. There are a variety of sneaky techniques to charge you additional interest on loans. This will be a recurring theme throughout this book. Reading the fine print is boring and hard on the eyes, but a necessary task for financial safety. And watch your APR. They may try to raise it on you, while hoping that you do not notice the letter they sent informing you of the change. This is why you need to open mailings

[3] Offers to transfer balances to a new card can also carry these fees.

from your credit card company, even if you think they are promotions. You can opt out of a rate increase, but only by shutting your account down. If you feel your rate is too high, call them and complain. You may get them to lower your rate. As an alternative you can switch to a different card.

Pizza and Credit Cards Don't Mix

Big, athletic, sandy-haired Scott Doolley was hungry. When he saw the line for free pizza snaking through the biology building on campus at the University of Indiana, he immediately cued up. He had time to kill before class. Once Scott got inside, though, he realized the Dominos Pizza® wasn't exactly free. He had to sign up for a credit card to get a slice. What the heck, he thought. He was starving.

Scott was a freshman on a partial scholarship thanks to his good grades in high school. He was working part-time, too, in the cafeteria to help pay for his books. He'd never had a credit card before – mainly because he didn't feel he needed one. But a lot of his friends had them and he thought he should have one too.

I'll just use it once in awhile, he thought. At first that's exactly what he did. He charged a meal when he didn't have cash or when he needed some groceries to stock his dorm room frig. But then it got easier for Scott to pay for things with his credit card: a shirt, new running shoes, an iPhone. Before long the bills on his credit card were bigger than his bank account. Scott was $1,900 in debt.

While it felt great to have a credit card, Scott was embarrassed to acknowledge that he really didn't understand how it worked. He didn't know that if he didn't pay his bill the credit card company tacked on a 17% interest rate to his existing debt. Worried and ashamed, he asked his dad, an accountant, for help. When he came home on the weekend, he and his dad sat down and went over his bills and the terms of the card. His dad didn't let him off the hook. Scott still had to foot the bill, but together they worked out a budget and a debt repayment plan. Within nine months, Scott had paid off the debt by cutting his spending and picking up more shifts at the cafeteria.

Scott still sees long lines for pizza in his biology building, but he always makes sure he has a snack in his backpack. He no longer has a credit card. Scott knows that in the future he may need one, but the next time he applies for one he'll take his time and skip the pizza.[4]

The laws concerning credit cards change constantly, particularly when there is a power shift in government between Republicans and Democrats, with Democrats typically enacting stricter rules on credit card companies.[5] It is important to realize that what is true today may not be true tomorrow. For information on credit cards and the Credit Card Act of 2009, go to: http://www.federalreserve.gov/creditcard/.

---

[4] Fictional account, loosely based on: "Majoring In Debt: Despite Crunch Credit Companies Keep Targeting Undergrads", *Newsweek*, February, 18 2009.

[5] I do not offer an opinion of credit card laws. Stricter laws can protect consumers, but they can also cause credit card companies to refuse to offer loans to some groups which drives them to paycheck lenders, or to raise rates in order to maintain profits. If credit card companies have to charge everyone the same rate, irresponsible borrowers get subsidized by responsible borrowers and are therefore encouraged to be irresponsible. There is also an issue of fairness.

If you have discipline and strong self-control, then you may wish to take out a credit card. But you should commit to paying it off every month, and making sure you pay on time. I recommend paying online each month (unless they charge a fee for doing so).

Using credit cards can also provide an advantage if they give cash back for purchases, or offer other inducements such as frequent flyer miles. For instance, a credit card may pay 2% for purchases on groceries, drugstore items, and gas. Every once in a while, you can call or go online and request the money that you have earned. These days I do not pay my credit card company - they pay me! If you are responsible about using your credit card, it can also improve your credit rating. **However, only take out a credit card if you have a will of steel. Remember that college will be a busy, distracting place, full of the temptation to spend.**

It is not a good idea to borrow to buy consumables. For each dollar you spend, you have to pay back what you spent, plus additional interest. Over the course of your lifetime, you will be able to enjoy yourself more — to consume more — if you save your money and wait to buy things until you can pay for them. With high interest rate loans such as credit cards, the consequences can be devastating. Remember that each time you borrow to consume something, you are stealing even more from your future. I will discuss this further when I cover forecasting.

Key Takeaway: College students often get into serious trouble with credit cards. Many college students are unaware of the consequences of having a bad credit record. Because they are so distracted with school and their new life on their own they forget to pay bills. They also borrow over their credit limit and overspend. Swiping a piece of plastic to buy something is deceptively easy. The result could be a massive debt burden after leaving school, a ruined credit rating, and years of high interest charges on loans.

Challenge

Will you take out a credit card in college? Why or why not? Are you truly prepared to remember to pay your bill every month?

8.7 Deceptive Lending Practices for Small Businesses

Businesses are not protected by the Truth in Lending Act. Yes, it requires the deceptive APR for consumer loans, but it also requires everyone to use the same method to quote interest rates. Lenders can quote interest rates in very "creative" ways to businesses. In Appendix A.2, I show how to calculate effective rates for several common, misleading ways that interest rates are quoted to businesses. There is a common theme. These quotations involve pretending that the lender is giving the borrower more money than they actually receive, and charging interest on the fake money.

Compensating balances are an example. The bank credits the borrower's bank account with money — money that the borrower cannot withdraw or earn interest on. This is actually pretend money that the bank says it is lending, which results in a lower quoted rate than what is actually being paid. The trick is to figure out the actual cash flows you receive when given a compensating balance loan, or any other business loan. Once you take into account how much cash you actually receive, and what your actual payments are, the calculator (or Excel) does not lie.

8.8 Conclusion

You now know the basics about interest rates. Hopefully, this chapter has been an eye opener. Abusive loan practices are all too common. Be sure to read the fine print in any loan contract. Borrowing is serious business, and inattention to detail can lead to disaster.

You can practice your new found adulthood by being firm with financial sales people. Many people only acquire this toughness with age because they have been taken advantage of repeatedly. It is also time to go slowly. Do not fall prey to aggressive sales pitches to lend you money. If you are not sure, tell him you need to take the paperwork home and think about it. Aggressiveness or excessive friendliness is a sign of trouble. Also, if you ask a question off the beaten track and they cannot answer, they may have been trained to just give a sales pitch and they may not understand the financial transaction. They are just mouthing the words they have been told to say.

In fact, you may very well notice something when you take out your first loan. Your lender may seem very pleased or happy when they see you (because he thinks you are young and naïve – easy pickings). Watch his expression change when you start asking him tough, well informed questions, and sales pitches bounce right off you. When taking out a loan, it is time to do your financial homework. You are in charge.

Key Terms:

APR (annual percentage rate)
APY (annual percentage yield)
Cash advances
Credit card checks
Deflating
EAR (effective annual rate)
Effective rate
Floating interest rate
LIBOR (London Interbank Offered Rate)
Lien
Nominal interest rates
Paycheck loans
Periodic rate
Prime rate
Real interest rates
Revolving loan
Secured loan
Stated rate
Truth in Lending Act
Unsecured loan
Usury laws
YTM (yield to maturity)

Formulas:

Converting one interest rate into another: $i_y = (1+i_x)^{\left(\frac{\text{\# times x compounds in a year}}{\text{\# times y compounds in a year}}\right)} - 1$

The relationship between the real rate of interest and the nominal rate is: $(1+i_{nominal}) = (1+i_{real})\cdot(1+\text{inflation})$, or, $i_{real} = \frac{(1+i_{nominal})}{(1+\text{inflation})} - 1$

The real rate of interest can approximately be found from: $i_{real} \approx i_{nominal} - \text{inflation}$.

Approximately, your after-tax, real interest rate is: $i_{left\ over} \approx i_{nominal}\cdot(1-\text{tax rate}) - \text{inflation}$.

The effect of inflation on your after-tax, real interest rate is: $i_{left\ over} \approx i_{real}\cdot(1-\text{tax rate}) - (\text{inflation}\cdot\text{tax rate})$.

End of Chapter Questions

1. You are quoted an APR on a loan of .10. The loan has semiannual compounding.
   a. What is the periodic semiannual rate?
   b. What is the equivalent effective monthly rate?

2. You are quoted an APR on a loan of .09. The loan has quarterly compounding.
   a. What is the periodic quarterly rate?
   b. What is the equivalent effective semi-annual rate?

3. What is compounding?

4. Which will be higher, a stated rate or an effective rate?

5. The effective quarterly rate is .02. What is the equivalent effective monthly rate?

6. The effective semi-annual rate is 8%. What is the equivalent effective monthly rate?

7. The APR on a credit card is 21.9%. The credit card has daily compounding. What is the periodic, daily interest rate? What is the EAR?

8. What interest rate represents how much your buying power increases with an investment? How do you calculate it?

9. If the rate of inflation is 5%, what will $100 in eight years buy you in today's terms?

10. If the rate of inflation is 6%, how much will your earnings and money need to grow in ten years in order to maintain your purchasing power?

11. How does inflation interact with taxes in determining what your ultimate buying power from an investment is?

12. What is a cash advance? How are you charged differently for a cash advance than for a typical credit card purchase?

13. Name a problem with the Truth in Lending Act, as well as a benefit.

14. What typical mistakes do college students make with credit cards?

15. In what ways do credit cards make money from consumers? How can they make a consumer money?

16. What are the "checks" that credit card companies send?

17. Are small businesses protected by the Truth in Lending Act?

18. What is a revolving loan? How is interest typically charged?

19. How are consumer loans quoted? What rate is quoted for savings accounts?

20. Why may credit card companies actually want you to make late payments?

Appendix

A.1

Southern Exposure: How Two Women Helped Unravel A Lending Empire --- A Retired Maid's Questions About Her ATM Card Led Lawyer to Georgia Scandal --- Investors' Missing $30 Million

By Carrick Mollenkamp

11 November 2004
The Wall Street Journal

UNION POINT, Ga. -- For decades, Ben Stewart Jr. ran this fading mill town. He was president of the Farmers Bank, owned much of the business district and served as mayor for a quarter century, defeating his own brother by 14 votes in one election.

In the 1990s, he built a lending company that made tens of thousands of small loans across the Southeast and Midwest and paid fat returns to hundreds of local investors who poured roughly $30 million into the enterprise. He built a personal fortune valued at millions of dollars that paid for a Southern gentry life of hunting, college-football box seats, and vacation homes in the mountains and on the coast.

But when Elsie Williams, a 68-year-old retired hotel maid, walked into the free legal-aid office in downtown Atlanta three years ago, Mr. Stewart's life and empire began to unravel.

Ms. Williams was one of 69,000 borrowers who obtained loans between 1998 and 2003 from Mr. Stewart's 60-outlet Stewart Finance Co., a lender specializing in customers who have bad credit or no credit history at all. Thousands of other small lenders market their services to the poor, but Stewart had an unusual angle: It took advantage of a federal push to persuade recipients of Social Security and other government aid to receive their payments via direct deposit. That gave it access to scores of elderly and African-American clients who had never had a bank account before.

The small-scale loans and the use of unregistered securities sold in one community allowed Stewart Finance to fly under the radar of regulators as the company tapped into this new client base. The company charged exorbitant interest rates and tacked on high fees to the accounts, often in violation of federal law, federal and state regulators allege. It also specialized, investigators say, in cajoling or tricking borrowers into buying questionable life-insurance policies and car-club memberships of little or no value.
Nicholas Lotito, an Atlanta criminal-defense attorney who represented Mr. Stewart, says Mr. Stewart maintained his innocence throughout the court proceedings that followed. Mr. Stewart acted in good faith and made attempts to maintain the profitability of his company, Mr. Lotito says.

Adrienne Ashby, a legal-aid lawyer in downtown Atlanta, wasn't sure where to begin when Ms. Williams walked into her threadbare office one morning in April 2001. Ms. Williams wanted help figuring out what was wrong with her ATM card.

That winter, Ms. Williams had taken out a loan for $204.84 from Stewart Finance to buy a couch for her publicly subsidized apartment. To obtain the loan, Ms. Williams agreed to have her $530 monthly government-aid check deposited directly into a new account set up for her by Stewart. Ms. Williams didn't understand why she couldn't withdraw all of her Supplemental Security Income funds with the ATM card the bank sent her.

Ms. Ashby, a then-28-year-old graduate of the University of Virginia law school, had recently left a six-figure salary as an associate in a private law firm to become a $39,000-a-year legal-aid lawyer. "I wasn't doing what I was supposed to

be doing," says Ms. Ashby, who grew up in a Norfolk, Va., public-housing complex, the daughter of a single, teenage mother. Her conscience, she says, "was picking at me."
With only Ms. Williams's bank statements in hand, Ms. Ashby had little to go on. Ms. Williams didn't understand the terms of her loan. It wasn't clear that any laws had been broken. The problem with the ATM, it turned out, was simply that Ms. Williams, unfamiliar with banks, didn't realize that there was a limit to how much she could withdraw in one day.

But this was one of Ms. Ashby's first legal-aid cases, so she decided to dig in.

Seventy miles east of Atlanta, among the pines and hardwoods of rural Georgia, Union Point is a faint image of itself in the heyday of the Southern textile industry. Incorporated in 1904 and named for the intersection of three early Georgia railroads, the town began to fade as the industry lost business to cheaper foreign imports. Mr. Stewart's businesses -- Stewart Finance's two-story brick office and a pawn shop -- dominated a small downtown strip. Today, the population of 1,600 is evenly divided between whites and African-Americans. One of the largest employers in town, the Chipman Union Inc. hosiery mill, closed in 2001, laying off hundreds of workers.

Amid the town's steady descent, Mr. Stewart increasingly seemed to offer the only hope. As his Stewart Finance business grew, hundreds of residents of the town and the surrounding county began investing their savings in the company's unregistered securities. In 2002, Stewart Finance's parent bought the town's shuttered hosiery mill and announced plans to reopen it and hire 150 people. It would never make good on that promise.

Mr. Stewart embraced his local investors like close friends, hosting cocktail parties and offering free Atlanta Braves tickets. When 80-year-old Mary Callaway, who had known Mr. Stewart from the time he was a toddler, was diagnosed with cancer in 1998, Mr. Stewart took her to the hospital. "We've been dear friends of his," says Mrs. Callaway, who says she and her husband lost about $174,000, their life savings, as investors with Mr. Stewart. "He had a generous nature and I think he loved his community."

In 1996, Mr. Stewart began a newsletter, "The Stewart Lender," that was filled with bon mots, employee dictums ("Eating at your workstation is a violation of company policy") and updates on the loan business. "I am very pleased to see the number of investors grow each year," Mr. Stewart wrote in 2001 after a cocktail reception for his backers. "We have big plans for the future and a successful investor program is certainly part of that."

Beginning in 1996, Lee Sweetapple, the retired former owner of a pipe-making company, invested a total of $700,000 in Stewart securities, some of which promised an 11% interest rate. Angela Deering, daughter of a retired Methodist minister in Union Point, invested the $300,000 she and her husband earned after restoring and selling a stately Southern home.

Nearly 900 individual investors, almost all of them locals, put their money into Stewart Finance securities and promissory notes, the latter of which were nothing more than Mr. Stewart's pledge to repay the investor. The Stewart securities weren't registered with the Securities and Exchange Commission as required by law once the company began to operate across state lines, according to federal regulators. Some $20 million poured into Stewart Finance during the 1990s. Between 2000 and 2003, a further $10 million came in, according to Gregory Hays, the court-appointed Chapter 11 trustee for Stewart Finance.
Elsie Williams was born in Atlanta, graduated from a vocational school, and then worked for years as a maid in New York City hotels including the Hilton. She later returned to Atlanta and moved into a subsidized public high-rise. When she took out her $204.84 loan on Jan. 9, 2001, she says cataracts made it difficult for her to read the paperwork. Ms. Williams says she didn't realize that Mr. Stewart's salesman also charged her an additional $73.50 for death-and-dismemberment insurance, as well as another $10 insurance-related fee. Including finance charges, the principal and insurance, Ms. Williams agreed to pay a total of $360 in five monthly installments of $72 -- an effective annual percentage rate of 94.63%, according to the loan document.

A year later, against Ms. Ashby's advice, Ms. Williams obtained a second Stewart loan of $165. Ms. Williams had undergone a mastectomy after being diagnosed with breast cancer and needed a special bra and a prosthetic breast. This time, the salesman added a car-club membership that cost $90 though Ms. Williams didn't own a car, couldn't drive and didn't realize she was buying the membership.

"Nobody never explained to me that I was getting any insurance," says Ms. Williams in an interview.
Ms. Williams had gotten caught in Mr. Stewart's effort to capitalize on the federal government's push in the mid-1990s to persuade recipients of Social Security and other government benefits to sign up for direct deposit.

The Comptroller of the Currency saw the electronic direct-deposit initiative as a way to serve the so-called unbanked -- inner-city households preyed upon by high-fee check-cashing outlets. In fiscal 2004, 78% of a total of 742 million government benefit payments were zapped into bank accounts, up from 54% of such payments in 1995. Beneficiaries typically withdraw the money using an ATM card. The program also reduced the government's administrative costs to 13 cents for each payment, down from about 75 cents to mail a check.

The program was a particular boon for Stewart Finance, streamlining the company's operations and giving it access to a new base of relatively unsophisticated borrowers. "Imagine that, a first of the month at [Stewart Finance] without long lines and crowded lobbies," trumpeted the company newsletter in March 2001. "SFC will benefit by not having to supply money, employ security guards, and service several hundred customers a day. The customer is going to enjoy the benefit of not having to come to the office or wait in line to receive their cash."

According to a complaint brought last year by the Federal Trade Commission, Stewart offered loans of $150 to customers if they signed up for direct deposit. Stewart Finance also trained its employees to tell the borrowers that the service was free, when they were actually being charged $4 to $6 a month, according to the complaint. The FTC also alleged that customers were pushed into buying car-club memberships or life insurance that resulted in commissions for Stewart Finance.

After Ms. Williams appeared in the legal-aid office, Ms. Ashby repeatedly called a toll-free number on Ms. Williams's financial statements. Her calls always ended up in "voice-mail hell," she says. Finally, a fellow legal-aid lawyer called the Social Security Administration and stopped any more checks from being deposited in Ms. Williams's account.

Then Ms. Ashby urged others in the legal-aid office to check new client "intake" sheets for complaints about Stewart Finance. Over the next several months, they identified other Stewart clients who had their loans financed with the same pattern of apparent extra fees and improper charges.

Ms. Ashby called in help from the Atlanta plaintiffs firm Bondurant, Mixson &Elmore, and sued Stewart Finance in July 2002 in Fulton County Superior Court in Atlanta. The complaint, on behalf of Ms. Williams and nine other Stewart borrowers, alleged fraudulent and predatory loan and sales practices.

After the lawsuit received local media coverage, Ms. Ashby began receiving tips from former Stewart Finance workers on how the company operated. One caller explained something that had baffled the lawyers: the widely varying charges on the car-club and insurance fees. The caller said these were automatic calculations by Stewart's computer system based on a percentage of a borrower's loan. A former midlevel Stewart Finance executive told Ms. Ashby how the company blanketed neighborhoods largely populated by people who received government benefits with fliers touting the company's loans.
"My personal goal was to bring Stewart Finance down," Ms. Ashby says. She says she sometimes wondered, "How does this man sleep at night?"

Nervous investors were told that a provision in the accounts that forced borrowers into binding arbitration for any complaints would shield the company from lawsuits. "There will not even be a court case," he wrote in the Stewart Lender newsletter.

But powerful forces were lining up against him. Democratic Georgia Gov. Roy Barnes, after his unexpected defeat in the November 2002 general election, decided to volunteer as a legal-aid lawyer, bringing to the case his expertise in banking and predatory-lending laws.

Investors began demanding their money back. Stewart Finance ran low on cash and then abruptly filed for bankruptcy-court protection in February 2003. Unbeknownst to investors, much of their money hadn't been used to expand the company. Instead, state and federal investigators say Stewart Finance had become a Ponzi scheme, in which old investors were being paid interest from the funds of new investors. According to state investigators and bankruptcy-court officials, Mr. Stewart plowed at least $1 million into gambling binges and millions more into vacation homes, a 1,000-acre quail-hunting plantation called Pinewood near Albany, Ga., sports memorabilia, firearms and a skybox in the football stadium at the University of Georgia, his alma mater.

Ms. Ashby also had contacted a former classmate who worked for the FTC, which launched its own investigation into Stewart. In September 2003, U.S. District Court Judge Jack Camp in Atlanta froze many of Mr. Stewart's assets. Then last May, the judge ordered Mr. Stewart to surrender to U.S. Marshals after he failed to pay a sanction for the sale of a family home in Hilton Head, S.C., after the freeze was in effect. At the same time, a special assistant attorney general representing the Georgia Secretary of State's office was wrapping up a planned criminal indictment against Mr. Stewart, alleging securities fraud and racketeering. On May 13, the day before Mr. Stewart was to report to U.S. Marshals, Andrew Ekonomou, the special assistant attorney general, was scheduled to present the indictment to a local grand jury.

But early that morning, Mr. Stewart got up and drove a few blocks through the fog to a rental home he owned, parked his Mercedes S500 and shot himself between the eyebrows with his Smith &Wesson .38 caliber revolver. A typed letter to his two adult sons, one of several notes left in his car, said: "I have a choice that I can make now that I will not have later. . . . I have lived a very good and happy life and I have very few regrets. Love, Daddy." Mr. Stewart was buried in a local cemetery three days later. He was 54.

Mr. Lotito, the lawyer who represented Mr. Stewart, says he planned a vigorous defense. "There were defenses and there was another story to be told on Ben's behalf," he says. Mr. Lotito says Mr. Stewart was hit with a "perfect storm" that included civil litigation, an investor run on the bank and the exit of a lender. All that saddled Mr. Stewart with nearly insurmountable challenges, the lawyer says.

Mr. Stewart's widow, Janice, insists her husband has been wrongly accused. Panicky investors who turned on the company were the real culprits, she says. "He never had been put before a jury or found guilty of anything," Mrs. Stewart says. "All the investors loved him to death as long as he was paying them the high interest."

Since Mr. Stewart's death, the Georgia Secretary of State, representing the interest of investors seeking to reclaim some of their $30 million, and the FTC, representing the company's thousands of borrowers, have been tussling over the remaining financial crumbs of his fortune. Lawyers for the two sides are attempting to negotiate a settlement. Altogether, about $5 million in assets remain, including the benefits of several life-insurance policies.

In late August, Mr. Stewart's personal property was publicly auctioned. The temperature touched 97 degrees as buyers and the curious, covered in sweat, drifted in and out of a Stewart Finance collection office, looking over vehicles, guns and office furniture, and bidding on his assets. The mill Mr. Stewart had hoped to reopen was among the items for sale.

A.2

A.2.1 Discount Interest

An annual loan has a discount interest rate of 9%. The discount interest is taken out up front, and the full principal of the loan paid off at the end. You need to borrow $460,000. Since 9% is taken out of the principal of the loan, principal·(1-.09)=Amount borrowed (received).

$$\text{Principal} = \frac{460{,}000}{1 - .09} = 505{,}494.51$$

To calculate your effective interest rate, realize that the loan amount is $460,000 and the future value is $505,494.51:

$$\text{Interest} = \frac{505{,}494.51}{460{,}000} - 1 = .0989$$

The trick is that they are charging you interest of 9% on the principal, but actually lending you less than the principal.

A.2.1 Trade Credit

Your supplier offers you the trade credit terms "3/15 net 40." In other words, if you pay within 15 days you will get a 3% discount off the list price. Otherwise the full list price is due within 40 days. You will not borrow until day 15, therefore the loan is for 25 days. Assume the list price is $100 (it does not matter). If you do not take the trade credit then the price of the product is actually $100·(1-.03)=$97, which is the present value. If you borrow you owe $100, which is the future value.

$$R_{25} = \frac{100}{97} - 1 = .0309$$

To calculate the number of 25-day compounding periods in a year:

$$\#\text{ Days} = \frac{360}{25} = 14.4$$

Therefore, to get the effective annual rate:

$$\text{EAR} = 1.0309^{14.4} - 1 = .55$$

A.2.3 Compensating Balance

You are considering taking out a loan with a compensating balance of 15%. You need to borrow $510,000. You are quoted an annual interest rate of 9%. It is a simple loan where you borrow today and pay back the loan in one year, along with interest owed. The compensating balance is not money and does not really exist, because you cannot withdraw it or earn interest on it. As in the discount interest example above, to figure out the principal on the loan:

$$\text{Principal} = \frac{510{,}000}{1 - .15} = 600{,}000$$

You will receive $510,000 as a loan. You will be charged 9% interest on the full principal when the loan comes due and will also have to return the $510,000.

$$t = 0:\ +\$510{,}000 \qquad t = 1:\ -\$510{,}000 - (\$600{,}000 \cdot .09) = -\$564{,}000$$

$$EAR = \frac{564{,}000}{510{,}000} - 1 = .1059$$

Once again, the trick is that they are pretending they are given you the compensating balance (and charging interest on it), when they are not.

A.2.4 Add-On Interest

This should be called "pile on" interest. You will borrow \$5,000, and the add-on interest rate is 15%. Compounding is monthly, with monthly payments for one year. The way it works is that they calculate the interest on the principal. The total is then chopped up into constant installment payments. In this example:

$$"Interest" = \$5{,}000 \cdot .15 = 750.$$

Chopping this up into installments, your monthly payment (for 12 months) is:

$$Payments = \frac{5{,}000 + 750}{12} = 479.17$$

You borrow \$5,000, then make 12 monthly payments of \$479.17:

$$The\ formula\ is{:}\ 5{,}000 = \frac{479.17}{R} \cdot \left[1 - \frac{1}{(1+R)^{12}}\right]$$

Using the financial keys: N=12, PV=5,000, PMT=-479.17, FV=0 I/Yr=2.22%. The monthly interest rate is 2.22%. The EAR=1.0222^{12} - 1 = .3015 The effective rate is more than double what they are quoting. They are pretending that you borrow \$5,000 for an entire year, when you are actually paying the loan off over time. This is called "amortization" which I shall cover in the next chapter. The trick is the same; they pretend that they are giving you more money than you actually receive.

9.1 Mortgage Basics

It is now time to turn to mortgages. Mortgages typically have a set number of monthly payments for 15, 20, or 30 years. Most people who get a good education buy a place to live at some point, and they borrow using a mortgage to make the purchase. A mortgage represents an enormous financial commitment, which can have a big impact over the course of a person's life. During the current financial crisis, many people got into trouble over their mortgages. Many will never financially recover.

There are three groups of mortgage borrowers: prime, alt-A, and subprime. Subprime borrowers have poor credit ratings. Alt-A borrowers are considered better, but their income has poor documentation for reasons such as self-employment. Prime borrowers have good credit ratings and are considered the best borrowers. One of the reasons why it is so important to maintain a good credit rating is that it can have a big impact on the interest rate that you will pay on your mortgage, which is where a large percent of your payments over the course of your life will go. The effect on your wealth will be considerable.

In order to understand mortgages, you will need to understand something called an amortization schedule. But first, it is helpful to revisit the issue of interest rates from a new perspective. Suppose you wanted to borrow $10 and never pay it back. In order to keep the lender happy, you would have to send her regular payments or she would demand her money back. Assuming that you (or your descendants) send her a payment every year forever, and the EAR is 6%, it is possible to work backwards to figure out how much your annual payments will have to be. From the lender's perspective, the present value of the payments must equal the loan amount. Referring back to the formula for the present value of a constant perpetuity:

$$PV = \frac{C}{i} \rightarrow \$10 = \frac{C}{.06} \rightarrow C = 10 \cdot .06 = \$.60.$$

In other words, as long as you send the lender $.60 every year, she will not get upset and demand her $10 back.

This illustrates another way of thinking about interest; it is a rental fee on money. Imagine that you rented a car. As long as you keep sending in rental payments, they will not have a reason to get upset with you and demand their car back.[1] When you borrow money, you can think of it as renting equipment. The dollar bills you are given (and coins) are the equipment. The interest that you pay is the rental fee.

Home Sweet Home

Robert and Amy Halprin were willing to wait for their first home. Recently married with a baby on the way, the Halprins wanted to put a full 20% down before buying a home, even though they were quickly outgrowing their one-bedroom apartment.

The couple had recently witnessed friends get sucked into "no-money down" home loans with low teaser rates that were eventually hiked up to higher rates they couldn't afford. The Halprins didn't want to fall into the same trap. So, while Amy managed their budget, setting aside all their extra money for a down payment, Robert studied every book on home buying he could find.

After the couple had a baby girl they made their move, buying a townhome in a new housing community 15 minutes from Robert's work. The couple cobbled together their savings and put down $50,000 on the $250,000 home. As a first-year lawyer, Robert knew how to read the fine print and insisted the lender take out a clause that required private mortgage insurance. He knew that given their high down payment, the lender shouldn't require it. That saved the couple thousands in loan costs. He also negotiated a lower interest rate, citing his and Amy's strong credit ratings.

In October they moved in and Amy started to nest – painting the baby's room a rose petal pink, hanging curtains in the kitchen and marveling at the townhome's honey colored hardwood floors. The best part for the Halprins was knowing they could afford it all.[2]

Amortization schedules distinguish the interest and principal portions of a mortgage payment. Figure 9-1 illustrates part of an amortization schedule for a 20-year, fixed-rate mortgage with an APR of 6%, and monthly payments of $2,500. The periodic rate is .06/12 = .005. In this example you start with the monthly payments that you can afford, and from that you determine the house price. The three green boxes are where you enter the mortgage information. A "t" column has been created in Column B. In this spreadsheet (see the supplemental materials for this textbook that you can download. Instructions are under "Internet Information" in the book appendix), you know the APR, the payment, and the percent down payment. (In the next spreadsheet in the supplemental materials, you know the house price and down payment, but not the monthly payment. The next two spreadsheets are for a thirty year mortgage.)

Since the monthly mortgage payments are an annuity, you can use the present value of a constant annuity formula to solve for the loan amount. The number of payments is 20·12 = 240:

---

[1] Actually, it would depend on the arrangement. They may have scheduled the car for use by someone else, and they may also want to verify that the car is still there.

[2] Fictional composite.

$$PV = \frac{2{,}500}{.005} \cdot \left[1 - \left(\frac{1}{1.005}\right)^{240}\right] = \$348{,}951.93.$$

Another way is to use the financial keys on your calculator: 240 n .5 i 2500 CHS PMT 0 FV PV. (Do not clear out the keys. You will see why in a minute.) The loan amount is $348,951.93. The formula in Cell F7 is the present value of a constant annuity. The principal outstanding at t=0 is the original loan amount. It is the "equipment" outstanding.

Figure 9-1
An Amortization Schedule

	A B	C	D E	F	G	H	I J	K
1	A 20 Year Amortization Schedule (Payment Known)							
2								
3	i_m=	0.005	APR=	0.06		Down Payment=	0.2	
4								
5	t=	Time Left	Payments	Principal Outstanding	Interest	Principal Payment	Principal Payment	Interest
6	Home Price With Down Payment=				436,189.91		Downpayment=	87,237.98
7	0	240		348,951.93				
8	1	239	2,500.00	348,196.69	1,744.76	755.24	-755.24	-1,744.76
9	2	238	2,500.00	347,437.67	1,740.98	759.02	-759.02	-1,740.98
10	3	237	2,500.00	346,674.86	1,737.19	762.81	-762.81	-1,737.19
11	4	236	2,500.00	345,908.23	1,733.37	766.63	-766.63	-1,733.37
12	5	235	2,500.00	345,137.78	1,729.54	770.46	-770.46	-1,729.54
13	6	234	2,500.00	344,363.47	1,725.69	774.31	-774.31	-1,725.69
14	7	233	2,500.00	343,585.28	1,721.82	778.18	-778.18	-1,721.82

F7: =($E$8/$C$3)*(1-(1/(1+$C$3)^C7))

G8: =F7*$C$3

J8: =PPMT($C$3,B8,240,$F$7)

Since 20% is typically required by the lender,[3] it must be true that: Home Price $\cdot(1\text{-}.2)$ = Mortgage Amount. With a little algebra: Home Price $= \frac{348{,}951.93}{1-.2} = \$436{,}189.91$. This is the value in Cell G6. The down payment is the purchase price minus the loan amount.

The next step is to figure out how much of each payment is principal and how much is interest. This is of vital importance because the interest portion of the payment is tax deductible and often represents a huge dollar savings. The first thing to realize is that the monthly payment does not change. It is only the fraction of the payment that is principal versus interest that changes. At the end of the year, the annual sum of the interest amount determines your tax deduction.

The best way to think about the interest portion is from the perspective of a rental fee. Consider the first payment at t=1. The "equipment" outstanding at the end of the previous month is $348,951.93. The rental fee is the

[3] In the current financial crisis, a sign that mortgages had gotten out of control was that lenders required no down payment on many loans.

monthly interest rate of .005. Therefore, the interest payment (rental fee) is $348,951.93·.005 = $1,744.76. This is the interest portion of the first payment, as seen in Cell G8.

However, your monthly payment is more than this. The extra amount of dollar bills paid must be equipment that you are returning. This is the principal portion of the mortgage payment. It is equal to $2,500 - $1,744.76 = $755.24. This is the amount in H8. Cell J8 contains the corresponding Excel function. However, in general I prefer to use my own financial formulas because I am confident of what they are doing.

There is another way of looking at the issue of principal versus interest. Consider your position at t=1 after your payment. You essentially owe on a mortgage with 239 payments. A mortgage with 239 payments has a value, which would theoretically be the loan amount if you were to borrow. What would the present value be? Just update n to 239. Solving for the principal, you discover that it is $348,196.69. In other words, if you take out a mortgage with 239 payments of $2,500 and an APR or 6%, you can borrow $348,196.69. (At any point in time, if you would like to know how much principal is outstanding, just put in the number of payments that are left into the financial keys and solve for the present value.) So how much of your first payment must have been principal? It is the previous amount of principal at t=0 minus this month's principal. The difference must be the amount that was used to pay down the principal. This is $348,951.93 - $348,196.69 = $755.24. Starting from the principal, to calculate the interest portion of the payment, just subtract out the principal payment. This is $2,500 - $755.24 = $1,744.76.

Now consider the next month. The principal outstanding at the end of the previous month has gone down. This in turn causes the "rental fee"; i.e., the interest portion of the payment to go down. And since the monthly payment remains the same, the amount of money being returned in the form of principal must have gone up. Over time, the interest portion of the monthly payment falls, while the principal portion of the payment rises. This means two things. The first is that the tax deduction associated with the mortgage payments falls over time. The idea is that as your income rises over time, you will be more able to afford the shrinking tax deduction. The other thing to consider is that at first the mortgage is not paid down very much. Over time, however, the amount that the mortgage gets paid off rises at an increasing rate.

Figure 9-2 illustrates what happens when you are about to pay your mortgage off, as seen at the end of the amortization schedule. At t=239, you will have one payment left. The mortgage is almost paid off, with principal of $2,487.56 remaining. The interest due on this is small, only $12.44. The rest of the payment at t=240 is principal, totaling $2,487.56. This happens to be the total principal amount left. With the final principal payment, the principal goes to zero and the mortgage is paid off. You will receive the bank's lien on your house, meaning that the bank can no longer claim your house as an asset if you fail to make your payments. It is time to have a party with your friends, complete with formally burning the bank lien!

When you shop around for a mortgage you will notice that two interest rates are often quoted: the APR and a lower interest rate. To untangle the difference, it is helpful to think of a mortgage in a very simple way. The bank gives you money, and then at certain times you give the bank money. It is all about what you are given, and what you have to give in return. The same is true of going to the grocery store. When you buy an apple, you give the store money and they give you the apple. It is that simple.

However, imagine that you went to the grocery store and the sign said that apples are $1 each. When you get to the cash register, you are charged $1.20 for the apple before sales tax. You point out the error to the clerk, but they reply with, "It is not an error. There is an extra fee for shipping the apple, stocking it on the shelf, and ringing it up at the register. These extra fees add up to $.20." You are annoyed for several reasons. The first is that it is difficult to know what you are going to pay as you shop, and you have to go through a lot more trouble to figure it out. The second reason is that you feel that they were trying to trick you into believing that you are paying less than what you are, only to spring the final price on you after you had already stood in line (and do not want to bother going somewhere else).

Figure 9-2
Final Mortgage Payments

t=	Time Left	Payments	Principal Outstanding	Interest	Principal Payment	Principal Payment	Interest
233	7	2,500.00	17,155.19	97.79	2,402.21	-2,402.21	-97.79
234	6	2,500.00	14,740.96	85.78	2,414.22	-2,414.22	-85.78
235	5	2,500.00	12,314.67	73.70	2,426.30	-2,426.30	-73.70
236	4	2,500.00	9,876.24	61.57	2,438.43	-2,438.43	-61.57
237	3	2,500.00	7,425.62	49.38	2,450.62	-2,450.62	-49.38
238	2	2,500.00	4,962.75	37.13	2,462.87	-2,462.87	-37.13
239	1	2,500.00	2,487.56	24.81	2,475.19	-2,475.19	-24.81
240	0	2,500.00	0.00	12.44	2,487.56	-2,487.56	-12.44

This is what the second lower interest rate is all about. Suppose the bank's fees for writing the mortgage are $3,000. When the bank quotes you the lower rate they pretend that they are lending you this extra amount, and that you are paying these fees yourself on the side, using the money they lent you. The difference is that they tack $3,000 onto the principal when they calculate the interest rate. Using the financial keys: 240 n 351,951.93 PV 2500 CHS PMT 0 FV i. The periodic rate is .491159. Multiplying by 12, the interest rate they quote is 5.89%, instead of the APR of 6%. They then presumably charge you an extra $3,000, which they do not mention in their advertising. (You presumably use the extra $3,000 they lent you to pay the fees.) The reason this interest rate is lower is because they are pretending that they are lending you more, while charging you the same monthly payment, which leads to a lower calculated interest rate. This is the calculated rate on the pure loan part (the apple) without the fees. But when you buy the apple, you would simply like to know how much you owe in total in one price with all of the store's costs/fees included. The APR is the better rate because the fees are built into it. This is a benefit of the Truth in Lending Act – fees have to be built into the interest rate. It is too bad the Truth in Lending Act mandated stated rates. The EAR on this mortgage (what you should really base your decision on) is $1.005^{12} - 1 = .0617$.

However, you can try to use the bank's behavior against them. Start with the lower rate they quote of 5.89% and then bargain over the fees: "I can hire my own people at a much lower rate to perform some of the functions that you are charging me fees for. I will take your interest rate (the lower one), but I will pay these other people the lower fees." I will discuss this again in more detail when I talk about buying a home in Volume 2.

Key Takeaway: The beginning principal on a mortgage is the loan amount. Over time, the tax deductible interest portion of mortgage payments falls, and the principal portion rises. Therefore, the principal balance on the mortgage gets paid down at an increasing rate. The mortgage is paid off when the principal goes to zero. Mortgage lenders will often quote two rates, an APR and a lower rate that does not include fees. The APR is more accurate because fees are included. To actually know what you are paying, you will have to convert the APR into an EAR. You can use the lender's lower rate against them by accepting that rate while negotiating lower fees.

Something called "points" also requires discussion. Some lenders offer the chance for the borrower to make a payment up front in return for a lower interest rate. These payments are referred to as points. A point is 1% of the amount borrowed. Whether it is in your interest to pay the points up front depends on how long you will keep your mortgage (how long until you sell or refinance). If you do not plan on having your mortgage for very long, it will not make sense to take points, because you have to make the large payment up front, but do not get to enjoy the benefit of the lower interest rate and payments for very long. If you plan on holding your mortgage for a very long time it can be worthwhile to take the points if you have the money available.

The best thing to do is construct a spreadsheet with the savings on your monthly payments projected out until you think you will get out of the mortgage. For instance, if you think your monthly payments will be $300 lower, and you plan on holding the mortgage for 10 years, then you would project out $300 for 120 payments. Take the present value of these payments and add them up, using the mortgage periodic rate. If the present value of the payment savings is greater than the upfront dollar cost of the points, take the points. Otherwise, skip the points.

9.2 Fixed Rates Versus Adjustable Rates

Some mortgages (and other kinds of debt) have interest rates that are periodically adjusted. Typically, they are fixed for some point of time (maybe three years) and then they adjust with market interest rates. These kinds of mortgages are called "ARMs" (Adjustable Rate Mortgages). A typical ARM quote may be 2.8% above the interest rate on a 1-year T-bill. The T-bill rate is the "index" rate, and the extra is the "margin." After three years the rate on your mortgage is adjusted every once in a while, possibly every six months. These terms will vary depending on the lender.

ARM quotations are typically lower than fixed-rate quotations for two reasons: The first is that a fixed rate is much riskier for the bank and safer for you. Imagine that you take out a mortgage with a fixed periodic rate of .5% per month. Soon after you take out the mortgage, interest rates jump up to .7% per month. The bank has just taken a loss. You are paying them below the market rate at which they make loans, and they are stuck. You on the other hand, enjoy the low interest rate and the security of knowing exactly what your payments are going to be. **When you take out a fixed-rate there are no surprises - your monthly payments are fixed for the life of the loan.** ARM rates tend to be tied to interest rates on short-term debt (short-term rates) because ARM rates can adjust frequently, just like the interest rates on short-term debt. Interest rates on fixed-rate mortgages tend to match interest rates on fixed long-term debt.

Someone may point out that the opposite could happen with a fixed-rate mortgage. What if interest rates fell? The bank would get to charge you the high rate, and this time you would be stuck. Actually, you can escape! All you have to do is go to another bank and refinance your mortgage at the lower rate. Refinancing is when you take out a new mortgage and use the proceeds to pay off the old mortgage. (Of course, you have to pay fees to refinance.) From the bank's perspective this is called "prepayment risk." The bank has to suffer if interest rates rise, but it cannot benefit if interest rates fall. As a result, they charge a higher rate for a fixed rate mortgage.

This is the reason, by the way, that people with mortgages should keep track of mortgage rates. Suppose you are starting your senior year in high school and interest rates have fallen. Your parents discover that their after-tax mortgage payment will fall by $150 each month if they refinance. Over the five years until you finish college, this will result in $9,000 more that can be set aside to pay for your college, just because they took a little effort to refinance their mortgage. It is almost like free money.

ARMs do not have prepayment risk. If interest rates rise, you have to pay more, and if interest rates fall, you do not have the incentive to refinance because your payment automatically comes down. The second reason that ARMs often have lower rates is because of "teaser rates," which I shall discuss below.

The choice between a fixed-rate mortgage and an adjustable one can be difficult. The fixed-rate mortgage offers security in knowing what your payments will be. The ARM will, at least at first, offer a lower rate. One important factor in making this decision is how long you expect to stay in your house. There is one situation that is a "no-brainer." Suppose that you know for sure that you will stay in your house for three years and then move. You are absolutely certain. Chances are high that you can find an ARM that does not adjust for three years, and the interest rate will be below any fixed rate that you could get. Since you are certain that you will move, take out the ARM and enjoy the lower rate, which is fixed for three years. However, this example begs another question: "Realtor fees for selling a house can be substantial. If you only plan on staying in a house a short time, would it not be better to rent a house?" In any event, the longer you stay in a house, the more you may tilt towards a fixed-rate mortgage that you can rely on.

> ***Key Takeaway:*** Mortgages come with adjustable and fixed interest rates. Which is best depends on how long you intend to hold a mortgage. Fixed rates tend to be a little higher because of prepayment risk, but offer the security of knowing what your payment will be. With a fixed-rate mortgage, it is important to keep track of mortgage rates, and refinance when they fall.

9.3 Other Mortgage Considerations and Housing Prices

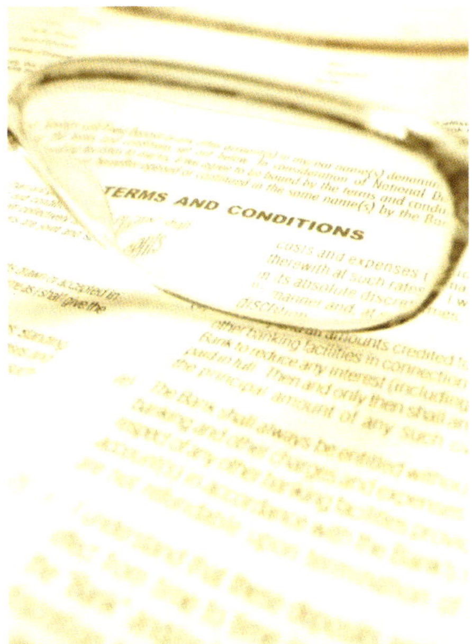

It is important to read the fine print on any contract, and that includes a mortgage. For instance, different banks will have different ways of handling extra payments. Suppose you decide to pay an extra $400 each month on your mortgage. You are paying down extra principal. Some banks will keep your payment the same, but shorten the length of your mortgage, while others will keep the length of your mortgage the same and reduce your payments. Banks may also charge a penalty for prepaying.

It is also important to understand whether your mortgage is full recourse. This means that if you default on the mortgage, in addition to seizing and selling your house, the bank will be able to come after other assets that you own and possibly garnish your wages. This is analogous to not having limited liability. Whether mortgages are full recourse will vary by state and bank. Also, you may automatically be subject to full recourse by law if you refinance your mortgage, even if your first mortgage was not full recourse.

This can be an especially important consideration when you are just starting out and do not have a lot of equity built up in your home. Imagine that you bought a house with 20% down two years ago. You just lost your job and cannot make your mortgage payments. The answer is to sell your house and pay off the mortgage, while planning on buying another place when you are back on your feet. However, suppose the value of the house has fallen. Realize that at the beginning you pay off the principal on your mortgage at a slow rate, and you will still owe a substantial amount on the mortgage. The house's value is now worth less than you owe on your mortgage. You are insolvent and may end up defaulting. As painful as this is (the default will stay on your credit rating for ten years or more) at least you can walk away from the payments.

With full recourse you will be stuck making payments to cover the difference. Actually, during the financial crisis, many people who did not have full recourse loans and were able to make their mortgage payments strategically decided to walk away from their homes because the value of their house had fallen below their mortgage. They were "underwater" and decided it was worth it to take a hit to their credit rating to be able to walk away. In any event, you do not want to end up in a situation like this, and should exercise caution when buying a home - it is an enormous commitment that can affect you for the rest of your life.

There are second mortgages, also known as home equity loans. Your home equity is the difference between your home value and what you owe on your mortgage. A home equity loan allows you to borrow against this equity (which is negative when a house is underwater. This is analogous to negative net worth.) Home equity loans have advantages over other kinds of debt because the interest on up to $100,000 of home equity borrowing can be deducted for tax purposes. (If you use the home equity loan to improve a home or buy a home it gets regular mortgage treatment.) And since home equity loans are secured on your house, you will pay less interest than on other types of consumer loans. For instance, you may have to pay 6% on a car loan, while you can pay 5.5% on a home equity loan.

The difference with credit cards is much greater. This means that you should consider taking out a home equity loan rather than other types of consumer debt. In the car loan example, your borrowing costs are lower if you take out a home equity loan rather than a car loan to purchase a car. If you do not pay your balance off on your credit card each month, it will be better to take out a home equity loan and pay off the card. (Better yet, do not run up credit cards in the first place.)

The problem with home equity loans is that they create the temptation to keep borrowing against your home to purchase impulse items that are not investments. An important part of planning for retirement involves paying off your home, or at least acquiring assets in greater amounts than liabilities. During the financial crisis, as people saw their home prices rise (and therefore their home equity) they borrowed money using home equity loans. When their home prices subsequently fell, they became insolvent. They discovered that they could lose their house for failing to pay a home equity loan just as easily as with a regular mortgage.

There is something called a "reverse mortgage." This is something that retired people sometimes use if they need money. Imagine someone has paid off his home and is retired. He has a health problem that is not fully covered by medical insurance and needs money for an expensive prescription every month. He can arrange for the bank to send him money each month. As the bank does so, the principal on his loan rises over time. (This is the reverse situation of a typical mortgage where regular payments get sent to the bank and the principal falls.) There is a guarantee by the government that if the principal rises to the value of the house, the bank cannot make the borrower move out. Offsetting this is the fact that reverse mortgages tend to have high fees and rates.

A better alternative may be to take out a small mortgage in excess of what is immediately needed, and use the excess to make the regular payments over time. The interest rate may be lower, although the guarantee will not be there. In either case, upon the retiree's death the bank has to be paid off first from the sale of the home, and only then can the heirs receive anything that is left over. Reverse mortgages cause less to be left to beneficiaries. However, this kind of arrangement may be the only way that a retired person can cover their expenses.

Key Takeaway: Be sure to read a mortgage's fine print. Also consider if the mortgage is full recourse before borrowing with a low down payment. Try to have enough of a down payment to avoid going underwater if the housing market declines. Home equity loans can be an inexpensive way to borrow to fund purchases. However they create the temptation to borrow irresponsibly. A reverse mortgage is a way for a retiree to receive payments from owing their house, but it causes their heirs to receive less.

Home prices and interest rates are closely related. Many people decide to buy a home based on a calculation similar to the one in Figure 9-1. They estimate out how much they can afford to pay each month, and from there decide how much of a home they can buy. Interest rates determine how much they can borrow, given what they are able to pay each month. The higher the interest rate, the less they can afford. The lower the interest rate, the more they can afford. As a result, home prices and interest rates move in opposite directions. When interest rates rise, potential buyers can borrow less and home prices fall, and vice-versa. However, in order to understand this further, a distinction needs to be made between real rates and nominal rates.

With inflation, salaries and home prices will rise along with other prices. When people think about what interest rate (and therefore payment) they can afford, they will take into account that their salary will rise. Therefore, people will reduce the cost to them of the payments if the payments are coming from inflation, rather than from a high real interest rate. House prices will still fall, but they will fall at little less if the rise in interest rates comes from inflation rather than an increase in real rates.[4]

In fact, as a homeowner with a fixed-rate mortgage, you hope for unexpected inflation. When you first buy your house, the interest rate you are charged reflects what the bank thinks inflation will be in the future. Suppose that later inflation skyrockets. Your house price will track the price level, along with your salary. However, your payments to the bank are fixed. The inflation is wiping out the cost to you of making the mortgage payments. This works to your benefit in a big way, but harms the bank and its owners. The banks will also pass their costs on to new borrowers. High unexpected inflation creates a massive transfer of wealth in the economy towards homeowners with fixed-rate mortgages, and away from others. It can also seal people in their homes. If they move, they give up their mortgage payments that are based on below market rates. They will have to pay full interest rates on a new mortgage. This can contribute to unemployment because people do not want to move to find new employment.

Just as inflation can go up, it can also come down. Imagine that you just bought your first house in a high inflation environment with a bare twenty percent down. You borrowed at a high nominal rate as a result. The economy then goes into recession. The Fed will typically respond by lowering rates. You enthusiastically look forward to refinancing, only to have bank after bank refuse to lend to you because your house price has fallen below the value of your mortgage, thanks to the poor economy. You are stuck with the high rate until you can pay your mortgage down. This could take a long time because your mortgage will get paid down slowly at the beginning.

Buying a house in a high interest rate environment can bring big risks and rewards. If interest rates come down while the housing market remains strong, your house price goes up and you can refinance into lower payments. This is an ideal situation that can really boost wealth. If interest rates come down while the housing market falls, you may be unable to refinance because your house has gone underwater. What should be clear from this discussion is that it is important to think about general economic conditions before taking out a mortgage.

Key Takeaway: Interest rates and house prices tend to move in the opposite direction, but not always. Two situations can significantly boost the wealth of borrowers of fixed-rate mortgages. If inflation unexpectedly rises along with house prices and salaries, the real cost of the mortgage payments declines. If interest rates fall and house prices rise, you can refinance into the lower interest rate and get the benefit of a higher house price. However, if housing prices decline along with the economy, interest rates fall, and you did not put much down on your house, you may not be able to refinance into a lower rate, all the while suffering from a decline in the value of your house. Careful attention should be paid to economic conditions before buying a house using a mortgage.

[4] The higher nominal rate (and payment) will not be offset by a higher salary at first because inflation has not caused their salary to rise yet.

Challenge

Do you think current conditions are good for borrowing to buy a house? Would you take out a fixed-rate mortgage, or an ARM?

9.4 Abusive Practices and Mortgage Games

The Roots of the Financial Crisis Can Be Found in the Mortgage Market.

Often ARMs have teaser rates. You pay a very low rate, possibly for two or three years, then the rate adjusts to either a high base index and/or a large margin. (After all, the bank has to charge high payments later to make up for charging you the low teaser rate.) Unfortunately, uneducated people were often unaware that their mortgage payments would skyrocket in the future. In the past, some savvy borrowers took out teaser rate mortgages, then refinanced them to another teaser rate mortgage before their rate readjusted. These days, any bank that offers a teaser rate mortgage will create a substantial penalty for prepayment.

Credit card companies also offer teaser rates. They charge a 0% APR for a year, before adjusting the rate upward. I was told by a student that he came up with the down payment for his house by taking out 0% cards. Right before the rate was going to adjust up, he would switch to a different 0% card. This certainly seemed to be a cheap source of funding, but there are several problems. The first is that he is not making any down payment. If the value of the house falls he is insolvent. He may also lose his job and have trouble with the payments. The second problem is that he is relying on being able to refinance into a new credit card. If conditions turn worse, he may not have access to new borrowing at a 0% rate, and will have to pay a high rate. The third problem is that this may affect his credit rating.

Before the financial crisis hit, two quasi government agencies, Fannie Mae and Freddie Mac, bought mortgage loans from the banks at the urging of the United States Congress. (Eventually, private institutions also got into the act.) They would then package and sell the loans in the financial markets with taxpayer backed guarantees against default. Fannie and Freddie enjoyed government subsidies on their own borrowing, and had taken over a huge amount of the mortgage market as a result. In turn, they funneled money back to congressmen so that their taxpayer protection would remain. There is also evidence that private institutions bought the most problematic mortgages of all and resold them. These institutions realized that the mortgages had problems, but sold them to investors anyway.

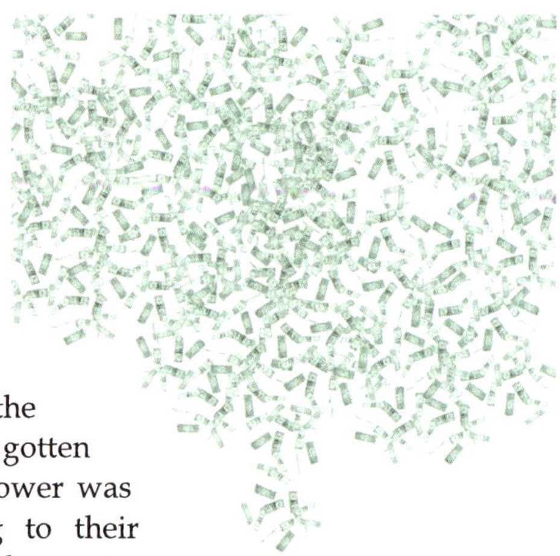

In earlier times, banks would have to provide their own money to the borrower. But since the bank could sell the mortgage contract to someone else and get their money back, they were no longer in a position of risk with regards to the borrower. Since the banks no longer held the loans, they did not care if they defaulted. The bank made money through the fees that they received when they sold their mortgages. They may have also gotten fees for servicing the mortgages (keeping paperwork on whether the borrower was paying, and collecting the payments). Often banks would pass along to their employees the incentive to generate loans, without concern for loan quality, by paying them generous commissions based on the number of loans written. All of this was exacerbated by the Fed, which had pumped money into the financial system after September 11th. This money needed a place to go, and ended up funding mortgages.

Let the Games Begin

Something called "liar loans" began to happen. Banks would look the other way when borrowers falsified their circumstances on their mortgage application, or loan officers would actually encourage them to lie. Sometimes, the loan officer would explain that this was the correct way to fill it out, using twisted logic. Sometimes it was clear that the information was false. These loans were mostly in the subprime market where borrowers had the most difficulty getting loans. Unfortunately, it also turned out that uneducated borrowers who took out subprime loans at high interest rates were often unaware that they had good credit ratings and could qualify for a prime mortgage at a low rate. The bank did not bother to point this out.

Because credit was so freely available, it fueled a housing boom because of the large number of people who could pay for houses with borrowed money. Housing prices skyrocketed. People began to borrow to buy houses that were way beyond their means. Their reasoning was that even though they could not afford to pay the mortgage payments for very long, they would sell the house in a couple of years at a much higher price and pay off the mortgage, leaving themselves a hefty profit. Even high income people got involved in this "house flipping." Unfortunately, when the unsustainable housing prices began to fall, many could not make their payments, while others walked away because the house was under water.

The banks facilitated flipping by using their own appraisers. (An appraiser is someone who estimates the value of property.) Banks are regulated, and are required to have an appraiser certify that the house is worth an amount that justifies the loan. This way, if the borrower defaults, the bank can sell the house and get its money back. However, the banks did not care if the borrower defaulted because they were selling off the loans. And since the appraiser relied on the bank for payment, they would go along and give the house a high appraised value. Financial regulators looked the other way, because they did not wish to upset all of the people who were happy with the way things were going before the crash hit. There was no interference by the Fed, other financial regulators at the state level, Congress, or the executive branch of government.

Lenders facilitated flipping with teaser rates on ARMS. A spectacle began to happen—people with little income buying huge houses that were five times too expensive for them. These people reasoned that by the time the teaser rate readjusted to a high rate and their mortgage payments hit the roof, they would be able to sell the house at a higher price and get out. Other people with less education did not understand that their rates would adjust up significantly in the future.

Even worse were "option ARMS." With these loans you could decide whether or not to make your monthly payment. If you failed to pay, the principal on the mortgage rose, leading to even higher payments in the future. It was these loans in particular that encouraged house flipping. (The buyer could avoid making any payment at all on an enormous house, while hoping that their house price rose. In addition, some uneducated people failed to understand the consequences of not paying.)

Unfortunately, unethical lenders and realtors (realtors help homeowners sell their house) often pretend to be friends. Here is a situation a friend of mine faced (with a hypothetical house price and name inserted). The house was worth $200,000. Sue did not have the 20% down payment. Her "friend," who was a realtor, told Sue about a "technique" to make the deal go through. The realtor would specify that the house was worth $250,000, and the owner of the house would "give" Sue a $55,000 down payment (which the owner would get back from Sue when the house was sold - they were not giving Sue anything).

In other words, rather than buy a $200,000 house with no money down, the owner would give Sue $50,000, but sell it to her for $50,000 more, getting the money back in the process. The bank would get to claim to regulators that the house was sold for $250,000, with a 20% down payment, when in fact she was buying the house for $200,000 with no down payment. This would make it easier for the bank to justify to regulators making a $200,000 loan on the house.[5] Sue was encouraged to buy a house that she thought was worth $250,000. In reality, she would have ended up buying a house for $200,000 with no money down, while putting herself at risk if housing prices fell — which they did. Fortunately, Sue's true friends talked her out of it.

Horrors in Housing

Glenda Ortiz's story reads like a dramatic play of the housing market collapse, complete with a predatory lender, a hapless homebuyer and easy credit that fueled greed all around.

According to the Washington Post, Glenda was a Best Western hotel chain cook that left her homeland of Honduras after a hurricane ravaged the country in the late 1990s. She landed in the Washington, D.C. area, looking for a better life and a piece of the American dream. Even though she didn't have much in savings or very good credit, a lender readily set her up with a high-interest home loan. Ortiz and her husband, an air conditioner installer, happily signed the loan documents, though the Spanish speaking couple couldn't understand the English they were written in or the fees that got piled into the loan.

The couple wound up buying a home for $430,000, three times the amount the property previously sold for and $5,000 over the asking price, according to the Post. The loan ate up more than half of the couple's monthly income and it wasn't long before they fell behind on their mortgage and their home landed in foreclosure. A broken-hearted and disillusioned Glenda Ortiz went back to living in an apartment.

But Ortiz's story continued to ring bells among government officials. Secretary of Housing and Urban Development Alfonso Jackson called Ortiz's home purchase and lending debacle a "nightmare of horrors in housing."[6]

---

5 Regulators like to see banks make loans to borrowers who contribute a large down payment. This means that the value of the house is significantly higher than the amount of the loan. If the borrow defaults, after the bank seizes the house and sells it, the bank is more likely to receive more from the sale than what was owed on the mortgage.

6 Brigid Schulte, "My Dream House was an Illusion: Latina's Loss in Va. Epitomizes Mortgage Crisis," The Washington Post, March 22, 2008; Secretary of Housing and Urban Development Alphonso Jackson, prepared remarks, meeting of the National Association of Hispanic Real Estate Professionals, Washington, DC, March 27, 2008, http://www.hud.gov/news/speeches/2008-03-27a.cfm.

Key Takeaway: If something sounds too good to be true, it is just that. Stay away from "incredible offers," super-low introductory rates, convoluted special arrangements, and get rich quick schemes. Unfortunately, when it comes to business dealings and a lot of money is at stake, "friends" may try to suck you into something harmful. Look out if there seems to be a frenzy about buying houses, or anything else for that matter.

Challenge

Suppose a friend was wildly excited about getting involved in a get rich scheme. What would you do about it?

What Happens When a Congresswoman Calls the Bank? She Gets an Earful of Muzak.

When home values started to plummet, homeowners rushed to call their bank to see if they could renegotiate or modify their home loans. Plenty of them got put on hold. So maybe Congresswoman Maxine Waters shouldn't feel so bad.

But what happened to Waters sure didn't look good for Bank of America. With ABC News cameras rolling, Waters called the bank to help one of her constituents modify their mortgage payments. Waters was put on hold, transferred, disconnected and redirected to unhelpful automated recordings. "This is absolutely horrible," she said, as ABC News filmed her on hold in her Washington, D.C. office.

Nearly two hours after she first attempted to get a loan officer on the phone, Waters got transferred to a refinancing department, only to be cut off, according to the ABC News Nightline investigation. Representatives from Bank of America apologized to Waters, saying they typically respond to calls within two to three minutes and that her experience wasn't how they wanted to treat homeowners.

Maybe so. But Waters said she believes that if this is the way she gets treated then the average homeowner has no chance.[7]

[7] Brian Ross and Avni Patel, "On Hold: Even Congresswoman Gets the Runaround on Bank Help Lines. Rep. Maxine Waters Dials and Redials Attempting to Get Help for Constituents." World News Tonight, ABC, Jan. 22, 2009.

Ethics

Many mortgages borrowers were financially destroyed by the mortgage crisis. The greater financial crisis was precipitated by the mortgage crisis, throwing many out of work and wreaking financial devastation.

One Side:

Uneducated people do not understand mortgages. Some do not even speak English. Many were given teaser rates, and did not understand that their payments were going to skyrocket in the future. They were manipulated by loan officers greedy for commissions, and banks that were greedy for fees. Eventually, these people had their financial future destroyed.

The Other Side:

Anyone should be able to understand that lying is wrong. Lying on a loan application can rightfully bring a felony charge. We should also expect adults to take responsibility for themselves and know what they are getting into. If we don't, then people will never bother to take responsibility for their own actions. And many of the people who defaulted were trying to flip houses, and they knew exactly what they were doing. They took a big risk to get rich quick and got burned, and now taxpayers who behaved responsibly have to pay big-time for their misconduct.

9.5 Final Thoughts

It is very tedious to read the fine print on financial documents. Unfortunately, it is absolutely necessary. Many mortgage documents have mistakes in them (or fraud), in addition to onerous terms that you may not be aware of. It is also important to arm yourself with information when you make financial decisions. The Internet contains a wealth of information on financial transactions.

I will discuss the finer points of buying a house in Volume 2. Buying a house is a major decision that requires hard work researching the best deal, and careful thought about whether the deal is in your best interest. Homeownership can be vital in establishing financial security and prosperity. It can also cause your downfall. Caution is required. Do not be shy about questioning the "helpful" person you are doing business with. Their feelings should not be hurt if you ask detailed questions. It is what any responsible person would do. You are not there to be their friend. You are there to conduct business. Finally, if something requires slight-of-hand, a "special arrangement," or if it is too good to be true, then it probably is. Use your common sense, and stay away from "getting rich quick," which just may land you in the poor house.

If you are diligent about only buying a house under the right circumstances, your house can be a source of great happiness. It can also be a place where you grow wealth along with your family. If you exercise self-control and wait until the time is right, you will lay the foundation that your happy home needs. And when you finally retire, your home will be a very valuable asset that can free you from worry, along with a store of memories.

Key Terms:

Adjustable rates
Appraiser
ARMs
Bank regulator
Fixed rate
Flipping
Full recourse
Home equity loan
Index rate
Liar loans
Margin
Mortgage
Option ARMs
Points
Prepayment
Prepayment risk
Principal
Refinance
Reverse mortgage
Second mortgage
Teaser rates
Underwater

End of Chapter Questions

1. A mortgage has an APR of 6.84%. Payments (and compounding) are monthly.
   a. What is the periodic monthly rate?
   b. You decide that you can afford monthly payments of $1,650 and wish to take out a 30 year mortgage. How much can you borrow to buy a townhouse in Whittier, California?
   c. How much of your first payment will be principal? How much will be interest?

2. A mortgage has an APR of 8.88%. Payments (and compounding) are monthly.
   a. What is the periodic monthly rate?
   b. You need to borrow $552,761.48 to buy a condo in Culver City. You plan on taking a 20 year mortgage. What will your monthly payments be?
   c. How much of your first payment will be principal? How much will be interest?

3. Construct an amortization schedule for a 15-year mortgage with an APR of 6.24%. Your monthly payments are $2,000, and you put 20% down.

4. Why does it matter how much of a mortgage payment is principal versus interest?

5. What is the difference between the APR on a mortgage, and the other "rate" they offer?

6. What are points?

7. Name the trade-off between taking a fixed-rate mortgage and an adjustable rate mortgage.

8. If you do not plan on staying in your home for long, does this increase or decrease your incentive to take out an ARM versus a fixed-rate mortgage?

9. What does it mean if a mortgage is full recourse?

10. How is a home equity loan different from a mortgage?

11. What are the advantages and disadvantages of a home equity loan?

12. How do real interest rates and inflation affect home prices?

13. What is a teaser rate?

14. What does it mean to "flip" a house?

15. What is a reverse mortgage?

16. What is an option ARM?

17. Who is an appraiser?

18. What economic conditions would you hope for with a fixed-rate mortgage?

19. If you are just getting started, what would you think about before buying?

20. When should you refinance a mortgage?

THE BASICS OF PLANNING

It is now time to discover the art of prognostication in the form of financial planning. Without the use of financial planning you are flying blind without an autopilot. You cannot discern if you will reach your destination—or smash into a financial cliff. With a little forewarning you can change direction and avoid that cliff. Financial planning takes effort, but it also provides a peek into the future, and the confidence of knowing where you are going. You just may end up in a place you really want to be.

Chapter 10

Budgeting in Excel

10.1 A Basic Beginning Budget

Spreadsheets are a powerful tool for financial forecasting. And this may sound odd at first, but they can bring a lot of comfort. Most people have no idea where they are headed. The can see how much they are saving (which is often not very much), and they have a rough idea of some of the things they need to save up to buy — but that is about it. They do not know if they will have enough to live on in retirement; they do not know if they will be able to fund their children's college, and on and on. They are financially lost in the woods with a vague idea of which way is north.

Forecasting in Excel will give you a map and compass. Not only will you have a very good idea of where you are headed, you will also be able to strategize about taking the best route. You will cut out unnecessary side trips and delays, and get to the place you value most.

There are two ways in which spreadsheets are a powerful tool for financial forecasting. They can be used to construct a short-term budget, or they can be used to create long-term forecasts, years into the future. Long-term forecasting will be discussed a later chapter where you will plan to save for retirement. I begin here by constructing a short-term budget using Excel. With a short-term budget you can do some precise pruning. You will be able to control where your money goes very effectively to promote your own happiness and well-being. This is also a chance to peek at what kind of lifestyle you will be able to lead.

Figure 10-1 shows how an annual budget could be constructed for Richard Wilson, who is a recent graduate from law school and an attorney.[1] (The full spreadsheet is in the supplemental materials of the book that are available on the Internet.) Richard makes an impressive income and is enjoying his new career. He happily looks to other lawyers at the firm, including higher earning senior attorneys, when setting his lifestyle. Richard has something else to look forward to: he is planning on proposing to his girlfriend. His life is headed in a whole new direction.

[1] Richard Wilson is a fictional character created for expository purposes.

Figure 10-1
Richard Wilson's Budget

	A B	C	D	E	F	G	H	I	J	K	L	M	N	O	P	Q	R	S
1		Inflation=		0.030	Monthly=	0.002466												
2		t=		0	1	2	3	4	5	6	7	8	9	10	11	12		Year
3																		
4	**Cash Inflows**																	
5																		
6		Take Home Pay		6,100	6,100	6,100	6,100	6,100	6,100	6,100	6,100	6,100	6,100	6,100	6,100	6,100		79,300
7		Interest																
8		Dividends																
9		Liquidated Investments																
10		Miscellaneous Income and Reimbursements		400	401	402	403	404	405	406	407	408	409	410	411	412		5,278
11	**Total Cash Inflows**			**6,500**	**6,501**	**6,502**	**6,503**	**6,504**	**6,505**	**6,506**	**6,507**	**6,508**	**6,509**	**6,510**	**6,511**	**6,512**		**84,578**

G1: =(1+E1)^(1/12) - 1

You will first focus on the rate of inflation and cash inflows. By the way, if inflation is low and you want to save time, you can leave inflation out for short-term forecasting (but not long-term). However, if inflation is high or you want to take a couple of extra minutes to be precise, then include inflation. Go to the Bureau of Labor Statistics website at http://www.bls.gov/data/ to look up the consumer price index (CPI). Take this year's index for December, divide by last year's December index, then subtract 1. You have the rate of inflation for the year.[2] Enter this number into Cell E1. In Cell G1 calculate the monthly inflation rate. The monthly inflation rate is $1.03^{1/12} - 1 = .002466$. This is what is in the formula bar.

Next, set up a time period row (Row 2). This short-term budget is for twelve months. However, at t=0, the last month's amount was put in as a starting point. After that, create rows for cash inflows. The biggest in this example is take-home pay. (Which is, as you recall, much less than starting pay.) You may wish to include interest, dividends, and investments that were sold. However, if you plan on saving, you may want to leave these out as being untouchable, and not something that you will live off of in daily life. (Richard Wilson had the good sense to max out contributions from pre-tax income to his company retirement plan.)

The final category is miscellaneous income and reimbursements. This could include a large variety of cash inflows. In this example it will consist of company reimbursements. Richard works as an attorney and takes prospective clients of his employer out to lunch and dinner, and the company reimburses him. (Unfortunately it takes two months. Richard is making his employer a two month, interest free loan.) Other possibilities may include royalties, or part-time work income.

Finally, sum down over cash flows in Row 11. Sum across each row into Column S to obtain yearly totals. Richard is happy to see that he has impressive income that he has earned for the year. Most graduates, even lawyers or MBA students, do not earn nearly as much.

Once all sources of cash inflows are entered, you have the good news. Now it is time to look at the bad news: cash outflows. Figure 10-2 illustrates how you could forecast rent, with the forecast shown only through month 9. Richard's current rent is $1,800. He is not sure what his new rent will be when it is increased in July. However, he has noticed that rent seems to be going up faster than the general rate of inflation of 3%. He decides to guess that rent will increase by 4%. Multiply the previous month's rent by 1.04 to get the new rent of $1,872. This is what is in the formula bar.

Figure 10-2
Rent Price Increase

	A B	C	D	E	F	G	H	I	J	K	L	M	N
1		Inflation=		0.030	Monthly=	0.002466							
2		t=		0	1	2	3	4	5	6	7	8	9
17		Rent		1,800	1,800	1,800	1,800	1,800	1,800	1,800	1,872	1,872	1,872

L17: =K17*1.04

Automobile expenses are next, as seen in Figure 10-3. Richard's annual car insurance contract will expire in April. He assumes that at that point it will rise by the rate of inflation, and then remain constant for another year. Each

[2] I used a hypothetical number. Of course, as I discussed in Chapter 2, there are real shocks to prices, which can bump around the CPI for reasons having nothing to do with inflation. Some economists prefer to look at the index without energy and food prices.

year in August he pays $46 for road service, so that he can get his tire changed if he has a flat, or his door opened if he accidentally locks himself out.

Fuel is the next item. This month he spent $120 on gas. As can be seen in the formula bar, the following month he assumed that gas would go up by the monthly rate of inflation. (Since you have the display set to round up to the nearest dollar, you do not see a change right away.) Drag and drop the formula across to get a steady increase in fuel costs. Richard expects to pay $185 to register his gar in April with his state government. Every three months he has minor maintenance done on his car, and the oil replaced if necessary. This is expected to be $20 in February. In August it will be higher by six months of inflation as seen in the formula bar for Cell M25. (It appears to have the same value because of rounding, but it is actually higher.)

His maintenance in November (not shown) was similarly increased by six months worth of inflation. Include his auto loan payment, and sum up the total in Row 27. However, as you shall see, this does not include the $30 he must set aside for unexpected repairs. Even ignoring this, the total for the year is $8,199 (see the spreadsheet), which must be paid in after-tax dollars. The pretax income needed to cover this is much higher. An automobile is a major expense. Even after his auto loan is paid off, Richard must save to have the down payment on a new car (less the resale price he gets for his old car). This is not a happy thought because an automobile provides the freedom to go where you want and a lot of extra convenience, to boot. However, at first it may be necessary to wait. You will be rewarded for waiting later.

Figure 10-3
Automobile Expenses

	A	B	C	D	E	F	G	H	I	J	K	L	M
1			Inflation=		0.030	Monthly=	0.002466						
2			t=		0	1	2	3	4	5	6	7	8
20			Automobile										
21			Insurance		120	120	120	120	124	124	124	124	124
22			Road Service										46
23			Fuel		120	120	121	121	121	121	122	122	122
24			Registration						185				
25			Maintenance				20			100			20
26			Loan		350	350	350	350	350	350	350	350	350
27			Total		590	590	611	591	780	695	595	596	663

F23: =E23*(1+$G1)

M25: =G25*(1+$G1)^6

Figure 10-4 has more cash expenditures by Richard Wilson. These include regular bank charges for his checking account, including online banking fees and regular haircuts (personal hygiene). Petty cash includes all small cash expenditures that are not made on a debit or credit card, and where a receipt is not collected. There are a number of small items that can fall into this category such as tips to parking attendants. Other budget items include clothes (including work clothing), clubs (health club), computers and peripherals, and credit card payments. Richard seems to be living a high life style just like the partners at his law firm. There is just one problem. As you are about to see, Richard does not have the income to support it.

Figure 10-4
More Expenditures

	A	B	C	D	E	F	G	H	I	J	K	L	M
1			Inflation=		0.030	Monthly=	0.002466						
2			t=		0	1	2	3	4	5	6	7	8
28			Bank Charges		15	15	15	15	15	15	15	15	15
29			Personal Hygiene					120			121		
30			Petty Cash		140	140	141	141	141	142	142	142	143
31			Charity/Political Contributions										
32			Clothing					800					
33			Clubs					1,000					
34			Computers, etc.									400	
35			Credit Cards***		600	595	590	585	580	575	571	566	561
36			Dining		360	361	362	363	364	364	365	366	367
37			Electronics								120		
38			Entertainment		100	100	100	101	101	301	101	102	102
39			Gifts		35	35	35	155	35	35	81	36	36
40			Groceries/Drug Store		600	601	603	604	606	607	609	610	612
41			Home Office Expenses		40	40	40	40	40	40	41	41	41
42			Household										
43			Decorating						400				
44			Dry Cleaning		55	55	55	55	56	56	56	56	56
45			Furnishings										
46			Misc.		35	35	35	35	35	35	36	36	36
47			Total		90	90	90	91	491	91	91	92	92
48			Insurance										
49			Life		25	25	25	25	25	25	25	25	25
50			Renters		20	20	20	20	20	20	20	20	20
51			Umbrella		40	40	40	40	41	41	41	41	41
52			Disability		20	20	20	20	20	20	20	20	20
53			Long-term Care		10	10	10	10	10	10	10	10	10
54			Total		115	115	115	115	116	116	116	116	116

Key Takeaway: Spreadsheets are a powerful financial tool. A short-term budget spreadsheet will help you focus your spending on where you want it, to achieve your own happiness as you know best. A car is extremely expensive and should be thought about carefully.

Challenge

How do you feel about owning a car? Do you think you will need one when you graduate from college?

10.2 Borrowing to Consume

Richard Wilson's use of credit cards deserves extra attention. Everywhere you look people are using credit cards. It seems like the normal thing to do, and it makes buying something quick and easy. To the extent that you pay the credit card off each month, simply list purchases under their own expense category. However, many people do not have the will to pay them off, and Richard Wilson is one of them. He has old credit card debts.

Consider the consequences of borrowing to make purchases. Figure 10-5 illustrates the purchase of a $5,000 high-end entertainment system using a credit card. (Only the earlier time periods shown. For the full spreadsheet, see the supplemental materials.) Richard, not surprisingly, is very popular with his buddies, who come over regularly to watch sports and movies.

Unfortunately, Richard Wilson was late on several payments and is paying the default APR of 30%. At t=0 he spent $5,000 on the system. Assuming that he makes constant payments over eight years to pay the credit card off, his constant monthly payment will be $141 (rounded up to the nearest dollar). The next column shows how his balance declines (an amortization schedule).

The next column shows what the entertainment system would cost in the future taking inflation into account. This will come in handy because you will consider what would have happened if Richard Wilson had waited to buy. The value is $\$5{,}000 \cdot (1 + monthly\ inflation)^n$. The next column represents how much he would have saved had he not purchased the entertainment system right away, but rather invested the same amount as the credit card payments in a savings account with an APY of 4%. (This column shows what would have happened had he foregone buying the entertainment system right away and put his money into a savings account instead.) The cumulative amount is last month's balance times one plus the monthly interest rate, plus the current contribution for the month.

At t=37, by putting the payments into a savings account, Richard would have saved enough to buy the entertainment system for $5,477, with $68 left over. If he continued to put the same payments into the savings account, at the end of eight years (when the credit cards payments would have stopped) he would have saved $9,258. Deflating these savings to today, this is worth $7,308.34. This is additional consumption, in today's terms, that he could enjoy over the space of the eight years in addition to the entertainment system. What this means is that if he had invested the same payment amount as the credit card payments, and also waited until he could buy the entertainment system without borrowing, in today's terms he could have enjoyed $5,000 + $7,308.34 = $12,308.34 instead of $5,000. His consumption would be almost 2½ times more.

Borrowing to consume results in a very large reduction in lifetime consumption. Borrowing at high credit card rates makes this problem much worse. Instant gratification is not good for the waistline, and it is certainly not good financially. With a little patience, Richard Wilson's paychecks will buy him a lot more. There can be justification for borrowing to invest in an asset that increases in value over time, such as a house. The interest on the loan may be offset by an increase in the value of the asset. However, borrowing to buy anything that has its value go away destroys wealth.

Figure 10-5
Entertainment System Purchase and Borrowing

Monthly Inflation=	0.0024663	Monthly Credit Card Interest=	0.025796093	Monthly Interest on a Savings Account=	0.0032737

Month (t)	Entertainment System	Payments	Balance	Cost of Entertainment System with Inflation	Cumulative Savings if Payments Invested	Real Value of Savings	Real Consumption
0	5,000					7,308.34	12,308.34
1		141	4,988	5,012	141		
2		141	4,975	5,025	283		
3		141	4,962	5,037	425		
4		141	4,949	5,050	568		
5		141	4,936	5,062	711		
6		141	4,922	5,074	854		
7		141	4,907	5,087	998		
8		141	4,893	5,100	1,143		
9		141	4,878	5,112	1,288		
10		141	4,862	5,125	1,433		
11		141	4,846	5,137	1,579		
12		141	4,830	5,150	1,726		
13		141	4,814	5,163	1,872		
14		141	4,797	5,175	2,020		
15		141	4,779	5,188	2,168		
16		141	4,761	5,201	2,316		
17		141	4,743	5,214	2,465		
18		141	4,724	5,227	2,614		
19		141	4,704	5,240	2,764		
20		141	4,685	5,252	2,914		
21		141	4,664	5,265	3,065		
22		141	4,643	5,278	3,216		
23		141	4,622	5,291	3,368		
24		141	4,600	5,305	3,520		
25		141	4,577	5,318	3,673		
26		141	4,554	5,331	3,826		
27		141	4,530	5,344	3,980		
28		141	4,506	5,357	4,134		
29		141	4,481	5,370	4,289		
30		141	4,455	5,383	4,444		
31		141	4,429	5,397	4,600		
32		141	4,402	5,410	4,756		
33		141	4,374	5,423	4,913		
34		141	4,346	5,437	5,070		
35		141	4,317	5,450	5,228		
36		141	4,287	5,464	5,387		
37		141	4,256	5,477	68		
38		141	4,225		210		
39		141	4,193		352		
40		141	4,160		494		

Returning to Figure 10-4, Richard Wilson is slowly paying off his credit cards. His first payment is $600 and declines over time. These payments go straight out of his pocket and to the credit card company. If possible, he should try to find a credit card with a lower rate. It will also help to pay it off as soon as he can, as long as he has enough savings to cover emergencies.

Temporary, extreme belt tightening can get this monkey off his back. He made a terrible mistake by borrowing on a credit card during college, rather than taking out student loans at a much lower interest rate. He thought he did not need to borrow for school, but then used a credit card. He did not pay attention to paying on time, or the balance he was running up when purchasing textbooks and other school supplies. Legal books are quite expensive. He also indulged on the entertainment system. Had he planned carefully, this item would be for student loans instead, and the payment would be much smaller.

Key Takeaway: Borrowing to consume can significantly reduce your overall lifetime consumption, as well as your lifetime wealth. Avoid borrowing in general, especially avoid using credit cards in college, and use student loans if necessary to finance your education.

10.3 Finishing Richard Wilson's Budget

Other expenses include dining and entertainment. These increased by the monthly inflation rate. Also, in May, Richard plans on spending $200 to attend a U-2® concert, and in November, $250 for good seats at a basketball game. Add these amounts on top of the regular amount. Gifts, Groceries and Drug Store, Home Office Expenses, Household Dry Cleaning and Miscellaneous increase by monthly inflation. Gifts needs extra amounts for birthdays and holidays.

Richard Wilson also has insurance payments. Insurance payments are typically increased once a year by the insurance company. His term life insurance is constant, but the other payments increase on the annual anniversary of taking out the insurance.[3] Each of these is increased by the annual rate of inflation.

He has renter's insurance. (When there is a fire, people are shocked to discover just how much it costs to replace everything.) Umbrella insurance covers any losses due to lawsuits not covered by other insurance, such as housekeepers falling off ladders. It is also an effective way to pay for part of his car insurance. Disability insurance pays him if he becomes disabled and is unable to work. Richard's state provides inadequate disability payments, which he decided to supplement with a small policy. Long-term care insurance covers payments for nursing home care when he is older. This may seem like money wasted, but it is absolutely essential. Imagine what would happen if he had a serious medical condition and could not work for an extended period of time. He would be bankrupt and destitute. I will discuss these insurance products among others in Volume 2. His total insurance payments are $115 the first month, then increase.

Figure 10-6 contains the last of Richard's expenditures. These include insurance copayments on doctor's visits[4] and medicine, miscellaneous expenses, pet expenses, recreation, miscellaneous fees and taxes, and travel. He is

[3] Term life insurance just means that he is only buying life insurance. This is not a combined policy for life insurance and retirement savings. Richard just took out term life insurance because of his plans to marry.

planning on taking his honeymoon in December, which adds $3,500 (not shown), as well as $200 in boarding fees for his dog. Utilities are a major area of expense. Cable, Internet access, cell phone, telephone landline, and electricity add up to $320 in the first month. Most of these increase once a year. The electricity varies by season. He does not use natural gas. Add up all cash expenditures, and you have the total cash outflows in Row 78. Over the course of a year, Richard's expenditures add up to $82,013, as can be seen in Figure 10-7.

Figure 10-6
The Last of Richard Wilson's Expenditures

	A	B	C	D	E	F	G	H	I	J	K	L	M
1			Inflation=		0.030	Monthly=	0.002466						
2			t=		0	1	2	3	4	5	6	7	8
55			Medical										
56			Doctor Copay		15								15
57			Medicine		15	15	15	15	15	15	15	15	15
58			Other										
59			Total		30	15	15	15	15	15	15	15	30
60			Miscellaneous		120	120	121	121	121	121	122	122	122
61			Pet										
62			Food and Supplies		50	50	50	50	50	51	51	51	51
63			Veterinarian								80		
64			Other										
65			Total		50	50	50	50	50	51	131	51	51
66			Recreation		40	40	40	40	40	40	40	40	40
67			Misc. Fees and Taxes										
68			Travel/Vacation										
69			Utilities										
70			Cable		45	45	45	45	45	46	46	46	46
71			Internet		45	45	45	45	45	46	46	46	46
72			Cell Phone		115	115	115	115	118	118	118	118	118
73			Landline		35	35	35	35	35	35	35	35	35
74			Electricity		80	80	60	60	60	60	80	80	80
75			Gas										
76			Total		320	320	300	301	304	305	325	325	325
77			Work Expenses		402	403	404	405	406	407	408	409	410
78			**Total Cash Outflows**		5,447	5,432	5,433	7,453	6,007	5,722	5,809	5,916	5,598

His net cash flow equals total cash inflows minus total cash outflows. This totals $2,564. Below the cash flow total are line items for savings that need to be set aside. Since Richard needs to set aside $30 each month for unexpected car repairs, this leaves $2,174 in savings for the condominium down payment. (This is net cash flow minus the $30 car repair amount.) Richard will never buy anything at this rate. He had been hoping to save $80,000 in five years, which works out to about $1,333 per month.

[4] His medical insurance company requires that he pay for part of his medical bills.

Figure 10-7
Richard Wilson's Net Cash Flow and Deficit

t=	0	1	2	3	4	5	6	7	8	9	10	11	12	Year
Total Cash Outflows	5,447	5,432	5,433	7,453	6,007	5,722	5,809	5,916	5,598	6,915	5,661	6,674	9,946	82,013
Net Cashflow	1,053	1,069	1,069	(950)	497	783	697	591	910	(406)	849	(163)	(3,434)	2,564
Saving Set Aside														
First Home	1,023	1,039	1,039	(980)	467	753	667	561	880	(436)	819	(193)	(3,464)	2,174
Kid's College														
Retirement														
Car Repairs	30	30	30	30	30	30	30	30	30	30	30	30	30	390
Home Repairs														
Property Taxes														
Total														
Surplus/Deficit	(310)	(294)	(294)	(2,313)	(866)	(580)	(666)	(772)	(453)	(1,769)	(514)	(1,526)	(4,797)	(15,155)
Unexpected Expenses														
Auto Repairs	390													
Medical	7,000													
Veterinary	1,500													
Catastrophic	6,000													
Job Loss	36,600													

The Surplus/Deficit row is the difference between what he saved each month and $1,333. Over the course of the year this amounts to a deficit of $15,155. He does not have any children, which can create substantial expenses, but he cannot afford any in the future at this rate. He also needs sufficient savings to cover unexpected expenses. These are auto repairs, medical problems that may require surgery or other treatments (some of which may not be covered by insurance), veterinary costs for his dog, catastrophic losses such as a fire, and enough money to cover losing his job and not finding another for six months.

This last item is referred to as a safety reserve. Unfortunately, in today's environment job loss is not uncommon. Without savings, Richard may be forced to borrow using a credit card at a very high rate. To make things worse, he may hit his borrowing limit and find himself unable to borrow more without a demonstrated source of income. He could also find himself in bankruptcy court.

Compounding this disaster, employers often ask to access the credit report of a job applicant, which will reveal his financial mistakes. (I shall discuss credit reports in a later chapter.) His financial troubles could result in him being unable to find a good job, leading to a long slide into a true lifetime disaster.

It is absolutely essential to build up enough savings to cover yourself in the event of job loss as soon as possible upon entering the workforce. Some unemployment insurance may be available, but it will not be nearly enough under typical circumstances. It is also essential that Richard have adequate insurance for other kinds of trouble. This is a topic that I take up in Volume 2.

Richard Wilson is like a car stuck in the mud. He keeps spinning his wheels and getting nowhere. Unless he goes through his budget and slashes spending everywhere he can, he will never dig himself out. After cutting spending in a major way, the next thing he should do is sell the fancy entertainment system and pay off his debt. His situation is all the more shocking because of his high income.

If only he had been more careful. If he had watched his borrowing and spending, and had taken on a roommate after he left college, he would not be stuck in the hole he is in. There is also something very painful that Richard faces — explaining himself to his future fiancé. Imagine the discomfort of having to explain to a future spouse that you are carrying a heavy debt burden that they will have to bear along with you and even help pay off—all because *you* were irresponsible. It is not a happy thought. (By the way, Richard gets married and solves his problems. See if you can spot him later in the book.)

I remember seeing a gut wrenching news story on television. A girl from a family of modest means had been determined to go to an expensive Ivy League college. She piled on nearly $90,000 in debt, while graduating with a nursing degree that paid very little. She tearfully asked the television news reporter how she could find someone to share her life with; someone who would be willing to shoulder such a huge burden. Because of the news story, the college decided to forgive some of her debt. How many others are not so lucky?

In fact, many people, even those with supposedly high earning power, find themselves in bad situations. They do not wake up to their problem because they do not financially plan. They can often be seen making no progress at all until their thirties or even forties, after their dreadful position has finally sunk in.

> ***Key Takeaway:*** Financially responsible people need to have adequate insurance, including car, umbrella, medical, apartment, home or condo, disability, and long-term care. A safety reserve needs to be built up as soon as possible in case of job loss, inability to work, medical or veterinary expenses, unexpected car repairs and expenses, and catastrophic loss. It can be a big mistake to base your spending on senior people at your company. Eating out, health clubs, travel, entertainment, dry cleaning, cab hopping and other expenses can wipe out savings, even if the person makes a large salary.

10.4 Myles Green's Budget

Richard's college friend, Myles Green, is in a different situation. Myles has a similar job and income. However, Myles resisted the temptation to spend the way his friends did when they got their first job. While they enjoyed their new found "sophistication" with dining out, traveling, and joining health clubs, Myles squirreled away his money and recently purchased a condominium. Figure 10-8 depicts how Myles' budget is different from Richard's, and only shows the line items that are different. An important difference is that Myles' take-home pay is substantially larger. Since Myles has a mortgage, he is having much less withheld from his paycheck, as mortgage interest is tax deductible. Of course, he will have to pay property taxes.[5]

[5] Some banks offer to collect tax payments as part of the mortgage payment and pay the property taxes for the owner. However, they are capable of making mistakes, and they may not offer interest on the money you gave them ahead of the payment date. Some banks require this, and may charge large fees.

Figure 10-8
Myles' Budget Differences with Richard

t=	0	1	2	3	4	5	6	7	8	9	10	11	12	End of Year
Take Home Pay	6,800	6,800	6,800	6,800	6,800	6,800	6,800	6,800	6,800	6,800	6,800	6,800	6,800	88,400
Mortgage/Condo Fees	2,000	2,000	2,000	2,000	2,000	2,000	2,000	2,000	2,000	2,000	2,000	2,000	2,000	26,000
Property Taxes										7,150				7,150
Automobile														
Insurance	100	100	100	100	103	103	103	103	103	103	103	103	103	1,327
Loan	320	320	320	320	320	320	320	320	320	320	320	320	320	4,160
Personal Hygiene				100			101			101			102	404
Petty Cash	120	120	121	121	121	121	122	122	122	123	123	123	124	1,583
Clothing				600						1,000				1,600
Clubs														0
Credit Cards***														0
Dining	175	175	175	175	175	175	175	175	175	175	175	175	175	2,275
Entertainment	70	70	70	71	71	271	71	71	71	72	72	72	72	1,124
Gifts	35	35	35	155	35	35	81	36	36	121	55	36	436	1,131
Groceries/Drug Store	630	632	633	635	636	638	639	641	643	644	646	647	649	8,312
Household														
Decorating					800									800
Furnishings												1,200		1,200
Insurance														
Homeowners	40	40	40	40	40	40	40	40	40	41	41	41	41	525
Recreation	35	35	35	35	35	35	35	35	35	35	35	35	35	456
Travel/Vacation													2,200	2,200
Utilities														
Cell Phone	70	70	70	70	72	72	72	72	72	72	72	72	72	929
Landline														0
Electricity	70	70	50	50	50	50	70	70	70	50	70	70	70	810
Total Cash Outflows	4,717	4,706	4,731	5,515	5,691	5,010	5,080	5,139	4,845	13,066	4,895	6,062	7,767	77,226

Myles avoided a major utility expense by forgoing being able to search the Internet when he is out. He has a simple cell phone and he has not found it to be much of a problem. Myles also cut out his landline telephone altogether. Finally, he watches his electricity usage, turning off lights when he leaves the room, not leaving chargers running, and cutting back on air-conditioning and heating.

As can be seen in Figure 10-9, Myles is in a much better position than Richard. Despite the need to set aside money for home repairs, property taxes, and homeowner's insurance (which is more than renter's insurance), Myles is saving more in order to have a happy, comfortable retirement. He also has a surplus of $7,157 for the year. Eventually, when he has children, he will be in a better position to pay their expenses and save for their college. Myles is relaxed and confident about his future. As his salary rises he accumulates wealth and can weather any problems that come up. Over time he increases his spending on enjoyment, while Richard struggles and makes no progress.

Figure 10-9
Myles Superior Financial Performance

t=	5	6	7	8	9	10	11	12	End of Year
Total Cash Outflows	5,010	5,080	5,139	4,845	13,066	4,895	6,062	7,767	77,226
Net Cashflow	2,195	2,126	2,068	2,362	(5,857)	2,315	1,149	(555)	16,452
Saving Set Aside									
First Home									
Kid's College									
Retirement	340	340	340	340	340	340	340	340	4,420
Car Repairs	25	25	25	25	25	25	25	25	325
Home Repairs	350	350	350	350	350	350	350	350	4,550
Total	715	715	715	715	715	715	715	715	9,295
Surplus/Deficit	1,480	1,411	1,353	1,647	(6,572)	1,600	434	(1,270)	7,157

Much of the reason for Myles's success comes from the fact that he understands his finances and plans ahead. Because he keeps a budget, he knows what spending targets he has to aim for. He also understands the consequences of spending, and can make informed decisions about doing with less now in order to have more later. Myles is confident because he can see where he is headed, and happy with himself for taking charge of his life. He does not spend on things that are unimportant, only to forgo things that will really matter to him later. And as you have seen, it is not difficult to maintain a budget. Once a year (perhaps around New Year's resolution time or tax time) it takes about an hour or less to update the budget for the next year. The reward for this is control: control over your money, control over your life, control over your future.

Key Takeaway: Even though Myles' salary was comparable to Richard's, his take-home pay is significantly higher because his mortgage interest is deductible. He therefore does not have to withhold as much from his paycheck for taxes. By being more frugal, Myles now owns his own condominium and is building wealth. He is relaxed and confident. Richard is stuck in a financial rut and getting nowhere.

Challenge

Do you naturally tend to spend or save? Do you think you can stick to a budget? What kind of lifestyle do you think you will be able to have after you graduate from college?

10.5 Conclusion

The first time you set up a budget in Excel it will take a little time. However, each year it will take very little time to update it. Inattention to spending can lead to financial stagnation, or worse. With a budget, you take charge of your money. You decide where to best spend your money to promote your own happiness. You are confident in knowing where you are headed and what to expect.

Budgeting has another benefit. Financial disagreements are a major cause of marital tension, even divorce. Chances are you are not married yet. However, when that happy day comes, consider getting your spouse involved in the budgeting process. It is all too often true that one spouse is frugal while the other is not. The frugal spouse simmers with anger at the self-indulgent and reckless spending of the other. She watches with growing frustration as the other squanders their joint future without a care in the world. If you both participate in the budgeting process, you can discuss spending limits and the future rewards that come from self-control. Not only will you be relaxed about your money and your future, you will have a happier marriage, too.

Key Terms:

Bureau of Labor Statistics
Car insurance
Car registration
Copayment
CPI (Consumer Price Index)
Credit report
Disability insurance
Expense reimbursement
Homeowner's insurance
Life insurance
Long-term care insurance
Medical insurance
Renter's insurance
Safety reserve
Umbrella insurance
Withholding

End of Chapter Questions

1. Based on the following table for the CPI from the Bureau of Labor Statistics, what was the monthly inflation rate from January to February in 2009? What was the inflation rate for calendar year 2009?

U.S. Department Of Labor, Bureau of Labor Statistics
07-16-2010
Consumer Price Index, All Urban Consumers, U.S. City Average, All items

Year	Jan.	Feb.	Mar.	Apr.	May	June	July	Aug.	Sep.	Oct.	Nov.	Dec.
2008	211.080	211.693	213.528	214.823	216.632	218.815	219.964	219.086	218.783	216.573	212.425	210.228
2009	211.143	212.193	212.709	213.240	213.856	215.693	215.351	215.834	215.969	216.177	216.330	215.949

2. Assume annual inflation is 3.5% and applies to all expenses. Based on the following information, construct an annual budget with total cash inflows, total cash outflows, and net cash flow.

Item	When	Last Amount	Price Change Frequency
Take home pay	Monthly	$4,600	Same for year
Mortgage payments	Monthly	$1,400	Fixed
Property taxes	Annual in September	$3,400	Increased annually
Automobile insurance	Monthly	$90	Annual increase in April
Road service membership	Annual in August	$45	Annual
Fuel	Monthly	$85	Monthly
Automobile registration	Annual in August	$120	Annual
Automobile Maintenance	Semi-annual in May and November	$80	Semi-annual
Automobile loan	Monthly	$290	Fixed
Bank charges	Monthly	$12	Fixed
Personal hygiene	March, June, September, December	$80	Every 3 months
Petty cash	Monthly	$80	Monthly
Charity	Annual in December	$150	Annual
Clothing	Semi-annual, March and September	$400	Every 6 months
Dining	Monthly	$85	Monthly

Continued

Item	When	Last Amount	Price Change Frequency
Electronics	Monthly	$10	Monthly
Entertainment	Monthly	$120	Monthly
Gifts	Monthly	$30	Monthly
Groceries/drug store	Monthly	$700	Monthly
Household decorating	Annual in February	$500	Annual
Dry cleaning	Monthly	$25	Monthly
Home furnishings	Annual in February	$600	Annual
Life insurance	Monthly	$20	Fixed
Homeowner's insurance	Monthly	$40	Annual increase in June
Umbrella insurance	Monthly	$35	Annual increase in March
Disability insurance	Monthly	$32	Annual increase in July
Long-term care insurance	Monthly	$14	Fixed
Doctor's appointment copayment	February and September	$15	Fixed
Medicine	Monthly	$10	Fixed
Miscellaneous	Monthly	$95	Monthly
Recreation	Monthly	$30	Monthly
Travel	Annual in July	$800	Annual
Cable	Monthly	$42	Fixed for year
Internet	Monthly	$44	Fixed for year
Cell phone	Monthly	$48	Annual increase in July
Electricity	Monthly	$80	Monthly
Gas	Monthly	$35	Monthly

3. Why is budgeting using spreadsheets so helpful? What is the benefit of short-term budgeting?

4. Why is owning an automobile so expensive?

5. Why is borrowing to consume so damaging to wealth?

6. What insurance payments will a financially responsible person expect to pay?

7. What kinds of medical payments can a person with medical insurance expect to pay?

8. At a minimum, how much of your salary should be set aside in case of job loss?

9. What kinds of emergencies should money be set aside for?

10. If Myles' salary was similar to Richard's, then why was Myles' take home pay so much more?

11. What additional expenses are associated with home or condo ownership?

12. As an exercise, look up the typical starting salary of a career you may consider. You can try: http://swz.salary.com/salarywizard/layouthtmls/swzl_salaryrangenarrow_10.html. Take Richard Wilson's budget and modify it, based on that starting salary. How much credit card debt do you think you will have when you graduate, and what will your payments be?

Chapter 11
Retirement

Enthusiasm, optimism, and adventurousness are common characteristics of youth. Preparing for old age is the last thing that comes to mind. Still, when you are with elderly people (your grandparents, for example), it is important to be especially considerate. They may be frail, or battling health problems or a number of other difficulties that come with age. And one day you, too, will be old. Imagine being confronted with an elderly version of yourself. How will the conversation go? Will your elderly self tell you that you should be proud, or that you let him or her down to face terrible suffering? Will you watch your elderly self hold up the checkout line at the grocery store for ten minutes arguing over a 10¢ coupon, or will you visit the beautiful boat that your elderly self intends to sail around the world? Just as you are kind to the elderly, be kind to your elderly self. The seeds of happiness in old age are planted in youth. And the good news is that it does not take a lot to make sure your far-off future is a golden one. As you start in life, keep that elderly person in mind. Some day you will look back with a smile of gratitude and thank yourself.

You may also wish to set ambitious goals for retirement. We all have to work hard during our lifetimes, either for a paycheck or as a homemaker. It is at retirement that you will finally have plenty of time to devote as you wish. Retirement can be filled with travel, entertainment, a special hobby or pursuit, philanthropy, or any number of possibilities limited only by the imagination. But these things require a strong commitment to taking the financial steps necessary to make them happen.

An important caveat needs to be emphasized before you start. Your retirement is likely many years away. Tax codes, laws governing retirement plans, your healthcare benefits, and a variety of other factors relevant to retirement can very easily change before the time comes for you to retire. The only thing predictable about government policy is that it is unpredictable. Keep this in mind.

Wisdom from the Ages

There are people alive today who did amazing things. Their stories are there for you to find. When you are out and about and see a senior citizen, imagine what they could tell you. Maybe they:

Stormed the beaches at Normandy.
Walked with Martin Luther King Jr.
Liberated Paris.
Were marched out as an American soldier on Enewetak Atoll to watch a hydrogen bomb go off.[1]
Were part of the team at NASA that landed the first men on the moon.

Not long ago, a friend of mine handed me a ceramic angel (she said she had two), given to her by Dorothy. She wanted me to have one. I always felt that my angel was very special and I kept it on my desk. One day I decided to ask about Dorothy, and was fortunate enough to be able to speak with her. Dorothy is a happy, optimistic, kind person; always ready to help others. Just by looking at her, you may never know that she took on the Nazis as a child and won.

Dorothy Greenstein

When Germany invaded Poland, blue eyed, blonde, pigtailed Dorothy was not quite nine years old. She had eight siblings (one had died while young), and three of her sisters and two brothers still lived with her and her parents. Dorothy's father was a veterinarian, judge — and a rabbi. Dorothy's family was Jewish.

Eventually the Jews were rounded up and put in a ghetto in Otwock. Brave, clever, polish-looking Dorothy would sneak through a hole in a wall to bring back supplies from outside the ghetto to keep her family alive. She was lucky not to be detected. Finally the Nazis decided to "resettle" the Jews and Dorothy and her sisters were told by her father to escape.

Dorothy was occasionally helped by sympathetic Poles. However, she was most often completely alone and without money, and had to rely on her own wits to stay alive. Many days she went without food. She managed to get a false identity by finding the grave site of a child who had died, and with identity papers in hand, she would answer want ads so that she could feed herself. She once had to flee when an employer asked her if she was Jewish. At times she hid in the woods or farm fields from soldiers or Nazi sympathizers with their guard dogs. This struggle went on through her 14th year.

After Poland was liberated by the Russians Dorothy cleverly found a way to contact a married sister and they eventually ended up in an American camp for displaced persons in Germany. There she learned the six languages she speaks and the piano. Dorothy and four siblings survived the Holocaust. He parents and brother had been taken to Treblinka.

What is most remarkable about Dorothy is that she did not let her experiences make her bitter or angry. She told me "I believe in angels." To this day she thinks that angels come to her aid in times of trouble.

When you see a senior, they may just be another Dorothy. And keep a lookout for one of her angels.

[1] Just as my father was.

11.1 Retirement in America

It is difficult to imagine, but about a quarter of your life will likely be spent in retirement. It is not something that most people like to dwell on. About of third of those heading into their golden years would rather clean the bathroom than financially plan for old age.[2] But consider this: Planning ahead can make the difference between buying a dream beach house in Hawaii or touring the world in search of ancient ruins, and wearing the same hole filled socks day in and day out or taking the bus everywhere.

Some people seem to be naturals at building a happy retirement. Most Americans, unfortunately, are not. Nearly half of those over the age of 55 have just $50,000 in retirement savings.[3] Shockingly, about a third of workers have saved nothing at all. Those numbers become all the more sobering when you consider the changing landscape of retirement benefits. Increasingly, many of us will have to rely on a larger portion of our own savings to secure our retirement. The average monthly Social Security payout, for example, is just $1,153.50, enough to live a starvation existence.

What is the good news in this otherwise dreary state of retirement in America? Youth and time. When you are young you have plenty of time to save and plan what kind of retirement you want - both financially and personally. You can wind up with plenty of money to play with. Maybe you want to backpack in the Bernese Alps in Switzerland or bask poolside in Cabo, San Lucas. Chances are that you are hardworking and ambitious. Why not be ambitious about how you will cap a life of achievement? To do so, you have to start early.

Yucatan Breezes

The eastern Mexico city of Mérida had a lot of competition when Ron and Sylvia were looking for the perfect place to retire: Ron, after all, visited more than 70 countries around the world in his travels as head of a resort properties company. But in 2004, he and his wife, Sylvia, picked Merida, just west of the famed resort town of Cancun.

The pair, who are in their sixties, bought a 200-year-old hacienda and spent a year having the home renovated. And in Mexico, the retirement savings Ron and Sylvia put away offer them the luxury of a maid, a cook, and a gardener - and the time to bask in Yucatan's warm sunshine, to explore the region's fascinating Mayan ruins - including the magnificent pyramids of Chichen Itza, and to enjoy Merida's Spanish-influenced gardens and architecture.

"You could think you're in a European city,"[4] says Ron, whose neighbors include Americans who can afford a part-time getaway home. "We quite enjoy it."[5]

---

[2] According to a study from insurance giant Aetna Inc. and the Financial Planning Association.

[3] According to the Employee Benefit Research Institution. See "Tough Problem: What To Do With a $1.7 Million Nest Egg," Kelly Barron, *Los Angeles Times*, March 18, 2008.

[4] Randy Myers, "Great places for a rich retirement," Corporate Board Member, May-June 2008, http://www.boardmember.com/MagazineArticle.

[5] Myers, Corporate Board Member, May-June 2008, http://www.boardmember.com/MagazineArticle. Ellen Florian Kratz, "Paradise found: Where to retire abroad," Fortune, July 11, 2005. Merida attractions, http://travelyucatan.com.

There are two reasons why you will need to consider retirement when you are young, instead of putting it off until far in the future as something hypothetical. First, it is essential to start saving for retirement in the most advantageous way possible as soon as you begin to earn income. I will walk you through how to do that. Second, when you graduate from college and start receiving job offers, retirement benefits can make a huge difference in identifying the best one. If one company offers you a big paycheck and meager retirement benefits, another offer that pays less but has better benefits just may be the smarter deal for you. (New, uninformed workers often make the mistake of taking the worse offer with the higher salary.) Retirement is something that you must commit to while young. People who have wonderful retirements have one thing in common — they worked at it from the very beginning. If you can muster the will to look far into the future and make plans, you can truly accomplish the remarkable. Whatever your dreams are for retirement, this textbook will provide a road map for how to get there. Every journey has a beginning. Yours will begin auspiciously while you are young.

11.2 Retirement Income and Expenses

A simple rule that people often use is that ten percent or more of income should always be invested towards retirement. Ideally this number should be 15, or even 20%. However, with the forecasting skills that you are about to acquire, you can plan more exactly.

A common goal that people have for retirement is to maintain the same standard of living in retirement that they had immediately before retirement. A well known rule to do this is to have 80% of the income in retirement that you had before retirement. This level may seem surprising, but it turns out that when you retire, your overall expenses can be expected to go down. So before I discuss income, it is necessary to take a look at how some expenses go up in retirement while many others go down. Table A11-1 in the appendix provides a summary.

Unfortunately, taxes cannot be ignored, and they are very important in retirement. (Yes, taxes are a recurring nightmare.) If you are taking income from a retirement account that you accumulated tax-free, then you will probably have to pay income taxes on any money that you withdraw when you retire, including principal. (Of course, future tax laws can be hard to predict.) On the other hand, if you are living off personal investment income, you will only have to pay taxes on capital gains or losses, interest, and dividends—not the principal you withdraw. Currently taxes on capital gains and dividends are lower than income taxes. (Recall that interest is taxed at the income tax rate. I will discuss retirement plans and their tax implications below.) You may also be in a lower income tax bracket when you retire, which will lower your average taxes paid due to progressive tax rates. Some of your Social Security benefits may not be subject to income taxes.[6]

Healthcare expenses are another important factor in retirement. Most likely you now enjoy the good health of youth, but you can expect higher medical bills when you get older. It is important to realize that at the moment healthcare is in a state of political flux, and costs could change substantially. As discussed in the tax chapter, the government currently provides Medicare Part A, which covers hospital expenses. However, you will need to purchase Medicare Part B and any supplemental plans to fill in gaps in coverage, including the cost of prescription medicine.

---

[6] According to the Social Security Administration, if you file a federal tax return as an individual and your combined income is between $25,000 and $34,000, you may have to pay taxes on 50% of your Social Security benefits. If your combined income is more than $34,000, up to 85% of your Social Security benefits are subject to income tax. If you file a joint return, you may have to pay taxes on 50% of your benefits if you and your spouse have a combined income of between $32,000 and $44,000. If your combined income is more than $44,000, up to 85% of your Social Security benefits are subject to income tax. If you are married and file a separate return, you probably will pay taxes on your benefits.

Another important expense is long-term care, possibly in a nursing home. Not all elderly people need this, but there are many who do. (I will discuss healthcare in retirement, including insurance for long-term care, in Volume 2.)

Paying off the mortgage on your home before retirement will mean substantial savings, although you will still have to pay property taxes, insurance premiums, and repairs and upkeep expenses. On the other hand, you will no longer need to save for retirement, and may choose not to make life insurance payments. If you have stopped working, commuting and clothing expenses will go down. Many retirees save money by moving to less expensive areas of the country: Florida and Arizona are filled with retirees. On the other hand, if you want to spend all of your leisure time traveling or enjoying entertainment and recreation, your expenses will be higher. If you would like to leave an estate to your heirs or help pay for your grandchildren's college, you will need more. Overall, if you have paid off your home and have adequate long-term care insurance you can expect the income that you will need to maintain a comparable lifestyle to go down.

Key Takeaway: Many expenses will go down in retirement while some will go up. Generally people see their taxes go down in retirement because they no longer work, and taxes on the money they withdraw from investments will generally be less (except for interest). Hopefully their home is paid off, and retirees do not have to worry about saving, or making contributions to life insurance. They also do not have commuting and other work related costs. Healthcare expenses typically go up. A rough rule is that 15%-20% of income should be set aside for retirement, and retirement income should be 80% of pre-retirement income to maintain a steady standard of living.

Judy and Steve Haibach

They were simple souls, high school sweethearts married for 35 years. Fit and active, they took loving care of their sparkling-clean home. Silver-streaked Steve worked as a technician for Southern California Gas Co. and Judy, bright and young-looking for her age, worked as a nurse. They never expected to become millionaires in their fifties. But after years of saving, the pair squirreled away nearly $2 million for their retirement.

How could a gas company technician and nurse become multimillionaires? They saved. The pair pinched pennies by eating bagged lunches. They took simple vacations, camping with their kids and friends at state parks, and enjoying each other's company and the beauty of the outdoors in a way that a ritzy vacation package could never match. Steve had served in Vietnam as an aircraft mechanic, and put that practical training and self-reliance to work repairing the couple's one car and home, and putting in his own landscaping. Along the way, they invested their money wisely. Now, the Haibachs are poised to retire early and fulfill their dreams. Steve would like to buy a Lexus hybrid. Judy wants to travel. They would also like to spend some of their free time volunteering to help others.[7]

[7] Barron, Los Angeles Times, March 18, 2008.

The question isn't at what age I want to retire, it's at what income. ~ George Foreman[8]

A big part of planning for retirement involves insuring that you have adequate resources to live on. The thought of running out of money in old age is a scary one indeed. Fortunately there are a number of ways to create income for a prosperous retirement. Creativity and careful planning are needed to tap into these sources and use them to their fullest advantage. Figure 11-1 illustrates where most income in retirement comes from. You shall now consider each in turn.

Figure 11-1
Retirement Income Sources

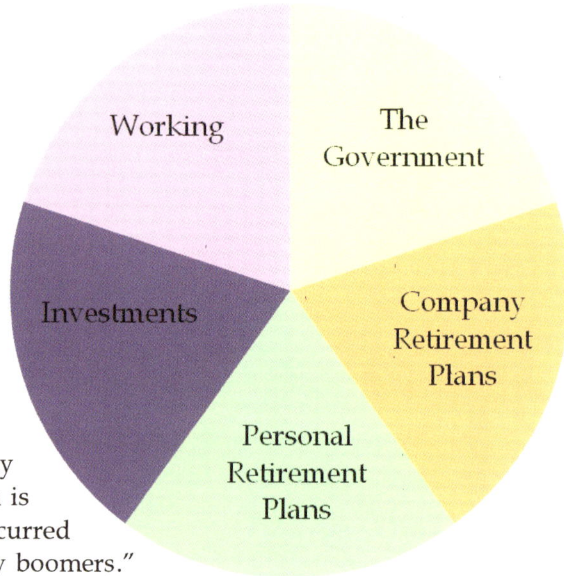

11.3 The Government

The main source of retirement income from the government is Social Security. (Social Security also provides disability insurance and Medicare, which I shall discuss in Volume 2.) Social Security is a "pay as you go" system, where taxes taken from current workers go to pay the retirement benefits of current retirees. (A summary of benefits from the Social Security Administration is in the Appendix.) Unfortunately, a big wrench is being thrown into that system. A large population boom that occurred after World War II produced the generation known as the "baby boomers." Since then, birth rates have gone down. All of these baby boomers are now heading for retirement and there currently are not nearly as many workers to support a retiree as there used to be because there are not nearly as many children born from these retirees. People are also living longer in retirement. In 1960 there were five workers for each Social Security beneficiary. The Social Security Administration expects that by the middle of this century, there will only be two workers for each Social Security beneficiary. This means that our youth, including you, will carry a heavy tax burden to support retirees, complete with large intergenerational transfers of wealth from young to old. Some even call Social Security a "Ponzi scheme."[9]

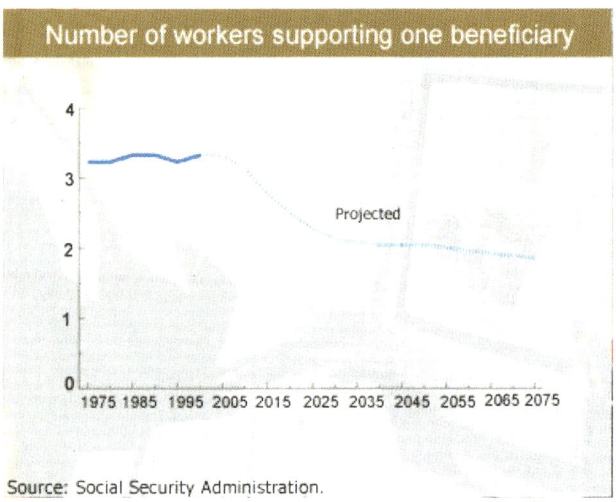

Money from Social Security taxes was spent, rather than invested, by the government. Research suggests that each dollar contributed to Social Security will yield 71¢ in present value terms.[10] This is quite a financial loss. And this issue is commonly referred to as the "third rail" of American politics - if you touch it, you are "dead" politically.[11]

[8] Quote Garden.
[9] As an example of a Ponzi scheme, imagine someone who sold debt. They get money from selling the debt and pocket most of it. When they have to pay interest on the debt, they sell more debt and use the proceeds to pay the interest. Since the amount of interest that they have to pay keeps rising, they have to keep selling more and more debt. Eventually the whole thing falls apart. The problem is that money from new investors is being used to pay the principal and profits of old investors.
[10] O. Mitchell and S. Zeldes, "Social Security Money's Worth," in *Prospects for Social Security Reform*, ed. O. Mitchell, R. Myers and H. Young (Philadelphia: Pension Research Council, The Wharton School, University of Pennsylvania Press, 1999), 79-151.

Eventually something will have to give. Social Security and Medicare are insolvent and will default if something is not done. It is important to be cautious when receiving projections of future Social Security benefits because they may be cut back, possibly drastically, or offset by taxes before or during retirement. Upset yet?

To be eligible for Social Security payments you will need forty quarters of credit. Most graduates of a good college earning a solid income can achieve this standing on their head.[12] The maximum income subject to Social Security in 2009 was $106,800 (the Medicare component of F.I.C.A. does not have a maximum income). If you earn more than this, you will notice that your take-home pay will suddenly bump up at a certain point during the year because Social Security retirement taxes are no longer being withheld. This is a good time to stash a little extra away in a retirement account.

There are maximum benefits you can collect in retirement no matter how much you contributed. In 2009 this was $2,323 per month - by itself, a pittance to live on. Unfortunately for retirees, "the Social Security Administration says that about a third depend on Social Security for more than 90 percent of their income; another third get half to 90 percent of their money from the program; and a third rely on it for less than half."[13,14]

> ***Key Takeaway:*** You will be taxed for Social Security on income up to a maximum limit each year. Your payments in retirement from Social Security will be small, and they should not be relied upon because expected Social Security tax collections cannot cover expected payments.

11.4 Employer Retirement Plans

Employer retirement plans are where most of the action is. They are typically qualified under the law for special tax status and are known as "qualified plans." (If employees are unionized, the union may be in charge of the pension plan rather than the employer.) These plans are usually a highly advantageous way to save for retirement. The federal government uses these plans to encourage saving for retirement, and allows for tax benefits to businesses that provide the plans, usually in the form of tax deductions. Individuals contributing to the plan also receive strong tax advantages.

There are numerous rules that the government puts in place to see that the plans are used as intended. For instance, there are restrictions on early withdrawal before retirement. Also, there are often rules requiring that funds be withdrawn after a certain age; this is to prevent people from using the fund as a way to leave money to heirs in a tax-advantaged way instead of to fund retirement. There can also be rules requiring that plans be widely available to employees, so that they are not used primarily as a tax-advantaged method to compensate top executives in a company. Retirement plan rules can be very complex. Business owners often regard these rules as a contorted horror story, and resort to hiring outside consultants (which can be quite expensive) to manage their plans for them.

---

[11] People walking along the rails of electric trains will sometimes accidentally electrocute themselves because they do not realize that the third rail has current running through it.

[12] Over the course of a year, a quarter of credit in 2009 is earned if you made a little over $1,000,[12] updated for inflation each year. You can earn a maximum of four quarters of credit in a year.

[13] Robin Toner and Marjorie Connelly, "Poll Finds Broad Pessimism on Social Security Payments," *The New York Times*, June 19, 2005.

[14] If you qualify for benefits, you can find out what your estimated benefits are by visiting the Social Security Website at: http://www.socialsecurity.gov/estimator/. You can also expect to receive a statement from the Social Security Administration once a year that lists your Social Security income, and expected future benefits.

Typically individuals can contribute pretax dollars to qualified plans (except for FICA), and their money grows without taxes on capital gains, dividends, and interest. When the money is finally withdrawn, those withdrawals are taxed as income. As you shall see in a later chapter, this is a small price to pay to invest money pretax and have it grow without tax. The benefit is enormous. There are strict rules under the Employee Retirement Income Security Act (ERISA) and the Tax Reform Act (TRA) about which plans qualify, and what the funding requirements are for employers. If you end up in personal bankruptcy, retirement money is generally not accessible to creditors.

Recovering from O.J.

O.J. Simpson may have been acquitted of murder at his criminal trial in the deaths of Nicole Brown Simpson and Ron Goldman, but a wrongful-death judgment in a 1997 civil suit ordered him to pay millions in damages to Goldman's family.

Twelve years after the slayings Simpson was living large, boating on Florida's beautiful waterways, and dining at the finest restaurants. He could enjoy his luxurious home because in Florida typically, homes cannot be seized by unsecured creditors. His outsized NFL pension, a whopping $300,000 a year, was also off limits. O.J. enjoyed the sunshine while the Goldmans struggled to collect.

However, the story did not end there. O.J. was eventually arrested and found guilty of kidnapping and assaulting a sports memorabilia dealer with a deadly weapon in a Nevada hotel room and sent to prison.[15]

You may need to work for your employer for a while before you can participate in a plan (become eligible), and not all plans are available to all employees. It is also important to consider the issue of vesting, which means that you qualify for payouts from the plan. In other words, when your retirement plan vests, you now have rights to payouts from the plan, although these payments may not occur for a long time. If you leave before vesting, you lose the benefit of your payments made to the plan. There are different rules for vesting that depend on the plan.[16]

This is why it is so important to understand retirement benefits right from the start. After you graduate from college and get a job offer, the issue of vesting is critical. These days people frequently switch jobs (or lose them). You can expect this to be especially true if you are new to the workforce. It can take awhile to discover where you want to be in your career, both in terms of what company you work at, and what profession you pursue. Imagine taking job after job where you contribute faithfully to retirement, but leave before your benefits vest. You are paying a fortune and getting nothing! This is why vesting can lock you in a kind of retirement jail. Losing money contributed towards retirement can be an impediment to taking a better position at a different company. From an employer's perspective, it is a useful way to keep employees from leaving.

Key Takeaway: Employer retirement plans are a major source of income for retirees. This is not surprising since they have highly valuable tax advantages for saving. When you initially start a job, you may not be eligible to participate in a retirement plan. Vesting is also an important consideration. Switching jobs can cause the repeated loss of retirement contributions, while concerns about losing unvested benefits can lock a person into a job.

---

[15] Sonya Geis, "Goldman Seeking to Squeeze O.J.," *The Washington Post*, Sept. 10, 2006. Stephanie Green, "Teary Simpson Sentenced to Prison for Role in Robbery," *The Washington Times*, Dec. 6, 2008.

[16] You may qualify for full vesting after five years at the same company, you may gain 20% vesting each year after three years of service (with full vesting in seven years). If you are in a "top heavy" plan, which has a large proportion of top earners, vesting occurs after three years, or 20% vesting begins after two years. For other kinds of plans, immediate, full vesting may occur.

11.4.1 Defined Benefit Plans

There are two broad categories of retirement plans: defined contribution plans and defined benefit plans. In a defined benefit plan, the plan document specifies the benefit amount. As you work, your employer makes contributions to the plan and they are not taxable to you. You do not get involved in the process—just sit back and let the employer worry about it. At retirement, the payments that you receive from your employer are considered income for tax purposes.[17] Before retirement it may be possible to borrow from the plan, but as I discuss in a later chapter, this is generally a very bad idea.[18]

Your employer sets the formula for benefits. Benefits may be a flat amount received by all employees, a percentage of their salary, or based on a combination of salary and length of service. Defined benefit plans often reward longer periods of service (and penalize shorter terms of service), so that it is costly to switch jobs. Unlike with vesting, it is older, long-term employees who can get locked in. Their many years of service allow them to accrue high benefits according to their employer's formula, which they will lose if they start over somewhere else.

It is also important to take the financial pulse of the company. If the company suffers financial heart failure, the Pension Benefit Guarantee Corp. (PBGC)[19] may have to step in to make the employee pension payments. However, employees can expect to receive pennies on the dollar, even as low as 60¢ for each dollar of pension owed.[20] If a company is not making enough contributions to a pension plan (think of it as a savings account for employees) to cover future payouts that the company has committed to (the plan is not "fully funded"), this can be a sign of trouble.

If a company cancels a plan (called a "pension reversion") it is only required to provide the employee with up to the amount that the plan was funded, which can create a shortfall for the employee if the employer was irresponsible about contributing enough. In fact, underfunded plans are a ripe target for pension reversions.

The issue of pensions can also play a role in a company's decisions to terminate employees. If there is an increasing scale in pension benefits as an employee gets older, the company may be tempted to lay off older workers to avoid the pension expense. This can also be a problem after a corporate takeover, when the new acquirer may not feel the same loyalty to older employees that the previous owner did. The idea behind accelerating compensation with years employed (including retirement benefits) is to bind workers to the company. However, this arrangement can also make older workers targets during layoffs.[21] Imagine the feeling of betrayal: after working for a company loyally for years while building up benefits from an initial low level, you are targeted for a layoff when you are older and less able to find another job. Unfortunately, these kinds of episodes happen all the time.

[17] After your retirement, employers are generally required to make regular payments to you rather than paying out a lump sum, unless you (and your spouse) sign a waiver.

[18] Employees can borrow restricted amounts from these plans, which they must pay back into the plan with interest. The interest is not deductable, and borrowing from these plans has the unfortunate aspect of spending before-tax dollars and replacing the balance with after-tax dollars. In general, it is a bad idea to borrow from retirement accounts. One exception might be using the balance for the down payment on a house, in which case there are tax-deductable interest payments on the mortgage. However, remember that the loan needs to be paid back with after-tax dollars, and there are serious penalties for failure to repay.

[19] The PBGC is a federal corporation created under ERISA; taxpayers can be on the hook for a failed pension plan.

[20] Another important consideration is how the benefits of the plan will be paid out at retirement. There can be significant differences.

[21] There is an active debate about whether these practices are justified and just part of the way things are done, or whether there has been a "breach of trust."

Now that you have received some finance training, you can show off your savvy when bargaining over a job offer. A host of questions need to be asked about a defined benefit plan. When will you become eligible? When will you become vested? What happens if you are laid off or leave voluntarily? Can you retire early or late? What is the formula used for accruing benefits; what role does years of service play? Is the plan fully funded and is the company experiencing or anticipating any problems covering its obligations? Do not be shy. Go ahead when you are at the "brass tacks" stage of negotiating your compensation with a potential new employer and ask respectfully.[22]

Al and Bonnie

Al was really sweating it. It was Labor Day in Cape Girardeau, Missouri, but it wasn't the weather that was making him perspire. Bonnie, the dark-haired beauty that was the girl of his dreams was in the parade, and she was a sight to see. He later confided, "I thought I was going to lose her that day."

It turns out that Al did manage to hang onto her, and they spent many happily married years raising their two sons. In 1990 Al was 56 and heading into the homestretch at his job. His golden years with Bonnie loomed ahead. That's when the trouble started. His employer began to humiliate him in the hopes that he would quit. (If they fired him their tax contributions to unemployment insurance would go up.) When that didn't work the hammer finally fell and he was fired.

After long years of service he received a scant $50,000, barely enough to live off for a couple of years, and a pittance of $200 a month. The prosperous retirement that he had worked so hard for from his employer's defined benefit plan was snatched from his grasp. Al worked at temporary jobs and eventually got a regular job at much lower pay. Retirement now meant hard work. At least he still had his Bonnie.[23]

Key Takeaway: With a defined benefit plan, the company does the saving for the employee's retirement. It uses a formula to decide how much it will contribute to each employee's retirement, which may depend on years of service. If so, longtime employees tend to get locked in to the company, or they can become the targets of layoffs. Underfunded pension plans can be subject to reversions, and are also a sign of company trouble. If a company fails and the pension plan is not fully funded, the PBGC may have to step in, but will pay retirees pennies on the dollar.

Challenge

Do you know anyone whose family was hurt by trouble with a defined benefit plan?

---

[22] You can look up the bond rating for companies with public bonds at http://cxa.marketwatch.com/finra/BondCenter/Default.aspx. Click on "corporate" an include the company's ticker symbol, which can be found from the company or on the Internet. Bond ratings tell you how save a company is from defaulting. For an explanation of ratings, go to the rating company's website. An alternative is to look up the company with Dunn and Bradstreet. A small fee may be necessary.

[23] Relatives of the author.

11.4.2 Defined Contribution Plans

With a defined contribution plan there is no more sitting back. You are in the driver's seat. Contributions typically are based on a percent of your income,[24] and may be paid by your employer, you, or both. Your employer may limit the kinds of investments that you can make with the money (because they are required to ensure that you act prudently), but that is it. You own the plan, and your employer cannot touch it. You can move your money around from one investment to another (those allowed by your employer), and you decide where to put the money at retirement.

Of course, because you own the account, it is not guaranteed by the PBGC. You account will rise or fall with contributions, investment gains or losses, expenses and fees, and forfeitures. (Forfeitures will be explained in a minute.) It is the contribution that is defined, not the ultimate payout.

It is time to hone your investing prowess. (I will discuss investing in Volume 2.) How you invest can have a huge impact on what you end up with. However, moderation is the key. Your retirement savings should not be used in get rich schemes. (See the Enron story box below.) With a few exceptions, employee contributions are pretax except for FICA. Withdrawals at retirement are subject to income tax. As you may imagine after seeing what happened to Al and Bonnie, these plans are becoming the most widely used and are very popular.

401(k) and 403(b) Plans

A popular type of plan is called a 401(k) plan. You may have even heard people discussing their "401k." A similar plan, called a 403(b), is available for employees of nonprofits. Employees make contributions to the plan based on a percentage of income. Employers are also responsible under ERISA for restricting investment options so that plan participants make prudent choices, and can be held liable if they do not.[25] It is common for employers to make matching contributions, and some even make double matching contributions, up to the total limit allowed.[26] For instance, suppose an employee makes the maximum contribution they are allowed of 5%. With matching, the company also contributes 5%, so that contributions total 10%. With double matching, they make a 10% contribution, so that total contributions are 15%.

If your employer matches your contribution, you should always try to make the maximum contribution. If you do not, you are turning down a sizeable chunk of money that is being handed to you outright. This would be true even if you feel that you are in an inhospitable investing environment. For instance, suppose that your employer matched your contributions. You would have to believe that your investments are going to fall by more than 50% before you would take a loss on your contribution when combined with your employer's. Note that you will also have forfeitures contributed to your account. These are employer matching contributions forfeited by employees who left the company before their contributions were fully vested. Employee contributions vest immediately, but employer contributions may not.[27]

[24] The exception is money purchase plans.
[25] In a 404(c) plan the employee is considered to be independently making investment decisions, and plan officials are not liable.
[26] In 2009, the maximum employee contribution was $16,500. If you are 50 or older, your employer may let you make "catch up" contributions (which were limited to $5,500 in 2009). The limits are increased each year.
[27] They are subject to the same minimum vesting rules as top-heavy plans.

Profit Sharing Plans

A number of companies have profit sharing plans. The company decides each year how much of its profit will be distributed to the employee retirement plan. A formula is then used to distribute the profit among employees. The formula may place emphasis on older employees. The amount in an employee's account is equal to contributions, plus (possibly) forfeitures, plus investment gains and losses.[28]

ESOPs

In an employee stock ownership plan, or ESOP (pronounced "E-sop"), the company arranges for shares of stock to be contributed to the employee plan.[29] (Employee stock option plans are used more for short to medium-term compensation and I put off a discussion of them until Volume 2.) Allocations of shares among employees are based on a formula. When employees leave the company, they receive their shares that have vested.[30]

ESOPs present unique risks. It is painful enough to have a company go under and lose your job. Imagine also losing your retirement savings because the stock has become worthless. All of your eggs are in one basket - and that basket can get run over by a bus. This makes ESOPs much less desirable as a retirement plan.[31]

There are a number of other defined contribution plans, which I will not go over in detail. Some plans are intended to be simpler and less expensive for employers to manage than typical plans. Table A11-2 in the Appendix contains a summary of most plans. Some of these plans contain IRAs, which I will discuss next. Table 11-2 below summarizes important considerations for employer plans.

> ***Key Takeaway:*** 401(k) and 403(b) plans are owned by the employee. Employers restrict what investments are available to "prudent" ones, and may match contributions by employees. If the employer makes matching contributions, it is extremely important for the employee to contribute as much as possible. Employees need to invest wisely to keep their retirement savings in these plans intact. With ESOPs, the employer contributes company stock for the employee's retirement. These plans are problematic: if the company goes under, employees could lose their jobs and retirement savings at the same time.

---

[28] The employer decides what investments will be available for the account. A profit sharing plan may include a 401(k) plan. The employer must make regular, substantial contributions for a profit sharing plan to remain in effect.

[29] These can be offered by public or private corporations, but generally not partnerships or professional corporations. There are several ways that this can be done. The company can contribute new shares of stock or use its cash to buy existing shares for the ESOP. An alternative method is for the ESOP to borrow money to buy shares on behalf of employees. The company must then make cash contributions over time to the ESOP to pay off the principal and interest on the loan.

[30] If the company is private, the company must buy back the shares. It must get the shares valued each year for ESOP purposes by an appraiser. If the company is public the employee can sell the shares in the stock market.

[31] It is important to realize that ESOPs have a variety of uses for companies. Common uses of ESOPs are to provide a broader market for the shares of owners of closely held companies who want to cash out and sell their shares, to motivate employees, and to take advantage of being able to borrow money for acquiring shares using pretax dollars. Other uses include using an ESOP as a defense against a hostile takeover by another company, as a way for employees to buy out a failing company from an owner in order to preserve their jobs, and as compensation for accepting concessions in union negotiations. Employees can vote their shares in public corporations, and have some voting rights in private ones.

Table 11-2
Summary of Important Considerations for Employer Retirement Plans

Consideration	Impact
All Employer Plans	
Tax advantages	Very helpful
Restrictions on early withdrawal	Not helpful
Forced regular withdrawals upon retirement	Not helpful
Contributions may go up with time of service	Could go either way
Defined Benefit Only	
Employer may become bankrupt	Devastating
Pension reversions.	Very costly to devastating
Delay before vesting.	Not helpful
Defined Contribution Only	
Immediate vesting.	Helpful
Employer contributions may not vest immediately and could be stock	Not helpful
Retirement savings can be lost at the same time as a job with an ESOP	Devastating

11.5 Personal Tax-Advantaged Retirement Plans

There are life insurance plans that include an important retirement investment component. I will put off discussing these until I cover insurance in Volume 2. However, there are other kinds of personal tax-advantaged retirement accounts as well. These are known as Individual Retirement Accounts, or IRAs. There are also Keogh plans (pronounced "KEY-oh") for self-employed people. I shall start with IRAs.

IRAs

There is a good chance you have heard people discussing their IRAs. There are even TV commercials about them. One way to invest in an IRA is by purchasing an annuity with an insurance company.[32] Otherwise, you can choose where you wish to invest your IRA. You can invest with a bank or other qualified company that will give you investment options to chose from.[33]

There are two types of IRAs: a traditional IRA, and a Roth IRA. A traditional IRA allows you to invest pretax dollars into a retirement account where the money grows without tax. The money is subject to income tax when withdrawn. Traditional IRAs have a penalty for individuals who make early withdrawals, and require withdrawals to begin by a certain age (more on this later).[34]

[32] In this case, regular withdrawals (the annuity) must begin by age 70½.
[33] However, the trustees of the account are required to prevent the saver from making highly risky investments.
[34] By age 70½.

Enron

During the 1990s Enron was an energy trading powerhouse. It's shiny new skyscraper – a monument to Enron's prowess - was almost completed. Money seemed to flow from the water fountains. According to one former employee, "On bonus day, a whole bunch of car dealers parked their most expensive cars outside the building there. I'm talking Jaguars, Mercedes, Lexus. And I guarantee you that they sold a lot of them."[35]

Enron had an ESOP for its employees, but that was not all: it also had a 401(k) plan, and the company would match employee contributions with Enron stock. Of course, the employee could not sell the stock until age 50. Apparently, people also have a tendency to follow the lead of their employers when it comes to their retirement investing. If employers invest their retirement money in the company stock, employees will, too. Enron employees certainly did, and they were also striking it rich, which only added to the stock buying frenzy. By one estimate, Enron's 401(k) plan earned 326% over three years.[36]

It seemed too good to be true, and it was. Enron's results were based on phony accounting schemes and the energy giant collapsed into bankruptcy. Its stock became worthless. Employees under age 50 were unable to sell the stock as the crisis unfolded, and Enron even temporarily froze the 401(k) plan, locking all employees into the stock. Well, not all employees: it turned out that top executives had been selling their stock all along, even though they were supposedly restricted from doing so.

Not only did Enron employees lose their jobs, many had their retirement savings wiped out; by over 300,000, 900,000, even more than a million.[37] The combination was devastating. Former Enron employee Kenneth Parrish saw his retirement savings fall from $200,000 to a couple of thousand dollars: "This ruined me," he said. He had to sell his house and move into a trailer with his two teenage daughters.[38]

Enron announced that it did not have money to take care of the building's potted plants and said employees could take them. A mob of reporters held vigil outside the building, hoping to get a story from a plant-toting employee. One wretched victim shouted, "I just want whatever's left that I can get!" Another victim got sweet satisfaction from selling his Enron training manual on EBay. It brought in a hefty $1,025.[39] Like travel like brochures for the Titanic or pieces of the Hindenburg dirigible, which went down in flames, Enron memorabilia became a hot item.

Years later, The Washington Post ran a story on forgiveness, using Enron employees as a subject. Kenneth Lay, chairman of the board of Enron, had died before he could be sentenced to jail, robbing some of their revenge. "He got off easy by dying," Lois Black told the Post. "You are gone, boom! You die and you are out of here. Of course, who knows what is on the other side?"[40]

---

[35] Brian Hutchinson, "New Tower a Monument to Enron's Avarice: In Houston, Everyone Hates the Energy Trader," *National Post* (Canada), Jan. 19, 2002.

[36] Albert B. Crenshaw, "A 401(k) Post-Mortem; After Enron, Emphasis on Company Stock Draws Scrutiny," *The Washington Post*, Dec. 16, 2001.

[37] Albert B. Crenshaw, "All the Nest Eggs in One Basket; Enron Shows What Can Happen to Undiversified 401(k) Plans," *The Washington Post*, Dec. 23, 2001.

Relatively small contributions are allowed for IRAs, and if your income is too high you may not be able to invest at all.[41] However, IRAs may be of particular interest to you when you are just getting started. The reason is that people tend to make less when they are young, and have a better chance of qualifying to invest in an IRA.[42] The Appendix contains a summary of these limits. A good strategy is to invest the maximum amount that you can as early as possible during the year, to earn the maximum interest tax-free. Savvy people will line up to buy IRAs at the beginning of the year.

Roth IRAs are different from traditional IRAs. Contributions to Roth IRAs are made after-tax. However, contributions grow tax-free, and as long as the contributions remain for five years, withdrawals are not subject to tax upon reaching age 59½. Roth income limits are also different.[43]

When comparing a traditional IRA with a Roth IRA, several considerations must be kept in mind. Suppose that you intend to withdraw your money at exactly the same time regardless of which IRA you have invested in. For instance, suppose you invest $5,000 on a pretax basis, you leave the money in for 30 years, and it accumulates at a rate of 7%. For a traditional IRA, you will get the initial investment, times accumulated interest, minus taxes at withdrawal. Call taxes at withdrawal "t_w." The amount withdrawn is $\$5{,}000 \cdot 1.07^{30} \cdot (1-t_w)$.

On the other hand, if you take the same initial pretax dollars and invest in a Roth IRA, you get the pretax amount, minus immediate income taxes when the money is earned (and the contribution is made) "t_E," times accumulated interest. This is $\$5{,}000 \cdot (1-t_E) \cdot 1.07^{30} = \$5{,}000 \cdot 1.07^{30} \cdot (1-t_E)$. To compare which is better, compare the two equations: $\$5{,}000 \cdot (1-t_w) \cdot 1.07^{30} \leftrightarrow \$5{,}000 \cdot 1.07^{30} \cdot (1-t_E)$, or, $(1-t_R) \leftrightarrow (1-t_E)$, or $t_R \leftrightarrow t_E$. Whether you should invest in a traditional IRA or a Roth IRA depends on your tax bracket at the time you are making the contribution versus when you are withdrawing the money at retirement. A successful strategy may involve switching contributions from one to the other depending on your circumstances.

Generally, Roths are considered better than traditional IRAs, at least if you leave your money in for five years. The reason is that you are not forced to make withdrawals from a Roth IRA at a certain age, and the money can continue to accumulate tax free (more on this below). It is also easier to get money out of a Roth IRA before retirement— just make sure you leave it in for five years. A big drawback is that Roth IRAs require burdensome paperwork - not most people's idea of entertainment.[44]

---

[38] Ellen E. Schultz, "Enron Workers Face Losses on Pensions, Not Just 401(k)s," *The Wall Street Journal*, Dec. 19, 2001.

[39] Hutchinson, *National Post* (Canada), Jan. 19, 2002

[40] Shankar Vedantam, "Forgive and Forget: Maybe Easier Said Than Done," *The Washington Post*, July 10, 2006.

[41] In 2010, a person who would not reach age 50 by the end of the year and who did not participate (or whose spouse did not participate) in a qualified plan could contribute $5,000 ($10,000 jointly). For the IRS limits, go to http://www.irs.gov/retirement/article/0,,id=202510,00.html. If you participate in a qualified plan with your employer, your contributions start being phased out at a low income level and are eliminated at a relatively modest income level.

[42] When their income becomes too high their previous investments can remain. If one person is not participating in a qualified plan but their spouse is, there is another set of rules phasing out contributions.

[43] Roth IRAs have an income limit when a person does not participate in a qualified plan, while a traditional IRA does not. However, the income limit is higher than for a Roth IRA when an individual does participate in a qualified plan than for a traditional IRA. The contribution limits are the same ($5,000 in 2009). The combined traditional and Roth limit is $5,000.

[44] There are also IRAs that are not tax deductable - you have to use after-tax dollars, and withdrawals are taxed. However, money can accumulate tax free. Given the restrictions on IRAs, these taxable ones may be inferior to other alternatives such as annuities, which we shall discuss later in the book. For a summary of IRAs, go to http://www.smartmoney.com/personal-finance/retirement/an-ira-primer-7957/.

Key Takeaway: IRAs only allow small contributions, and if your income is too high you may not be able to invest at all. They can be particularly beneficial to young people, just getting started. A traditional IRA allows money to be invested before tax and accumulate tax free. Money is taxed at withdrawal. After-tax money is invested in Roth IRAs, but the money can accumulate tax-free and is not taxed at withdrawal. Which is better depends on your tax bracket now versus at retirement. Roth IRAs are generally considered better because they have fewer restrictions about withdrawals, and also allow money to stay in at retirement—but they require a lot of paperwork.

Keogh Plans

Keogh plans allow self-employed people to invest in a qualified plan. There are defined benefit and defined contribution plans. Limits on these plans are similar to other kinds of business-qualified plans. However, a Keogh plan can provide a unique opportunity for the owner of a business to funnel large sums of money into a tax-advantaged retirement account late in the game.[45]

11.6 Distributions from Retirement Plans

A key retirement plan consideration is how accumulated money can be distributed to the owner, or a surviving spouse or beneficiaries. I will not go into detail about withdrawals because you are years away from having to worry about it. However, as was discussed above, you want to invest in IRAs in the best way now, and withdrawal rules matter. As a young person, you may also be the beneficiary of an estate, and how much you get will depend on distribution rules. For a substantial inheritance, this could be a big deal. And in an emergency, you may also need to withdraw retirement savings early.

Withdrawal issues fall in three broad considerations: 1. Are early withdrawals possible, and under what circumstances will early withdrawals be penalized or taxed? 2. When do withdrawals need to be made in retirement, and can tax-free transfers be made to surviving spouses and beneficiaries? 3. What transfers into other accounts are possible, and are there difficulties with doing this?

Early withdrawals are generally a bad idea. You are often taking pretax money that is accumulating without tax to pay for immediate needs at the expense of retirement. Also, it can be the case that you are required to return the "loan" and if you do not, there are substantial penalties. Each kind of retirement account will have its own rules, and it is important to do research on your account before making a withdrawal. There are certain circumstances that may allow for forbearance with penalties and taxes. Table A11-3 in the Appendix lists most withdrawal reasons that may exclude or reduce penalties or taxes. A final possibility is to borrow from an account. However, just like with defined benefit plans, the loan will have to be paid back (although you are paying back yourself), and failure to do so could cause a substantial penalty. If you leave your employer, the loan may come due immediately. Also, until you repay the loan, your money is not accumulating tax free.

---

45 The amount payable during retirement has a ceiling in 2009 of the lesser of 100% of the participant's average compensation for his or her highest three consecutive calendar years, or $195,000. See IRS publication 560: http://www.irs.gov/pub/irs-pdf/p560.pdf. The employer can then make quite large contributions to see that the plan is funded, based on actuarial calculations about the recipient's death. The need for actuarial calculations can cause extra expense and headache.

Most retirement accounts - such as traditional IRAs, 401(k)s, and 403(b)s - require that withdrawals begin by a certain date during retirement.[46] An exception is a Roth IRA. If you have sufficient funds, it can be a big advantage during retirement to keep money accumulating in a tax-sheltered retirement account. I will give a specific example of this in a later chapter. Another important concern has to do with how payments get made to a surviving spouse or beneficiaries, or to an employee who becomes disabled and cannot work. I will discuss these topics in Volume 2 when I cover disability and life insurance. Different qualified plans are subject to different distribution rules upon retirement, and also depend on the mix of pretax and after-tax contributions, investment gains versus principal, and employer versus employee contributions. Generally, defined benefit plans are the most restrictive.[47] "Rollovers" and "transfers" refer to moving money from a qualified plan or IRA to a new IRA. There are tricky issues surrounding rollovers and transfers as well as other issues concerning withdrawals, which are left to the Appendix.

Key Takeaway: There are tricky issues surrounding withdrawing money from retirement plans. Early withdrawals are generally a bad idea because they can involve penalties and taxes. Most retirement accounts require minimum withdrawals at a certain age, which is a disadvantage.

11.7 Investments

It is better to save additional amounts above those allowed in tax-advantaged retirement plans because the limits for these plans are low. How good an investor you are can make the difference between being wealthy and leaving others in the financial dust, and being poor. There are two types of investments that can yield cash for retirement: financial investments and real investments. Financial investments include securities such as stocks and bonds; real investments can include a house and other real estate, as well as antiques, jewelry, or art.

Some real investments can yield a steady cash flow, such as ownership in an apartment building, while others must be sold to provide cash. I have already discussed the different tax laws concerning dividends, interest, and capital gains. If a person sells a home and moves to a cheaper area after retirement, there is an additional break they can take advantage of. As long as the retiree owns the home and lived in it for a minimum of two years, there are no capital gains taxes on the first $250,000 in profit from the home if the home has a single owner; the exempt amount is $500,000 if the owners are a married couple. Investing is one of the main topics for Volume 2.

11.8 Working During Retirement

A final option is working in retirement. But it can be dangerous to rely on wages earned during old age. Young people do not like to think about being in poor health when old, but unfortunately, it is a common state of affairs. It can also become more difficult and unpleasant to work when old - which can be difficult for a young, fit person to imagine. Older people can also have a much more difficult time finding employment and typically earn much less than when they were younger. There are many exceptions to this, of course: many people of retirement age enjoy their work, or use it as a way to keep active or supplement their income. But it is dangerous to assume that you will be able to work in old age.

---

[46] This will also happen with annuities.

[47] The rules are also different depending on whether the distribution is a lump sum or is put into an annuity.

Don't underestimate the value of Doing Nothing, of just going along, listening to all the things you can't hear, and not bothering. ~ Pooh's Little Instruction Book, inspired by A.A. Milne.[48]

Where's Waldo?

Playing a jagged rendition of "Yankee Doodle Dandy" on his harmonica, Ralph "Waldo" McBurney of Kansas sat on his couch wearing a comfy blue and white checkered shirt and broad smile. His eyes twinkled even though he wasn't exactly happy with his harmonica playing. Humming on the harmonica, though, was merely McBurney's avocation. At 104 years old, the gray-haired and bespectacled centenarian still had another job: Beekeeper.

McBurney spent the better part of his career in agriculture. But it was his turn as a beekeeper that earned him the title of America's Oldest Worker several years ago. He kept as many as 100 bee colonies and made honey as well, shuffling from the hives to his beekeeping factory. During the hot summer months when the bee business wasn't busy, McBurney still buzzed about. He showed up at his desk bright and early to sign copies of his book *"My First Hundred Years."* Later in the day, donning a baseball cap and a cardigan, he'd drive to the local post office and faithfully mail out the books to customers. Yes, he still had a driver's license!

Few things slowed him down. He was married—to his second wife for 43 years. Agile and quick minded, McBurney could joke with the best of them, saying he lived by the motto: "Use it or lose it." Up until he was 101 he was running 10-mile races. He even set a few records in the Senior Olympics in long jump, discus throwing and shot put. Aside from phenomenal genes and an enviable work ethic what else kept McBurney going? He never smoked and always ate his vegetables.[49]

11.9 Conclusion

Retirement plans are complicated, but the massive tax savings they offer make them worthwhile. Issues surrounding retirement plans can be grouped into a few categories. Vesting and the formulas used to calculate contributions can make switching jobs difficult or costly, and can leave a longtime worker vulnerable to layoffs. Plan eligibility and being able to transfer retirement savings when switching jobs are other considerations. Forced withdrawals at retirement reduce the benefits of retirement plans. The safety of retirement savings is very important.

---

[48] Quote Garden.

[49] http://www.cbsnews.com/stories/2006/12/08/assignment_america/main2243516.shtml, http://www.thaindian.comnewsportal/world/ralph-mcburney-americas-oldest-worker-dead_100216401.html.

Another issue is who decides how the money is invested, and whether it will be held in company stock or other securities tied to the company.

One Long Party on the Sea

A round-the-world cruise can be the trip of a lifetime. Unless, of course, you'd rather spend the rest of your life on a cruise. Retirees Cornelis and Terry have taken four around-the-world cruises in seven years - and they couldn't care less about seeing the sights. "It's just fun to be on a ship," says Cornelis, a retired filmmaker. For him, three-month voyages are an escape from the cold back home in Toronto. Think of a ship as a floating winter home - and you can still keep in touch with friends with cell phones, on-board Internet and BlackBerries®.

And three months are nothing for some passengers. Cornelis met a traveler who was on his fiftieth sea voyage - an endless cruise that was a deluxe alternative to a retirement home. Such cruises don't come cheap. A high-end room on a world cruise can cost as much as $200,000 per person, and is largely the privilege of wealthy people who are used to fine living and excellent service. But one travel agent recalls a 51-year-old teacher who saved for years to pay for a long, $40,000 cruise.

For the person who has worked hard, saved money, and made smart investments, a long cruise can be a well-deserved reward and an opportunity to indulge a lifelong fantasy: exotic ports of call, pampering spa treatments, luxurious evenings of four-course dinners, and a dance floor filled with passengers in tuxedos and glittering evening gowns. Even on the sea, however, a traveler's desires can be more down to earth: spending days doing little more than lounging in the sun, reading a novel, or playing pool. For Cornelis, it's as simple as "a total absence of responsibility. At home when I drop a towel on the floor after a shower, it's still there at the end of the day. Here, it disappears."[50]

Employer retirement plans are either defined benefit or defined contribution. With defined benefit plans the employer is in charge of putting money aside for their employees' retirement. In this case, the financial health of the employer and the funding of the plan are vital. With a defined contribution plan such as a 401(k), the employee owns the retirement account and decides where to put the money. This is supervised by the employer, who determines which investments to make available to the employee based on prudence. Unfortunately, an employer may decide to make matching "prudent" contributions in company stock.

Retirement income can come from other sources too. Social Security is intended to help out with retirement, although it is on shaky legs. Personal investment accounts should supplement employer accounts, and it may be possible to invest in personal retirement accounts such as IRAs. Finally, it may be possible to work during retirement, but this should not be relied on.

Saving for retirement means freedom from fear. While it is a bad idea to spend retirement savings early, knowing that you have a large nest egg available to you in emergencies is a source of great comfort. You will also not have to worry about being old and unable to work, with nothing to live on—a terrifying thought indeed. With each

[50] Gene Sloan, "Travelers Round the Globe on Luxury Cruises," USAToday.com, Feb. 1, 2007, http://www.usatoday.com/travel/destinations/2007-02-01-queen-mary-two_x.htm; Alison Linn, "Around the World in 123 Days? Long-Term Cruises Growing in Popularity," The Associated Press, 2005, http://www.msnbc.msn.com/id/ 9831679/from/RSS; The Independent Traveler Inc., "World Cruises 2010 and 2011," cruisecritic.com, http://www.cruisecritic.com/articles.cfm?ID=514 (accessed June 1, 2010).

paycheck, regard some of the money as off limits. It does not belong to you. You do not steal from the elderly. Do not steal from your elderly self.

If you have the gravitas to plan for retirement when young, you can be one of those carefree people with a beautiful life. The trick is to pace yourself. Runners with big egos set a fast pace out of the starting blocks, then watch other runners who timed themselves pass them by. When the big egos start spending right from the beginning, your steady, measured approach will get you much farther.

Planning for retirement is a chance to dream. You will have worked all your life and then, finally, you have all the free time in the world. You could build exquisite stained-glass windows for your home or build a dam in Africa. Will you pursue the whimsical, frivolous, or deeply meaningful? How will you add a flourish to a life of accomplishment?

Key Terms:

401(k) plan
403(b) plan
Annuities
Defined benefit plans
Defined contribution plans
Disability insurance
ERISA
ESOP
IRA
Keogh plan
Long-term care insurance
Medicare
PBGC
Pension reversions
Plan eligibility
Profit sharing plan
Retirement plan funding
Rollover
Roth IRA
Social Security
TRA
Traditional IRA
Transfer
Vesting

End of Chapter Questions

1. Name major factors to consider when thinking about how much cash you will need during retirement.
2. How does someone qualify for Social Security? What can be expected in the future from Social Security?
3. Is all income subject to Social Security taxes?
4. What are the main benefits of qualified retirement plans?
5. What is the PBGC?
6. What is the main difference between a defined benefit plan and a defined contribution plan?
7. What questions should you ask a potential employer about a defined benefit plan?
8. Describe a 401(k) plan.
9. Why is employer matching so valuable?
10. What is the difference between a profit sharing plan and an ESOP?
11. What is an IRA?
12. What are the main differences between a traditional IRA and a Roth IRA?
13. What are the main considerations when comparing a traditional IRA with a Roth IRA?
14. What does it mean to say that a retirement plan is not fully funded?
15. Why are early withdrawals from retirement plans generally a bad idea?
16. Why are ESOPs problematic?

17. What is vesting, and what issues surround vesting?

18. How do formulas for retirement contributions play a role in career plans?

19. Name the ways that you can provide income for yourself upon reaching retirement age.

20. What are the problems with relying on working during retirement?

Appendix

A.1 Summary Tables

Table A11-1
Factors That Increase and Decrease Expenses in Retirement

Increase
Contributions to Medicare Part B and supplemental plans
Increased deductable payments due to hospital visits and other care
Possible expenses for long-term care
Travel and leisure expenses
College contributions for grandchildren or leaving an estate
Decrease
Withdrawal of principal is not taxed
Capital gains and dividends currently have a lower tax rate
You may be in a lower tax bracket, and therefore pay lower average taxes
Part of Social Security benefits may not be taxed
Medicare Part A is provided by the government
Mortgage paid off
No need for continued contributions to retirement savings
Reduced work-related expenses, such as commuting and clothing costs
Moving to a cheaper area
No contributions to life insurance

Table A11-2
Summary of Retirement Plans

Plans Covered in This Chapter
Social Security: A small amount to live off, and the system is currently insolvent.
Defined Benefit Plans: Can be taken over by the PBGC or have a reversion; can also give an employer the incentive to fire older employees.
401(k) and 403(b) Plans: Employees own their contributions and contributions from their employer that have vested. Employer matching can be especially beneficial.
Profit Sharing Plans: Several varieties. Profits are invested on behalf of employees.
ESOP: Employees receive shares in their company; plans can have high risks.
Traditional IRA: Can be done as an annuity or through a qualified institution that allows investment in prudent securities. Income and contribution limits. Pretax dollars are invested and accumulate without tax. Distributions at retirement are taxed as income.
Roth IRAs: After-tax dollars are invested and accumulate tax free. Withdrawals are not taxed and do not have to begin at retirement.
Keogh Plans: Employer can make quite large contributions at a late age.
Other Plans Available to Small Businesses
Simplified Employee Pension (SEP)
Savings Plan (Simple Retirement Plan)
Stock Bonus
Money Purchase Pension

Table A11-3
Possible Reasons for Early Withdrawal Penalty and Tax Forbearance

Higher education expenses for family members

"First-time" home purchase for you or family members (did not own home within last two years)

Death or disability

Large medical expenses

Withdrawals are put into an annuity

Unemployment combined with the need to pay for health insurance

You were over 55 and left your job

You "rolled over" the account (to be explained)

The withdrawal was part of a divorce decree or separation agreement

A.2 Early Withdrawals

There are differences between a rollover and a transfer. When funds are transferred, plan administrators manage the transfer and no taxes result. Rollovers start by the saver receiving a lump-sum distribution from a qualified plan. They must then place these funds into an IRA or possibly an annuity within 60 days to avoid paying taxes. There are limitations on the number of rollovers within a year. (One reason is that a person can use a rollover if they have a short-term funding problem - they can withdraw money from a retirement account and as long as they roll it over within 60 days they will not get a penalty.) A qualified plan can be rolled over into an IRA, put into an annuity, or received as a lump-sum distribution. Rolling over the plan into an IRA, however, can present difficulties and should be thought out ahead of time. The Internal Revenue Service makes the qualified plan withhold 20%. This can create a tricky situation. The 20% is withheld from you, but if you don't contribute that amount to an IRA you will have been considered to have not rolled it over, and it can become subject to taxes and penalties. You have to come up with the amount yourself, while waiting for the 20% that was withheld to be released to you later. An alternative is to ask (and possibly cajole) your plan trustee into transferring the money for you.

If a person has been a participant for five years, that employee can receive a lump-sum distribution from a qualified plan. However, assuming that you are young now, your reported income at the time of retirement and distribution will be enormous for the year because the huge distribution is added to income, forcing you to apply a high tax bracket to the withdrawal. You can move your retirement account to an annuity to avoid this. Distributions are taxed as income, unless they came from after-tax dollars. I will discuss annuities in more detail in Volume 2.

A.3 Social Security Administration

Social Security Administration
SSA Publication No. 05-10035
October 2008

Social Security and your retirement plans

Social Security is part of the retirement plan of almost every American worker. If you are among the 96 percent of workers who are covered under Social Security, you should know how the system works and what you should receive from Social Security when you retire. This booklet explains how you qualify for Social Security benefits, how your earnings and age can affect your benefits, what you should think about in deciding when to retire and why you should not count only on Social Security for your retirement income.

This booklet provides basic information on Social Security retirement benefits and is not intended to answer all questions. For specific information about your situation, you should talk with a Social Security representative.

Your retirement benefits

How do you qualify for retirement benefits?

When you work and pay Social Security taxes, you earn "credits" toward Social Security benefits.

The number of credits you need to get retirement benefits depends on when you were born. If you were born in 1929 or later, you need 40 credits (10 years of work).

If you stop working before you have enough credits to qualify for benefits, the credits will remain on your Social Security record. If you return to work later on, you can add more credits so that you qualify. No retirement benefits can be paid until you have the required number of credits.

How much will your retirement benefit be?

Your benefit payment is based on how much you earned during your working career. Higher lifetime earnings result in higher benefits. If there were some years when you did not work or had low earnings, your benefit amount may be lower than if you had worked steadily.

Your benefit payment also is affected by the age at which you decide to retire. If you retire at age 62 (the earliest possible retirement age for Social Security), your benefit will be lower than if you wait until later to retire. This is explained in more detail on pages 7 and 8.

Note: *Each year, about three months before your birthday, you receive a* Social Security Statement. *It can be a valuable tool to help you plan a secure financial future. It provides you with a record of your earnings and gives estimates of what your Social Security benefits would be at different retirement ages. It also gives an estimate of the disability benefits you could receive if you become severely disabled before retirement, as well as estimates of the survivors benefits Social Security would provide your spouse and eligible family members when you die.*

You can get retirement benefit estimates

You can use the online Retirement Estimator to get immediate and personalized retirement benefit estimates to help you plan for your retirement. The online Retirement Estimator is a convenient, secure and quick financial planning tool, since it eliminates the need to manually key in years of earnings information. The estimator also will let you create "what if" scenarios. You can, for example, change your "stop work" dates or expected future earnings to create and compare different retirement options.

For more information, ask for *Online Retirement Estimator* (Publication No. 05-10510) or *How To Use The Online Retirement Estimator* (Publication No. 05-10511) or visit our website at ***www.socialsecurity.gov/estimator***.

Full retirement age

The "full retirement age" is 65 for people who were born before 1938. But because of longer life expectancies, the Social Security law was changed to gradually increase the full retirement age until it reaches age 67. This change affects people born in 1938 and later.

Early retirement

You can get Social Security retirement benefits as early as age 62, but if you retire before your full retirement age, your benefits will be **permanently** reduced, based on your age. For example, if you retire at age 62, your benefit would be about 25 percent lower than what it would be if you waited until you reach full retirement age.

Some people stop working before age 62. But if they do, the years with no earnings will probably mean a lower Social Security benefit when they retire.

Note: *Sometimes health problems force people to retire early. If you cannot work because of health problems, you should consider applying for Social Security disability benefits. The amount of the disability benefit is the same as a full, unreduced retirement benefit. If you are receiving Social Security disability benefits when you reach full retirement age, those benefits will be converted to retirement benefits. For more information, ask for* Disability Benefits *(Publication No. 05-10029)* .

Delayed retirement

You may choose to keep working even beyond your full retirement age. If you do, you can increase your future Social Security benefits in two ways.

Each additional year you work adds another year of earnings to your Social Security record. Higher lifetime earnings may mean higher benefits when you retire.

Also, your benefit will increase automatically by a certain percentage from the time you reach your full retirement age until you start receiving your benefits or until you reach age 70. The percentage varies depending on your year of birth. For example, if you were born in 1943 or later, we will add 8 percent per year to your benefit for each year that you delay signing up for Social Security beyond your full retirement age.

Note: *If you decide to delay your retirement,* ***be sure to sign up for Medicare at age 65****. In some circumstances, medical insurance costs more if you delay applying for it. Other information about Medicare is on* *pages 17-18* .

Deciding when to retire

Choosing when to retire is an important but personal decision. Regardless of the age you choose to retire, it is a good idea to contact Social Security in advance to see which month is best to claim benefits. In some cases, your choice of a retirement month could mean higher benefit payments for you and your family.

In deciding when to retire, it is important to remember that financial experts say you will need 70-80 percent of your preretirement income to have a comfortable retirement. Since Social Security replaces only about 40 percent of preretirement income for the average worker, it is important to have pensions, savings and investments.

It may be to your advantage to have your Social Security benefits start in January, even if you do not plan to retire until later in the year. Depending on your earnings and your benefit amount, it may be possible for you to start collecting benefits even though you continue to work. Under current rules, many people can receive the most benefits possible with an application that is effective in January.

You should apply for benefits about three months before the date you want your benefits to start. If you are not quite ready to retire, but are thinking about doing so in the near future, you may want to visit Social Security's website to use our con-venient and informative retirement planner at ***www.socialsecurity.gov/retire2/***.

"Working beyond full retirement age can increase your benefits."

Retirement benefits for widows and widowers

Widows and widowers can begin receiving Social Security benefits at age 60, or at age 50 if they are disabled. And they can take a reduced benefit on one record and later switch to a full benefit on the other record. For example, a woman could take a reduced widow's benefit at 60 or 62 and then switch to her full (100 percent) retirement benefit when she reaches full retirement age. The rules vary depending on the situation, so you should talk to a Social Security representative about the options available to you.

Family benefits

Benefits for family members

If you are getting Social Security retirement benefits, some members of your family also can receive benefits. Those who can include:

Spouses who are age 62 or older;

Spouses who are younger than 62, if they are taking care of a child entitled on your record who is under age 16 or disabled;

Former spouses, if they are age 62 or older (see "Benefits for a divorced spouse" on page 11) ;

Children up to age 18, or up to 19 if they are full- time students who have not yet graduated from high school; and

Disabled children, even if they are age 18 or older.

If you become the parent of a child (including an adopted child) after you begin receiving benefits, let us know about the child so we can decide if the child is eligible for benefits.

NOTE: *Children's benefits are available only to unmarried children. However, in certain situations, benefits are payable to a disabled child who marries someone who is also eligible as a disabled child.*

Spouse's benefits

A spouse who has not worked or who has low earnings can be entitled to as much as one-half of the retired worker's full benefit. If you are eligible for both your own retirement benefits and for benefits as a spouse, we always pay your own benefits first. If your benefits as a spouse are higher than your retirement benefits, you will get a combination of benefits equaling the higher spouse benefit.

If you have reached your full retirement age, and are eligible for a spouse's or ex-spouse's benefit and your own retirement benefit, you may choose to receive only spouse's benefits and continue accruing delayed retirement credits on your own Social Security record. You may then file for benefits at a later date and receive a higher monthly benefit based on the effect of delayed retirement credits.

If you are receiving a pension based on work where you did not pay Social Security taxes, your spouse's benefit may be reduced. Additional information on pensions from work not covered by Social Security can be found on page 15 and 16 of this publication.

If spouses want to get Social Security retirement benefits before they reach full retirement age, the amount of the benefit is reduced **permanently**. The amount of reduction depends on when the person reaches full retirement age.

For example:

If full retirement age is 65, a spouse can get 37.5 percent of the worker's unreduced benefit at age 62;

If full retirement age is 66, a spouse can get 35 percent of the worker's unreduced benefit at age 62;

If full retirement age is 67, a spouse can get 32.5 percent of the worker's unreduced benefit at age 62.

The amount of the benefit increases at later ages up to the maximum of 50 percent at full retirement age. If full retirement age is other than those shown here the amount of the benefit will fall between 32.5 percent and 37.5 percent at age 62.

However, if your spouse is taking care of a child who is under age 16 or disabled and gets Social Security benefits on your record, your spouse gets full benefits, regardless of age.

Here is an example:

Mary Ann qualifies for a retirement benefit of $250 and a spouse's benefit of $400. At her full retirement age, she will receive her own $250 retirement benefit, and we will add $150 from her spouse's benefit, for a total of $400. If she takes her retirement benefit before her full retirement age, both amounts will be reduced.

NOTE: *Your current spouse cannot receive spouse's benefits until you file for retirement benefits.*

Maximum family benefits

If you have children eligible for Social Security, each will receive up to one-half of your full benefit. But there is a limit to the amount of money that can be paid to you and your family—usually 150-180 percent of your own benefit payment. If the total benefits due to your spouse and children are more than this limit, their benefits will be reduced. Your benefit will not be affected.

Benefits for a divorced spouse

Your divorced spouse can get benefits on your Social Security record if the marriage lasted at least 10 years. Your divorced spouse must be 62 or older and unmarried.

The amount of benefits he or she gets has no effect on the amount of benefits you or your current spouse can get.

Also, if you and your ex-spouse have been divorced for at least two years and you and your ex-spouse are at least 62, he or she can get benefits even if you are not retired.

What you need to know when you are eligible for retirement benefits

How do you sign up for Social Security?

You can apply for retirement benefits online at *www.socialsecurity.gov* or you can call our toll-free number, **1-800-772-1213** . Or you can make an appointment to visit any Social Security office to apply in person.

Depending on your circumstances, you will need some or all of the documents listed below. But do not delay applying for benefits because you do not have all the information. If you do not have a document you need, we can help you get it.

Information needed:

Your Social Security number;
Your birth certificate;
Your W-2 forms or self-employment tax return for last year;
Your military discharge papers if you had military service;
Your spouse's birth certificate and Social Security number if he or she is applying for benefits;
Children's birth certificates and Social Security numbers, if you are applying for children's benefits;
Proof of U.S. citizenship or lawful alien status if you (or a spouse or child applying for benefits) were not born in the United States; and
The name of your bank and your account number so your benefits can be deposited directly into your account.

You will need to submit original documents or copies certified by the issuing office. You can mail or bring them to Social Security. We will make photocopies and return your documents.

Right to appeal

If you disagree with a decision made on your claim, you can appeal it. For an explanation of the steps you can take, ask for *The Appeals Process* (Publication No. 05-10041).

You have the right to be represented by an attorney or other qualified person of your choice. For more information, ask for *Your Right To Representation* (Publication No. 05-10075) .

If you work and get benefits at the same time

You can continue to work and still receive retirement benefits. Your earnings in (or after) the month you reach your full retirement age will not reduce your Social Security benefits. However, your benefits will be reduced if your earnings exceed certain limits for the months before you reach your full retirement age. (See chart, page 6, to find your full retirement age.)

Here is how it works:

If you are younger than full retirement age, $1 in benefits will be deducted for each $2 in earnings you have above the annual limit.

In the year you reach your full retirement age, your benefits will be reduced $1 for every $3 you earn over an annual limit until the month you reach full retirement age. Once you reach full retirement age, you can keep working, and your Social Security benefit will not be reduced no matter how much you earn.

If, during the year, your earnings are higher or lower than you estimated, let us know as soon as possible so we can adjust your benefits.

If you want more information on how earnings affect your retirement benefit, ask for *How Work Affects Your Benefits* (Publication No. 05-10069) , which has current annual and monthly earnings limits.

A special monthly rule

A special rule applies to your earnings for one year, usually your first year of retirement. Under this rule, you can receive a full Social Security check for any **month** you earn under a certain limit, regardless of your yearly earnings. If you are self-employed, the work you do in your business is taken into consideration as well.

If you want more information on how earnings affect your retirement benefit, ask for *How Work Affects Your Benefits* (Publication No. 05-10069) , which has current annual and monthly earnings limits.

Your benefits may be taxable

About one-third of people who get Social Security have to pay income taxes on their benefits.

If you file a federal tax return as an "individual," and your combined income* is between $25,000 and $34,000, you may have to pay taxes on 50 percent of your Social Security benefits. If your combined income* is more than $34,000, up to 85 percent of your Social Security benefits is subject to income tax.

If you file a joint return, you may have to pay taxes on 50 percent of your benefits if you and your spouse have a combined income* that is between $32,000 and $44,000. If your combined income* is more than $44,000, up to 85 percent of your Social Security benefits is subject to income tax.

If you are married and file a separate return, you probably will pay taxes on your benefits.

At the end of each year, we will mail you a *Social Security Benefit Statement* (Form SSA-1099) showing the amount of benefits you received. You can use this statement when you complete your federal income tax return to find out if you have to pay taxes on your benefits.

Although you are not required to have federal taxes withheld, you may find it easier than paying quarterly estimated tax payments.

For more information, call the Internal Revenue Service's toll-free telephone number, **1-800-829-3676** , to ask for Publication 554, *Tax Information For Older Americans* , and Publication 915, *Social Security Benefits And Equivalent Railroad Retirement Benefits* .

**On the 1040 tax return, your "combined income" is the sum of your adjusted gross income plus nontaxable interest plus one-half of your Social Security benefits.*

Pensions from work not covered by Social Security

If you get a pension from work where you paid Social Security taxes, that pension will not affect your Social Security benefits. However, if you get a pension from work that was not covered by Social Security for example, the federal civil service, some state or local government employment or work in a foreign country—your Social Security benefit may be reduced.

For more information, ask for *Government Pension Offset* (Publication No. 05-10007) , for government workers who may be eligible for Social Security benefits on the earnings record of a spouse; and *Windfall Elimination Provision* (Publication No. 05-10045) , for people who worked in another country or government workers who also are eligible for their own Social Security benefits.

Leaving the United States

If you are a U.S. citizen, you can travel to or live in most foreign countries without affecting your Social Security benefits. There are, however, a few countries where we cannot send Social Security payments. These countries are Cambodia, Cuba, North Korea, Vietnam and areas that were in the former Soviet Union (other than Armenia, Estonia, Latvia, Lithuania and Russia). However, exceptions can be made for certain eligible beneficiaries in countries other than Cuba and North Korea. For more information about these exceptions, please contact your local Social Security office.

If you work outside the United States, different rules apply in determining if you can get benefits.

For more information, ask for *Your Payments While You Are Outside The United States* (Publication No. 05-10137).

A word about Medicare

Medicare is a health insurance plan for people who are age 65 or older. People who are disabled or have permanent kidney failure or have amyotrophic lateral sclerosis (Lou Gehrig's disease) can get Medicare at any age.

Medicare has four parts

Hospital insurance (Part A) helps pay for inpatient hospital care and certain follow-up services.

Medical insurance (Part B) helps pay for doctors' services, outpatient hospital care and other medical services.

Medicare Advantage plans (Part C) are available in many areas. People with Medicare Parts A and B can choose to receive all of their health care services through a provider organization under Part C.

Prescription drug coverage (Part D) helps pay for medications doctors prescribe for medical treatment.

If you are already getting Social Security benefits when you turn 65, your Medicare starts automatically. If you are not getting Social Security, you should sign up for Medicare before your 65th birthday, even if you are not ready to retire. For more information, ask for *Medicare* (Publication No. 05-10043).

Help with Medicare expenses for people with low income

If you have a low income and few resources, your state may pay your Medicare premiums and, in some cases, other "out-of-pocket" medical expenses, such as deductibles and coinsurance.

Only your state can decide whether you qualify for help under this program. If you think you qualify, contact your state or local medical assistance (Medicaid) agency, social services or welfare office. You can get more information about this program from the publication, *If you need help paying Medicare costs, there are programs that can help you save money* (Publication CMS-10126). To get a copy, call the Medicare toll-free number, **1-800-MEDICARE (1-800-633-4227)**. If you are deaf or hard of hearing, you may call TTY **1-877-486-2048 .**

"Extra help" with Medicare prescription costs

If you have limited income and resources, you may qualify for extra help to pay for your prescription drugs under Medicare Part D. Social Security's role is to help you understand how you may qualify and to process your application for extra help. To see if you qualify or to apply, call Social Security's toll-free number or visit our website.

Retirement Benefits

Contact Social Security

Visit our website

Our website, ***www.socialsecurity.gov***, is a valuable resource for information about all of Social Security's programs. At our website you also can:

Apply for certain kind of benefits;

Get the address of your local Social Security office;

Request a *Social Security Statement* or a replacement Medicare card; and

Find copies of our publications.

Call our toll- free number

In addition to using our website, you also can call us toll-free at **1-800-772-1213** . We treat all calls confidentially. We can answer specific questions from 7 a.m. to 7 p.m., Monday through Friday. We can provide automated phone service 24 hours a day. If you are deaf or hard of hearing, you may call our TTY number, **1-800-325-0778** .

We also want to make sure you receive accurate and courteous service. That is why we have a second Social Security representative monitor some telephone calls.

Social Security Administration

SSA Publication No. 05-10035

ICN 457500

Unit of Issue - HD (one hundred)

October 2008 (Destroy prior editions)

What's inside

A.4 2009 IRA Contribution Rules

2009 IRA Contribution Rules

2010 Roth IRA Contribution and Deduction Limits - Effect of Modified AGI on Contributions

This table shows whether your contribution to a Roth IRA is affected by the amount of your modified AGI as computed for Roth IRA purpose.

If You Have Taxable Compensation and Your Filing Status Is...	And Your Modified AGI Is...	Then...
married filing jointly or **qualifying widow(er)**	Less than $167,000	you can contribute up to the limit.
	at least $167,000 but less than $177,000	the amount you can contribute is reduced.
	$177,000 or more	you cannot contribute to a Roth IRA.
married filing separately and you lived with your spouse at any time during the year	zero (-0-)	you can contribute up to the limit.
	more than zero (-0-) but less than $10,000	the amount you can contribute is reduced.
	$10,000 or more	you cannot contribute to a Roth IRA.
single, **head of household**, or **married filing separately** and you did not live with your spouse at any time during the year	less than $105,000	you can contribute up to the limit.
	at least $105,000 but less than $120,000	the amount you can contribute is reduced.
	$120,000 or more	you cannot contribute to a Roth IRA.

2010 Traditional IRA Contribution and Deduction Limits - Effect of Modified AGI on Deductible Contributions If You ARE Covered by a Retirement Plan at Work

If you are covered by a retirement plan at work, use this table to determine if your *modified AGI* affects the amount of your deduction.

If Your Filing Status Is...	And Your Modified AGI Is...	Then You Can Take...
single or **head of household**	$56,000 or less	a full deduction up to the amount of your contribution limit.
	more than $56,000 but less than $66,000	a partial deduction.
	$66,000 or more	no deduction.
married filing jointly or **qualifying widow(er)**	$89,000 or less	a full deduction up to the amount of your contribution limit.
	more than $89,000 but less than $109,000	a partial deduction.
	$109,000 or more	no deduction.
married filing separately	less than $10,000	a partial deduction .
	$10,000 or more	no deduction.

If you file separately and did not live with your spouse at any time during the year, your IRA deduction is determined under the "single" filing status.

2010 Traditional IRA Contribution and Deduction Limits - Effect of Modified AGI on Deductible Contributions if You are NOT Covered by a Retirement Plan at Work

If you are not covered by a retirement plan at work, use this table to determine if your *modified AGI* affects the amount of your deduction.

If Your Filing Status Is...	And Your Modified AGI Is...	Then You Can Take...
single, **head of household**, **or qualifying widow(er)**	any amount	a full deduction up to the amount of your contribution limit.
married filing jointly or **separately** with a spouse who **is not** covered by a plan at work	any amount	a full deduction up to the amount of your contribution limit.
married filing jointly with a spouse who **is** covered by a plan at work	$167,000 or less	a full deduction up to the amount of your contribution limit.
	more than $167,000 but less than $177,000	a partial deduction.
	$177,000 or more	no deduction.
married filing separately with a spouse who **is** covered by a plan at work	less than $10,000	a partial deduction.
	$10,000 or more	no deduction.

If you file separately and did not live with your spouse at any time during the year, your IRA deduction is determined under the "single" filing status.

12.1 Introduction

Going to college is one of the most exciting times of a person's life. College will transform your worldview, along with your understanding of who you are. You may meet your spouse in college, begin a career, start on a journey of self-discovery, and set the foundation for a lifetime of learning. Everything will radically change.

Getting to college requires great effort. If you are not in college yet, hopefully you have devoted yourself to your studies and developed a strong record that you can be proud of. If you are applying for college, possibly for the first time you are faced with selling yourself, your accomplishments, and your potential. Fortunately, there are an enormous number of colleges and universities to choose from, all with their own unique strengths and weaknesses, history, and personality.

All colleges require an investment of time and money. Some, such as state colleges, are fairly affordable; many elite private universities can be extremely expensive. Where you go must be tempered by what you can afford. Some of you are lucky enough to have parents who can pay your entire way, including room and board. Most are not. By being savvy, you can open up the range of colleges that you can attend, or if you are already in college, put yourself in a more sound financial position when you graduate. You have already seen how much of a burden debt can be, especially when you are first getting started. Remember that college is a first step. A critical goal should be to graduate with manageable debt.

Even if your parents intend to pay your way, there are important strategies that can save them a substantial sum. Any loving child should be willing to expend some effort to save their parents a possibly enormous amount of money, or it just may be *your* parents arguing over that 10¢ coupon at the grocery store in retirement. A number of these strategies are available if you are already in college. I can also tell you personally that it is a source of great pride to tell your parents that you have come up with some of your own funding. It is time for a little initial practice at raising money to support yourself. And do not forget you may be a parent one day and will have to contend with sending your own children to college. Since a university education can be a massive investment, it makes sense to treat that investment with due respect and to take the time to find all resources at your disposal.

Even if you are not from a wealthy family, if you are highly energetic and proactive there is no reason you should not be able to afford a high quality college that you can be proud of. It is up to you. Look at paying for college as a job, and use your smarts. (This chapter will help, too.)

The best helping hand that you will ever receive is the one at the end of your own arm. ~ Fred Dehner[1]

College costs have been rising steadily above the inflation rate, something that I will discuss in the next chapter. Hopefully at some point, college costs will level out in comparison with other costs in the economy. There is no way to know if this will happen, so it is important to plan accordingly. The good news is that there are a variety of ways to finance college. Many require careful planning, starting even before a child is born. Table 12-1 summarizes the most common ways that college can be financed.

There is substantial need-based aid, and many families (not just "poor people") can qualify. Even if your family seems relatively well off, do not assume that you do not qualify for need-based aid. In addition, college savings plans can be a highly effective way to save and they are available to anyone. Savvy investing may help pay for college, along with friends and family. Every year thousands of merit-based scholarships are awarded by the government, colleges, and private individuals and institutions – and you do not have to be a straight-A student to get one.

There are some tax breaks for college students and their parents. Loans to students and parents are available directly from the government, and private loans can also finance college. Many opportunities to pay for college through work exist. Testing out of college courses or transferring from a community college can save a bundle. The important thing to remember is this: with determination and careful planning, anyone can go to a good college.

It is important that parents and children discuss how they will pay for college long before the time comes to apply to schools. The child needs to know what resources are available so that they can set their expectations early about what kind of college is affordable. There are also many things a child can do from a young age to increase the amount of money they have for college, but from the beginning the child needs to know that they will be required to come up with funding. Coaching by parents can also increase a child's ability to bring in needed money. If you have not discussed funding with your parents, do not assume that because your friends can afford to go to an expensive college that you can, too. It is time for a parent-child talk.

How did it get so late so soon?
It's night before it's afternoon.
December is here before it's June.
My goodness how the time has flewn.
How did it get so late so soon?
~Dr. Seuss[2]

[1] Quote Garden
[2] Quote Garden.

Table 12-1
Common Ways of Financing College

Need-based aid:	
	Federal government (FAFSA)
	Federal government (other)
	State governments
	Institutional "need-based" aid
College plans:	
	Section 529 college savings plans
	Section 529 prepaid tuition plans
	Coverdell Education Savings Account
	Savings Bonds (EE and I) & Roth IRAs
Private resources:	
	Investing and miscellaneous
	Relatives
Merit-based scholarships:	
	Government
	Institutional
	Private individuals/organizations
Taxes:	
	Credits and deductions
Loans:	
	Subsidized/unsubsidized Stafford, Perkins, and PLUS loans
	Private
Work study:	
	Government subsidized
	Military
	Working colleges
Testing out and transfers:	AP courses
	CLEP and DSST
	Finishing early
	Combined programs

12.2 Need-Based Aid

FAFSA

The Free Application for Federal Student Aid (FAFSA) is used to determine if you are eligible for aid from the federal government. Many colleges also use the application in determining their need-based aid awards.[3] Federal aid comes in three forms: grants, loans, and work-study programs. I shall discuss loans and work-study in more detail later. Aid in the form of a grant does not have to be repaid; loans must be paid back with interest. Unless your family has relatively low income, much of the aid that you are likely to receive if you qualify, will be in the form of loans. The needier you look on your applications, the more likely it is that you will receive grants or subsidized loans, which have much better terms than standard private loans.

The base year from which financial need is calculated is generally the calendar year before you fill out the FAFSA. The award year is the academic year starting in the year after the base year. For example, when you apply for aid for your senior year in college, your base year is the calendar year you finished your sophomore year and started your junior year, and the award year is for the following academic senior year.

Income that is considered available to pay for college is called AI (or "available income." As you prepare to apply for aid, get ready for a sea of acronyms). AI plus the fraction of assets included in calculating your contribution is called adjusted available income (AAI). Your cost of attending college is your COA. Your expected family contribution is your EFC. Your aid will be the difference between your COA and your EFC. You will find out your EFC by accessing your Student Aid Report (SAR), which will also summarize the information in your FAFSA.

Your parents must complete the FAFSA (they can do so online) and will have to include information about you as well. If you have been abandoned by your parents and declared an emancipated minor by the courts, you alone will be responsible for filling out the FAFSA (there are a few other exceptions under which you become responsible for the application). Make sure your parents have all the necessary information, including tax forms and asset figures, before they begin. (They should try to do their taxes as soon after January 1 as possible.) They should also have applied for and received a personal identification number, or PIN. The FAFSA web address and other useful websites are listed in the book appendix under "Internet Information."

I will now give a broad explanation of how aid is calculated assuming that you are a dependent, and give suggestions for maximizing your aid. These suggestions are intended to prevent you or your parents from making mistakes that will harm your chances for aid. Be sure when considering any aid-increasing method to consult with appropriate advisors and to stay within the law. The admonishments I gave when discussing tax codes apply here as well. Also realize that the various amounts I am about to give change constantly, as do financial-aid laws. The Internet address for EFC instructions and the EFC formula is listed in the Appendix.

---

[3] Until recently, the strategies people used to save for college crucially depended on whether they could qualify for financial aid. There were tax-advantaged investment choices that were very beneficial except that they reduced financial aid. People who could not qualify for financial aid would take advantage of those investments while those who could qualify for aid would not. However, because of tax code changes, many of the tax advantaged methods people used to finance college have gone away, and the best ways to invest are now often the same, whether you qualify for aid or not. In any event, starting with a discussion of financial aid is the logical first choice because other kinds of college financing activities can reduce financial aid.

It's Easy to Have Impressive Credentials

Adam Wheeler's credentials were unbeatable. He had perfect SAT scores, straight "A"s at the Massachusetts Institute of Technology, glowing recommendations from four MIT professors, and superlative recommendations from a prestigious private high school. His credentials were so impressive they got him into Harvard as a transfer student.

It's too bad he made them up. It seems that Adam did not attend MIT, but rather Bowdoin College, where he was expelled for academic dishonesty. He also attended a public high school in Delaware. The glowing MIT recommendations were fakes; the names on them matched those of some Bowdoin professors. The SAT transcript was allegedly forged.

Adam got caught when he took it upon himself to apply for a prestigious Rhodes Scholarship and a Fulbright award. His application claimed he had received perfect "A"s at Harvard (far from the truth), co-authored books, and given lectures. A Harvard professor caught him when he noticed that Adam's essay was similar to the writings of a colleague who was a Renaissance literature expert. The discovery of plagiarism led to the unraveling of his hoax, and Adam left Harvard rather than face an inquiry.

A student or alumnus who falsifies admissions documents can have their course credits and degree taken away - and that's only the beginning. When Adam's dismissal prompted him to apply for transfer to Yale, he landed in court. A suspicious official at Yale called his parents, who admitted his application contained "falsehoods." The police were notified and Adam was arrested and faced 20 counts, including larceny, identity fraud, falsifying a recommendation, and falsifying a degree credential. It seems that Adam received $45,000 in scholarship money based on his falsified credentials, and he even applied for an internship at McLean Hospital, an affiliate of Harvard. Adam isn't looking too impressive anymore as he finally devotes himself to studying something — serious jail time[4]

Parents and students must list their income, including any scholarships or work-study earnings. A certain amount of the parents' income is disregarded (sheltered): for instance, for the 2010-11 academic year, two parents with one child going to college may subtract $20,210 from their available-income total. Only $4,500 of the student's income is sheltered, after that, 50% of it is counted. Of course, by the summer of your senior year you will no longer have to file forms. There is also an important exception to this—work-study. In this case the student's income is exempt. Unless your parents have low income, their contribution from AAI (AI + available assets) will be $7,926 plus 47% of AAI over $29,300.

There are three ways to reduce reported income: by directly avoiding actions that increase reported income, by shifting income to assets (which have a lower contribution rate), and by trying to qualify for the simplified EFC formula (which shields all assets from consideration). Parents should avoid capital gains, as they are considered income. (If they must sell assets, they should try to sell ones that had a capital loss.) They should not convert a traditional IRA to a Roth IRA; that can create an enormous spike in reported income. Postponing bonuses will reduce income for one year, and push one higher bonus earned later out of the calculation (earned after your final base year). If your parents can shift when they pay taxes - for example, choosing to move for work-related reasons in January of

---

[4] Jacques Steinberg and Katie Zezima, "Campuses Ensnared By 'Life of Deception'," *The New York Times*, May 19, 2010; James Bone, "Honestly, I Got Into Harvard With Genius Grades ...," *The New York Times*, May 19, 2010; "The Not-So-Talented 'Mr Ripley'; Student Faked Academic Results to Land Place in Harvard," *Today*, NBC, May 20, 2010; Matt Rocheleau, "Harvard Hoax: Adam Wheeler Case Points to Rise of Student Fraud," *The Christian Science Monitor*, May 19, 2010.

your junior year in college rather than the previous December - they should try to pay the most taxes during a base year because federal taxes are an allowable expense taken out of income. That is a move that will make most accountants flinch because it is the exact opposite of the usual strategy of delaying taxes.

Qualifying for the simplified EFC formula is very beneficial because all assets are excluded.[5] Currently, if parents file an IRS Form 1040A or 1040EZ and their income is less than $50,000, they qualify for the simplified formula.[6] They could own multimillion-dollar investment accounts, a stable of Arabian purebreds, and a ten-car garage full of race cars and none of those assets would be considered for federal aid (aid from a college is another matter). Taking unpaid leave will reduce salary and mean real economic loss, but if it tips the family into the simplified EFC formula it may be worth it (and enjoyable) to take that leave. If the parents own a C corporation, they could try reducing their salary (which they still keep as part of the C corporation assets). Withdrawals from retirement accounts as well as earnings put into retirement accounts are considered income, but increased contributions to a retirement account may allow the parents to qualify for the simplified EFC formula.

There are two kinds of assets for federal financial aid purposes: included and not included. Think of assets as chess pieces - shifting them in the right way can make you and your parents a winner. You have already seen that shifting income to assets will reduce your parents' EFC, since less is taken from assets than from income. Currently, only 5.64% of assets go toward the EFC each year. Your parents should also try to shift assets so that they are not included. In fact, they may not have to do anything. Up to $80,300 of assets are not included, depending on the age of the oldest parent. If the older of two married parents has reached age 45, then $46,600 in assets will not be included. This means that they may not have to worry about assets at all. If so, shifting income to assets will result in fully shielding that money from your EFC.

All assets owned by the student are included in the EFC, and 20% each year must go toward it. For financial-aid purposes, it is better for the parents to own assets than the student. (A new rule requires that a student-owned 529 college savings plan be considered an asset of the parents.) For this reason, grandparents or others who wish to make contributions for your college should try to avoid putting assets in your name. Also, any payments they directly make will count against your aid. It is better for them to invest in a college plan for you that is held in their name. The other thing they can do is commit to paying off your student loans once you graduate.

Parents should maximize their contributions to retirement plans. This will not lower their AI, but in the following year it will shelter these contributions because retirement savings are not included as assets. Parents should also pay off consumer debt such as credit cards or car loans. That will reduce their cash, which is an included asset. (If they must borrow to put you through school, there are better ways.) They should also accelerate spending on excluded assets. Cars, computers, furniture, boats, and other personal assets are not included. (Your parents could own a multimillion dollar yacht and it would not be included.) If your parents are already planning on purchasing these kinds of assets, sooner is better than later. Students should use their own savings if possible to purchase their own personal assets (such as a dorm refrigerator) before submitting the FAFSA. That reduces the student's reported assets, which are included at a higher rate rather than the parents. In the same vein, student's assets should be spent as quickly as feasible, possibly even to the point of refusing student loans and using up the student's savings, instead. Parent assets, which are included at a lower rate or not included at all, should be used last.

---

[5] A very low income may also qualify a student for a zero EFC.

[6] Your parents' accountant may not like the 1040A or 1040EZ form, but may be unaware of the implications of using these forms in qualifying for federal financial aid.

Students at Sea

It isn't uncommon for a college student to spend a semester abroad. Maybe your sister went on safari in Botswana to document herd behavior among the blue wildebeest. Perhaps your brother joined a professor's archaeological dig in Peru, excavating an ancient tomb near the Andes.

But for some students, a foreign land isn't quite exotic enough. Instead, they opt for a floating classroom – a semester aboard a ship. A number of accredited programs draw adventurous students from top colleges and universities around the country who earn credit for courses ranging from marine life and environmental studies to ancient history, economic development - even the fine arts. Some trips let you delve into the riches of small coastal waterways; others take you on a voyage halfway around the world or farther. When your classroom docks, you may explore Shanghai or Cape Town. It is a welcome change of pace to arrive in Bermuda or Istanbul via the deep blue sea instead of a cramped and crowded jet!

An education, like life, is a journey. Whether you sail the Caribbean or the South Pacific, whether your destination is North Africa or Nova Scotia, seeing the world from the unique vantage point of the sea can give you a better view of all that your life can hold.[7]

Parents' equity in their primary residence - even if it is the Hearst Castle - is not included in the EFC. One way of shifting assets would be to use cash to pay off part or all of the mortgage. On the other hand, your parents may decided to use a home equity loan to help pay for your college (although student loans are typically better—this should be carefully investigated, including tax implications). If they do, they should get a home equity line of credit, which they can withdraw and use immediately to pay for your school expenses. Otherwise, the cash withdrawn goes into included assets.[8] If your family owns at least 50% of a business with 100 or fewer employees, the net worth of the business is not included. This is rather remarkable, since some types of businesses could be extremely valuable but not have a lot of employees. Hedge funds come to mind.

Carefully choose the date to submit the FAFSA, because assets and marital status are listed as of the application date. In addition, the EFC for each child goes down quite a bit the more children are in college. If you have a very bright sibling following behind you, it may be worthwhile for her to go to college a little early. Since the custodial parent fills out the FAFSA, there is an advantage to living with the lower-income parent in the

[7]Semester at Sea, http://www.semesteratsea.org, accessed June 6, 2010; Sea Semester: Field Programs in Marine and Environmental Studies, http://www.sea.edu/home/index.aspx, accessed June 6, 2010; Sea|Mester, http://www.seamester.com, accessed June 8, 2010.

[8] For AMT purposes, the interest is not deductible on home equity loans used for college expenses.

case of divorce. Also, when you get your SAR back, be sure to check it: mistakes can be made. If you have unusual circumstances, such as a sibling with a medical condition that requires large expenditures, try to appeal. In fact, send the college financial aid office detailed documentation on any unusual circumstance, such as a one-time bonus at work.

Now that you have learned the ins and outs of how the EFC is calculated, it is time to estimate whether you will get aid. You can do this directly by going to the web addresses for the EFC formula and EFC instructions. On the other hand, there are estimators designed to make the process easier. The web addresses for all these resources can be found in the Appendix. With some clever planning, you just may be surprised that you qualify.

Key Takeaway: Federal government aid comes in the form of grants, loans, and work-study. Unless your family has low income, most aid will come in the form of loans and work-study. In order to qualify for aid your parents will have to fill out a FAFSA, which requires their financial information and yours. Your EFC is your expected family contribution. The more income and assets of the parents and student, the higher the EFC. It is important to avoid making income and assets appear greater before applying for aid. Also, a student's income and assets are counted much more heavily toward the EFC than parent income and assets. If at all possible, assets should be in the parents' name. Parents should pay down debt to reduce reported cash. Their primary residence and personal assets, such as furniture or a small business, are not included. Other assets, such as investment accounts, are.

Challenge

If you are not in college yet, have you discussed financing college with your parents? Do you have ideas for increasing your chances for aid? If you are in college, have you discovered strategies for increasing your aid?

Other Federal and State Government Aid

If your family has a low EFC, you may be eligible for a Pell Grant. The maximum grant for the 2010-11 year is $5,550. Remember that grants are particularly desirable because you do not have to pay them back. Also, if you qualify for a Pell Grant, you may be eligible for other grants, which you must apply for. These include Academic Competitiveness Grants (ACGs) and the National Science and Mathematics Access To Retain Talent Grants (National SMART Grants). The Teacher Education Assistance for College and Higher Education (TEACH) grant does not require Pell eligibility, and the Iraq and Afghanistan Service Grant is available to any student whose parent died due to military service in Iraq or Afghanistan and who is not eligible for a Pell Grant. If you believe you qualify for one of these grants, be sure to check for any further restrictions.

Each state will have its own financial aid and grants. Check with your state—you may qualify for state aid even if you do not qualify for federal aid. You may have to fill out a state form. If your parents are divorced and live in different states, try both states. A web address to locate state agencies is in the Appendix.

Institutional "Need Based" Aid

I am sure you have noticed the quotes in the section title. Many colleges dress up merit aid and call it need-based aid, or they jointly take merit and need into account. What this means is that your parents could have substantial income and you could still qualify. Unless your family is very wealthy, you should always apply for aid. In fact, some schools hate to admit it but they like to encourage wealthy students to attend because they make large donations as alumni. Schools use need-based aid to price-discriminate (they give more aid to lower-income students who are more sensitive to price) and to lure the more sought-after students.

Many colleges look at the FAFSA in determining merit-based aid, while others (mostly private) look at the College Board Profile, or CSS. Some look at both, while some have their own application. This means that colleges may look at assets or income that is not considered by the federal government such as equity in a primary residence or retirement savings. (Many still exclude some or even all of home equity.) They may also look at small-business income. The Appendix contains the web address of a CSS-based aid calculator (the same address as the EFC calculator). It is very important to realize that colleges and universities provide aid on a first-come, first-served basis. **Make sure your parents fill out their taxes and apply as soon as possible after January 1.**[9]

If you are not in college yet, unless the sky is the limit, you will need to consider the costs of a particular college before you apply. But tuition alone will not tell you how much you will pay or what assistance you will get in the form of grants versus loans. Before you cross off that quaint but pricey liberal arts college, consider that many colleges like to create the impression they are elite by advertising a high price tag, but they also give substantial need-based aid. Think of it as a high list price – there is almost always a coupon. The College Board website has statistics on grants and loans by college. For instance, tuition at Sarah Lawrence College in New York is listed as $41,968. This is in the top range. However, 261 students applied for financial aid from the college and 235 received it. The average financial-aid package was $34,623, and the average need-based grant award was $32,318. The percentage of undergraduate aid awarded by Sarah Lawrence as scholarships or grants was 83%, compared to 17% for loans and jobs. The average indebtedness of students at graduation was $17,246.

Some colleges give a lot of "aid" that is mostly in the form of loans. You could end up with a heavy debt burden when you graduate, so when you're looking at prospective colleges, be sure to look at the indebtedness of their students upon graduation. Colleges may also charge high fees that are not listed as part of tuition; some schools do not charge tuition at all. Something should be very clear from this discussion: **It is imperative to research schools before deciding which ones are too expensive.** Fortunately, there is a lot of information readily available to do just that.

There are a number of strategies that can increase your chances at need-based institutional aid. Before you start, try googling "Common Data Set." I was absolutely astounded at the amount of information that is available (in conjunction with the College Board website). There are two major tactics: be as desirable as possible and appeal to the college's competitive instincts with rivals. You can find out what the typical SAT scores are of students, even by percentiles. You can also find out what characteristics the school is looking for in their applicants. Some may emphasize test scores, while others care about community involvement or religious affiliation and activities. If you are willing to consider a range of colleges, with careful research you can find ones you like that are a good fit and will offer you generous aid.

[9] They do not have to actually file the taxes early.

In addition, by tailoring your application to what the college is looking for, your chances for admission and aid go up. Try to apply to colleges where you are in the more desirable group. If SAT scores are important to the college, try to be in the top group. If you are actively involved in your religious organization, play that up with colleges that are seeking that characteristic. If you are a phenomenon at badminton, there just may be a school that prizes its badminton team. High school counselors may be able to steer you in the right direction based on how similar students have done. If your high school has "Family Connection" you can look at statistics.

Many colleges have competitor schools. The movie *The Blind Side®* makes this point beautifully (in addition to being wonderfully entertaining). Try to get offers from competitor schools. Their desire to outdo each other may just land you a big funding package. If you are not sure what the competitor schools are, the College Board shows for each college, other schools researched by the same website visitor.

There are many high-quality state colleges and universities, and if you are an in-state resident you may pay very low tuition or receive state grants. Many states also have reciprocity agreements. This means that you can get in-state tuition even if you go out of state, and you may be able to use grants awarded by your state. You will need to ask.

Once you receive financial aid offers from different schools, you can compare them using a calculator (see the Appendix). Some schools are in the habit of offering generous aid to freshmen and letting the aid evaporate in later years. Ask if you can expect similar aid for all four years. Avoid early decision, because the school does not have to compete for you with other schools and will give you less aid. Early action does not pose this problem, since you are free to go elsewhere.

If a school's aid offer is simply too small and you cannot attend, try discussing the situation with one of the school's financial-aid officers. You have nothing to lose, and you just might persuade him to give you more.

Finally, and this cannot be emphasized enough: graduation rates for colleges are very important. Some state schools are being squeezed for funding. Many required classes fill up, significantly delaying when students can graduate. Suppose that you take one year longer to graduate, and that you will earn $60,000 upon graduation. After-tax, you could lose $48,000 or more in income and retirement benefits every year that you do not graduate! According to the College Board, California State University at Long Beach has a 9.7% four-year graduation rate. At UCLA, it is 66.2%. Low graduation rates can also signal other kinds of problems with the school.

Obstacles are those frightful things you see when you take your eyes off your goal. ~ Henry Ford[10]

[10] Quote Garden

Key Takeaway: Many colleges use the CSS when considering aid. Much "need based" aid is actually based on a college's desire to attract students, and students from families with considerable income can still get aid. The listed tuition of colleges is only a small part of the picture, as many give large grants and scholarships. If you are applying to colleges, if you think strategically and research colleges, you can find one that is a good fit and that will provide generous aid. Try to be in the top category of students that they want, and play them off colleges they compete with. A college with a low graduation rate can cost you a year or more in salary and benefits.

Challenge

If you are applying to college, are you rethinking your approach to picking a college? If so, how?

12.3 College Plans

Since the time to pay for college is quickly approaching or already here, it is a little late to begin investing in a savings plan for college. If your parents did invest in a college plan, you are in a much better position to fund college. However, you will need to coordinate with your parents and manage how you spend money from the plan as well as from your other funding sources. And keep in mind that you may have children one day, and you will need to immediately invest on their behalf if you wish to pay for their education.

Section 529 refers to a section of the tax code that allows for the creation of tax-advantaged investment plans. There are two types of 529 plans: college savings plans and prepaid tuition plans. There are no income limits to these plans, so that even wealthy individuals can invest. Federal law also allows rollovers once a year between different 529 plans. Other types of savings plans with education tax benefits include Coverdell Education Savings Accounts and savings bonds. However, these plans have federal income restrictions.

Section 529 College Savings Plans

Each state has its own 529 college savings plan, and most are available to residents of other states. Investments in these plans have tax advantages that are similar to a Roth IRA. Put in after-tax money, and the money grows and can be withdrawn without federal tax, as long as the withdrawals are used for qualified educational purposes. These include tuition, room and board, and required enrollment expenses. Generally, the money is also not taxed at the state level if you invest in your own state, but is taxed if you invest in an out-of-state plan. (There are exceptions to this.)

As long as a family stays within the gift-tax exclusion, contributions to a college savings plan are not considered part of an estate. This means that on an annual basis, very large tax-advantaged contributions can be made toward a child's college expenses. In addition, up to five years of contributions can be made at once. From a tax perspective, it is better to put as much in, as soon as possible, so that the money can grow without tax. For instance, based on the $13,000 gift-tax limit in 2010, a married couple could donate $13{,}000 \cdot 2 \cdot 5 = \$130{,}000$ every five years. There is no limit per student, so relatives and even friends can set up their own 529 plan for a student.

It is extremely important to research state 529 plans. State plans are notorious for charging enormous fees that wipe out any tax advantages. These fees will vary depending on whether the state or an advisor is administering the plan. Some state plans do have reasonable fees. State plans also restrict investment offerings, with some having more restrictions than others. Most allow you to choose from a menu of investments once a year.

Stay away from high-fee plans and ones that lack a variety of good options for investing your contributions. I recommend getting on the Internet and finding which plans tend to be recommended by a variety of different sources. Then select a list of top candidates and do your own research, combing through the fine print of each plan. Try to pay fees lower than 1% (maybe as low as 0.8% or less). Also look out for state restrictions on contribution limits and how the money can be spent.[11] Some state plans will not charge you state income tax, even if you are not a state resident.

I will discuss in more detail the game of Twister® that must be played to avoid tax penalties upon withdrawal when you have multiple plans, grants, tax credits, and financial aid. There is a 10% penalty for nonqualified expenses, and if the plan is owned by your parents, they will also pay income taxes.

Section 529 Prepaid Tuition Plans

Prepaid tuition plans typically allow in-state residents to pre-purchase college credits, and at the federal level the money accumulates tax free and is not taxed at withdrawal. The idea behind these plans is that they will guarantee that your investment will keep up with the cost of college tuition. Investment returns are based on an index or other measure of college costs within the state. While this may eliminate some risk associated with college costs, these plans have a number of drawbacks due to their many restrictions. They are generally available only to state residents, and the number of credits that can be purchased is restricted. Withdrawals must also be reduced by other grants, scholarships, and payments from tax-advantaged plans. If the student chooses to go out of state to college there could be penalties. Private institutions are allowed to have their own prepaid tuition plans. However, this could lock the student into going to a specific school.

Coverdell Education Savings Accounts, Savings Bonds, and Roth IRAs

Coverdell Education Savings Accounts (ESAs) used to be referred to as "Education IRAs." They have income phase-outs for contributions. The maximum contribution is $2,000. These accounts allow withdrawals for more expenditures than 529 plans, such as tutoring and computer equipment, and they may be more useful for private K-12 expenditures. Parents must contribute, and contributions stop when the child turns 18.

Two kinds of U.S. savings bonds can be used for education purposes in a tax-advantaged way: Series EE bonds and Series I bonds. Only people age 24 and over can purchase the bonds and use them later to get a tax break for educational purposes. The first step is to elect to defer taxes until withdrawal, or until the bonds mature. If the withdrawals are used for qualified education expenses they are not taxed, but, unfortunately, this tax advantage has low-income phase-outs. These bonds use different methods to determine interest. Series EE bond interest is based on other federal bonds, and Series I bond interest is based on a combination of inflation and other bond interest.

[11] Due to Financial Wisdom Prep's strict no-conflict-of-interest policy, I will not recommend specific plans. However, with a little research it should not be difficult to find the best plans.

With a Roth IRA, as long as you leave your money in for five years you can withdraw the principal for educational purposes. Any earnings in a Roth IRA can continue to grow tax free. (Of course, this begs the question of why you are not keeping that money in even longer and enjoying the even greater tax benefits for retirement.)

Key Takeaway: Section 529 plans have considerable tax advantages and do not have federal income phase-outs. There are 529 college savings plans and 529 prepaid tuition plans. Contributions can grow tax free, and withdrawals are also tax free if used for qualifying educational expenses. Every state has a college savings plan, and generally allows residents of other states to contribute. It is important to carefully research these plans because they may have high fees and they may heavily restrict investment. Prepaid tuition plans have many restrictions, however their investment earnings track the expense of in-state tuition. In addition to 529 plans, there are other tax-advantaged savings accounts and bonds, including Coverdell Education Savings Accounts, Series EE and I bonds, and Roth IRAs. These, however, have income phase-outs and restrictions.

12.4 Private Resources

There is a grab bag of private resources for funding the costs of a college education. Of course, you are free to invest on your own. One strategy is to buy and hold stocks that do not pay a dividend. You will not have to pay taxes until the money is withdrawn, and you will be taxed at the low long-term capital gains rate, assuming tax rates do not change. However, stocks are riskier than bonds.

Many colleges will reduce or eliminate tuition for employees or their children. I met an enterprising parent who took a job at an expensive private college specifically so he would not have to pay tuition for his son. Many colleges have agreements with other schools, so you may be able to get a tuition break at a "sister" school. The University of Chicago has a very generous benefit for their professors – it will pay 80% of tuition at *any* accredited college. These kinds of benefits can be particularly advantageous for large families. Some non-educational employers pay for employees (or even for their children) to take college courses.[12]

If your parents' credit card pays them back a percentage of purchases, or allows them to earn points for travel, etc., they should use the card to pay those big tuition bills. They may just earn enough points for you to fly home for spring break. However, they do not want to damage their credit rating by having a high debt level on their card. (I will discuss credit ratings in a later chapter.) With such a large purchase, I recommend prepaying on the credit card, or paying it off immediately, to keep the balance down.

If you are lucky enough to have relatives who want to help, be sure to coordinate with them. They could unintentionally reduce your aid or create tax problems. Unfortunately, trusts are generally not helpful and could even cause trouble. Trusts are counted as assets of the student, and if money cannot be withdrawn during college, they could harm the ability of the student to pay for college.

---

[12] At the moment, you can exclude up to $5,250 of employer tuition assistance from income.

"He Makes You Have a Dream"

John U. Bacon is a journalist who contributes articles on sports and business to ESPN, Time, Sports Illustrated and a dozen other publications. His commentary is regularly featured on Michigan Public Radio and AnnArborChronicle.com. He's the author of four books - his most recent, "Bo's Lasting Lessons: A Legendary Coach Teaches the Timeless Fundamentals of Leadership," about University of Michigan football coach Bo Shembechler, was on the New York Times and Wall Street Journal bestseller lists. Oh, yeah - he's a teacher, too.

You'd probably assume that a guy this busy wouldn't have much time for his students. But you'd be wrong. The waitlists for Bacon's classes at Michigan - "The Rise and Fall of the American Sportswriter" and "The History of College Athletics" - set records for length. In 2009, students lucky enough to get a seat in his classroom helped win him the annual Golden Apple award, which recognizes outstanding Michigan faculty and is presented by a student group on campus.

"He is an excellent person, a great motivator, the type of person who makes you have a dream," an engineering major said of Bacon.

Bacon's advice to students? "If you hate what you do, it will never be enough, never enough money, never enough awards."[13]

12.5 Merit-Based Scholarships

Government and Institutional

The federal government has the Supplemental Educational Opportunity Grant (SEOG), which is administered by colleges. States also have merit awards, which may or may not be portable. Colleges have the most merit-based grants. Much of what I wrote before about persuading a college to give you need-based aid applies here. Research schools carefully, be strategic about where you apply, and try to be as desirable to a college as possible. Ask if a school awards merit scholarships and if you can apply.

Private

There are an enormous number of private scholarships, with awards totaling in the millions. You can apply for many scholarships while already in college. Even better, they are not just for straight-A students. There are awards for left-handers, tall people, short people, obese people, Star Trek fans, vegetarians, beef eaters, knitters, people with blue eyes, birdwatchers, animal lovers, badminton players, accordion players, and people who are talented at shooting marbles. If you and your date wear outfits make out of Duck brand duct tape, you can enter the Stuck at Prom contest.

---

13 Jennifer Zobel, "They're Lining Up for Bacon," The Michigan Daily, Jan. 9, 2008, http://content.michigandaily.com/content/theyre-lining-bacon; Asa Smith, "Golden Apple Recipient John U. Bacon Discusses Lessons in Life, Sports," The Michigan Daily, March 31, 2009, http://www.michigandaily.com/content/2009-04-01/golden-apple-award-winner-john-bacon-discusses-his-experiences-part-his-ideal-las; Kathleen Kingsbury, "America's 10 Hottest Classes," The Daily Beast, Sept. 8, 2009, http://www.thedailybeast.com/blogs-and-stories/2009-09-08/americas-10-hottest-classes/2/.

Do not let fee-based scholarship advisors get your hopes up that you can win a full ride. However, you may very well be able to win significant scholarships and there are a lot of them out there. Your parents could be struggling to save for their own retirement as well as putting you and your siblings through college. Imagine being able to tell them that you took it upon yourself to win a scholarship to help pay for the costs. What a feeling of accomplishment and pride!

Scholarships may reduce any aid you are eligible for, but unless your family has very low income, scholarships will most likely reduce loans. Remember that loans have to be paid back with interest. You are reducing the debt burden you will face when you graduate. Colleges do not want to discourage students from seeking scholarships, and many will not reduce your aid by the full amount of a scholarship.

You will also make yourself more attractive to colleges because winning scholarships looks good (and takes the burden off cash-strapped colleges). They may even decide to give you more "need based" aid. Some schools match scholarships. If you are ambitious and apply for a lot of scholarships, you will become an application genius, armed with multiple, carefully crafted essays, meticulously compiled and refined lists of accomplishments, and real savvy about looking good on paper—not a bad thing to be before you sit down and fill out those all-important college applications. On the other hand, if you have already applied for college you are now armed to apply for scholarships.

The difference between try and triumph is a little umph.
~Author Unknown[14]

There are scholarships available to kids in elementary school. This may be a little late for you, but your siblings and future children should give it a try. They will start the process of becoming savvy and well-funded early. However, most scholarships are for teens and for college students. Do not give up applying for scholarships once you start college.

Regard the hunt for scholarships as a part-time job with a potentially large payout - and one that has significant tax advantages if used for school expenses. It is time to get organized and go on a treasure hunt. Try making a list of your attributes, accomplishments, and talents. This could be your ethnic heritage, religion, political beliefs - even your last name. (There are surname scholarships: are you a Zolp?) There are scholarships based on your location. Do you have an unusual interest such as accordion playing? Do you have a flair for Latino art? Are you asthmatic and involved in community service? There is a scholarship. Some are awarded to students who have triumphed over difficulties. Have you overcome trouble such as abandonment or having an alcoholic parent?

The next step is to list any organizations that you or your parents are associated with. For your parents, it could be their employer, credit union, savings and loan, professional organization, or country club. Have a talk with your parents and get them on board. They will be happy to assist you in your search for money! Perhaps it is time for you and your parents to think about joining various organizations. Learning secret handshakes may just be fun —and lucrative. It is also a good time to think about expanding your extracurricular activities. They will also come in handy in applying for college and financial aid.

[14] Quote Garden

Scholarship Superstars

There are many students out there who have paid a large portion of their way through college by winning scholarships. Here are some big winners listed at scholarships.com.[15] Ivy won the $80,000 Passion for Fashion Scholarship. Ryan, whose mother could not afford to put him through college, won $111,800 for four years at an Ivy League college. He credits hard work applying for as many scholarships as he could during the summer before his senior year. He even returned $20,000! Jacob won a total of $70,300 from five different scholarships.

Perhaps the biggest scholarship winner is Ben Kaplan. Not only did he win almost $90,000 and graduate from Harvard debt free, he turned his ability to win scholarships into a career. Ben became an award-winning author of several highly popular books packed full of useful advice on winning scholarships.[16] He even toured the country in a 40-foot bus, giving workshops and promoting his books. He has appeared on numerous television and radio shows, including Oprah.[17] As Ben tells it:

"It's about not letting current financial circumstances dictate our destinies. It's about accepting risk and having faith: the risk of putting yourself on the line, and the faith that comes with believing in yourself."[18]

Inspiring words.[19]

Finding scholarships requires hard work and determination. The Internet is a good place to start, and there are several scholarship search engine web addresses in the Appendix. However, this is only the beginning. Many scholarships require legwork. You will have to ask, or go directly to institutional, corporate, or association Web sites. Your high school counselor may be aware of many.

Also, many private scholarships are administered by college financial aid offices (you are not given the money directly). Once you attend college, the financial aid office can provide a wealth of information about potential scholarships. Many organizations give scholarships, including corporations, associations, civic organizations, veterans groups, unions, and those created by wealthy individuals. Search through lists of associations and philanthropic foundations.

---

[15] http://www.scholarships.com/financial-aid/college-scholarships/success-stories/success-stories.aspx.

[16] Ben's books include *How To Go To College Almost For Free*, HarperCollins Publishers, New York, 2nd edition, 2002, and *The Scholarship Scouting Report*, HarperCollins Publishers, New York, 2003.

[17] http://www.cityofcollegedreams.org/content/about-ben-kaplan.

[18] Michelle Singletary, "Through College Avoiding Debt," *The Washington Post*, January 7, 2007.

[19] Mary Beth Marklein, "An Education 'Almost For Free': Recent Grad Helps Kids Find Scholarships and Grants," *USA Today*, October 9, 2000; Stacy A. Teicher, "Think You Can't Afford College in 2005? Think Again, Experts Urge," *Christian Science Monitor*, December 30, 2004.

Now that you are ready to hunt for scholarships, it is time to access your inner bulldog. Applying for scholarships is a numbers game. If your chances of winning are small, then you will need to apply for a lot of them. Stubbornness is key. Decide ahead of time that you will not let rejections bother you. The more you apply, the better your chances of winning. When you apply for the best-known ones, your chances will be lower. However, there are many little-known scholarships, and some receive no applications at all. The harder the scholarship is to find, the better your chances. Dig like a dog after a precious bone.

A note of caution is in order about athletic scholarships. Their renewal is not guaranteed and the training required could be very time consuming. You could also get injured and lose your scholarship. However, they can get you into a selective school, and you do not necessarily have to be a top athlete. There are many scholarships for less common sports such as badminton and lacrosse.

Does college pay? They do if you are a good open-field runner.
~Will Rogers[20]

When it comes time to write the essay and fill out the scholarship application, there are a number of principles for success, many of which I will go over in detail in future chapters. Research is a very important principle. Be sure to understand the goals of the organization providing the scholarship and research what they are looking for in an applicant, just as if you are applying for a job. If you can discover who will be judging your essay, try to find out about them. Create a story about yourself (as you do with a résumé, which describes who you are to employers). Let your unique personality shine through. Try to think about what is compelling about you and your background, and bundle it up in a vivid way. Finally, just like a résumé, your essay and application should be free of errors and beautifully formatted.

Key Takeaway: There are an enormous number of private scholarships available, and not just for A students. Scholarships may reduce the aid you receive, but most of that aid will be in the form of loans. Some colleges match scholarships. The hunt for scholarships should start in elementary school and continue through college. Finding and applying for scholarships will be a lot of work. Think of it as a part-time job with a potentially big, tax-free payout. Try to apply for many scholarships, and do not get discouraged by rejections. Try to create a compelling and vivid picture of yourself in your essays and applications, and do your research on what the organization giving the scholarship (and the judge) are looking for. Think of applying for scholarships as training for applying to college. By applying for scholarships, you could turn yourself into an application genius by the time you turn your attention to college admission. It can go the other way too – you have already filled out college applications, making it easier in college to apply for scholarships.

[20] Quote Garden.

Challenge

Are you ready to dig in and hunt for scholarships? What is unique about you? What are your greatest accomplishments? Do you have a compelling story and interesting personality that you can present?

12.6 Taxes

The topic of taxes, once again, cannot be avoided. (The Appendix contains the web address for IRS publication 970, Tax Benefits For Education.) I have discussed taxes throughout the chapter, but there are several aspects worth discussing on their own. There are several tax credits available to students or the parents of students. The new American Opportunity Credit (AOC) is intended to replace the older Helping Outstanding Pupils Educationally, or HOPE, tax credit. The AOC has a higher maximum credit of $2,500 per eligible student or dependent student. The income phase-out limits are also higher.[21] One hundred percent of the first $2,000 of qualified education expenses and 25% of the next $2,000 can be claimed; 40% of the credit is refundable.[22] Qualified expenses include tuition and fees, equipment, and books required for enrollment. The credit can be used for only four tax years.

The AOC is replacing the HOPE credit. However, a larger HOPE credit of $3,600 is available for students meeting rules for Midwestern disaster areas (see IRS publication 970 for more information). The Lifetime Learning Credit has no limit on the number of years it can be claimed. The maximum credit is $2,000 ($4,000 for students in a Midwestern disaster area). Income phase-out limits are low[23] and the credit is nonrefundable, but it is available for all years of postsecondary education. Another possibility is taking an adjustment to income for tuition and fees (you do not have to itemize). Remember that deductions (or, in this case, an adjustment to income) are generally less desirable than credits because credits come directly out of taxes, while deductions reduce the reported income that is used for computing taxes. Phase-outs for the tuition-and-fees adjustment to income is also low.[24]

Unfortunately, if you have ESAs, savings bonds, grants, scholarships, or 529 plans, coordinating for tax purposes can be like a trying to juggle while finding your way out of a maze. Generally, payments used for a tax break for one purpose cannot be used for another, but what qualifies as an expense is different for different plans. It is important to coordinate withdrawals from 529 plans versus ESAs, and you must carefully calculate how much you should withdraw from each account. You also have to be careful about spending money in December for January tuition.

Also, you cannot use more than one adjustment to income or credit at the same time. It becomes more complicated when there are multiple children and more than one tax method is used, or methods are switched. You can either go through IRS publication 970 carefully and do scenarios (hopefully using tax software), or take the less painful route and ask a competent accountant to give you advice.

In the past, parents who did not qualify for aid would put assets in their child's name. The Uniform Gifts to Minors Act and Uniform Transfers to Minors Act

---

[21] In 2009 the phase-outs begin at modified AGI of $160,000 for a married couple and $80,000 for a single parent, and the maximum income is $180,000 for a married couple and $90,000 for a single parent. You cannot claim the credit if you file as "married filing separately."

[22] This means that you can get a check in the mail for as much as 40% of the credit if your calculated taxes before the credit were not as much as the credit.

[23] In 2009 the phase-outs begin at modified AGI of $100,000 for a married couple and $50,000 for a single parent, and the maximum income is $120,000 for a married couple and $60,000 for a single parent.

[24] With modified AGI of $130,000 or less ($65,000 if filing single) you can take a maximum deduction of $4,000. If it is more than this but less than $160,000 ($80,0000 if filing single), then the maximum deduction is $2,000. No deduction is allowed over these limits.

specified the amount of assets that could be put in a custodial account for a child, which would be controlled by a custodian but owned by the child. At a certain age, the account would terminate and the child would have access to the account. As long as the amounts were under the gift-tax exclusion, they would not be included for estate-tax purposes.[25] These accounts were considered advantageous because assets could accumulate at the child's income tax rate. However, with the advent of the "kiddy tax," investment income over a relatively small amount is taxed at the higher of the parent's or child's rate in most situations, eliminating nearly all of the advantage.[26]

12.7 Loans

The federal government is now the only lender of federally guaranteed loans. Private lenders are no longer involved. (Although you can take out a private loan without the federal guarantee.) There are unsubsidized and subsidized Stafford loans and Perkins loans, which you can defer paying until six months after you graduate. (Perkins loans are made and administered by the college.) These loans tend to have very low interest rates (so in a sense, they are all subsidized), and the student does not need a good credit rating because the loans are provided by the government.

Unsubsidized Stafford loans begin accruing interest as soon as they are taken out, while subsidized Stafford loans do not begin to accrue interest until six months after graduation. Depending on your FAFSA, you may qualify for the subsidized loans, which is another reason to fill out the FAFSA even if you do not expect to receive a grant. The amounts that you can borrow are limited each year and depend on your year in school. If you are having difficulty making payments, you may be able to receive forbearance or a deferral on your payments.

Parents may be able to take out PLUS loans provided by the Department of Education, but their credit score will be taken into account. Generally, the student can borrow more cheaply than the parent. Also, when considering a PLUS loan, parents should look into private alternatives, such as a home equity line of credit, which may be tax deductible.

The interest on student loans that is used to pay for qualified school expenses can be taken as an adjustment to income for tax purposes, subject to limits and income phase-outs.[27] As per my discussion on taxes, qualified expenses must be reduced by other tax-advantaged methods to pay for expenses. The maximum deduction is $2,500.

Two payment programs are available for lower-income borrowers: the Income Contingent Repayment (ICR) program and the Income Based Repayment (IBR) program. Depending on your income and the number of people in your family, you may qualify to have your loan payments reduced.

Your loans may even be forgiven after 25 years, or 10 years if you are in government service. Congress may enact legislation to cease taxing loan forgiveness under these programs. If you are in the military, you may be able to defer loans as well as the interest on subsidized loans. You may even be able to have your loans paid off.

---

[25] The law varies by state.

[26] In 2009, the limit was $1,900.

[27] In 2009, income phase-outs will kick in if the modified AGI of jointly married filers is between $120,000 and $150,000 (between $60,000 and $75,000 for a single filer).

Key Takeaway: The AOC tax credit is replacing the HOPE tax credit for educational expenses. The AOC can be used for four years of education and has limits as well as income phase-outs. The Lifetime Learning Credit can be used for any number of years. Education expenses can also be used as an adjustment to income. The combination of tax-advantaged college plans, savings bonds, and credits and deductions can create complex tax issues, and withdrawals from plans along with the use of credits should be considered carefully. The federal government makes subsidized and unsubsidized Stafford loans available to students. Subsidized loans have the advantage that interest does not accrue right away. Both can be deferred until after college. Perkins loans are made directly by colleges. Parents can take out PLUS loans, but they should weigh all loan options carefully.

12.7 Work-Study

The federal government subsidizes colleges to offer jobs to students, most of which pay minimum wage. The advantage of work-study to the student is that the wages are not added to FAFSA income. You will find other job opportunities as well. When I was a graduate student at Harvard I was surprised to find that Harvard undergraduates were interested in babysitting jobs: one wanted to be a pediatrician, another was studying language development in children.

As I shall discuss in the career skills chapter, there are also many opportunities for internships (temporary jobs offered to college students by employers). Internships can provide a number of benefits, including being helpful for building a résumé. Some internships offer the chance to become known to an employer, or to get experience and a leg up for a very competitive job after graduation.

The military offers the opportunity to fund college through work. If you are not interested in the military, then the commitment required will not be worth it. But if you have an interest in joining, you could have a substantial amount of your college expenses paid for through the Reserve Officer Training Corps (ROTC). The more time you serve, the more your college expenses get paid. The Montgomery GI Bill can also be a means of funding college, during and after duty. Military colleges will pay for the tuition, room, and board of their students, but a substantial commitment to the military is required. There are also non-military "working colleges" that offer students reduced or free tuition but require that their students work.

12.9 Testing Out and Transfers

You could save up to a year's worth of college expenses by placing out of college courses through the Advanced Placement (AP) Program; you will need to take AP courses in high school and pass required exams. Placing out of courses does not mean that you cannot attend college for the full four years. You could enjoy a reduced course load (while focusing on getting high grades) or spend extra time working to avoid a pile-up of student loans. The College Level Examination Program (CLEP) also offers the opportunity to place out of courses, depending on the college. The DSST Program (formerly called the Dantes Subject Standardized Test) is a way for military and eligible civilian personnel to learn in a non-standard way and get course credit.

There are numerous programs that allow students to combine courses for multiple degrees, potentially saving them a bundle. I graduated from the University of Chicago with a combined bachelor's and master's degree simply by taking graduate courses rather than undergraduate courses. The Graziadio School of Business and Management at

Pepperdine University has a joint business program that offers graduates of a community college the chance to earn a bachelor's and master's degree in business in an accelerated program. Finally, graduating early can save a bundle. I have already discussed the costs that some colleges impose because students cannot graduate in four years and begin full-time employment. A strategy to save costs is to take extra courses and graduate early, saving on room and board and accelerating the chance to earn employment income.

12.10 Getting Advice

Planning for college can be complex, but the good news is that you can get advice from a certified college planning specialist (CCPS). The web address for the National Institute of Certified College Planners is in the Appendix. However, a note of caution is in order. Be very careful about who you get advice from. Some "advisors" receive commissions from selling a limited number of products, such as a few 529 plans, and they will steer you only to those. Many of them may have very limited knowledge and are not much more than salespeople. Other advisors may be very sophisticated when covering tax and estate issues, but know very little about FAFSAs, or funding college in general.

Since you have learned a great deal from reading this chapter, you are better trained to spot a bad advisor. Try asking questions when you already know the answers. Research 529 plans. If an advisor tries to steer you into a poor one, you know they are trouble. If you have the chance to qualify for aid and your accountant boasts of knowledge about college planning, ask if there are situations where you should accelerate paying taxes. An informed accountant will understand that you are trying to reduce available income for FAFSA. A badly informed one will blanch at the very thought.

12.11 Conclusion

There are many ways to fund college. No matter who you are, with determination and hard work you can receive a quality degree and experience the joys of attending college. The earlier you start planning the better, and parents *and* children need to be involved. This is a team effort. The student can help by working hard to get scholarships and pursuing other funding possibilities. Once you are in college, there are many opportunities for funding.

You can expect college to have a profound effect on your life. You have new horizons before you that you have not even begun yet to explore. College is a wonderful opportunity and a precious gift. Be sure to use every moment to the fullest.

Key Terms:

Academic Competitiveness Grants (ACGs)
Adjusted available income (AAI)
Advanced Placement Program (AP Program)
American Opportunity Credit (AOC)
Available income (AI)
Award year
Base year
Certified College Planning Specialists (CCPS)
College Board
College Level Examination Program (CLEP)
College Savings Plans
Common Data Set
Cost of Attendance (COA)
Coverdell Education Savings Accounts
DSST Program (formerly Dantes Subject Standardized Test)
Education IRAs (See Coverdell Education Savings Accounts)
Expected family contribution (EFC)
Free Application for Federal Student Aid (FAFSA)
Helping Outstanding Pupils Educationally (HOPE) credit
Included asset
Iraq and Afghanistan Service Grant
Kiddy tax
Lifetime Learning Credit
Merit-based aid
National Institute of Certified College Planners
National Science and Mathematics Access To Retain Talent Grant (National SMART grants)
Need-based aid
Pell Grant
Perkins loans
Plus loans
Prepaid tuition plans
Roth IRAs
Savings Bonds (EE and I)
Section 529 plans
Stafford loans (subsidized and unsubsidized)
State agencies
Student Aid Report (SAR)
Teacher Education Assistance for College and Higher Education (TEACH) grants
Uniform Gifts to Minors Act
Uniform Transfers to Minors Act

End of Chapter Questions

1. What is the FAFSA? Who should apply?
2. What are your COA, AI, AAI, EFC, and SAR?
3. Describe strategies to get your reported income down for the FAFSA.
4. Describe strategies to get your reported assets down for the FAFSA.
5. Are there differences in the methods used to apply for federal and institutional need-based aid? If so, what are they?
6. What is a Pell Grant?
7. Discuss strategies for getting more institutional need-based aid.
8. What resources can you use to increase your chances of institutional aid?
9. What are Section 529 plans? What are their advantages? What are the two types of plans and what are their differences?
10. What is a Coverdell ESA? How does it compare to Section 529 plans?

11. How do scholarships typically reduce aid? Are they worthwhile?
12. What is the best way to approach getting scholarships?
13. What principles can increase your chances of winning scholarships?
14. What tax breaks are available for education?
15. What tax challenges are associated with education?
16. What kinds of educational loans are available, and what are their advantages and disadvantages?
17. What is work-study?
18. How can you test out of college courses?
19. What important issue surrounds graduating early or late?

It is time for prognostication. Come one. Come all. You will amaze your friends and confound your enemies with your remarkable ability to see into the future. Actually, there is no hocus pocus involved. Spreadsheets are a powerful tool for forecasting your finances. And you WILL be able to amaze your friends. When you tell them, "Based on how home prices are rising, I will need to earn 7% on my money to buy the house that I want in six years," they will ask in admiration, "How did you know that?!" I will leave the confounding your enemies to you.

13.1 Saving for a House

Now that you have reviewed retirement and college plans, you can use the spreadsheet techniques you have learned to make long-term forecasts for a variety of goals, such as saving for a house, saving for a child's college, and of course, retirement. Be sure to follow along in the supplemental spreadsheets for the textbook. You shall begin by forecasting to save enough money to buy a house, since this is most likely what you will save up for first. Much of the spreadsheet modeling you used before for budgeting will come in handy. Also, you now have a better understanding of how taxes play a role in saving. Figure 13-1 illustrates a financial model that forecasts saving to buy a house.

The time periods are now annual, rather than the monthly time periods previously used in budgeting. Each assumption that you make you will enter into a red box. Later if you wish, you can change your assumptions and the spreadsheet will automatically readjust. This spreadsheet will also make a handy template for tracking savings over time, and can be used in a variety of situations.

Assume the EAR is 6.4%. This translates into a periodic monthly rate of $1.064^{\frac{1}{12}} - 1 = .005183$. Notice that in the following example numbers are rounded in the underlying formulas so that what appears in the cell compounds up correctly based on what is seen. Your current savings is $1,000, the value that you put in Cell G2. Next assume that each year you make constant monthly contributions to an investment account, and that these contributions go up at the beginning of each year by the constant amount of 3% (perhaps your assumed wage increase). Enter this amount into Cell E1. Next is your marginal tax rate in Cell G1, which you assume to be 28%. (Note that if your income rises, you may have to create a row with a tax rate for each year that matches your income.) The kind of house that you would like to buy costs $500,000 right now (t=0). Enter this into I1. The next assumption is about house prices. These can rise more or less than inflation, depending on the area. You assume housing prices in your area rise by 5% per year, which you enter in Cell K1. Finally, your first contribution in one month will be $1,000.

Figure 13-1
Saving to Buy a House

	A	B	C	D	E	F	G	H	I	J	K
1	Annual:	Interest=	0.064	Contribution Increases=	0.03	Tax Rate=	0.28	t=0 House Price=	500,000	House Price Increases=	0.05
2	Monthly:	Interest=	0.005183			Beginning Savings=	1,000				
3	t=	1	2	3	4	5	6	7	8	9	10
4	Monthly Contribution	1,000.00	1,030.00	1,060.90	1,092.73	1,125.51	1,159.27	1,194.05	1,229.87	1,266.77	1,304.77
5	Cumulative Annual Savings	12,348.06	12,718.50	13,100.05	13,493.06	13,897.85	14,314.78	14,744.23	15,186.55	15,642.15	16,111.41
6	Total Cumulative Savings Before Tax	13,412.06	26,866.17	41,325.32	56,847.40	73,493.26	91,326.95	110,415.84	130,830.75	152,646.20	175,940.50
7	Taxes	115.38	338.66	578.76	836.67	1,113.40	1,410.02	1,727.68	2,067.55	2,430.89	2,819.02
8	Other Withdrawals	-	-	-	-	-	-	-	-	-	-
9	Total Cumulative Savings After Tax and Other Withdrawals	13,296.68	26,527.51	40,746.56	56,010.73	72,379.86	89,916.93	108,688.16	128,763.20	150,215.31	173,121.48
10	End of Year House Price	525,000.00	551,250.00	578,812.50	607,753.13	638,140.79	670,047.83	703,550.22	738,727.73	775,664.12	814,447.33
11	21% of End of Year House Price	110,250.00	115,762.50	121,550.63	127,628.16	134,009.57	140,710.04	147,745.55	155,132.82	162,889.47	171,033.94

C4: =ROUND(B4*(1+$E1),2)

B6: =ROUND((G2*(1+$C1))+B5,2)

C6: =ROUND((B9*(1+$C1))+C5,2)

B5: =ROUND(FV($C2,12,-B4,0),2)

B7: =G1*(B6-(12*B4 + G2))

C7: =$G1*(C6-(12*C4 + B9))

Looking at Row 4, enter your constant monthly contributions for the first year of $1,000 into Cell B4. In the second year (Cell C4), the constant monthly contribution is higher by 3%, based on the contribution rate of increase put into Cell E1. Now drag and drop the formula across. After having made your first 12 contributions starting the next month, your savings for the first year is $12,348.06, as seen in Cell B5. This is the future value (as of the end of the year) of the twelve constant payments. (Be sure to check the blue formula boxes above.) Continuing down, Cell B6 has your calculated total savings by the end of the year. You set this equal to your beginning savings of $1,000 at t=0 which compounded interest (interest was compounded once using the annual interest rate) plus your cumulative savings coming from your contributions for the year (Cell B5). The total is $13,412.06.

Next comes taxes in Cell B7. The interest you earned is just the total amount that you have for the year minus principal contributions. Your principal contributions are the initial savings that you had at the beginning of the year, plus your monthly payments multiplied by 12. This totals $13,000. The difference between your principal contributions and the total amount must be the interest earned. This is $412.06.

Finally, to calculate taxes, you multiply interest earned with your income tax rate. Taxes in the first year are $115.38. (For simplicity, do not bother taking into account that you do not have to pay taxes until April, and could earn interest on your tax payment for another 4 ½ months - this is a small amount.)

If you took out withdrawals at the end of the year, these amounts would go in Row 8. In this example there are no withdrawals at the end of the year, and these amounts are set to zero. Row 9 contains your total savings after taxes and withdrawals have been removed. For year 1, this is $13,412.06 - ($115.38 + 0) = $13,296.68. Several cells for year two deserve discussion. For the total cumulative savings before tax in Cell C6, you now add in the initial amount from the end of the previous year (Cell B9) rather than starting savings (Cell G2). Likewise, you base taxes on the previous year's principal contribution (Cell B9) in addition to contributions for the year. Using column C, cells in Rows 4-9 can be dragged across and dropped, since you added "$" place markers where necessary.

The next step is to keep up with housing prices. You set Cell B10 equal to the current housing price (Cell I1), multiplied by one plus the assumed rate of growth in housing prices (Cell K1). Each year thereafter, the house price will reset to be 5% higher than the year before. In Row 11 you assume that a down payment of 20% is needed to buy a house, plus 1% in fees. Looking across, it will take until year ten to have enough saved. In year ten you will finally have $173,121.48 (Cell K9), which will just cover the down payment needed (Cell K11).

It is important to realize that since the house price is a moving target, this makes it more difficult to save a sufficient amount, and may call for targeting a less expensive home, which you can move into sooner. There can also be substantial expenses associated with moving into a new home. You may want to increase the percent contribution above 21% to account for these extra expenses.

Your forecast contains assumptions about interest rates, the growth in housing prices, and how much you will be able to contribute. These are guesses. You may end up with more or less than you planned. As circumstances change your forecast will need to be updated. Human nature is also an issue. People seem to have a tendency to be too optimistic when they forecast. When my graduate business majors hand in forecasts to me, most are wildly optimistic. Finding one that is realistic or even conservative is like finding a giant pearl in the sand. When I was a student at the Harvard Business School a professor told us that an executive of a company presented an overly optimistic forecast, and that as a member of the corporate board, the professor made sure he was fired!

Key Takeaway: When planning to buy a home, remember that housing prices are a moving target and adjust your expectations for the kind of house you can afford accordingly. There are also fees and expenses associated with moving into a new home. People are almost always too optimistic when they forecast.

Challenge

What kind of house do you think you will be able to live in? Do you think you can be realistic about forecasting what you can afford?

13.2 Saving for a Child's College

Our next example seems like something that you will not have to worry about for a very long time. At your stage in life, the thought of having children is probably way out there. I can certainly understand how you feel. However, when you have a child you will need to start saving for college right from the beginning, and even better yet—before. The next example demonstrates this and provides a chance to think about the expense of putting a child through college. Many people have children before they reach thirty. Your own child may be less than 10 years away. I know this is a startling thought for a young person.

Some parents put themselves through college and feel that their child should do the same. That is fine. You can use the following example to help plan for a number of other goals. This example is one of the more challenging ones to learn, but it is a useful template for financial planning because it demonstrates how to figure out how much extra funding is needed to reach a goal that you may have. In the last example your contributions were fixed, and you then determined how long it would take to save. In this example, you have to spend a set amount of money at a certain time. It is then necessary to figure out how much money needs to be contributed.[1] This problem adds the extra twist that the money needed in the future will be spread out over multiple years.

Private tuition in the last decade has risen at about 2.4% above inflation. (See the College Board "Trends in College Pricing" at http://professionals.collegeboard.com/profdownload/trends-in-college-pricing-2008.pdf.) Public tuition has risen at about 4.2% above inflation. The cost of a private college is over $37,000 per year on average, while the average cost of an out-of-state public college is above $29,000 per year. Suppose that you can save money in a Section 529 plan. (Your money grows tax free, and withdrawals are not taxed as previously discussed.) Assume you will be married. As of 2009 you can contribute up to $26,000 to your child each year as a married couple without the

[1] You could also modify the last example to figure out the payment that would give you a certain amount of savings by a certain time. You would do this using solver. I shall explain solver below.

contribution being added to the basis for a child's estate. You could also make a large contribution every five years: 5·$26,000 = $130,000. (Cut this amount in half for a single parent.) You may not wish to contribute too much to the account, because if you do not spend it on eligible college expenses, any withdrawals will be subject to a substantial penalty.[2]

After looking at your savings and other factors, you decide to start with a contribution of $65,000 every five years. (You can always change this amount later if you wish.) It may be difficult to initially come up with this large amount. On the other hand, the full $65,000 would be able to grow tax-free immediately, saving money in the long-run. If you have after-tax investments when a child is born, put as much of it as you can into a college savings plan right away. Figure 13-2 illustrates this.

You assume that inflation is 3%, that college costs rise 4% above inflation each year, and that the nominal interest rate is 5%. With a marginal tax bracket of 33%, your after-tax interest rate is .05·(1-.33) = .0335. So instead of taking out a dollar amount of taxes each year, you will adjust your interest rate earned. In general, realize that your tax rates will change, so that one after-tax rate will not be appropriate (requiring a tax column). In the following example, assume that you contribute at the end of the year and that you have the same tax rate. You can use the simplifying assumption that an after-tax interest rate is appropriate for budgeting taxes, and apply this rate to taxable contributions outside the college savings plan.

Assume that you will send your child out-of-state to a public college or to a private college. You split the difference between the two and set annual college costs as of today at $33,000. (Cell G3 – this is what you would have to pay for a child to attend college the next year, and you are assuming that you would have to pay today for the following year.)

Notice that time periods go down the spreadsheet instead of across. (Either way is acceptable.)You assume that you will be relatively well off, so that you can afford to make large lump-sum contributions to the college plan and send your child to an expensive college. Your child will begin college at the end of their 17th year (they just turned 18). At that time, looking at Cell G20, the annual cost of college is $104,240.90. (You are back to not bothering to round inside the cell formula again.) Next, drag and drop down to get college costs for the three years after this. Also notice that your child will finish college at the end t=21. However, payments are due before the beginning of each year.

In celebration of your child's birth, you put $65,000 into a college savings plan today. Every five years after that, another $65,000 goes in. In year 15, you put $26,000 in, because when your child has their 18th birthday (the end of year 17) you will begin making withdrawals to pay for tuition (which is due before the start of college). At t=0 your cumulative savings will equal the $65,000 just put in. The next year you will simply earn interest on this amount (Cell C4). You then drag and drop down through Row 7. Cell C8 will be different because a new contribution is made. The cumulative savings will include the cumulative amount saved from the year before with interest, plus the new contribution. Cell C9 has the same formula as Cell C4, and so forth, repeating the process through Cell C20.

[2] Your child may go to an inexpensive state school or not go to college at all. If you have another child you could roll the plan over and use it for them, but you are not sure you will.

Figure 13-2
Saving For Your Child's College

	A	B	C	D	E	F	G	H
1	i= 0.05		College Cost Increase=	0.07			After Tax Interest Rate=	0.0335
2	t=		Cumulative Savings	Payments From Plan	Extra Required		Annual Cost of College	
3	0	65,000	65,000.00				33,000.00	
4	1		68,250.00					
5	2		71,662.50					
6	3		75,245.63					
7	4		79,007.91					
8	5	65,000	147,958.30					
9	6		155,356.22					
10	7		163,124.03					
11	8		171,280.23					
12	9		179,844.24					
13	10	65,000	244,844.24					
14	11		257,086.45					
15	12		269,940.77					
16	13		283,437.81					
17	14		297,609.70					
18	15	26,000	323,609.70					
19	16		339,790.19					
20	17		356,779.70	-	104,240.90		104,240.90	
21	18		374,618.68	111,537.77	-		111,537.77	
22	19		276,234.96	119,345.41	-		119,345.41	
23	20		164,734.03	127,699.59	-		127,699.59	
24		Left Over	37,034.45		Extra Annual Payment=			

C4: =C3*(1+B$1)

C21: =(C20-D20)*(1+B$1)

G20: =(G$3*(1+D$1)^A20)

C8: =C7*(1+B$1)+B8

E20: =G20-D20

Cell C20 gives you a starting point to think about how much you will have saved. Looking at Column G, you will need over $400,000 to pay for your child's college. However, you are starting with about $357,000. Additional savings are needed, which you will cumulate in a taxable account. You realize that it is better to use the savings plan as late as possible to pay for college, because you want your money to cumulate free of tax as long as it can. Therefore, you will use the outside taxable account to pay for college first. After staring at the amounts you are confident that you can use the college plan to pay for the second through fourth year of college.

Column D represents amounts that you will use from the college plan. For these years, put in the amount of the college costs seen in Column G. You will also contribute money from the plan the first year, but you do not know the amount yet. Leave Cell D20 blank. Cell C21 is what is left over in the college plan after withdrawals from the previous year, but before taking money out for the current year. It is equal to what was left in the plan from the previous year (after withdrawing money) plus a year's interest. Drag and drop this formula down to Cell 22 through Cell 24. Cell C24 is money left over after you are done paying for your child's college. In a minute this will become zero.

Next, create your contributions from an outside plan. This is Column E. Cell E20 is equal to Cell G20 - D20. This is equal to the cost of college for the year, minus contributions from the plan. Drag and drop this formula down. Cells E21 - E23 should be zero, since full funding will come from the plan.

You now have everything set up. It is time to figure out how much you will contribute from the savings plan for the first year of college so that you end up with nothing left over in the plan at the end. A quick way to do this is to use "solver" if you are using Excel as your spreadsheet software. You may have to install it as an add-on, but it is not difficult, and you can search for instructions under Excel help.

You need to set your withdrawal in year one so that you have nothing left over. You can simply ask solver to do this. As seen below in Figure 13-3, you set the target cell, Cell C24, equal to zero (be sure to click the "radio button"), by changing Cell D20. Then click solve. After a solution is found, accept the solution. Notice that Cell C24 has to be a formula that ultimately depends on Cell D20. Figure 13-3 shows the result, along with additional cells that you are about to add.

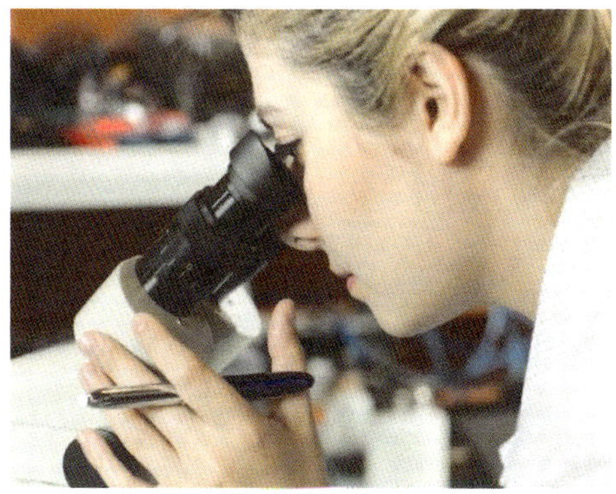

Solver found that you would withdraw $31,991.75 (Cell D20) to pay for year one of college. (In reality, you may want to withdraw a little more to make sure you do not have any difficulty withdrawing all of the plan amount at the end, since there are restrictions on how the money can be spent.) The amount needed from the outside account has also reset. Cell E20 is now $72,249.15.

There are two steps left: figure out how to fund the outside account, and fully understand the cost of sending a child to a top college of their choice. Column F contains the present value of the contribution from the taxable account (the "Extra Required"). Looking at Cell F20, this is Cell E20 divided by 1.0335^{17}, since the interest is being taxed. One way to fund the extra amount would simply be to put this amount in at t=0.

There are other alternatives that you could consider. One would be to put in a constant amount each month and increase the contributions each year by your assumed wage increase. This was what was done in Figure 13-1 to save for a house. However, since you do not know what your initial payment is, you would have to use solver to set the initial payment so that you have enough saved at the end. (By the way, you could have done something similar with saving for a house: set a concrete goal to have a certain amount saved at a certain time, have future payments grow based on the first payment, and use solver to figure out what the first payment should be.)

You decide to take a different approach and assume that you will make a constant annual contribution at the end of each year. You would like to know what this contribution is. Cell F24 provides the answer assuming that your last contribution to the plan will occur at the end of year seventeen. Using the Excel payment formula, you discover that if you contribute $3,222.97, at the end of each year you will have enough.

Figure 13-3
The Solution to Saving for Your Child's College

	A	B	C	D	E	F	G	H
1	i= 0.05		College Cost Increase=	0.07			After Tax Interest Rate=	0.0335
2	t=		Cumulative Savings	Payments From Plan	Extra Required	PV	Annual Cost of College	PV College
3	0	65,000	65,000.00				33,000.00	$251,048.04
4	1		68,250.00					
5	2		71,662.50					
6	3		75,245.63					
7	4		79,007.91					
8	5	65,000	147,958.30					
9	6		155,356.22					
10	7		163,124.03					
11	8		171,280.23					
12	9		179,844.24					
13	10	65,000	244,844.24					
14	11		257,086.45					
15	12		269,940.77					
16	13		283,437.81					
17	14		297,609.70					
18	15	26,000	323,609.70					
19	16		339,790.19					
20	17		356,779.70	31,991.75	72,249.15	41,262.41	104,240.90	59,533.30
21	18		341,027.35	111,537.77	-		111,537.77	61,635.83
22	19		240,964.06	119,345.41	-		119,345.41	63,812.62
23	20		127,699.59	127,699.59	-		127,699.59	66,066.28
24		Left Over	(0.00)		Extra Annual Payment=	$3,222.97		

F20: =E20/((1+H$1)^A20)

F24: =-PMT(H1,17,F20,0)

H20: =G20/((1+H$1)^A20)

Set Target Cell:	$C$24	Solve
Equal To:	• Value of: 0	
By Changing Cells:	$D$20	

In order to gain some understanding, it is worth asking what the expense of college for a child means. Try a thought experiment: suppose that you did not have a child. Instead, you signed a debt contract promising to make the same payments in the future that you would have made for college for a child (Cells G20-23). How much would the lender give you today?

To start, you need to know the present value of the payments using the interest rate after tax of 3.35%. Cell H20 has the present value of the first payment, which you can then drag and drop down. Cell H3 has the final amount that you could borrow based on the present value of all the payments. If you sign a debt contract promising to make the equivalent of the college payments, you will be handed $251,048.04, based on an after-tax interest rate. This can be thought of as the cost in present-day terms of sending a child to a good college (the average of private and out-of-state public schools), taking into account that interest on savings accounts are taxable. If all of your contributions could be put into a college savings plan, you would use the before-tax interest rate, and the cost would work out to be $187,183.87. See the benefit of college savings plans?

Some may find this amount a little sobering. And to make it worse, it represents contributions that must be made after taxes, retirement savings, medical insurance, and other withdrawals are taken from your salary. One would hope that college costs do not keep increasing above the rate of inflation.[3] If you assume that college costs will start to track inflation (Cell D1 is .03), then the present value of college falls to $123.971.49 without a savings plan, and $92,504.09 if all contributions are put into a plan. Clearly, what happens with future college costs is very important.

Of course, many children are able to go to college. However, some are not able to afford the college of their choice. Some pursue other strategies to fund college. They may go to a community college first before transferring to a four-year college, work full time for a while before attending, work during high school and college, or borrow heavily. Sadly, almost 50% of college students do not finish,[4] and financial hardship is often the cause. This is not true of good colleges, but there are many colleges that are nothing more than failure mills. They are happy to take student loan money for tuition, but do little to help their students succeed and graduate. (I discuss the devastation that can be caused by dropping out in later chapters.)

It is important to understand what kind of commitment is required if you wish for your child to not face these conditions. Some parents feel that it is important for a child to be aware of the expense of college and contribute to this expense (even if the parents can afford it), to teach their children about reality and the need to save and budget. And as you have seen, families do typically receive substantial assistance unless they are fairly affluent. This example took a conservative approach by assuming no assistance. The child can also help by actively seeking scholarships and working.

Key Takeaway: College tuitions have been steadily rising above the rate of inflation. The cost of sending a child to a top college without aid is quite large, although many families qualify for aid. It is important to start saving as soon as possible for a child's college, even before they are born. College savings plans are an important way to fund college, due to tax advantages.

Challenge

If you plan on having children at some point, do you intend to pay for their college?

[3] There is some evidence that grants have been going up so that net costs have declined in comparison to inflation.

[4] http://www.nytimes.com/2009/09/09/business/economy/09leonhardt.html; http://www.msnbc.msn.com/id/ 10053859. To see graduation rates by college, go to: http://www.collegeresults.org.

13.3 Saving for Retirement

Anytime long-term planning is involved, it is essential to keep inflation in mind. The next example gives you a chance to think about the importance of inflation in long-term forecasting. Of course, it is also a chance to learn how to plan for your retirement; one of the most important financial planning activities you will ever undertake. Figure 13-4 illustrates this.

Imagine that you are 35 years old and would like to retire in 30 years at age 65. In addition, you would like for your retirement income to keep up with inflation. There is good news and bad news. The good news is that people can expect to live much longer than they used to. The bad news—people can expect to live much longer than they used to, making it much more difficult to retire at 65.

Assume that inflation will be 3%, and the real rate of interest will be 2%. This makes the nominal rate of interest $1.02 \cdot 1.03 - 1 = .0506$. The monthly nominal rate is $1.0506^{1/12} - 1 = .0041219243$. Assume that your salary will rise 1% above the inflation rate. (This is actually conservative if you expect promotions throughout your career.) Your current annual income is $120,000, which is $86,400 after tax (assuming a 28% tax bracket and no state taxes; you should include estimated state taxes if you are in an income tax state). You assume that the tax bracket you will fall in will rise over time, and adjust the marginal tax rate up when your income hits a higher tax bracket. (See Row 7.) This is actually a conservative assumption because of inflation. Hopefully, tax brackets will be adjusted upward in the future with inflation.

You have two places where you save for retirement: a pre-tax employer provided retirement plan, and an after-tax investment account. Currently you have $50,000 in your retirement plan (Cell B11). Between your own contributions and your employer's, you put away 15% of pre-tax income into your retirement plan, which will grow 1% above inflation (Cell B4). You have $10,000 in an after-tax investment account (Cell B15), and currently contribute $6,000 after-tax to the account (Cell B14).

Note that you could put in a different contribution for each year (Row 14) if you wanted to. You currently assume that your contributions rise at the same rate as your salary. In a more detailed forecast, you may put in forecasted money left over after all of your expenses at the end of each year. This would come from your annual budget forecast, like the one constructed for Richard Wilson in Chapter 10.

Focusing on the pre-tax retirement plan, Row 9 is seen to have monthly pre-tax income, which rises by 1% above the inflation rate per year. Your monthly contributions are 15% of this. Each year (see Row 11) your savings will be the amount you had at the end of the previous year plus interest, plus the future value of an annuity from your monthly contributions for the year (see Cell C11). By the year that you retire (t=30) you will have saved $2,303,333.13 in the retirement plan.

At that point, assume that you take money out from the retirement plan to live on immediately (you will consider the money coming from the private plan in a minute), and once every year after that. Your withdrawals will grow by the rate of inflation. (Assuming monthly withdrawals is more complicated, and will require a much more detailed forecast using solver. I will discuss this later.)

Figure 13-4
Saving for Retirement

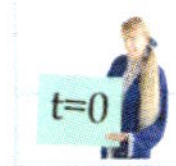

	A	B	C	D	E	F	G	AF	AG
1	Inflation=	0.03				Current Annual Income=	120,000		
2	Real Rate=	0.02				Current After-Tax Annual Income=	86,400		
3	Nominal Rate=	0.0506				Monthly Nominal Rate=	0.0041219243		
4	Salary Increase Above Inflation=	0.01							
5									
6	t=	0	1	2	3	4		30	Retirement
7	Tax Rate	0.28	0.28	0.28	0.28	0.28		0.35	0.25
8	**Retirement Plan:**								
9	Monthly Pre-tax Income	10,000	10,400.00	10,816.00	11,248.64	11,698.59		32,433.98	
10	Monthly Contributions	1,500.00	1,560.00	1,622.40	1,687.30	1,754.79	● ● ●	4,865.10	
11	Savings Before Tax	50,000.00	71,680.28	95,223.59	120,754.85	148,406.50		2,303,333.13	
12	After-Tax Income	35,739.16							
13	**Private Plan:**								
14	Annual Contributions	6,000.00	6,240.00	6,489.60	6,749.18	7,019.15		19,460.39	
15	Savings	10,000.00	16,604.32	23,698.85	31,311.43	39,471.32		561,999.18	
16	After-Tax Income	8,720.14							
17	**Real Total After-Tax Income Before Retirement**	104,226.47							
18	**Real Total After-Tax Income Starting Retirement**	44,459.30							
19									
20	Real Rate=	0.07							
21	**Real Total After-Tax Income Starting Retirement (tax=.33)**	165,591.54							

C11: =(B11*(1+$B3))+FV($G3,12,-C10,0)

C15: =(B15*(1+$B3*(1-C7)))+C14

B12: =AF11*((1+B$1)^(-AF$6))*(1-AG$7)*((1+((1+B$1)/(B$3-B$1))*(1-((1+B$1)/(1+B$3))^24))^(-1))

B16: =AF15*((1+B$1)^(-AF$6))*(1-AG$7)*((1+((1+B$1)/(B$3-B$1))*(1-((1+B$1)/(1+B$3))^24))^(-1))

B17: =12*AF9*(1-AF7)/((1+B1)^AF6)

It is time to review the time value of money. Imagine that you are standing in the future at t=30. At this point, t=30 becomes your "t=0." You will withdraw money immediately. (There is a cash flow at "t=0.") Each year your withdrawal rises by the rate of inflation of 3%. Assume you make your last withdrawal 24 years later when you are 89, which you will live off until you turn 90. (You are in effect assuming that you will live until your 90th birthday.) In reality, you do not know how long you will live.

There are several approaches that you may take. One is to make an assumption for money saving purposes about how long you will live, but have plenty of cash and assets that you can sell or mortgage if you live longer. Your children then get anything that is left over. Another approach is to buy an annuity from a life insurer. You pay them a big sum, and then get an agreed upon payment until you die. (You can also arrange for your spouse to continue getting payments.) You decide to take the first approach. It is interesting to note that in calculating the annuity you would get, a life insurer would make a similar calculation to the one that you will be making, using actuarial tables about life expectancy.[5]

Standing in the future, given your savings, how much can you withdraw, where your withdrawals grow by 3% and your first withdrawal is "today?" Think of yourself as making a loan to the bank of your retirement savings. From the bank's perspective, they are borrowing money (PV) and have to pay it back with a growing payment. This is the present value of a growing annuity where there is a cash flow at "t=0":

$$\text{"PV"} = \text{"}C_0\text{"} + \left(\frac{\text{"}C_0\text{"} \cdot (1+g)}{i-g}\right) \cdot \left[1 - \left(\frac{1+g}{1+i}\right)^n\right]$$

Solving for C_0,

$$\text{"}C_0\text{"} = \text{"PV"} \cdot \left[1 + \left(\frac{(1+g)}{i-g}\right) \cdot \left[1 - \left(\frac{1+g}{1+i}\right)^n\right]\right]^{-1}$$

To understand what you get, multiply this by one minus your tax rate during retirement since you will pay income taxes. (This is one place where it may be appropriate to use an average rate rather than a marginal rate, since you are removing taxes on all of your income.) Also, to understand what your income will buy you since these payments are very far out, it is very important to deflate the payments. The final equation is:

$$\text{After-Tax, Real "}C_0\text{"} = \frac{\text{"PV"}}{(1+\text{inflation})^n} \cdot (1\text{-retirement tax rate}) \cdot \left[1+ \left(\frac{(1+g)}{i-g}\right) \cdot \left[1- \left(\frac{1+g}{1+i}\right)^n\right]\right]^{-1}$$

"PV" is $2,303,333.13, "g" is .03 and "i" is .0506. This represents the after-tax amount that you can withdraw at the year of your retirement to live upon, inflated to today's terms. The messy formula is in Cell B12. It takes a while to construct, but it is not difficult if you do it in steps. Start with $\frac{1+g}{i-g}$ and slowly add to the formula, checking the mathematical result each time as you go. Alternatively, you can create multiple cells. Start by putting the formula in brackets in a cell. Then create another cell that is (1 − retirement tax rate) divided by the previous cell, etc.

---

[5] An actuarial table lists the probability of something happening to someone such as death or ill health, based on their characteristics.

There is a different approach to forecasting retirement withdrawals. The idea is to create a spreadsheet that includes your withdrawals after retirement. Those withdrawals depend on C_0, where C_0 is undetermined. The next step is to use solver to specify C_0. Spreadsheet 13-4b in the supplemental materials has an example of this method. A plus to this method is that you can specify an amount to be left over for your heirs.

The method for determining the real value of savings from the private investment account is similar to that of the retirement plan. There are two differences. Looking at Cell C15, interest is reduced by the tax-rate (assuming that taxes are paid on interest at the end of the year). In Cell B16, retirement payments are not reduced by taxes (unlike Cell B12), because earnings on this account have already been taxed, and withdrawals of principal are not taxed. Of course, you are ignoring possible capital gains taxes as securities are sold.

Cell B18 contains the total real value of your first withdrawal from both accounts to cover a year's expenses at year 30, and is the sum of B12 and B16. You will only be able to live off of $44,459.30 in retirement each year in present value terms. This amount is far below the $104,226.47 found in Cell B17, which represents the inflation adjusted value of your last monthly after-tax salary payment before retirement, multiplied by 12 - a measure of your real income right before retirement. It is also well below your current annual after-tax salary.

This helps to illustrate an important point: the retirement plan had $2,303,333.13 at retirement, and the private plan had $561,999.18. This may sound like a lot, but with inflation and the need to live off this money for years, it turns out that it is not very much. I once had a retiree complain to me that her bother-in-law bragged that he had $1 million saved for retirement, while she had a relatively modest pension from her company. I pointed out that as a practical matter, she was much better off than he was!

This brings up another important point: looking at Cell B21, if the real interest rate is set to 7%, then your real annual withdrawals at retirement will be $165,591.54. This is about 59% above your real after-tax income before retirement, and given that expenses tend to go down in retirement, is a very nice amount. It should be clear from this that rates that are earned on investments are extremely important for determining how comfortable you will be in retirement. I shall talk about investments in Volume 2.

Each year, it is important to compare how you did with your goals, in order to readjust your forecasts as well as your expectations for the future. This should not be terribly time consuming. First, put your actual current savings into Cell B11 and Cell B15. Then eliminate one column to reduce the number of years to retirement. You may have to drag and drop formulas across the column that was eliminated. Poof! It takes minutes. Finally, update the values at the top, including inflation, real rates, etc.

> ***Key Takeaway:*** A million dollars or more may sound like a lot for retirement, but it is not. Plan carefully for retirement or you could be left in poverty. When doing long-term forecasts, it is vital to include inflation. Forecasting in real dollars tends to be more difficult and less helpful. The rate of return on your investments will have an enormous impact on how much you have in retirement and it is essential to be a wise investor.

The forecast did not take into account an important tax strategy that you could make use of. This has to do with withdrawing after-tax dollars first. After all, you have two accounts: a retirement account that accumulates tax free, but is subject to income taxes upon withdrawal, and a personal account that accumulates with tax but is tax-free upon withdrawal. (Note that this will be somewhat different if you have capital gains, which can accumulate tax-free until sale. I put off this discussion until Volume 2.) If you withdraw from the personal account first, this allows your funds in the retirement account to accumulate tax-free. Your personal funds cannot. Also, you do not get taxed on your withdrawals from your personal account. This allows you to put off paying income tax on your retirement account as long as possible. Figure 13-5 illustrates the difference between pulling out money from your retirement account first, versus pulling money out from your personal investment account first.

Figure 13-5
Pulling Out Money from Your Retirement Versus Personal Account First

	i= 0.05				i after tax= 0.0325			
	tax rate= 0.35							
	t=	1	2	3	4	5	6	7
				Withdrawing Pre-Tax Money First				
Pre-Tax Account:	10,000.00	10,500.00	6,178.85	1,641.64				
	Withdrawal	4,615.38	4,615.38	1,641.64				
	After Tax	3,000.00	3,000.00	1,067.07				
After Tax Account:	10,000.00	10,325.00	10,660.56	11,007.03	9,369.01	6,576.00	3,692.22	714.72
	Withdrawal			1,932.93	3,000.00	3,000.00	3,000.00	714.72
				Withdrawing After-Tax Money First				
Pre-Tax Account:	10,000.00	10,500.00	11,025.00	11,576.25	12,155.06	10,771.02	6,463.42	1,940.44
	Withdrawal				1,896.95	4,615.38	4,615.38	1,940.44
	After Tax				1,233.02	3,000.00	3,000.00	1,261.29
After Tax Account:	10,000.00	10,325.00	7,563.06	4,711.36	1,766.98			
	Withdrawal	3,000.00	3,000.00	3,000.00	1,766.98			
	Difference							546.57

Assume the nominal interest rate is 5%, and your tax rate is 35%. Your after-tax interest rate will be $.05 \cdot (1 - .35) = .0325$. Start with $10,000 in a pre-tax account, and $10,000 in an after-tax account where interest is taxed. You will withdraw, after-tax, $3,000 in total each year until your funds are exhausted. If you start by withdrawing money from the pre-tax account, you will have to withdraw $4,615.38 to get $3,000 after tax. In year three, you remove the last of those funds and need to begin withdrawing money from the after-tax account. You can withdraw funds until year seven, when you make a final withdrawal of $714.72. On the other hand, if you start by withdrawing from the after-tax account first, you will not need to start withdrawing from the pre-tax account until year four. Eventually, at year seven you will be able to withdraw $1,261.29. The difference is $546.57.

With the stroke of a pen, simply by being financially wise and choosing to withdraw money from the after-tax account first, you end up with a sizeable extra amount available from the original $20,000 you started with. This is similar to the idea behind why a Roth IRA may be better than a traditional IRA, which requires that you begin withdrawals at age 72½. As long as you have other after-tax savings you will want to withdraw them first because Roth investments are not taxed until withdrawn. Of course, this benefit is diminished if the after-tax account has been accumulating capital gains on stock or other securities that is payable when the securities are sold. However, even in this case, the relative benefit is still there because capital gains taxes are typically less then income taxes, and the capital gains may be small. This all depends on your tax rate at retirement.

> ***Key Takeaway:*** A savvy strategy is to withdraw after-tax savings first, rather than pre-tax savings. Roth IRAs usually have an advantage over traditional IRAs because they do not require withdrawals at age 72½.

13.4 Other Forecasting

Once you have your retirement forecast set up, it will take minutes to update it each year. Your annual budget should take less than an hour to update. There are then two items left. Go over your assets and liabilities to make sure you will be solvent and liquid, even in a bad downturn. If you are like most people you will have a simple personal balance sheet. (Nicholas James had a complicated one for exposition purposes.)

Then do one last forecast—a simplified balance sheet at retirement, ignoring small assets and liabilities. Take big items and forecast them. For most people, their only major long-term asset will be their house. You may have other valuable assets, such as art, antiques, and jewelry. Guess at how much their value will go up. Hopefully you will not have liabilities at retirement if you have been diligent about paying off your house and other loans. Your net worth at retirement is your cushion. A common strategy is to save enough to live upon for a long period of time. Then, if you live even longer, you can reverse mortgage your house, or sell it and move into a smaller one. Otherwise, the house and other property can go to heirs. Your house can also be a source of funds if you have non-reimbursable health expenses or other unexpected expenses.

13.5 Conclusion

This chapter has presented advanced concepts of financial modeling. When you first get started supporting yourself, it is vital that you set up financial models; right after college graduation is a good time. This will take a solid day to accomplish, and will require some additional refinement as you discover the unanticipated in your finances. However, the initial set-up only happens once, and there are many templates that accompany this book to make your job easier. Once this task is done, you only need to update your forecast once a year, unless circumstances change dramatically, and updating will take much less time.

You can use the templates provided to do other planning, if you wish, such as saving to buy a house. The reward is that you will be in charge of your destiny. You will understand where you have been and where you are headed.

Of course, there are no guarantees in life. However, you will be traveling on your life's journey with a powerful and detailed map to guide you. Having this map will lend confidence. You may not be able to anticipate every event in your life, but you will have the tools for dealing with many of them, and the knowledge to see in what direction you are headed. Without this roadmap, you are stumbling around in a maze, not understanding where you came from and not knowing where you are going.

Once you have set up your financial models you will also become more aware of those around you, and in many cases you will notice that they are headed for trouble. You will observe friend, after colleague, after family member, making one mistake after another. You will be better able to resist the temptation to spend excessively in order to look as affluent as your friends ("keeping up with the Joneses"), only to fall off a financial cliff later.

You will also be able to avoid the effect of heavy stress that comes with financial fears and problems, the shame that comes with difficulty supporting your family, and the shock of having unrealistic expectations that are later dashed. Those around you will wonder at your ability to stay happy and achieve progress, year after year. As time goes by, you may find yourself constantly being asked for advice by worried friends and relatives, who will see that you have control over your life, while they seem to have little over theirs. It really comes down to something very simple. If you are in command of yourself, you will live a better life.

End of Chapter Questions

1. Using the template in the supplemental materials, forecast when you can buy a house. Assume the following:

EAR	5%
Contribution increase rate	2%
Marginal income tax rate	25%
Initial house price	$230,000
House price increase rate	3%
Beginning savings	$7,700
Monthly contribution	$880
Percent of house price needed for down payment, fees, and moving expenses	26%

2. Using the template in the supplemental materials, forecast paying for a child's college. Assume the following:

EAR	4%
College cost rate of increase	5%
Marginal tax-rate	28%
Initial annual cost of college	$27,000
Lump sum amounts contributed to 529 plan	$45,000/$18,000

3. Using the template on the supplemental materials, forecast your retirement savings and income in retirement. Assume the following:

Inflation	4%
The real rate of interest	1%
Your salary rises above inflation each year by	2%
Your current annual income	$75,000
You will pay the married tax-rate	Depends on bracket
Contribution rate to pre-tax retirement plan	10%
Taxable private plan annual contribution	$7,500
Initial savings	$5,000

4. What factors need to be considered when forecasting buying a house?

5. What was the important difference between the housing forecast and the forecast of saving for college?

6. What has been happening with college tuition rates?

7. How can solver come in handy with forecasting?

8. If you want to send a child to an exclusive private, or out-of-state public college, do you expect your 529 plan contributions will cover it?

9. What strategy should you use about withdrawing funds from a college savings plan?

10. How do you treat retirement plan contributions differently than private investment accounts when forecasting?

11. How big a difference can the rate of return on investing make?

12. What factors will reduce your ability to live off of future retirement income?

13. Does $2 million dollars sound like a lot of savings for retirement in 30 years?

14. Should you pull money out of a pre-tax account first, or an after-tax account? Why?

15. Besides a budget and retirement forecasting, what other financial planning is essential?

16. As an exercise, forecast retirement by plugging in what you expect your potential career starting salary to be. Assume inflation is 4%, the real interest rate is 3%, and your salary rises by 2% more than inflation. You will set aside 15% in a retirement plan, and you plan on retiring in 40 years.
    a. How much will you have saved when you retire?
    b. If you assume that you will live for 30 years after retirement, what constant amount can you withdraw?

17. Repeat exercise 14, except add a personal investment account and assume your contributions are 5% of your take home pay.

Chapter 14

Spending Money

14.1 Introduction

I have devoted a great deal of time to discussing how to save money, and the dangers of borrowing. It is now time to focus on spending money. It turns out that how much money you make is not the only factor in determining your wealth. How that money goes out when you spend is equally important. Throughout the chapter you will notice a theme about power. Will you let other people and forces control you, or will you control your own life?

In order to spend money wisely, there are two things that you will need. The first is a framework for spending so that you make the most of the money you have; the second is perspective. It is not a cliché that money cannot buy happiness; it is a demonstrated fact. In order to find true contentment of the heart, money must be put in its philosophical place.

Some consumption is necessary to live; food, clothing, and shelter are all needed for survival. However, consuming just enough to live on would be considered by most to be a very harsh existence. Clearly, making wise choices about consumption is important. So often, people look back with regret at the choices they have made regarding their consumption. Some of these people are financially destitute, but all too often they are typical people in all walks of life and levels of wealth who regard their past choices as mistakes. They tell themselves, "If only I had understood the consequences of what I was doing, I would not have caused myself such harm." One of the purposes of this chapter is to help you make the best choices about consumption that you can, based on your own individual feelings. In other words, to give you information so that you can make decisions that are in your personal best interest.

14.2 Reducers

We begin with a framework for spending money. With a bit of practice, this framework will become a habit that you may not even consciously think about, like buckling your seatbelt. The effect on your happiness and well-being could be profound.

Each dollar that you consume reduces future money available to you by more than a dollar. The reason for this is clear; the dollar would have grown in value had it been invested. That future money could be used for a variety of purposes such as consumption, the down payment on a house, or to live on in retirement. The money scale illustrates that choice. As you are contemplating buying something, in order to make the best decision you will need to know how much you are giving up in the future. Armed with this knowledge, you can make the tradeoff between current consumption and future consumption that is best for you.

One approach is to think about what you are saving for. Depending on where you are in life, you may be saving to buy a house, saving for your children's college, or saving for retirement. If you are saving for multiple purposes, pick the one that "has to give." For instance, if you are saving for your children's college and retirement and any reduction in savings will come out of money for retirement, then pick retirement as the goal. The next step is to create something that I have named a "reducer." This could be a "home reducer" or a "retirement reducer." Since most young people initially save to buy a home, let us call ours a home reducer.

Suppose you would like to buy a house in eight years. Also, you expect to earn 7% on money you invest. With a marginal tax-rate of 25%, your after-tax interest rate is .07·(1-.25)= .0525. The next step is to specify the frequency of payments. This will depend on the situation. For instance, suppose that you enjoy going to a high-priced coffee shop every day, and you typically spend $8.00. If you drink your own coffee bought at a grocery store, it will cost you .50, so the extra amount is $7.50. If you pretend that it is yesterday and the first payment will start today, then the number of payments is 365·8 +1=2,921. (This is the short-cut for future value problems when there is a cash flow at t=0. Remember that this short cut does not work for present value problems.) The daily periodic rate is $1.0525^{\frac{1}{365}} - 1 = .000140197$. The future value of all the extra coffee payments is:

$$FV = \frac{\$7.50}{.000140197} \cdot [1.000140197^{2,921} - 1] = \$7.50 \cdot 3,609.53 = \$27,071.44.$$

This is the amount you are giving up for a down payment on a house in order to go to the coffee shop. The house reducer is 3,609.53. A reducer is how much you lose by spending $1 regularly, and in this case equals $27,071.44/7.50. (To keep it simple you could round to 3,600.) What this means is that for every $1 purchase that is made every day, multiply by 3,600 to figure out how much less down payment will occur in eight years.

Another example may be eating out at a restaurant once a week. Suppose you currently eat out on a Saturday night and Sunday afternoon. You decide to apply a house reducer to the Sunday afternoon meal. You typically pay $35, including tip and tax. If you ate at home you would pay $5 in groceries. Now the frequency is weekly. The number of payments is 52·8 + 1 = 417, and the periodic weekly rate (assuming even 52 week years) is $1.0525^{\frac{1}{52}} - 1 =$ .000984490. The future value of the restaurant meals is:

$$FV = \$30 \cdot \left\{ \frac{1}{.000984490} \cdot [1.000984490^{417} - 1] \right\} = \$30 \cdot 515.31 = \$15{,}459.24,$$

The reducer part of the equation is in yellow. With rounding, your home reducer for weekly purchases is 515. This tells you how much less you would have per dollar spent if you made a habit out of a particular purchase. Table 14-1 lists different home reducers based on frequency of purchase, as well as an approximate number that is easier to remember.

Table 14-1
Eight-Year Home Reducer, 7% Interest, 25% Tax Bracket

Frequency of Purchase	Approximate Home Reducer for $1	Home Reducer for $1
Daily (365 days)	3,600	3,609.53
Weekly (52 weeks)	515	515.31
Monthly	120	119.88
Annual	10	11.14
Once	2	1.51

Now that you have your reducer, you are in a position to make better decisions on a day-to-day basis. For instance, before stepping into the restaurant, after a quick calculation, you decide that you are better off saving more than $15,000 towards a house – or not. (By the way, with 20% down, having $15,000 extra will mean that you can buy a house that is worth $75,000 more.) The point is that because you can see more clearly the consequences of your decision, you can make the decision that is in your best interest.

A typical example where using a reducer would come in handy would be getting a cell phone with Internet service. You are at the counter in a store, and the clerk is saying that if you buy an Internet capable phone, then for only $40 per month you can surf the Internet from that phone. After insisting repeatedly on being quoted fees and taxes, the total turns out to be $47. You then apply your house reducer and discover that you will have approximately $5,640 less for a down payment, and will buy a house worth $28,200 less.

You can now make an informed decision. After taking a minute to mull the matter over (despite the impatient clerk), you realize that you spend most of your time at work or home where the Internet is available anyway. You skip the Internet phone. On the other hand, if you travel a lot as part of your business, you may decide that it is worth it. You are in charge of your money in an informed way. To keep things even simpler, in this example you can even remember numbers that are close to the reducer like 3,650, 520, 120, and 10, that correspond to the number of payments in a year multiplied by ten.

The longer the time period, the larger the reducer. Table 14-2 presents a retirement reducer, for retirement occurring in twenty years with the same interest rate and tax bracket as before. It is assumed that you invest in a taxable account.

Table 14-2
Twenty-Year Retirement Reducer, 7% Interest, 25% Tax Bracket

Frequency of Purchase	Approximate Retirement Reducer for $1
Daily (365 days)	12,717
Weekly (52 weeks)	1,813
Monthly	420
Annual	37
Once	3

What is immediately apparent is that the consequences of spending magnify the longer the time period. Skipping the coffee shop every day would result in having $7.50·12,717 = $95,363 at retirement, enough for a typical person to live off of very nicely for an entire year or more! However, there is an expression that you "cannot take it with you when you go." A reducer helps illustrate the tradeoff between spending now and consuming later. Just remember that it is also alright to have fun once-in-a-while. Just do so on your terms, in the way that is best for your own happiness.

Key Takeaway: Reducers tell you how much you are giving up in the future when you spend now. Based on the frequency of purchases, multiply the amount spent by the reducer to tell you how much less you will have. You can then make a better decision about whether to spend.

Challenge

What is your reducer? Would using a reducer change your spending behavior?

14.3 A Rational Approach to Spending

Constructing a reducer is the first step in learning to take a rational approach to spending money. All too often, purchases are made based on impulse, emotion, or weakness in the face of a sales person with the personality of a pit bull. The result is regret. An important part of controlling your financial life involves acquiring the habit of using a rational framework when thinking about spending, and learning to get tough when pressured.

Going on vacation provides an excellent place to start. Suppose that you have been working very hard at your job for several years and have just received a promotion and large raise. You decide to celebrate and spend $3,000 on a three day vacation in Cozumel Mexico, scuba diving and sightseeing.

After a long plane trip with an unpleasant stopover in the Mexico City airport, you have landed on the beautiful island and face the choice of paying for a cab or taking the hotel shuttle. A cab will cost

$15 and the hotel shuttle is free. However, the shuttle does not run very often, and you will have to wait 30 minutes. A rational approach may involve thinking about the cost of the cab ride in the context of time. If you sleep 8 hours per day on vacation, then you are awake 16 hours per day. Multiply this by 3 and the number of hours on vacation is 48. Divide the total cost of the trip by the number of hours ($3,000/48) and the cost per hour of vacation is $62.50.

According to this, you should be willing to pay $31.25 to save yourself a half-hour of waiting for the shuttle. This is why people seem to spend extravagantly on vacation— they pay a lot for the time. The flip side of this is that people can also lose their inhibitions about spending while on vacation. People will often pay a fortune on some souvenir that they do not even like very much, when a simple memento on a shelf will serve the purpose of reminding them of their joyful trip. On the other hand, goods can sometimes be purchased much more cheaply overseas and shipped back home (but beware of fakes).

Another example is home computing. Imagine that you are a software engineer and sometimes work at home. You are considering buying the slower Internet connection speed from your Internet service provider. You will save $15 per month. Since you plan on buying a condominium in eight years you apply your house reducer and come up with a total of $1,800. You are about to take the slower speed when you realize that you can work faster when at home and that you will be able to work from home in the morning and avoid rush hour. Not only do you save on gas and wear on the car, your time is also freed up, allowing you to spend less time eating out and more time cooking. You decide to buy the faster connection. A note of caution is needed: these savings will not appear if you sleep in instead! It is important to be realistic about whether money will really be saved.

A different conclusion should be reached by a dance instructor at a college, who has an active, physically demanding lifestyle. She spends little time on her computer, mostly emailing and shopping. The instructor should skip the fast connection and also buy a modestly priced computer. The money will bring her greater happiness elsewhere.

We have already discussed how damaging it is to borrow to consume. Anything that has its value go away can be considered consumption in the long-term, because it does not grow wealth. Only borrow to consume if something is extremely important to you.

There are a variety of techniques that salespeople use to get you to buy. They may try to play you off of someone you are with by intimating that "you need to show her you care by spending money on her." Another technique is to try to convince you that if you do not buy immediately, you will lose some unbelievable one-time deal that is about to go away. Do not believe it. Sometimes they will convince you to buy something, and then add on "little" extras, hoping that you will not notice that your bill is becoming huge.

Ego is often used as a lever: "Only smart, savvy people buy —." Stockbrokers in expensive suits are particularly adept at using this. They try to convince you that only great, wise people really know how to invest, and therefore you must buy their investment product if you want to be one of those great, wise people. The biggest ego booster of all is being impervious to manipulation. Rather than be a dupe to aggressive and manipulative sales people, determine to be the master of your own behavior and money. Strength of character is required. If you are kind they will try to convince you that you will hurt their feelings, or their family will starve if you do not buy. Really successful salespeople brag about being able to size people up and figure out which lever to pull.

Hidden fees and costs are very commonplace. There always seem to be hidden fees when purchasing a car, buying cell phone service, buying cable or Internet service, and a host of other purchases. Demand to know what the final bill will be. Insist they tally it all up before you buy. Of course, other costs may be involved. When you buy a sofa, what will the delivery fees be? If you pick it up yourself, what will the rental cost of a towing trailer be?

Printers are a notorious place for hidden costs. The initial printer seems remarkably cheap (and it is to get you to buy it). However, they gouge you on the ink. (The price of the printer pales in comparison to the cost of using ink over the life of the printer.) That silk blouse may seem like a steal until you realize that dry cleaning will multiply its cost by a factor of ten. Some cars need much more expensive gas and have very large servicing fees and insurance costs. Long-term commitments are a big problem. Health clubs can require a year-long contract. Many people stop going after a couple of months, but have already paid for an entire year. Arm yourself with information, and consider all costs and fees. There may be more desirable or cheaper alternatives. You could buy a monthly subscription to watch movies, or instead buy used DVDs from Internet resellers and trade DVDs back and forth with friends.

These are only a few of the many situations individuals face every day. Reducers are a useful first step in understanding the tradeoff between current consumption and future savings. As you have seen from the computer engineer example, spending money in one place can also free up money in another. The vacation cab ride example illustrates how purchases can be irrationally inconsistent unless thought about carefully. When thinking about spending, ask the ultimate question, "Is this the best thing I can do with my money, or should I put it elsewhere?"

Table 14-3 summarizes six typical spending considerations. Practice using this table as a framework. Eventually, it will come naturally without even trying.

Table 14-3
A Spending Framework With Six Considerations

Reducers	Spending money today may mean less money tomorrow.
Spending to Save	Spending money in one place may free up money in some other way.
Consistency	Is one spending decision inconsistent with another?
Emotion or Pressure	Do you really want the item or service, or are you responding to emotion or sales pressure?
Information	Do you know about all of the taxes, fees, and other costs? Is there a long-term commitment?
Better Alternatives	Can you find something better?

Once you get in the habit of thinking about purchases rationally, you will make major strides in increasing your own happiness. It is remarkable the amount of effort that people will put into earning an extra 1% raise for the year at work. At the same time, they put little to no thought into how they spend money, while sending huge quantities of the stuff down the drain. If you are smart about how you spend, you can make much less than someone else, yet have substantially more.

It takes practice to get good at spending wisely. Imagine a football team that spent all of its time working on team spirit, complete with self-awareness building and pep rallies – but no time practicing. Despite a high level of effort and enthusiasm the result would be embarrassing to watch, and worthy of comedy segment on television. A framework and practice are needed to prevent your financial life from ending up like that football game. It is time to build financial muscle.

Key Takeaway: You can take charge of your spending if you develop a habit of considering: your reducer, spending to save, being consistent, being informed, resisting emotion or pressure, and thinking of better alternatives. Every hard earned dollar will go much further, and you could even move your wealth past someone with much higher earning power.

Challenge

Have your spending choices been good ones? Are there any that you regret? The next time you buy something will you remember to apply the spending framework?

14.4 Tales from Life

There are a variety of potential situations that you as a reader may face; from being in an ultra-rich family to being a favored son or daughter in a family of modest means. Most likely you will have had the good fortune to come from a middle or upper class environment, with material comfort and protection from worry. However, a common problem for students when they leave home is their unexamined world view that they can continue to own fancy electronics, expensive clothes, and other things that they are accustomed to. If this is your perspective, then at some point life just might disabuse you of this notion in a very cruel way.

A major source of trouble can come from living with success. How so? Young people from very affluent backgrounds can be especially set-up for terrible suffering in the future because they have not learned to base their spending on the resources that they have. Money has "grown on trees for them." The result is tragedy and pain. Most of you reading this book will have the opportunity to live the lifestyle your parents enjoy or even better, but not at first. That is why it is so important to create budgets. Plan and assess your financial circumstances regularly.

There are three times in a person's life when the exhilaration of new-found freedom can lead to trouble. The first is when a young person leaves home for the first time for college. As part of the "creating your own space" process it is easy to overspend. Making the situation worse, college students are often confronted with aggressive advertising that targets their lack of financial experience. I have already discussed the $80 sandwich.

Speaking of college, it is worth taking a moment to discuss an issue that is becoming very common. Putting the "newfound freedom" and "trouble from being protected" themes together, a second problem in college can come from being nurtured. Often college is the first time that a student is on their own. While many plunge in and start making their way, some feel lost. They can become what is referred to as a "boomerang kid." In other words, they drop out and return home. A surprisingly large and growing number of college students fall into this category, many at very prestigious colleges. I shall discuss this in more detail in the next chapter, however, it is worth mentioning here.

For most, college will be the "time of their life." Unfortunately, for some it is a time to feel lost. Without the usual assistance of parents, many feel overwhelmed with planning their course or study, or dealing with problems involving professors and other college students. Learn to plan ahead early on, including financial planning, to create a sense of having a rudder to steer by. By doing so, the need to stay in college will also be reinforced when the damaging consequences of dropping out are revealed. These consequences include not being able to earn a significant salary at a job, while owing a large amount on student loans and possibly credit cards.

Beyond the financial devastation is the humiliation of dependency. Imagine living as an adult with your parents who become increasingly frustrated and upset with you at your lack of direction. You then suffer a deepening depression and loss of self-esteem. That is why college students who are struggling should proactively seek help and counseling from parents, college counselors, and elsewhere. I will return to this topic when discussing career skills.

When a Boomerang Returns

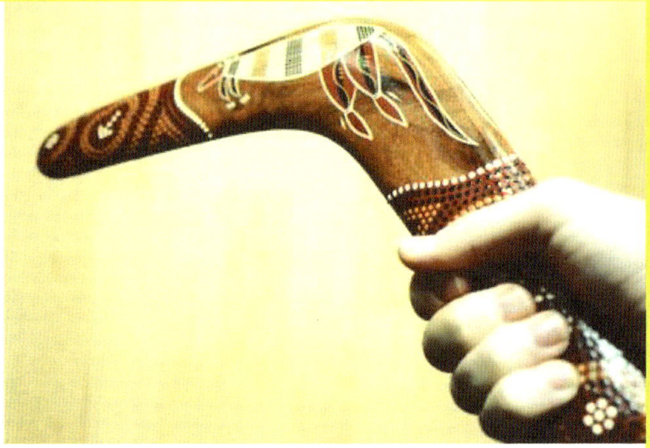

Nate seemed to have it all. Tall and strapping with sandy blonde hair and a winning smile he'd been a star tennis player in high school and won a partial scholarship to Northwestern University. When he wasn't playing tennis, Nate hung out with girls in his dorm or at various sororities. It seemed like he always had a date and often had to squeeze in his studies to make room for his social life. Nate was having the time of his life.

But now, sitting on the couch in the den of his parent's house, aimlessly flipping channels on the television, those memories seemed remote to him. Two years at Northwestern were over. After a great start, Nate had torn ligaments in his shoulder and had to sit out his sophomore year. Without tennis to ground him, his grades slid and he started skipping classes. Meanwhile, without his tennis scholarship he was getting deeper in debt, eating out, going to movies and buying gadgets like a new iPad. He owed nearly $3,000 on his credit cards. On top of that he had $20,000 worth of student loans. Unable to cope with school or his finances, he dropped out and moved back home.

Nate's mom was on his back to get a job, but he didn't know where to start. Most days he just sat in front of the television. His friends were all at school and he was too embarrassed to reconnect with them, especially with girls he once dated. When Nate looked into the mirror he did not recognize the sunken eyed stranger who stared back at him. He drifted deeper into his slump. Then, his parents gave him an ultimatum: get a job and go back to school. Not knowing what else to do, he reluctantly agreed.

Nate got a weekend job teaching tennis with a program that helped inner-city kids. He loved working with kids and making them feel as though they could accomplish something. In the process he discovered that he needed to tell himself the same thing. During the week he worked at a Radio Shack near his parents' house. At first he was embarrassed, but he liked earning money and he started to pay down his credit card debt.

Nate even started taking a class at night on personal finance at a local community college. He liked the class so much he decided that one day he wanted to become a certified financial planner. In the fall he planned on going back to school to study finance. He wasn't going back to Northwestern and he wasn't going to play on the tennis team. But that was O.K. He was back on track and doing what he wanted to do.[1]

The second time that can lead to trouble is when a person moves into their own place for the first time. It is very easy to overspend when stocking an apartment with furniture, decorations, and supplies. Try writing down everything that you may need to stock a new place. Just buying cooking utensils and other items for the kitchen will fill a page; the sum total is enormous. (People also underestimate how much it would cost to replace their belongings, and do not buy enough home or renter's insurance.) When starting out, look for used items, and family castoffs. Some of my happiest memories are of taking castoff furniture at a flea market and refinishing them into something beautiful. To this day, I cannot bear to part with a floor lamp that I made from an old coat rack.

---

[1] A fictional composite, based on newspaper stories.

The final time that can lead to trouble—perhaps the worst trouble, is when someone takes their first job. Imagine that you have just graduated from a good college and are working in an urbane environment. There are people there who have been in their career for a long time and have large incomes and personal wealth. They look and act very sophisticated. You will naturally consider these people to be role models and will be inclined to imitate them. You may say to yourself, "Of course I am supposed to eat out for lunch, hop a cab everywhere I go, join a health club, own a designer watch and briefcase, and take dates to top restaurants." Or you may tell yourself, "Of course I am supposed to wear expensive jewelry, have my nails done at a salon once a week, own silk garments that need to be dry cleaned constantly, and completely update my wardrobe with each new season."

As I will discuss in the next chapter, it is important to dress appropriately at work. However, it is especially true of young people that they can take it too far because they do not understand the consequences of their spending. This inclination can be reinforced by competition, one-upmanship, a perhaps, unconscious attempt to create the impression of being better paid than coworkers, and the desire to be "sophisticated."

Now that you are receiving financial training you are in a much better position to counter these temptations. Do not let the brinksmanship of others control you. When coworkers brag about their designer clothes, cab hopping, and extravagant trips, and then turn their gaze on you, a calm "I'm saving up to buy my own place" is a devastating response. It will immediately become clear that they do not have a clue about what they are doing and are completely out of control of their lives, while you are in charge of yours. You will see them deflate like a punctured tire. So who one-upped whom? And in a proper spirit of concern, you may just save them from themselves. Who knows? Because of those few simple words, you may have rescued someone from years of financial hardship.

Unfortunately, many people experience a lost decade, or worse. They wake up in their mid-thirties and realize that they are in debt, and do not own any assets of long-term value. The high life-style they were leading was an illusion – they were simply stealing from their own future.

Just How Easy Is It to Lose Money?

When some people get money for the first time they act like kids in a candy store, oblivious to the severe bellyache that awaits them. It is a story as old as time, dancing down a path strewn with coins that lead to a financial cliff. Using money wisely requires a head tightly screwed on. And if you think it is easy to blow the small amount of money that comes from a first job, it is nothing compared to what some people have done. Many lottery winners end up in bankruptcy, or even dead. They are the ultimate example of how easy it is to squander money, and why financial training is so important.

William Post won $16.2 million in the Pennsylvania lottery. Within just two weeks of winning he had already spent $300,000. He bought business ventures that failed while spending lavishly, and he eventually declared bankruptcy. Post was living off of food stamps when he died.

Michael Carroll, a garbage collector known as the "lotto lout," won $15 million. He bought four houses including a villa in Spain, demolition-derby cars, and jewelry, burning through almost his entire winnings within eighteen months. Carroll went back to receiving support from the government.

Michael Antonucci was a musician when he won the British National Lottery. After spending his money on cars, yachts, failed businesses, and extravagant vacations, he became broke and ended up sleeping on an air mattress in the office of a pub he worked at.

Keith Gough worked in a bakery when he won $9 million. Spending freely on cars and racehorses, he eventually wound up as a divorced alcoholic. After becoming the target of a swindler who robbed him of $700,000, Gough eventually died broke.[2]

Key Takeaway: When young people first get started on their own, they cannot expect to have the same standard of living that they enjoyed with their parents. However, with careful financial management they can accumulate wealth and prosper, just as their parents did. There are three points in a typical young person's life where they are at high risk of getting into financial trouble. The first is when they go to college, where they can overspend, or even worse, drop out. The second is moving into their own place for the first time. The third happens when starting a new job. Peer pressure, competition, and the desire to emulate higher ups at a company can lead to a financial lost decade.

Challenge

Do you currently face peer pressure that is not helpful? How do you respond to it?

---

[2] Jane Ridley, "Reversal of Fortune", *Daily News*, Wednesday July 29, 2009; Araminta Wordsworth, "After the Windfall; One of U.K.'s Youngest Lottery Winners Found Dead After Living Life of Recluse", *National Post*, Friday January 8, 2010; Julie Carpenter, "We Blew the Lott", *The Express*, Tuesday February 9, 2010; Rod Chaytor, "Broken Man; Five Years Ago Keith Gough Won Pounds 9M On the Lottery. But His Cream Turned Into a Nightmare. He Drifted Into Alcoholism, His Wife Left him and He Was Conned Out of Pounds 700K. He Died A..", *The Mirror*, Saturday April 3, 2010.

14.5 Gaining Perspective

As you prepare to start out in life, it is an opportune time to explore your values and reflect on what you find important. In the context of this textbook, it is important to ask what money or wealth will mean to you. After all, money is nothing by itself – it is simply paper or metal. It cannot bring happiness on its own. It only has value because it can be used to obtain something else. So the question becomes, "What do I value in life, and what role does money play in helping me obtain that which I value?"

Perhaps the best place to start is with asking what having too little money would mean. Some people are happy with almost none. They may find fulfillment in helping others around the world, while making just enough so that they can pursue a life of service. What can make this kind of lifestyle not only livable, but also enjoyable, is having a family or a community to rely on in times of trouble.

Otherwise, a hand to mouth existence can be mean and filled with fear: fear that the next paycheck will not come, fear of becoming sick and not being able to pay for medical care, fear of incapacitation. As I discuss in Volume 2, there are important safety nets that can reduce these risks, but some require (possibly substantial) payments.

We will cover the burden of financial distress later, but it also bears discussion here. Financial distress is its own special kind of nightmare. Every day is a desperate struggle to pay the debt. Any spare activity that costs money is curtailed. Fear moves in, and life revolves around struggling to bring in coin. Debt can be a truly harsh taskmaster. It can obtain power over your life in a way that would gain the admiration of the most brutal dictator. Many divorces and endless family conflicts revolve around financial problems.

So what *can* money bring? It can bring a host of opportunities. Travel takes money, as do many other experiences. Having wealth can open doors to the famous, powerful, or noteworthy. It can widen your horizons in terms of whom you know and whom you work with.

Realize, however, that money is only one path to these things. Many poor people and people of modest means have also found greatness and access to rarefied doors. Money can bring protection from need and lessen the threat of poor health, though it cannot guarantee good health. Money can also help with accomplishment. New businesses typically need funding and many individuals have found success and fulfillment through creating a business, whether they are a famous filmmaker or a successful banker.

Of course, money can bring possessions. Many beautiful objects can be acquired with money: clothing, jewelry, houses, antiques, cars, artwork, etc. The list goes on and on. Some find satisfaction in acquiring rare collections; anything from rare historical documents to rare paintings or coins. However, at the risk of sounding clichéd, possessions are not a substitute for the love of a family and friends, or the respect of the community.

Do You Rule Your Money, or Does Your Money Rule You?

How you relate to your money can determine whether you feel empowered and free, or powerless and imprisoned. And it doesn't matter whether you're a miser or a freewheeler. In these examples, consider how both misers and spenders can be ruled by their money.

A Tiger Tamed

In his prime, Mike Tyson was one of the most menacing boxers in the history of the sport. He certainly looked the part with his gold teeth and tattooed face. He mauled opponents, racked up knockouts and heavy weight championships, and even bit off part of an opponent's ear.

Tyson could earn as much as $30 million for a single boxing bout, and brought in as much as $400 million over his career. But out of the ring Mike wasn't in control, and the good times really began. Mike went on wild spending sprees that included hosting extravagant parties, buying jewelry, cars, clothes and cell phones. He even bought a sleek, beautiful, Siberian tiger.

Apparently, to live like Mike cost $400,000 a month and $8,100 to care for his tiger. (It cost $65,000 just to be ferried around in limos.) All of that spending wreaked havoc on Mike's finances. When he filed for bankruptcy in 2003, the list of debtors was as long as the Las Vegas strip where he earned his fame. The champ said that he'd been struggling with his money since the late 1980s.

Nowadays, an accountant controls Mike's money, and he's pursuing other forms of competition. Believe it or not, the former heavyweight champion, who has raised pigeons all his life, is going to try his hand at pigeon racing. But it's doubtful that his feathered flock will bring him a big payday.[3]

The Witch of Wall Street

Back in the 19th century she was known as the "Witch of Wall Street" not just for her financial prowess, but also for her horrid temperament and zealous frugality. Hetty's looks could have earned her that title as well. As the story goes, Hetty only had one dowdy black dress. She sometimes showed up for dinner with dirty hands. (Maybe she was trying to save on soap and water!) And she reportedly scared children with her scowl.

The Guinness Book of World Records called Hetty Green the world's greatest miser. Hetty was so cheap she used to carry around a pail of dry oatmeal so it could be mixed with water and cooked on a radiator for an inexpensive meal. What makes this so strange is that she had amassed a $150 million fortune, equal to about $2.5 billion in today's dollars, by buying up real estate and investing in bonds. If she were alive today, she'd still be the richest woman around—outdoing celebrities such as Oprah and Madonna.

But unlike Madonna, Hetty didn't enjoy her money much. Instead of living in a mansion, she lived in an apartment in Hoboken. She once dressed as a pauper and tried to get free medical care for her son's broken leg. The ruse didn't work and her son's leg didn't get immediate attention. Eventually, his leg worsened and was amputated.[4]

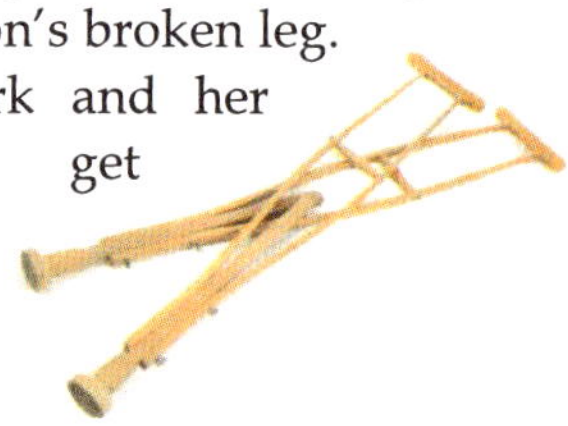

[3] Richard Sandomir, "Tyson's Bankruptcy Is a Lesson in Ways to Squander a Fortune," *The New York Times,* Aug. 5, 2003; "Mike Tyson 2008 Interview – Addicted to Money, Girls & Chaos," www.myspace.com/emceet., May 6, 2008; The Associated Press, "Tyson Enters the World of Pigeon Racing," posted on http://www.TysonTalk.com, March 24, 2010.

Money can bring its own set of troubles. Wealth can draw false love and false friends. The wealthy can be a target for theft, fraud, abuse, even murder. The wealthy can also fall into a cynical lifestyle. They can become detached from the feelings of others or the struggles that others go through. The absence of struggle can lead to an aimlessness of purpose. While many wealthy people accomplish great things and use their wealth to further accomplishment, others come to live simply to consume.

At the end of a long life's journey, it would be tragic to realize that you have worked hard for something your entire life that you did not really value after all. So it is time to gather perspective, and consult parents and others who you look to for guidance.

An Errand Boy Turned Billionaire Gives Back

Frank Batten Sr. once said that as a kid he was part of a prankster gang that did things that would have made him blanch if his own children tried them. Batten even once burned down a building, according to his son. He tipped buckets filled with water against the doors of houses so their owners would be doused when they opened the door, and he routinely skipped school.

All of that may have been true. But the cotton-haired gentleman, with the quick wit and bright blue eyes eventually made good. Starting out as an errand boy for his uncle who owned several Virginia newspapers, Batten worked his way up to become one of journalisms most respected publishers and a pioneering media mogul of Landmark Media Enterprises. It was Batten who came up with the idea for the Weather Channel.

A stint at a military academy gave Batten much needed discipline, and an education at the University of Virginia helped create a commitment to giving back to the schools he loved and fostering education in others. Batten wound up giving UVA the largest charitable gift in its history—$100 million to start a school in leadership and public policy. Batten fondly remembered the time he spent in Charlottesville walking underneath the leafy green trees where the university's founder, Thomas Jefferson, once traveled. Much like Jefferson, Batten said he hoped to inspire students to take on the responsibilities of leadership and public service.

Batten could afford to be generous to his alma mater. At the time of his death at age 82, he was worth about $2.5 billion. Not bad for a former mischief-maker![5]

---

[4] Constance Rosenblum, "Hetty: Scrooge in Hoboken," *The New York Times*, Dec. 19, 2004; "Hetty Green Biography," Bio True Story, www.biography.com; *Investopedia.com*, "Hetty Green: "The Witch of Wall Street" (by Andrew Beattie), http://www.investopedia.com/articles/financialcareers/09/hetty-green-witch-wall-street.asp; Jen O'Neill, "Happy Birthday, Hetty Green, The Witch of Wall Street," Nov. 21, 2009, *Finding Dulcinia, the Librarian of the Internet*, http://www.findingdulcinea.com/features/profiles/g/hetty-green.html; "The List: History's Greatest Misers," *The Sunday Telegraph (UK)*, Jan. 11, 2009; "The Witch of Wall Street," by Murphy, Puma P.A.C., People United Means Action, March 2, 2009.

[5] Phillip Walzer, "Frank Batten Sr. Remembered as Low-Key But Extraordinary," *The Virginian Pilot*, Sept. 18, 2009; "UVA Benefactor Frank Batten Sr. Dies," *UVA Today*, Sept. 10, 2009; Earl Swift, "Frank Batten Sr., Retired Landmark Chairman, Dies at 82," *The Virginian-Pilot*, Sept. 11, 2009; Dennis Hevesi, "Frank Batten Sr., Media Executive and Founder of the Weather Channel, Dies at 82," *The New York Times*, Sept. 11, 2009.

Once you become married, you may also find that your spouse has a different view of spending than you do. Unfortunately, as I have pointed out, spending is a major source of conflict in marriages. The good news is that you can spare yourself years of arguments by discussing spending, possibly even before you get married. Emphasize that marriage involves teamwork. Show your spouse a reducer. Get him or her involved in financial planning. Agree ahead of time when it is appropriate to spend and when it is not, and stick with the plan. You will "spend" a lot more time laughing and smiling with your spouse, and a lot less time bickering.

One of the purposes of this book is to help you take whatever resources you have earned through the sweat of your brow, be they modest or great, and use them in the most effective way to achieve your goals. This book also has a second purpose. You have seen that many different kinds of financial situations can drive people's lives, such as financial distress. Money can also drive a person's life by dazzling him to all else, so that he looks with blinders on at how many zeros he is accumulating at the end of his bank balance. As a finance professor, my students are often surprised to hear me say that money is not everything. Another purpose of this book is to help you learn how to rule your money, rather than letting money rule you.

Key Terms:

Boomerang kids
Reducers

End of Chapter Questions

1. Assume that you are saving for a child's college in 15 years. You can invest your money at an annual rate of 6% and your marginal tax rate is 25%. Construct a college reducer. After seeing this, what do you think of your parent's penny pinching?

2. Assume that you are saving to buy a boat in 10 years. You can invest your money at an annual rate of 5% and your marginal tax rate is 28%. Construct a boat reducer.

3. Assume that you are saving to buy a new car in 3 years. You can invest your money at an annual rate of 8% and your marginal tax-rate is 15%. Construct a car reducer.

4. Name examples of inconsistent spending.

5. Think of examples of how spending money can save money. How would this consideration require extra honesty with yourself?

6. What techniques have you noticed salespeople using?

7. Think about hidden costs. Can you name situations where hidden costs could be a big problem?

8. List three purchases that you or someone you know made lately, and go over how the six spending considerations apply.

9. There are three times in a young person's life when they are tempted to overspend. Name those three times.

10. How important do you think earning money is? Where do you see money fitting into your life?

Career Skills

In college you will learn a great deal about the technical requirements of your future career. If you are a computer engineering student you will learn how to program software and design circuit boards. If you are a medical student you will learn how to treat medical conditions. But this is only the half of it. Success at a career requires a vast amount of knowledge and skills that are not typically taught in college. Some young adults are fortunate enough to have highly successful parents that give them insight into what it takes. The success of these young adults may partly be due to their parents' impressive list of contacts, but much of it comes from the coaching they get. Most people start from scratch with very little career coaching. It is time to level the playing field.

Chapter 15
Career Skills

The thought of picking a career is both exciting and daunting. The good news is that there are a wonderful variety of careers available to suit any kind of personality. Each career has its own unique rewards and drawbacks, sources of inspiration and difficult challenges, times of excitement, and spells of tedium. All careers have something in common in that they require business skills. Even in the artistic professions, opportunities need to be negotiated, artistic mediums purchased, and property rights protected. Education and training are key elements to success, but there are other essential ingredients as well. These include a savvy outlook, business skills, and "street smarts."

We shall discuss a number of principles for success. One of the most important has to do with attitude. Perhaps the best analogy is being on a sports team. There are certain rules that have to be followed. You have the best chance of winning if you have a clear view of your goal and a strategy for getting there. You will make friends and those friendships will matter, but while on the field those friendships are also tempered by the larger exigencies of the game. Despite competing against another team, the members of that team are not your enemies. An attitude of professionalism is required (characterized by not taking things personally—it is part of the game), along with good sportsmanship. Succeeding depends on self-control, hard work, and focus.

15.1 Getting Started

The first step is to think about possible occupations. This is also relevant, by the way, to which college you pick. Any college will be better for some occupations than others. There are no government statistics available on switching careers, but one government study found that a group of baby boomers switched employers more than 10 times between the ages of 18 and 42.[1] (Imagine what this did to their retirement savings due to the failure of their pension contributions to vest! Apparently *they* did not.)

Since changing careers can be costly, a great deal of attention needs to be paid to picking a career and an employer. Part of the problem is that certain careers can be glamorized in movies and television. The dull and unpleasant aspects are not conducive to an exciting story. (Police detectives spend a great deal of their time filling out paperwork; college professors suffer through grading giant stacks of papers and having their research torn up by colleagues at presentations.) A career with a lot of foreign travel may sound wonderful until you find out that the novelty wears off quickly and it devolves into long, tedious hours at airports and on crowded planes away from family.

[1] Bureau of Labor Statistics, http://www.bls.gov/nls/nlsfaqs.htm#anch41.

Making a Living Underwater

Jill Heinerth has descended into deep waters to swim through what she calls "the veins of mother earth." She's traveled into caves in Antarctica and through volcanic lava tubes. In doing so, she's mapped some of the planet's unknown regions and discovered its secrets, including Mastodon bones and tusks from Jurassic era beasts.

But you won't find Jill's career in many job postings. And you won't find many people whose job descriptions include filmmaking, photography, scientific exploration, motivational speaking, technical advisory, teaching and one more: cave diving.

Blonde, blue-eyed Jill is one of the world's foremost authorities on underwater caves. It's an expertise that's taken the Canadian born adventurer into some of the world's darkest corners and most unusual discoveries.

Jill says her parents fostered a love of exploration by never placing artificial boundaries in her way, such as telling her she couldn't do certain things because she was a girl, and encouraging her to pursue her dreams. Ever since, she's been on an "endless pursuit of wondering where the lifeblood of the planet comes from."

She once followed underground caves throughout Florida, filming her travels below while another crew filmed above. The underground caves traveled beneath a golf course and restaurants. The documentaries from her underground forays helped people see that their activities on land deeply affect the source of water coursing underneath their feet.

When she's not submerged, Jill speaks about her exploits, trains others to cave dive and even advises Hollywood. She served as a technical advisor for the movie "The Cave," and worked as a stunt double for some of the male actors. You've got to be strong to cave dive. Jill typically wears hundreds of pounds of equipment, but it never weighs her down.[2]

---

[2] Jill Heinerth, National Geographic Radio interview: http://cdn3.libsyn.com/rebreatherpro/Jill_NatGeoRadio.mp3?nvb=20100504190313&nva=20100505191313&t=0d153ffcd2ae731e1d1b6; Corie Russel, "Six Women With Unusual Careers," *She Knows Living* Web site: http://www.sheknows.com/articles/811378/6-women-with-unusual-careers.

The technical training that comes out of textbooks can lead you astray. You may discover that you love archaeology after studying the topic. However, after looking into pursuing archaeology as a career you find that it is close to impossible to get a job. There may be three or four in the entire United States that open up each year that pay next to nothing.

This leads to a principle of success – research. Some supposedly "glamorous" careers are intensely political, with fierce competition and backstabbing. Start with an open mind and consider as many careers as possible. Read about each one. This can include informational books on careers or autobiographies of successful people in the field. Realize, of course, that successful people will have had an unusually positive experience in their careers, but their autobiographies will also tell you about overcoming the great odds that people typically have to face. The best way to get information is to talk with people pursuing the career. This may require networking, which is another principle of success. Ask your parents, or anyone else that you can, if they know people in the career that you are considering and whether it can be arranged for you to talk with them. Ask these people about all aspects of the career, both good and bad.

There are some careers that very many people want to be involved in that have few positions available. Examples are acting, screenwriting, dancing, writing novels, sports, etc. It can be very difficult to break into one of these careers as a result, and many people never succeed. We have all heard stories of extreme things people try to do to get noticed in some of these professions. Success may also require just plain, old, random luck. If you are determined to pursue that kind of career, you can reduce your risk by having a backup. For instance, if you would like to become a screenwriter, getting a double-major in advertising or business communications could provide a paying "day job" to fund your ambitions, as well as a backup career if your first choice does not pan out.

There are other careers that people find very enjoyable, which have more positions available. However, those careers do not pay very much. Other careers will pay a lot, but they are very demanding or unpleasant in some way, and can be very competitive and difficult to succeed in. Some careers typically pay a lot, but the income can be unreliable. No career offers everything – all have drawbacks which you will not know enough about just from reading textbooks. The key is to approach the subject determined to be realistic. Ask yourself how your potential career, in all of its aspects, will fit with your personality, the lifestyle you want to lead, and your plans regarding a family.

Key Takeaway: Every career has pluses and minuses. Some get glamorized in movies and television. The technical aspects of a career found in a textbook are only part of the story. It is important to research a career carefully to see if it fits with who you are and your future plans regarding a family. It is particularly helpful to speak with people who are pursuing that same career, and to keep an open mind concerning the good and bad. Professionalism, research, and networking are principles of success.

Challenge

Have you thought about a career yet? If so, based on what? Is there more research that you can do? If you have not thought about a career, consider what you would want in a career. Do you want to have plenty of time to be with a family? Do you want to be intellectually challenged? Do you want prestige or wealth? How do you feel about competition?

The Success and Saga of the Supremes

As a camera slowly pans across a glittering stage, Diana Ross and the Supremes® come into view wearing gold, sequined pantsuits, and swaying in unison to the beat of one of the groups hit songs, "Someday We'll be Together."® The televised performance from the 1960s was one of many that helped make the Supremes one of the most successful and glamorous female bands of all time. The trio's lilting voices, along with a string of hit songs, catapulted them to international fame, as did their strikingly feminine looks. Diana Ross, Mary Wilson, and Florence Ballard always appeared on stage wearing matching outfits and perfectly coiffed hairdos; their timing choreographed in harmony with the music. It was a rocket ship ride for three girls from poor Detroit neighborhoods, who were eventually discovered by Motown records® and molded into cultural icons.

But behind the scenes the Supremes weren't always supreme. As their fame grew Diana Ross became the front person for the trio, creating hard feelings within the group; within Motown other artists began to resent the attention given to the Supremes. Unable to deal with the pressure and feeling pushed aside, Florence Ballard slumped into depression and turned to alcohol. She was fired from the group and continued to spiral downward. Tragically, she died broke at age 32.

While the Supremes carried on, the group eventually disbanded as Diana Ross sought to succeed on her own. Later, when she embarked on a reunion tour with the group, Mary Wilson didn't join and publically ridiculed Diana Ross for snubbing her. The tour embarked with replacements, but it was a flop. Despite the group's saga, the public only wanted to remember the success of the Supremes.[3]

15.2 College

There certainly have been numerous people who have had very successful careers without ever going to college. However, times have changed and these days it is much more difficult to succeed without a college education. Gary Becker, winner of the Nobel Prize in Economics, pioneered the concept that investments are made in human beings, just as they are made in financial securities or machines. These investments are called "human capital."[4] In making an investment, money or other resources are put into buying something in anticipation of receiving payouts from the investment in the future. (A publisher's printing press is an example.) It turns out that investments are made in people, with college providing a great example.

The high cost of college has already been discussed. Today, four-year college tuition exceeding $100,000 is not uncommon, and tuition has been rising steadily. However, the room and board part of the cost is not a relevant aspect of the investment decision. A student would need room and board regardless of whether they attended college or not, and these costs should not be attributed to attending college. There is another enormous cost that has not even been discussed yet that is directly attributable to college—time. If a student was not spending time in college, then they

---

[3] http://www.vocalgroup.org/inductees/the_supremes.html; http://www.classicbands.com/supremes.html; http://www.independent.co.uk/news/people/profiles/exsupremes-singer-saddened-at-comeback-tour-snub-720625.html; http://www.foxnews.com/story/0,2933,287637,00.html.

[4] Gary S. Becker, *Human Capital, a Theoretical and Empirical Analysis With Special Reference to Education* (Chicago: University of Chicago Press and the National Bureau of Economic Research, 1993).

could have earned a living working at a job. This foregone income is an example of an "opportunity cost." In fact, four years of skipping work could be as costly as tuition, doubling the cost of college, if not more. It is clear that in total, college is a tremendous investment of time and money in human capital. There are even human capital websites that rate colleges in terms of payout for each dollar invested in college.[5] (Of course it goes without saying—there is more to a college than just its ability to help you earn a higher income.)

The loss from dropping out of college is gigantic. Suppose that a student drops out of an expensive college in their third year, and they earn $25,000 less each year as a result until they retire 44 years later. With an interest rate of 5%, in present value terms, this represents a loss of $441,569. This is in addition to the $90,000 in tuition spent, and the $75,000 over three years of foregone, after-tax income from not working.

Clearly, dropping out of college can have a devastating effect on lifetime wealth. The situation can be even worse if debt in the form of student loans or credit cards has piled up. The person dropping out can find herself struggling to make debt payments on a non-college graduate salary, and even wind up in financial distress. The painful process of bankruptcy will not help, as student loans are not reduced or forgiven in bankruptcy.[6] Any college student who is considering dropping out should proactively seek out counseling and follow another important principle: advice. There are many places a student can go, including college counseling services, residence hall supervisors, friendly professors, parents, etc. The important thing is to actively seek out guidance and support.

Most students find college an exhilarating time. It will also set the foundation for the rest of your life. You may discover your future spouse there, make friends for life, and begin your journey as an independent adult. You will meet an enormous number of people. Many people use the connections they make in college for the rest of their life. Later on, college contacts can get you jobs, customers, etc. In fact, good colleges try to make this process easier, and set up forums for alumni to network. At business schools, the quality of access to alumni can be a major factor in deciding which school to attend, because getting high-level jobs involves networking.

College is also where you will make a significant investment in what you know, which will have a profound effect on your ability to succeed. Use it wisely. After all, it is your future. It would be impossible to even begin to describe how college changes people. You will have the opportunity to learn many subjects deeply, including information that you will use throughout your career. Your world view will be shaped by your college experiences. As a professor, the most gratifying thing that I could possibly hear from a student is, "you changed my life." College could possibly be the biggest investment you ever make in yourself. Regard it as such and use it wisely. You may very well decide on your career when in college. If you are not sure about a career when you start, try sampling classes related to possible careers. Colleges offer a remarkable number of opportunities to grow. Actively seek out the best courses, interesting programs, and friendly professors. College can determine if you get off to a fast start or a stumbling one, which brings us to another principle of success—strategizing. Plan your time in college well, and use each resource and moment of your time to the fullest. Consider carefully each course you take. Will it further your career? Will it provide some other important kind of personal fulfillment or development? Try to get to know your professors. Drop by their office or chat them up after class. They just might

[5] See http://www.humancapitalscore.com and http://www.payscale.com/best-colleges.
[6] Laws concerning student loans are in flux.

have that invaluable tip, networking connection, or remarkable insight that makes all the difference in your future career. I would also like to think that we professors are interesting to talk to.

Karl Weintraub

Professor Karl Weintraub was in high demand at the University of Chicago. How could you tell? By taking a look at the quadrangle the night before registration. There you would see students camping out. To make sure they got in his class, the students staked out their spot at the registration window. It became quite a party late into the night, complete with sleeping bags and plenty of food, and students with all kinds of majors were there, not just history majors.

Professor Weintraub was a bear of a man, and a bit of a campus celebrity. Students would trade stories about his classroom theatrics and colorful tales, delivered in a staccato German accent. He didn't teach history—he made it come alive. Forget dull recitations of events and dates; his class was designed to transport the student into the minds of historic figures, as well as the common man. He wanted to show his students how differently people in the past viewed themselves, both as human beings and as part of the greater context that they were in, and how these views changed over the course of human history.

Professor Weintraub hid from the Nazis in a Dutch attic during World War II. However, it was his opportunity to become a director in Britain that he most enjoyed musing about. He turned it down, of course, but he always wondered if he might have become an Alfred Hitchcock.

Luckily for his students he chose to become a history professor. Start with a dramatic tale, throw in some peppery language, stir the students up, and you have a recipe for becoming a beloved and fondly remembered purveyor of knowledge.

Key Takeaway: College is an exhilarating time. College can also be the place where you make the biggest investment in your human capital. Building human capital is a principal of success, as is seeking advice and strategizing. Use your college time wisely. The loss from dropping out is enormous and could even land you in financial distress. Seek out help if you are having trouble.

Challenge

Have you thought about how you can use your college experience in the most effective way?

Internships, or other kinds of work during college, can be an enjoyable opportunity with careful planning. An internship is a temporary job offered by employers for college students, typically over the summer. Some students have to work to pay the bills, while others do not. But in either case, having a job during college (either over the summer or during school) can be an opportunity to develop, as well as an exciting first look into a future career. In fact, it can be helpful to start the process early. Some students work during high school. This may be necessary in order to fund college, but it can also provide an opportunity to acquire business skills early and begin a résumé. (A résumé is a document that you create to tell others about your career abilities.) Building an impressive résumé and maintaining a good public record are extremely important principles of success. (We will cover this in more detail in the last chapter of the textbook.)

I have already discussed internships and work-study as a way of funding college. However, it is not uncommon for college students who can afford it to take low paying, or even nonpaying, summer internships because they provide several benefits: a chance to learn about a potential career's plusses and minuses, a chance to build a résumé before taking your first post-college job, a chance to acquire skills, a chance to network with people who can lead to a better post-college job, and a chance to learn about a potential employer for later. The first job out of college can have a big impact on a person's career. An internship may provide a leg up to that first job. In some professions that are difficult to get into, like investment banking, having an internship under your belt can make a big difference. Of course, it is also important to get sufficient rest over the summer in order to fully take advantage of what college offers.

In some professions, it can be very advantageous to develop skills on your own. An example is computer programming. Many students learn how to program off of the Internet, and show up for college with a basic grounding in the subject. Becoming a reporter for the college newspaper will help hone interviewing skills.

Working is also a chance to find out about the real world and adjust your expectations. People who start their first job out of college expecting too much can damage their career with unreasonable demands of their employer. Some have a strongly differing view about working during college. Because an education is so important, "college should be a student's full-time job." Nothing should interfere in the slightest way. In any event, good grades in college are important for future employment. If you are planning on going to graduate school, they are absolutely essential. Maintaining your health and getting sleep are also essential. You may think you are young and invincible, but too many days of staying up late will eventually catch up with you. I thought I was invincible, getting four hours of sleep a day while taking care of a new baby and roaring through my graduate school classes at Harvard – until I became chronically ill and was not able to accomplish much of anything for a year until I recovered.

How Do I Get a Job Like That?

If you don't see yourself dressing in a pin-stripe suit, or wearing high heels every day and sitting behind a desk, you don't have to. Here's a look at some unusual careers that go beyond the typical 9 to 5 job.

Video Game Tester: Believe it or not, people can make a living playing video games. The job, though, isn't all fun and games; it's hard work. Video game testers need to have excellent computer and observational skills to spot software bugs that can ruin the success of a game. They also need stamina. After all, playing video games can be exhausting.

Pet Psychologist: Even doggie can get depressed. And that's when you need a pet psychologist. Like people, animals have an emotional life. They can also be taught to modify their behavior. No one likes it when Fido chews the leg off the dining room table. Training for this profession will force you to hit the books, though. You'll need a psychology degree, and maybe one in animal behavior, too.

Stylist: Not everyone knows how to look their best. Fortunately, you can pay someone to tell you how to dress. A stylist is your go-to person for honest feedback on whether saddle shoes go with a miniskirt. Fashion consultants generally work with well-heeled clients, helping them shop for clothes and even giving them makeup advice.[7]

---

[7] Tim Crosby, "How Video Game Testers Work," *How Stuff Works*: http://electronics.howstuffworks.com/video-game-tester4.htm; Gabby Hyman, "6 Unusual High-Paying Careers," *HotJobs.Yahoo.com*: http://hotjobs.yahoo.com/ career-articles-6_unusual_high_paying_careers-600.

Before you start your career, do your research and find out what is expected. In some professions, such as ones requiring artistic ability, it is helpful, or even required, to have a portfolio of work developed during college. Also, think about how you can be notable. In addition to good grades, is there something that you can do in college to help you stand out from the pack? Find whatever networking opportunities are available. This brings up another principle for success—push yourself. If you are naturally shy, it is time to find your inner courage. Brush your teeth, stick your chin up, and go shake hands. You will never get ahead hiding in a corner.

Key Takeaway: Internships and other kinds of work can give you a leg up on a career. It may also be necessary with some careers to develop a portfolio of work in college. There are other ways to obtain skills and stand out as well. Some have the differing view that college is vital, and therefore a student's focus should remain on doing well in school. In any event, good grades are very important, as is maintaining your health and wellbeing. An essential principle for success is pushing yourself, as is building a résumé. If you are naturally shy it is time to learn to be more outgoing and network.

Challenge

Do you have to work before or during college? If not, how do you feel about working in order to get a head start on a career? How do your parents feel about it?

15.3 Interviewing

Most college graduates will start by taking a position with a business; even those who eventually start their own. It is important to begin looking early in your senior year. If you wait until the spring all of the best jobs may be gone. Find out in the early fall when companies that you are interested in are interviewing. I will go over applying for a job in a later chapter.

Hopefully your efforts have paid off and job interviews are approaching; it is time to prepare. The first step is carefully researching the company. There is nothing that will kill an interview sooner than showing up without knowing anything about the company. If possible, try to research the people you will be speaking with as well. When notified of an interview, ask who you will be interviewing with, their titles and responsibilities.

On the day of the interview be sure to dress appropriately. If you are living on a slim budget in college this may be difficult, but it is essential that you have a good appearance. Since you are just graduating from college, they will probably give you slack for not having an expensive suit. However, you will not be forgiven for wrinkles or a sloppy appearance. In the corporate world you will generally have to wear a suit. However, this is not true in all business professions where a "hip" image is cultivated. Be sure to fit in with the attire of the people you are interviewing with, but err on the side of being conservative. You can always relax your attire later. If the office has a "casual Friday" wear business casual, which is just short of a formal suit. It is also generally better to dress simply without an excessive amount of jewelry or other distractions.

Go to the interview armed with a list of questions in mind. If you first can talk to other people who have already interviewed there it will help in preparation. Do not ask about how much you will get paid, or other benefits. (Save this for after you get an offer.) Also, be careful with your questions. They will be looking at what kind of questions you ask in order to learn about you. Questions about job responsibilities and opportunities for advancement, and comments that express enthusiasm for coworkers can signal to the interviewer that you are focused on getting to work and being a team player. Avoid anything negative. Employers want people with positive attitudes. Give the impression that if a difficulty occurs you will regard it as an opportunity – to shine.

Another impression to avoid is that of the prima donna. A friend of mine who had a high position in an accounting and consulting firm once told me that above all else, they valued the employee who did not complain and did whatever was necessary to get the job done. The interviewer may try to throw you a curve ball at some point. One tactic is to ask you to name a weakness that you have, but remember to always keep it positive. A weakness may be that "sometimes I work too hard," or "I am insatiably curious." If you have a weak spot in your résumé, be sure to plan on how to explain it without seeming defensive or dwelling on the subject.

Finally, try to practice ahead of time and remember that you may have a series of interviews where each person is looking for something different in you. The human resource person may be concerned with checking off a list of needed skills, and avoiding someone who is odd or who will cause trouble. Your potential boss will want someone who helps him look good and saves him work. Coworkers will want someone they feel comfortable with and who will cooperate and pull their weight on a team. After the interviews, be sure to send thank you letters on nice stationary. (See an example of a cover letter in the last chapter.) Yes, letters are old fashioned, but in the context of interviewing they demonstrate good business etiquette and professionalism. Remember the names of the people you interviewed with. Hopefully, they will hand you a business card, but they may not. If not, when you get a spare moment write their names down.

Whoops! Job Interview Blunders and Bloopers

Job interviews are nerve-wracking events. If you don't repeat the mistakes of some of these hapless interviewees, you may land the job despite the jitters.

Late for a job interview, a woman raced in traffic only to find a slow poke blocking her way into the garage. She beeped and honked, sharing dirty looks with the other driver. The woman then took it a step further by shouting obscenities. Bad move. Turned out the other driver owned the company where she was interviewing.

It was allergy season, and this interviewee had terrible hay fever. During the interview she sneezed so hard that a button on her blouse flew off and shot across the room.

It's a clever idea, but not terribly fashionable: nevertheless, one interviewer reported that an interviewee showed up without socks to match his dark suit. His solution: color his ankles with a black marker.

One interviewee was so nervous, that as he shook hands with the gentleman who was interviewing him a wad of gum shot from his mouth and smacked the man in the face.[8]

[8] Washingtonian.com, "Great Places to Work: Interview Horror Stories: The Funniest Job Interview Mishaps," Nov. 1, 2005, http://www.washingtonian.com/articles/businesscareers/2159.html; Anthony Balderamma, "Worst Interview Faux Paus,"

Once you have a job offer it is time to ask questions about compensation. What forms of compensation will be paid? What will compensation such as bonuses depend on? What retirement plans are available, and what eligibility and vesting requirements do they have? What medical insurance is available? In addition to compensation and benefits, there are a number of other considerations, such as the cost of living in the area and the availability of transportation. This can also be the time to bargain for a signing bonus, or other wants such as a office with a window. If you have competing offers you will be in a much stronger position. However, be careful not ask for too much. Once you start, having something that other coworkers do not could breed resentment.

Hopefully you have competing offers and it is time to make a decision. The potential for career advancement is very important. Your first job out of college will be a stepping stone, and it is important to make sure it is a good one. Think strategically about how the job will affect your entire career. Sometimes, first jobs pay more because they have career drawbacks such as limited opportunity for advancement. Keep in mind the value of future jobs that can come from the current one. There are jobs out there that pay very little and require incredible work hours because they can lead to a very desirable future position. At small companies, people tend to have to fill multiple functions. If you work at a small company you may have a variety of tasks, which is a chance to develop your skills. However, there may be limited opportunity for advancement. A small company will also be less known to future employers if you want to switch jobs (and whether the employer is impressive or not). At a large company your job may be more specialized, but there will be more advancement opportunities and your employer will be better known.

You do not want a company to "own you." For instance, suppose that a company has its own proprietary software for its accounting, payroll, and inventory systems. Most other companies use standard packages provided by well-known software producers. You work diligently and become an expert at your company's system over a number of years. Guess what? They do not have to pay you very much! If you switch jobs you will have to start over from scratch at another company that will not give you a very good beginning salary because you do not know their system.

Another example has to do with developing a reputation outside the company. Suppose you are given very difficult and demanding work because of your company's unique circumstances. Outsiders do not know this, however. Again, your company does not have to pay you very much. Try to build skills that are marketable to other employers, as well as a reputation with outsiders. Hopefully your company rewards employees who perform. However, as a practical matter they only need to be nice enough to you to keep you from quitting. If you do not look good to other companies, your rewards could be meager. Always view what you are doing from the perspective of developing yourself over a long career. Think strategically about the skills you are building, and the record you are creating for the outside world to see. Regard yourself as a work in progress. The position you hold is always a stepping stone to something else.

Think about visibility – another principle of success. You may be offered a position in a company that does not seem to be the most appealing–until you realize that you will get the chance to work with the CEO or someone else who is very powerful or successful. Half the battle is getting noticed both inside and outside of a company.

It is not possible to list all considerations associated with job opportunities here, especially since each career path is different. In making your decision, be sure to ask as much advice as possible from people with experience in the profession. Some executives even hire career coaches, which could be a good investment with the right coach. If you take a sophisticated approach to managing your career from the very beginning, your career just may start out in overdrive. Table 15-1 lists important factors to consider when thinking about a new job or a new position within a company.

CNN.com, October 28, 2009; http://www.cnn.com/2009/LIVING/10/28/worst.interview. tips/index.html; http://www.cnn.com/2009/LIVING/10/28/worst.interview.tips/index.html.

Table 15-1
Important Factors Relating to a New Job or Position

Will the opportunity develop your skills?
Is the opportunity a valuable stepping stone to something else?
Does the opportunity look good on a résumé?
Will the opportunity allow an employer to "own" you?
Does the opportunity give you visibility with a key person or the general public?

> ***Key Takeaway:*** Before interviewing, be sure to research the company thoroughly. Also try to find out as much as you can about the people you will be interviewing with. Come armed with a list of careful questions, and always be enthusiastic, positive, and professional. Remember that different interviewers will be looking for different things in a candidate. Do not seem demanding. A whole host of issues are important when deciding on a job offer. Career advancement and the ability to learn new skills are very important. Another big issue is whether a position is highly specialized, and if you will be able to develop an outside reputation and switch jobs easily if necessary. Avoid getting in a situation where your company "owns you." Think strategically about building a reputation and strong résumé.

15.4 Working at a Company

Once you start work, be sure to maintain a professional attitude at all times. Take on responsibility readily, and focus on succeeding in whatever task you are given. At first, you may sometimes feel frustrated being given a dull or low-level task, but that is the price of being new. Be sure to do that task well without complaining, and always maintain a pleasant demeanor. Performance is a principle of success. I remember hearing a CEO of a major corporation give a talk about why he was successful. He told the audience that if he was given a broom, he made sure to do a really good job sweeping the floor. Mistakes and poor performance follow people. In order to stand out, it is important to not have blemishes on your record. Remember that you are building a story about yourself to present to the world. You will be given increasing responsibility as you build your employer's trust.

You are what you know. Your value to an employer comes from what you know how to do. When I first graduated from college, I started at a company performing simple research tasks such as collecting data from the library, entering the data into the computer, etc. However, I took it upon myself to learn a complicated statistical package that was being used by my employer. I would take the simplest programs written by people above me and figure them out using the manual. I then asked to be given uncomplicated programming tasks where I would continue to add to my programming ability. Over time I was able to take on increasingly difficult projects. It may be hard to believe, but the first spreadsheet programs were also just coming into use. (Yes, I am that old.) I taught myself these as well, and started incorporating them into my work. By the time I left the company four-and-a-half years later, I had received several promotions, and my compensation had well more than tripled.[9] Find things out for yourself. Do not be reliant. Bosses do not like it when they have an employee who constantly wants to be told how to do things. At the other extreme, do not exceed your authority. Be absolutely dependable and keep learning. You succeed based on what you know. It should be common place for people to hear you say, "Can I try that?" or "How can I help?"

Consider taking on tasks that develop your résumé, even if they do not give you much of a benefit otherwise. Think of a diploma as a piece of paper that is an entry ticket into a game. To win you have to have a reputation and the knowledge to back it up. Focus on building yours. Finally, the best time to work hard and put in the long hours is when you are young, as family responsibilities may call as you get older.

Early Jobs of the Rich and Famous

Everyone has to start somewhere, and every job is a step toward something else. Even if it is working at a deli counter, or washing dishes at a Chinese restaurant. Before you turn your nose up at those humble occupations, take a look at who landed them first.

Sylvester Stallone was thirty years old, worked at a deli counter, and didn't appear to be going anywhere fast. But it was what Stallone did with his off time that rocketed his career. As the story goes, Stallone banged out the script to Rocky when he wasn't wrapping bologna. The rest is the stuff of Hollywood legends.

Michael Dell didn't wake up running a computer empire. One of his early jobs was as a dishwasher at a Chinese restaurant making $2.30 an hour.

Here's a look at how some other notable personas got their start:

Bill Murray sold chestnuts outside of grocery stores.
Rush Limbaugh shined shoes.
Jack Nicholson worked in the mailroom of MGM.
Jerry Seinfeld sold light bulbs over the phone.
Former Secretary of State, Madeleine Albright, sold bras at a Denver retailer.[10]

One of the most common problems that stifles people's careers is that they get stuck in a rut. They learn how to perform a job well, and then they just keep doing the same thing over and over again. To succeed it is necessary to always push yourself to try new things and to always do better. An important career skill is to embrace change. If your job is going well, then good. Get your feet off the desk and figure out what the next step is, or it will be someone else passing you by. A job is not a machine that you can sit back and enjoy once it is well oiled. It is a living organism. It will wither if you do not continue to improve and grow it. You have the latest technology for running your business. Great. What will the next innovation be? How can you stay in front?

The advent of the PC and the Internet created a dramatic laboratory for what can go wrong with people's careers. It used to be a status symbol for an executive to dictate what they wanted into a machine, and have a secretary

[9] Of course, you may eventually hit a glass ceiling if you do not have a certain credential. For instance, some companies will not promote people past a certain level unless they have an MBA. I eventually left that job because I needed a Ph.D. to advance further.
[10] Tom Van Riper, "First Jobs of the Rich and Famous," *CNN/CareerBuilder.com,* Sept. 6, 2005; Van Riper, "Celebrity First Jobs," Forbes.com, May 24, 2006, ://www.msnbc.msn.com/id/12959265; MidLifeCrisis Blog: http://midlifecrisisblog.org/?p=1564.

type it up for him *on a typewriter.* Any executive worth their salt would not do their own typing. I know, this sounds positively Stone Age, but this was the way it used to be until the 1990s. When PC computing came along it had the power to dramatically transform businesses. It completely changed the way they were operated and controlled.

However, upper level executives fought back because they did not know how to use computers, or even how to type. They considered typing beneath them. They had years of valuable wisdom built up, but with the new technology, new upstart employees knew more about something important than they did. Executives fought back against introducing technology into their company in order to maintain their own personal power. Of course, this was not sustainable. Many companies were run out of business by new competitors who took advantage of technology, or they were taken over by hostile raiders who fired middle and upper level management. Those upper level executives who were willing to learn the new technology and incorporate it were the winners. They had the advantage of their many years of hard won experience and street smarts, along with the ability to use a powerful innovation that had come along. When Wal-Mart was first founded with its one store, people were managing inventory using pieces of paper stuffed in file cabinets. However, Wal-Mart embraced a new, highly efficient computerized inventory system and became the biggest retailer in the world.

It must be very hard to believe at your age, with all of the changes that you are going through, that you will get stuck in your ways. But it is the natural tendency of all people who become successful. They want to keep what they have, rather than risking it by doing something different. This is a false sense of security. If a shark stops moving it drowns. Be like a shark. The world is constantly changing. What works well today will not work tomorrow. It is those people who continually embrace the new as they gain experience, who continue to learn and develop their skills, that reach the very highest levels.

Key Takeaway: To succeed at a company, always try to add to your knowledge and skills, and build your résumé. Never sit back while successful. Always try to improve what you do. Consider a job a continuing process. Embrace change, seeking out new training if necessary. Do every task well without complaining. Do not expect to be given high-level responsibility when you first start.

15.5 Starting a Business

Starting a business is an enormous subject and it is not possible to cover it here. If you are considering starting a business, you should collect a variety of readings on the topic and talk to as many people as possible. However, there are a number of general principles that I shall discuss.

Starting your own business requires a broad set of skills. Perhaps it is best to work as an employee at a business first and "learn the ropes" before striking out on your own, although there are certainly contrary examples (such as Steven Jobs). Having experience in a family business, or access to a caring mentor can help.

Some professions involve working as an independent contractor. Examples of independent contractors are people who provide consulting services to businesses: ghostwriters, people who create photographs or illustrations for authors, people who come into a businesses to help solve computer problems, etc. The idea is to widely sell your expertise at something. In some ways being an independent contractor can be simpler than founding a traditional business since you can start out with just yourself, or maybe a few employees, and you may not have to buy or manage a lot of physical assets at first. However, many of the difficulties of traditional businesses remain. While the failure rate for new businesses is in dispute, most would agree that it is quite high, maybe even well above fifty percent. There is a tradeoff. It is better to start a business after you have gained needed experience. This takes time. However, once you start a family you will have mouths to feed, and it will be difficult to take on too much risk. This is an argument for starting early. One of the reasons that the United States creates so many new businesses is that failure is not frowned on to the extent that it is in other countries, where failure brings deep shame. In the U.S. it is considered an opportunity to grow. Thomas Edison failed 10,000 times before discovering the light bulb.

I have not failed. I've just found 10,000 ways that won't work.
~Thomas Edison[11]

How Failure Breeds Success

Billionaires Bill Gates and Paul Allen were just a couple of nerdy high school students with big glasses and messy hair when they cooked up their first company. The idea began with something as boring as traffic. Ever since he was thirteen years old, the machines that counted and compiled traffic data for governmental agencies had fascinated Gates. He and Allen, along with another classmate Paul Gilbert, thought they could design a computer to tally up the data more efficiently. It wasn't a bad idea, but the business, called Traf-O-Data, flopped. "It wasn't a rocket taking off," Allen later said about the company. "It was an underwhelming failure. It landed with a thud."

Traf-O-Data may have been a dud, but what it eventually spawned wasn't. Allen said that their failed entrepreneurial effort helped him and Gates understand micro processing, and that what later followed was a "natural evolution of everything we learned." From the failure of Traf-O-Data Gates and Allen went on to found Microsoft, one of the most successful companies of the personal computing era.[12]

Famous Failures

Successful people are almost evangelistic about the benefits of failure. Why? Most all of them have failed—sometimes spectacularly. Few, if any of them, let their setbacks deter them. In fact, it was because of their failures that they succeeded. Many learned vital information and gained valuable experiences from their mistakes, and were spurred on to achieve greater things. So, the next time you make a blunder, take heart. You're in fine company.

·Michael Jordan was cut from his high school basketball team because of his "lack of skill."
·Winston Churchill failed the sixth grade.
·Albert Einstein's parents thought he was retarded and a teacher encouraged him to drop out of school because his grades were so poor.
·Harry Truman ran a haberdashery (a men's outfitter) in Kansas City that went bankrupt.
·Hillary Clinton failed the District of Columbia bar exam.
·John F. Kennedy Jr. failed the New York bar exam—twice.[13]

Many things need to come together. Funding has to be available, there has to be demand for the product or service, costs have to be low enough for the business to be viable, the business has to be able to fend off competitors,

---

[11] http://www.quotationspage.com/quote/30392.html.
[12] http://www.youtube.com/watch?v=b_Yr-7FBCk4.
[13] Kenneth Foo, "The 16 Most Inspiring Famous Failures," *eZine Articles*, http://ezinearticles.com/?16-Most-Inspiring-Famous-Failures&id=862208; "Famous Failures," *Businessweek.Com*: http://images.businessweek.com ss/06/08/failures/index_01.htm; David Lat, "The Bar Exam: A List of Famous Failures," *Above the Law.com*, July 17, 2007; http://abovethelaw.com/2007/07/the-bar-exam-a-list-of-famous-failures.

the business has to be able to keep the benefits of what it produces, the business has to be able to make what it offers known to potential customers, and the business has to have a workable accounting system and legal compliance.

For many, one of the main sources of suffering when starting a new business has to do with managing the books. Bringing in customers, planning marketing campaigns, designing your next product or service, or planning your next artistic performance may be where your heart is. Trying to keep track of the accounting numbers while paying taxes is for many the nightmare side of things. If you do think you may start a business at some point then brace yourself—you will be better off if you gut out an accounting course in college. Some pain now will mean a lot less later.

It is helpful to break successful new businesses down into one of three categories listed in Table 15-2. Starting an established kind of business and running it well generally involves lower risk, but also lower reward. The viability of the business model is well established, and the founder's task is to do a better job than competitors. This kind of business typically has lower reward because it has lower risk, and is open to many individuals to try. Sam Walton may disagree, however.

Table 15-2
Types of New Successful Businesses

An established kind of business run well
An established kind of business with a beneficial new twist
A radically new kind of business

The second category still has relatively low risk. The idea is to take an established business and add a valued modification. That is what made KB Homes successful. When KB Homes was founded, it was common practice for homes to have basements, which could add significantly to the cost of construction. KB homes sold much less expensive houses without basements, and they found that there was a large demand by price conscious consumers. KB homes is now one of the largest home builders in the United States.

The third category is high risk. Since something very different is being tried, it is easy to overlook one of the many elements needed for a successful business (an element that does not actually work in your case). Sometimes a new entrepreneur thinks something has not been tried, only to find out that it has been tried and was not viable for some unforeseen reason. However, when a radical new idea succeeds, that is where the biggest rewards can come from, such as the founding of Apple.

This category is also risky because it can be difficult for an unestablished entrepreneur to keep the benefits of their idea. Powerful people or businesses can say, "Thank you for the idea. Now I will take my money and other advantages to create it myself without you." This often happens as the result of a new entrepreneur having to solicit funding from a large number of potential backers in order to get the business started.

If you are considering starting a business as a career, self-assessment is very important. Are you outgoing enough to meet people and pitch your new product or service? Are you highly self-reliant? Can you live with risk and high stress? Are you able to motivate yourself, and live with competing possibilities and uncertain outcomes? Are you willing to work extremely long hours? Do you have a limitless amount of drive and the ability to overcome past failures? Successful entrepreneurs often fail many times before they succeed. Tenacity is needed. Even with successful businesses, many roadblocks had to be overcome.

There are myriad difficulties. Unless you are wealthy, you will probably need to convince others to give you funding. This can be especially difficult without a track record. As you start your business, you may have to go without sufficient funds to pay your living expenses, and debt may pile up. Some businesses have the advantageous aspect that they can be started with little money and built up over time, such as the Chocolate Factory in Chapter 2. If you do receive funding, you will be giving away ownership in your business, as Steve Jobs found out when he was fired from his own company. Finally, even if you are successful, your entire family wealth can be tied up in the success of the business. Enron employees are a good example of why this is a big problem. If you work as an employee of a company, hopefully you can take your savings and put it into a variety of investments. If you lost your job your savings would still be safe. If one of the investments failed the others would retain value. This concept was introduced in Chapter 2 and is called diversification. Entrepreneurs are notoriously undiversified. Their career and their life savings rise and fall as their business does.

Three Guys and an Idea

It was your typical dinner party among twenty-something-year-old friends at Steve Chen's home in San Francisco on a crisp January 2005 evening. In the background, the click and whir of digital cameras continued throughout the party as individuals took photos and videos, promising to download and share them with each other later. Sharing the photos was easy; however the videos were a problem. The Videos were too large to email, and different cameras required different codecs, thereby different software to download. There was no way to share them. Chen and his friends, Chad Hurley, and Jawed Karim realized that with camera phones and the increase of ways to take videos, this problem would increase.

The three friends had all worked together at Paypal, but they were now unemployed after eBay purchased the company. In February 2005, they got together to create a website where their friends could share videos. They began working on the idea in Hurley's garage in Menlo Park, creating an architecture for the site that would allow them to expand and simplify the process, with each taking on the role they were best suited for. Karim had opted out of the management role and minimized his involvement since his plans were to go to Stanford to earn his master's degree. In May, they had the site up and running to share clips with their friends, but then the site became viral. By December they launched their official website with over 300 million videos served on a daily basis. Along the way they had secured funding from Sequoia Capital, a venture capitalist, in order to expand.

Some twenty months after the idea, and less than a year after their official launch, YouTube was purchased by Google for $1.65 billion dollars. Three entrepreneurs saw a problem, used their expertise to solve the problem, and from that came an industry that has launched innumerable other entrepreneurs, and changed the industry of creating videos, television, and making movies.[14]

Finally, success seems to involve several ingredients. Protect your ownership. Do not give away a stake in your business readily, and protect your rights to intellectual property (inventions, written work, art, music, etc). If you bring in a partner, make sure they are compatible and will pull their weight. (Although it is often true that new entrepreneurs try to do too much on their own.) Make sure everything possible is written down. If not, trouble can really start. What happens if one of you wants to get out of the business? What happens if one of the partners dies? Can the spouse make decisions? Do they get a cut of the profits, or does their half of the business have to be sold? If you do not write everything down, you could end up suing each other in court for years.

---

14 Chad Hurley and Steve Chen, interview by Charlie Rose, Aug. 9, 2007, http://www.youtube.com/ watch?v=7E6E9q8Jebw; Jim Hopkins, "Surprise! There's a Third YouTube Co-Founder," *USA Today*, Oct. 11, 2006; http://www.usatoday.com/tech/news/2006-10-11-youtube-karim_x.htm; Associated Press,
"Google Buys YouTube for $1.65 Billion," MSNBC, Oct. 10, 2006, http://www.msnbc.msn.com/id/15196982.

It is essential to set up your business properly at the beginning. (See Chapter 2 for business entities.) Make sure that you hire a good lawyer and get your accounting system in place before you open your doors. Find a good accountant that works well with small businesses and does not charge excessive fees. And last, but definitely not least—pinch pennies with a vengeance. Make every cent count.

A Wrong Guess

The Marciano brothers and the Nakash brothers seemed like the perfect pair. Both families were immigrants who founded clothing companies selling jeans to the American public; the four Marcianos founded Guess?®, and the three Nakashes founded Jordache® Enterprises. The Marcianos were struggling to make their hot new jeans company grow, while Jordache was already a half-billion dollar company. It was a natural fit. The Nakashes bought a 51% stake in Guess? for $5 million, and Guess? got the funding it needed.

That's when the trouble began. The Marcianos said that the Nakashes promised them they could avoid taxes on the sale, only to find out the tax avoidance scheme was illegal. They also claimed the Nakashes stole their jean designs to use in their own Jordache collection. The accusations flew back and forth, everything from customs law violations to kickbacks. Lawsuits and criminal charges were filed, and spanned Los Angeles, Delaware, and Hong Kong. At one point, as a result of the accusations, customs agents and the IRS raided Jordache and carted away millions of documents.

A jury finally found that the Nakash brothers fraudulently gained control of Guess?, leading to the Marcianos regaining 100% ownership. The unseemly battle took 6½ years. According to a lawyer for the Nakashes, "With the amount both sides are paying in legal fees, they could buy another jeans company."[15]

The Marcianos weren't done. They accused one of their attorneys of bad faith and refused to pay him a $10 million bonus. The attorney promptly filed a $17 million lien against proceeds that the Marcianos got from getting Guess? back.[16]

---

[15] Lisa Belkin, "When the Honeymoon Ended," *The New York Times*, May 1, 1986.

[16] Belkin, The New York Times, May 1, 1986; Michael Marlow, "After Verdict, Guess Battles Go On," *WWD*, March 24, 1989; Jim Schachter, "Victors See Red in Blue-Jeans Feud; 'Guess' Founders and Lawyer Still Squabbling After Settlement," *The Washington Post*, June 1, 1990; Michael Lev, "Jeans Makers Settle 7-Year Fraud Case," *The New York Times*, May 31, 1990.

Key Takeaway: Starting a business is not all that it is frequently made out to be. Many businesses fail. It requires coping with stress, uncertainty, and roadblocks that get in the way. Very long hours are required, and unless you are already wealthy, your savings and most of what you own will be tied up in the business. Seeking funding creates its own challenges. Business owners should pick who they work with carefully, protect their rights, sign legal contracts, write everything down. Entrepreneurs should set their business up properly at the beginning, including finding a good lawyer and accountant. Legal protection and ownership are principles for success.

15.6 General Principles for Success

Whether you plan on a career employed by a business or start your own, there are general principles of success. Research is an important principle. Always be prepared by researching the businesses and the people with which you will be dealing. In law, a lawyer is never supposed to ask a witness a question unless he already knows how the witness will answer. That same principle can be helpful in so many other ways. Our system of business is based on contracting; however it is important to know about people. When disputes get resolved by lawyers and courts they become very expensive, tremendously time-consuming, and nerve wracking, and they often do not work out as desired. It is better to find ethical, constructive people who keep their word and are willing to compromise. It is often true that people's reputations precede them, although it is not always possible to know about someone and their reliability.

In the same vein, be absolutely reliable yourself. If you give your word, keep it. Many highly successful people regard this as an absolute must. Perhaps the most common failing of the multitudes who do not get ahead in this world is that they make promises that they do not keep. The damage they cause is enormous. Imagine that you are trying to get a book published. This is very difficult to do—the competition is fierce. You get a publisher to agree to take a look at your book, but they want to see it by a certain deadline. Your business partner is in charge of providing pictures. As the deadline looms you discover that they are doing something else and the pictures are not ready. You scramble, paying many extra thousands of dollars to someone to take pictures at the very last moment. If you do not make the deadline, the publisher may decide that you are unreliable and drop you. Approaching that particular publisher again in the future will be unlikely, and getting that kind of a contact is very hard to do. You may not find another one.

When you give your word, someone relies on you and may make other major commitments. The damage from reneging can be severe, and that someone will not be shy about telling anyone and everyone about what you did. You could also be sued for breach of contract. A reputation for unreliability is the kiss of death. I cannot count how many successful business people have said that the main thing they look for in someone is whether they keep their word. Circumstances may change, and it may become very costly, but make your word your sacred duty.

I think that very many people make promises they cannot keep because they do not want to make someone feel bad by saying no. However, the damage they cause when they renege is much, much worse. Some may string you along. They do not think they can do what they are committing to, but they cynically keep you on the hook in the off chance that they will be able to. It takes a spine to be honest with someone. If you do not have time, tell him, "I have X, Y, and Z commitment. If I were to promise you that I could do it and then I did not, that would be really unfair to you. It is better for you to find someone right from the beginning who will get it done." Moral courage is the best answer.

Donald Trump's Word

Mark Burnett shared the importance of keeping one's word at a college graduation speech. It seems that Burnett was tired of producing the TV show Survivor®; just about everything in the jungle could kill him. Burnett was headed down the Long Island Expressway and decided to call Donald Trump's office and make an appointment to pitch a new reality TV show, maybe in one week's time. The show would be about business people competing to get hired by Trump.

To his amazement, Donald Trump answered the phone. Burnett thought about hurriedly hanging up, but he plucked up his courage and told Trump he wanted to make a pitch to him. Before Burnett could say, "in about a week" Trump told Burnett to drop right by.

Burnett made his pitch on the fly and Trump loved it. He instructed Burnett to go to the next room and contact his agent Jim at William Morris to inform him about the agreement. However, Jim was incensed that Burnett had contacted Trump directly, instead of going through the agency. He listened to Burnett's pitch over the phone and then told him he could not approve the deal.

Disheartened, Burnett told Trump's assistant Norma that he had been turned down. Then he went in to deliver the news to Trump. According to Burnett, this was Donald Trump's response:

> Didn't I just shake your hand before and say we're doing this? Norma! Come in here. Take a letter to William Morris from me. Dear Jim, "You're fired!"[17]

Always keep your integrity. Sometimes whole businesses are dishonest, and it happens because people have a natural tendency to take their cues from the people around them. It is a common theme that someone got into trouble because everyone else was doing the same thing. As the fallout from the financial crisis unfolds, I believe we will see plenty of "respectable" businesspeople going to jail; and many others who were involved in shady practices will have their careers ruined. No employer will want to touch them. Besides, what kind of life does someone have if it revolves around cheating others? There are so many ways to be successful while contributing to the good of society. I believe that happiness requires self-respect, and self-respect will never happen with dishonesty.

---

[17] From a commencement speech by Mark Burnett for the Graziadio School of Business and Management, Pepperdine University: http://www.youtube.com/watch?v=dbTZSbrb_yw

Research will come in handy in many other ways. You will have a much better chance of success in selling a product or service, or closing a business deal, if you understand the circumstances and desires of the person you are conducting business with. What is it that they are looking for? Avoid "cold calling" (contacting someone without a referral by a mutual acquaintance) if possible. Before a job interview, find out as much as possible about the company and people you will be speaking with.

A White Collar Criminal Looks for Redemption

Sam E. Antar isn't shy about telling people he's a crook. He uses other adjectives to describe himself and his crimes as well: a low life, vile, ugly, and vicious. The bespectacled, cigar smoking, convicted felon goes even further, saying his life has been a "mistake of history."

So just what did Antar do? Back in the 1980s, the former chief financial officer of electronics chain Crazy Eddie helped mastermind one of the largest securities frauds of its day. The chain gained fame by advertising its "insaaaannne" prices. But what were really insane were its finances. Antar and other family members who ran Crazy Eddie bilked investors out of hundreds of millions of dollars by skimming profits, money laundering, and playing fast and loose with inventories. Antar avoided jail by testifying against others, including his cousin.

It's a tough past to live down, but Antar is trying to make good by preaching against white-collar crime, and lecturing about how to spot it. One of his main takeaways is that "unexamined acceptance" is an investor's worst nightmare. Verify everything, he says.

Antar spreads his anti-crime message through his blog and countless lectures around the country with various law enforcement agencies, universities, and other professional organizations. He says he takes no fees for his speaking engagements and pays for his own travel. But even Antar would recommend you verify that.[18]

Actively manage your career. This will include building a résumé over time that tells a positive story about yourself, as well as building a reputation for accomplishment and trustworthiness. Do every task well, and never show work until it is polished (legitimate excuses do not matter, people still remember shoddy work). Regularly take stock of where you are, and where you would like to be. Manage your career just as you would manage a project at work. Get advice whenever possible, and look for mentors if you work in a corporation. As your mentor moves up the ladder, she may pull you up with her. Seek out jobs with visibility to influential people. Keep as many contacts as possible; even maintain a list. Network with people to gather information, find new opportunities, and meet new people.

---

[18] Sam Antar's blog: http://whitecollarfraud.blogspot.com/p/about-me.html. Press clippings from Antar's blog: http://whitecollarfraud.blogspot.com/p/media-commentary-and-mentions.html; Herb Greenberg, "What Two Crooks Told Me Over Lunch," *The Wall Street Journal*, March 5, 2007, http://www.marketwatch.com/story/what-2-crooks-told-me-over-lunch; Aaron Einstein, "Crazy Like a Fox," *Crain's New York Business*, Oct. 4, 2009, http://www.crainsnewyork.com/article/20091004/SUB/910049995.

Pushing Myself

So how did I push myself? I am an academic, and prefer the quiet world of numbers and research. But in order to start Financial Wisdom Prep and promote my textbook, venturing out from the college campus was absolutely necessary. I had to extensively network and sell people on my idea. I definitely left my comfort zone.

Always seek to expand your knowledge. Do not get in the bad habit of resting on your laurels. Always learn new things, and push yourself outside your comfort zone. You do not get ahead by only trying what is easy. Attempt the difficult. Constantly experiment. The price of trying something on a small scale that does not work will be modest, while the reward for discovering something new can be great. Consider your career a constant journey of improvement.

In a similar vein, make sure that your human capital is marketable. Being highly specialized can be lucrative, but also risky. Technologies change all the time, and whole industries move overseas. Invest in specialized skills with caution, or be prepared to retrain if necessary. When change happens, embrace it rather than fight it. With change comes opportunity. There is a common misperception that the Chinese characters for the word "crisis" can be decomposed into danger and opportunity; however, I like to think of them this way. Sometimes the best chance to break into something new happens during times of turmoil. If you are experiencing a crisis, ask yourself how you can use the situation to move yourself forward.

危机

Threat of Extinction

Round-faced, quiet, unassuming Phil Tippet was living his boyhood dream. He had risen to become the head of the animation department for Industrial Light and Magic (ILM), moving models of animals and other creatures to make them come to life on the silver screen. It was a fantasy job in every sense of the word. His work on the movie *The Empire Strikes Back®* earned him an Oscar.

His next step was to create his own animation studio, called Tippet Studio. He started it in his garage. When Steven Spielberg asked Phil to help with his next movie, which was about dinosaurs brought to life through the discovery of ancient DNA, the sky seemed to be the limit.

Phil set right to work. Then he received a tremendous shock. Spielberg had become convinced that the creatures created by computer-generated imagery (CGI) appeared more realistic on film than did Phil's physical models. Phil was a master in the art of manipulating models. It seemed that his career was over.

But Phil knew a lot about what it took to create successful animation for movies, from how animals moved to managing teams of creative people, to the many other things needed to create successful animation for movies. Spielberg decided to put Phil in charge of directing ILM's computer animators. Phil even discovered a new technology: the digital input device, which allows computers to capture movement from physical models. Phil went on to win a second Oscar for his work on *Jurassic Park®*.

Phil contributed something else to *Jurassic Park* — his reaction to Spielberg's decision to go with CGI for the movie. When Dr. Grant, the paleontologist in the film, remarks that live dinosaurs have put him out of a job, Dr. Malcolm replies, "Don't you mean extinct?"[19]

---

[19] http://www.tippett.com/studio/phil.html; http://features.cgsociety.org/story_custom.php?story_id=4534; "Bonus Footage," *Jurassic Park*, DVD, directed by Steven Spielberg (1993, Universal City, CA: Universal Studios Home Entertainment, 2000).

The rung of a ladder was never meant to rest upon, but only to hold a man's foot long enough to enable him to put the other somewhat higher.

~Thomas Henry Huxley, Life and Letters of Thomas Huxley[20]

Be open to advice. There seems to be a natural process that controls skin thickness. (No, I am not discussing a medical condition.) Young people tend to have very thin skins, but their skin thickens over time as they achieve success and self-confidence. Skin thickness tends to peak in the mid to middle-late years, and then thins out again with old age. If you can listen carefully to advice, and yes, even criticism, you will be miles ahead. It is easy to spot a badly run business. I bet that you have seen a dozen of them. When customers complain, these employees immediately become combative and try to win the argument. It devolves into an ego-laden jousting match. They refuse to listen.

The best businesses take every customer complaint and consider them carefully. Some may not have merit, but some do. They continually do things better as a result. Be the same way as a person. When someone offers you advice, or even criticism, there is a good chance that their motive is not simply to make you feel bad. They are trying to tell you something. They may be wrong. But even if they are, if people are getting the wrong impression of you, is that not useful information? The nice thing about advice is, once you have mulled it over, you can throw it out with no harm done. If there is valuable information in the advice, you have been handed a gift.

Learn to protect yourself; your money, reputation, and property. Make sure that you sign contracts when necessary, and consult with attorneys when needed. Even when you trust someone very much, it is better to write things down to prevent misunderstandings and cover every possibility. It is not personal—it is simply professional behavior.

Finally, no discussion about success would be complete without discussing leadership. Leadership is an amorphous concept that is bandied about all the time. Here is my take on it: leadership is about being aware of the greater context. It is about having a vision. When someone tries to take advantage of every angle and he is one hundred percent out for himself, people know it. Leaders see what they are doing in the greater context of something important, and devote themselves to promoting that. They also share their vision. Ultimately, they get ahead because others look to them for guidance.

Leadership is also about inspiration. You do not rise by rising above. At first glance, George Washington appears haughty in the painting, choosing to stand in the boat while others row. Actually, they were being shot at! Washington was demonstrating the need to be brave by making a very large target of himself.

There is a famous expression that "a rising tide lifts all boats." If you bring out the best in those below you, if you show them that they can accomplish more than they ever thought they could, and if you make them feel that what they are doing is important, they will lift you up.

Leaders make sure that their employees get full credit and praise for their accomplishments. Leaders are also assiduously fair. In order to gain the admiration of those below you, you must first gain their trust. Table 15-3 summarizes general principles for success.

[20] Quote Garden.

The Greater Context

This seems like an opportune time to talk about the greater context of Financial Wisdom Preparatory Institute and this textbook. The introduction already gave historical context. In the 20th century we lost the ability to hand down vital knowledge that people need for happiness and success. Children used to learn necessary skills to support themselves and manage their money through working at the family business. These days, young people are sent out the door without the basic training required to take care of themselves and assume adulthood. I believe that most people lose a significant amount of their wealth to financial mistakes. The suffering is terrible and can lead to depression and divorce. If I can prevent some of that, I will be rewarded indeed. Please let me know in the future if something in this textbook has saved you from a horrible mistake. I would love to hear about it, along with anecdotes you would care to share, or your own pearls of wisdom.

There is more to it, however. The situation has brought on abuse. Everywhere I look, I see predators circling hapless victims. Our very economic safety is at risk. During the recent financial crisis we came to the brink of a full financial collapse. Another great depression with bread lines and 30% unemployment became a real possibility. I have already discussed the heart of the crisis—people being egged on by ruthless lenders, or greedily speculating into taking out mortgages that they could not afford. If there was a general understanding of the nature and unyielding demands of debt, if the risk associated with borrowing had been understood, the crisis never would have happened.

Even more important, if people are better stewards of their money then they will be better citizens. The government is the biggest borrower in the United States and takes a large portion of our earnings. With financial training we will all be more informed, independent, self-reliant, and capable watchdogs, demanding that our elected leaders borrow responsibly and spend *our* money wisely. It is up to us to hand the next generation a better world.

15.7 Conclusion

Heading for college is one of the most exciting times in a person's life. College is also the first stepping stone in your career. However, the technical knowledge that you will learn in college is only part of what you will need to know in order to have a flourishing career. There are general principles of success that the accomplished seem to have in common. Some lucky individuals receive this training and go on to high success. Most however, do not. They haphazardly stumble across a few of these principles here and there, often because of costly mistakes. There are no guarantees in life. But if you constantly try to apply these principles, you will be many steps ahead of the game. The end result just may be triumphant.

Table 15-3
Sixteen Principles for a Successful Career

Professionalism	Do not take business situations personally.
Performance	Do every task very well, no matter how small. Never show your work until it is polished.
Integrity	Stay honest. Do not get sucked in if "everyone is doing it."
Research	Gather information about businesses and people. Knowledge is power. Know what you are getting into in any situation before you even show up.
Networking	Meet with as many people as possible who may be of assistance at some point. Try not to "cold call."
Advice	Seek out suggestions from successful or well-informed people. Do not be defensive about advice or even criticism when it is offered.
Human capital	Invest in knowledge for a future payoff. This includes college, as well as a lifetime of on-the-job training and self-improvement. Try to develop skills that are generally marketable.
Strategizing	Periodically take time to assess where you are and how to best get to where you want to be. Actively manage your career.
Résumé and public record	This is the first look that people will get of you. Make sure it is a good one. Try to create a "story" about yourself and develop a public reputation.
Visibility	Try to take on tasks that will get you in front of influential people who can help you.
Work with reliable people/relationships	It is better to work with trustworthy people than to end up in court, or with no legal recourse at all.
Keep your word	Always follow through on commitments, even when it is not convenient. Your reputation will follow you.
Push yourself	Do things outside your comfort zone and take carefully considered risks.
Embrace change	Keep up with a changing world. Get in front of change.
Leadership	Keep the greater context in mind, inspire others, and set an example. Engender trust.
Legal protections and ownership	Sign contracts and protect property rights, even with people you trust.

Key Terms:

Cold calling
Human capital
Networking
Opportunity cost
Professionalism
Résumé

End of Chapter Questions

1. What does "professionalism" imply?
2. How may school learning lead you astray with regard to a career?
3. What sorts of concerns should you worry about when considering a career?
4. What sort of activities will help in finding a career that you are happy with?
5. Why is it so costly to drop out of college? What are the consequences?
6. What are the pros and cons of working during college? What is an internship?
7. When can networking help?
8. What kind of preparation is important before an interview?
9. What sorts of things should you consider with a new job offer, or a new position in a company?
10. What is an opportunity cost?
11. What is a résumé?
12. Name a common problem that stifles people's careers.
13. Name difficulties with starting your own business.
14. What should you do at the very beginning if starting a business?
15. There are three broad categories that new businesses fall into. What are they?
16. Why is breaking your word such a problem?
17. Why is it important to find people who are honest, cooperative, and reliable?
18. What legal protections are needed in business?
19. What does it mean when a company "owns" you?
20. How do people commonly get involved in unethical behavior?
21. What role does failure play in people's careers?

22. What kind of a personality do people who start new businesses need?

23. Why is your first job out of college so important?

24. As an exercise, go through each principle for success and think about a situation where the principle would come in handy.

Risk

Chapter 16
Leverage and Risk

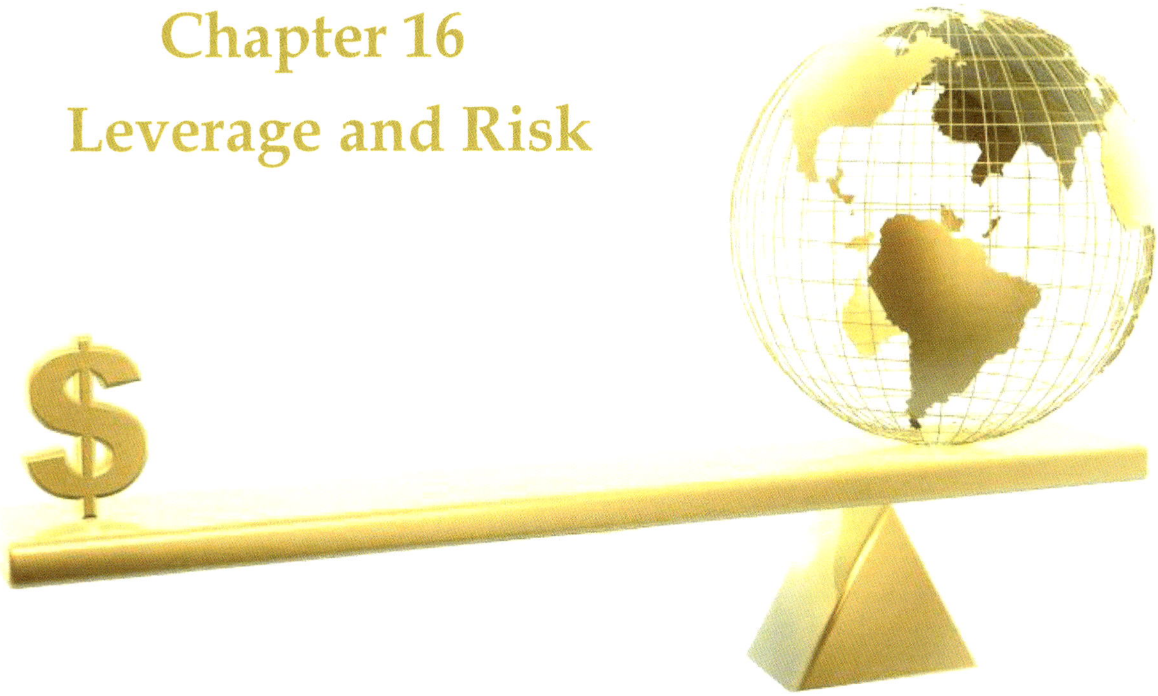

Leverage is a concept in physics. The use of leverage allows a person to lift an extremely heavy object many times their size. Leverage multiplies the force being applied to an object. In finance, understanding the concept of financial leverage is essential. Financial leverage can be a powerful tool for growing wealth. It can also lead to disaster because leverage magnifies risk. Unfortunately, leverage can also be used as a mechanism to mislead investors.

16.1 The Principle of Leverage

There is a very good chance that you will use financial leverage at least once in your life. Financial leverage happens when a person borrows in order to make an investment. For example, consider a hypothetical stock portfolio. A portfolio is a collection a securities. The portfolio is called "The Young Stocks One Thousand," or just "Young Stocks" for short. It consists of one thousand stocks of new public companies. On a regular basis, companies are removed as they age and new ones added.

As a young and optimistic investor, Rosie Specs is considering buying shares in a mutual fund that tracks the performance of Young Stocks. However, the minimum investment is $10,000, and she does not have the needed cash. She does have equity in a new townhouse and decides to take out a home equity loan in order to invest. She borrows $5,000 and provides the other $5,000 herself for a total investment of $10,000. The interest rate on the loan is 5%. One year later she decides to liquidate, or in other words, sell off her investment and pay off the loan (cash out her investment). Table 16-1 compares two situations: Rosie's current situation, and one where she had come up with the total investment herself without borrowing. It also looks at two possibilities: one in which Young Stocks grew in value by 30%, and one where Young Stocks fell in value by 30%.

With Rosie's situation that involves leverage; if Young Stocks rose by 30%, then the initial $10,000 would be worth $13,000. After selling her shares, Rosie has to pay back the money she borrowed. She also owes 5% interest on the loan. Subtracting these out, she has $7,750 left over. Considering that she put in $5,000 of her own money, the percentage gain on her money is 55%. This is a very impressive amount. If she had invested the entire amount from her own savings, she would have made 30%, the same percent increase that Young Stocks went up. Rosie is feeling pretty good about her investing dexterity.

Problems start if Young Stocks does not do well. Suppose the fund falls by 30%. Then Rosie gets $7,000 from selling her shares. However, she still owes the $5,000 in principal and $250 in interest. Her creditors do not care about how her mutual fund did; she owes the money regardless. After paying back the loan she is left with $1,750. Her percentage loss is -65%. This is also very impressive, but not in a good way. Had she invested the $10,000 without borrowing, she would be down -30%. You have now seen a financial lever in operation. Leverage takes whatever the investment does and makes the effect stronger. Rosie's upside potential is bigger, but so is her downside potential.

Table 16-1
Rosie's Investment Result in Young Stocks

	Young Stocks Up By 30%	Young Stocks Down By 30%
Using Leverage		
Money from selling mutual fund shares	$13,000	$7,000
Principal owed on debt	$5,000	$5,000
Interest owed	$250	$250
Total money left	$7,750	$1,750
Percentage gain or loss on Rosie's investment	$\frac{7{,}750 - 5{,}000}{5{,}000} = 55\%$	$\frac{1{,}750 - 5{,}000}{5{,}000} = -65\%$
Without Leverage		
Money from selling mutual fund shares	$13,000	7,000
Percentage gain or loss on Rosie's investment	$\frac{13{,}000 - 10{,}000}{10{,}000} = 30\%$	$\frac{7{,}000 - 10{,}000}{10{,}000} = -30\%$

Table 16-2 shows what Rosie's investment results would be for different levels of leverage (percent borrowed). The gains and losses clearly get bigger as leverage rises. In fact, at 70% leverage, Rosie's loss is over 100%. What does this mean? She owes money. Not only is her investment wiped out, she has to come up with extra cash to pay off her loan. If she has not planned well, she could end up in financial distress. During the housing crisis, people were using home equity loans for a variety of purposes, including investment. Some found themselves in this situation.

Table 16-2
Rosie's Investment Result for Different Leverage Levels

Leverage	Young Stocks Rises By 30%	Young Stocks Falls By 30%
0	30.0%	-30.0%
10%	32.8%	-33.9%
20%	36.3%	-38.8%
40%	46.7%	-53.3%
50%	55.0%	-65.0%
70%	88.3%	-111.7%
90%	255.0%	-345.0%

Unfortunately, Young Stocks went up by 30%. Why would this be unfortunate? The answer makes for an interesting cautionary tale. After Rosie made such a killing in the stock market, she attended a picnic where she could not help but crow to her friends about what an incredible amount she made on her investment. Rosie's friend Louise had invested in Young Stocks, but she did not borrow and could not match Rosie. They all decide to borrow to invest in Young Stocks for the following year.

After a year, Young Stocks has fallen by 30%. Rosie and her friends are shocked that a strategy that worked so well the year before has now caused them to lose 65% of their investment. They have fallen victim to a common investing mistake. Leverage magnifies investing results, but it does not always work to *improve* results. Rosie and her friends did not understand that they were taking on more risk.

Key Takeaway: Borrowing to invest, also known as "leverage," increases gains, but also increases losses. An investor has to put less of their own money into an investment. This magnifies gains when the investment does well. However, they have to pay back the money they borrowed with interest, regardless of how the investment does, which magnifies losses when the investment does not do well. Therefore, leverage increases risk.

Dot.Com Mania

The advent of the Internet brought on a whirlwind of excitement. The Internet was going to change the world. How the economy functioned and the very way that people lived their daily lives was about to change. The new dot.com companies just getting started were going to be the next GM or GE. Venture capital firms began popping up everywhere in response to the flood of money pouring into Internet startup companies. A wave of IPOs hit the stock market, with startups selling their stock for the first time at spectacular prices— even though they had not made a dime in profit. Investors put as much money as they could into the new dot.com stocks, as well as established companies that jumped onto the Internet bandwagon. People began using their credit cards to invest, and even took out home equity loans. Leverage soared.

And so did the stock market. The NASDAQ index, which was heavily weighted towards technology stocks, took off, rising by well over 500% between 1995 and 2000. However, something started to become apparent. Many dot.coms did not have a business model that fit well with the Internet. One dot.com, that raised millions in an IPO, had a business model of selling basic items like toothpaste on the Internet and quickly went bust.

Worse yet, while the Internet was fabulously valuable and did transform the economy, it was hard for companies to make profits off the Internet. Yes, the Internet became wildly popular and did transform the economy. However, that did not mean that it was easy for a company to make money off the Internet. Any time a company came up with a clever idea, others could instantly see what they were doing and immediately copied them, driving their profits down. It was very difficult to gain from a new Internet idea. It was the consumers who received the benefit and not the companies selling to them. Prices were driven down to rock bottom as consumers could easily comparison shop. In the space of a little over a year, the value of Yahoo's stock fell by almost 118 *billion*. As the bubble burst, the NASDAQ plunged by almost 78%. Many investors who had borrowed heavily to invest in the frenzy learned a hard lesson.[1]

Figure 16-1 compares the results for investing in an S&P 500 index fund on an annual basis without using leverage, and with a strategy of borrowing 50% at 2% interest. (From Chapter 2, the S&P 500 index numerically tracks the performance of a hypothetical portfolio of big company stocks, selected by Standard and Poor's. Mutual funds create portfolios that track indices including the S&P 500. Their results may not exactly match the index.) The vertical axis is the percentage gain or loss on the investment for a year. For instance, if someone invested in the S&P 500 at the very end of 1989 using an unlevered strategy, their percentage gain or loss as of the end of 1990 would be -6.56%. A leveraged investment would have earned -15.12%. Looking at the time period of the financial crisis, an unlevered

---

[1] Larry Black, "America's National Debt: It's Becoming Personal: Millions Could Lose Out If A Credit-Fuelled Boom Hits The Buffers, Says Larry Black" *Sunday Business*, February 20, 2000; Jane Bryant Quinn, 'Borrowed Money, Borrowed Time" *The Washington Post*, Sunday May 28, 2000; "Us Consumers Drowning In Debt" *Sunday Business*, February 4, 2001.

investment made at the end of 2007 would have earned -38.49% in 2008. A levered investment over the same time period would have earned a horrific -78.97%.

Figure 16-1
Leveraged Versus Unleveraged Portfolio Reversals

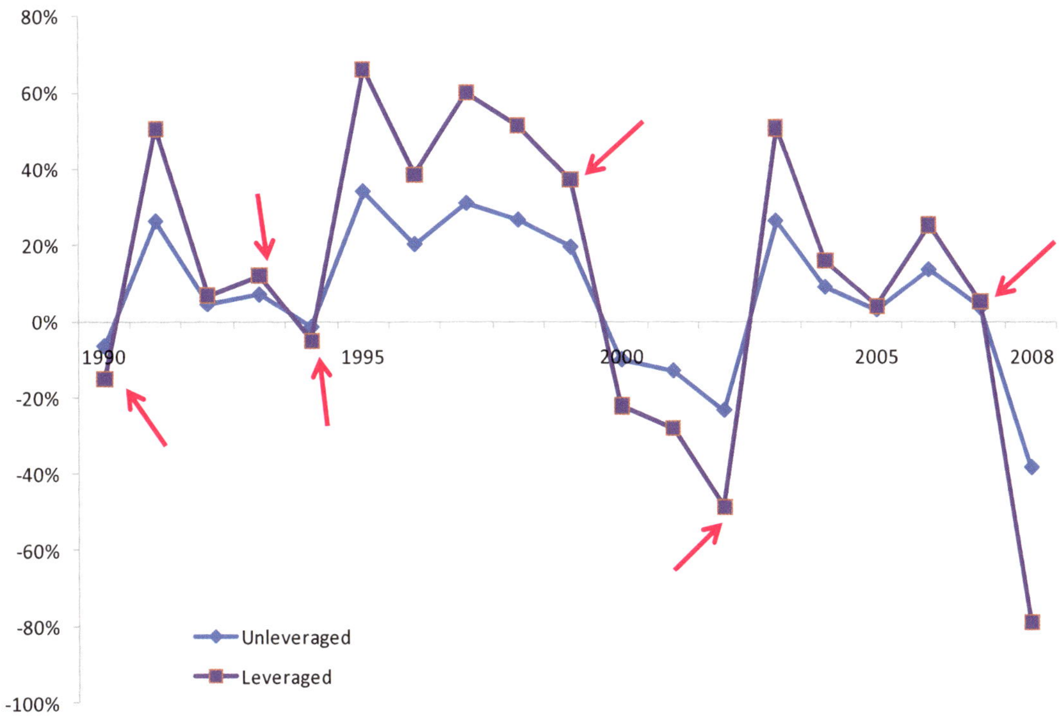

When the S&P 500 does well, the levered investment is better (as long as the S&P rises enough to cover the interest on the borrowing – usually a small amount). When the S&P 500 loses value, the unlevered investment does better. This can cause a reversal in fortune. (The red arrows indicate the start of a time period when the portfolios switch in terms of which one does better.)

It is important to emphasize that you do not know what will happen in the future; you can only see what happened in the past. For instance, Figure 16-2 shows what the graph would look like at the end of 1999. Not knowing any better, it may be natural to pick the levered strategy that previously did better. Going back to Figure 16-1, this would create a loss of -22.28% for the year 2000, along with increasing losses for 2001 and 2002. Imagine feeling frustrated at the end of 1999 because you earned less on your unlevered strategy, and you then decide to switch to the levered strategy – just in time to earn less than the unlevered strategy.

Of course, switching back and forth like this does not make any sense. Since you do not know what the stock market will do in the future, it is better to decide which strategy seems best and stick with it. Typically, the stock market rises. However, there have been a number of times when it did not. In other words, the stock market is risky. Because the stock market typically rises, a leveraged strategy will typically do better. However, there is no guarantee of this. Also, people often invest for short time periods, such as someone who is relatively young and saving up to buy a house. If they take a leveraged strategy and the market falls, their investment could lose much of its value. Most retirees cannot afford to take big risks with their retirement savings because they could be left destitute.

Figure 16-2
Leveraged Versus Unleveraged Portfolio Reversals Before 2000

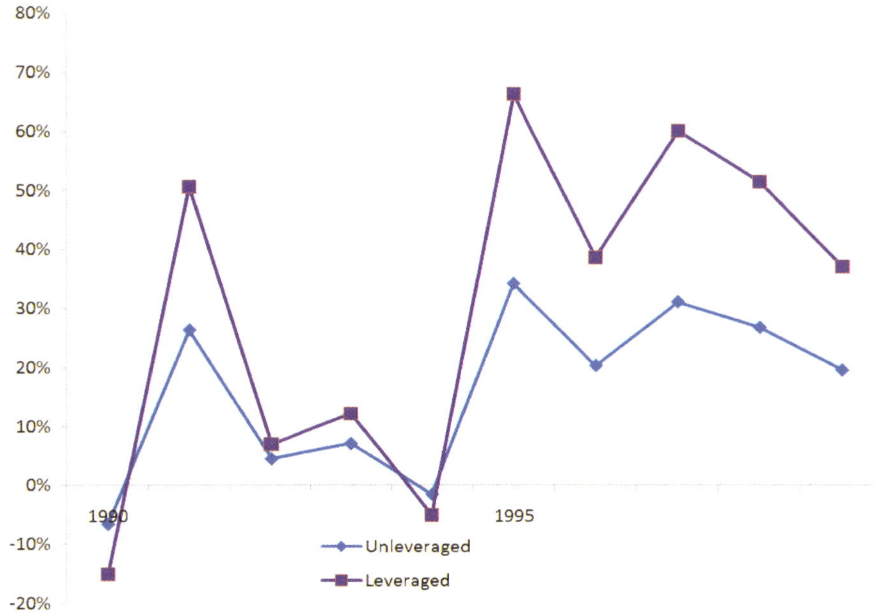

Investing involves a tradeoff— that of risk versus reward. Typically, risky investments earn more, but they are also riskier, meaning there is a greater chance of having things turn out very badly. (I shall discuss investing in greater detail, along with risk versus reward in Volume 2.) In the S&P example above, it would make more sense for an investor to think about how much risk they can tolerate in order to be able to expect more, and then stick with the amount of leverage that is appropriate based on their investing horizon (length of time to hold an investment) and tolerance for risk. In fact, there are plenty of people who consider the stock market risky enough, without piling on leverage.

Fees are charged for switching accounts back and forth, and the effect of fees on investments can be enormous (which is a topic that will also be covered in great detail in Volume 2). Imagine someone creating a maze of roads that track along a major highway, crisscrossing back and forth along that highway. They advertise the roads as a shortcut. The owner charges a fee each time the person abandons one road and switches to another in a vain attempt to make better progress than on the main highway. The person who charges the toll gets rich, while the travelers on the road switch back and forth, going slower than people on the main highway because of all the switching.

People who switch back and forth between accounts based on past performance are like these hapless victims. Brokers and others can sit back and get wealthy on the fees they charge, while the investor's switching does nothing for them. Even worse, many brokers encourage investors to switch back and forth since they make fees when investors buy and sell investments. They tout the latest "hot" stocks and other investments that have had recently good performance. Hapless investors are then shocked when the "good" investment they made does badly.

Key Takeaway: A leveraged investment strategy will do better when the market is rising (except for very small increases), while an unleveraged strategy will do better when the market is falling. Switching back and forth between the two strategies based on past performance does not make sense, and creates fees, which can have a very deleterious effect on investment performance. Since brokers make money when investors buy and sell investments, many brokers encourage investors to switch investments frequently, making hefty fees in the process.

16.2 Leverage Differences in Investment Funds

By now you may be telling yourself that you will not switch back and forth between investing strategies based on leverage. However, investors can be fooled because different investment funds have different amounts of leverage. (I will discuss this topic in more detail in Volume 2.) Consider the three hypothetical investment funds in Table 16-3.

Table 16-3
Three Investment Funds

	Upcoming Stocks Fund	Golden Oldies Fund	Middle-of-the-Road Fund
Last Year's % Gain	5%	7%	24%
Typical % Gain Over the Last Five Years	6%	9%	14%

Unlike Young Stocks, these funds are not index funds. A person called a "portfolio manager" buys and sells stocks, so the stocks held in the portfolio change. This is referred to as an "actively managed" fund. As can be seen from the names of the funds, each manager tends to buy certain kinds of stocks. It may be tempting to conclude that the portfolio manager of Middle-of-the-Road Fund is the best at picking stocks. After all, they generated the biggest gains for their investors.

What is not shown is whether these funds use leverage. There are many investment funds that borrow. For each $1 that Middle-of-the-Road Fund receives from an investor, they borrow $2 and invest $3 in total. Instead of the investor taking on leverage, the fund is doing it for her. The fund's results will be magnified.

Suppose that stocks in general had risen over the last five years, so that most funds had a positive gain. This last year was a little weaker with a more modest rise. The results for Upcoming Stocks and Golden Oldies, which are not leveraged, reflect the general market outcome. Middle-of-the-Road had higher gains because of its leverage. Another thing to notice is that last year's gain is higher than over the past five years, unlike the general stock market. It is possible that Middle-of-the-Road took on more leverage within the past year so that it achieved a higher gain than over the past five years.

An uninformed investor may choose Middle-of-the-Road, confident in the fact that they researched investment funds carefully and picked the best one. Not only were its returns higher, but it was showing an upward trend in performance as well. The next year when the market has a downturn, Middle-of-the-Road takes a huge plunge and the investor is flummoxed. How could it be that after carefully picking the best performing fund, they ended up with the worst results? What they did not understand was that they were picking the fund based on leverage and not the ability of the portfolio manager. This is a very common investing mistake, and illustrates why it is important to read a fund's prospectus to find out if the fund uses leverage, along with other information. A prospectus gives investors information about the fund and is required by law.

New funds can have a difficult time attracting investors. They need to stand out from the pack. This can create the incentive for them to take on leverage, since the market typically goes up. If the market goes up and they had very high leverage, they get to stand out as the new "hot" investment fund. In fact, even established funds need to stand out.

In many circumstances in life, when being at the top or standing out is important, it creates the incentive to take risks. An Olympic skier may know that he has average talent and should not expect to win a medal. The solution is to take big risks so that he has at least a small chance of winning. A similar thing happens when employees fight for a single job promotion. They will take risks to create the chance that they will outperform everyone else.

Returning to investment funds, the opposite will happen if the stock market has been doing poorly for a while. Funds with the least leverage will typically do better. Investors who pick these funds will be confused when their results lag behind because the market had a good year.

I shall discuss investment funds in more detail in Volume 2. However, these funds bear some discussion here in the context of leverage. There is a large diversity of leverage in investment funds. Many have none, while the leverage in others can be substantial. Mutual funds can take on leverage, but they are highly regulated and their leverage is legally limited. Hedge funds are lightly regulated, and can have leverage of 90% or more. During the time leading up to the financial crisis when the market was soaring, hedge funds typically (but not always) created very high gains for investors. Because of the large quantity of money that flowed in from investors (who may not have fully understood the impact of leverage), and the large fees hedge funds could charge investors, new hedge funds began opening their doors. When the markets turned south during the financial crisis, hedge funds experienced historic declines, with a number of them racking up huge losses. Some funds dropped out.[2]

What is key is that if the market has been doing well, then leveraged funds will typically look better. When the market has been doing poorly, unleveraged funds will typically look better. When the market changes direction, which happens all the time, do not expect funds to maintain their ranking in terms of performance. And when the market is doing well, it encourages funds to take on leverage. If there is a bubble, where the market seems to be irrationally rising at a high rate, expect severe reversals in fortune when the bubble bursts.

[2] Zachery Kouwe, "Hedge Funds Rebound, Gaining 5% In a Month," *The New York Times*, June 9, 2009.

Tulip Mania

Beautiful tulip flowers were imported into Europe from Turkey in the 16th century, and became prized in the gardens of the wealthy. Dutch farmers stopped growing food and planted tulips. People began investing their life savings, and a tulip futures market was established. The price of one flower bulb rose more than 800%.

The speculation was so fierce that it "led some investors to pay up to 2,500 guilders for a single bulb. The same money would have purchased 27 tons of wheat, 50 tons of rye, four fat oxen, eight fat pigs, 12 fat sheep, two hogsheads of wine, four turns of beer, two tons of butter, three tons of cheese, a bed, a new wardrobe and a silver beaker."[3]

Finally, the tulip market crashed and tulip prices fell by 90%. It brought about a depression with much pain and anger. A botany professor went about beating tulips with his stick.[4]

Private equity investments also involve leverage. The private equity companies borrow heavily in order to buy the stock of a public company and turn it into a private company. Historically they have earned high profits. However, they have been suffering due to the financial crisis, and a number of their companies are in financial distress or have gone bankrupt. Investors in private equity companies are pulling out, and some have experienced substantial losses.

Key Takeaway: Different kinds of funds will have different leverage. Past fund results can be driven by what the market was doing and the leverage of the fund, rather than the ability of the portfolio manager. Private equity and hedge funds tend to have high leverage.

16.3 Going on Margin

People who go on margin tend to be the daredevils of the investing world. Going on margin involves borrowing money from a broker, unlike the example where Rosie borrowed on her own using a home equity loan. Like home equity loans, margin interest is also tax deductible under some circumstances. The terms of margin loans are regulated, and the terms can also vary by the broker, who can impose even stricter conditions than regulators.

Different kinds of investments will also have different margin rules, and not all securities can be bought on margin. According to Regulation T of the Federal Reserve, an investor can borrow up to 50% of the value of stock that they are purchasing.

[3] Sandra Block, "Book Takes A Long Look At The Rich and Poor History Of Speculation", *USA Today*, Monday September 20, 1999.
[4] Sandra Block, *USA Today*, September 20, 1999; "Tulip Mania Led To 16th Century Crash", *Courier Mail*, Saturday December 27, 1997; Troy Lennon, "Why Crowds Go Mad", *The Daily Telegraph*, Friday January 31,2003.

This is referred to as the "initial margin." FINRA then requires that as the price of the stock changes, borrowing cannot exceed 75% of the value of the stock. This is referred to as a "maintenance margin" or "maintenance requirement."

For example, an investor who purchases $20,000 of stock can borrow up to $10,000 (the initial margin). The equity in the stock is the difference between the value of the stock and the amount borrowed, similar to the idea of net worth. As long as the value of the stock does not fall below $13,333, the maintenance requirement of 75% is not violated. On the other hand, suppose the value of the stock plunges to $12,000. The investor will get a "margin call" from their broker, asking that they supply another $1,000 of their own money, and likely more, to reduce their borrowing below 75%.

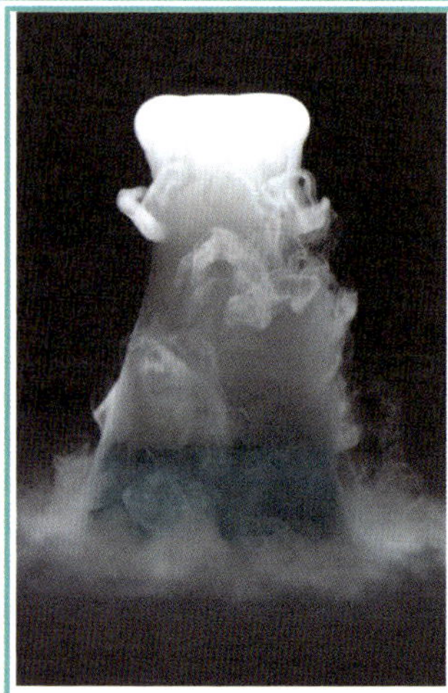

The Alchemy of LTCM

Long Term Capital Management (LTCM) was an early hedge fund. Two of its founders were Nobel Prize winners in economics who were widely credited with discovering the mathematics of derivatives (see "I've Been Trapped!" in Chapter 2). Robert Merton and Myron Scholes were financial wizards whose alchemy came from complex and mysterious mathematics, which would yield the secret to obtaining vast wealth. Investors begged for the honor of investing with them. At first, LTCM's results were fantastical. They earned their investors approximately 40% after fees, for two years running, then 20%. Their genius was established.

However, they began to struggle to reproduce the same results. Something was wrong. Their secrecy was imperfect and others began to peer into their realm and discover their magic. They decided to call upon the artifice of leverage to increase their power, eventually borrowing more than 96% to buy a vast array of securities worth $125 billion. After all, their investment results had been consistently positive.

In 1998, a financial earthquake began. Financial markets around the world were thrown into turmoil. Despite the epic efforts of its founders, LTCM was shook to its core. It perched on the brink of insolvency. The empire that Merton and Scholes had created became so large that had they defaulted, they could have threatened the world financial system. In ignominious defeat, and with the oversight of the government, they had to be bailed out by a consortium[5] of investment banks – the very kind of investor who used to beg to invest with them.[6,7] Their troubles were a precursor to the current financial crisis.

[5] A consortium of investment banks is a coordinated group.

[6] The President's Working Group on Financial Markets, "Hedge Funds, Leverage, and the Lessons of Long-Term Capital Management," April 1999.

[7] Nova Documentaries, "Trillion Dollar Bet," 2000.

If the investor does not answer the call, or provide the required money, the broker will sell off their stock without getting their permission, in order to pay off the debt. The broker then returns what is left over. The investor will have to suffer whatever loss taken at that point. However, as long as the broker acts quickly enough, and the drop in the value of the stock is not too severe, the investor will not end up owing money on their borrowings after all of their investment has already been used to pay off borrowings (although the possibility still exists).

Key Takeaway: Going on margin means borrowing from a broker to invest. This involves taking on leverage. The daredevils of the investing world go on margin.

16.4 Borrowing to Buy a Home

Before you congratulate yourself for deciding to never go on margin, consider that most people with good incomes end up borrowing heavily to make at least one very large investment – they borrow to buy a house. I have already discussed mortgages and how house prices relate to interest rates, but now it is time to have a general discussion about house prices and the risks associated with buying a house.

Historically, housing prices have risen fairly reliably, but there have been times when housing prices have fallen, with our recent situation being a dramatic example. Also, local areas can experience falling real estate prices, even when national housing prices are rising. When buying a home, it is important to consider whether real estate prices are stable or rising.

To illustrate the point in the context of leverage, imagine that you have been working for seven years and have been diligently saving to buy your first home. You earn $80,000 per year and your take-home pay is $45,000. You are particularly pleased with how you have budgeted and forecasted, and you are now ready to buy just like you planned. You have $90,000 hard earned dollars. Table 16-4 illustrates two strategies for home ownership; an aggressive one and a more conservative one.

Table 16-4
Aggressive Versus Conservative Home Buying Example

	Aggressive	Conservative
House Price	$600,000	$325,000
Down Payment / Loan	15%: $90,000 / $510,000	25%: $81,250 / $243,750
25% Loss / New House Price	-$150,000 / $450,000	-$81,250 / $243,750
Net	-$60,000	$8,750

In the aggressive strategy you buy the biggest house you can using the entire $90,000 as a 15% down payment on the house price. This means you buy a $600,000 house. In the conservative strategy, you buy a smaller, $325,000 townhouse with 25% down. This requires $81,250, and you have $8,750 left over in cash. By the way, with the conservative strategy you are able to take points and pay less interest on the mortgage.

Now imagine that house prices take a plunge, as they recently did. Your house price falls by 25%. In the aggressive strategy you lost $150,000 on your home, which is now worth $450,000. This means that as a practical matter, you have lost $3\frac{1}{3}$ years of take-home pay. (The loss has wiped out the equivalent of three years of hard work at a job.) Ouch! The house is also now worth less than what you owe on the mortgage by $60,000. With the conservative approach, your house is now worth the same as the mortgage, and you lost 1.8 years of take-home pay. You still have the cash of $8,750 that you set aside.

The aggressive approach has caused your house to go "underwater." The idea is similar to net worth. The value of your house is less than the value of the mortgage. You are now in trouble. You can try to ride it out, paying your mortgage each month and waiting for house prices to recover. However, what if you lost your job? You could not sell the house to pay off your mortgage and move into a less expensive place. You are in deep and could default. Not only that, you are a prisoner in your own house. You cannot sell it and move. At best you may be able to rent it out if you want to move. However, the rent would not cover the mortgage payments on the house (you would have to come up with the difference), and renting is difficult. There can be a lot of work to renting; the renter could fail to make their payments, give you trouble, or damage the house. Renting can be complicated for a number of reasons, and there are often strict laws for landlords to follow.

You are in a much better position with the conservative strategy. Your loss is painful, but not nearly as painful as in the aggressive approach. You can sell your house and move, using the extra cash to pay the realtor's fees (you will need some more as well). The process for saving to buy a home can begin again.

Key Takeaway: New home buyers face an especially risky situation because they have not built up enough savings to weather losing their job in addition to a housing downturn. Putting more money down and buying a less expensive first home can mitigate risk. If a house is under water it is worth less than the mortgage. This can trap a person in the house, and they could even default if they become unemployed.

It is not possible to cover all of the factors that influence real estate prices, but we shall spend at least some time on the topic. I leave a more detailed discussion to Volume 2. When buying a home, it is worthwhile to do additional reading on real estate prices before making a decision. The quality of public schools in an area is important. If they are not of good quality, parents will have to pay, possibly a substantial amount, to send their children to private schools. This will depress the price of houses. Of course, the crime rate is important, in addition to the attractiveness of the house and neighborhood, access to transportation, commuting distance to commercial areas, the weather, and local and state taxes. As long as these factors are stable, then housing prices would not be expected to plunge— but they can. There have been municipalities that got into financial trouble and had to dramatically raise taxes, lowering real estate prices. Crime rates in neighborhoods have also been known to change. It is better to look for "improving" neighborhoods.

Entire regions can experience a housing price collapse. In the 1980s, Texas's economy was heavily dependent on the oil industry. With the price of oil booming, home prices soared. Then OPEC (an oil organization that influenced oil prices) fell apart and oil prices plunged. The effect on home prices was dramatic, and eventually lead to the failure

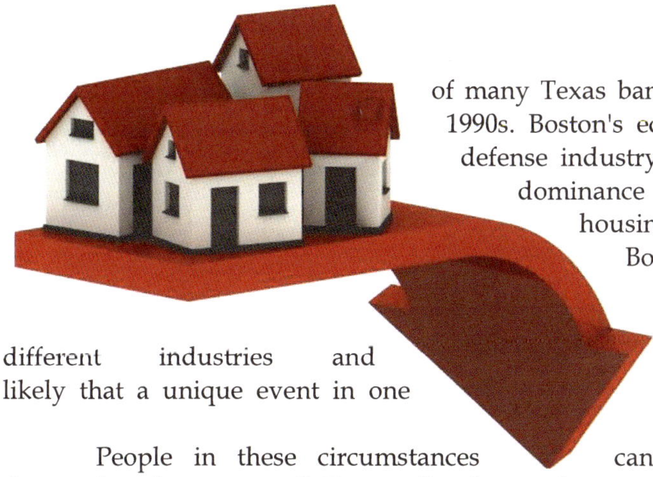

of many Texas banks and thrifts. Boston experienced a similar situation in the 1990s. Boston's economy was heavily dependent on minicomputers and the defense industry. With the collapse of the Soviet Union and the emerging dominance of servers, Boston's economy took a turn for the worse and housing prices fell dramatically. The common theme with Texas and Boston was that their economy was heavily dependent on a few industries. There are even areas where the economy is heavily dependent on a single company. When an area has many different industries and businesses that depend on different circumstances, it is less likely that a unique event in one industry will have a large effect on housing prices.

People in these circumstances can also fall into a trap. They refuse to bring their house price down when they try to sell. Eventually, their realtor gets tired of showing their home when no one is willing to pay the asking price, and does not bother bringing people by. The owners are forced to drop the price drastically. It would have been better to set a lower, more realistic price at the beginning to avoid even deeper price cuts down the line.

On the national level, there are several factors that can have a strong influence on real estate prices. I have already discussed how home prices move in the opposite direction of interest rates. (The lower the interest rate, the more a buyer can borrow, and the more they offer for a home.) A depressed economy will also dampen home prices. A combination of a bad economy and high interest rates will be particularly devastating, as home owners discovered in the late 1970s and early 1980s.

Another situation of concern is a housing bubble, as has been recently experienced in the United States. The problem is, it is not always easy to tell when a bubble is happening. (I will discuss bubbles in securities prices in Volume 2.) However, there are certain characteristics to look for. If housing prices suddenly start rising rapidly it can indicate a bubble, but only if other indicators are there as well. This could include a strong shift in government policy to encourage home buying that is not sustainable, such as keeping interest rates artificially low. House flipping indicated a bubble. If real estate is a popular topic of conversation among people, it is another sign of a bubble.

There are good numeric measures that indicate a bubble. One is the ratio of what it would take to rent a home for a year versus the price to buy a similar home. Rental rates reflect what people can really afford to live in a place. If housing prices soar compared to rental rates, it suggests trouble. Another measure is the typical amount that people contribute as a down payment. The lower this number, the more likely that buyers are borrowing beyond their means and home prices are too high. Finally, the ratio of family income to home prices can indicate a bubble if this number is low, because a family's income determines how much they can afford to buy.

Key Takeaway: Local conditions such as crime and the quality of the public schools affect housing prices in addition to national factors. Beware of a housing bubble. If housing prices seem to be getting above what people can reasonably afford, this is a sign of trouble.

It is especially important to be cautious when you are just getting started, and to make sure you have enough of a down payment and extra savings to weather a housing downturn. You can also turn to the futures market to protect yourself. (I will discuss this in Volume 2.) Realize that you have received a lot of warnings, not to discourage, but to protect. I do not want to turn you away from home ownership. Housing prices do typically go up, and since people borrow substantially to buy, this leverage can create a major boost in wealth over their lifetime. Home ownership may very well be the biggest contributor to your net worth, as well as a major source of security in your retirement. By investing carefully you can create a prosperous future. Just be cautious, and do not buy based on emotion or pressure. Thoroughly research market conditions and wait if you are unsure.

~Guess the Mystery Woman~

Chances are that you know who the mystery woman is. (The answer is at the end of the chapter.)

The mystery woman was in chaos as she surveyed the people sitting with her at the table. She came from humble beginnings, but her young husband had just taken an exciting new position at the Harvard Business School. However, real estate prices in the Boston area were very high. So high in fact, that they were beyond the means of typical new professors who had just graduated as a Ph.D. students and had a mountain of student loans to pay off.

The Harvard Business School, in its usual fashion, had come up with a practical solution. They offered new professors a loan program where they would lend the 20% needed for the down payment on a home, secured by the home as collateral. Since the bank, lending the 80% for the mortgage, would get paid first from selling the home if the borrower defaulted, they were unconcerned that the 20% down payment was being borrowed.

Every instinct in the woman said it was a bad idea, but she faced formidable opposition. She and her husband were at the venerable Harvard Business School, seated at a table with some of the biggest luminaries in the profession of finance. These were famous people who had made their names by being at the top of the field. She couldn't possibly compete, as she was just a student.

The mystery woman took a stab at arguing that it was a bad idea. "I do not think it is a good idea to buy such an enormous undiversified asset, essentially on margin," she told them. The professors at the table gave patronizing smiles at her use of finance terms to make her point. She was reassured that real estate always goes up as more and more people need houses, and that there was nothing to worry about. It was the verbal equivalent of a pat on the head. Her husband was convinced, and she stood alone, finally caving in.

Soon thereafter the Boston real estate market collapsed. When she and her husband sold their home and moved, the sales price did not cover the loans. Their house was "under water." They had to borrow additional money at a high interest rate to pay off both the mortgage and the loan from the business school. They spent several years paying off the new debt while they rented.

The situation could have been worse. They had aggressively negotiated a very good price on their home and the price did not fall as much as other homes in the area as a result. In addition, they had not bought as big a home as they could have. The lesson hurt, but she walked away a wiser woman about being "helped" with debt, and she avoided the current real estate crisis. She is also not into having her head patted anymore, and after reading this textbook you shouldn't be either.

16.5 Conclusion

You have learned what financial leverage is and how it magnifies investing results for better or worse. Leverage can also be used to fool investors. Leveraged funds do better when the stock market is rising, while unleveraged funds do better in a downturn. This does not mean the portfolio manager of one fund has more talent than the manager of another fund. Going on margin is a way for daredevils to borrow to invest. Borrowing to buy a house involves taking on leverage and risk, and it is important to analyze the direction of housing prices first. There are many factors that drive housing prices. Investing wisely in a house can lead to a lifetime of growing wealth and prosperity. Just use your head. And when you do buy your first home, be sure to celebrate.

The Mystery Woman: Yours truly, of course, the author of this textbook. (The woman in the photo is a model and not the author.) Most people make a serious financial mistake at some point in their life. It is time I fess up to mine. If you do make a mistake, regard it as a learning experience. My losses in the Boston housing market were relatively small, and helped me to recognize the housing bubble that popped recently.

Key Terms:

Actively managed fund
Cash out
Going on margin
House flipping
Initial margin
Investing horizon
Investing on margin
Leverage
Liquidate
Maintenance margin or requirement
Margin call
Portfolio manager
Speculating
Under water

End of Chapter Questions

1. What is financial leverage?

2. Suppose you borrow $40,000 and invest $60,000 of your own money in a portfolio of stocks. The interest rate on the loan (after tax) is 3% per year. After one year, how much do you owe on the loan, and what is your profit if the portfolio of stocks rose by 12%? How would your answer be different if the portfolio fell by 12%? Compare your results with the alternative of investing $60,000 of your own money without borrowing.

3. Under typical conditions, when will a leveraged investment do better? When will an unleveraged investment do better?

4. What is the difference between investing in an index, and investing in an actively managed portfolio?

5. What is a prospectus?

6. The market has been falling over the last three years. In the most recent year, the market fell by the least. Of the three portfolios below, which do you think had the most leverage, (at least at the beginning)? Which had the least? Suppose one of the portfolios changed its leverage in the most recent year. Which one do you think it was?

Portfolio Returns

	Fund A	Fund B	Fund C
Past Three Years	-.04	-.11	-.08
Past Year	-.02	-.03	-.04

7. Given the leverage discussion, what is the problem with picking funds based on past performance? What steps could you take to not make this mistake?

8. How important are fees to investing results?

9. What is going on margin?

10. Why is buying a house particularly risky for someone who is just getting started?

11. What does it mean for a house to "go underwater?" What are the problems with going underwater?
12. Name several important local factors that determine home prices.
13. Name several signs of a housing bubble.
14. In general, is home ownership a good idea?

Your Credit Score and Good Name

Chapter 17

Credit Scores

You will carry a grade of your financial performance around with you for your entire life, just as everyone does. Gawkers are many. Anyone from a potential employer to a mortgage lender may take a look. Every time you engage in a financial transaction it can be added to your record for countless others to see. The consequences of having a bad grade can be severe and long lasting. Given how important this grade is, you would expect that people would pay it tremendous attention. High school students carefully manage their record when applying for college, athletes give laser-like attention to their performance statistics, but the reality for credit scores is shockingly different. It is astonishing how unaware or indifferent individuals are to their credit score. People routinely fight for every dollar of pay raise at work while putting in long hours, yet they do not bother to take just a few minutes each month to pay their bills on time when the result is thousands of extra dollars spent. This ignorance is particularly tragic for the poor.

17.1 Credit Reports

At the moment you probably do not have much, if anything on your credit report, but that will change very soon. Your credit report contains a history of your financial activities, and forms the basis for your credit score. There are three major credit reporting agencies ("CRAs" or "credit bureaus") that collect information on individuals and compile it into credit reports. These are Experian, TransUnion, and Equifax.[1] They gather information that is voluntarily supplied to them by a variety of individuals and businesses, and they sell it. The CRAs do not extend credit themselves.

CRAs collect information from public records such as court documents. In addition, individuals and businesses that you have owed money to in the past can provide information, such as banks, credit unions, thrifts, landlords, utilities, phone companies, and hospitals. Information may be reported to one CRA but not another, which results in inconsistent credit reports across the three agencies. Also, not everyone that you have owed money will bother to report, which could be an advantage or a disadvantage.

Sometimes your permission is needed to access your credit report. However, individuals or businesses that are considered to have a legitimate need can access your credit report without your permission. These can include creditors, landlords, insurers, and various government agencies. Employers must ask for your permission, except

[1] Experian PLC, TransUnion LLC, and Equifax Credit Information Services Inc.

possibly in the trucking industry. A business or lender may only access one credit report, or they may access all of them.

In order to have a credit report you must first be identified. In a country with millions of people this can be a challenge. Unless you have a very unusual name, there will be many other people with your name (excluding possibly your middle name). A major identifier is the Social Security number that the government assigns to individuals in order to track them for Social Security benefits. The same number is used for tax identification purposes, and often private businesses also use it to identify customers. This is unfortunate in that it leads to identity theft, which I shall review in a later chapter.

Your credit report will include your name, date of birth, address, past addresses, past names (such as before marriage), names you may also be known by, and phone numbers, including unlisted numbers. Your employment history will be included. Being sued, going bankrupt, being subject to a tax lien, or failing to make timely child support payments can become a part of your credit report. Currently the three major CRAs do not report criminal conviction information in credit reports, but they are allowed to under federal law, and they may collect it separately and provide it in background checks. Credit reports do not contain your medical history. Also, some states have more restrictive laws governing what can be collected or reported than other states have. Realize, however, that credit reports are not the only information that will be available on you. I will discuss your public record in a later chapter.

Your credit report will contain a history of your accounts such as loans. Accounts, past and present, are reported, including ones that have been paid off and closed. The account type is also tracked. For instance, credit card debt is a "revolving" loan that does not have a maturity, while a car loan is "installment" debt that is paid off. Any actions that were taken to collect from you due to late or insufficient payment will be reported. The debt available to you, and the debt that you use, is also reported. For instance, you may have a $10,000 credit limit on a credit card (debt available), but you have only borrowed $480 (debt used). The age of accounts is recorded, which is the difference in time between when you first opened the account and the present. Finally, your bill paying history will be included, along with any late payments.

Key Takeaway: Credit reports contain identifying information including your Social Security number. They also include information from public records, and information supplied by individuals and businesses. A history of your account activity is given, including any loans that you took out and your bill paying history.

Challenge

Do you think you have a credit report? If so, are you happy with what would appear?

17.2 Credit Scores

A credit score is a number that is calculated to measure your creditworthiness. The first score was calculated by the Fair Isaac Corporation, and is called a FICO score. There is a specific mathematical formula for the FICO score. The original formula was derived by performing statistical analysis on whether consumers repaid their loans. (I will discuss statistical analysis in Volume 2.) The statistical analysis indicated that certain information about a consumer was important for predicting whether they would pay what they owed, and gave the numeric relationship between that information and the likelihood of payment. A formula was then created from the analysis. The end result of this is that information will be taken on you and plugged into the formula to come up with a number. However, to be assigned a credit score you must have had an account open for six months that was updated in some way (such as by recording an on-time payment). Otherwise there will not be enough information to construct a credit score. Like it or not, in very short order you will have a credit score, if you do not have one already, and many will access it.

FICO scores range from 300-850; the higher the score the better. Generally, a score above 700 is a good sign that you will pay, while a score below 600 indicates that you could be a problem for a lender. The formula used to calculate FICO scores is not publicly available because they are afraid consumers may try to game the system. FICO scores are calculated from information in credit reports. Table 17-1 provides general information on scoring, and Figure 17-1 shows the distribution of FICO scores.[2]

Your payment history includes information about whether or not you make your payments on time. The longer a payment is overdue, and the larger the amount, the worse the effect. The number of overdue payments also matters. Other adverse information is included, such as bankruptcies, tax liens, and collections by collection agencies.[3] The farther in the past a negative item is, the better. This means that your credit score can improve over time as old mistakes fade in importance.

Table 17-1
Determinants of FICO Scores

Percent of Score	Information
35%	Payment history
30%	Credit usage and availability
15%	Length of credit history
10%	New credit
10%	Other factors

The "credit usage and availability" category measures how much credit you are using in comparison to how much credit you have available. If you have substantial credit available to you that you are not using, this is considered a sign that you are financially stable. Avoid running your credit card balance above 20% of the limit. Take out another card if necessary and keep them both below 20%. (Or even better, pay them off every month!)

[2] http://www.myfico.com/CreditEducation/WhatsInYourScore.aspx.

[3] A collection agency is a business that specializes in collecting money from people who have failed to make payments. They will be discussed in more detail in a later chapter.

Figure 17-1
FICO Score Distribution

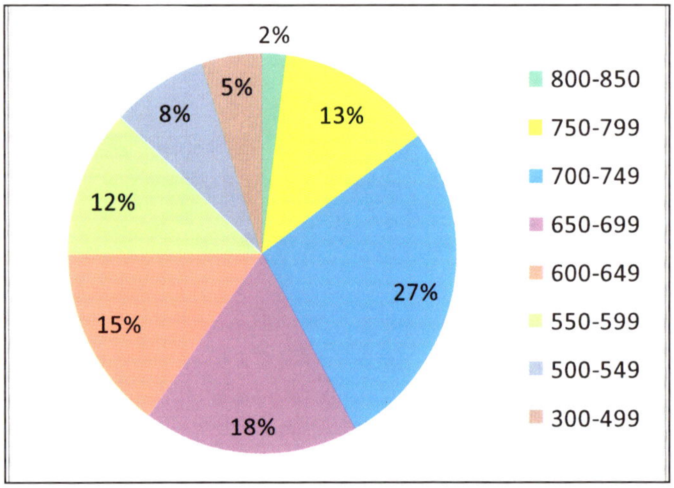

The "length of credit history" category is not good news for young people. The time since each specific account was opened, and the time since the last activity was recorded is considered. The more history a CRA has on you to base their score on, the better your score will be. To make it worse, new credit is a factor. The number of recently opened accounts, and the time since they were opened matters in a negative way. Fresh borrowing can lower a credit score, and a flurry of new borrowing is worse. This is a double whammy for new college graduates. They do not have a credit history, and they start borrowing to buy things. Because of this, an argument can be made to open credit accounts as early as possible, but this can also lead to trouble (more on this later).

"Hard hits" also lower a FICO score. A credit inquiry (when someone purchases your report) can be either a hard hit or a "soft hit." A soft hit typically involves a consumer inquiring about their own credit. This will not lower their score. Also, some lenders buy limited credit report information (without the person's permission) in order to make "pre-approved offers." (I consider these pre-approved offers to be a problem, and I will discuss them again later.) This also does not lower scores. However, in the pre-approved offer fine print, it may say that upon the person applying, the applicant will have their credit report accessed (a hard hit), and they can still be turned down—so much for pre-approved. A hard hit happens when the business making the credit inquiry is conducting a transaction with the consumer, such as a bank considering making a loan. The number of hard hits matters in a negative way, as well as the time since the hit.

It can be beneficial to shop around for the best interest rate on a loan. However, try to do your shopping within a reasonably short period of time instead of spreading it out. Within 30 days is a good target. It may also matter if you have hard hits for the same type of loan, versus different loans. A number of hard hits, all by mortgage lenders, will indicate that you are shopping for a mortgage, which is a perfectly reasonable thing to do. A flurry of hard hits across a number of different types of loans will indicate something else, possibly that you are desperately trying to get credit any way you can.

The "other factors" category includes the types of accounts you have. Some accounts are considered better than others (revolving versus installment, etc.). Borrowing from "consumer finance companies" is a negative. Consumer finance companies tend to not be bank affiliated and serve subprime borrowers.

CRAs may report your FICO score, or report a different score that they choose to calculate themselves. Other scores will have a different range than the 300-850 range of the FICO score. Remember that the FICO score was the first score, but it is not the only one. Businesses use a variety of methods in assessing a customer's creditworthiness. Some may rely on FICO scores, while others may start from scratch and use their own methods. Others may combine FICO scores with other information. As an example, when you apply for a mortgage the bank can ask detailed questions about information that is not available in your credit report. The bank can take into account your income and employment history, whether you currently rent or own, and the amount of the down payment. Other factors considered in deciding whether to grant you credit may include other assets you own, and the type of home being purchased.

17.3 The Consequences of a Poor Credit Score or Record

The consequences of a poor credit score can be severe. Assume that with a FICO score above 800, the APR on your 30-year mortgage would be 4.74%, and with a FICO score of 630, the APR would be 6.33%[4]. With a mortgage of $350,000, you would have monthly payments of $1,823.66 if your FICO score is above 800. With the low FICO score, your monthly payments would be $2,173.25. The difference is $349.59.

Of course, the interest part of this payment will be tax deductible and will change over time. The supplemental materials for the chapter contain a spreadsheet that calculates the difference in after-tax savings assuming a tax rate of 28%, and a 7% effective annual rate on an investment account. In present value terms, the savings from having a good credit score comes to $44,370. This could easily be one year's take-home pay or more for someone just starting.

Car loans make another good example. Assume that you replace your car every five years, and always take out a $20,000, five year car loan. This means that you will always have a car loan outstanding. With a FICO score of 800, assume the APR is 6.309%, and with a FICO score of 630, assume the APR is 13.668%. The monthly difference in your payments is $461.93-$389.54 = $72.39. Over the course of 30 years, with a 7% interest rate, the present value is $11,121.10 Between the mortgage and the car loans, in present value terms, over $55 thousand in after-tax take-home pay has been lost. Of course, credit card debt at high interest rates will add substantially to the loss.

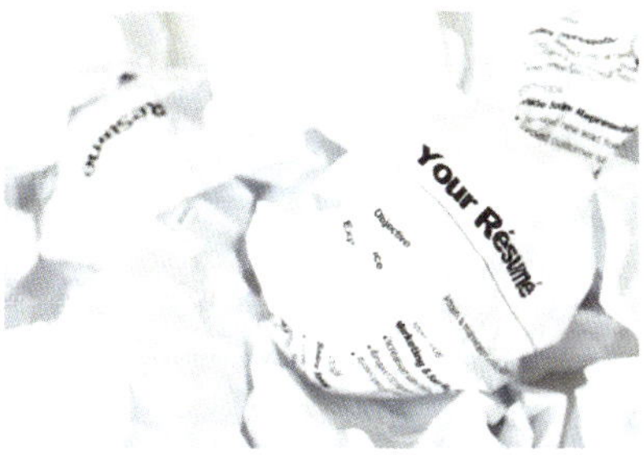

Now consider that you may have to pay more for life insurance and car insurance. There is something called a "credit-based insurance score" or "insurance score" that insurers use to set prices. Your insurance could cost more with a poor rating. Unfortunately, the bad news keeps on going. Include the fact that you could lose a job offer or take a job with less pay, have trouble renting an apartment, have to put more down on deposits, etc., and it keeps piling up. Your credit score can affect just about every aspect of your financial life.

It is terribly sad that so many people are capable of maintaining a good credit score, but fail to because they do not understand its importance. It only takes a minute to remember to pay bills on time, and the savings could be thousands of dollars. Someone who consistently makes late payments due to casual indifference could pay a default APR of 30%, or more. The credit card company gets paid, albeit a little late, and makes an enormous amount of interest on the card balance. Recurring late fees add to the hefty profits. A credit card company's favorite customer is one who faithfully pays a few days late each month.

Even worse, many people are unaware that they have a good credit score. The poor in particular have been known to take out subprime interest rate loans when they do not have to. Of course, the lender does not bother to explain this to them. Credit card companies and other lenders benefit from their ignorance of credit scores.

[4] For rates with different FICO scores, see: http://www.myfico.com/myfico/CreditCentral/LoanRates.aspx.

What Do Librarians and Credit Reports Have in Common?

It turns out municipalities aren't the only ones tracking your overdue books. Laura Tropea found that out the hard way. When the civil rights lawyer pulled her credit report to see what a prospective landlord might find, she expected to see some late credit card payments from her undergraduate days.

But Laura was surprised to find overdue library fines, instead. It turned out she owed about $160 to a library in Ann Arbor, Michigan, a town she hadn't lived in for five years. She wondered if the fines had anything to do with an application for a credit card being rejected.

They very well could have. As municipalities look for every nickel and dime to pour into their ailing budgets, they're turning to collection agencies. That raises the chances for late fees to show up on your credit report.

If you have an overdue book, though, take heart—you're in fine company. It turns out George Washington checked out a book from the New York Society Library and never returned it. The overdue book went undetected for 221 years until a librarian found the original ledger in a garbage heap. The fines would have amounted to $300,000. However, the library is forgiving the founding father the fines.

Nonetheless, George Washington's credit score probably would have taken a hit.[5]

Key Takeaway: Your credit score will depend on your payment history, how much credit you use and have available, the length of your credit history, the amount and number of new credit accounts, and other factors such as the type of credit you have. The financial consequences of a bad credit score are enormous. You could pay very high rates on loans and insurance, and fail to get a job or apartment.

Challenge

Do you have any strategies for building a high credit score?

[5] "That Unpaid Library Fine Could End Up On Your Credit Report" *The Baltimore Sun*, August 12, 2005, courtesy of http://archive.mailtribune.com/archive/2005/0812/biz/stories/03biz.htm; "George Washington Owes $300K in Overdue Library Books," NBC News, May 19, 2010, courtesy of http://www.nbcnewyork.com/news/local-beat/George-Washington-Owes-300K; "Mount Vernon Presents Overdue-Library Book to the New York Society Library 221 Years Later", PR Newswire, May 17, 2010, courtesy of http://www.prnewswire.com/news-releases/mount-vernon-presents-george-washingtons-overdue-book-to-the-new-york-society-library-221-years-later-93988589 .html.

17.4 Consumer Rights

There have been a number of laws passed concerning credit reports and credit scores. The Equal Credit Opportunity Act (ECOA) disallows using certain characteristics in credit reporting and scoring. Credit reports cannot contain information on your race, sex, religion, country of origin, marital status, or whether you are receiving public assistance. However, there are roundabout ways that companies may try to get around these requirements. I saw a guest on a news program tell a perhaps, spurious story that if a woman buys cheap motor oil, her credit score assigned by some (not necessarily her FICO score) may drop. The reason is that the cheap motor oil purchase is being taken as an indicator that she may be getting divorced, and the CRAs are not allowed to collect information on marital status directly.

If you are denied credit, the creditor must give you the specific reasons why, or they must inform you that you have the right to find out the reasons within 60 days of being denied. "Your credit score is not high enough" is not specific enough. Insist on more detailed reasons like, "you had too many late payments."

The Fair Credit Reporting Act (FCRA) contains a number of requirements of CRAs and the purchasers of credit reports and scores. If you are denied credit or insurance, the company that denied you must give you contact information for the CRA that supplied the report they used. You can contact the company to get a free report if you apply within 60 days of being denied. Do not contact the CRAs directly, or you may end up paying.

In addition, you are entitled to a free credit report from all three CRAs once a year. There is a website that handles free requests. You do not have to order all three reports at the same time, and a savvy strategy may be to order one from each CRA every four months, although this is more work. You can also receive a free report if you are unemployed and plan to look for a job within 60 days, or if your report has incorrect items due to identity theft.[6] When you order your credit report, for a small fee you can also get your credit score. Table A17-1 in the appendix contains helpful websites and contact information.

It is all too common to find errors in credit reports. While monitoring my credit score, I was shocked to see that it had fallen precipitously. My three credit reports revealed that phantom late payments to Neiman Marcus (a high-end department store chain) had appeared. I was listed as being overdue by many months. I had not shopped there in years, and did not own a credit card with them. After calling Neiman Marcus I discovered that they had no record of me. I then went through the process as dictated by the FCRA to dispute the items with all three CRAs. Within several months the negative entries were removed from my reports, and my credit score recovered. It is heartbreaking to think of all the people who are losing jobs and paying high interest rates because of negative, false information in their credit reports. All they have to do is check their reports and correct the errors. If they only knew better.

The FCRA requires the CRAs and the companies or individuals who supplied information to them to correct inaccurate or incomplete information. You can dispute information free of charge. Some CRAs allow online disputes, while another requires a letter. They must investigate any disputed items, usually within 30 days, and forward the dispute to the information provider. The information provider then has to investigate and report back to the CRA, and if any information is inaccurate or incomplete they must send corrections. At the conclusion of the investigation, the CRA must notify you of any corrections and give you a free copy of your report if the dispute results in a change.

[6] Also if you are on welfare.

The Busboy Master Criminal

Abraham Abdallah, a restaurant busboy and "pudgy, convicted swindler and high-school dropout,"[7] was leading a secret life. Not content to rob the ordinary, he decided to steal from the very rich and famous. Armed with a well-thumbed copy of Forbes' "400 Richest People in America," he managed to obtain sensitive information on notables such as Oprah Winfrey, George Soros, Warren Buffet, Ted Turner, and George Lucas. Abraham had rented several mailboxes to facilitate the fraud, using the credit card number of Paul Allen (Microsoft cofounder) and James Cayne (the head of a large investment bank). When he was arrested, Abraham had a credit card with Steven Spielberg's name.

Abraham allegedly collected credit reports by impersonating large financial firms, faking their stationary and using custom made rubber stamps (which the credit reporting agencies deny happened). He used a web of cell phones, virtual voicemails, and drop boxes to avoid detection. He would buy expensive merchandise using stolen credit card numbers, and then send couriers to pick up the packages. They in turn would be directed to multiple locations, or other couriers, before he took the merchandise in order to avoid arrest.

Abraham's willingness to think big eventually brought about his undoing. Abraham impersonated billionaire Thomas Siebel (founder of Siebel Systems), and requested that $10 million be transferred out of Siebel's account and into an offshore account. Unfortunately for Abraham, there wasn't $10 million in the account, and Siebel's broker, Merrill Lynch, started asking questions. According to Richard Smith, chief technology officer at the Privacy Foundation, "If he'd just transferred $500,000, he'd have been fine."[8]

The NYPD set up a sting operation to catch the elusive Abdallah. After intercepting a courier who was sent to pick up stolen merchandise, the police did their own impersonating. Acting as the courier, the police were redirected to different locations, and eventually to an auto repair shop, where they arrested the auto mechanic who picked up the package. Then they lay in wait. When Abraham drove up, he realized the game was up and took off. A detective leaped through his sunroof and held him in a headlock, slapping the cuffs on Abraham while still upside down.

It is not clear how much Abraham had stolen — at least $100,000 worth of computer equipment and gold coins. However, there was a limit to his ambitions. He decided not to try to steal from Bill Gates — because he was just too famous.[9]

You can also request that the CRA send notices of any corrections to anyone who received your report within the last 6 months. This can be especially helpful if you were turned down for credit or insurance. For employment purposes, you can request that a corrected copy be sent to anyone who received an incorrect report within the last two years. Do not sit back and let your reputation become ruined. I discussed in the Career Skills chapter how the world is

---

[7] Murray Weiss, "How NYPD Cracked the Ultimate Cyber Fraud, Brooklyn Busboy Busted in Theft of 200+ Tycoon IDs," *New York Post*, March 20, 2001.

[8] "Scam Targeted Rich and Famous", *St. Petersburg Times*, Wednesday, March 21, 2001.

[9] Murray Weiss, *New York Post*, March 20, 2001; *St. Petersburg Times*, March 21, 2001; Mike Claffey, Robert Gearty, and Dave Goldiner, "Celeb Hack Had Knack", *Daily News*, March 21, 2001; Jayson Blair and William K. Rashbaum, "Man Broke Into Accounts of Celebrities, Police Say", *The New York Times*, Wednesday, March 21, 2001.

a surprisingly small place. Your reputation will follow you with employers. If your dispute is not resolved to your satisfaction, you can ask that a statement of the dispute be put in your report. For a fee you can request that the CRA provide your statement to anyone who received a copy.

It is commonly reported that late payments are not removed from a credit report for seven years, and bankruptcies are not removed for ten years. However, there is something very important to realize that is generally not mentioned. There is no time limit for late payments or bankruptcies if you are applying for a job over $75,000 per year, or for credit or life insurance over $150,000 (including a mortgage). Many college graduates who go to good schools will face these situations, and negative information stays **forever**. There is also no time limit on criminal convictions. If you have an unpaid judgment against you,[10] it will not be removed until the maximum of seven years, or when the statute of limitations for the judgment runs out (they can no longer collect). However, courts can renew judgments after the statute of limitations has run out. You are about to become an adult. It is time to start protecting yourself. Your credit score is a good place to start.

> ***Key Takeaway:*** Consumers have numerous rights concerning accessing their credit reports, correcting errors, and getting information if they have been denied credit. It is common wisdom that late payments stay on credit reports for 7 years, and bankruptcies for 10 years, but this is not true for the kinds of jobs, insurance, or mortgages that successful people apply for. In many cases, negative information stays forever.

17.5 Building Good Credit and Credit Repair

Having a good credit score can be particularly difficult for someone who is just getting started because they do not have a credit history. Parents can take out a credit card for their child, but this is controversial. Having "free money" in the form of a credit card can build the wrong habits. It is time for some introspection. When you are in college you face a flood of distractions. It is very easy to forget to pay a bill. There are also many temptations to run the balance up. When you graduate, the last thing that you need is to have a horrible credit record that takes seven years to overcome. You will be competing with many other graduates for college level entry positions with employers. Having a bad credit score will help you stand out, and not in a good way. Realistically consider whether you want to handle the responsibility. It is time to be honest with yourself. If you are distracted easily, the alternative is to have the bills sent to your parents. Set up an arrangement where you send them an email telling them you know the bill needs to be paid. If you forget, they can scold you. What is essential is that you do not take out credit and forget to pay.

There is another problem that can happen to young adults. Your credit rating depends not only on whether you pay on time, but also how much of your credit you are using. If you have a high balance on a card, or worse, run over the credit limit, your score will fall. A will of steel is required or unfortunate consequences will follow. So many college students ruin their credit. However, out of difficulty comes opportunity. Now that you are armed with information about your credit report and can manage it carefully, you have the opportunity to stand way out from the pack with an employer. (Never forget there can be a silver lining!)

[10] A judgment is made by a court, and indicates that you owe money.

One approach that is sometimes taken is to cosign with a parent on a loan of theirs, such as their car loan. Your credit report should reflect the regular payments they make; however, be cautious. You will be as responsible as they for the payments. A careful discussion is needed at a minimum. Later on after you graduate from college, if your parents are willing they could cosign on your car loan. Their good credit will bring your interest rate down since they are committing to the payments, but now it is the parents who must be cautious. There are plenty of stories about children defaulting and leaving their parents stuck with the payments. Think carefully about whether you want to ask your parents to take this on. It may be more "character building" to go it alone. And there is no guarantee your parents will agree. Some loving parents feel very strongly that children should learn to stand on their own feet for their own good.

At least once a year check your credit report. It is also a good idea before applying for a job, an insurance policy, or a loan. Make sure to leave several months to have errors corrected. In filing a dispute, include the information suggested in the appendix. If you are denied credit or insurance, ask why. If necessary, exercise your right to receive information, and take steps to fix errors in your report.

If you have accounts that would improve your credit score that are not in your credit report, try to have them added. The company who provided the account is not obligated to do so, but they may be willing to for a fee. However, do not expect these accounts to get updated over time.

Remember to keep loan balances low. Rather than running up a credit card, get another card and spread the balance around. Avoid the reverse of this. Do not run up a balance on one account while canceling another. It can be better to leave an unused account open rather than cancel it, because your available credit will fall relative to borrowings. Paying off debt helps. Do not have too many accounts open, and be careful about which kind they are. A dozen department store cards may be considered negative (not to mention expensive).

There are fee-based services that provide access to your credit reports on a regular basis. Some services notify you if there is an inquiry on your credit report, even going as far as texting or emailing you. This can give you prompt warning if someone is trying to steal your identity by applying for a credit card or other loan in your name. (I will discuss identity theft in a later chapter.) Needless to say, the consequences of someone taking out loans in your name, and then defaulting, could be disastrous. The fees for these notification services tend to be low, but be careful and shop around. There are more expensive services that provide regular credit reports and scores. It may be excessive and expensive to get an updated report every month, although the result can be reassuring. It can also be a convenient way to look up information. If you are not using a service provided by a CRA, be sure that accessing your credit report is not considered a hard hit. If you are given a credit score by a service, or in response to being turned down for credit, ask if the score is the actual score or an estimate. If you were turned down for credit, demand the actual score.

You can "freeze" your credit report. When you freeze your credit report, you are given a pin. You can use the pin to temporarily unfreeze your credit report or allow access to specific entities. This can prevent identity theft. However, if you are applying for credit, or need to give someone access to your report, you will have to unfreeze your account and then refreeze it after your report has been released, or give him temporary access. Freezing and unfreezing your report will cost money. If you are the victim of identity theft, you can have your report frozen for free. We will return to this in the identity theft chapter. My experience with freezing my report was unpleasant. I had repeated technical difficulties with all three agencies. This is in contrast to the ease with which I could access the system of one of these agencies to buy their credit monitoring service. Be prepared to do battle.

If your credit score is poor it may be tempting to contact a credit repair service. However, they charge a fee for doing very little that you cannot easily do for yourself, and some even engage in illegal activities. It may just be better to stay away. The Credit Repair Organizations Act requires that credit repair services give you a copy of "Consumer Credit File Rights Under State and Federal Law" before you sign a contract with them, and the contract must disclose your rights and obligations. Credit repair companies cannot make false claims about what they are capable of, or perform services without your signature on a contract. Afterwards, there is a three day waiting period where you can change your mind. The contract has to spell out all fees, provide a description of the services, specify the time needed to achieve results, and list any guarantees they offer. An important protection is that they cannot charge you until they achieve the results promised.

Beware of any service that demands payment upfront, or does not follow the requirements of the law. Other warning signs of illegal activity include suggesting that you try to create a different credit report by applying for an Employer Identification Number to use to open accounts, rather than your Social Security number. (Employer Identification Numbers or EINs, are a unique number assigned to businesses that employ people, including sole proprietorships.) Trying to falsify a credit report through creating a new identity, or other tactic, is illegal. If you go along with the idea, you could also be breaking the law. Another suspicious tactic involves granting you "credit" and then reporting it to the CRA. The credit repair service has no intention of supplying you funds, but the reported access to credit can improve your score. Such activities are of dubious legality and should be avoided.

Repairing Your Credit the Old Fashioned Way

Taking the easy way out of a jam never seems to work. And the same goes for repairing your credit. At least that's what Beverly White, a fifty-eight year-old foster mother and behavioral therapist in Charlotte, North Carolina learned.

Beverly desperately wanted to provide a stable home for her teenage girls. There was only one problem— she had a low credit score that was between 400 and 500. With her score in the basement Beverly couldn't get a mortgage. So, she turned to a credit repair company for help. For $1,400, the company promised to raise Beverly's credit score by hundreds of points in just two months.

But the only thing that improved was the credit repair company's cash flow. They got Beverly's money, but Beverly got gypped. The credit specialist who took her check disappeared, and she was out her money.

It's become a common scenario. With lots of people struggling with bad credit, scam artists are taking advantage. After a litany of complaints, the Federal Trade Commission has begun to crack down on the swindlers.

The truth is, if you have a low credit score there's no quick fix. You need to pay off your debts and slowly build your credit score back up by getting your financial house in order. That's what Beverly did and in the end she wound up buying her dream home.[11]

[11] Sid Kirchheimer, "Scam Alert: Credit Repair's Dirty Business," *AARP Bulletin*, May 1, 2009; http://bulletin.aarp.org/yourmoney/scamalert/articles/credit_repair_s_dirty_business_.html; http://marketplace.publicradio.org/display/web/2009/03/27/mm_freecredit/; http://www.ftc.gov/bcp/edu/pubs/consumer/credit/cre13.shtm.

Be sure to manage your credit report carefully to avoid a bad report. When there is a problem, take action to fix it. If you have legitimately negative items, the older the negative item is, the more your credit score will improve. Ultimately, the best repair is the resolve to avoid the same mistakes in the future and time.

Key Takeaway: Be sure to stop and think carefully before taking out a credit card, either before or during college, and be cautious about the kind and the amount of debt you take on. Parents can help with credit, but this is controversial. Be sure to check your credit reports at least once a year. Approach a credit repair service with caution.

17.6 Conclusion

Maintaining a good credit report is not difficult. It just requires that attention be paid. Many young people are completely unaware that they are building a history of irresponsibility until they apply for a job or try to take out a loan. This is when the consequences become apparent— and painful. The good news is that a strong credit report can do a lot to help you build wealth and stand out from the crowd, including with employers. You now have the tools to do just that. Others will marvel at how you seem to be able to grow money on trees. Your green thumb is not a mysterious talent— it is because of your good credit score. When you borrow your interest rate is less; when you buy insurance your price is less; and on and on. In a world filled with Cs and Ds, you will carry an A+. Out there in the greater world, grades really do matter.

Key Terms:

Collection agency
Cosign
CRA
Credit inquiry
Credit limit
Credit repair organizations act
Credit report agency (CRA)
Credit-based insurance score, or insurance score
Employer identification number (EIN)
Equal Credit Opportunity Act (ECOA)
Fair Credit Reporting Act (FCRA)
FICO score
Freezing and unfreezing credit reports
Hard hit
Installment loan
Revolving loan, or revolver
Soft hit

End of Chapter Questions

1. What is a CRA?
2. What is the main way that people are identified for credit reporting purposes?
3. What kind of information is included in a credit report?
4. Who might access your credit report?
5. What is a FICO score? How is it calculated? What information is used to calculate it?
6. What is a hard hit, and what is a soft hit?
7. In what ways can a poor credit score cause you difficulty?
8. What kinds of information are not allowed in a credit report?
9. How long does it take for a late payment to disappear from a credit report? What about a bankruptcy?
10. How often do you have the right to obtain a free credit report?
11. What does it mean to freeze your credit report? What would you have to do if you needed to allow someone access to it?
12. Why should you approach a credit repair service with caution?
13. Why may it be better to have two credit cards, rather than one? Can you have too many credit cards?
14. What types of credit may lower your credit score?
15. When shopping for credit, such as a mortgage, how can timing come into play in terms of your credit score?
16. What does cosigning on a loan mean?

Appendix

A.1 Useful Websites and Contact Information

Table A17-1
Useful Websites and Contact Information

Annual Free Credit Report **Be careful to copy this exactly to avoid "phishing."**
To order online: https://www.annualcreditreport.com/cra/index.jsp, 1-877-322-8228
To order by mail: http://www.ftc.gov/bcp/edu/resources/form/requestformfinal.pdf
The Three Main Credit Reporting Agencies
Experian: http://www.experian.com/
TransUnion: http://www.transunion.com/
Equifax: http://www.equifax.com/home/en_us
Helpful Websites
Federal Trade Commission: http://www.ftc.gov/bcp/menus/consumer/credit.shtm
Consumer Federation of America: http://www.consumerfed.org/finance/credit_scores_report.asp
Privacy Rights Clearinghouse: http://www.privacyrights.org/Credit-and-Credit-Reports

A.2 Sample Dispute Letter

Sample Dispute Letter

Date
Your Name
Your Address,
City, State, Zip Code

Complaint Department
Name of Company
Address
City,State, Zip Code

Dear Sir or Madam:

I am writing to dispute the following information in my file. I have circled the items I dispute on the attached copy of the report I received.

This item (identify item(s) disputed by name of source, such as creditors or tax court, and identify type of item, such as credit account, judgment, etc.) is (inaccurate or incomplete) because (describe what is inaccurate or incomplete and why). I am requesting that the item be removed (or request another specific change) to correct the information.

Enclosed are copies of (use this sentence if applicable and describe any enclosed documentation, such as payment records and court documents) supporting my position. Please reinvestigate this (these) matter(s) and (delete or correct) the disputed item(s) as soon as possible.

Sincerely,
Your name

Enclosures: (List what you are enclosing.)

Do not send original documents, but do send backup documentation of your dispute. Send your letter by certified mail with a return receipt requested in order to document when the CRA received your letter. Provide as much detail as possible, including what you want the CRA to do to fix the problem.

Financial distress can be a very difficult topic to read about. One of the goals of this textbook is that it will never be something that you experience. The possibility of financial distress is something that cannot be ignored. It may come as a surprise that financial distress is all too common, and it does not just happen to poor people. In Chapter 4 you saw Nicholas James get into trouble because of a simple mistake. Had Nicholas witnessed financial distress for himself through a friend or relative, he may have avoided that mistake. The goal of this chapter is to instill an awareness of the particular torment that is financial distress, and to warn against common reasons for falling into financial distress. However, financial distress is not always something that can be avoided, and I finish with a discussion of how to recover.

18.1 Causes of Financial Distress

There are many causes of financial distress, and experts disagree about which factors contribute the most. However, several factors are typically pointed to as being important. Overspending, borrowing, and a lack of control lands many in bankruptcy court.[1] This is one reason why keeping a budget and tracking your financial circumstances is so important. Updating your personal financial statements can provide a early warning about trouble heading in, giving you needed time to act.

Borrowing to consume not only destroys wealth, it can also land you in financial distress. When you borrow to buy assets, at least you can sell those assets if necessary to get out of trouble. Things you consume do not keep their

[1] I will discuss filing for bankruptcy in more detail below.

value. In general, it is important to consider carefully whether it is in your best interest to borrow, and to understand the terms of loans. Subprime borrowers often did not understand that their payments were going to increase in the future because of teaser rates and ARMs. Variable rate debt such as ARMs had unpredictable payments that could go up substantially; option ARMS were much worse. As borrowers skipped making payments, the principle on their loans rose rapidly, leading to major increases in their payments later on.

Health problems are a major contributor to bankruptcies. Medical bills can pile up, especially without health insurance. (I shall discuss the importance of maintaining health insurance in Volume 2.) What is even more devastating is that illnesses can cause someone to stop working or running their business. Again, there is insurance (long-term disability) that can help with this situation. It is also important to have an employee who can take over if you are unable to run your business. Even without health problems, job loss is a major contributor to financial distress. It is important to build up a safety reserve and use it only in emergencies. Ideally, six months' worth of after-tax income should be invested in reasonably liquid investments, if not more. The alternative is living in fear. The combination of a job loss and an underwater house is particularly difficult because the underwater house prevents people from moving to take a new job — something to consider before stretching to purchase a house.

Driving without liability insurance is a big contributor to financial distress. Unfortunately, car accidents are quite common, and the damages you could owe can be quite high. In addition, liability for a host of other reasons can cause financial distress. This is something that umbrella insurance can help with. (I will discuss this in Volume 2.)

Divorce also seems to be a factor. A person goes from sharing the cost of a house, utilities, and other expenses to having to cover them alone. Sometimes a newly divorced or widowed person who has not been in the workforce has trouble earning a sufficient income. Having a child or adopting can create the same kind of stress to support an extra person.

There are a variety of mistakes which lead to financial distress. In Nicholas James's case, he committed to making an investment without considering the reliability of the money he would need. His problem was made worse because someone who owed him money defaulted. In addition, the value of assets can fall, including a house, while liabilities do not go away. I shall discuss something called "overconfidence" in Volume 2. There is evidence that the typical person is overconfident in their ability both to invest and to control situations. Recklessly speculating by investing on margin, without the resources to sufficiently absorb losses, can bring financial distress. There are tax "ticking time bombs" such as the one described in Chapter 3. Be sure to consult with tax or financial advisors before making big financial decisions, and get tax checkups when getting started or when your circumstances change. Identity theft is becoming an increasing problem, as well as other kinds of theft and fraud, and can lead to financial distress. Sometimes people start a business unsuccessfully and do not have enough back-up resources to support themselves until they find employment, or they start a business without sufficient resources to keep going until the business makes money. Any new business is going to require a large upfront investment, and people are typically much too optimistic about when the business will be able to make money. Also, beware of unforeseen tax consequences of starting a business or having a business fail. Finally, self-destructive behavior such as an addiction to gambling and alcoholism can lead to financial distress. Table 18-1 summarizes major reasons for financial distress and needed precautions.

Key Takeaway: There are many reasons for financial distress, but several factors are commonly cited. It is important to budget and keep updated personal financial statements, although it is not always possible to avoid financial distress. Consider carefully before borrowing and have adequate insurance to cover a variety of serious problems. Try to save at least six months of after-tax income as a safety reserve against job loss. Make sure you have adequate resources before trying to start a business, and do not be overly optimistic about when the business will make money.

Table 18-1
Major Reasons for Financial Distress

Reason	Precautions
Overspending and borrowing	Avoid borrowing to consume and keep a budget.
Borrowing unwisely	Understand the terms of loans and make sure you can cover payments under a variety of circumstances. Keep a worst case balance sheet and liquidity schedule.
Health problems	Maintain health and long-term disability insurance, and try to have back-up help at a personal business.
Job loss	Maintain at least a six month safety reserve, and avoid buying a house in conjunction with low job security and low savings.
Being sued	Keep sufficient car, umbrella, and other kinds of insurance, and behave cautiously.
Insufficient resources for divorce, widowhood, or a new child	This is a difficult situation. Controlling expenses, financial planning, and financial advice can help.
Financial commitments	Keep track of personal financial statements, and make sure resources will be there when needed. Maintain a liquidity schedule.
Speculating on margin and borrowing to invest	Do not borrow to invest unless you can absorb large drops in the value of the investment. Going on margin is risky and not for many. Consider carefully before buying a house.
Ticking time bombs	Consult with advisors before making important financial decisions. Get tax "checkups" when needed.
Theft and fraud	Keep insurance against theft, and take other measures to protect yourself. Have a variety of assets.
Business failure	Before starting a business, make sure you have sufficient resources in the beginning to cover your expenses before the business makes money or possibly fails. Understand tax consequences.
Self-destructive behavior	Get counseling and treatment for addiction to gambling, alcoholism, etc.

18.2 Financial Distress

There is a theory in physics that the universe contains "dark matter" that accounts for unexplained movement in the cosmos. Dark matter, the theory goes, is invisible but has a powerful effect that changes the progression of whole galaxies. There is no known way to directly measure dark matter. It can only be perceived by its effect on celestial bodies around it.

Human beings have their own dark matter. This force is everywhere, and the power that it exerts is dark indeed. It causes violence, suicide, divorce, depression, and isolation. Families seem to pick up and disappear, anger swirls for no apparent reason, fruitful activities suddenly wither, hope evaporates.

Given how destructive this dark matter is, you may be surprised to be hearing about it for the first time. How could it be that something so dangerous and harmful is not discussed? What is it that allows this dark matter to remain hidden? The answer is: fear and shame. People keep secret from each other that they are in financial trouble. While the results of financial distress are all too visible, the reason is concealed in the shadows.

Financial trouble is a major contributor to suicide. Some experts believe financial distress is the number one reason for divorce. It is a source of tremendous stress. For people who support a family it can mean deep shame. Imagine having to tell your spouse and children that look up to you, that they will lose everything they own, and have to move to a new place with greatly reduced circumstances. It becomes excruciating to meet the looks of relatives and friends. If you are alone, your isolation increases. The pressure is enormous. *Will I end up on the street? How will we feed ourselves; get by? Yesterday my life was full of pride and possessions. Today I am an abject failure.* These are the kinds of thoughts that run through people's minds. Exposing themselves to public humiliation by admitting they are in financial distress is unbearable.

The response to this can be to strike out. Every small disagreement becomes something worth a major battle. Charming eccentricities of spouses become insufferable annoyances. In response to the imagined disillusionment of a spouse, self-defense involves lashing out and pointing out all of *their* faults. These fights seems to spring out of nowhere. Where two people once lived in happiness and harmony, they now inexplicably cannot tolerate each other and agree on nothing. Withdrawal is a common response. They refuse to talk to each other while anger builds. Children suffer in silence and begin to act out in their own way. Trouble starts at school. Friends watch helplessly, offering advice that goes nowhere.

Divorce is prevalent and easy to see. In 2008, for every two couples getting married, almost exactly one was getting divorced.[2] What is not obvious is the underlying reason that people argue; they do not admit they are in financial trouble.

Parents also feel that they should "protect the children" and not talk to them about their problems. We see families breaking up or moving away, but we do not see the invisible reason. We see the gravitational pull of financial distress into depression, isolation, and even suicide,[3] but not the force itself. While a very visible bankruptcy sometimes results from financial distress, often financial distress involves years of trying to pay off backbreaking debt with multiple jobs or other kinds of suffering that are not apparent to others. Troubled people, ensnared by their problems, invisibly wander among the happy, laughing crowds.

Challenge
Do you know someone who has experienced financial distress? Could they have avoided it with proper precautions? How many people that you know may have experienced financial distress that you are unaware of?

18.3 Facing Financial Distress

Hopefully, you will never face financial distress. Now you have an extra reason: it is a matter of protecting yourself and your family. But to err is human, and even with every precaution it is not always possible to avoid financial distress. A confluence of difficult circumstances, from ill health to job loss, can overwhelm anyone. People who are relatively young and unestablished are particularly vulnerable. The chance of bankruptcy seems to peak around the ages of 35 to44. This age bracket suggests that trouble typically starts in early adulthood, piles up over a period of years, and eventually overwhelms.[4]

When financial problems start, many fool themselves that the situation will turn around because they are afraid. So many deceive themselves into thinking that the problem will go away— only to watch it grow. As the bills keep mounting, the worst mistake you can make is to pretend that there is not a problem. The quicker you acknowledge the problem and take action, the less your troubles will be. Your best protection is to be decisive and proactive. Taking immediate steps will also build your self-confidence. Everyone makes mistakes, but it is how they react to them that is most telling about who they are. Act forcefully as soon as you realize you have a problem and you will be on road to rebuilding your self-esteem *and* your pocketbook.

---

[2] Centers For Disease Control and Prevention, *FastStats Home Page*, for 44 states and the District of Columbia, http://www.cdc.gov/nchs/fastats/divorce.htm.

[3] See the CDC Web site, http://www.cdc.gov/ViolencePrevention/suicide/riskprotectivefactors.html.

[4] Institute for Financial Literacy Inc., *Who Went Bankrupt in 2006? A Demographic Analysis of American Debtors*, May 2007, http://ssrn.com/abstract=1084873.

If you are experiencing financial difficulties, the first thing to do is focus on what is most important. Possessions can be replaced, but you and your family cannot. It is time to concentrate your efforts on connecting with family. If times are difficult it is especially important to communicate with loved ones. Go over with each other the effects of financial distress on families and resolve not to let financial distress harm your relationships with one another. Reiterate that you care about and value each other. Provide emotional support. Forgive mistakes in yourself and others, and focus on what you admire and cherish in each other.

It is time for "all hands on deck." This is when families can prove their worth by fighting for each other. You are in this together. Do whatever it takes, including getting counseling from family, friends, and community. Do not hold things inside and withdraw; talk. It can also be a time to admit that you need someone else. This is not weakness; it will make you stronger. You just may discover that you have grown as a person and in your relationships. In fact, as you have seen in the Career Skills chapter, successful people often became successful after overcoming hardship and mistakes. If you are single, seek out parents, siblings, friends, and those you go to for guidance. Do not become isolated or let hardship turn into real tragedy.

Having a spouse actively involved in financial planning is especially beneficial in the context of financial distress. Not only are two heads better than one in preventing distress, but if problems do arise, both spouses can shoulder responsibility for what happened. They can also share equally in what needs to be done.

After committing to take care of yourself and your family, it is time to take stock of the situation. Accept that you will have to make sacrifices, and make sure the entire family is prepared to do the same. Write down what the problem is. Carefully create a personal financial statement and put together preliminary financial projections. Do not panic. This is just a starting point.

With everything laid out in front of you, a solution may present itself. Creating a plan will also reduce stress and provide reassurance about what the future will bring. The solution may involve selling assets along with cutting expenditures. It would be better to sell a car and payoff the car loan, than default and have the car seized. At least your credit score will be intact. Another possibility is getting a second job or having a spouse go to work, possibly part-time.

Explore what assistance is available. If you have lost your job you may be entitled to unemployment benefits. If you have a liquidity problem, you may be able to talk your creditors into waiting until you can sell assets. Alternatively, you may be able to borrow against assets to meet short-term bills. Careful assessment of the situation, and a personal financial plan, will help. If creditors can see that you have a specific and carefully thought out plan of action, they will be more willing to cooperate. Remember that if you default your creditors will typically take a loss. It may be in their best interest to give you some relief in order to assure future payments. You should negotiate on delayed or reduced payments, as well as what gets reported to the CRAs.

An insolvency problem is a more difficult situation than a liquidity problem because you do not have enough assets that you can sell to pay off your debts. Finding extra sources of income is one way of working your way out; however this may not be possible. If you seem to have a difficult or complicated problem, seek out financial advice.

There are free credit counseling services. If you have relatively high income, or a lot of assets, your money may be well spent getting the help of a qualified fee-based financial advisor, but beware of scams. Even supposedly nonprofit companies can charge high fees or be illegitimate. Some charge excessive fees while pressuring you to make additional contributions. Others may try to steer you into bankruptcy where they can make bigger fees. Try to receive in-person counseling. Many organizations operate nonprofit credit counseling programs such as universities, military bases, credit unions, housing authorities, and the USDA Cooperative Extension Service.[5] Your local consumer protection agency could also be a good place to get a referral for credit counseling.

Key Takeaway: Financial distress is very prevalent, yet it is hard to recognize because people do not talk about it. The effects of financial distress are all too apparent: anger, divorce, depression, even suicide. Unfortunately, it is not always possible to avoid financial distress. If you have a problem it is vital to act immediately and forcefully. Gather with family and decide to fight the problem together. Seek advice; do not panic. Create personal financial statements and a budget. If a solution does not present itself, seek help from a reputable advisor.

Challenge

Suppose you were in financial trouble. Is it your natural tendency to hide, or would you act decisively as soon as you realized there was a problem?

18.4 Dealing with Creditors and Your Rights

Do not let late payments pile up. Contact creditors as soon as there is a problem.[6] Be as specific as possible about your circumstances and what is needed to resolve the situation. Realize that various creditors will be in different positions. Some will be secured. This means that if you default they can seize any assets that were pledged as collateral. Seizing your assets will be expensive. First the creditor has to go through the process of seizure. They then have to find a buyer for the asset and may have to take a large loss, especially if they do not want to hold the asset for a long time while looking for a higher-priced buyer. Lenders are in the business of writing loans. They do not like to deal with actual physical assets and the process of selling them. As long as you offer to pay them more than what they could get from seizing your assets, net of their costs, they will usually (but not always) be willing to negotiate. It never hurts to try.

There is something called a "short sale" that can be a solution if you are having trouble making mortgage payments. (Note that this is completely different from short selling stock, which I will discuss in Volume 2.) In a house short sale, you "sell the house" to your mortgage holder, who then sells it back to you at a lower price. The principal on your mortgage is reduced in the process. Principal reduction is referred to as "debt forgiveness." Typically, debt forgiveness is considered income for tax purposes. This means that if you were forgiven $20,000 on your mortgage, the amount would be considered income by the IRS and you could owe substantial taxes. This would make debt forgiveness, as a solution, out of reach in most circumstances. However, in response to the financial crisis, Congress made debt forgiveness on mortgages not subject to income tax in order to facilitate the reworking of distressed mortgages. However, if you have debt other than mortgage debt, any forgiveness you receive may still be subject to income taxes.

---

[5] U.S. Department of Agriculture Cooperative Extension Service: http://www.csrees.usda.gov/financial security.cfm.

[6] Although, according to some federal laws, you need to be behind on mortgage payments for a certain length of time before federally mandated relief can kick in.

From Spendthrift to Cheapskate

Mary Hunt prided herself on being an up-and-comer. And when her husband, Harold, landed a job as a manager at a well-known California bank, she felt she had arrived. To go with her husband's fancy new job, Mary wanted the lifestyle to boot. So she started spending, basking in feelings of being nurtured and cared for — and she didn't stop.

For 12 years she went on a shopping spree, buying a blouse here, or toys for the kids there. She piled up debt on credit cards too numerous to mention. Meanwhile, her husband and two kids were oblivious to her free-wheeling ways.

Eventually the spending became too big to ignore. Mary had gotten her family into $100,000 worth of debt. The couple also made financial blunders together. They refinanced their home to pay off their bills but kept spending. In the process they had added even more to their mortgage. They also thought they could get rich quick by starting a business they knew little about. The business went belly-up.

In debt and desperate, Mary finally vowed to change her ways and get her family back on track financially. She explains in her website: "Our difficult financial situation prompted Harold to consider a career change. An ordinary man would have considered something quite different, but this extraordinary man refused to give up on me."[7] Mary got a full-time job and several part-time jobs. She ironed men's shirts at home and cleaned houses on the side. The family cut back drastically. It took 13 years, but the Hunts got out of debt. Mary got a new job, too. She now makes a living advising others how to become debt free.

Her "Cheapskate Monthly" newsletter and "Debt-Proof Living" website are huge hits. Mary has written 13 books on how to live within your means. Today she travels the country speaking about her experience and encouraging others to stay out of debt. As Mary says on her website: "Cheapskate. Who me? You bet!"[8]

Unsecured creditors do not have a specific asset that they can seize, but they still have the right to expect payment. It could eventually get to the point where they do begin taking assets, garnishing your wages, or both. When a court orders your wages to be garnished, part of your salary is sent to your creditors. Also, creditors, both secured and unsecured could report that you have defaulted to the CRAs. The resulting damage to your finances has already been discussed.

Debt consolidation is a possible option if you own a home or other large, valuable asset. Debt that is secured tends to carry lower interest rates than debt that is not secured. Mortgage debt is also tax deductable. For example, suppose you have credit card debt with an interest rate of 14%. Home equity loans are running at 6% and the interest is tax deductable so long as the debt on the house is less than what the house is worth. (Interest on the portion of a home

---

[7] http://www.debtproofliving.com/MeetMary/MarysStory/tabid/212/Default.aspx.

[8] "She Made the Most Out of Getting Out of Debt: One Woman's Story of Massive Debt and How She Turned It Into Green," *Evening News*, CBS, May 7, 2008; http://www.debtproofliving.com/MeetMary/MarysStory/tabid/212/ Default.aspx; http://www.amazon.com/Everyday-Cheapskates-Greatest-Debt-Proof-Living/dp/0762423358; Michelle Singletary, "Learning From the Cheapskate Queen," *The Washington Post*, July 3, 2005.

equity loan that is above the value of the house is not tax deductible.) By taking out a home equity loan and using the proceeds to pay off the credit card debt, you could substantially lower your debt payments and taxes. Of course, this begs the question of why you did not do this in the first place, financial problems or not. (I will discuss "spreads" between different kinds of debt and investments in Volume 2.) The downside of debt consolidation is that your assets are now secured and can be seized more easily.

There is another kind of creditor that has a great deal of power — tax authorities, including the IRS. (See "Even if the President is Your Brother" in Chapter 3.) Tax authorities have been known to freeze bank accounts, seize assets, and garnish wages. (When your bank account is frozen, you cannot access your money.) You will then have to scrape together funds somehow (without access to most of your money) to hire an attorney to go to court and argue that the IRS must give your assets and wages back. Returning to the theme of being proactive, hire a tax attorney for help before you get to the point where the IRS begins pursuing you.

Beware of scams promising to get you out of all or substantial taxes. (See "Who's the Vampire" in Chapter 3.) However, if you have had particularly difficult circumstances, such as poor health or a death in the family, the IRS may be willing to forgive substantial amounts of tax liabilities. Sometimes the courts may side with you.

Many creditors do not want to deal with borrowers who are very late on their payments. They will sell the rights to the payments to collection agencies, receiving pennies on the dollar in the process. The collection agencies specialize in going after delinquent borrowers. In the past they would use very unpleasant methods to collect. However, The Fair Debt Collection Practices Act gave debtors relief from harassment. For instance, debt collectors cannot call before 8:00 a.m., or after 9:00 p.m. They also cannot call you at work if they know that your employer does not approve. In addition to other restrictions, they must honor a written request from you to stop further contact.

Key Takeaway: Contact creditors as soon as you realize you have a problem. Creditors typically take a large loss if they seize assets. If you have a clear plan of action they may be willing to make concessions. Get help from a tax attorney as soon as possible if you are having trouble with tax authorities. If your debts have been referred to a collection agency, you have a number of rights including the right to not be harassed.

18.5 Bankruptcy

Bankruptcy is a system in which courts arrange to help debtors who are in over their heads get relief from paying debts. Bankruptcy was not available during Victorian England, and defaulters ended up in "debtor's prison." There they would sit indefinitely, unable to pay their debts since they were prevented from working. Charles Dickens, one of the most famous authors of the period, had his father end up in debtor's prison. Dickens' works, such as *Oliver Twist* and *Little Dorrit*, chronicled the difficult conditions for indigent children and debtors.

Consider the decision to apply for bankruptcy carefully. Bankruptcy should be a last resort. Get advice before you file with the court. A bankruptcy is not removed from a credit report for ten years, and it is never removed for jobs paying over $75,000, or insurance or credit over $150,000. For someone that has received a good education, this could mean a lifetime stigma. Major changes were made to the bankruptcy laws in 2005 with the Bankruptcy Abuse Prevention and Consumer Protection Act. Periodically, depending on the composition of Congress, bankruptcy laws are changed to make them either friendlier to debtors or friendlier to creditors.[9]

[9] I make no political statement. Bankruptcy can help desperate people who got in debt over their heads. It can also reward irresponsible behavior and drive up the borrowing costs for people who responsibly pay their bills.

Charles Dickens' Victorian Tale of Debt

When Charles Dickens was a mere lad of twelve, his world was turned upside down. His father John, a clerk in the Naval Pay Office, spent beyond his means to maintain his social stature in intensely socially conscious Victorian England. When he could not pay his debts, John was sent to debtors' prison at Marshalsea Road. Charles, a sensitive boy with delicate health who loved reading, was forced to work in squalid conditions at a blacking warehouse. There, amid the rats, he pasted labels on shoe polish jars for ten hours a day, six days a week, for six shillings a week.

John was unable to pay off his debts from prison, as his family was incapable of making enough. Eventually, the entire family lived with the father in debtors' prison, with Charles and his older sister staying on Sundays. Finally, John received word of a legacy due from his paternal grandmother. Because he was expecting the inheritance he was able to apply for release under the Insolvent Debtors Act.

Charles Dickens eventually became one of the most famous authors of his time. Dickens' many stories contain tales from his time of servitude as a child and his family's experience with debtors' prison. He remained very bitter about his ordeal, and worked to bring the plight of the poor to the attention of the public.[10]

There are typically two ways that a person can file for bankruptcy: under Chapter 7 or Chapter 13 of the bankruptcy code. (Some may file under Chapter 11.) Chapter 7 involves the sale of most of a person's assets. Some assets are exempt, meaning that the debtor gets to keep them. This may include basic personal items and a car.

The alternative is Chapter 13. With Chapter 13, if you have sufficient income you can keep most property, which is an advantage over Chapter 7. However, this comes at a cost. Generally, you will be required to make regular payments to creditors over the space of three to five years. If you do not have significant assets, Chapter 7 is preferable because future payment is not required. It is over and done with very quickly. If you have significant assets, Chapter 13 is preferable because you can keep most assets. The option to file under Chapter 7 may not be available if you have too much income.

In order to file for bankruptcy, you must first have received pre-bankruptcy credit counseling within six months of filing. After the bankruptcy proceedings, you must complete debtor education before your debt is discharged (no longer held against you). See the FTC website for information. Generally, with either type of bankruptcy, unsecured debt becomes discharged (but with payment in Chapter 13) and various actions may be stopped, including foreclosure. You will still lose your home in Chapter 7, but you may be able to keep it in Chapter 13. This is an involved topic. Both types of bankruptcies can stop repossessions, wage garnishments, utility shut-offs, and other debt collection activities. However, there are a number of payments that may remain, including child support, alimony,[11] fines, taxes, and student loans. The fact that student loans are usually not discharged is particularly tragic for students who drop out of college.

---

[10] Pam Hobbs, "Dickens' London Is a Rare Blend of Fact, Fiction," *The Globe and Mail* (Toronto), March 1, 1980. "Education: The story continues," *The Guardian*, June 4, 1991; http://www.charles-dickens.com.

[11] Alimony is payment to one former spouse by the other, as ordered by the court, after a divorce.

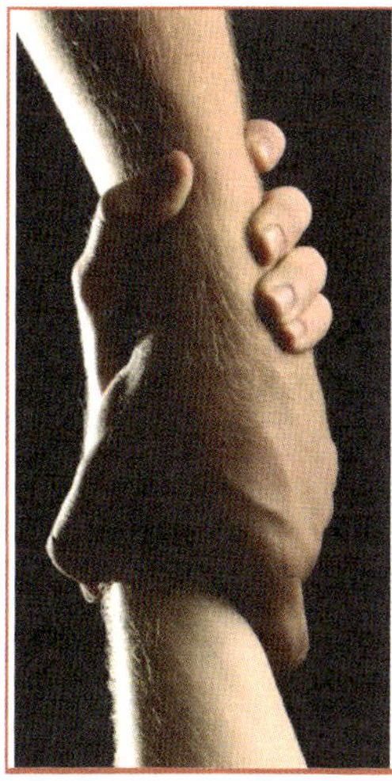

A Humbling Experience

I recently volunteered to give personal finance workshops at PATH, an organization that helps the homeless get back on their feet. The experience has been both humbling and educational. My initial reaction was surprise at the sophistication of many of the homeless. Some had held impressive jobs, while others were graduates of good colleges. Many were very well spoken.

I was asked a number of tough questions. I also learned that there are people who try to exploit the homeless. At least one college tries to get the homeless to take out student loans to pay for classes, when their changes of graduating are slim. Once you finish this textbook you will have the skills to give personal finance seminars to the homeless. It would be a way to contribute to the community through service, and you just might change someone's life.

Key Takeaway: Bankruptcy should be a last resort. It will stay on your credit record for 10 years, and if you apply for a job paying more than $75,000, or borrow or buy insurance over $150,000 it will stay forever. There are two ways that people typically file for bankruptcy, under Chapter 7 and Chapter 13. You will lose more property in Chapter 7 than in Chapter 13, but you will get more of your debt discharged. Many debts cannot typically be discharged, such as student loans and child support.

Challenge

Suppose someone you care about displays signs of being in financial distress, such as arguing with a spouse or withdrawal. What, if anything, would you do?

18.6 Conclusion

What should be clear is that financial distress is something to be avoided if at all possible. The consequences of financial distress on individuals and families can be devastating. However, it is all too common. Since people do not talk about it, others are unaware of how prevalent the problem really is. This only compounds the situation.

The first priority should be protecting oneself and one's family. The next step is taking stock of the situation. There are a number of approaches that can be taken, none without sacrifice. I have not spent a lot of time dwelling on all the possible things that can be done. If a solution does not become readily apparent after careful analysis, it is important to seek help.

There are many people who have gone through financial distress, even bankruptcy, and grew as a result. A famous personal finance author found his second calling after surviving financial distress. Difficult situations may not be pleasant, but they can be regarded as a chance to become a stronger person, as well as a stronger family. Your wallet may be lighter, vacation may be walking in the woods rather than sailing in the Caribbean, you may have to rent rather than own, but happiness can resume.

Key Terms:

ARMs
Asset seizure
Chapter 7
Chapter 11
Chapter 13
Collection agencies
Debt collection agencies
Debt discharge
Debt forgiveness
IRS
Overconfidence
Secured debt
Short sale of a house
Teaser rates
Unsecured debt
Wage garnishment

End of Chapter Questions

1. List major reasons why people end up in financial distress.
2. Why is borrowing to consume particularly problematic?
3. What steps can people take to protect themselves financially from health problems?
4. How should people prepare for job loss?
5. How can investing lead to financial distress?
6. How do taxes relate to financial distress?
7. What precautions against financial distress are needed when starting a new business?
8. Why do we not tend to see financial distress?
9. What is most important when dealing with financial distress?
10. Name important steps to take to cope with financial distress.
11. Name financial tactics that you can use to cope with financial distress.
12. Which is worse, an insolvency problem or a liquidity problem?
13. What is the difference between a secured creditor and an unsecured creditor?
14. In the context of housing, what is a short sale?
15. What is a debt collection agency?
16. What is debt consolidation?
17. What is bankruptcy?
18. There are two ways that people typically file for bankruptcy. What are they, and how are they different?
19. What types of obligations are typically not discharged in bankruptcy?

20. Can contacting a credit counseling service be helpful? What do you need to look out for?

21. What is the best approach to contacting creditors?

Chapter 19

Identity Theft

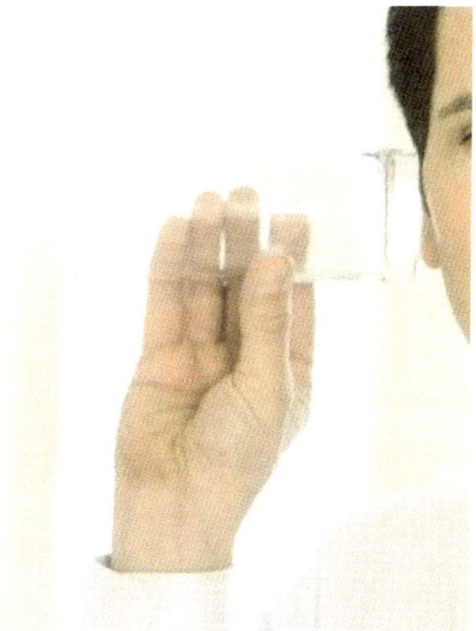

Identity theft takes many forms. At its core, identity theft involves impersonating another for gain— usually financial gain. Identities are stolen in order to take out loans, and then the borrower and the money disappear. Investment and bank accounts get emptied. Phone charges are run up. Apartments rented.

However, there are other, highly insidious forms of identity theft. People steal identities in order to get medical care. Their victims may end up receiving incorrect treatment in an emergency, or have health insurance denied during times of ill health. Criminals sometimes claim to be someone else, and when they skip bail and disappear, an arrest warrant goes out — for the identity theft victim. Also, people steal identities in order to get a job or have income tax obligations placed on someone else.

The suffering caused by identity theft is enormous. Criminal identity theft can cause repeated false arrests and unnecessary detention when attempting to travel. Financial identity theft does not usually result in the victim having to pay the obligations created by the perpetrator— but there are other costs. Victims must spend many hours filling out paperwork, making phone calls, and filing police reports. The victim may also have to spend money on attorneys, commuting, etc. Businesses owners are frequent victims of identity theft when they mistakenly give money, goods, or services to identity thieves. They lose the full amount they gave away. Others lose jobs or entire careers can be ruined. Approximately eight million people per year fall victim and the numbers are rising.[1]

19.1 Information

Information about a victim must be obtained in order to impersonate her. The grand prize is a Social Security number. Since many people have the same or a similar name, and often change their name (particularly with marriage), a number is needed to identify each unique individual. The number that is used most is a Social Security number. It was originally assigned early on by the Social Security Administration for the purpose of tracking Social Security contributions and benefits. Other government agencies and private businesses began to "piggyback" on their efforts and also used the Social Security number for identification. This became particularly handy when different government agencies or private businesses needed to coordinate about an individual.

You may be asked for your Social Security number when you borrow, subscribe to a cell phone service, or rent an apartment. Unfortunately, a Social Security number is heaven for identity thieves. With one number they can access multiple accounts of hapless victims. Once your Social Security number is stolen you can be victimized over and over again for the rest of your life. (Your Social Security number can even be sold on a black market.)

---

[1] Federal Trade Commission statistics for 2007. http://www2.ftc.gov/opa/2007/11/idtheft.shtm.

To make things worse, Social Security numbers are relatively permanent, and changing them is difficult. And even if a Social Security number does get changed, credit files and other types of files often keep the old number to link it up with the new one. If you succeed in getting a new credit report under the new number (without the old one listed), you will not have a credit history and will start over building a credit score from scratch.

In order to steal from a person's accounts, it is also necessary to identify those accounts. This requires knowing the account numbers for checking accounts, credit card accounts, medical insurance accounts, etc. Passwords or pins are sometimes necessary to access accounts. However, people are forgetful and need to be able to access their accounts. Security questions are created to solve the problem. Answer the security questions and you can reset the password for the account. Several common questions are your mother's maiden name, your place of birth, and birth date. Starting to see the problem?

19.2 Types of Identity Theft

There are several well-known types of identity theft that this chapter will cover. Just keep in mind that criminals are always coming up with new ways to steal identities and it is important for you to keep up, too.

Private Accounts

There are two types of account fraud: "account takeover" and "application fraud," also known as "new account fraud." Account takeover happens when someone gains access to a legitimate account taken out by the victim, and the thief uses that account for personal gain. Examples include using a credit card number to buy items over the Internet, using the actual physical credit card for a purchase, using a counterfeit card, or using an ATM or debit card to withdraw funds from a checking account. New account fraud involves using personal information about someone to open new accounts. This could involve applying for a credit card in a victim's name, and running up expenditures, or getting a cell phone account and running up charges.

Good, old-fashioned pocket picking, purse snatching, and opportunism with a lost purse or wallet, accounts for a significant amount of identity theft. Purses and wallets can provide a veritable thieves' paradise of Social Security numbers, private account numbers, and personal information, in addition to ready cash.

Another common problem involves stealing laptops. During the last three years, I have known of at least four students and one fellow employee who have had a computer stolen out of their car. In all cases except one, the laptop was left within view in a car. In two of these cases it was for only minutes. If you leave a laptop or other electronic device in your car in plain sight, you are begging to have it stolen. There have been a number of incidents with businesses or government employees having laptops stolen with more than a hundred thousand records of customers, employees, or citizens. (By the way, this is not a good way to endear you to an employer or further your career. There may even be crushing legal liability involved.)

"Dumpster diving," in addition to being an unpleasant image, is also a common identity theft technique. Dumpsters and trashcans can be a veritable cornucopia. (Sorry, I could not resist.) People throw out Social Security statements that contain their Social Security number. Into the trash go bank statements, credit card statements, cell phone bills, and so on, all containing account numbers.

Moving on to a similar but more hygienic idea, mailbox theft is also a common identity theft technique. Most things arrive first in the mailbox, before moving on to the trash, and many mailboxes are unlocked. Thieves will also intercept outgoing mail, and even steal entire postal service mail drop boxes (possibly at night, and involving a pickup truck and chains).

Table 19-1
Types of Identity Theft

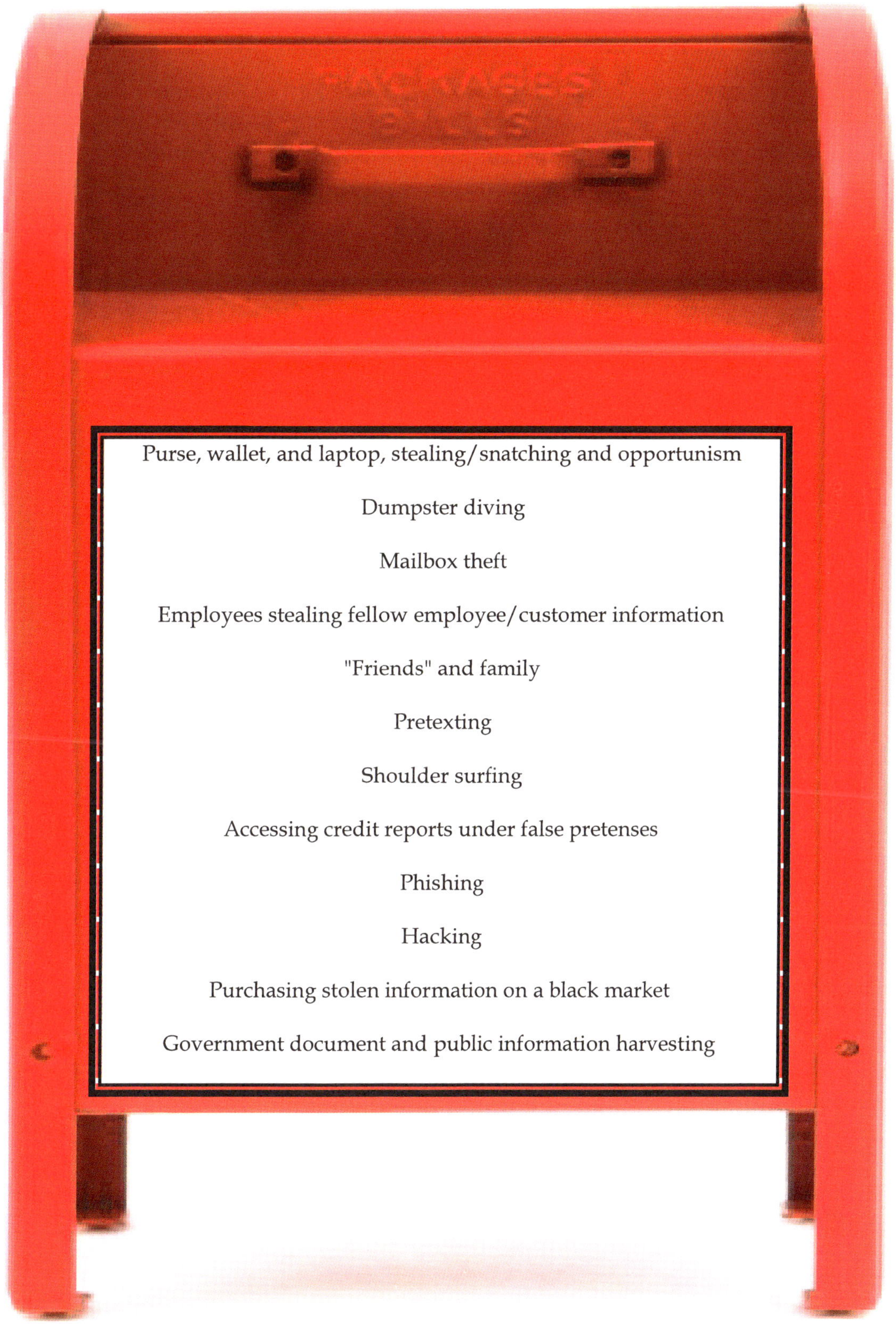

Purse, wallet, and laptop, stealing/snatching and opportunism
Dumpster diving
Mailbox theft
Employees stealing fellow employee/customer information
"Friends" and family
Pretexting
Shoulder surfing
Accessing credit reports under false pretenses
Phishing
Hacking
Purchasing stolen information on a black market
Government document and public information harvesting

LOCK YOUR DOOR AND YOUR MAILBOX

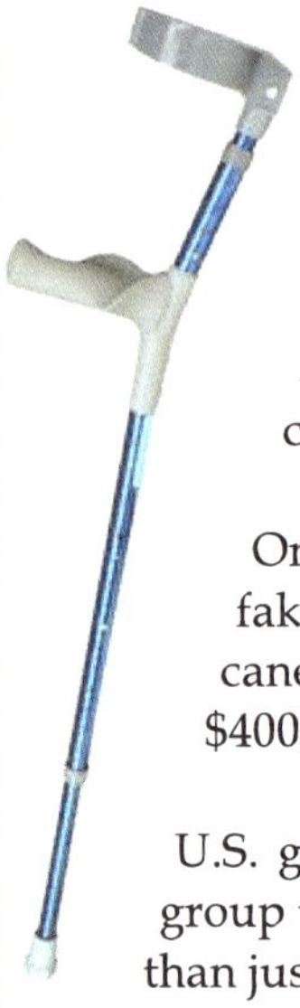

What do medical scrubs and mailboxes have to do with identity theft? For a band of Baltimore thieves, disguises such as medical scrubs, canes, and wheelchairs were the tools of a 30-year identity theft ruse. Mailboxes were where all the scams began.

The thieves pretended to stuff mailboxes with advertising circulars, but instead fished for anything they could use to cobble together a new identity— Social Security checks, credit card bills, even DVD mailers.

Once the crooks had names and vital information such as a Social Security number, they faked new identification cards and headed in costume to the banks, shuffling along with their canes or rolling up in their wheelchairs. Over several decades, the Baltimore gang cashed up to $400,000 worth of checks by impersonating folks like you and me.

U.S. government officials eventually caught up with the criminals, sentencing the leader of the group to 11 years in federal prison. But if you want to protect your identity, you'll need to do more than just lock your door. Padlock your mailbox, too.[2]

All of those juicy Social Security numbers, account numbers, and other information are created and used by the government and businesses. Banks, credit card companies, merchants (retail stores such as grocery stores and department stores), and a host of others, store and process your personal information. This means that the number of employees that come into contact with your information is quite large — not a reassuring thought. You will also have to provide your Social Security number, date of birth, and other information to employers. This information is a tempting target for personnel employees with sticky fingers who have access to personnel records.

Key Takeaway: Identity theft happens when someone pretends to be someone else for personal gain. Common forms of identity theft are financial, medical, or criminal in nature. A Social Security number is particularly valuable to an identity thief. Account numbers and personal information used in security questions are also a prize. Private accounts can be taken over, or an identity thief can take out a new account in the victim's name. Purses and wallets are a common source of identity theft, along with dumpster diving and stealing from mailboxes.

The next type of identity theft I find particularly painful, and reflects the growing phenomena of stealing children's identities. I had a neighbor who played with my son while growing up. She was intermittently abandoned by her mother and father, who had serious drug addictions. I was told her father was a heroin addict. (Drugs are a scourge everywhere, even in supposedly "well-to-do" neighborhoods.) The young girl mostly stayed with her grandmother, who lived next door. A group of us ladies circled the wagons; encouraging her to study hard and plan for college, tutoring her in math, and helping her and her grandmother in various ways. Her mother had died from an overdose the girl's senior year in high school, but her father was still alive just as she was preparing to go to college.

---

2 U.S. Department of Justice; http://creditidentitysafe.com/idtheft/the-ad-man-stealing-mail-and-identities.htm; http://www.identitytheftblog.info/identity-theft/thirty-year-identity-theft-career-ends/, U.S. Department of Justice, June 5, 2009; http://www.justice.gov/usao/md/PublicAffairs/press_releases/press08/BaltimoreFraudster SentencedtooverI3YearsinSchemetoStealIdentityInformation,html.

She told me that she applied for student loans but discovered that she could not get credit. Someone had used her Social Security number to get gas station credit cards in her name and then defaulted after using them. Gas station credit cards can simply be inserted into most gas pumps. The thief does not have to present the credit card personally and have their appearance compared with the name on the card. Despite her being a child without financial transactions, the thief was able to obtain her Social Security number.

Friends, family, roommates, and even perfect strangers can get enough information to answer those security questions previously mentioned. When it is a stranger, it is called "pretexting." Imagine that you are on the ski vacation of your life in Colorado. You are totally relaxed. Fun is the only thought on your mind. You meet a fellow skier who seems to spend more time in the air than on the ground. Back at the lodge you get into a conversation that naturally involves discussions of where you are from, where you were born, your age, your favorite pet, where you went to high school, your best friend, and the hottest investments. Later on you discover that he had a plan for financing his expensive vacation – using your information to get into your investment account and empty it out.

Fortunately, pretexters are usually less personal. Their most common technique is to call on the phone pretending that they are from a bank or other business that you have an account with. They come up with some excuse for needing your account information, password, or Social Security number. It may be to verify your account, sell you new "high value" products, or "protect" you against theft.

"Shoulder surfing" includes peeking at computer screens and ATMs. Clever thieves place brochure boxes next to ATMs, and even fill them with the bank's brochures. They also place a small camera inside that tapes the customers' keystrokes. A high tech and insidious version of this involves intercepting transmissions of insecure or not very secure wireless networks. This can happen at cyber cafes, hotels, business centers for travelers, etc.

The Fair Credit Reporting Act requires that CRAs only provide credit reports to businesses or persons who have a legitimate need to see your credit report. Among others, this can include businesses with which you are applying for a loan, landlords, or employers. CRAs also sell abbreviated information to credit card companies that make "pre-approved" credit card offers. Unfortunately, they may not always check carefully. Identity thieves pretend to be legitimate businesses and request credit reports, which are a jackpot full of Social Security numbers and account information.

Key Takeaway: Many forms of identity theft are up close and very personal, with family members and children often being the victims. A common way that personal information is obtained is through phone calls from a supposedly legitimate business with a valid reason for calling. Other ways may be through casual conversation, shoulder surfing, or intercepting unprotected computer communications at cyber cafes, hotels, and airports.

Victimizing Victims

The old adage, "kick 'em when they're down," apparently applies to defrauded Bernie Madoff investors. At least that's what a group of sadistic identity thieves thought.

Bernie Madoff ran one of the largest investment scams in U.S. history, losing roughly $20 billion for thousands of investors. Some investors were well-healed investment funds. Others were retirees who lost their life savings. Cruelest of all, some of the victims were charities, including a children's hospital and a fund for holocaust victims. All were eager to recoup their money and that's what a new group of con artists were counting on.

Here's how the vicious hoax worked. Identity thieves set up a website claiming to have recovered $1.3 billion of investors' money. To spice up the story they said that Madoff had squirreled away the recently found funds in Malaysia. For some street credibility, the identity crooks named their phony website the International Security Investors Protection Corporation - a name that mimicked a legitimate site sponsored by various governmental agencies. The scamsters also claimed to be located in ritzy Geneva and to be associated with the United Nations.

Did anyone fall for it? It's hard to tell. But the Securities and Exchange Commission swooped in to warn investors not to fall prey to the scam and to guard their personal information. Meanwhile, you can add victimizing the victims to the list of ploys of identity thieves.[3]

"Phishing" involves impersonating a person or business, on the Internet or in mailings, in order to get your information so that they can then impersonate *you*. There are several methods. A common method is to send an email that appears to be from a reputable company saying that you either need to verify account information, or respond to some other kind of situation. When clicking on the link in the email, you will go to a log in page that appears to be at the company's website. Once you log in, they have your username and password. They can then go to your real account and steal from it, or use information in the account to steal from other accounts you have. For instance, your account at a mutual fund may contain bank account numbers needed to transfer funds back and forth.

Another phishing method involves setting up fake websites, often with "incredible deals" for consumers. When the consumer buys something, the identity thief has their credit card number, as well as security information if the victim sets up an account. If the consumer uses the same user name and password for other accounts, they can access those as well. Old-fashioned mail (the mailbox kind) is a method for delivering fraudulent "preapproved" credit offers that require you to fill in information, including your Social Security number, and send the form in. Other scams include requests for charity, etc.

Computer hackers write software that invades the information systems of financial institutions and other businesses. Just about any business has sensitive information of some sort, whether it is employee information or customer information. Hacking allows for the possibility that thousands, if not hundreds of thousands, of identities can be stolen at the same time.

---

[3] U.S. Security and Exchange Commission. "Apparent web-site scam targets victims of Madoff's Ponzi Scheme," *The Wall Street Journal*, March 10, 2010.

A "black market" for information has sprung up. (A black market is a market that operates outside of the law.) There are websites (maintained overseas) that criminals can access in order to buy information. For instance, "carding sites" sell credit card information. Unfortunately, this facilitates identity theft by putting information into the hands of a potential horde of thieves. It also elevates identity theft to a global scale. It is not a comforting thought that a ten-year-old in Thailand could exercise his prowess at hacking and sell your Social Security number and other account numbers on a black market.

Unfortunately, there are publicly available sources of information that do not require skill to obtain. Shocking as it is, there are counties in the United States where Social Security numbers and other information are available to the public on court documents and other records. These could include documents regarding property ownership (for the purpose of property taxes, etc.), divorce decrees, and lawsuits. These documents are a matter of public record and can be obtained by anyone who simply asks! Clearly, something needs to be done about it. There are also non-secure private business websites that take customer information and can be accessed by outsiders.

Key Takeaway: Computers are vulnerable to identity theft. Hackers may invade the computer systems of financial institutions and businesses. There is a black market for sensitive information, where Social Security numbers and other sensitive information are sold around the world. There are even publicly available government sources of sensitive information.

Challenge

Have you given out information that could lead to identity theft? In which ways is your identity most vulnerable to theft?

Medical Insurance Accounts

There are people who impersonate someone else in order to obtain medical care. They may convince a hospital that they are you when they are in the emergency room. Later, you receive an enormous bill for services. Another possibility is that they acquire your health insurance information and seek out treatments. Many people carry health insurance cards around in their wallet or purse. Even worse, some insurers use your Social Security number as your account number. The thought of having a thief's medical problems put on your medical records may sound embarrassing. However, the consequences of medical identity theft can be harmful, or even deadly.

Imagine being rushed to the emergency room. There the hospital administers medications to prevent a blood clot from forming because they have medical records indicating that you have a problem with this condition. Unfortunately, someone with the condition claimed that they were you. In fact, you have a bleeding problem (your blood does not clot easily, leading to excessive bleeding that cannot be stopped easily). The consequences could be deadly.

Some identity thieves impersonate medical providers and file false claims with your insurance company, saying that they gave you medical goods or services. Your insurance company then sends them money. (I shall discuss medical insurance in Volume 2.) However, for the purpose of understanding identity theft, it is important to know that medical insurance has deductibles and coverage limits. A deductible means that you may have to pay a certain amount of money on health payments before your insurance will begin to pay. If an identity thief does not pay at the time of treatment and you have not gone over your deductible, you will get a bill from the medical provider. Even worse, the identity thief may create so many medical bills that they cause you to hit your coverage limit for the year. (A coverage limit is the total amount that the insurance company will spend on you.) Despite relatively low medical claims to the insurance company legitimately made on your behalf, the insurance company may refuse to pay, saying that you have hit the limit. You also may get turned down for life insurance because the life insurance company looked at your medical records and thinks that you have a life-shortening medical condition. You may not be able to get new medical insurance because of a "pre-existing condition" that you never had. (Laws regarding whether insurers can deny you coverage for pre-existing conditions are in flux at the moment.)

Criminal and Civil Court Records

Imagine that you are driving down a beautiful highway in your home state of California, when you are pulled over for a taillight that is out. Suddenly the officer orders you out of the car, throws you spread-eagle against the hood, frisks you, handcuffs you, and hauls you off to jail. At the jail you are told that you have an arrest warrant issued in Texas against you. You are accused of skipping bail and failing to appear for trial after being arrested for drug trafficking. (When people post bail, they are in jail accused of a crime, and in order to get released, they give the court money as a pledge to return for trial.) You have never been to Texas in your life, and your most risky behavior was chancing a parking ticket. (Actually you thought about it, and then felt guilty and put the quarter in the meter.) You spend the night in jail with repeat violent felons.

Unfortunately, criminals sometimes have been successful in convincing justice authorities that they are someone else. This can be aided with the use of false or stolen identification. They post bail and then disappear. They may even serve their full time in jail, but under someone else's name. When they get out, their record, unlike their victim's, is clear.

Civil judgments can also involve identity theft. In a civil judgment, someone broke the law and is liable for some kind of damage to someone else, but they have not committed a crime. Failing to fulfill a contract would be an example. Sometimes, someone found liable under a civil judgment has given a false identity. They disappear when it is time to pay up, leaving the victim to prove their innocence.

Other Kinds of Identity Theft

There is a grab bag of miscellaneous identity theft. An example is an illegal alien using a U.S. citizen's Social Security number for the purpose of obtaining employment. The victim could be accused of filing false Social Security information, illegally receiving Social Security benefits, or falsely claiming a tax refund. They could also spend a considerable amount of time clearing up their records. Another example is stealing student loans.

> ***Key Takeaway:*** There are insidious forms of identity theft that can get people jailed or killed. Medical identity theft involves someone receiving treatment under your name. This can lead to a host of problems, including receiving the wrong treatment. Criminal identity theft happens when an accused or convicted criminal pretends to be someone else. They could get the victim falsely arrested.

Battling Identity Theft

Walter was a tough, hard-bitten veteran trained to deal with the enemy. After his honorable discharge, he was filled with hope and anticipation on starting his new life as a contract software developer for several financial firms. He was twenty-nine years old and ready to move on with his life. Walter had a roomy apartment in a hip part of Austin, Texas, and had saved nearly enough money for a shiny new BMW 3 Series convertible.

Walter had no trouble landing contracts for new jobs. He had great references, and when one job ended he quickly began another. His résumé continued to grow. On dusky Austin evenings, Walter would sit back in his chair on the balcony and dream of the software development company he hoped to create.

But then, inexplicably, Walter's career went off the tracks. Suddenly, no one wanted to hire him. Over several months, interview after interview soured. Even firms he had worked at before deserted him, despite his doing a great job.

Walter was puzzled and disheartened. Unable to find work as a software developer, he wound up toiling away as a store clerk during the day and a server at a restaurant at night. He took on a buddy as a roommate to help him shoulder the rent. More and more of his bills ended up on his credit card, and his debt started to soar.

It wasn't until he asked for a copy of the background check one firm had run on him that he realized someone had stolen his identity. He found himself fighting an enemy he could not even see. The thief had assumed Walter's identity when he had been arrested for drug charges and shoplifting. No wonder Walter couldn't get hired.

Walter is still battling to untangle the mess. After two years he has managed to repair his credit. Fortunately, one of Walter's previous employers stood by him and hired him back. But the fake criminal record still exists, and for now, his career ambitions are broken down by the roadside.[4]

19.3 Recovering from Identity Theft

Dealing with identity theft is never pleasant. The first step is to take a deep breath and gather perspective. Having someone pretend to be you in order to commit crimes can be very upsetting. However, realize that it is a matter of putting one foot in front of the other. Usually a step by step process will clear up the problem. For additional emotional support, see the website in the book appendix.

Time is your enemy; act immediately to limit damage. Pretending the problem does not exist will only make it worse. In any dealings you have over identity theft, be sure to keep detailed records, including copies of all correspondence, the names of people spoken with, dates, etc. The best thing to

[4] This fictional account is based on a composite of actual cases reported in these sources: http://www.privacyrights.org/ar/wcr.htm; http://g27radio.blogspot.com/2007/04/think-youre-safe.html.

do is start a file, which you will add to any time you take action or have dealings in clearing up the problem. Mail all such letters using certified, return receipt mail.

If the stolen information can be used for obtaining credit or opening fraudulent accounts, the first step is to notify the three major credit bureaus and establish fraud alerts. You will only need to notify one, who will notify the other two. With the fraud alert, creditors are required to call you before extending credit, although, unfortunately, not all follow the law and make that call. Try to supply a phone number where you can always be reached.

The next step is to file a police report and obtain a copy, along with evidence of attempts to open fraudulent accounts. After gathering as much information as possible on what happened, file a report with a local police department, and also with the police department in the area where the fraud happened, being sure that the report includes a list of the fraudulent accounts. Keep contact information on the officer handling your case.

Most police will cooperate in creating a report. However, if they are unwilling, you may have several options. If the fraud involved the U.S. mail, you can file a report with the U.S. Postal inspector. If a phony driver's license or driver's license number was used, report it with your state Department of Motor Vehicles and get a new license with a different number.

The first fraud alert will only last ninety days. After receiving a notice of your rights from the credit bureaus, contact all three and request a free copy of your credit report and an extension of the fraud alert for seven years. You will also need your police report. Go through your credit reports and note any additional problems. Mail the credit bureaus and anyone who granted a fraudulent account informing them that the accounts are fraudulent. The FTC has a sample letter that can be used. The credit bureaus will then be required to block the negative information associated with the fraudulent accounts from your credit report.

You should also ask the credit bureaus to remove any inquiries associated with granting the fraudulent accounts, and ask them to notify anyone who has received an incorrect report within the last six months, or any employers within the last two years. You may have to fill out a fraud affidavit and send it to anyone who granted fraudulent credit. Be sure to ask them for a letter stating that they have closed the account and discharged any claims against you. Report any stolen credit or ATM cards immediately by phone, along with fraudulent use of your phone account or other types of accounts. You may have to follow up in writing. If you are the victim of check fraud, you may have to contact the check verification companies. (Check verification companies are used by merchants to verify that checks they receive are covered and legitimate.) You can also get a free report once a year from them. If their report is not cleared up, you may have difficulty writing checks or opening bank accounts.

It will be necessary to monitor your credit report and other accounts frequently from then on. Most states will allow you to obtain additional free reports, in addition to the annual report, if you are an identity theft victim. Many states will also allow you to freeze your credit reports for a small fee, and for free if you are an identity theft victim. With a freeze, your credit report cannot be accessed by someone contemplating granting credit. This will cause him to deny credit to an identity thief who is impersonating you. If you would like to take out credit, you can unfreeze your report temporarily, and then refreeze it again. However, I had a student tell me that it took almost three months, for some unfathomable reason, before he could get his credit report unfrozen. All the while he was unable to finance the purchase of a house he wished to bid on. This suggests leaving plenty of time to unfreeze your account before applying for credit. Another possible way to avoid identity theft is to sign up for a service that sends you alerts if your report is accessed.

There are very few protections for identity theft of brokerage accounts, mutual fund accounts, and other kinds of investment accounts. To make things worse, these accounts can hold substantial amounts of wealth, and even a person's entire retirement savings. If you are a victim, contact your broker or other entity keeping the account for you immediately, and go through your investment account agreement carefully. File a report with the police and contact the SEC and FINRA, as well. As I will discuss below, it is vital to use all possible measures to protect these accounts.

For other kinds of identity theft, contact the involved party. If your Social Security number has been misused, contact the Social Security Administration. However, as already discussed, changing your Social Security number can create numerous problems and should only be attempted in very serious cases. Even then, it may not work.

If your passport has been stolen or misused, contact the U.S. Department of State's Passport Services. Report student loan theft to the school that opened the loan and request that the account be closed. (The laws regarding student loans are in flux.) Medical identity theft will require cleaning up medical accounts and medical records. This can be quite involved. (See a suggested website in the book appendix.) If you are the victim of a false criminal or civil judgment, contact the police department and the court in the jurisdiction involved. If the problem is criminal, contact your state department of justice and the FBI about clearing your name.

If debt collectors try to collect from you as a victim of identity theft, explain to them you are a victim, get all information about the account, find out what paperwork they require from you, and confirm your conversation in writing. Ask them to confirm in writing that you do not owe the debt. They are required by law to inform the person who issued the debt that you are a victim of identity theft, although you should do so as well. Creditors are also not allowed to sell fraudulent debt accounts to debt collectors. Point this out to them if necessary.

As a last resort, it may be necessary to hire an attorney to gain the cooperation of anyone who granted credit, or provided other kinds of consideration or services to an identity thief. What you should never do is give in and make payments. It was their responsibility to verify the identity of the person they dealt with. The reasons are clear. Imagine that the victim of identity theft was responsible for making payment. Someone could take out an account claiming they are a famous and wealthy personality such as Oprah Winfrey. The person granting the credit would have no incentive to make any effort to verify the identity of the person they are lending money to because they know that Oprah will make good on the payment. It should be clear that it is necessary that the person granting the credit or other services should be the one responsible for verifying the identity of the person they are dealing with, and this is in fact how the law works. They are the person "on the spot," in the best place to prevent fraud. If a credit grantor is not cooperating, point this out to her.

It may be worthwhile to perform some sleuthing. You may be able to uncover who stole your identity and hand over your findings to a prosecutor. In writing, ask anyone who granted fraudulent credit to hand over any documentation they have to you, and also to law enforcement. This could include the loan application with the perpetrator's handwriting and photocopies of the driver's license that may have their picture. Federal law requires them to turn it over. Other companies involved in providing goods or services to the identity thief may also be willing to cooperate. If the thief is prosecuted, offer to give a Victim Impact Statement to ensure that they are given a sentence that reflects the true harm that they have caused.

BY THE NUMBERS

- Between 7 million and 10 million people have their identities stolen annually.
- The Federal Trade Commission says identity theft is the fastest growing crime of our time.
- The average amount of time it takes from when an individual uncovers that someone has been using his or her identity to when they obtain credit is 14 months.
- On average it takes two years to clear up your credit records after your identity has been stolen.

Key Takeaway: What do you do if a 57-year-old mechanic from Dubuque pretends to be you? Do not panic, but act quickly and get organized. Notify all the major credit card bureaus and establish a fraud alert. Make a note of every conversation you have, and file every record you receive in a dedicated folder. File a police report. Depending on the theft, you may need to contact other agencies. Contact the credit bureaus again to extend your initial 90-day fraud alert for seven years. Thereafter, continually monitor your credit reports.

19.4 Precautions and Good Habits

It is not possible to completely protect yourself from identity theft. Someone may do everything right with their health including exercising, eating right, and getting regular checkups, and yet still suffer a serious illness. However, just as in protecting your health, taking precautions against identity theft can significantly reduce the chance of a problem. Well-armed is well protected.

I will start with a discussion of investment accounts since the amount of money subject to theft can be substantial, while protections are few. If you log in to your account online, be sure to log out when you are finished, or someone may be able to continue your session if you leave your computer. The website should also be secure, with "https" at the beginning of the address. Your password should be completely different from any other passwords you have and should not reflect anything about yourself, such as a friend's name Each should be a strong password with plenty of capital and lower case letters, along with numbers and symbols. An easy way to do this is to create an expression such as, "Be a star. Save a percent of your money for life at retirement." The password would then be "Ba*Sa%oy$4l@r".

Watch out for shoulder surfers. If you are using Wi-Fi, your keystrokes may be intercepted. Do not send sensitive information over unsecured networks. If you are accessing your account at work, it may be an employee who steals from you. A keystroke tracking virus could also copy your password. I am so worried about investment accounts that I have a text file on my computer. I copy and paste in the password characters when accessing my account. Also, be sure to never have your computer remember your passwords. Type them in each time.

Do not use a computer that is not your own. If you cannot avoid it, clear the temporary Internet files and browsing history afterwards. You may be able to use a security token to access your account. These are small, number generating devices that change your password frequently. Check with your broker or investment manager if they are available. It may also be possible to request from your broker or investment manager to have a cookie placed on your computer. Your accounts can then only be accessed from that computer.[5] However, any time you erase cookies or change computers, you will have to remember to access your account online and remove this feature first. Afterwards, you can go online again and have it put back. In general, these kinds of measures may be too time consuming, but investment accounts are worth it. Protect these accounts like a junk yard dog.

Get a shredder and shred sensitive documents that have personal or account information, such as investment statements and phone bills. Get a locking file cabinet for sensitive documents that you cannot shred. Pictures of documents inserted into text files are better than text copies. Scan them if necessary, and encrypt anything that is a text file. Better yet, buy software that allows you to store sensitive information in encrypted folders on your computer. Be sure to have good antivirus and firewall protection for your computer, and keep its operating system and browser updated. (It is also a good idea to keep other software up to date to prevent hacking.)

If you use a wireless system, make sure it is password protected. Never reveal your passwords to accounts. Avoid businesses (especially small ones) that take your information and transmit it, but do not have good security in place. Unfortunately, many businesses do not take appropriate steps to insure the security of their systems. Be careful to not transmit sensitive information at "hot spots" that are not secured. Review website security policies, and if insufficient or nonexistent, consider going elsewhere.

Avoid responding to emails by clicking on links. For instance, if you receive an email from your bank asking that you update your account, access the bank website separately in your browser using the known IP address. Do not respond to the email by providing information. (This is also true of an "employee" of a businesses that calls. Ask to call her back using the publicly listed number for the business.) Avoid downloading "free" software such as free games. Avoid opening files sent to you by strangers and using file sharing programs. Use a different password for each account.

One trick is to use a rule to modify a root password based on the account being accessed. Try not to use your mother's maiden name, your birthday, place of birth, or other personal information that may be publicly available as security questions. It may be a good idea to make up answers to security questions at websites. For instance, your favorite dog Rex becomes "Toto" for a security question.

Give your Social Security number reluctantly. Ask if an alternative number will suffice. Take credit card receipts with you, and do not permit your credit card number to be written on checks. Whisper sensitive information when in public, or write it on a piece of paper that you take back. Be stingy about revealing information about yourself that can be used for security questions.

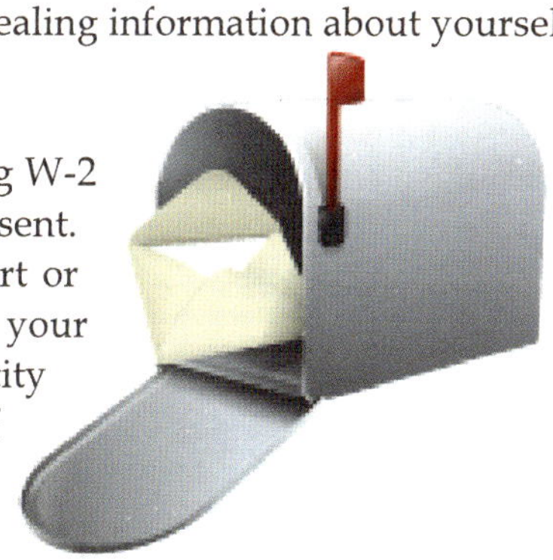

Tax time can be trouble. All sorts of sensitive information is mailed, including W-2 forms with your Social Security number. Double-check when any documents will be sent. If they do not show up, start monitoring your credit regularly, or place a fraud alert or freeze on your credit reports. Try to file your tax returns electronically, or drop off your mail at the post office. Do not leave your tax filings in a mailbox overnight. Identity thieves know that the day before taxes are due mailboxes are a goldmine of information.

---

[5] No system is perfect. At least some security tokens have been hacked, and cookies can be gotten around.

While on vacation make sure your mail is held at the post office, or have a friend pick it up, and do not leave sensitive mailings in your mailbox. If your address changes, make sure you update your address with businesses, employers, the post office, and the credit bureaus. If you discover an incorrect change of address, correct the problem. (Someone may be trying to intercept your mail to get their hands on sensitive information or credit card offers.) Remove your name from marketing lists of the three credit bureaus, and sign up for the FTC's national do not call registry. Opt out of having your information shared whenever possible. Try to pay as many bills as possible online, and opt to receive statements electronically.

Keep an eye on your credit card when you hand it to someone. A cashier may try to use a small, hand-held "skimmer" to record your card information. If someone such as a restaurant server leaves with your card, be sure to check it when they bring it back. A trick is to return an old expired card of someone else that looks the same. The victim is unaware that their card is stolen and fails to cancel it promptly.

Check your wallet and make sure there is no unnecessary information in it such as your Social Security number. (Photocopy identification cards with your Social Security number and mark out your number in indelible ink.) Keep track of what is in your wallet in case it is stolen. Report stolen cards immediately, and change passwords if there is a problem. Do not leave sensitive information in hotel rooms.

Unfortunately, friends and relatives all too commonly turn out to be identity thieves (as well as victims). Dealing with this can be especially painful. Several websites are listed in the book appendix that offer advice. Roommates can be a very effective way to save money when young. However, roommates require extra precautions with regard to identity theft. Try to have one person in charge of accounts such as cable television service. If possible, have separate locking mailboxes, or get a post office box and have sensitive material such as W-2 forms and bills sent there. It will require an extra trip to the post office once in a while, but will be worth it. Try to go paperless, and have a log-in for your computer. Do not leave it unattended. Restrict access over a network. Keep careful control of documents.

Children can be particularly vulnerable to identity theft. More than likely you do not have children yet, but at some point in the future they may rely on you to protect them from having their identity stolen – with a lifetime of unpleasant consequences to follow. The Children's Online Privacy Protection Act (COPPA) restricts what information websites can collect from children under the age of 13. Websites are also required to have a privacy policy detailing what information they collect from children, and what they do with that information. In the future, if you have children, check websites your children visit, and be selective about giving permission for your child's information to be collected or used. Talk with them frequently about which websites are acceptable, and what information they are allowed to reveal, not only at websites, but in general.

Social networking websites are a particularly good place to look for personal information that can be used to answer security questions. (They can also provide a permanent source of trouble for someone in the future. I will discuss this in the next chapter.) Regularly check your child's credit report. They may not have one. However, when they do, put a freeze on it. There are thieves who try to guess children's Social Security numbers, and then sell them on a black market. (Unfortunately, Social Security numbers are not completely random. They are based on the age of the person when they received the number and where they were born.)[6]

---

[6] Id Thieves Now Targeting children, Fox News, http://www.foxnews.com/scitech/2010/08/03/id-thieves-targeting-children/.

Finally, monitor your credit reports. There are services that will send you alerts through a variety of mechanisms if your credit report is accessed (including by text message). You may want to have a freeze put on your credit report. If you are away on military duty, have an active duty alert put on your credit reports to prevent access while you are away. Check your credit reports at least once a year, and more often if you have reason to believe that your data has been compromised, or you are already a victim of identity theft. The book appendix has useful websites regarding identity theft.

Key Takeaway: It is vital to develop good habits to protect your identity. Investment accounts must be diligently guarded. Use strong passwords for accounts and do not reveal them. Shred documents and keep your virus protection and firewall up to date. Do not respond to emails asking for sensitive information. Go to the company's website using your own link. Be stingy about giving out information.

Challenge

What habits can you work on to protect your identity? It is time to start practicing them.

19.5 Conclusion

Identity theft is a serious and growing problem. Victims may expend considerable time and money fixing the problem, with the possibility of permanent damage. It is vital to develop good habits to minimize the chance of becoming a victim. People naturally try to avoid visiting dangerous places and leaving valuable possessions unprotected. The same kind of good habits need to be ingrained to prevent identity theft. An identity thief who accesses investment accounts can rob someone in a way that a burglar could only dream of. Children also need to be protected. It is time to start practicing. Is there a sale on shredders?

Key Terms:

Account takeover
Active duty alert
Application fraud
Black market
COPPA
Credit freeze
Criminal and civil record identity theft
Dumpster diving
Fraud alert
Hacking
Medical account identity theft
Merchants
New account fraud
Phishing
Pretexting
Private account identity theft
Security questions
Shoulder surfing
Social networking websites

End of Chapter Questions

1. Why are Social Security numbers so valuable to identity thieves?
2. What are common security questions that should be avoided?
3. What is account takeover and new account fraud?
4. When is it particularly important to monitor the mail?
5. What is dumpster diving?
6. What is pretexting?
7. What is shoulder surfing?
8. What is phishing?
9. What kinds of problems are associated with medical identity theft?
10. What is criminal identity theft?
11. Name the basic steps for dealing with credit fraud.
12. What does it mean to freeze a credit report? How does it work?
13. Why is it so important to monitor investment accounts?
14. What is a skimmer?
15. What does a credit monitoring service do?
16. What is a security token?
17. Name extra precautions to be taken with a roommate.
18. What is a fraud alert?

19. What rights do you have if you are a victim of identity theft and are contacted by a collection agency?

20. What extra precautions need to be taken around tax time?

21. If a server takes your credit card out of your sight, it is important to remember to do what?

22. If a bank employee contacts you because they think your account has been accessed, what should you do?

23. How should you respond to emails from businesses that you deal with asking for information?

Chapter 20

Looking Good for A Lifetime

Most people take care with their appearance. After all, that is how they first get judged—fairly or not. Someone's appearance can speak volumes about who they are. These signals are not always correct, but in our fast paced world people often resort to quick, superficial judgments. An inappropriate appearance can mean the difference between acceptance and rejection.

In a formal business setting, too much makeup or a wrinkled tie can tell people you are not up to a challenge. In an artistic setting, formal attire tells people you are stiff and uncreative. Your appearance signals whether you are aware of the sensibilities of those around you, which is crucial for success. Your appearance can also be a way to sparkle and stand out, and a way to express your individuality.

However, your physical appearance is only a small part of what people see. You also have a persona that is presented to the public over the Internet, through public records, and in your résumé. It is ironic that people who spend tremendous amounts of time on their physical appearance often pay little attention to how they look elsewhere. Success in a career depends on the entirety of how you look. You have already seen that a poor credit score can cost a fortune, and in some cases the negative information never goes away. A poor public appearance can be just as harmful to your career, your standing in the community, and your reflection in the eyes of family and friends.

It is also important to realize that you will change over time. Your tastes and goals, habits, and view of the world will change as you gain experience. I do not know many older adults who do not consider themselves to be very different people from when they were young. Keep your older self in mind, and respect that future person's feelings about how they should be presented to the world.

In the not-so-distant past, before the Internet and electronic records, people could get a second, third, or even a fourth chance. However, we have entered an era where information sticks to people from a young age. Your parents did not have to face this when growing up. In today's environment, a new set of wisdom needs to be handed down, or

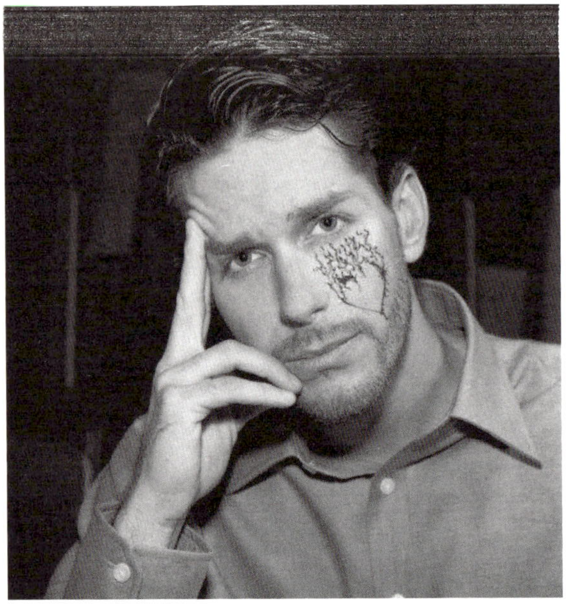

The tattoo was added to the model.

serious blunders can maim for a lifetime. A bad mistake while young can be just like an enormous, hideous tattoo, or some horrible, disfiguring scar. It can be repellant to those around you, a constant reminder of something you wish you could forget, *and* impossible to get rid of.

20.1 Online

Cautious conduct on the Internet and over cell phones, iPads®, and other electronic communications is an enormous subject. Dangerous predators in search of young victims troll chat rooms and social networking sites posing as someone else. (For every K-12 school there are multiple convicted sex offenders, and these are the ones who were caught. In 2007, in New York, 670 sex offenders lived within 2 blocks of a school.[1])

The people in the photograph are models.

Another problem that is becoming increasingly common is brutal cyber bullying with sometimes tragic results. Hopefully, you have been warned about the physical danger that the Internet poses, and take the appropriate care. Be sure to never reveal personal information about yourself on the Internet that could allow someone to locate you, such as your address, phone number, or birthday. Better yet, only interact with "eyeball friends" that you personally know. Do not post pictures or send them electronically, if at all possible. Do not meet people in person who you first meet on the Internet.

If you are under-age and an adult online asks you to keep him a secret, do the opposite—report him. Any adult that asks someone under-age to keep something secret is doing something wrong. Any responsible adult knows better than to tell teens to keep secrets from their parents and others. Even if you are 18 or over, you can still be a tempting target. Create usernames or online profiles that do not identify you. Avoid websites that entrap young people. Trouble can come from excessive spending online (and online auctions), gambling, and getting involved in hate groups. Helpful websites are included in Table 12-1 to keep you safe and happy.

Table 20-1
Online Safety

http://www.webwisekids.org/
http://www.netsmartz.org/index.aspx
http://www.safekids.com/

---

[1] Office of Rep. Anthony Weiner, *Sex Offenders Near Schools: A Review of the Sex Offender Database*, Jan. 28, 2007, http://weiner.house.gov/reports/01.28.07Sex%20Offenders.pdf. Ironically, representative Weiner was caught in his own scandal involving the Internet.

Key Takeaway: It is important to have a good appearance in all ways, including on the Internet. Since the danger of having negative information recorded on the Internet is a new phenomenon, wisdom about maintaining a good appearance on the Internet is not yet being handed down in a systematic way. Once information is recorded, it may never go away. Also, protect yourself from predators by not revealing information that can lead to your physical location, and do not visit with people in person that you meet over the Internet.

Challenge

When you are on the Internet, are you in the habit of thinking about your public image and safety?

Lisa Jones Résumé

Wonderful college record.

Impressive portfolio.

Terrific part-time work experience.

Fantastic references.

Online: Uses profanity.
Viciously bullied several other teens with her friends.
Steals music and videos.
Posts "steamy" pictures.
Likes to drink and smoke.
Has a _____ political position, and thinks others who do not share her views are stupid.

Chances are that you have been warned about Internet predators. What you may have received less warning about is the record you are creating online—a record that will follow you for the rest of your life. If the public has access to something, chances are good that it will be preserved. When something is taken off the Internet, it is often still available because it gets archived. "Snap-shots" are constantly being taken of the Internet through the use of "crawlers"; software that patrols the Internet and preserves information.[2] This can include social networking pages, postings on blogs, comments in chat rooms, files posted at various websites, etc.

Once information about you is publicly available, it typically never goes away. You may also think that information you supply to a website is private, only to discover it is not. Websites have varying policies about revealing user data, and it is important to check a website's privacy policy if you are revealing sensitive information to them. Some websites actually sell customer information. In fact, they will sell information they promised to keep secret after switching their privacy policy.

There are many ways that information can be collected on an individual. An easy way is an online search, which can turn up a surprising amount. It is important to periodically track what comes up under your name. Businesses sell information on customer purchases and activities. It may be possible to find out what food you buy and if you consume alcohol, especially if you use a grocery store customer card. A plethora of government records are available.

There are also services that specialize in gathering information for a fee. They can dig into all sorts of clever and unexpected places. Employers are steadily increasing their use of these services to do background checks on potential employees. Before making something about yourself publicly available, realize that college admissions officers, potential employers, family, friends, future children, and the community (including the press) will be able to see it too—forever.

[2] For an example, see the Wayback Machine: http://www.archive.org/

Facebook

Facebook was in the habit of repeatedly changing its privacy settings, making previously private information public. Its privacy controls had become increasingly complex, with almost 150 options, so "that even privacy experts find them bamboozling."[3] And they were set up to assume you wanted to share as much information as possible unless told otherwise. A group of Google engineers bailed out on Facebook because large amounts of public information were made available by default. Some information was shared with other companies such as Yelp, Pandora, and Microsoft, without the user's permission. User activities were broadcast to multiple websites through a notification tool called Beacon. Facebook's behavior even caught the attention of international regulators. Officials from 30 European countries complained in a letter to Facebook, and 15 consumer groups filed a complaint with the FTC.

Why was Facebook so interested in making user information public? Could it be because they sell advertising? Advertisers like to target their ads to people with specific characteristics that make them the most likely to buy— they don't want to pay for advertising to people who won't be interested.

Several senators called on Facebook to improve its privacy policies. In response, Facebook updated its controls to make them simpler. However, as one person put it, "I'm considering deactivating my account. Facebook is a handy site, but I'm freaked by the idea that my information is in the hands of people I don't trust. That is too high a price to pay."[4] I can tell you that the author of this textbook did just that.[5]

Young people routinely post horrible things about themselves that can seriously haunt them. On social networking sites, they regularly post swear words, inappropriate photos and videos, and admissions of smoking, drinking, or taking drugs. Postings also include vitriolic tirades against people with different political views. The typical person changes their political views over time. At some point in the future, someone who is considering hiring you for a very desirable job may see a tirade you made against their political beliefs that you do not even hold anymore.

This is a model.

Bullying online can be extremely damaging to the perpetrator. The reason is that there are a variety of behaviors that are an enormous problem for employers, and this is true in any kind of profession. It is often the case that the most important thing an employer tries to discern in a job applicant is whether they will be a "team player." Free-riding, backstabbing, bullying, gossiping, and office politicking cost employers a veritable fortune. After Empower Public Relations instituted a "gossip-free" office policy, their sales doubled in one year.[6] Anything that indicates that you are the kind of person who would engage in this kind of conduct will seriously impede your ability to get a job. Employers want people who are friendly, optimistic, cooperative, responsible, hard-working, and trouble avoiding. Anything you project about yourself

---

3 "Dicing With Data; Facebook, Google and Privacy," *The Economist*, May 22, 2010.

4 Daniel Lyons, "The High Price of Facebook; You Pay For It With Your Privacy," *Newsweek*, May 31, 12010.

5 Jessica Guynn, "Facebook Alters Site To Ease Privacy Concerns; Settings Will Be Simplified To Allow Users To Shield Their Personal Information," *The Los Angeles Times*, Thursday May 27 2010; Miguel Helft and Jenna Wortham, "Facebook Bows To Pressure Over Privacy," *The New York Times*, Thursday May 27, 2010; Lyons, *Newsweek*, May 31, 12010; *The Economist*, May 22, 2010; Jon Swartz, "Senators Request Facebook Change; New Feature Raises Issues With Privacy," *USA Today*, Wednesday April 28, 2010.

6 Marilyn Gardner, "Some Employers Get Tough on Workplace Gossip," *Christian Science Monitor*, June 3, 2008.

online that goes against this is a serious problem. This is also true when applying to colleges, that carefully avoid students that they think will cause trouble.

Humiliation and the Internet

Anonymity is increasingly hard to achieve in our hyper-connected society. And to prove it, professor Lanier Holt of the University of Indiana does a little "scouting report" on his students. Holt recently googled 104 of his incoming students in his Principles of Public Relations class to find out what's on the Internet about them.

Some students still had untarnished web reputations, but Holt found embarrassing Internet photos of other students. One student appeared smoking marijuana; another picture showed a student posing half-undressed.

Holt's point is that in the Internet age information is an easily accessible commodity. And for high school students applying to college and future job hunters, what's on the Web is just as important as their college essays and resumes.

A Career Builder survey recently showed that about 45% of prospective employers check out social networks such as Facebook when reviewing job candidates. The real kicker: about a third of the employers rejected candidates after checking them out online. How come? Embarrassing photos is just one of the reasons. The Internet is also a showcase for shoddy writing, poor communication (including bad mouthing others and spreading rumors), and for lying about your qualifications.

A word to the wise: If you really want a job, carefully hide your social networking page from public view (or don't have one at all), edit your blog to prevent unflattering postings, and use your online manners.[7]

Another source of major trouble has to do with illegally downloading or file-sharing music and videos (also known as stealing). Of course, it can lead to legal problems and financial losses. It can also be a guaranteed way of getting doors slammed in your face by employers, colleges, etc., because you generated a public record indicating that you are dishonest.

The best way to avoid a bad online persona is to avoid posting anything that indicates something negative about you. It is also helpful to use generic "usernames" or online profiles. Control access to your accounts as much as possible. When leaving your home, you first make sure your appearance is acceptable. It is important when dealing with the online world to take the same care. Think of yourself as posing for a portrait that the world sees. If you would not feel comfortable with something being posted on a sign above your head, or printed in the newspaper, then do not put it online. Of course, this begs the question: If you are embarrassed or ashamed about something coming out in public, then why do it in private? If you had the

[7] Jeffrey Zaslow, "Surviving the Age of Humiliation," *The Wall Street Journal*, May 5, 2010; Kim Eaton, "If You're Applying For a Job, Censor Your Facebook Page," *FastCompany*, Aug. 19, 2009, http://www.fastcompany.com/blog/ kit-eaton/technomix/if-youre-applying-job-censor-your-facebook-page.

reaction to reading this that you need to stop posting things that you do online, then it is time to look in a mirror and honestly ask yourself if you should be doing them at all.

Unfortunately, files and pictures that you send electronically can be posted on the Internet by the recipient, even if that is not what you intended. It is also a simple matter to scan paper photos and documents into electronic form and post them as well. Being conscious of everything you write down or every picture taken of you may seem to be too much, but this does not mean that you cannot practice caution. Even if you do not keep your guard up at all times, you can develop habits that help. As is true with many things in life, practice creates improvement.

A Double Tragedy

The two young teenage girls had a lot in common. They were intelligent, attractive, and planning on a bright future. They both had loving families. But it was something else they had in common that led to tragedy. Hope Witsell and Jesse Logan had sent inappropriate pictures of themselves over their cell phones, and those pictures became widely distributed to high school classmates. What was intended to be very private became very visible to all. That was when the vicious bullying began. Public shaming and brutal taunts went on day after day. There was a special agony to being humiliated in front of a jeering crowd. The pain was unbearable. Tragically, instead of reaching out for help, both shared a final fate by hanging themselves.

These are models and not the actual people being discussed.

Legal problems associated with these situations can be severe. Bullying can lead to legal liability. People who keep or distribute the photos, even if they are minors, could face child pornography charges. Surprisingly, minors who send pictures of themselves may even face child pornography charges; receiving payment for the pictures is not required. In addition to possible jail time, they may be required to publicly register as sex offenders for a long period, if not their entire life. The result is a permanent brand as one of the lowest members of society.[8]

Key Takeaway: Publicly available Internet information gets stored by crawlers and never goes away. Many young adults post damaging information about themselves on social networking sites and make it publicly available. Individuals and organizations are increasingly investigating people now that information is so readily available electronically, including college admissions officers and employers. Any evidence of unwanted personality traits can seriously damage a person's chance at employment.

Challenge

Is your social networking site available to the general public? If so, does it show you in a positive light? Imagine a college admissions officer or prospective employer looking at your site. Do you feel good about that?

[8] Mike Celizic, "Mom Shares Grief Over Teen 'Sexting' Suicide," NBC San Diego, March 6, 2009, http://www.nbcsandiego.com/news/archive/Her_teen_committed_suicide_over__sexting_.html; Andrew Meacham, "Sexting-related bullying cited in Hillsborough teen's suicide," Tampabay.com, Nov. 29, 2009, http://www.tampabay.com/news/humaninterest/article1054895.ece.

20.2 Public Records

There are a host of public records that can be accessed through background checks and other means. According to one survey, for some positions, 47% of employers check the credit history of applicants.[9] Clearly, criminal records are very damaging. Most young people in nurturing circumstances do not think of themselves as someone who can have a criminal record. However, young people get into trouble all the time, and the law is increasingly allowing teens to be prosecuted as adults. If you are a minor, that does not guarantee that something will not permanently end up on your record. As an adult, your record will stick.

Dangerous driving is a major source of trouble. More young people die from car crashes than anything else. The most common causes are driver error, speeding, distracted driving, and drinking or drugs. Being distracted can be deadly. Having friends carrying on loud conversations in the car, or talking on cell phones or other electronic devices, pulls attention away from the road, when a split second can make the difference between life and death. The other causes should be clear.

Remember that young people often have a feeling of invincibility that is not justified. Young people can die just like anyone else. A car is a multi-ton juggernaut of steel moving down the road. When you get behind the wheel you are taking on the grave responsibility of protecting other's lives. Imagine the crushing guilt of being responsible for maiming or killing another human being. That guilt could be accompanied by financial destitution from a lawsuit, and the burden of carrying a negative public record for a lifetime. If you were driving dangerously, or under the influence, you could also spend a long time in jail.

Young people from nurturing circumstances are used to being protected— and also forgiven. The legal system is not so kind. If you have broken the law, police and prosecutors will not be on your side. You may be nothing more than a statistic, and prosecuting you may be just another feather in their cap as they build their own record. Know the law and do not assume that something is not important, or that you will get away with it. Jail or probation is not something abstract that happens to "bad" people. Break the law at your peril.

Some offenses of minors stay on their record forever, just like offenses for those eighteen and over. A small brush with the law can mean a lifetime of reduced career opportunities and low esteem by the community. That one infraction could mean three months of probation (supervision by law enforcement), but it also means a permanently damaged record and major destruction of a once bright future. There is no substitute to taking pride in yourself and following a path of integrity.

---

[9] Kristen McNamara, "Bad Credit Derails Job Seekers," *The Wall Street Journal*, March 16, 2010.

Destiny and a Texas Highway

It was an onyx black night on a lonely, two-lane stretch of West Texas highway, when the boom of metal bashing into metal rang out.

Two cars crashed on that dark night in 1963. One went through a red stop sign barreling into the other. One teenage driver died instantly; a life extinguished. The surviving teenager grew up to become First Lady Laura Bush.

At the time, Laura Bush was an ordinary 17-year-old girl driving with a friend to the movies. She ran a stop sign and wound up killing her long-time friend, Mike Douglas, who improbably was driving the other car. Laura had known Mike since they were children. And although she says they didn't date in high school, they were close friends who talked on the phone almost daily.

While Mike's life ended that night, what became of Laura is well known. She went on to get an advanced degree in library science, and worked as a librarian before marrying George Bush and serving eight years in the White House as First Lady.

But Laura's polite demeanor and polished appearance during her White House years has belied a lasting guilt that she's felt since that fateful night long ago. Only recently, with the advent of the publishing of her book, *Spoken From the Heart*, has she openly talked about her private anguish.

"I felt terrible guilt," she recently told Larry King during an interview. Perhaps compounding Laura's guilt was that she never spoke to Mike's family after the accident, or knew whether Mike's parents ever forgave her. "I dealt with it by not talking about it," she said. "No one suggested going to get help. It was just how it was in 1963 in West Texas. You just sort of swallow your troubles and went on."

Laura said that the accident taught her a very difficult lesson about life. There are some tragedies that you can't change no matter how much you may want to.[10]

Key Takeaway: An arrest or conviction can be devastating to a career, even for a relatively minor crime. Dangerous driving is also a major source of trouble for young adults. It can create legal, financial, and career trouble—not to mention devastating guilt over harming another.

[10] Rebecca Traister, "Laura Bush: More Interesting Than Her Husband," *Salon.com*, May 12, 2010, http://www.salon.com/life/broadsheet/2010/05/12/laura_bush_on_larry_king; Laura Bush on Childhood Accident, CNN with Larry King, May 12, 2010; Anahad O'Connor, "Laura Bush Opens Up About Car Crash," *The New York Times*, April 27, 2010, http://www.nytimes.com/2010/04/28/books/28laura.html.

As you face adulthood, it is time to commit to taking on the responsibility that comes with it. Not just responsibility for others, but also responsibility for yourself. You are assuming the role of guardian for yourself. Put down this textbook for a moment and get a mirror. You may be skeptical at first, but give it a try. You may be surprised at what you learn. Take a look. There is a new person there who is responsible for you and holds your life in their hands. What do you expect of that person? What would you tell him or her?

What $40 Bucks Can Ruin

Goateed, barrel-chested Joe Hyer was born and raised around Olympia, Washington. A life-long lover of the outdoors, Joe was an Eagle Scout as a kid and worked as a summer camp staffer for the Boy Scouts. For years, he volunteered with various organizations in Olympia and became a prominent businessman, founding a store based on his passion for mountain climbing and Washington's beautiful vistas.

Joe parlayed his interests and connections to the community into a successful business and political career. In fact, Joe was so popular that he was elected to Olympia's city council and served as the city's mayor pro tem. He was poised to serve as Thurston County treasurer, too – until he was arrested on drug charges.

It was a surprising fall from grace for Joe. In the end, he pleaded guilty to one felony charge of selling about 5 grams of marijuana for about $40. He was sentenced to 10 days in jail and 240 hours of community service, including talking to school kids about his mistake. "I made a serious mistake in judgment," he told a judge. "I screwed up."

The $40 drug deal turned out to be far more costly for Joe, though. It ruined his rising political career and reputation.[11]

20.3 Building Your Story and Résumé

Many famous people have written biographies full of fascinating tales of triumph and tragedy, personal growth and regrets, ignorance and realization. You are at the beginning of building your own story. There will be a private story and there will also be a public one. It is your public story to which we turn.

---

11 "Hyer Will Quit Council," *The Olympian* (Washington), April 10, 2010, http://www.theolympian.com/2010/04/10/1201481/hyer-will-quit-council.html; Matt Batcheldor and Christian Hill, "Former Councilman Hyer Sentenced," *The Olympian* (Washington), April 27, 2010, http://www.theolympian.com/2010/04/27/1219832/ex-councilman-sentenced.html; "Former Councilman Sentenced," KOMOnews.com, April 26, 2010, http://www. youtube.com/watch?v=vPYjPegGARg; Joe Hyer biography: Olympia City Council Web site, http://olympiawa. gov/city-government/city-council-and-mayor/city-council-contact-and-meet-us/joe-hyer.aspx.

An Unlikely Hero

Greg Mortensen never expected to become the leader of a worldwide movement, or an international humanitarian. He didn't expect to become the co-author of a No 1. New York Times best seller, or a nominee for the Nobel Peace Prize, either.

That's partly because Greg's amazing achievements began with a dangerous failure. In 1993, Greg was an avid mountaineer and set out to climb Pakistan's K2, the second highest peak in the world. But his ascent up the dangerous mountain, with air too thin to breathe for long and frigid temperatures, went terribly wrong and Greg wound up getting lost.

Weak and desperately hungry, Greg stumbled into the remote village of Korphe and was nursed back to health by its caring people. When he regained his strength, he asked the villagers how he could return their kindness. They asked for a school. Greg had no resources and few ideas of how to make the villagers dream come true, but he promised he would.

What transpired thereafter was a heroic effort to build a single school that turned into an international movement. Back in the U.S., Greg sold his possessions, including his prized mountain gear, wrote hundreds of letters seeking money from notable people (only Tom Brokaw sent a $100 check), accepted pennies as donations, and lived in his car to keep his cause afloat. Eventually Greg received funding from a wealthy, high-tech philanthropist to build his first school and from there a movement was born.

The few schools that existed in the region were often backed by the same radical Islamic factions that fed al-Qaeda and the Taliban. Greg came to believe that his efforts to create non-secular schools was vital in stemming terrorism. Others agreed, and poured millions into his non-profit organization.

A book about Greg's journey, *Three Cups of Tea*, has sold more than 3 million copies in 39 countries. His Pennies for Peace charity has encouraged school children from around the world to collect pennies to help educate kids in Pakistan and Afghanistan. Over 3,000 schools globally have contributed. Greg's Central Asia Institute has built more than 100 schools, and now works to create programs to support them. Greg told Parade Magazine: "I have observed with my own eyes how America's welfare is tied to that of our brothers and sisters on the other side of the world - and, in particular, that of our youngest sisters. Their dreams of progress rest in our hands; our desire for peace rests in theirs."[12]

[12] "Greg Mortensen Promotes Peace Through Girls Schools," *U.S. News and World Report*, Oct. 22, 2009, http://www.gregmortenson.com/2009/10/usnews-oct-22-09; Maria Speidel, "Critic's Choice," *People*, March 20, 2003, http://www.gregmortenson.com/2006/03/people-magazine-critic-choice; "Putting Pennies to Good Use," *Oakland Tribune* (California), Jan. 4 , 2010, http://www.gregmortenson.com/2010/04/oakland_tribune; "Fighting Terrorism With Schools," *Parade Magazine*, Nov. 22, 2009, http://www.gregmortenson.com/2009/11/parade-nov-22-09; https:// www.ikat.org/projects/regional-map.

When you apply for college or employment, they will want to know your story. What are your accomplishments? What kind of person are you? Chances are you have been focusing on presenting a strong picture to colleges. However, you are also creating a story that will affect your career. Getting a good start can be essential in many careers. The Career Skills chapter covered career building activities such as getting internships. Here I focus directly on creating a record.

In order to get hired, you will more than likely have to provide a résumé. It is up to you to decide what information is relevant, and how to present it. There are a number of views on what a good résumé should look like, and this will also vary depending on the type of job being sought. Figure 20-1 shows an example of a résumé.

There are a number of things that your résumé needs to communicate. It needs to account for your time and show that you keep busy. If you have graduated from college and begun to work full time, it is especially important to avoid unexplained gaps where you seem to disappear. If you do have a gap, there are two approaches to the problem. One is to simply explain it in a cover letter briefly. (I was hit by a car and required six months to recover.) The other approach is to not organize your résumé chronologically, but by skills or some other method, and hope they do not notice.

A résumé also needs to highlight your skills. You can do this directly with a "skills" section, or sprinkle your skills throughout. A skills section is particularly useful if you are applying for a technical job, as Darren Jefferson is doing, but for non-technical jobs it may be distracting. (More on Darren Jefferson later.) A small skills section at the bottom may be useful if, for instance, a job requires knowledge of Excel.

Many industries use keywords. You can go to job search websites and look for what kind of specific key words employers seem to mention and then use those key words in your job descriptions if applicable. Many companies have employees who specifically search for job candidates. They are called Human Resource Management ("HRM") personnel. They may look for keywords based on specifications given to them by the people who need to do the hiring from within the company. They themselves may not understand perfectly the needs of the person doing the hiring. If the words you use to describe your job experience do not match these keywords, they may pass you by. Remember that there are several layers you may have to get past. The HRM employee may do the first pass, culling through large numbers of résumés and picking the few who seem to fit the template. This illustrates the career principle of networking. It is much better if you have a direct contact at a company than allow yourself to be subjected to this process.

Your résumé must show that you are making progress and have a proactive strategy for your career. As the reviewer works chronologically through your experience, it is ideal for her to see that each experience has led to a better one, and that you have been steadily acquiring skills. Darren Jefferson started with a simple information technology support job in high school. The next summer he got a more demanding job with a website development company, and over the course of two summers his duties grew in importance and difficulty, signaling that the company thought he could handle more responsibility, and that they wanted to continue hiring him over the summer months. The same was true of his next job at the social networking company.

Figure 20-1
Résumé Example

Darren Jefferson

321 Hannover Street, Apartment 11
Los Angeles, CA 90045
(310) 555-1234
darrenjefferson56@ispprovider.com

SKILLS

- Linux
- Microsoft Office
- Python
- SQL
- PHP
- Speaks fluent Spanish
- HTML
- C/C++
- Quicken
- Gimp

EDUCATION

Excellent University, *Summa Cum Laude* **September 2006 - June 2010**
B. S.: Majored in Computer Engineering and Computer Science, and minored in Applied Math.
Courses included Operating Systems, Distributed Computing, Network Security, and Cryptology.

WORK EXPERIENCE

Red Cap Resources LLC, New York, NY (Computer Security) **Summer 2009**
Security Technician

- Wrote a report entitled "Vulnerabilities Through Symlinks In Temporary Directories" that was included with company research publications. https://redhatresources.com/publication517.html
- Gave a presentation on security tokens and account password protection techniques as part of a technology seminar provided to brokers of a large securities brokerage company.
- Assisted with penetration testing of a bank's servers. Discovered a vulnerability that allowed penetration of customer accounts, that required the immediate attention of the bank.

Social Network Nouveau, Inc., San Jose, CA (Social Networking Website) **Summer 2008 & 2007**
Database Specialist, Summer 2008

- Reduced server load from queries by five percent through database restructuring.

Developer, Summer 2007

- Backend programmed using Hybernate.
- Frontend programmed to optimize AJAX queries.

WebResources, Inc., Los Angeles, CA (Website Development) **Summer 2006 & 2005**
Technical Assistant, Summer 2006

- Maintained package for Linux.
- Applied security patches to the Linux kernel run by the server.

Technical Assistant, Summer 2005

- Fixed bugs in mail servers and troubleshot other problems.

School Spirit High School, Los Angeles, CA **September 2005 - May2006**
Information Technology Technical Support Person

OTHER

President, Excellent University Chapter of The Association of Computing Machines, 2009-2010
Package Maintainer for Gentoo Linux, 2004 - 2005
Volunteer creator of the Computer Boost For Youth charity website. http://computerboostforyouth.com
Member violin player of the National Honor Society for Orchestra.

http://dj111.socialnetworknouveau.com

Darren Jefferson's job descriptions are very specific. This is extremely important. Anyone can make vague, overstated claims about what they have done. People reviewing the résumé will want specifics. In the case of computer programming, anyone can say that they know a computer language, but programming successfully is another matter. Darren Jefferson gives hard facts. For instance, he tells the reviewer that he reduced server load by five percent.

Darren's experience at Red Cap Resources is particularly well done and helpful. He can point to a specific success with penetration testing. Even better, he can demonstrate that he will look good to customers, make presentations, and write well enough that the company would want to post his report on the Internet. Stockbrokers can be a particularly tough crowd to impress with a presentation.

Darren can also point to his work online, allowing reviewers to take a look. It is difficult to find people who can truly write well, and being able to show an impressive writing sample is a plus. Keywords such as "presentation" and "wrote" are included in the résumé. Everything is specific. Overall, he demonstrates a record of growing responsibility and skills, and employers who are happy to have him back.

Darren chose to put his education before his work experience because he has an impressive college record to present. He is also emphasizing that he graduated from college recently. This makes his work experience all the more impressive, and also explains why he only worked over the summer. Someone who has been out of college for a long time may want to list their education later. Most people will not want to list courses, but Darren did because he is applying for a technical position and wants to highlight specific skills that he has.

The "Other" section contains other accomplishments and should not be overdone. In Darren's case it has parallel structure based on listing roles that Darren has played. The volunteer work says something positive about his personality and attitude. The violin membership is a judgment call. It suggests creativity and an active personality that seeks personal improvement outside of work.

It is very important that the résumé be visually appealing. Imagine what it would be like to go through giant stacks of them. A résumé that is well organized and uncluttered is a relief for weary eyes. If a physical one is sent, make sure the résumé and cover page are on matching, high quality stationary. Bold type and italic type can help to distinguish different kinds of information. Darren Jefferson's address is in italic, as well as the impressive "summa cum laude" after his college name.

The formatting can also be used to bring out certain things. Darren Jefferson put the dates on the right and used a bold font to highlight that he looks very good from a chronological perspective. Breaking information up into different sections helps. It also helps that there is a great deal of indenting to distinguish different types of information. The information in each section is indented from the section title, and lines break up each section. Looking at the work experience section, the job title is indented further, and the job descriptions even further still.

Do not clutter your résumé up with unimportant information, or overstate your accomplishments. Most reviewers will see right through this, and will either question your honesty or think that you are arrogant. Someone just graduating from college should probably not have more than one page for their résumé unless they have an unusually high level of work experience. Never lie or distort on a résumé; it is too easy to check information. Occasionally, people have been hired and a lie was later discovered. They were promptly fired, which had a terrible impact on their career. Lying about credentials, such as passing professional certification tests, can even bring jail time. Better to be honest from the beginning.

Everything needs to be consistent. The formatting should match, at least within each section. If some sentences use periods, they all should. Everything should be in the same tense. Darren Jefferson's work experience is always in the past tense. Be extremely diligent about removing errors of any kind. Even one error on so important a document sends a signal that you are sloppy, and stands out like a sore thumb to HRM personnel. All of this concern with formatting may seem like "nit picking," but it can mean the difference between getting your résumé passed up the ladder, and getting it tossed in the "circular file."

When sending a résumé you will have to include a "cover page," or if emailing, add an introduction to the email. If you send a cover page, be sure to use a business format for the letter. (An example is included in the appendix.) Keep the letter simple and formal. Explain why you are contacting her, why you think that you would be a good fit for the position (this is where you can also demonstrate that you have researched the company), and when you will be available to fill the position. In Darren Jefferson's case, he found out from his professor that in addition to required technical skills, they also needed someone with writing and communications skills to interact with their clients. Mentioning their South American customers also had the added benefit of demonstrating that he had researched the company carefully. If there is something negative in your résumé (such as a couple of months off after college), quickly explain why without dwelling on it. Finish by saying that you will follow-up with a phone call in a week.

Key Takeaway: Your résumé should tell a story about you that shows steady progress over time. It should highlight your accomplishments and skills, without overstating anything. Try to be specific about what you have achieved. Since your résumé is so important and will initially be one page, you should spend considerable time making it easy to follow, visually appealing, and error free. Try to find important key words to include.

Another strategy may be to create an online presence with carefully crafted information at a website or social networking site. While many people show themselves in a bad light, you can turn the tables and strategically show yourself to the world in a good light. Darren Jefferson has his website listed at the bottom of his résumé. However, it is important to stay safe and carefully control the information presented. Do not reveal your full name or how to contact or find you. Be sure to consult with your parents if you are underage.

This can also be a risky strategy. It is easy to create the wrong impression, and people tend to have difficulty judging how they are being perceived by others. A website lacks human interaction. Some professions are relatively conservative, and just the fact that you have a webpage may be viewed negatively.

Use the online page as a marketing tool to sell yourself, and not a place to interact. An online page should put your best foot forward while creating a "personality." It could contain updates on your hobbies or interests. It may even be alright to include interactions with friends, depending on who your potential employers are, but it is important that you control what gets posted. Show "fresh faced" friends posting cheerful, tasteful comments. If you do post pictures, keep your attire very tasteful. For instance, having fun on a sailboat in nice sailing clothes creates an appealing picture.

Your résumé and accomplishments can go on your page. Try to create the right impression. Generally, there are a lot of characteristics that employers are looking for. Think of words like confident, cheerful, optimistic, personable, hardworking, motivated, cooperative, intelligent, creative, honest, responsible, decorous, trouble avoiding, and undemanding.

Focus on the impression your page creates to someone who does not know you, but who just may hire you. Nothing negative should be included. Be especially careful to avoid certain impressions. Employers typically detest employees who care only about themselves, are arrogant, demanding, inflexible, combative, negative, or unethical.

Research the career that you are interested in. What kind of person is most successful? What personality characteristics seem to be appreciated? How do successful people in the profession present themselves in public? Use them as examples, but also remember that you do not have the success that they have yet, and you should take a different tone. If it is a sales position, they will want someone who is outgoing and interacts with people well.

In Darren Jefferson's case, putting the social networking site at the bottom may have been a mistake because he wants to enter the security field where circumspection and discretion are paramount. They will be looking for people who are quiet and not particularly social. On the other hand, the job he is applying for requires an outgoing personality to deal with clients. It is a judgment call.

20.4 Carrying Yourself and Your Reputation

I have already pointed out that it is important to protect yourself with contracts, but legal recourse is expensive and a last option. It is better to find people who are reliable and keep their word. This is something others will look for as well. By developing a reputation for integrity and doing what you say, people will seek you out. Keeping your word will sometimes be costly, but it is a short-term cost. You are investing in your reputation.

People accumulate a reputation in their personal lives and in their careers. When seeking employment, it is common to have the employer ask to speak with your colleagues – if not in your current job (if your interviewing is a secret), then in an older job. References are also typically required. Many careers involve a surprisingly small community. There is a very good chance that someone knows you, or knows someone who does. How you carry yourself, and the reputation that you develop will follow you.

20.5 Conclusion

Most people are in the habit of checking their physical appearance when they are in public. It is time to develop good habits about your entire appearance, on the Internet and elsewhere. What do people see? Are you creating the right impression? There are so many ways that information about you can be accessed. Your ability to succeed will depend on the persona you present. The good news is that you are the individual who has the most ability to influence what others see. Given your career plans, is it most important that you seem creative, or responsible?

When you start on a journey you do not leave the door and walk randomly about. You create a roadmap and follow a plan. As you go through life you are building a story. A story that wanders without a plan from one place to another is confusing, jumbled, and unsatisfying. It does not take the reader to an interesting place. A story that is well thought out is enjoyable, interesting, and leads to a satisfying conclusion. As you go through life, the story you are building will be viewed by others. Think about the story you are creating. Make it appealing— something that you can use as a resource to achieve your goals. Hopefully, your story will be a tale of happiness and success that you will one day look back on with pride.

Key Terms:

Crawlers
Eyeball friends
Human resource management (HRM) employees
Résumé
Social networking websites

End of Chapter Questions

1. Name important ways to protect yourself from online predators.

2. What is a crawler?

3. How do you find out about a website's use of your personal information?

4. Name major sources of information about you.

5. Who may access your social networking webpage?

6. Name issues surrounding bullying.

7. What are the major factors that cause young adults to get into automobile accidents?

8. Suppose you have a "minor" criminal offense on your record. Why may it not be "minor?"

9. What is the purpose of a résumé? Who decides what goes in it?

10. What is a cover page?

11. List important considerations when creating a résumé.

12. What exactly is an HRM employee?

13. Why would you want to create a webpage site to show to potential employers? Why would you not want to?

Appendix

September 22, 2010

Mr. Darren Jefferson
321 Hannover Street, Apartment 11
Los Angeles, CA 90045
(310) 555-1234
darrenJefferson56@ispprovider.com

Ms. Maria Hernandez
Security Systems Supervisor
Computer Security, Inc.
444 Wilson Street
Suite 500
Washington, D.C. 21344

Dear Ms. Hernandez,

Professor John Smith at Excellent College mentioned that you are a former student of his and suggested that I contact you. Professor Smith also sends his regards. I am interested in applying for the senior security analyst position that you described to Professor Smith. I just finished a two month tour of Europe after my recent graduation from college, and can begin work within several weeks.

I believe that I would be an excellent fit for the position for several reasons. In addition to a background in security programming and penetration testing, I have also interacted with customers in a variety of situations. This includes presenting at a seminar, fielding technical support questions, and collaborating on website design. Since I speak Spanish fluently, I will be able to speak with your South American clients. I also have experience in written communication to the public through producing seminar materials and writing a publicly posted research report.

I will call you in a week to discuss the position further. I look forward to speaking with you.

Sincerely,

Darren Jefferson

Darren Jefferson

~BOOK APPENDIX~

FINANCIAL WISDOM™
PREPARATORY INSTITUTE

Good Habits for a Lifetime

At the Start

Get a filing cabinet or file container of some kind, preferably one that locks, and set up a filing system for documents. Encrypt computer documents. Set up initial forecasts and balance sheets/income statements. Find a good accountant and have an initial visit. Try to build up a safety reserve.

Once a Quarter:

Reevaluate your investments and risks.

Once a year:

1. Update your annual budget.
2. Update your long-term forecast.
3. Update your balance sheet.
4. Check your credit history with the three main bureaus for free.

Periodically:

Visit an accountant for a checkup and to update tax strategies.

At All Times

Apply the consumption discounter and think carefully before spending. Take a rational approach and consider cheaper alternatives.

Consider a service to monitor hard hits to your credit records.

Read reports and statements such as bank statements and phone bills.

Keep a safety reserve.

Consider getting financial advice periodically, or before important decisions.

Before getting financial advice or assistance, research your rights and research your advisor/lawyer/accountant/broker's history. (Use government agencies and the Internet.)

Before signing documents read the fine print.

Keep all financial, investment, and medical records.

Before making an important financial decision, research the "ins" and" outs" of the decision on the Internet. Fully consider options.

Shred financial documents, get a locking mailbox, and keep up with identity theft techniques to protect yourself. Protect your computer from viruses and malicious software.

Control privacy settings, and be cautious about what you put on the Internet.

INTERNET INFORMATION

To access chapter spreadsheets and other electronic information including the links below:

1. Go to http://financialwisdompi.com/textbook.html
2. Click on the download button for Financial Wisdom Volume 1
3. Enter the code: "successandhappiness"

*The files are large and will take a while to download.

Chapter 3
IRS tax rates and other information: http://www.irs.gov/
To figure out withholding: http://www.irs.gov

Chapter 5
FDIC Website: http://www.fdic.gov/index.html
To find out if your deposits are insured: https://www.fdic.gov/edie/index.html

Chapter 8
For information on the credit cards and the Credit Card Act of 2009: http://www.federalreserve.gov/creditcard/

Chapter 10
Consumer price index (CPI): http://www.bls.gov/data/
To find starting salaries for various careers:
http://swz.salary.com/salarywizard/layouthtmls/swzl_salaryrangenarrow_10.html

Chapter 11
Social Security Estimator: http://www.socialsecurity.gov/estimator/
For a summary of IRAs: http://www.smartmoney.com/personal-finance/retirement/an-ira-primer-7957/
Small business and Keogh plans: http://www.irs.gov/pub/irs-pdf/p560.pdf
To check the bond rating of a company with public bonds:
http://cxa.marketwatch.com/finra/BondCenter/Default.aspx

Chapter 12
U.S. Department of Education college student aid: http://federalstudentaid.ed.gov/
Instruction worksheet for EFC:
https://studentaid.ed.gov/students/attachments/siteresources/CompletingtheFAFSA10-11.pdf
The EFC formula: http://ifap.ed.gov/efcformulaguide/attachments/111609EFCFormulaGuide20102011.pdf
EFC Estimator (Dept. of Ed.): https://fafsa4caster.ed.gov/F4CApp/spring/login?locale=

Another EFC and institutional estimator provided by a helpful website:
http://www.finaid.org/calculators/finaidestimate.phtml
Financial Aid Resource Publications from the U.S. Department of Education (unfortunately this is out of date. Exclude any discussions of private lending.): http://studentaid.ed.gov/students/publications/student_guide/index.html
Available Federal Grants: http://studentaid.ed.gov/PORTALSWebApp/students/english/grants.jsp
Federal Student Aid Financial Aid and Scholarship Wizard:
https://studentaid2.ed.gov/getmoney/scholarship/scholarship_search_select.asp?13817/.
State Higher Education Agency listings:
http://wdcrobcolp01.ed.gov/Programs/EROD/org_list.cfm?category_ID=SHE
A Very Helpful Website: http://www.finaid.org/
Techniques to maximize federal aid: http://www.finaid.org/fafsa/maximize.phtml
IRS scholarship webpage and link to tax pamphlet: http://www.irs.gov/govt/tribes/article/0,,id=185504,00.html
College Board website with college information: http://www.collegeboard.com/
College Board resources and calculators: http://apps.collegeboard.com/cbsearch_ss/welcome.jsp
Compare college results: http://www.collegeresults.org/
NICCP: National Institute of Certified College Planners; to find Certified College Planning Specialists (CCPS):
http://www.niccp.com/
Student Loan Income Based Repayment Calculator:
http://studentaid.ed.gov/PORTALSWebApp/students/english/IBRCalc.jsp
Student Loan Income Contingent Repayment Calculator:
http://www2.ed.gov/offices/OSFAP/DirectLoan/RepayCalc/dlentry2.html
Federal Student Aid Scholarship Search Engine: https://studentaid2.ed.gov/getmoney/scholarship/v3browse.asp
Scholarship search: http://www.scholarships.com/
Scholarship search Fast Web: http://www.fastweb.com/content/college-freshmen-sophomores
Scholarship search scholarship coach:
http://edu.fastweb.com/v/w_regp/flow/?utm_source=lc_fwreg&utm_medium=cpa&utm_campaign=lc_text&utm_content=35458&aid=15065
Military aid for students: http://www.finaid.org/military/
Military education benefits: http://www.military.com/education/

Chapter 13
College Board: Trends in College Costs: http://professionals.collegeboard.com/profdownload/trends-in-college-pricing-2008.pdf
To see graduation rates by college: http://www.collegeresults.org/

Chapter 15
Human Capital Calculator: http://www.humancapitalscore.com/
Colleges' Expected Pay: http://www.payscale.com/best-colleges

Chapter 16
Credit counseling: http://www.cccsstl.org/
Your rights with collection agencies: http://www.ftc.gov/bcp/edu/pubs/consumer/credit/cre18.shtm

Chapter 17
To order a free annual report online: https://www.annualcreditreport.com/cra/index.jsp
To order a free annual report by mail: http://www.ftc.gov/bcp/edu/resources/form/ requestformfinal.pdf
Experian: http://www.experian.com/
TransUnion: http://www.transunion.com/

Equifax: http://www.equifax.com/home/en_us
Federal Trade Commission Credit Page: http://www.ftc.gov/bcp/menus/consumer/credit.shtm
Consumer Federation of America Credit Score Page: http://www.consumerfed.org/finance/credit_scores_report.asp
Privacy Rights Clearinghouse, Credit Reports: http://www.privacyrights.org/Credit-and-Credit-Reports

Chapter 19

For emotional support: http://www.idtheftcenter.org
For information on opting out of credit card offers: http://www.ftc.gov/bcp/edu/pubs/consumer/credit/cre35.pdf
For getting on the do not call list: http://www.donotcall.gov
For a sample letter to the credit bureaus and fraudulent account issuers:
http://ftc.gov/bcp/edu/pubs/consumer/idtheft/idt04.pdf
For a fraud affidavit form: http://www.ftc.gov/bcp/edu/resources/forms/affidavit.pdf
FTC advice: http://www.ftc.gov/idtheft
A useful website for identity theft victims: http://privacyrights.org/print/fs/fs17a.htm
Deceased Person Identity Theft:
http://www.idtheftcenter.org/artman2/publish/c_guide/Fact_Sheet_117_IDENTITY_THEFT_AND_THE_DECEASED_-_PREVENTION_AND_VICTIM_TIPS.shtml
Family & Acquaintances Perpetrating Identity Theft:
http://www.idtheftcenter.org/artman2/publish/v_fact_sheets/Fact_Sheet_115_When_you_personallyknow_the_identity_thief.shtml
Child Victims: http://www.idtheftcenter.org/artman2/publish/v_fact_sheets/Fact_Sheet_120.shtml
Medical: http://www.worldprivacyforum.org/medicalidentitytheft.html

Chapter 20

Online safety: http://www.webwisekids.org/; http://netsmartz.org/index.aspx; http://www.safekids.com/
Privacy Rights Clearinghouse: http://www.privacyrights.org/fs/fs16-bck.htm

Formulas

The future value of a single cash flow: $FV=PV\cdot(1+i)^n$

The future value of multiple cash flows:

$$= C_0\cdot(1+i)^n + C_1\cdot(1+i)^{(n-1)} + C_2\cdot(1+i)^{(n-2)} + C_3\cdot(1+i)^{(n-3)} +...+ C_n$$

The present value of a single cash flow: $PV = \frac{FV}{(1+i)^n}$

The present value of multiple cash flows: $PV = C_0 + \frac{C_1}{(1+i)} + \frac{C_2}{(1+i)^2} + \ ... + \frac{C_n}{(1+i)^n}$

The present value of a constant annuity: $PV= \frac{C}{i} \cdot \left[1- \left(\frac{1}{1+i}\right)^n\right]$.

The present value of a growing annuity: $PV= \left(\frac{C_1}{i-g}\right) \cdot \left[1- \left(\frac{1+g}{1+i}\right)^n\right]$.

The future value of a constant annuity: $FV= \frac{C}{i} \cdot \left[(1+i)^n- 1\right]$.

The future value of a growing annuity: $FV= \frac{C_1}{i-g} \cdot \left[(1+i)^n- (1+g)^n\right]$.

The present value of a constant perpetuity: $PV= \frac{C}{i}$.

The present value of a growing perpetuity: $PV= \frac{C_1}{i-g}, i > g$.

Converting one interest rate into another: $i_y=(1+i_x)^{\left(\frac{\#\text{ times x compounds in a year}}{\#\text{ times y compounds in a year}}\right)}- 1$

Deflating a dollar amount in the future: $\text{Today's Buying Power}=\frac{\text{Future Dollar Amount}}{(1+\text{inflation rate})^{\text{number of time periods}}}$

The relationship between the real rate of interest and the nominal rate is: $(1+i_{nominal})=(1+i_{real})\cdot(1+\text{inflation})$, or, $i_{real} = \frac{(1+i_{nominal})}{(1+\text{inflation})} - 1$

The real rate of interest can be found from: $i_{real} \approx i_{nominal}$ - inflation.

Approximately, your after-tax, real interest rate is: $i_{left\ over} \approx i_{nominal}\cdot(1-\text{tax rate}) - \text{inflation}$.

The effect of inflation on your after-tax, real interest rate is: $i_{left\ over} = i_{real}\cdot(1-\text{tax rate}) - (\text{inflation}\cdot\text{tax rate})$.

CHAPTER ANSWERS

2. BUSINESSES, INSTITUTIONS, & FINANCIAL SECURITIES AND MARKETS

1. Owners and creditors both have given the company money. However, owners have the right to make decisions for the company; creditors do not. The company writes a debt contract with creditors, which specifies the timing and amount of money due. Other restrictions on the company may also be included. Creditors must receive their money before the owners can be paid. If the company fails to live up to the debt contract, the company could end up in court and be taken away from the owner and given to the creditors.

2. A typical owner has direct control over the business. Stockholders exert control by voting for the board of director, who represent them and oversee management. Typically, one share has the right to cast one vote.

3. C corporations have shareholders, as do S corporations. This is a more rigid form of ownership. Partnerships and LLCs involve individuals coming to their own arrangement about ownership, which is more flexible. C corporations, S corporations, and LLCs have limited liability, while partnerships do not. C corporations have the disadvantage of double taxation, while the other forms have flow-through taxation. C corporations also have enormous amounts of regulation, while S corporations have significant restrictions on who can own their shares. However, institutions can own shares in a C corporation, cannot own a partnership or shares in an S corporation, and are discouraged from ownership in an LLC.

4. The chairman of the board leads board discussions and calls meetings. The CEO is the chief executive officer - the top manager of the company, and is sometimes also the chairman of the board. The CFO is the chief financial officer and reports to the CEO.

5. Stockholders are considered the owners of the company. Bondholders are lenders; they own a debt contract with the company. They get paid principal and interest, and get paid before shareholders. Companies can give shareholders money in two ways: by paying them dividends or by buying back the shares. Dividends are taxed at the capital gains rate, while interest is taxed as income. In the event of bankruptcy, lenders get paid first and shareholders may end up with worthless shares. Stocks do not mature, but bonds do.

6. The Federal Government.

7. The money market is debt that matures in a year or less. The capital market is debt that matures in over a year, and stock. Money market securities are typically safe from default. Debt in the capital market can be relatively safe or risky.

8. Mutual funds own portfolios of securities and issues shares (that provide ownership) in these portfolios. The main advantage of mutual funds is to allow individuals to own diversified portfolios without having to spend large amounts on brokerage fees.

9. A venture capital company takes money from individuals and institutions and invests in new businesses. Their goal typically is to take the business public after it becomes established.

10. A hedge fund invests in a variety of often complex securities. They have qualified investors and are currently loosely regulated, although they may become more regulated in the future.

11. C corporation have double taxation. The profits of the corporation are taxed. Then, when the leftover earnings are distributed to the owners, the owners pay a tax again. With flow-through taxation, only the owners are taxed on the earnings.

12. Nonprofits have special status with the IRS that exempts them from federal income tax. Nonprofits are usually organized for a special purpose, such as philanthropy.

13. Municipal bonds are not subject to federal income tax. (The exception to this is the AMT to be discussed later.) Municipal bonds often have third-party guarantees and low default rates.

14. A capital loss or gain represents money made or lost on the sale of securities and real assets.

15. Bankruptcy happens when someone cannot fulfill their debt obligations and ends up in court proceedings.

16. Stockbrokers buy and sell securities on behalf of clients. They must have a license.

17. Derivatives are financial securities that get their value from other financial securities. Options are a kind of derivative.

18. Futures and forwards are contracts that arrange for the purchase price and delivery of commodities and financial securities at some point in the future.

19. The Federal Reserve is an independent government agency responsible for overseeing the financial system.

20. An open market operation is when the Federal Reserve buys or sells T-Bills. The Fed tries to keep inflation in check, while avoiding depressing the economy.

21. Inflation is caused by an increase in the money supply.

22. Inflation confuses people about prices, which are essential for the efficient functioning of the economy. It also causes wealth transfers between different groups of people.

23. When people sign contracts with fixed dollar amounts, some get harmed and some benefit from unexpected inflation. People who promise to pay money, such as employers or borrowers, are helped, while people who are owed money, such as employees or lenders, are harmed.

24. Limited liability means that if a company is sued, the personal assets of the owners cannot be taken.

25. When forming a partnership, it is vital to write everything down in a contract to avoid costly litigation; an unintended consequence after the business has started.

26. When you sell a bond, you are borrowing. They give you money and you give them the bond, which is a debt contract that you signed.

27. Bulls are optimistic and believe securities prices will rise; bears are pessimistic and believe securities prices will fall.

28. Private equity companies typically buy up the stock of public corporations and take them private. They make a profit by improving the companies they buy.

29. You could lose your limited liability if you mix your personal life with your business.

30. A stock exchange is a physical location or network of computers where stocks are traded. The NYSE Euronext and NASDAQ are the two best known ones in the United States. A stock is listed if it is traded on the exchange. Over-the-counter stocks are not listed on an exchange, and are traded among brokers and dealers.

3. Tax Codes

1. Your average tax rate is your taxes paid, divided by taxable income. Your marginal tax rate is the rate applied to the next dollar you earn. For decision making purposes, emphasis is placed on the marginal tax rate.

2. $Taxes = [11{,}950 \cdot .1] + [(45{,}500 - 11{,}950) \cdot .15] + [(117{,}450 - 45{,}500) \cdot .25] + [(180{,}000 - 117{,}450) \cdot .28] = 41{,}729.$

3. Active income occurs from the direct participation of an individual in generating income. Passive income happens when someone has an interest in a revenue stream, but is not actively involved in generating that revenue stream.

4. The basis for a financial asset is the purchase price. The basis for real assets is the purchase price plus expenditures for improvements (minus depreciation). Increases in the basis reduce capital gains, which are the sales price minus the basis.

5. Short-term capital gains are for assets held for a year or less. Long-term capital gains are for assets held over a year. Short-term capital gains are taxed as income (a higher rate) than long-term capital gains, which are taxed at 15% (5% for low-income tax individuals.)

6. Gross income includes all compensation and income received. Business income has expenses removed first, so that profits (income minus expenses) go into gross income.

7. Adjustments to gross income include, among others, educator expenses, health savings accounts, moving expenses for employment, and some student loan interest.

8. The standardized deduction is a fixed amount. There is a large list of possible itemized deductions, and the taxpayer must determine which they can claim. The taxpayer has the choice of whether to take the standard deduction, or to itemize.

9. FICA pays for Social Security benefits and Medicare. Social Security benefits include retirement payments, disability, and payments to survivors if you dic. Medicare provides for hospitalization benefits after you reach retirement age. Your employer must match the FICA taxes that you pay. After a certain income level, Social Security is not taxed on extra earnings. If you are self-employed, as your own employer you have to come up with the extra FICA taxes.

10. Exemptions are amounts that you are allowed to deduct from your taxable income for yourself and dependents. They are inflation adjusted.

11. Tax credits come directly off of your taxes. Examples include foreign income taxes and the EIC. Some tax credits are only allowed for a certain percent and can be phased out for higher income individuals. Deductions are subtracted from income, and therefore only save you your tax rate multiplied by the deduction.

12. The AMT is a parallel method of computing taxes. It generally includes more income as taxable, but has a bigger exemption and a lower tax rate than the top bracket.

13. The AMT was not inflation adjusted; therefore, as people's income rises with inflation, they qualify for the AMT.

14. Business expenses are subtracted from revenue (sales) before being included in gross income; therefore they reduce gross income.

15. An adjustment to income is better because a person does not have to itemize to receive the benefit. This will be especially true for lower income people who are better off not itemizing.

16. The first stock had a long-term capital gain of 110-100 = 10. The second stock has a short-term capital gain of 62-50 = 12. The third stock had a capital loss of 10-2 = 8. On net, your capital gain was 10+12-8 = 14. Since you had more short-term capital gains than long-term capital gains, you will pay your income tax rate on the net capital gain.

17. The first stock had a capital loss of 6,000 - 4,000 = 2,000. The second stock had a capital loss of 8,000 - 3,000 = 5,000. The third stock had a short-term capital gain of 6,000 - 5,000 = 1,000. The fourth stock had a long-term capital gain of 13,000 - 11,000 = 2,000. On net you had a capital loss of (2,000+5,000) - (1,000+2,000) = 4,000. You can only deduct $3,000 off your income for this year, but you can carry forward the $1,000 remainder for future years.

18. An employer withholds money from your paycheck and sends it to the government, so that your estimated taxes get paid on a regular basis.

19. A W-4 form is used to determine how much to withhold. Your employer gives it to you in order to receive instruction about how much they need to withhold from your paycheck. You specify the number of personal allowances from which withholding is calculated.

20. Yes. You need more withholding because your income bracket with a working spouse or second job will be higher than the one based on your paycheck from the employer who gave you the W-4 form.

21. Stock dividends are taxed at the long-term capital gains rate of 15% (5% for lower income filers).

22. As long as you own a house for two years, you can avoid capital gains taxes on up to $500,000 for married filers, and $250,000 for single filers. It is important to keep records to document any expenditures that increased the basis of the house (which lowers the calculated capital gain.)

23. If you itemize, state and local income, along with property taxes are a deduction. In states with no income taxes, sales taxes can be deducted.

24. If you are head of household, your tax bracket is higher than for a single tax payer, except in the top tax bracket.

25. Charitable contributions are deductible up to 50% of AGI.

26. Medical expenses above 7.5% of AGI are deductible.

27. There are many tax credits; including credits to encourage energy efficiency, the working parent of a disabled dependent, a child tax credit, or credits for foreign income.

28. There can be income phase-outs for tax credits.

29. A W-2 form is sent to you by your employer and summarizes your compensation, withholding, and other information relevant to calculating your taxes.

30. Interest on mortgage payments is tax-deductible.

4. Personal Financial Statements

1.

Trudi's Balance Sheet 12/31/2009			
Assets			
Current Assets			
	Cash	6,500	#4
	Short-Term Financial Assets	13,500	#7 + #5 + #12
	Short-Term Personal Property	500	#10
	Other Short-Term Assets	350	#6
	Total	20,850	
Long-Term Assets			
	Long-Term Financial Investments	124,000	#1 + #11
	Retirement Accounts	310,000	#2
	Long-Term Property	253,000	#8 + #3
	Other Long-Term Assets	35,000	#9
	Total	722,000	
	Total Assets	742,850	
Liabilities and Net Worth			
Current Liabilities			
	Payments Due	222	#4 + #3 + #11
	Accrued Expenses and Obligations	1,200	#12
	Short-Term Debt Due	700	#5
	Current Portion of Long-Term Debt	6,180	(#1·12) + (#8·12) + (#9·12)
	Total	8,302	
Long-Term Liabilities			
	Long-Term Debt Obligations	214,000	#2 + #10 + #7
	Other Long-Term Obligations	27,000	#6
	Total	241,000	
Total Liabilities		249,302	
Net Worth		493,548	
Liabilities and Net Worth		742,850	

2.

Trudi's Worst Case Balance Sheet 12/31/2009			
Assets			
Current Assets			
	Cash	6,500	#4
	Short-Term Financial Assets	13,200	#7 + #5 + #12
	Short-Term Personal Property	100	#10
	Other Short-Term Assets	350	#6
	Total	20,150	
Long-Term Assets			
	Long-Term Financial Investments	92,000	#1 + #11
	Retirement Accounts	280,000	#2
	Long-Term Property	188,500	#8 + #3
	Other Long-Term Assets	28,000	#9
	Total	588,500	
	Total Assets	608,650	
Liabilities and Net Worth			
Current Liabilities			
	Payments Due	222	#4 + #3 + #11
	Accrued Expenses and Obligations	1,200	#12
	Short-Term Debt Due	700	#5
	Current Portion of Long-Term Debt	6,180	(#1·12) + (#8·12) + (#9·12)
	Total	8,302	
Long-Term Liabilities			
	Long-Term Debt Obligations	214,000	#2 + #10 + #7
	Other Long-Term Obligations	27,000	#6
	Total	241,000	
Total Liabilities		249,302	
Net Worth		359,348	
Liabilities and Net Worth		608,650	

3.

Trudi's Asset and Liability Liquidity Schedule

Assets By Liquidity Sale Time

Time	Asset	Amount
Immediate	Cash	6,500
	Savings Account	500
	Total	7,000
One Week	Mutual Fund Shares	85,000
	Car	3,500
	Money Market Account	7,700
	Stocks at Brokerage	7,000
	Total	103,200
One Month	Assignable Trust Fund	28,000
	Heavy Statuette	100
	Total	28,100
Two Months	Employer Reimbursement	350
Six Months	CDs	5,000
Nine Months	Condominium	185,000
Long-Term	Investments in a 401(k) plan	280,000

Liabilities by Time Due

Time Until Due	Liability	Amount	Surplus (Deficit)
One Week	Cell Phone Bill	95	110,105
Two Weeks	Cable Bill	45	
	Mattress Payment	700	
	Electric and Gas Bill	82	
	Total	827	109,278
One Month	Mortgage	415	
	Car Loan	45	
	Credit Card	55	
	Total	515	136,863
Six Months	Mortgage	2,075	
	Car Loan	225	
	Credit Card	275	
	Taxes Due	1,200	
	Total	3,775	138,438
One Year	Mortgage	2,490	
	Car Loan	270	
	Credit Card	330	
	Total	3,090	320,348
More Than One Year	Mortgage	200,000	
	College Tuition Payment	27,000	
	Credit Card	12,000	
	Car Loan	2,000	
	Total	241,000	359,348

4.

Trudi's Income Statement for 2009		
Revenues		
	Salary	125,000
	Net Capital Gains	12,500
	Dividends and Interest Payments	4,000
	Prize Winnings	600
	Total Revenue	142,100
Expenses		
	Recurring Personal Expenses	12,000
	Interest Expense	14,000
	Kitchen Fire	2,500
	Taxes	65,000
	Total Expenses	93,500
Income		
	Net Revenue	48,600

5. An asset is something that has a market value (can be sold for money). Real assets are physical objects that are valued by people because they provide enjoyment, such as a chair which can be sat upon. Financial assets are documents that entitle the owner to receive payments in the future. Assets can also include a number of situations, such as winning a lawsuit and being entitled to a future payment.

6. Current assets will be held for a year or less. Long-term assets will be held for more than a year.

7. An asset is liquid if it can be sold quickly without having to offer a discount (take a loss) because of the speed of the sale. Some current assets may not be liquid. If your house is up for sale it is a current asset if you expect to sell it within the year. However, houses are not liquid. It takes time to sell a house, and the need for a speedy sale reduces the price of the house.

8. A liability comes from owing money. Liabilities can come from loans, taxes owed, or cell phone bills, just to name a few possibilities.

9. The current portion of long-term debt is the principle owed within the next year on a long-term debt contract. Paying principal means returning money that was borrowed. Some long-term debt contracts involve paying back money owed over time, and some of this repayment may occur during the next year, leading to a current portion of long-term debt.

10. New worth is the difference between total assets and total liabilities, and is a measure of wealth. It represents what you would have left over if you sold off all your assets and paid off your debt. Having a high net worth at retirement is an important target, since most retirees live off their net worth.

11. A cash flow is money coming in or going out. Getting paid a salary is money coming in and is a positive cash flow. If money is spent, it is going out and is a negative cash flow.

12. Changes in net worth come from changes in assets or liabilities. This can happen because of cash flows, changes in market value of assets or liabilities, or incurring unexpected assets or liabilities.

13. The purpose of an income statement is to tell someone how much they have added to or taken away from their wealth over a period of time.

14. A balance sheet is a snapshot of one period in time. An income statement tells what happened over a period of time, such as a year.

15. Because the act of investing does not immediately change wealth. The cash item declines while a different asset item rises.

16. Revenue is anything that adds to net worth; therefore, anything that makes assets go up or liabilities go down is revenue. Receiving a salary is revenue, along with prize winnings or capital gains.

17. Revenue adds to net worth.

18. When you buy something that retains value; *that* is investing. When you buy something that does not keep its value, such as groceries, that is an expense.

19. Expenses make net worth go down.

20. This could include capital gains and losses, or winning a raffle while still waiting to receive the prize money.

21. Revenue adds to net income, while expenses take away from net income. Revenue minus expenses is equal to net income.

22. Net income is equal to the change in net worth on a balance sheet from one time period to the next.

23. You need to determine if you will become insolvent (and therefore in danger of becoming bankrupt) in a serious economic decline.

24. A debt ratio is equal to $\frac{\text{Total Liabilities}}{\text{Total Assets}}$. The higher the ratio, the more likely it is that you can become insolvent. The more volatile your assets are, the lower you want this ratio to be. If assets could decline by 40%, then you want a debt ratio below 60%.

25. The balance sheet cannot tell us everything about whether we will remain solvent. For one thing, it only breaks out assets and liabilities by whether they are resolved within a year or over a year. Even if you are solvent, you may have liabilities become due before you can sell assets to cover your liabilities. You could become bankrupt, even though the value of assets is greater than the value of liabilities.

26. In addition to the value of assets falling which reduces solvency, liquidity can dramatically drop during a financial crisis.

27. Capital gains (losses) cause income to rise (fall). They do not affect cash flow. Asset sales (purchases) do not affect income, but cause cash flow to rise (fall).

28. Financial statements address our financial safety and our progress towards accumulating wealth.

29. The liquidity of assets tends to fall during a financial crisis or recession.

30. A house is illiquid. The seller must fix the house and find a broker to sell the house. A buyer must receive financing and investigate the house. The buyer's bank must also investigate the buyer and determine the value of the house.

31. Paying interest is an expense that causes net worth to fall. Borrowing does not change net worth. (Cash balances go up by the same amount as the loan liability.) Paying down debt is the opposite; it does not affect net worth. But cash balances fall, as does the value of the loan liability.

5. Managing Your Cash and Budgeting

1.

Number	Date	Transaction Description	Payment		X	Deposit		$Balance
105	8/1/2009	Burton's Shoe Repair	44	13	c			3492.58
ATM	8/5/2009	Cash	100	00	c			3392.58
106	8/5/2009	Cell Phone Co.	47	44	c			3345.14
107	8/12/2009	Natural Foods	224	95				3120.19
D	8/14/2009	Paycheck			c	3871	72	6991.91
AP	8/19/2009	Better Car Insurance	104	13	c			6887.78
108	8/22/2009	Cash	40	00	c			6847.78 ***
Dep	8/24/2009	Birthday Check from Grandma				150	00	6997.78
AW	8/6/2009	Clear Cable	46	85	c			6950.93

***Math mistake fixed

Reconciled balance = 6950.93 + 224.95 - 150.00 = 7025.88. This matches the bank statement and the account is reconciled.

2. A checking account is an account at a bank, or other financial institution, that allows you to deposit and withdraw money, either directly at the bank, by writing checks, or using debit cards. Typically, checking accounts do not pay interest, although NOW accounts do. A savings account is an account at a financial institution that pays interest. However, it is typically necessary to go to the financial institution to make deposits and withdrawals. Some allow online transfers to and from checking accounts at the same financial institution.

3. The most common places to get a checking account are banks, savings and loans, and credit unions.

4. The FDIC insures most checking and savings accounts up to a limit. It is important to verify that your account is insured.

5. No. Other investments, such as insurance offered by an FDIC insured bank, do not have the backing of the FDIC and you could lose your entire investment.

6. Bank customers panic because they think the bank is failing. They may all rush to the bank at the same time to try and get their money out, causing immediate failure of the bank.

7. Do not write a check in pencil or something else that is erasable. Before signing the check, always fill in the amount and the name of the person or entity that the check is being written to, and always make sure the check is covered.

8. "Postdating" is when you sign a date on a check that is in the future. The person who receives the check can cash it immediately, regardless.

9. "Float" is when someone is able to earn interest off of money that is technically not theirs. Banks legally enjoy float off of their customer's checking accounts.

10. When a check is on "hold" it has been deposited in your account, but the bank is not allowing you access to the money.

11. When a check "clears," it means that your bank has debited or credited your account. In other words, the check has been officially recognized by your bank.

12. A PIN number is a secret number given to you to use for your accounts so that only you can access your money. Never tell it to anyone else.

13. An ATM is an automatic teller machine. They will be located at your bank. Your bank and other banks will have ATM machines located in a number of places as well. If your bank has an agreement with the bank providing the ATM machine, you will be able to use the machine to make withdrawals, but with a higher fee.

14. When you use a credit card, the credit card company pays the merchant who you are purchasing goods or services from and lends you the money. If you do not pay the money back within a given amount of time you are charged interest.

15. Check "kiting" is a felony. It involves someone who is allowed to withdraw money from their checking account before it has cleared. That person writes checks back and forth between checking accounts at two different banks, which allows him to take out money and earn income on it.

16. Reconciling involves matching your check register with your bank's statement. You add up amounts in your register that have cleared, and compare this with the bank balance. Hopefully the two match.

17. A safety stock is extra money kept in your checking account in order to make sure you do not accidentally bounce a check.

18. Overdraft protection is provided by some financial institutions. For a large fee they will either automatically move money from your savings account (if it is with the same institution), or extend you a loan to cover a check.

19. There is financial software that allows you to download transactions from your bank, and send instructions to the bank to send checks from your account. Various merchants also have websites that allow you to pay online from your checking account.

20. Budgeting helps you to understand your financial situation, control your spending, set aside needed funds for a home, retirement, etc., and avoid financial disaster.

21. This will depend on your taxes and deductions, but your take-home pay could be substantially lower than your salary.

22. You will need to make substantial up-front investments in things like apartment deposits, home furnishings, and business attire.

23. Cars are expensive to purchase, costing in the thousands of dollars. Add to this insurance, registration and fees, gas, maintenance, and repairs.

24. A signing bonus is an up-front payment when someone starts a new job. It is an acknowledgement that someone straight out of school may not have enough money for the suits and other expenditures needed.

25. Job benefits are very important, such as retirement benefits and medical insurance. The value of these benefits must be included when comparing jobs. The cost of living in the area where the job is located should also be considered. Jobs in expensive cities need to pay more so that people can afford to live there.

26. There are two reasons: the first is that banks borrow using short-term debt, but their loans (loans are assets to the bank) are long-term, such as mortgages. If people do not trust them, they cannot continue to borrow new debt to pay off old debt, and they cannot sell assets in time to pay off their debt — they are illiquid. The second reason is that banks lend out most of the money that customers deposit in their checking accounts. If customers all come in demanding their money, the bank cannot cover it.

27. Getting a roommate, using public transportation, cooking more and eating out less.

28. You are agreeing to make payment. In that sense, it is. Also, depending on the state and the situation, a check may be regarded by the law as a contract.

29. You can tell online banking software to automatically send a check to someone on a regular basis for the same amount.

30. This is when you authorize someone to automatically remove money from your checking account. You are relying on their integrity not to make excess withdrawals.

6. Compounding Interest

1. In the case of debt, the original loan amount and the price of a security are the same thing. When borrowing, we are in effect selling a financial security; the amount we sell it for is equivalent to receiving a loan.

2. Future value tells us the future amount that we are owed by someone or the bank (if we have a savings account), or how much we owe someone else.

3. The time value of money refers to the fact that people do not like waiting for their money, and will demand interest payments as compensation.

4. Discounting involves taking the present value of a cash flow. We are, in effect, multiplying by something less than one.

5. Compounding refers to earning interest on interest previously received. Compounding makes savings grow faster and faster, similar to exponential growth.

6. $5{,}000 \cdot 1.03^6 = 5{,}970.26$ Keystrokes: 1.03 ENTER 6 y^x 5000 X.

7. $1{,}000 \cdot 1.04^2 + 2{,}000 \cdot 1.05 = 1{,}081.50 + 2{,}100.00 = 3{,}181.60$. Keystrokes: 1.04 ENTER 2 y^x 1000 X 1.05 ENTER 2000 X +

8. $\frac{3,087}{1.05^2} = 2,800$. Keystrokes: 1.05 ENTER 2 y^x 1/x 3087 X

9. $\frac{540.80}{1.04^2} + \frac{210}{1.05} = 500 + 200 = 700$. Keystrokes: 1.04 ENTER 2 y^x 1/x 540.80 X 210 ENTER 1.05 ÷ +

10. $i = \frac{5,000}{4,651.16} - 1 = .0750$

11. The first two loans can be combined: $FV = 300 \cdot 1.05^4 = 364.65$. The future value of the second loan is: $FV = 400 \cdot 1.05^3 = 463.05$. In total, you are owed: 364.65+463.05 = 827.70.

Financial Key Problems

12. Answer: 561.02 Keystrokes: 5 n 7 i 400 CHS PV 0 PMT FV

13. Answer: 4,381.48 Keystrokes: 3 n 4.5 i 0 PMT 5000 FV PV

14. Answer: 2,191.24 Keystrokes: 6 i 500 CF_j 800 CF_j 1200 CF_j NPV

Excel Problems. Look at the full solutions in the Excel supplemental materials for the textbook, downloadable from the Internet.

15.

Question 12

i=	0.03		
0	1	2	3
8,000.00	8,240.00	8,487.20	8,741.82
	9,000.00	9,270.00	9,548.10
		10,000.00	10,300.00
			28,589.92
0	1	2	3
8,000.00	9,000.00	10,000.00	
8,741.82	9,548.10	10,300.00	28,589.92

16.

Question 13

i= 0.04					
0	1	2	3	4	5
Cash Flow	350.00	450.00	580.00	0.00	640.00
Cash Flow Present Value	336.54	416.05	515.62	0.00	526.03
Total Present Value	1794.24				

Keystrokes: 4 i 350 CF_j 450 CF_j 580 CF_j 0 CF_j 640 CF_j NPV

17.

Question 14

(Underlying numbers not rounded)

0	1	2	3	4
Cash Flow	1,000	5,000	0	10,000
Cash Flow Present Value	980.39	4,712.98		8,227.02
Total Present Value	13,920.40			

7. Annuities and Perpetuities

Annuities

1. Whenever you compare two offers, you need to put them on the same time basis, i.e., the present value. This problem is the present value of a growing annuity with a cash flow at t=0:

$$PV = 5{,}000 + \left(\frac{5{,}000 \cdot 1.0025}{.0042 - .0025}\right) \cdot \left[1 - \left(\frac{1.0025}{1.0042}\right)^{25 \cdot 12}\right] = \$1{,}179{,}933.25.$$

The present value of the payments is better than the offer of $1,000,000. Keep the payments. By the way, suppose that you do not want to wait for the payments. You still should not take the $1,000,000. The present value of the payments represents what you could sell them for. You will get $1,179,933.25! (Minus any fees paid.)

2. You are saving for the future. This is the future value of a constant annuity with a cash flow at t=0.

$$FV = (1{,}850 \cdot 1.004^{4 \cdot 12}) + \frac{1{,}850}{.004} \cdot \left[1.004^{4 \cdot 12} - 1\right] = \$99{,}923.77.$$

You will be just short of the $100,000 needed. Volunteer for some overtime at work perhaps?

3. You need to compare two offers, and therefore should put payments on a present value basis. There is a cash flow of $50 at t=0. From there, you have the present value of a constant annuity:

$$PV = 50 + \frac{20}{.005} \cdot \left[1 - \left(\frac{1}{1.005}\right)^{8}\right] = \$206.46.$$

The string of payments are better.

4. You are making a comparison, so put everything on a present value basis. There is no payment today. You have the present value of a constant annuity with no payment at t=0:

$$PV = \frac{400}{.005} \cdot \left[1 - \left(\frac{1}{1.005}\right)^{3 \cdot 12}\right] = \$13{,}148.41.$$

Pay the IRS the $10,000 now.

5. What you pay for the annuity is the present value of the payments that you will receive in return. Your first payment is one time period from today. Therefore, you have the present value of a growing annuity with no payment at t=0.

$$PV = \left(\frac{120{,}000}{.05 - .03}\right) \cdot \left[1 - \left(\frac{1.03}{1.05}\right)^{22}\right] = \$2{,}069{,}881.78.$$

See the supplemental materials:

i= 0.05

t=	0	1	2	3	4	5	6
Cash Flows		120,000.00	123,600.00	127,308.00	131,127.24	135,061.06	139,112.89
Present Value of Each Cash Flow		114,285.71	112,108.84	109,973.44	107,878.70	105,823.87	103,808.18
TotalPresent Value	2,069,881.78						

6. You need to know how much you will have accumulated in the future. Your first contribution is at t=1. This is the future value of a constant annuity, with no cash flow at t=0.

$$FV = \frac{160}{.0075} \cdot \left[1.0075^{12} - 1\right] = \$2001.21.$$

You will just have enough.

7. Since you are asking how much you will have accumulated in the future, this is a future value problem. You have a cash flow of $6,000 at t=0 and your payments grow by 3%. Therefore, this is the future value of a growing annuity with a cash flow at t=0:

$$FV = (6{,}000 \cdot 1.06^{12}) + \frac{6{,}000 \cdot 1.03}{.06 - .03} \cdot [1.06^{12} - 1.03^{12}] = \$132{,}878.91.$$

See the supplemental materials:

t=	0	1	2	3	4	5	6
Cash Flows	6,000.00	6,180.00	6,365.40	6,556.36	6,753.05	6,955.64	7,164.31
Future Value of Each Cash Flow	12,073.18	11,731.49	11,399.46	11,076.84	10,763.34	10,458.72	10,162.72
Total Future Value	132,878.91						

You will not have saved enough. It is time to tighten your belt and spend less. The reward is a serene cabin in the woods.

8. This is about saving for the future and is a future value problem. Your first payment is one month from today, so there is no cash flow at t=0. This is the future value of a growing annuity with no cash flow at t=0:

$$FV= \frac{190}{.005-.0033} \cdot \left[1.005^{2\cdot 12} - 1.0033^{2\cdot 12}\right] = \$5{,}016.01.$$

Those little indulgences add up.

9. The present value of the payments is:

$$PV = 50 + \frac{20}{.005} \cdot \left[1 - \left(\frac{1}{1.005}\right)^8\right] = \$206.46.$$

Take the string of payments.

10. The present value of the payments is:

$$PV = 30{,}000 + \left(\frac{30{,}000 \cdot 1.01}{.07 - .01}\right) \cdot \left[1 - \left(\frac{1.01}{1.07}\right)^7\right] = \$197{,}825.63.$$

Take the up-front $300,000.

11. The present value is:

$$PV = \frac{400}{.004} \cdot \left[1 - \left(\frac{1}{1.004}\right)^{36}\right] = \$13{,}386.35.$$

Pay right away.

Perpetuities

12. Using the present value of a constant perpetuity formula: $PV = \frac{3{,}000}{.05} = \$60{,}000$. Permutation: with the extra cash flow at t=0, just add it in: PV = $60,000 + 3,000 = $63,000.

13. Using the present value of a growing perpetuity: $PV = \frac{200}{.0023-.001} = \$153{,}846.15$. If the first cash flow is at t=0:

$$PV = 200 + \frac{200 \cdot 1.001}{.0023-.001} = \$154{,}200.00.$$

8. INTEREST RATES

1. a) $.10/2 = .05$ b) $1.05^{1/6} - 1 = .008165$

2. a) $.09/4 = .0225$ b) 1.0225^2 -1 .0455

3. "Compounding" is when interest is earned on prior interest. Compounding makes money grow at an ever increasing rate. The longer money is invested, the bigger it gets at an increasing rate.

4. The effective rate.

5. $1.02^{1/3} - 1 = .006623$

6. $1.08^{1/6} - 1 = .0129$

7. $.219/365 = .0006$ $EAR = 1.0006^{365} - 1 = .2447$

8. This is the real interest rate. It is equal to [(1+nominal rate)/(1+ inflation)] - 1, or approximately the nominal rate minus the inflation rate.

9. It will buy you what $\frac{100}{1.05^8} = \$67.68$ will buy you today.

10. $1.06^{10} - 1 = .7908$. You money and income will need to increase by 79.08% in 10 years to maintain your buying power.

11. Inflation magnifies the effect of taxes, as can be seen by: $i_{\text{left over}} \approx i_{\text{real}} \cdot (1\text{-tax rate}) - (\text{inflation} \cdot \text{tax rate})$. Inflation can even drive this negative.

12. A cash advance is when you receive money from your credit card (rather than using your card for purchases.) Interest accrues immediately, unlike the typical situation with a credit card purchase. Also, cash advances usually come with large fees.

13. The problem with the Truth in Lending Act is that it mandates stated rates, which causes interest rates on loans to be quoted below the true interest rate being charged. A benefit of the Truth in Lending Act is that everyone has to quote rates the same way.

14. Taking a card out if they are not prepared to pay the bills regularly every month, forgetting to pay on time, overspending with credit cards because they do not see money changing hands, and running over credit card limits.

15. Besides charging interest, they charge fees for late payments and for borrowing over the limit if the borrower has opted in. They typically charge interest immediately on cash advances. Some cards charge an annual fee. They can raise rates with prior notice to the borrower, or if the borrower is late on payments. They can actually be a source of cash if they get paid off every month, and they offer discounts on purchases or benefits such as frequent flyer miles.

16. These are documents that look like regular checks. Typically, if you spend them you are taking out a cash advance and will get charged fees. You will usually start accruing interest immediately.

17. No. Interest rates are quoted in a variety of ways to small businesses. Some ways are quite deceptive.

18. A revolving loan has a maximum amount that you can withdraw, but you can choose to withdraw less. Typically, you will be charged interest on the amount you withdraw, and a smaller charge on the amount you do not withdraw.

19. Consumer loans are quoted using an APR (annual percentage rate), which is below the true, effective rate consumers are paying. Savings account interest is quoted using an APY (annual percentage yield), which is an effective rate and is above the APR.

20. They can charge you fees for being late, and can raise your interest rate to the very high default rate. Interest still accrues on the late payment as well. You will also be charged fees if you run over your limit.

9. MORTGAGES

1. a) .0684/12 = .0057
b) $PV = \frac{1650}{.0057} \cdot \left[1 - \left(\frac{1}{1.0057}\right)^{360}\right] = \$252{,}065.46$. Financial Keys: 360 n .57 i 1650 CHS PMT 0 FV PV.
c) Interest=.0057·$252,065.46=$1,436.77 Principal=$1,650-$1,436.77 = $213.23

2. a) .0888/12 = .0074
b) $\$552{,}761.48 = \frac{C}{.0074} \cdot \left[1 - \left(\frac{1}{1.0074}\right)^{240}\right]$. You can use algebra to solve for C, but the easiest way is to use the financial keys. Financial Keys: 240 n .74 i 552761.48 PV 0 FV PMT. The answer is 4,930.76 You can then plug the payment into the annuity formula to see if you can get the present value back.
c) Interest = .0074·$552,761.48=$4,090.43 Principal = $4,930.76-$4,090.43 = $840.33

3. See the supplemental materials for the amortization schedule.

4. Interest is tax deductible.

5. The rate does not have the fees built into it, and therefore does not reflect what you actually pay. The APR includes everything in one interest rate quotation.

6. A point is 1% of the amount borrowed. The idea is that you put more money down to get a lower interest rate. There is a break even time. If you do not expect to hold your mortgage until this time (because you sell your house or refinance) you should not take the points. After this time you should.

7. You know what your payments will be with a fixed-rate mortgage. This provides security. If interest rates rise, your payment does not go up; if they fall you can refinance. However, the interest rate on a fixed-rate mortgage is typically below that of an ARM.

8. If you do not intend to keep a mortgage for long, then the ARM will seem better because the rate will be lower and will not adjust right away.

9. If you default on a mortgage is full recourse, the lender can still come after your personal assets and your wages.

10. They are similar. However, only interest on up to $100,000 of a home equity loan is tax deductible.

11. A home equity loan can be a cheaper way to borrow than other consumer loans. For instance, it may be preferable to getting a car loan to buy a car. However, a home equity loan can lead to the temptation to borrow against your house. This can reduce your financial security and reduce wealth if you are not borrowing to buy long-lived assets.

12. If real rates rise, house prices fall. It is harder for borrowers to buy a house. House prices tend to track inflation. However, if there is unexpected inflation, this can work to the benefit of homeowners, who find it easier and easier to make their mortgage payments as wages rise with price levels.

13. A "teaser rate" is when an ARM offers a very low starting rate; however the rate eventually adjusts higher.

14. Buy a house in the hopes that housing prices increase so that it can be sold in the near future at a higher price.

15. The bank sends you money while the principal rises. This causes less to be left to heirs, but may be the only way to cover expenses. A traditional mortgage may work better, but does not have the guarantees of a reverse mortgage.

16. An option ARM allows the borrower to skip payments. The principal on the loan goes up and can easily lead to financial distress.

17. An appraiser is someone who values property for someone else.

18. There are two situations. If unexpected inflation is causing housing prices and salaries to rise, the value of your mortgage payments will fall. Also, if interest rates fall while the housing market responds by going up, you can refinance your interest rate while enjoying an increase in the price of your house.

19. With a low down payment, the fear is that housing prices will fall. You could end up underwater and you may default. If the mortgage is full recourse, other assets could be taken, along with having your wages garnished. Also, if interest rates are falling, you will not be able to refinance.

20. When interest rates are falling. Be sure to watch mortgage rates.

10. Budgeting in Excel

1. From January to February 2009, inflation in the United States was: $= \frac{212.193}{211.143} - 1 = .4973\%$.

From December 2008 to December 2009, inflation in the United States was: $= \frac{215.949}{210.228} - 1 = 2.7213\%$.

2. (See the supplemental materials)

Question 2 Budget

Inflation= 0.035 Monthly= 0.002871

t=	0	1	2	3	4	5	6	7	8	9	10	11	12	End of Year
Cash Inflows														
Take Home Pay	4,600	4,600	4,600	4,600	4,600	4,600	4,600	4,600	4,600	4,600	4,600	4,600	4,600	59,800
Total Cash Inflows	4,600	4,600	4,600	4,600	4,600	4,600	4,600	4,600	4,600	4,600	4,600	4,600	4,600	59,800
Cash Outflows														
Mortgage Payments	1,400	1,400	1,400	1,400	1,400	1,400	1,400	1,400	1,400	1,400	1,400	1,400	1,400	18,200
Property Taxes										3,519				3,519
Automobile														
Insurance	90	90	90	90	93	93	93	93	93	93	93	93	93	1,198
Road Service									47					47
Fuel	85	85	85	86	86	86	86	87	87	87	87	88	88	1,124
Registration									124					124
Maintenance						81						83		164
Loan	290	290	290	290	290	290	290	290	290	290	290	290	290	3,770
Total	465	465	465	466	469	551	470	470	641	470	471	554	471	6,428
Bank Charges	12	12	12	12	12	12	12	12	12	12	12	12	12	156
Personal Hygiene				81			81			82			83	327
Petty Cash	80	80	80	81	81	81	81	82	82	82	82	83	83	1,058
Charity	150												155	305
Clothing				407						414				821
Dining	85	85	85	86	86	86	86	87	87	87	87	88	88	1,124
Electronics	10	10	10	10	10	10	10	10	10	10	10	10	10	132
Entertainment	120	120	121	121	121	122	122	122	123	123	123	124	124	1,587
Gifts	30	30	30	30	30	30	31	31	31	31	31	31	31	397
Groceries/Drug Store	700	702	704	706	708	710	712	714	716	718	720	722	725	9,258
Household														
Decorating		518												518
Dry Cleaning	25	25	25	25	25	25	25	26	26	26	26	26	26	331
Furnishings		621												621
Total	25	1,164	25	25	25	25	25	26	26	26	26	26	26	1,469
Insurance														
Life	20	20	20	20	20	20	20	20	20	20	20	20	20	260
Homeowners	40	40	40	40	40	40	41	41	41	41	41	41	41	530
Umbrella	35	35	35	36	36	36	36	36	36	36	36	36	36	467
Disability	32	32	32	32	32	32	32	33	33	33	33	33	33	423
Long-term Care	14	14	14	14	14	14	14	14	14	14	14	14	14	188
Total	141	141	141	143	143	143	144	145	145	145	145	145	145	1,868
Medical														
Doctor Copay			15							15				30
Medicine	10	10	10	10	10	10	10	10	10	10	10	10	10	130
Total	10	10	25	10	10	10	10	10	10	25	10	10	10	160
Miscellaneous	95	95	96	96	96	96	97	97	97	97	98	98	98	1,256
Recreation	30	30	30	30	30	30	31	31	31	31	31	31	31	397
Travel/Vacation								828						828
Utilities														
Cable	42	42	42	42	42	42	42	42	42	42	42	42	42	546
Internet	44	44	44	44	44	44	44	44	44	44	44	44	44	572
Cell Phone	48	48	48	48	48	48	48	50	50	50	50	50	50	634
Electricity	80	80	80	81	81	81	81	82	82	82	82	83	83	1,058
Gas	35	35	35	35	35	36	36	36	36	36	36	36	36	463
Total	249	249	250	250	250	251	251	253	253	254	254	254	255	3,273
Total Cash Outflows	3,602	4,595	3,475	3,953	3,473	3,558	3,564	4,317	3,664	7,527	3,501	3,588	3,747	52,564
Net Cashflow	998	5	1,125	647	1,127	1,042	1,036	283	936	(2,927)	1,099	1,012	853	7,236

3. Budgeting will help you see where you are headed financially and to understand the consequences of your financial actions. Short-term budgeting will allow you to focus your spending on the way that best suits your own tastes and welfare.

4. An automobile must be purchased. If you borrow, there will be car payments with interest. In addition, there is car insurance, maintenance, fuel, and repairs. You may also buy road service.

5. You pay interest; and if you have been irresponsible about paying on time, it will be very high interest. Not only are you spending on something that does not grow wealth (consumption), you are creating the extra interest expense along with it.

6. Car, umbrella, apartment or home owners or condo, life, disability, medical, and long-term care.

7. Copayments will be required. You may also have uncovered prescription expenses and medical treatments.

8. Enough to cover your living expenses for six months.

9. Job loss, auto repairs, and major medical expenses that are not covered by insurance. Also, catastrophic losses from events such as fire.

10. Myles had less withheld from his salary for taxes. This was because the interest portion of his mortgage payments were tax deductible.

11. For a home or condo, property taxes and repairs. In addition, a condo will require condo fees.

12. To find a potential starting salary, try: http://swz.salary.com/salarywizard/layouthtmls/swzl_salaryrangenarrow_10.html. Be sure to think through whether you will own a car, whether you will be married, have children, and own or rent a place to live.

11. Retirement

1. Medical expenses and insurance costs, having a mortgage paid off, possible long-term care, no need to save for retirement, different taxes, costs of travel and leisure, the need to pay for college for grandchildren, or leaving an estate.

2. It takes 40 quarters of sufficient work income to qualify. Payouts are based on income. Social Security is heading for insolvency, and it is unclear what will happen to benefits in the future.

3. Medicare is taxed on all income. However, the rest of Social Security has a maximum income that gets taxed.

4. The employer typically gets a tax deduction, and the employee gets to contribute pre-tax earnings (except for Social Security). Typically, the employee's money can grow tax-free until it is eventually withdrawn. At this point it gets taxed as income.

5. The PBGC is a Federal corporation that partially insures some retirement plans.

6. Defined benefit plans specify what benefits employees will receive. In general, these types of plans are partially insured by the PBGC. Defined contribution plans are owned by the employee. Their savings will rise or fall with investment results, as well as contributions and forfeitures. Usually, the plan sponsor of a defined contribution plan has a fiduciary duty to prevent the employee from making bad investments, except for 404(c) plans.

7. Eligibility, vesting, plan funding, future solvency, rules if you separate from the company early, the formula used for accruing benefits, and the role of years of service.

8. A 401(k) plan is a defined contribution plan where the employee contributes a percentage of their income. Employers frequently match contributions by employees.

9. When an employer matches 401(k) contributions, they are contributing money to your retirement from their own pocket - not yours. It is important to take advantage of matching.

10. In a profit sharing plan, the employer decides how much profit to share (and can even make contributions if profits are negative) and allocates contributions to employees according to a formula. These contributions can potentially be invested in a number of things. In an ESOP, employees are given stock in their companies. The employer can borrow money to contribute to an ESOP, and they are used for a variety of purposes.

11. An IRA is an individual retirement account. These accounts have various tax advantages, but there are also restrictions as to who had how much can be contributed to an account.

12. A traditional IRA allows pre-tax contributions, but withdrawals are subject to income tax. Contributions to a Roth IRA are after-tax, but withdrawals are not taxed. Generally, Roth IRAs are considered to have better tax advantages. Roth IRAs also have several other advantages. They do not have mandatory withdrawals after a certain age, and they have less restrictions on withdrawals without penalty.

13. Your tax rate when contributing versus when withdrawing money, the need for early withdrawals, the timing of withdrawals in retirement given that traditional IRAs have withdrawal requirements, Roth IRA paperwork.

14. The employer has not been making enough contributions to ensure that the retirement plan will be able to pay promised payments to future retirees. This is a sign of trouble. The employer could default on the retirement payments.

15. You lose the tax benefits of a retirement account, you are taking from retirement to fund current expenditures, and you may be subject to substantial penalties.

16. Company stock is contributed to the retirement plan. If the company goes under, employees lose their jobs and retirement savings at the same time.

17. You may work for a company for a while before you are eligible to receive retirement benefits that have been contributed on your behalf. This will create a loss from switching to a new job before benefits vest.

18. Sometimes employers use a formula where they contribute more (and the employee, therefore, receives more in retirement) based on years of service. This creates the incentive for older workers not to leave because they are accruing a lot of retirement benefits. They can also become a target for a layoff.

19. Social Security and other government programs, qualified and non-qualified company retirement plans, personal tax-advantaged retirement plans, investments, and working during retirement (if possible).

20. You may find working very unpleasant and taxing, you may not be able to work, and your wages may be substantially lower.

12. Financing College

1. The FAFSA is the Free Application for Federal Student Aid. Anyone who wants federal aid to attend college should apply (grants, loans, or work study). Many colleges also use the FAFSA in determining how much aid they give. Many people qualify for aid, not just poor people.

2. Your COA is your cost of attendance. AI is available income, and AAI is adjusted available income, which includes a portion of assets. The EFC is your expected family contribution, which is given in the SAR (student aid report.)

3. Avoid activities that increase reported income, shift income to assets, and take actions to allow for a simplified EFC formula. Activities such as selling assets for a capital gain, and rolling a traditional IRA over into a Roth IRA, will increase reported income. If your parents own a C corporation, they could pay themselves less salary, which would shift those payments to an asset (cash of the corporation). By qualifying for the simplified EFC formula, assets are ignored entirely.

4. There are included and not included assets. One strategy is to shift included assets to non-included assets. For instance, by using cash or investment accounts to pay down the mortgage on the house. It is better to have assets in the parents' name since their expected contribution is less. Personal assets are also not included.

5. Yes. Institutions often use the CSS profile and include home equity and retirement accounts, among other differences. Institutions have leeway to provide aid based on their own criteria, and often mix need with other considerations. This is one of the reasons why it is important to apply, even if you do not think you will qualify.

6. A need-based grant provided by the federal government.

7. To maximize your chances, research colleges. Find ones that give a lot of grants rather than loans. Find colleges that are looking for students with your attributes, and try to be in the top tier. Apply to colleges that compete with each other.

8. The College Board has statistics on colleges. Also, try googling "Common Data Set" and the name of the college.

9. Section 529 plans, according to the tax codes, give special incentives to save for college. They do not have income limits and are offered by state. There are two types: college savings plans and prepaid tuition plans (which can also be offered by private entities). College savings plans allow money to grow tax-free, and withdrawals are not taxed if they are used for qualified expenses, which include tuition, room and board, and enrollment expenses. Out of state residents can often invest in a state plan, while state tax rules vary by state. These plans may charge large fees and highly restrict investment choices; they should be researched carefully. Generally, states do not tax residents. Pre-paid tuition plans generally allow state residents to purchase tuition credits, and their investment grows by a measure of in-state tuition expenses. These plans may be subject to portability problems, and can lock a student into a specific school.

10. These plans are similar to 529 plans, but they allow for more qualified expenses. However, they have a low contribution limit and income phase-outs.

11. Typically, scholarships will mostly reduce loans, which have to be paid back with interest. Some colleges match scholarships. Applying for scholarships will hone your application skills before applying for college.

12. Regard getting scholarships as a part-time job. Think of it as a numbers game where you will get a lot of rejections. Apply to a lot of scholarships to increase your chances. Go on the hunt. Search Internet sites, but do not stop there. There is no substitute for shoe leather. Make a list of all of your affiliations, as well as your parents', and ask. Consider joining new groups and increasing your extracurricular activities. Search for corporate scholarships and look at

association and philanthropic directories. Ask high school counselors, and if you are in college, ask at your college financial aid office.

13. Compile a list of your accomplishments and unique characteristics. Research the organization giving the scholarship to find out what they are looking for in a candidate. If possible, find out who the judges will be and research them as well. Try to create a coherent, vivid, and compelling story about yourself that lets your personality come through. Carefully craft your essay and make sure it is completely error free.

14. The American Opportunity Credit for qualified education expenses is replacing the HOPE credit. It has income phase-outs, and the maximum credit is $2,500 in 2009. One-hundred percent of the first $2,000 in expenses can be taken; 25% of the next $2,000. It is 40% refundable and can only be used for four years. The Lifetime Learning credit can be used for any number of years, but it is smaller with lower income phase-outs. Qualifying education expenses can also be used as an adjustment against income, which is less desirable than a tax credit that comes directly out of taxes.

15. Education expenses cannot be used for more than one tax advantaged purpose. Therefore, withdrawals from 529 plans, ESAs, and savings bonds must be carefully coordinated with each other, and with any tax credits or adjustments to income taken. This process can be complicated.

16. Subsidized and unsubsidized Stafford loans are available from the federal government. Perkins loans are given directly by colleges. Subsidized loans are better because they do not accumulate interest while the student is in school. These loans tend to have lower rates than private loans. Parents can also take out PLUS loans. However, they should compare these loans to other kinds of loans such as a home equity line of credit. Some student loan interest may be allowed as an adjustment against income, subject to income phase-outs. In 2009 the maximum amount is $2,500. Repayment programs may cause student loan payments to be reduced (but extended) or forgiven, depending on income, family size, and occupation.

17. The federal government subsidizes students to work at college jobs. These jobs tend to be low paying, but earnings are not used in FAFSA calculations. Students should also consider internships, which may pay better (but get included in AI) and give the student a leg up on a career. The military also offers the chance to get college expenses paid for in return for service. Another possibility is working colleges, which offer reduced or zero tuition in return for working.

18. There are a number of ways to test out of college courses. If a student completes AP courses and passes the follow-on tests, they can test out of up to one year of college. CLEP examinations are also recognized by many colleges. The DSST program allows military and eligible civilians to earn credit for non-standard kinds of learning.

19. Graduating early will save room and board (and tuition for summer school classes may be cheaper) and allow the student to start earning a salary earlier. On the other hand, many state schools are strapped for cash, and required courses fill up, delaying graduation. Lost wages from this can be enormous.

13. Forecasting in Excel

1.

Annual:	Interest=	0.05	Contribution Increases=	0.02	Tax Rate=	0.25	t=0 House Price=	230,000	House Price Increases=	0.03
Monthly:	Interest=	0.004074			Beginning Savings=	7,700				
t=	1	2	3	4	5	6	7	8	9	10
Monthly Contribution	880.00	897.60	915.55	933.86	952.54					
Cumulative Annual Savings	$10,799.86	$11,015.86	$11,236.18	$11,460.90	$11,690.12					
Total Cumulative Savings Before Tax	18,884.86	30,680.94	43,141.13	56,294.77	70,172.39					
Taxes	156.22	295.27	442.21	597.37	761.13					
Other Withdrawals	-	-	-	-	-					
Total Cumulative Savings After Tax and Other Withdrawals	18,728.65	30,385.67	42,698.92	55,697.40	69,411.26					
End of Year House Price	236,900.00	244,007.00	251,327.21	258,867.03	266,633.04					
26% of End of Year House Price	61,594.00	63,441.82	65,345.07	67,305.43	69,324.59					

2.

i= 0.04		College Cost Increase=	0.05			After Tax Interest Rate=	0.0288
t=		Cumulative Savings	Payments From Plan	Extra Required	PV	Annual Cost of College	PV College
0	45,000	45,000.00				27,000.00	$157,549.14
1		46,800.00					
2		48,672.00					
3		50,618.88					
4		52,643.64					
5	45,000	99,749.38					
6		103,739.36					
7		107,888.93					
8		112,204.49					
9		116,692.67					
10	45,000	161,692.67					
11		168,160.37					
12		174,886.79					
13		181,882.26					
14		189,157.55					
15	18,000	207,157.55					
16		215,443.85					
17		224,061.61	34,814.92	27,069.57	16,705.33	61,884.49	38,190.52
18		196,816.55	64,978.72	-	-	64,978.72	38,977.50
19		137,111.35	68,227.66	-		68,227.66	39,780.69
20		71,639.04	71,639.04	-		71,639.04	40,600.43
	Left Over	0.00		Extra Annual Payment=	$1,256.58		

3.

Inflation= 0.04
Real Rate= 0.01
Nominal Rate= 0.0504
Salary Increase Above Inflation= 0.02

Current Annual Income= 75,000
Current After-Tax Annual Income= 56,250
Monthly Nominal Rate= 0.0041059936

t=	0	1	2	3	4	5	6	• • •	29	30	Retirement
Tax Rate	0.25	0.25	0.25	0.25	0.25	0.25	0.25		0.35	0.35	0.25
Retirement Plan:											
Monthly Pre-tax Income	6,250	6,625.00	7,022.50	7,443.85	7,890.48	8,363.91	8,865.74		33,864.92	35,896.82	
Monthly Contributions	625.00	662.50	702.25	744.39	789.05	836.39	886.57		3,386.49	3,589.68	
Savings Before Tax	50,000.00	60,652.01	72,328.81	85,111.32	99,086.29	114,346.72	130,992.26		1,272,484.77	1,380,680.42	
After-Tax Income	14,353.35										
Private Plan:											
Annual Contributions	7,500.00	7,950.00	8,427.00	8,932.62	9,468.58	10,036.69	10,638.89		40,637.91	43,076.18	
Savings	5,000.00	13,139.00	22,062.65	31,829.24	42,500.97	54,144.19	66,829.74		869,589.78	941,153.73	
After-Tax Income	9,784.10										
Real Total After-Tax Income Before Retirement	86,327.75										
Real Total After-Tax Income Starting Retirement	24,137.45										

4. How quickly housing prices are rising, nominal interest rates, your marginal tax rate, your monthly contribution, how much you intend to put down, the price of the kind of house you want today, and fees and expenses of purchasing.

5. In the housing forecast, you set how much you would contribute each month, and then looked to see how long it would take to buy a house. With the "saving for college" example, you figured out how much you would have to spend at a set point in the future, and then solved for how much you would have to contribute.

6. College tuition rates have been rising more rapidly than inflation. Private tuition has risen 2.4% above inflation, and public tuition has risen 4.2% above inflation.

7. If you know how much you will need to spend at a set point in the future, you can use solver to figure out how much you will have to contribute. Also, if you have a set amount you want to leave to heirs, you can figure out how much you can withdraw to live on in retirement. If you set a specific goal for retirement, you can solve for how much needs to be contributed.

8. Based on the forecast covered in the chapter it will not be enough, but this depends heavily on what happens to the rate of increase in college tuition and 529 contribution limits.

9. Since the contributions accumulate tax-free, withdraw them last. However, there are restrictions on how the money can be spent, and it is important to make sure nothing is left.

10. With retirement plans, contributions are typically made pre-tax, and withdrawals are taxed at the income tax rate. Private investment contributions come from after-tax money, and earnings are taxed. However, withdrawals of principal are not taxed. Any capital gains will be taxed at the capital gains tax rate.

11. As seen by the retirement planning forecast, having the real rate go from 2% to 7% increased retirement income by 272%. It has a huge effect and therefore wise investing is very important.

12. Inflation and taxes. Since retirement is many years away, taking inflation into account is extremely important.

13. According to the retirement forecast, it is not a lot.

14. Pull money out of the after-tax account first. Let the money in the pre-tax account continue to grow without tax, and delay paying income tax on the withdrawals.

15. Look at your balance sheet to make sure you are solvent and liquid. Also, create a simple forecast of your retirement balance sheet, only including large items. This is your cushion. You may also want to forecast goals that you have, such as saving to buy a house and putting a child through college.

14. Spending Money

1. Your annual after-tax interest rate is $.06 \cdot (1 - .25) = .045$.

College Reducer for 15 Years, with a 6% Interest Rate and 25% Marginal Tax Bracket

Frequency	Number of Payments	Periodic Rate	Formula	Reducer
Daily	$15 \cdot 365 + 1 = 5{,}476$	$1.045^{\frac{1}{365}} - 1 = .000120601$	$\frac{1}{.000120601} \cdot [1.000120601^{5{,}476} - 1]$	$7,757.07
Weekly	$15 \cdot 52 + 1 = 781$	$1.045^{\frac{1}{52}} - 1 = .000846837$	$\frac{1}{.000846837} \cdot [1.000846837^{781} - 1]$	$1,106.38
Monthly	$15 \cdot 12 + 1 = 181$	$1.045^{\frac{1}{12}} - 1 = .003674809$	$\frac{1}{.003674809} \cdot [1.003674809^{181} - 1]$	$256.45
Annual	$15 + 1 = 16$	.045	$\frac{1}{.045} \cdot [1.045^{16} - 1]$	$22.72
Once	1	.045	1.045^{15}	$1.94

2. Your annual after-tax interest rate is $.05 \cdot (1 - .28) = .036$.

Boat Reducer for 10 Years, with a 5% Interest Rate and 28% Marginal Tax Bracket

Frequency	Number of Payments	Periodic Rate	Formula	Reducer
Daily	$10 \cdot 365 + 1 = 3651$	$1.036^{\frac{1}{365}} - 1 = .000096901$	$\frac{1}{.000096901} \cdot [1.000096901^{3651} - 1]$	$4,379.99
Weekly	$10 \cdot 52 + 1 = 521$	$1.036^{\frac{1}{52}} - 1 = .000680369$	$\frac{1}{.000680369} \cdot [1.000680369^{521} - 1]$	$625.04
Monthly	$10 \cdot 12 + 1 = 121$	$1.036^{\frac{1}{12}} - 1 = .002951609$	$\frac{1}{.002951609} \cdot [1.002951609^{121} - 1]$	$145.17
Annual	$10 + 1 = 11$	.036	$\frac{1}{.036} \cdot [1.036^{11} - 1]$	$13.21
Once	1	.036	1.036^{10}	$1.42

3. Your annual after-tax interest rate is $.08 \cdot (1 - .15) = .068$.

Car Reducer for 3 Years, with an 8% Interest Rate and 15% Marginal Tax Bracket

Frequency	Number of Payments	Periodic Rate	Formula	Reducer
Daily	$3 \cdot 365 + 1 = 1096$	$1.068^{\frac{1}{365}} - 1 = .000180257$	$\frac{1}{.000180257} \cdot [1.000180257^{1096} - 1]$	$1,211.64
Weekly	$3 \cdot 52 + 1 = 157$	$1.068^{\frac{1}{52}} - 1 = .001265949$	$\frac{1}{.001265949} \cdot [1.001265949^{157} - 1]$	$173.57
Monthly	$3 \cdot 12 + 1 = 37$	$1.068^{\frac{1}{12}} - 1 = .005497367$	$\frac{1}{.005497367} \cdot [1.005497367^{37} - 1]$	$40.91
Annual	$3 + 1 = 4$	.068	$\frac{1}{.068} \cdot [1.068^{4} - 1]$	$4.43
Once	1	.068	1.068^{3}	$1.22

4. There is an endless list. An example would be buying high definition movies and watching them on an old television. Buying a super-fast computer for doing work on the Internet, and paying for a low connection speed. Buying too large a house is an invitation for inconsistency. You will not have enough money left over for decent furniture, or to have fun.

5. There are many examples. If you work at a high-paying job, and your bonus heavily depends on hours spent at the office, it may be worth it to hire a housekeeper or have groceries delivered. If you use a lot of paper printing, it may be worth the extra cost to get a duplex printer (prints on both sides.) If you just have to drink espresso, an espresso machine may save you money in the long run if you are currently going to the coffee shop. Insulating a home can pay-off in lower heating costs. However, these kinds of calculations can be used to justify spending a lot of money, without truly receiving the benefit of lower costs.

6. One of the most obnoxious techniques is to latch onto you and refuse to go away until you buy something. Some unethical people will try to sneak in extra purchases on you, such as in a cell phone contract, or add an extra amount to what you think you are buying. Another technique is to offer you a "free" month's subscription to something. If you forget to cancel after a month you begin to get bills. Sometimes the advertised price includes you having to do something onerous, like mailing in a rebate form that requires large amounts of information about you. Something may be offered for "free," but you have to buy something else at an inflated price at the same time.

7. College is a good example. Students often have to repeatedly pay fees for such things as receiving transcripts, application fees, course fees for equipment, fees for registering late or dropping a course, and so on. Airlines charge fees for carry-on bags. Car rental companies are very creative at coming up with extra fees. Be sure to fill the tank when you return the car rather than letting them do it.

8. Someone I know signed up for martial arts training. This was a very large reducer because of the monthly checks. However, the training was expected to increase her energy level and productivity at work, which could result in more

income. She was suffering from being overweight, and was already spending a lot on medications and food. The martial arts training could save money if she could get her weight down, and was consistent with her spending money on health. Future medical bills from a serious medical condition could also be avoided. She was considering purchasing life insurance. If she could get her weight down her premiums would be lower. She took her time to decide, and did not bend to pressure from the martial arts instructor. After careful questioning, she learned that she would have to pay fees to test for each belt that she earned, and also purchase equipment. She decided that a health club was a less valuable alternative because the health club bored her and she would not keep going. The personal instruction and chance to move up in rank would help to hold her interest. She also thought the martial arts training would help her become more self-confident at work, and come in handy if she ever needed to defend herself. She decided she would also save money by reducing other recreational activities. Once she reached a certain rank, she could have her fees reduced by helping out with teaching newcomers. Finally, she could cancel her contract at any time. There was no long-term commitment required, which was another plus. She decided to see if she really did lose weight and continued to want to stick with it.

9. Going to college, moving into a new place for the first time, and starting a new job.

10. There is no correct answer to this question, but it still requires a great deal of thought.

15. Career Skills

1. Professionalism implies not taking things personally and not regarding rivals as enemies.

2. The technical aspects of a career may be quite enjoyable, but the other aspects of the career could be very unpleasant.

3. There are many concerns to consider. Is the career so highly specialized that if it goes away you will not be able to get employment elsewhere? Does the career require long hours of work or a lot of travel? Is it highly competitive or political? Is random luck important? Are there very few jobs? Is it low-paying? Is the income unreliable? Will you have time for a family? Could the industry go overseas or become obsolete?

4. Do research. Read books on the career. Better yet, find people who are pursuing the career to speak with. Discuss your career plans with professors.

5. You have invested a tremendous amount in college, which you will lose, including all of the tuition and the opportunity cost of your time. Since you were in college you were not working and earning money. Your lifetime earnings will be smaller, which will add up to a tremendous amount in present value terms. If you have student loans or other debt, you will be in the situation of owing on this debt while earning a low, non-college salary. Bankruptcy will not help because college loans are not forgiven in bankruptcy.

6. Working can bring in needed money. It can be a first look at a future career or a potential post-college employer. It is a chance to network and acquire skills. It will also look good on a résumé. An internship is a temporary job offered to college students, usually over the summer. The drawback of working during college is that is can interfere with learning and getting good grades. It is also important to be well rested.

7. Networking can help with everything. It can help with finding a job, finding customers, finding accountants, lawyers, and other companies to help with your business.

8. Be sure to research the company thoroughly. Also find out as much as you can about the people you will be interviewing with. Have a number of good questions prepared.

9. Can the job lead to a better job (within the company or outside)? Can you build a widely known reputation that makes you more marketable? Do you have a chance to build your skills? Does the job offer you visibility with someone important or with the public? Besides compensation, what benefits are offered? What promotion potential is there? How expensive is the area? Is commuting difficult? What are the details of the job? Will there be a lot of travel? How many hours are you expected to put in?

10. An opportunity cost is something that you give up for something else. An example is giving up working and making income to go to college.

11. A résumé is a document that you create which lists your accomplishments and demonstrates your abilities. It is used to gain employment, impress customers, etc.

12. When people become successful they get stuck in a rut. They do not want to risk what they have by trying new things, but this actually causes them to lose out. The result is that they do not keep up with change.

13. Starting a business is very risky. Many fail. You will need a broad set of skills. You will need funding, and you may go without a sufficient income to support yourself for a long time, piling up debt as a consequence. You will work long hours, face many roadblocks and frustrations, and live with ambiguity and uncertainty. You have to know how to do everything (at least to the point where you can supervise others), including your accounting books. Others with more money may take your idea and use it themselves before you can get established. You have to protect property rights.

14. Find a good attorney and lawyer, and get your business set up properly. This includes getting the necessary incorporation documents, getting licenses and registering with tax authorities, and setting up an accounting system.

15. 1.) An established kind of business run well, 2.) An established kind of business with a new twist. 3.) A radically new kind of business.

16. Breaking your word could do someone else enormous harm because they relied on you. This means that they did not find someone else, and spent resources and time based on your promise. They could fail to accomplish something, damaging their own reputation or future prospects. They may be able to sue you, and they will tell people about your lack of reliability.

17. Resorting to lawsuits is very costly. It is also very time consuming and often upsetting. The results can be unpredictable and subject to random events.

18. There are many legal protections needed in business. Agreements should be written into contracts, and intellectual property rights protected. It is important (though expensive) to consult with attorneys.

19. You have skills that are specific to the company. You cannot get good outside job offers; therefore, the company does not have to pay you very much or treat you well. A variation of this is having accomplishments that are not observable to outsiders.

20. People have a tendency to follow the behavior of others around them. Entire businesses can be dishonest. People will also rationalize unethical behavior.

21. Most successful people have past failures. In fact, they consider them a gift that they have learned from. Failure does not carry the stigma in the United States that it does elsewhere in the world, which is one of the reasons so many new companies get started in the U.S..

22. You have to live with uncertainty and risk, and not be discouraged by failures or roadblocks. A new business requires long hours with uncertain results and ambiguity. You may have your wealth tied up in your business.

23. It is a first stepping stone. Your first job attaches to your reputation, influencing future opportunities. It is also an important place to learn your trade.

24.

Professionalism	Employers will trust you to act in the best interest of the company, rather than acting on emotion.
Performance	Do every task very well, no matter how small. Never show your work until it is polished.
Integrity	You will feel better about yourself, protect your reputation, and avoid possible jail time.
Research	You could impress an interviewer with your knowledge about the company and get a job.
Networking	You could find an important customer.
Advice	You could avoid a pitfall in your career, such as taking a job where you cannot develop your outside reputation.
Human capital	Because you took the time to learn new things at your work, you were asked to fill in for someone in an emergency and ended up getting a promotion.
Strategizing	You realize that your career has stalled, and you get new training so that you can be promoted.
Résumé and public record	You carefully polish your résumé and get a great job offer.
Visibility	Try to take on tasks that will get you in front of influential people who can help you.
Work With reliable people/relationships	You avoid someone who will let you down at a critical moment. For instance, you do not hire someone after you find out that they are not willing to work hard.
Keep your word	Someone signs a contract with you to provide him with a big computer programming project which will take many months, because he heard you are reliable.
Push yourself	You volunteer to make a speech for a fellow employee who is sick, even though you are very uncomfortable talking in front of crowds. As a result, you are invited by several television news stations to comment on various issues. Eventually, you start your own successful business as a result of your increased public recognition.
Embrace change	When a new way of doing things arrives, learn to adapt, or even lead in creating change.
Leadership	Keep the greater context in mind, inspire others, and set an example. Engender trust.
Legal protections and ownership	Because you signed a contract, someone who did not contribute what they promised to your book cannot claim profits from your sales.

16. LEVERAGE AND RISK

1. When you borrow to invest you are taking on financial leverage, which increases gains and losses on investments.

2.

	Portfolio Rises by 12%	Portfolio Falls by 12%
	Leveraged	
Owed On The Loan	40,000·(1.03)=41,200	41,200
% Gain or Loss	$\frac{100{,}000 \cdot (1.12) - 41{,}200}{60{,}000} - 1 = .18$	$\frac{100{,}000 \cdot (1 - .12) - 41{,}200}{60{,}000} - 1 = -.22$
	Unleveraged	
Owed On The Loan	0	0
% Gain or Loss	$\frac{60{,}000 \cdot (1.12)}{60{,}000} - 1 = .12$	$\frac{60{,}000 \cdot (1 - .12)}{60{,}000} - 1 = -.12$

3. As long as the underlying investment rises enough to cover interest expense, then the leveraged investment will do better. If the investment falls, the unleveraged investment will do better.

4. Investing in an index involves buying shares in a portfolio that tracks the index. These portfolios are "passive," in that they simply try to track an index portfolio of stocks. An actively managed portfolio has stocks bought and sold to achieve gains; it does not simply track something.

5. A prospectus provides information on financial investments and is required by law.

6. Based on the previous three years, Fund A has the least leverage, and Fund B has the most since leveraged funds generally do worse when the market declines. Fund B appears to have reacted by lowering its leverage in the most recent year, since it declined less than Fund C, and is much closer to Fund A.

7. Past fund performance may simply depend on whether a fund is leveraged or not. As markets go up or down, leveraged and unleveraged funds will alternate in which one does better. Since you do not know what will happen in the future, it does not make sense to pick a fund based on the past, because you have to pay fees to switch back and forth. It is better to decide which strategy is better based on your tolerance for risk, and stick with it.

8. Over a long period of time, fees can have a huge impact on investment performance (covered in Volume 2.)

9. Borrowing from your broker to buy securities. You will have to fulfill margin requirements, and you could get a margin call.

10. You will not have a lot of savings at the beginning, and you could have your house go underwater and have negative net worth.

11. When a house goes "underwater" it is worth less than the mortgage. You could end up stuck in your house because you cannot sell it and pay off the mortgage. The alternative is trying to rent it, which is difficult and costly. Also, if you lose your job you could end up defaulting. From Chapter 8, you may not be able to refinance if interest rates fall.

12. Crime, weather, the quality of public schools, access to transportation routes or public transportation, and the proximity to business districts all play a role (among other factors).

13. A rapid rise in home prices, house flipping, and a lot of talk among the public about real estate. Also, extreme government policies, such as unsustainably low mortgage rates, can create or indicate a bubble. Another sign is when house prices get out of alignment with rental rates or people's income.

14. Homeownership can be a powerful way to grow wealth and provide for a secure retirement. However, it should be approached with caution to avoid buying in a down market. Also, if you move frequently, the realtor's fees associated with moving may suggest renting instead.

17. Credit Scores

1. A CRA is a credit reporting agency. They collect information on individuals in a credit report and sell that information.

2. Their Social Security number.

3. Identifying information is included, along with a history of your accounts, your employment history, law suits, bankruptcies, tax liens, and late child support payments. Your borrowings and available credit is listed.

4. Employers, lenders, landlords, insurers, government agencies, and various businesses.

5. A FICO score is the first credit score, calculated by the Fair Isaac Corporation. It is based on statistical analysis of the chance that someone will default. It uses information from your credit report. It is possible that other information is also used, such as purchases. The categories of information are: payment history, credit usage and availability, length of credit history, new credit, and other factors.

6. A hit occurs when your credit report is accessed. A soft hit does not affect your credit score. An example would be when you request your free report. A hard hit is done by someone you are conducting business with, and it can lower your credit score.

7. The consequences of a poor credit score can be enormous. You could pay a much higher interest rate on loans and insurance, and may be required to put down larger deposits on accounts. You could also lose job offers or apartments.

8. Medical history, race, sex, religion, country of origin, marital status, and if you are receiving public assistance.

9. A late payment takes 7 years; a bankruptcy 10 years. However, there is no time limit if you are applying for a job that pays over $75,000 per year, or for credit or life insurance over $150,000.

10. Once a year. You do not have to access all three reports at the same time.

11. Your report cannot be accessed. You can unfreeze the report to allow someone access, and then freeze it again.

12. They cannot do much more to repair your credit than you can. Some have illegal or unsavory practices.

13. You do not want to have a high balance in comparison to your credit limit. It would be better to spread out spending over two cards, than to have a high balance on one. On the other hand, having a large number of credit cards could be detrimental to your score.

14. Credit from consumer finance companies, and others that tend to lend to subprime borrowers.

15. Try to get your shopping done within 30 days. Your credit hits then appear to belong to the same borrowing activity.

16. When the primary borrower on a loan fails to make payments, the cosigner is responsible for making the payments.

18. Financial Distress

1. Overspending with borrowing, borrowing unwisely, health problems, job loss, being sued, and insufficient resources for divorce, widowhood, or a new child. Also financial commitments, borrowing to invest in risky investments, ticking tax time-bombs, theft and fraud, business failure, and self-destructive behavior.

2. When you borrow to consume, you take on debt without purchasing an asset that can be sold if necessary to pay off the debt.

3. Buy health, disability, and long-term care insurance.

4. Have savings to support you for at least 6 months, and avoid buying a house if you do not have substantial savings or have any doubts about your job security.

5. The value of the investment falls below the amount of the loan. In the case of a house, the house can become "underwater."

6. There can be unexpected taxes that lead to trouble, such as when the AMT kicks in with higher income. Also, there can be unexpected taxes when starting or shutting down a business.

7. Make sure you have enough savings to: 1.) Cover yourself if the business fails and you need to seek employment 2.) Cover you until the business makes money. Do not be overly optimistic.

8. People do not talk about their problems when they have financial distress.

9. Protect yourself and your family. Make sure the entire family supports each other.

10. Take action immediately when you realize there is a problem. Create a personal financial statement and put together preliminary financial projections. Talk with creditors as soon as you have a plan, and try to get them to make concessions. Seek counseling if necessary. Bankruptcy should be the last option.

11. Possible financial steps are selling assets, cutting expenditures, taking extra jobs, and refinancing debt into a lower interest rate loan, such as a home equity loan.

12. An insolvency problem is worse than a liquidity problem because your assets are worth less than your liabilities. With a liquidity problem, is it easier to convince a creditor to wait until you can sell assets.

13. If you fail to make payments, a secured creditor can seize specific assets named in the loan document. An unsecured creditor does not have specific assets listed as collateral in the loan document.

14. You sell the house to the bank, and the bank sells it back to you at a lower price. This is effectively loan forgiveness.

15. A company that buys unpaid debts and collects the money. In the past they used aggressive tactics, but legislation has been passed to give debtors rights against harassment.

16. Borrowing with secured loans to pay off unsecured loans. This lowers interest payments. This should be done even without financial distress, although it does create secured assets. You may also be able to find cheaper interest rate loans, secured or not.

17. Bankruptcy is a legal process overseen by the courts, where debtors are typically given relief from creditors.

18. Chapter 7 and Chapter 13. In Chapter 7 you lose more assets, but more debt is forgiven than in Chapter 13. Debts, such as student loans, fines, taxes, alimony payments, and child support payments, may not be forgiven.

19. Payments that may remain include child support, alimony, taxes, fines, and student loans.

20. Credit counseling services can be very helpful. However, some are illegitimate, while others charge excessive fees or steer debtors into bankruptcy to collect higher fees.

21. Before approaching creditors, be prepared to explain what happened and have a clear plan of action to solve the problem. Be proactive and contact them as soon as possible; do not wait until they are trying to collect.

19. Identity Theft

1. A Social Security number can be used to access many accounts because it is commonly used to identify people.

2. Your mother's maiden name, your birthday, and place of birth.

3. Account takeover is when an identity thief gains access to an existing account of a victim and uses it for their own purpose, such as using a credit card number in order to steal. New account fraud involves opening a new account under a victim's name, and using the account for purchases and other services such as cell phone service. The victim is then contacted to cover payments, or their credit rating becomes damaged.

4. At tax time. This is when sensitive information such as Social Security numbers on W-2 and other forms, travels through the mail.

5. Searching dumpsters and trash cans for sensitive information that is thrown out.

6. Pretending to be someone else, such as an employee of a business, to trick a victim into revealing information.

7. Looking over someone's shoulder as they type in passwords, etc.

8. Phishing involves impersonating a business on the Internet; sending fake emails from a company is an example. When a person clicks on a link they are taken to a fake website that collects their information. A variation is creating a fake website that offers "great deals," etc.

9. You could be given the wrong treatment, sent a bill for medical services you did not receive, or denied coverage for being over your limit. You could also have trouble getting new health or life insurance.

10. Someone who has been arrested or convicted pretends to be you. The arrest goes under your name and could cause you to be falsely arrested. You could also have career problems.

11. Do not panic, but act quickly and get organized. File a police report. Notify all the major credit card bureaus and establish a fraud alert. Make a note of every conversation you have and file every record you receive in a dedicated folder. Depending on the theft you may need to contact other agencies. Contact the credit bureaus again to extend the initial 90-day fraud alert for 7 years. Thereafter, continually monitor your credit reports.

12. When a credit report is frozen, your credit record cannot be accessed by others. In order to receive credit you will have to unfreeze your credit record, and then refreeze it after the lender has accessed your record.

13. Investment accounts can contain a large portion of your wealth, and they have few protections.

14. A skimmer is a small hand-held device that identity thieves can use to get your credit card information. Always keep an eye on your credit card ,if possible.

15. They send you a message if someone accesses your credit report using an email or a text message.

16. A security token is a small device that generates numbers. It updates your password frequently, and it can be very useful for preventing identity theft of investment accounts.

17. Try to have one person in charge of accounts, such as the cable television account. Try to have separate locking mailboxes, or get a post-office box to have sensitive mail delivered to. Try to go paperless and have secure Wi-Fi. Have your computer require a log-in. Get a locking file cabinet.

18. Fraud alerts are placed with the CRAs. With a fraud alert, creditors are required to call you before extending credit. You can have one placed for free for 90 days if you are the victim of identity theft. You can request an extension for an additional 7 years.

19. You can get information on the account, and on any required paperwork. They are required by law to inform the person who issued the debt that you are an identity theft victim. They cannot continue trying to collect from you.

20. Double-check when any tax documents will be sent. If they do not show up, take extra precautions with your credit reports. Try to file your tax returns electronically, or drop your tax return forms off at the post office. (Avoid leaving your tax return forms in a mailbox overnight.)

21. Check to see if it is your name on the card when you get it back.

22. Do not give him any sensitive information. He may very well be pretexting. Ask to contact him by calling the main number for the bank (which you get yourself), and being transferred.

23. Do not respond to the email. Go to your account using your own link. Alternatively, call the business using a phone number that you know.

20. Looking Good for a Lifetime

1. Do not reveal information that could lead someone to find your physical location. Restrict who can access your social networking page. Never meet someone in person that you first met over the Internet.

2. A crawler is software that trolls the Internet and records information. It is one of the reasons that information posted on the Internet can stay forever.

3. Read a website's privacy policy. However, their policy can change. If the website does not have a privacy policy, it is a good indication that they are not careful about information.

4. Anything posted about you on the Internet that is publicly available, information collected by businesses that you interact with online and offline, and government records and filings.

5. Anyone: employers, college admissions officers, etc.

6. Bullying can be considered a crime. If the bullying occurs online or makes it into the news, it can create a permanent public record indicating that you are vicious.

7. Driver error, speeding, distracted driving, and drinking or drugs.

8. It could become part of the public record and destroy your career. Employers routinely ask job applicants if they have been arrested. It is also a common college application question.

9. A résumé highlights information about you for the purpose of applying for jobs. It can also be used in other ways such as when applying for speaking engagements and the like. You decide what to include in your résumé.

10. A cover page should be sent with a résumé. It should explain why you are contacting her, any needed information (such as when you can start work), and why you are applying for the position.

11. A résumé should tell a story about you, and is often presented in chronological order. It should highlight your skills and accomplishments. A résumé should be beautifully formatted with consistent construction, error free, and printed on good quality stationary. Do not exaggerate or lie. Be as specific as possible, and try to include key words that employers seem to look for in the kind of job you want.

12. They are a human resource management person. They screen applicants for job positions.

13. A social networking page can be another place a potential employer can get a to look at you. If you are careful, this can boost your chances. On the other hand, some employers will view social networking pages negatively. It is also easy to unintentionally create a negative impression.

PHOTOGRAPH INFORMATION

Book Cover

Map and compass: pf-photos, courtesy of http://www.istockphoto.com, www.pf-photos.com, zulufriend, Lisbon (Portugal). File #5922474.

Chapter 1

High school graduates: This photo was modified. Andresr, courtesty of http://www.istockphoto.com, andresr.com, London, Blackheath. File #8312548.
Map and compass: pf-photos, courtesy of http://www.istockphoto.com, www.pf-photos.com, zulufriend, Lisbon (Portugal). File #5922474.
Farmer and son: SFB Photographics Inc., courtesy of http://www.istockphoto.com, seanfboggs, seanfboggs.com. File # 7637197.
Rock concert: This picture was modified. Stacey Newman, courtesy of http://www.istockphoto.com, www.thelazyactivist.com, Ontario (Canada), stacey_newman, file #6475268.
TV news reporter: claudiaveja, courtesy of http://www.istockphoto.com, www.claudiaveja.com, file #8306370.
Hands holding nest egg and magnifying glass: This is a composite picture with Microsoft clip art and dashed lines added. The hands and nest egg were modified. YinYang courtesy of http://www.istockphoto.com, file #4785101. The magnifying glass: Microsoft clip art j0433829.png.
Little Red Riding Hood with wolf: VisualKeys, courtesy of http://www.istockphoto.com, jcrosemann, file #11158982.
Happy family: This photograph was modified. Linda Yolanda, courtesy of http://www.istockphoto.com, file #9390684.
Creepy businessman with contract: attator, courtesy of http://www.istockphoto.com, file #5119272.
Lady with map: ZavgSG, courtesy of http://www.istockphoto.com, file #6975632.
David: Phooey, courtesy of http://www.istockphoto.com, file #4460956.
Flying books: LuisPortugal, courtesy of http://www.istockphoto.com, file #7235328.
Tunnel with a light at the end: sagaYago, courtesy of http://www.istockphoto.com, manuelvelasco.wordpress.com, file #3023641.
Women with map: mihaicalin, courtesy of http://www.istockphoto.com, www.mihaicallin.ro, file #3248859.

Chapter 2

New York skyline: André Viegas, courtesy of http://www.istockphoto.com, file #11222379.
Neon cup: Graffizone, courtesy of http://www.istockphoto.com, file#251553.
Art gallery owner: Composite picture. Photograph of woman: Chris Gramly Photography, San Rafael, CA, http://www.gramly.com . Art photograph: Branislav. Courtesy of http://www.istockphoto.com, chrisgramly file #896896; Branislav file #1627794.
Boardroom dreamer: Oleg Prikhodko, courtesy of http://www.istockphoto.com, Cimmerian, file #260863.
Hot dog stand: David Ritter, Phoenix, AZ. Courtesy of http://www.sxc.hu, dlritter, file #365822.
Stock certificate: MBPHOTO. Courtesy of http://www.istockphoto.com, DNY59, file #642276.
Construction business partners: Junial Enterprises, http://www.junial.com. Courtesy of http://www.istockphoto.com, junial file #7163579.
Chocolate: foodandwinephotography.com, 091 582180. www.foodandwinephotography.com. Courtesy of http://www.istockphoto.com, oscargalway, file #8840956.
Market bull: Myles Davidson, Dartford, Kent, UK, http://www.ebdesigners.com. Courtesy of http://www.sxc.hu, myles, file #30846.
Bond certificate: Mark Jensen, Seattle, WA, http://www.jensenphotography.org. Courtesy of http://www.istockphoto.com, jensenphoto, file #958988.
Orange tree: Kathryn McCallum, Orlando, FL. Courtesy of http://www.sxc.hu, lemon_drop, file #127516.

Executive on tightroap: RTimages, Alton, Hampshire, UK, http://rtimages.com. Courtesy of http://www.istockphoto.com, RTimages, file #4493767.

Chapter 3

Woman Face Down with Tax Forms: Arizonaphotographic.blogspot.com. Courtesy of http://www.istockphoto.com, sarrobi, file #2999139.

Vampire: http://www.walker1890.co.uk. Courtesy of http://www.istockphoto.com, duncan1890, file #1207683.

The Moon: Carolina Smith Photography. Courtesy of http://www.istockphoto.com, CarolinaSmith, file #1549911.

Time Bomb: mipan1.100webspace.net/index.htm. Courtesy of http://www.istockphoto.com, mipan, file #3998073.

Dollar and Computer: Henrik Jonsson Graphic Design, +44 20 7727 1852, http://www.henrikjonsson.com. Courtesy of http://www.istockphoto.com, Henrik5000, file #9600225.

New Job: Digital Planet Design, http://www.digitalplanetdesign.com. Courtesy of http://www.istockphoto.com, sjlocke, file #655128.

Chapter 4

"Nicholas James's" portrait: digitalskillet.com, courtesy of http://www.istockphoto.com, digitalskillet, file #6870909.

"Nicholas James's" house: Andrew Manley http://www.andrewmanley.com, courtesy of http://www.istockphoto.com, manley620, 3186024.

Home theater: VegaBlue, courtesy of http://www.istockphoto.com, EricVega, Fuquay Varina, NC , www.VegaBlue.com, file #2478383.

Housekeeper with rose colored glasses: The photograph has been modified. Henry Schmitt, http://us.fotolia.com, file# 23253327.

Vintage car: http://maksymenco.com, courtesy of http://www.istockphoto.com, alexmax, file #1486582.

Housekeeper on ladder: Modified composite picture. Lady on Ladder by Viorika Prikhodko Photography, courtesy of http:// www.istockphoto.com, Viorika, file #4884302. Bushes by Juan Gabriel Estey, http://krop.com/juanestey/, courtesy of http://www.istockphoto.com, juanestey, file #3553036.

Man on chair in the ocean: Oliver, courtesy of http://www.istockphoto.com, bowie15, file #9312505.

Dripping money faucet: ktsimage, courtesy of http://www.istockphoto.com, ktsimage, file #6204163.

Plumber: Kurhan, courtesy of http://us.fotolia.com, file# 20417799.

Flaming dollar sign: jokerproproduction, courtesy of http://www.istockphoto.com, jokerproproduction, file #8605077.

Net worth bathtubs: This picture was modified. Microsoft clipart, file# 00021388.wmf.

Sunrise: Ducky's Deluxe Business Cards, http://www.duckycards.com, courtesy of http://www.istockphoto.com, duckycards, file #3152015.

Chapter 5

Lady in Green with Budget: Ekaterina Monakhova, www.katemonaknova.com, Buenos Aires. Courtesy of http://www.istockphoto.com kate_sept24. File #10486280.

Crowd at Door: www.pixalot.de. Courtesy of http://www.istockphoto.com Pixalot. File #6066744.

Lady in Blue Sweater Who Wrote Check: 4X6. Courtesy of http://www.istockphoto.com, file #10554290.

Baker: YinYang Courtesy of http://www.istockphoto.com, file #10402330.

Juggler and Policeman Composite Picture: Juggler, Padagogische Hochschule www.jophil.at. Courtesy of http://www.istockphoto.com, file #2485775; Policeman, KD Photography & Design kdphotodesign.com. Courtesy of http://www.istockphoto.com KarenMower. File #7805757.

Money Vacuum: mipan.orgfree.com. Courtesy of http://www.istockphoto.com mipan, file #866777.

Jane Wright: Stock Photo NYC Courtesy of http://www.istockphoto.com Stockphoto4u, file #5654093.

Cookie: www.dorioconnell.com Courtesy of http://www.istockphoto.com DOConnell, file #6364766.

Moving Boxes: Sven Hoppe. Courtesy of http://www.istockphoto.com Heidelberg, BW(Germany), file #6014936.

"Jane Wright" Shopping Composite Picture: Jane's face, Stock Photo NYC, courtesy of http://www.istockphoto.com Stockphoto4u, file #6841849. Rest of picture, Inga Ivanova Moscow, courtesy of http://www.istockphoto.com, file #4182114.
"Jane Wright" on a Bicycle: Diego Cervo Bernareggio, Milano (Italy). Courtesy of http://www.istockphoto.com diego_cervo, file #9620824.

Chapter 6

Hourglass: Aggressive Entertainment, courtesy of http://www.istockphoto.com, file #1847192.
Three percent signs: This photograph was modified. Andrew Johnson, courtesy of http://www.istockphoto.com, file #10533103.

Chapter 7

Money: Composite picture. Background: Microsoft Word Clipart jo433118.jpg. Rolled bills: MsLightBox, courtesy of http://www.istockphoto.com, file #11795802.

Chapter 8

Exponential graph: fpm, www.grafikzeug.com, courtesy of http://www.istockphoto.com, file #3173238.
Mad scientist with equation: Equation was added to the photo. Fuzephoto, Kangah, www.fuzephotography.ca, courtesy of http://www.istockphoto.com, file #10558749.
Staring business man: Denis Pepin, Cybernesco, usefulimage.com, courtesy of http://www.istockphoto.com, file #1760395.
Burning dollar: Roman Sigaev, courtesy of http://us.fotolia.com, file# 5857794.
Wheelbarrow full of money: Zargon Studios Corp., courtesy of http://www.istockphoto.com, file# 6946090.
Woman with credit cards: Tadija Savic, courtesy of http://us.fotolia.com, file# 4581662.
Money sandwich: JBP, joebelanger, www.joebelanger.com, courtesy of http://www.istockphoto.com, file #11038669.
Pizza: arkpop, courtesy of http://us.fotolia.com/CheckoutOrder, file# 7781887.
"Trust Me" man: Studiovancaspel, mammamaart, Berlin, courtesy of http://www.istockphoto.com, file #118849.

Chapter 9

Mortgage and key: Modified photograph. Hidesy, www.hidesy.com Kippa-Ring, QLD (Australia), courtesy of http://www.istockphoto.com, file #1142031.
Apple: Olga Lyubkina, courtesy of http://us.fotolia.com, file #105674.
Money falling from the sky: 14ktgold, courtesy of http://us.fotolia.com, file #11907592.
Fine print and glasses: Janaka Dharmasena, courtesy of http://us.fotolia.co, file #9169580.
Foreclosure: Andy Dean, courtesy of http://us.fotolia.com, file #13247505.
Raining money on a businessman: Modified photograph. PictureArt, courtesy of http://us.fotolia.com, file #4997699.
Boy flipping through the sky: Composite photograph. Courtesy of http://us.fotolia.com; The sky: Luiz, file #8215336. The boy (modified photograph): Anchels, file #4016542.
House of horrors: Modified photograph, courtesy of http://us.fotolia.com, file #23361526.
Feet and fireplace: Monkey Business Images, courtesy of istockphoto: http://www.istockphoto.com, file #8333368.

Chapter 10

Coin jar: Modified photograph. Eric Spiegel, fallenposters, courtesy of http://www.istockphoto.com, file #11884986.
"Richard Wilson": Modified composite photograph. Richard Wilson's face: Snap!photo, courtesy of http://www.istockphoto.com, file #5899178; white shirt and yellow sweater (modified photo), Azndc, www.istockphoto.com/azndc, courtesy of http://www.istockphoto.com, file #8641805.

Girl gorging on cinnamon buns: Modified photograph. knape, courtesy of http://www.istockphoto.com, file #2067611.

Ugly monkey: Kristina Afanasyeva, courtesy of http://us.fotolia.co, file #20590223.
"Richard Wilson" worried at the computer: Snap!photo, courtesy of http://www.istockphoto.com, file #5896535.
SUV stuck in the mud: sleddogtwo, www.istockphoto.com/sleddogtwo, courtesy of http://www.istockphoto.com, file #4387133.
"Myles Green": Neustock, Neustockimages, courtesy of http://www.istockphoto.com, file #8364212.
Couple budgeting: Neustockimages, courtesy of http://www.istockphoto.com, file #10107319.

Chapter 11

Girl and Grandmother: Linda Yolanda, courtesty istockphoto: http://www.istockphoto.com, file #11543051.
Grandfather, Son, and Grandson: Key To My Heart Photography by Judy Lynn, courtesy istockphoto: http://www.istockphoto.com, JLBarranco, www.judylynnphotography.com, file #11138097.
Sr. Lady in Blue Car: Srabin, courtesy istockphoto: http://www.istockphoto.com, file #2652380.
Grandfather and Granddaughter: pamspix, courtesy istockphoto: http://www.istockphoto.com, file #3680747.
Speedboat: kirza, courtesy istockphoto: http://www.istockphoto.com, file #2341237.
Older male worker looking at a vista: Fenykepez, courtesy istockphoto: http://www.istockphoto.com, file #11575242.
Man handing cash: courtesy istockphoto: http://www.istockphoto.com, file #10339585.
Man scratching head holding money: Jerry Koch Photography, courtesy istockphoto: http://www.istockphoto.com, JerryPDX, photos.yahoo.com/jerrypdx, Portland, OR, file #4812540.
Enron tower: Jake Hellbach, courtesy http://us.fotolia.com/, file #3388493.
Bee and flower: Digihelion photostudio, courtesy istockphoto: http://www.istockphoto.com, www.digihelion.com, 421 908 214268, file #9943113.
Stained glass: Michael Shibler, courtesy http://us.fotolia.com/, file #1862019.

Chapter 12

University of Chicago: Modified photograph. Uschool University Images, courtesy http://www. istockphoto.com, file # 5424675.
Female student in White: mocker_bat, courtesy http://www.istockphoto.com, file #10995984.
University columns: chimpyk, courtesy http://www.istockphoto.com, file #9123512.
University building with autumn leaves: gregobagel, courtesy http://www.istockphoto.com, file #8651781.
Handcuffs: milosluz, courtesy http://www.istockphoto.com, file #2290694.
Woman playing chess: Yuri Arcurs, courtesy http://www.istockphoto.com, file #7008419.
Two college students sitting together: Take A Pix Media, courtesy http://www.istockphoto.com, file #9390768.
Magician: Myerson Photo, courtesy http://www.istockphoto.com, file #9452426.
College Old Mill: TheBiggles, courtesy http://www.istockphoto.com, file #5950836.
Female student with books and money: courtesy http://www.istockphoto.com, file #6487891.
Walker Museum at the University of Chicago: stevegeer, courtesy http://www.istockphoto.com, file #3744553.
Mother and daughter: La Fabrika Pixel, courtesy http://www.istockphoto.com, file #11454269.
Exploding firecracker: Microsoft clip art 00237339.wmf.
Fireworks: Microsoft clip art 00410595.wmf.
Bulldog: Shooting The World, courtesy http://www.istockphoto.com, file #3992686.
Man clasping head: flashgun, courtesy http://www.istockphoto.com, file #8060366.
Student eating pizza: YinYang, courtesy http://www.istockphoto.com, file #10900557.
Female soldier: Designs of Integrity, courtesy http://www.istockphoto.com, file #6293979.
Male soldier: DanielBendjy, courtesy http://www.istockphoto.com, file #12075537.
Red brick walkway and campus building: gregobagel courtesy http://www.istockphoto.com, file #11919735.

Chapter 13

Hands and crystal ball: Modified photograph. VallarieE, courtesy of http://www.istockphoto.com, file #11542873.

House under construction: pixelbrat, www.PixelbratImagery.com, courtesy of http://www.istockphoto.com, file #1770215.

Man and woman eating pizza: Sna;!photo, courtesy of http://www.istockphoto.com, file #5818467.

Baby girl: pphelsp, www.wix.com/paggre/My-Homepage, courtesy of http://www.istockphoto.com, file #11317555.

University of Florida: irinka-s, Gainsville, FL, courtesy of http://www.istockphoto.com, file #11198575.

College student looking through microscope: One Word Photography, www.onewordphotography.com, Calgary, Alberta (Canada), courtesy of http://www.istockphoto.com, file #12246436.

Female college student: Joshua Hodge Photography, blog.joshuahodge.com.au., courtesy of http://www.istockphoto.com, file #9072563.

Retirees at the beach: Amriphoto, www.amriphoto.com, Vienna, courtesy of http://www.istockphoto.com, file #6357953.

Senior lady with "t=0" sign: Modified photograph. Denis Pepin, Cybernesco, usefulimage.com, courtesy of http://www.istockphoto.com, file #9898605.

Lady with binoculars: Modified composite photo courtesy of http://www.istockphoto.com: Lady and binoculars: Dragan Trifunovic, www. dragantrifunovic.com, Zemun (Serbia), file #2006371; Lens: DSGpro, www.istockphoto.com/DSGpro, file #4312672.

Golden nest egg: Modified photo. Richard Clark, JamesWhittaker, www.richardclark.com, courtesy of http://www.istockphoto.com, file #11231120.

Chest with antiques: photozox, file courtesy of http://www.istockphoto.com, #5524980.

Maze: solarseven, www.jamesthew.com file courtesy of http://www.istockphoto.com, #8857422.

Man on couch: Yuri Arcurs, www.arcurs.com, Faarup (Denmark), courtesy of http://www.istockphoto.com, file #10171387.

Chapter 14

Money iceberg: cybrain, courtesy of http://www.istockphoto.com, file #11242544.

Scale with money. This photograph has been altered. Anyka, Wilrijk, Antwerp (Belgium), courtesy of http://www.istockphoto.com, file #1316626.

Scuba diver: Tammy616, Buddina, QLD (Australia) courtesy of http://www.istockphoto.com, file #5404970.

Cockleshell: Zinatova, courtesy of http://www.istockphoto.com, file #4583322.

Boomerang: Horticulture, courtesy of http://us.fotolia.com, file #1819869.

Group of business people: Arnau Design, Xaviarnau, www.arnau-design.com, courtesy of http://www.istockphoto.com, file #4353670.

Man burning money with cigar: Digital Planet Design, sjlocke, www.digitalplanetdesign.com, courtesy of http://www.istockphoto.com, file #1211130.

Woman looking at a quarter: Digital Property LTD, Shironosov, Chelyabinsk, Ural (Russia) courtesy of http://www.istockphoto.com, file #3315423.

Witch hat: IsraelMckee, courtesy of http://www.istockphoto.com, file #14162552.

Tiger: Stephen Meese Photography, www.steve-meese.co.uk/, Rotherham, South Yorkshire (UK), courtesy of http://www.istockphoto.com, file #4201967.

Boxing gloves: Himbeertoni - Büro für Gestaltung, www.himbeertoni.com, Berlin, courtesy of http://www.istockphoto.com, file #4284734.

Dove: Okea, courtesy of http://www.istockphoto.com, file #9052060.

Wooden Crutches: Michael Flippo, courtesy of http://us.fotolia.com, file #18196313.

Woman embracing man: Modified photograph. Yuri Arcurs, www.arcurs.com, Denmark, courtesy of http://www.istockphoto.com, file #3708733.

Chapter 15

Man on roof, Oliver bowie15, courtesy of http://www.istockphoto.com, file #11464907.

Cellist: Gaby Jalbert, gabyjalbert, (Canada) www.gabyjalbert.com, courtesy of http://www. istockphoto.com, file #1783111.

Photographer: Korhan Isik, Bus. Phone, +902324642265, courtesy of http://www.istockphoto.com, file #4811328.

Vertical coral reef: Metropolitan Marketing, johnandersonphoto.com, New York, courtesy of http:// www.istockphoto.com, file #11922737.

Red glove: This photograph was modified. TrudyWilkerson, courtesy of http://www.istockphoto.com, file #9631941.

Professor counsel: BartCo, courtesy of http://www.istockphoto.com, file #5806076.

College student; Rich Vintage Photography, www.richvintagephoto.net, courtesy of http://www. istockphoto.com, file #9617680.

Businessman offering a handshake: www.imabase.com, Imabase, courtesy of http:// www.istockphoto.com, file #10589658.

Business woman with red hair: Aldra, courtesy of http://www.istockphoto.com, file #3005859.

Ball and chain: Alex Staroseltsev, Kiev, (Ukraine), courtesy of http://www.istockphoto.com, file #10521954.

Aircraft engineer: 36Clicks Creative, 36clicks, www.36clicks.nl, courtesy of http:// www.istockphoto.com, file #5997907.

Success blocks: selensergen, Istanbul, (Turkey), www.presence.com.tr, courtesy of http:// www.istockphoto.com, file #8030660.

Vet: www.izabelahabur.com, izusek, London, courtesy of http://www.istockphoto.com, file #10483628.

Businessman leaping: PeskyMonkey, New York, courtesy of http://www.istockphoto.com, file #10602600.

Architects: www.rapideye.co.za, RapidEye, courtesy of http://www.istockphoto.com, file #6824271.

Denim patch: Vladimir & Dilyana, courtesy of http://www.istockphoto.com, file #4136686.

Man with fingers crossed behind back: Wish Me Luck, courtesy of http://www.istockphoto.com, file #5174438.

Conductor: Archivio, courtesy of http://www.istockphoto.com, file #9530565.

Fossil: Jeff Chiasson Photogaphy, jeffchiassonphotography.com, courtesy of http:// www.istockphoto.com, file #10574443.

George Washington crossing the Delaware: This photograph was modified. http://www.walker1890.co.uk, courtesy of http://www.istockphoto.com, file #9186301.

College students: Joshua Hodge Photography, blog.joshuahodge.com.au, pixdeluxe, courtesy of http://www.istockphoto.com, file #927860.

Chapter 16

Jumping goldfish: Irochka_T, courtesy of http://www.istockphoto.com, file #9872372.

Earth on a lever: modified photograph; sgame.shutterpoint.com, courtesy of http:// www.istockphoto.com file #3659012

Picnic: gollykim, courtesy of http://www.istockphoto.com, file#7426852.

Slalom: techno, technotr, courtesy of http://www.istockphoto.com, file #11154240.

Tulips: courtesy of fotolia.com, http://us.fotolia.com, file# 124611.

Motorcycle stunt: CJP Designs, www.cjpdesigns.com, courtesy of http://www.istockphoto.com, file #424422.

Smoky beaker: amridesign, www.amriphoto.com, courtesy of http://www.istockphoto.com, file #7433516.

Falling tower: www.brucemichaelbaillie.co.uk, courtesy of http://www.istockphoto.com, file #169390.

Falling houses on arrow: SwedeAndSour, www.swedeandsour.com, courtesy of http://www. istockphoto.com, file #9957402.

Mystery woman: Prill Mediendesign & Fotografie, courtesy of http://www.istockphoto.com, file #5485959.

Underwater house: vicnt, courtesy of http://www.istockphoto.com, file #5163261.

Couple in new home: www.pikselstock.pl, Warsaw, piksel, courtesy of http://www.istockphoto.com, file #8856923.

Chapter 17

Cheering crowd: pixalot, www.pixalot.de, Reutlingen, BW (Germany), courtesy of http://www.istockphoto.com, file #6187283.

Man with an "A" on his forehead: Modified photograph. Nicholas Monu, nico_blue, Providence, RI, courtesy of http://www.istockphoto.com, file # 1047370.

Woman with a "D" on her forehead: Modified photograph. www.stefanredel.de, Stefan_Redel, Messstetten, Germany, courtesy of http://www.istockphoto.com, file #10271020.

Man with a Social Security card: Composite photograph. Man: Komar, www.komargallery.com, file #11985202; Social Security card: Kameleon007, file #9686589. Both courtesy of http://www.istockphoto.com.

Man under a microscope: Composite photograph. Microscope: K.J. Pargeter Images, file #1887745; man: New Dawn Singers Inc., www.newdawnsingers.com, file #6566990. Both courtesy of http://www.istockphoto.com.

Rejected résumé: Nazdravie, courtesy of http://www.istockphoto.com, file #5229919.

Money on a hook: Vladyslav Danilin, courtesy of http://us.fotolia.com, file #11720483.

Librarian: Lisa F. Young, courtesy of http://us.fotolia.com, file# 2602124.

George Washington stamp: Inferna, courtesy of http://us.fotolia.com, file# 18149034.

Woman jumping with shopping bags (red circle and slash was added): Alexander Novidov, www.fotonovikov.com, Irkutsh (Russia), courtesy of http://www.istockphoto.com, file #6177515.

Soapy dishes: Yaroslav Pavlov, courtesy of http://us.fotolia.com, file #16855418.

Man in red sweater contemplating: soupstock, courtesy of http://www.istockphoto.com, file #3744930.

Woman standing out from the group: Modified photograph.. Phil Date Photography, phildate, www.phildate.com.sg, Singapore, courtesy of http://www.istockphoto.com, file #1525350.

Man frozen with money: New Dawn Singers Inc., joshblake, courtesy of http://www.istockphoto.com, file #2262449.

Hundred dollar bills and tools: Kapu, courtesy of http://us.fotolia.com, file #16566920.

Money tree: imagedepotpro, courtesy of http://www.istockphoto.com, file #12693551.

Chapter 18

Woman stepping on a banana peel: David Franklin, Hatman 12, courtesy of http://www.istockphoto.com, file #3569739.

People walking in "dark matter": Composite photograph. Running-man nebula, www.skyimages.de, skyimages, stmeca, file #11230756; people walking (modified photograph): www.urbancow.com, urbancow, file #4824782. Both images courtesy of http://www.istockphoto.com.

Arguing parents and daughter: TatyanaGl, courtesy of http://www.istockphoto.com, file #7325518.

Invisible man: VikaValter, courtesy of http://www.istockphoto.com, Helsinki (Finland), file #7884190.

Unhappy couple at the beach: Juanmonino, courtesy of http://www.istockphoto.com, file #2302407.

Woman financially planning: Norge Malo Sr., courtesy of http://www.istockphoto.com, file #11890394.

Charles Dickens lithograph: www.walker1890.co.uk, courtesy of http://www.istockphoto.com, duncan1890, file #7164277.

Jail door background: Modified photograph. Pack-Shot, courtesy of http://www.istockphoto.com, file #5887621.

Helping hand: jonhortondesign, courtesy of http://www.istockphoto.com, file #3602212.

Family strolling in the woods: www.abejonphoto.com, aabejon, courtesy of http://www.istockphoto.com, file #4649885.

Chapter 19

Eavesdropper: Microsoft clipart j0409717.jpg.

Purse-snatching martial arts defense: Gerville, courtesy of http://www.istockphoto.com, Leesburg, VA, file #3973395.

Mailbox (text inserted on top): Aggressive Entertainment, dem10, www.dem10.com, courtesy of http://www.istockphoto.com, file #5277472.

Forearm crutch: Accent, courtesy of http://us.fotolia.com, file #4182405.

Skiers: Modified photograph. Dave Long, dave9296, courtesy of http://www.istockphoto.com, file #4752478.

Shoulder surfer: Modified photograph. Ed Hidden Photography, MotoEd, New Cumberland, PA, edhidden.squarespace.com, courtesy of http://www.istockphoto.com, file #730563.

Computer code: kr7ysztof, courtesy of http://www.istockphoto.com, file #3290510.

Laughing doctors: Capture the Moment Photography LLC, Bryngelzon, courtesy of http://www.istockphoto.com, file #1877532.

Jailed man: Moodboard, courtesy of http://us.fotolia.com, file #11982956.

Army boots and glove: Jackie Smithson, courtesy of http://us.fotolia.com, file #1239180.

Rescue dog: PK-Photos, courtesy of http://www.istockphoto.com, file #8298201.

Woman at computer: peepo, courtesy of http://www.istockphoto.com, file #12006857.

Courthouse: Microsoft clipart j0400622.jpg.

Female detective: Arman Zhenikeyev, Zhenikeyev, Almaty (Kazakhstan), novic.photosight.ru, courtesy of http://www. istockphoto .com, file #10861308.

Terracotta warriors: hanhanpeggy, courtesy of http://www.istockphoto.com, file #9411919.

Man with login glasses: dcdp, dcdp.vox.com, courtesy of http://www.istockphoto.com, file #6326034.

Loose lips sink ships: From a United States of America instruction pamphlet for World War II soldiers.

Mailbox: Microsoft clipart j0433831.png.

Lost wallet: Carterdayne Inc., carterdayne, Seattle, WA, courtesy of http://www.istockphoto.com, file #10539357.

Chapter 20

Good-looking man and woman: Mlenny Photography, Mlenny, www.mlenny.com, courtesy of http://www.istockphoto.com, file #2728585.

Man with a tattoo: Composite photograph. Man, asiseeit, file #10322741; tattoo: Huck Productions, Dizzo, www.motion-gfx.com, file #309910. Both photographs courtesy of http://www.istockphoto.com.

"Predator" with sign (man is a model): Composite photograph. Man holding sign, Daniel Dunca, dundanim, file #9517239, man in the picture, foto pfluegl, starfotograf, www.fotograf.at, Wien, Vienna, file #1806229. Photographs courtesy of http://www.istockphoto.com.

Statue: Crossroads Creative, daniellesmith, crossroadscreative.com, courtesy of http://www. istockphoto.com, file #226463.

Female "bully" (woman is a model): Olga Sapegina, olga_sweet, St. Petersburg, Kolpino (Russia), courtesy of http://www.istockphoto.com, file #5349339.

Man at a laptop with thumbs down: Innovative Photography, courtesy of http://www.istockphoto.com, file #4809964.

Teens with cell phone: Modified photograph. Eric's Photo Lab, MrPants, courtesy of http://www.istockphoto.com, file #3394553.

Father and son: Modified photograph. digitalskillet, courtesy of http://www.istockphoto.com, file #7102177.

Mother and daughter: leezsnow, courtesy of http://www.istockphoto.com, file # 5480137.

Woman looking in mirror: DawidMarkiewicz, courtesy of http://www.istockphoto.com, file #11272706.

HRM employee: This photograph was modified. Adam Borkowski, courtesy of http://us.fotolia.com, file #8935318.

Female photographer: factoria singular sl, Brosa, Cambrils, Tarragona (Spain), www.factoriasingular.com, courtesy of http://www.istockphoto.com, file #8955738.

Man checking his appearance in window: Brasil2, Ile de France, www.istockphoto.com/Brasil2, courtesy of http://www.istockphoto.com, file #2625354.

KEYWORD INDEX

13468300R00285

Made in the USA
Lexington, KY
06 February 2012